Blacks in the New World
August Meier, Series Editor

A list of books in the series appears
at the end of this volume.

Black Property Owners
in the South,
1790–1915

BLACK PROPERTY OWNERS IN THE SOUTH
1790–1915

Loren Schweninger

UNIVERSITY OF ILLINOIS PRESS
Urbana and Chicago

For
John Franklin
Michael Ivan
James Lee
Emily Jean

Illini Books edition, 1997
© 1990 by the Board of Trustees of the University of Illinois
Manufactured in the United States of America
1 2 3 4 5 C P 5 4 3 2 1

This book is printed on acid-free paper.

Library of Congress Cataloging-in-Publication Data

Schweninger, Loren.
    Black property owners in the South, 1790–1915 / Loren Schweninger.
        p.   cm. — (Blacks in the New World)
    Includes bibliographical references (p.   )
    ISBN 0-252-01678-5 (cloth : alk. paper). — ISBN 0-252-06634-0 (pbk. : alk. paper)
    1. Afro-Americans—Southern States—Economic conditions.   2. Afro-
Americans—Southern States—Land tenure.   3. Property—Southern
tenure—Southern States—History.   6. Southern States—Economic
conditions.   I. Title.   II. Series.
E185.8.S39   1990
333.3'089'96073075—dc20   89-20361
                                                                            CIP

You know how hard it is to accumulate where there is nothing to begin with and when evrything was as dark as night in behalf of the coulerd race. but thanks to him whose name i am not worthy to mention he has given us the key to knolege and whosoever is found worthy will be able to open the Book and look thereon. the days of fugitives slave laws and missouri comprimises and dread scots deciscions are things of the past and the sheading of Blood was their doom. it is a truth that cannot be denied that without the sheading of blood there is no remission of sin. god grant that there may be no more sheding of blood amongst the american people. the only encouragement i had in the days of continual night was the coulerd people trying to improve their condition. there is no healthyer sighn of improvement than to see any people trying to do right. a great many are trying to do the very best and so long as they continue we have nothing to fear. . . . it indeed is remarcable what one man do when he has a cultivated mind and is careful, onnest, and fine in his motives. and as the good lord has blesd me in the times when all was so dark i do trust him that he will still continue hise blesing forever on all my ofsprings and our race for all time to come.

David Imes to Frederick Douglass,
March 29, 1869

Contents

Acknowledgments / xiii

List of Abbreviations / xv

Introduction / 1

CHAPTER ONE
Beginnings: Africans in a New Land / 7

CHAPTER TWO
Property Ownership among Slaves, 1800–1865 / 29

CHAPTER THREE
Free Negro Property Owners, 1800–1860 / 61

CHAPTER FOUR
Affluent Free Persons of Color, 1800–1861 / 97

CHAPTER FIVE
Property Ownership among Southern Blacks, 1860–1915 / 143

CHAPTER SIX
Prosperous Blacks in the South, 1862–1915 / 185

Epilogue / 233

A Note on Appendixes / 239

APPENDIX ONE
Correspondence / 241

APPENDIX TWO
Petitions / 247

APPENDIX THREE
Probate Court Records / 259

APPENDIX FOUR
Tax Assessment Rolls / 271

APPENDIX FIVE
The Manuscript Population Censuses / 281

APPENDIX SIX
Biographical Listing of Prosperous Blacks in the South,
1870s–1915 / 295

APPENDIX SEVEN
A Profile of Prosperous Blacks, 1870s–1915 / 301

Notes / 307

An Essay on Sources and Methodology / 371

A Selected Bibliography of Books and Articles / 393

Index / 411

List of Tables and Figures

Tables

1. Property Assessed to Negroes in Selected Maryland Counties, 1783–1818 — 19
2. Account: Mary Carrol to Dr. W. B. Cooper, 1855–1860 — 41
3. Rural Free Negro Realty Owners in the Upper South, 1850/1860 — 75
4. Urban Free Negro Realty Owners in the Upper South, 1850/1860 — 76
5. Rural Free Negro Realty Owners in the Lower South, 1850/1860 — 81
6. Occupations among Upper and Lower South Black Real Estate Owners, 1850/1860 — 82
7. Prosperous Farmers and Planters in Louisiana, 1850/1860 — 120
8. Real Estate Holdings among Affluent Free Persons of Color in the Upper and Lower South, 1850/1860 — 125
9. Rural Negro Landowners in the Lower South, 1870 — 146
10. Black Realty Owners in the Lower South, 1860/1870 — 148
11. Black Property Owners in the Lower South, 1860/1870 — 151
12. Rural Negro Landowners in the Upper South, 1870 — 153
13. Occupations among Upper and Lower South Urban Black Realty Owners, 1860/1870 — 156
14. Black Realty Owners in the Upper South, 1860/1870 — 158
15. Black Property Owners in the Upper South, 1860/1870 — 159
16. Black Farm Owners in the Lower South, 1870–1910 — 164
17. Black Homeowners in the Lower South, 1870–1910 — 170
18. Black Farm Owners in the Upper South, 1870–1910 — 174
19. Black Homeowners in the Upper South, 1870–1910 — 180
20. Prosperous Blacks in the Lower and Upper South, 1860–1870 — 206
21. Leading Black Wealth-holding Parishes in Louisiana, 1860–1913 — 273
22. Number of Owners and Acres of Farm Land Owned by Negroes in 56 Typical Counties of Georgia, by Classified Size of Holdings, 1899 — 274

23. Number of Owners and Assessed Value of Farm Land Owned by Negroes in 56 Counties of Georgia, by Classified Value of Holdings, 1899   276
24. Number of Owners and Assessed Value of Town and City Real Estate Owned by Negroes in 56 Typical Counties of Georgia, by Classified Value of Holdings, 1899   278
25. Distribution Analysis of Black Real Estate Owners in the Lower South, 1850   282
26. Distribution Analysis of Black Real Estate Owners in the Upper South, 1850   282
27. Distribution Analysis of Black Real Estate Owners in the Lower South, 1860   283
28. Distribution Analysis of Black Real Estate Owners in the Upper South, 1860   283
29. Distribution Analysis of Black Real Estate Owners in the Lower South, 1870   284
30. Distribution Analysis of Black Real Estate Owners in the Upper South, 1870   284
31. Occupations among Propertied Blacks in the South, 1850 and 1860   285
32. Occupations among Upper and Lower South Black Real Estate Owners, 1860/1870   286
33. Real Estate Holdings among Blacks and Mulattoes, 1850   287
34. Real Estate Holdings among Men and Women, 1850   288
35. Total Estate Holdings among Blacks and Mulattoes, 1860   289
36. Total Estate Holdings among Men and Women, 1860   291
37. Total Estate Holdings among Blacks and Mulattoes, 1870   292
38. Total Estate Holdings among Men and Women, 1870   293
39. A Profile of Prosperous Blacks: Black Wealth Holders with Minimum Estates of $20,000, Acquiring Bulk of Estate from 1870s to 1915   303

Figures

1. Leading Black Wealth-holding Parishes in Louisiana, 1860   119
2. Rural Black Realty Owners in the South, 1850–70   154
3. Total Value of Black-owned Real Estate, Upper and Lower South, 1850–70   158
4. Black Home Ownership in Arkansas, 1870–1910   171
5. Black-owned Farm Property in Virginia, 1891–1915   175
6. Percentage of Black-owned Farms by States in the South, 1910   176

Acknowledgments

A number of individuals and institutions have provided assistance in bringing this study to print. My debt to scholars in the field is a large one; Ira Berlin, John Blassingame, Robert Calhoon, John Hope Franklin, Richard Fuke, Willard Gatewood, Jr., Barry Hirsch, Robert Kenzer, Lester Lamon, Randall Miller, Sydney Nathans, Howard Rabinowitz, Lee Soltow, Walter Weare, and David Whitten generously answered questions, shared advice, and provided information. A list of the archivists, librarians, and courthouse employees who guided me to new material would require several pages, but their spirit of concern and friendly assistance added greatly to this book. Especially helpful in this regard were Rosemary Estes of the Museum of Early Southern Decorative Arts, Conely Edwards of the Virginia State Library, Michelle Neal of the University of North Carolina-Chapel Hill library, and James Thompson, Robert Gaines, and Gaylor Callahan of the University of North Carolina—Greensboro library. Our Academic Computer Center's Marlene Pratto, Dennis Funk, James Penny, Terri Kirchen, and Diane Case, and the University's Research Council, which provided eight separate grants (1978 to 1985), assisted this project in various ways. My three research assistants, Jeryl Rice, Mary Best, and James Lomax, gave unstintingly of their time and effort, especially in the tedious jobs of double-checking data lists and correcting footnote citations. The American Philosophical Society and the American Association for State and Local History provided financial assistance for travel, copying, and microfilming. A Senior Fellowship for College Teachers from the National Endowment for the Humanities allowed me the luxury of a year's uninterrupted writing. Richard N. Current read and offered many helpful suggestions for an early draft of this work. August Meier rigorously critiqued several drafts of the manuscript and assisted greatly in its structure, clarity, and organization. It is much better for their close scrutiny. My wife, Patricia, remained patient and supportive throughout, despite her own careers as a teacher, graduate student, and mother of four.

List of Abbreviations
and Short Titles

AER American Economic Review
AH Agricultural History
AHCSA Arkansas Historical Commission State Archives (Little
    Rock, Arkansas)
AHQ Arkansas Historical Quarterly
AHR American Historical Review
arph average real property holdings
ateh average total estate holdings
BHR Business History Review
BTHC Barker Texas History Center (Austin, Texas)
BTWP Booker T. Washington Papers
CC College of Charleston (Charleston, South Carolina)
CWH Civil War History
DB Dun and Bradstreet (New York City)
DU Duke University (Durham, North Carolina)
erph estimated real property holdings
etph estimated total property holdings
FC Filson Club (Louisville, Kentucky)
FSA Florida State Archives (Tallahasse, Florida)
GDAH Georgia Department of Archives and History (Atlanta,
    Georgia)
GHQ Georgia Historical Quarterly
GHS Georgia Historical Society (Savannah, Georgia)
GPO Government Printing Office
HNOC Historic New Orleans Collection

JAH Journal of American History
JMC-UMSHS Joint Manuscript Collection—University of Missouri and State Historical Society (Columbia, Missouri)
JMH Journal of Mississippi History
JNH Journal of Negro History
JSH Journal of Southern History
JSoH Journal of Social History
LC Library of Congress
LH Louisiana History
LHQ Louisiana Historical Quarterly
LSA Louisiana State Archives (Baton Rouge, Louisiana)
LSU Louisiana State University
MDAH Mississippi Department of Archives and History (Jackson, Mississippi)
MESDA Museum of Early Southern Decorative Arts (Winston-Salem, North Carolina)
MHM Maryland Historical Magazine
MHR Missouri Historical Review
MSA Maryland State Archives (Annapolis, Maryland)
MSRC Moorland-Spingarn Research Center (Washington, D.C.)
MVHR Mississippi Valley Historical Review
NA National Archives
NCDAH North Carolina Division of Archives and History (Raleigh, North Carolina)
NCHR North Carolina Historical Review
NOPL New Orleans Public Library
RACS Records of the American Colonization Society
RCC Records of the Claims Commissioners
RCPC Records of the County Probate Court
RG Record Group
RIR Records of Internal Revenue
RPPC Records of the Parish Probate Court
RSCDTC Records of the South Carolina Direct Tax Commission
RTD Records of the Treasury Department
SCDAH South Carolina Department of Archives and History (Columbia, South Carolina)
SCHM South Carolina Historical Magazine
SCL South Caroliniana Library (Columbia, South Carolina)
SHC Southern Historical Collection (Chapel Hill, North Carolina)
te total estate
THQ Tennessee Historical Quarterly
TI Tuskegee Institute (Tuskegee, Alabama)
trph total real property holdings
TSLA Tennessee State Library and Archives (Nashville, Tennessee)

TU Tulane University (New Orleans, Louisiana)
USMSAC United States Manuscript Agriculture Census
USMSPC United States Manuscript Population Census
USMSSC United States Manuscript Slave Census
VMHB Virginia Magazine of History and Biography
VSL Virginia State Library (Richmond, Virginia)
WMQ William and Mary Quarterly

Introduction

"Few today are interested in Negro history," W. E. B. Du Bois wrote in 1939, "because they feel the matter already settled: the Negro has no history."[1] Since Du Bois made that statement the study of Negro history has undergone an astonishing transformation. Influenced by World War II and the civil rights movement and racial unrest of the 1960s, historians have produced an entire new literature about blacks, an abundance of books and articles detailing how they coped with slavery and racism, molded a unique and separate community, and fashioned a new and vibrant culture. Much of this recent scholarship has focused on the cultural differences between the races. "Upon the hard rock of racial, social, and economic exploitation and injustice," Lawrence Levine writes in *Black Culture and Black Consciousness*, "black Americans forged and nurtured a culture: they formed and maintained kinship networks, made love, raised and socialized children, built a religion, and created a rich and expressive culture in which they articulated their feelings and hopes and dreams."[2] Insightful, innovative, and imaginative, Levine and other writers have greatly expanded our understanding of black Americans. In doing so they have silenced forever the assertion made a generation and a half ago that "the Negro has no history."

However stimulating and provocative, the emphasis on a unique black culture neglects, sometimes ignores, the most significant aspect of the black experience during the nineteenth and twentieth centuries—the struggle of Negroes to enter the mainstream of American life. My own study of this subject began at the Library of Congress during the academic year 1977–78. To prepare for an investigation of "the black elite," I immersed myself in the secondary literature as well as various manuscript collections. It soon became apparent, however, that I had started up the wrong path. The term "elite," at least as applied to blacks, appeared to have a myriad of vague and conflicting usages. To some it meant light skin color, to others wealth, to still others higher education or membership in social clubs. Also unsatisfactory were other contemporary phrases—"wealthy blacks," "middle-class blacks," "upper-class blacks," "the Negro aristocracy." During this time, I found myself referring again and again to several older studies (written between 1924 and 1943) that focused on black property ownership. These pioneer works—Carter G. Woodson's *Free Negro Owners of Slaves in the United States in 1830*, J. H. Harmon, Jr., Arnett G. Lindsay, and Carter Woodson's *The Negro as a Business Man*, Luther Porter Jackson's *Free Negro Labor and Property Holding in Virginia, 1830–1860* and "The Virginia Free Negro Farmer and Property Owner, 1830–1860," and John Hope Franklin's *The Free Negro in North Carolina, 1790–1860* and "The Free Negro in the Economic Life of Ante-Bellum North Carolina"—emphasized the great determination of blacks, despite many obstacles, to accumulate property. But, burdened by heavy teaching loads and lacking both research support and modern technological tools, the scholars of that time examined only two states, North Carolina and Virginia, and relied either on the United States census returns or on local tax records. What would a thorough analysis of other states, using both federal and county records, newspapers, manuscript collections, and other sources, reveal about black Americans?[3]

In the summer of 1979 I secured a microfilm copy of the 1850 population census of Louisiana—where a large group of propertied Negroes had resided—and used it to make up a list of real estate owners. I then set out to investigate local parish records. It was a disheartening experience. The New Orleans records had recently been moved from the district court building to the basement of the public library, and after three days rummaging through disorganized packets of estate papers, I reluctantly left without having found more than a half-dozen pertinent documents. In Plaquemines, Pointe Coupée, St. Landry, Natchitoches, and other parishes, the estate papers were in good order, but the travel and research proved exhausting, almost overwhelming. By the end of the summer, I seriously considered abandoning the project altogether.

Still, I could not rid myself of the feeling that an analysis of property ownership held the key to a better understanding of the black experience in America. And questions kept recurring: How significant was the acquisition of property for blacks? Did they, like most Americans, equate ownership with power, prestige, and status? Did property have anything to do with Du Bois's comment: "It is astonishing how the African has integrated himself into American civilization?" Again surveying the secondary literature I discovered that several older state monographs, a few recent urban investigations, statistical studies by economist and historian Lee Soltow, and census office publications provided comparative information for selected cities in the North and Northwest as well as for a few states and isolated counties in the South. Yet there was no general study of the subject, nor was there any analysis of ownership in the South as a whole (where 90 percent of the Negro population resided until World War I) during the vitally important middle period of the nineteenth century—the transition from slavery to freedom.[4]

Since the manuscript census returns for 1850, 1860, and 1870 provide fairly accurate property estimates (real 1850; real and personal, 1860 and 1870) as well as the racial identities (B = black; M = mulatto; W = white) for each head of household in the United States (excluding slaves), I began the time-consuming task of systematically combing the population schedules (on microfilm), recording the names, ages, occupations, and property holdings (along with eleven other variables) for blacks who owned at least $100 worth of real and/or personal property and who lived in the fifteen slaveholding (and former slaveholding) states and the District of Columbia. (A sampling procedure was used for owners of property worth $100 to $900 in 1870; see An Essay on Sources and Methodology.) These data for a total of nearly 41,000 names were then typed into the VAX (computer) and analyzed with SPSSX (Statistical Package for the Social Sciences) and SAS (Statistical Analysis System). By using these programs, I was able to obtain information about wealth among blacks and mulattoes according to age, occupation, location, and sex and to compare these data from one decade to the next.

Besides the manuscript census returns—which consistently identify a property owner's race—other records have been consulted: numerous state tax assessment lists for South Carolina (1865–67) and Louisiana (1893–1916), county tax assessment books, and when available, wills, probate records, estate inventories, and final judgments (see An Essay on Sources and Methodology). For the period after 1865, newspapers, periodicals, city directories, biographical dictionaries, manuscript collections, association records, and government documents were perused. In some cases, specific court documents were examined—land deeds, leases, mortgages, releases from mortgages, property assignments, and conveyances.

From these various sources, as well as a few secondary works, more extensive biographical information was gathered on blacks who reached the top of the economic spectrum, including name, color (black or mulatto), gender, place of residence, estimated property holdings, occupation, status at birth, color of parents, status of parents, social club membership, religious affiliation, political activity, and an individual's etph (estimated total property holdings) at various times during his or her life. These data—a Who's Who among Negro Wealth Holders—included information on, among others, 241 blacks who acquired the bulk of their estates (with minimum realty holdings of $20,000) during the last third of the nineteenth and/or the early twentieth centuries (see appendixes 6 and 7).

Preliminary results were startling. In Louisiana, for example, free Negro property owners (total number = 1,244) controlled an average of $3,646 worth of real estate in 1850. Within a decade this had risen to $4,370. Some of the real estate valuations included "slave property," which was listed in some parishes under "real" rather than "personal" property. Nevertheless, the average real estate holdings of $1,479 (including propertyless family heads) compared favorably with the average of $1,492 for white males in the nation as a whole. Though they were less likely than whites in the nation to own at least some real estate (34 percent to 43 percent), and though they owned less realty on average than other southerners, Louisiana's free people of color were slightly better off in economic terms than white adult males in the Northeast (mean real estate = $1,461) and the Northwest ($1,284) and nearly twice as well off as foreign born Americans ($833).[5] Even when the analysis was shifted to other Deep South states it was difficult to accept the contention of some historians that antebellum free persons of color in that region were "the poorest of the poor," "desperately poor," and mired in poverty.[6] The average real estate holdings among the nearly 7,000 free Negro families in the lower states stood at $742 in 1850, three-fourths of the average for white Americans. In South Carolina, about the same proportion of free black family heads (54 percent) as of whites in the nation owned property in 1860.

In some sections of the Deep South, of course, free persons of color were members of a highly privileged group, but in the fifteen southern states and the District of Columbia, approximately one of five free black heads of family owned at least some real property (total number = 9,640) in 1860, while slightly more than two out of five whites did so. By 1870, approximately 11,000 Negroes had acquired at least $1,000 in real and/or personal holdings and another 157,000 (according to the sample) had managed to move out of the propertyless group. A total of 43,268 had become landowners. By 1910, a generation and a half after freedom, this had risen more than tenfold, with 426,449 Negroes in the South owning their own farms or homes (out of approximately 1,741,019 families) and others owning various tracts of rural land and undeveloped city lots.

The significance of this study, however, transcends the statistical and biographical data on property holders. The how much, and where, and when tell only part of the story, although the evidence strongly suggests that in their determination to secure an economic stake, tens of thousands of blacks—far from being landless peasants—made impressive gains in their efforts to acquire land and personal holdings. Its importance lies in a fuller appreciation of American values and their impact on the lives of a people torn from their native land and thrust into an alien, sometimes hostile, environment. By focusing on propertied blacks themselves—their values, attitudes, ideals, their relations with whites—and by examining those who rose to the top of the economic ladder, as well as those who aspired to do so but failed, we can perhaps better comprehend the ambiguous tension between race consciousness and the strong impulse of so many blacks to "integrate" themselves into American civilization.

CHAPTER ONE

Beginnings:
Africans in a New Land

Only a generation ago the study of southern blacks during the seventeenth and eighteenth centuries was still in its infancy. The Johns Hopkins University studies on slavery notwithstanding, the historiography of the British colonies in America was still dominated by the prodigious works of Charles M. Andrews, who chronicled the political, economic, and social development of colonial America with a rigor and reliance on primary sources which are still greatly admired even today. But Andrews and his contemporaries virtually ignored blacks. They considered race prejudice, Negroes, and slavery of minor importance. During the past two decades this void has been substantially eliminated, as historians have examined the beginnings of slavery during the colonial era, shown how the institution developed differently in different colonies and in different sections of the same colony, and emphasized how the expanding economies in the southern colonies, and later states, relied primarily on the labor of enslaved Africans. In a sense the more recent scholars were simply viewing the period from the perspective of those who lived and worked in the South at the time. By the dawn of the nineteenth century, most observers who journeyed through any section of the region stretching from Chesapeake Bay, southward along the coastal plain, and westward to the mouth of the Mississippi River, were struck by how the life and labor of the region seemed to be dominated by blacks.

One of the most exciting and potentially most fruitful areas of inquiry in recent years has been an analysis of the interaction between whites and blacks, how slaves adjusted to their new environments, how white colonists came to rely on the expertise of Africans in certain areas, and how blacks maintained a cultural continuity with their past while adopting new values and attitudes more compatible with their New World experiences. These changes were slow and some-times almost imperceptible to contemporaries, but the "acculturation" process continued from generation to generation, as blacks arrived from the British West Indies, various other islands in the Caribbean, and West Africa, mingling with those who had been on American soil for many years. Our understanding of these complex processes of cultural change has only begun, but despite the brutal and oppressive nature of colonial slavery, some blacks were able to do more than merely survive in a new environment. They discovered ways to alleviate their drudgery, attain a measure of independence, and in some locations, even loosen the shackles of bondage. As the plantation system expanded, port cities grew to accommodate the trade among the colonies and the mother country and the West Indies. To service the hundreds of ships arriving each year, black workers were employed as shipwrights, ropemakers, and coopers. Gradually, some slaves entered the higher trades, working as gold beaters, silversmiths, and cabinetmakers. In the low country of South Carolina and Georgia, female slaves acquired control over much of the marketing network, selling slave-grown produce along the docks or through the streets of port cities. A few blacks attained the status of free men or women or paid their owners a portion of their earnings in return for de facto freedom.

Yet, circumstances varied considerably in different parts of the South, in rural and urban areas, in the British colonies and the areas colonized by the French and the Spanish. In some sections of the tide-water of Virginia, the low country in the Carolinas, and, by the early nineteenth century, the sugar parishes of Louisiana, only a minority of the black population came in daily contact with whites, but in towns and cities, and among those who worked as skilled hands and house servants on large plantations, just the opposite was true. Differences also evolved within the free Negro population, with the emergence of an urban, increasingly light-skinned elite in the Gulf region and South Carolina, and a rural, primarily dark-skinned free population in Virginia, Maryland, and other sections of the upper region. Similarly, there were regional contrasts among black freemen and women who entered the slaveholding class, with some acquiring relatives and friends and others purchasing laborers. This chapter traces the significant changes that occurred in the attitudes and lives of blacks as they adjusted to America by focusing on their changing views toward property ownership. It begins in West Africa, moves to seventeenth-century Virginia, proceeds to eighteenth-century South Carolina and Louisiana, and ends at the dawn of the nineteenth century. It seeks to understand the importance of property in the lives of those who were in the process of becoming Afro-Americans.[1]

From Africa to the New World

"Our land is uncommonly rich and fruitful, and produces all kinds of vegetables in great abundance," Olaudah Equiano, an Ibo from West Africa, said of his native village. "We have plenty of Indian corn, and vast quantities of cotton and tobacco." Deliciously flavored pineapples grew without cultivation, as did various spices, including pepper, while his people enjoyed gums, honey, and a great variety of other fruits. "All our industry," he said, "is exerted to improve those blessings of nature." The women of his village engaged in spinning, weaving, dying, sewing, cooking, and making pottery; the men "manufactured" tools—axes, hoes, shovels, "beaks" (pointed iron digging spears)—worked in the fields, and served as "Embrenche," or village elders and chiefs. The Ibos were known for their energy and intelligence, their dancing, singing, and poetry. They had little use for money. Nature provided them with most of their needs. Everyone— men, women, and children—helped clear the land and harvest the crops. "Our tillage is exercised in a large plain or common, some hours walk from our dwellings, and all the neighbours resort thither in a body," he recalled. "Everyone contributes something to the common stock."

In 1756, at the age of eleven, Equiano was kidnapped, transported to the coast, and carried on board a slave ship bound for the New World. It was a shocking experience, seeing white-skinned people for the first time—their long hair, odd complexions, strange voices—and witnessing his fellow blacks chained together, "their countenances expressing dejection and sorrow." The putrid smell of the tubs and the fetid air below deck made him so sick that he could not eat for several days. He often prayed that his "last friend," death, would end his suffering. But Equiano survived his ordeal to became one of the few blacks ever to write about the journey from Africa to the New World. In America, everything seemed different, the people, the houses, the cities, the dress, the manners, the mores, even slavery itself. In the Caribbean, he said, blacks were branded, chained, and tortured— "The iron muzzle, thumbscrews, etc. are so well known as not to need a description, and were sometimes applied for the slightest faults."[2]

Olaudah Equiano's wrenching experiences were shared by some ten million other Africans who found themselves torn from their native land and carried to the New World as slaves. They began their journey somewhere in the vast region stretching from the Senegal River, west and south along the great savannah and rain forests, to the mouth of the Congo River and far beyond, an area of enormous geographic and ethnic diversity, inhabited by the Fulani, Mandinka, Wolof, Ashanti, Fanti, Ibo, Yoruba, Bakongo, Nsundi, Ngala, and numerous other peoples. Despite their remarkable cultural and linguistic differences (more than three hundred languages were spoken), one common thread bound them together—the communal life of their villages. Whether Wolof, Hausa, or Bakongo, from birth through puberty, marriage, maturity, and old age, they passed through various rites and rituals binding themselves spiritually and culturally to others in their communities. Even in death they entered the spiritual world of "the living dead," remaining "alive" so long as they were remembered by one of their neighbors. This cultural web binding people together dominated every aspect of life among blacks in their native land—social, economic, political, and religious; it was, as historian Nathan Huggins has said, "a common imperative pulling all together to an insistent command that was above and beyond the individual self, the family, or the clan."[3]

Perhaps no concept was more alien to their African heritage than the idea of private ownership of property. Even such leaders as Sonni Ali and Askia Mohammed, who reigned over the great kingdom of Songhai, with its enormous wealth and power, did not perceive of themselves as *landowners* but rather as administrators over communal village properties. "Landed tenure in Africa is free," Virginia-born free black Martin R. Delany noted after visiting Liberia and Abeokuta, home of the Egba people, "the occupant selecting as much as he can cultivate, holding it so long as he uses it, but [he] cannot convey it to another." Jamaican-born mulatto Robert Campbell, Delany's companion who settled in Lagos, made the same observation: "every individual enjoys the right of taking unoccupied land, as much as he can use, whenever and wherever he pleases." But it was deemed his property only so long as he cultivated it; "after that it is again common property." In their homeland nearly everything was held in common—farmland, pasture, livestock, tools—and nearly everyone, as among the Ibos of Equiano's youth, worked to provide sustenance for those who lived in the village. Until the coming of Europeans, West Africans had little concept of the ownership of private property.[4]

Gradually, however, New World blacks began to drift away from their old ideas about the land and communal property. The transformation occurred everywhere slavery existed in the Americas. Even on isolated plantations of the Caribbean, where Africans continued to arrive in large numbers, slaves began to express their individuality through the acquisition of material wealth and property. "Torn from societies that had not yet entered into the capitalistic world, and thrust into settings that were profoundly capitalistic in character on the one hand, yet rooted in the need for unfree labor on the other," anthropologist Sidney Mintz writes, "the slaves saw liquid capital not only as a means to secure freedom, but also as a means to attach their paternity—and hence, their identity as persons—to something even their masters would have to respect."[5] It was not merely observing Europeans and envying their wealth and comfort, or seeing how their accumulations had made them independent and powerful, or even accepting new definitions for success and self-esteem, although all of these probably influenced to one degree or another the changing attitudes of blacks. In the brutal and exploitative new setting they found that survival depended not so much on communal harmony as on individual ingenuity. Even those who could never relinquish the hope of someday returning to the life they had been forced to abandon realized that perhaps the only way to make their dream a reality was to make adaptations to their new land.

Slaves in the Southern Colonies

In the southern mainland British colonies—Maryland, Virginia, South Carolina, later North Carolina and Georgia—black attitudes toward property holding also changed, but these changes came slowly and unevenly, depending on the period, conditions of labor, and number of blacks arriving directly from Africa. During the seventeenth century, a majority of the slaves who arrived in the colonies had already spent several years, sometimes longer, in the Caribbean, primarily on the islands of Barbados, Jamaica, and Antigua. They had already adjusted to the New World environment and had seen how their masters valued "liquid capital." Few in number, working on small farms or isolated cowpens, facing the same harsh frontier conditions and dangers from Indian or Spanish attack as their owners, they were allowed a large measure of autonomy. "The autonomy of the isolated cowpen and the freedom of movement stock raising allowed made a mockery of the total dominance that chattel bondage implied," historian Ira Berlin noted, describing the prestaple crop period in the low country of South Carolina. "Slaves set the pace of work, defined standards of workmanship, and divided labor among themselves, doubtless leaving a good measure of time for their own use." Some of them were able to convert this autonomy into actual freedom by acquiring small amounts of capital and purchasing themselves, or serving their master in such a way as to receive emancipation papers.[6]

During the eighteenth century, as planters turned to the production of staple crops and began acquiring large numbers of Africans, the lingering communal values toward property remained strong in some regions. On the largest plantations in the Chesapeake and among blacks arriving directly from Gambia, Guinea, and Angola in the Sea Islands of the Carolinas and Georgia there was a continual renewal of African ways. In both regions, African-born slaves were often put on separate plantations, assigned the most arduous jobs—clearing new land, topping and stripping tobacco, damming and planting rice—and sometimes rarely came in contact with creole slaves (those born on American soil) or even whites. Even toward the end of the century, many blacks who labored on the rice plantations of the Lower South remained "physically separated and psychologically estranged from the Anglo-American world and culturally closer to Africa."[7]

Yet, as recent historians have pointed out, several "black societies" emerged in various sections of the South during the period. One "society" contained those who had spent many years in the New World. Cast together with a great variety of different peoples, offered incentives—better treatment, special privileges, skilled jobs—if they mastered a new language, embraced a new religion, and learned new skills, they began to view property and its acquisition differently from when they had first arrived. Another "society" consisted of creole slaves, those born on American soil. In the Chesapeake region, where their numbers increased rapidly and whites remained a majority of the population, substantial numbers of creoles assimilated the property values of whites. In the lower regions, where the proportion of Africans remained high, a small group of native-born, urban, highly skilled, and often light-skinned Negroes embraced new attitudes. Living and working in close proximity to whites, they quickly perceived the connection between obtaining material wealth and the possibility of freedom. In all of these societies, including the one with native Africans, there was a gradual movement away from the idea that an individual could not possess his or her own property. In this respect, even on remote plantations, newly arrived slaves seemed strange to those who arrived earlier, and even stranger to those born in America.[8]

During the eighteenth century, some blacks who learned English and acquired new skills were able to loosen somewhat the shackles of

bondage. Generally, they lived and worked in towns and cities—
Baltimore, Norfolk, Williamsburg, Richmond, Wilmington, Beaufort,
Georgetown, Charles Town, Savannah—and had acquired skills as
carpenters, caulkers, coopers, and shipwrights. With fluctuating demands for their labor, these artisans were sometimes hired out by
their owners for wages. While most of their earnings went to the master, and while they could be separated from their families, or harshly
treated, they eagerly sought this type of work. At worst they would be
released from the supervision of their owners; at best they could obtain a measure of freedom. A few slaves were granted the privilege of
self-hire. They could contact potential employers, negotiate contracts,
and arrange for lodgings. Self-hired slaves usually paid "wages" to the
master. As early as 1733–34, a Charles Town, South Carolina, grand
jury criticized slaveholders for allowing their Negroes "to work out by
the Week," and "bring in a certain Hire" which was "not only Contrary to a Law now subsisting, but a Great Inlet to Idleness, Drunk-
enness and other Enormities." In 1782, a group of Virginia planters
complained that "many persons have suffered their slaves to go about
to hire themselves and pay their masters for their hire," and as a result
"certain slaves" lived free from their master's control. Some blacks
were so eager to work on their own that they neglected their regular
duties, became truculent, or lied about their activities. Two ambitious
Charles Town bricklayers, Tony and Primus, who spent their days
building a church under the supervision of their master, secretly
rented themselves to local builders at night and on weekends.[9] In
1741, South Carolina slaveholder Elizabeth Smith complained that
her "Negro-Man Lancaster" constantly earned money which he lost
"Gaming" or at "the little Punch Houses." This was despite her notices
in the local newspaper forbidding anyone to hire him "in white washing or any other kinds of Work whatever."[10] A few years later, Annapolis physician Alexander Hamilton issued the same kind of notice for
his slave Ben, a cooper who had been allowed "to increase his trade
for his own Benefit," but now had become almost completely independent, defiantly refusing to attend to his "regular duties."[11]

Even during these early years hiring was primarily (though not exclusively) confined to towns and cities. On the sprawling plantations
adjoining the inland waterways of the South, slaves sought other
means to diminish their dependency on the master. "There is no Master almost [who] will [not] allow his Servant a parcell of clear ground
to plant some Tobacco for himself," Virginia colonist John Hammond
observed as early as 1656, "which he may husband at those idle times
he hath allowed him."[12] The size of the parcel could range from one

to four or five acres, but even the smallest plot, Georgia planter Johann Martin Bolzius asserted nearly a century later, provided incentive for slaves. "They plant their tobacco on Sundays," Bolzius explained, "and thus buy something for themselves, their wives, and children." [13] In the Carolina and Georgia low country, planters relied on the "task system"—assigning blacks certain tasks such as hoeing, planting, weeding, draining, chopping. Once slaves completed the day's tasks, they were allowed to cultivate their own crops. [14] A visitor to North Carolina in 1771 described the daily routine: every morning the master or overseer assigned the tasks; the slaves worked diligently until about one or two o'clock in the afternoon; they spent the rest of their time "working in their own private fields, consisting of 5 or 6 acres of ground, allowed them by their masters, for planting of rice, corn, potatoes, tobacco, &c." On some plantations they also raised hogs, cattle, poultry, and horses. The most industrious among them made "a great deal." "They do not plant in their fields for subsist[e]nce," the visitor explained, "but for amusement, pleasure, and profit." [15]

How could slaves earn a profit? According to the rules on some plantations, slaves could grow their own crops and raise their own livestock only if they promised to sell (or trade) them to the owner. This rule gained the force of law in South Carolina in 1740, the General Assembly requiring that each item sold be listed on an inventory which was to be signed by the plantation owner. But such a law was difficult to enforce, especially among blacks who had acquired a knowledge of the marketplace. In the area surrounding Charleston, slaves established a trading network which became so extensive that the governor of the colony and other officials demanded that punitive action be taken. "We present as a very great Grievance and an intolerable Hardship on the several Inhabitants of Charles Town," a group of townspeople asserted, "that Negroes are suffered to buy and sell, and be Hucksters of Corn, Pease, Fowls &c. whereby they watch Night and Day on the several Wharfes, and buy up many Articles necessary for the Support of the Inhabitants and make them pay an exorbitant Price for the same." These black "Regraters" practiced "great Corruption and Fraud throughout the whole Province." [16] The same type of network sprang up in the Chesapeake region where bondsmen sold chickens, hogs, sheep, and produce to peddlers and merchants. One Prince George County, Maryland, planter lamented in 1770 that it was virtually impossible for him to raise sheep and hogs since the "Negroes are constantly killing them to sell to some white people who are little better than themselves." [17] In North Carolina, whites mounted a vigorous campaign to halt slave "dealing and Trafficking," enacting, in 1741, a strict law forbidding slaves to buy, sell, trade, barter, or borrow "any Commodities whatsoever" or to raise horses, cattle, or hogs "on any Pretense whatsoever." Similar statutes were passed in 1779, 1787, and 1788.[18]

From Slavery to Freedom

Most blacks who achieved a degree of autonomy during the colonial era did so as slaves. Even bondsmen who had gained a quasi-free status—by hiring their own time and arranging their own contracts—found it difficult to obtain deeds of emancipation. The law assumed that all blacks were slaves and, at least until the 1770s, few owners were willing to sign formal documents of manumission. Yet the path to freedom was never completely closed. A few blacks ran away, mingled with slaves and free Negroes in towns and cities, and eventually secured the status of freemen. Some gained the favor of a benevolent master, or performed an act of heroism, or betrayed a slave insurrection plot. Others were bought by free relatives or worked their way out of bondage by saving enough to purchase themselves. Still others were children of a white father who set them free. A few slaves received certificates of freedom from missionary and religious organizations.

As early as the 1630s (perhaps the 1620s) a few Virginia blacks had made the journey from servitude to freedom.[19] Some of the first Negroes brought to the colony were probably similar to white indentured servants who served a term of years and then received their "freedom papers." Whatever their original status, free blacks were soon acquiring land, constructing houses, building up herds of cattle and hogs, and planting crops of tobacco. By the 1650s, a number of free blacks—Sebastian Cane, Manuel Rodriggus (Emanuel Driggus), Philip Mongum, Francis Paine, Anthony Johnson, Anthony Longo, among others—had become freeholders. They spent most of their time planting, transplanting, weeding, topping, and curing tobacco, but they also raised corn, wheat, and vegetables, tended herds of livestock, constructed buildings, and cleared new land (by girdling trees). Several among them produced as much as 1,500 pounds of tobacco each year. Selling their crop for ten shillings per hundredweight, they could earn up to ten pounds sterling—this at a time when a few pounds could be traded for one hundred acres of uncleared land.[20] In a few localities, free black farmers comprised a relatively large proportion of the total black population. In Northampton County, nearly one-third of the Negroes (approximately 44 of 144) had gained their freedom by 1664, and some of these had become landowners.[21]

Hard working, self-reliant, and independent, Virginia's black free-holders of the seventeenth century were not hesitant to assert their rights as property owners and even slaveholders.[22] In 1655, Anthony Johnson, owner of a 250-acre farm, successfully petitioned the Northampton County Court for the return of a runaway slave. Johnson sued his white neighbor, Robert Parker, for detaining "one Jno Casor a Negro the plaintiffs servant under pretense that the said Jno Casor is a free man." The court ordered Parker to return the slave "unto the service of his master."[23] When another white neighbor, Philip Taylor, accused Johnson of doing less than his share in a joint crop venture, the black farmer retorted: "Now Mr. Taylor and I have devided our Corne And I am very glad of it [for] now I know myne owne. hee finds fault with mee that I doe not worke, but now I know myne owne ground and I will worke when I please and play when I please."[24] Even more defiant was Anthony Longo, who, when served with a subpoena to testify in court during the harvest season, told the deputy "shitt of your warrant." "Have I (said hee) nothinge to doe but goe to [testify], goe about your business you idle Rascall." The deputy later explained that Longo made "such noyse that I could hardly heare my owne words, reading the warrant to [him], which when I had done readeinge, the said Tony stroke att mee, and gave mee some blows."[25] As suggested by these bold acts of defiance, black farmers in early Virginia considered themselves equal to white colonists.

Black self-confidence derived primarily from the ability to acquire property. Owning sizable tracts of land, competing successfully with whites in the marketplace, building up impressive herds of livestock, and purchasing slave laborers themselves, some free black colonists acquired a sense of well-being. The importance they attached to owning property could be seen in the care with which they passed their holdings on to succeeding generations. During the 1660s, following a series of restrictive laws in Virginia designed to curtail the activities of free blacks, Anthony Johnson moved his family to Maryland. There his son John Johnson emerged as a prosperous farmer, acquiring more than 500 acres, and in 1677 his grandson, John, Jr., purchased a 44-acre farm, naming it Angola.[26] Thus, fifty-eight years after the arrival of the first slaves on American soil, a single free black family boasted three generations of property holders.

Despite this auspicious beginning, free blacks found it difficult to sustain their early gains. During the 1680s, as Chesapeake planters expanded their tobacco acreage and imported large numbers of slave laborers, whites became increasingly fearful of the free Negroes in their midst. In 1691, the Virginia Assembly banned future manumissions altogether. "And forasmuch as great inconveniences may happen to this country by setting of negroes and mulattoes free, by their either entertaining negro slaves from their masters service, or receiving stolen goods, or being grown old bringing a charge upon the country," the statute read, "*Be it enacted* . . . That no negro or mulatto to be after the end of this present session of assembly set free by any person or persons."[27] Even those emancipated for a heroic deed (such as revealing a conspiracy) were to leave the colony. In 1705, the assembly further restricted the activities of free Negroes and inaugurated penalties for any "Negro, mulatto, or Indian," bond or free, who lifted a hand against "any Christian." These proscriptive statutes, the open hostility of whites, and the arrival of shiploads of Africans weighed heavily on the minds of Negroes who had come to consider themselves essentially like white colonists. Just as these blacks had come to feel estranged from newly arriving Africans, so the whites had come to feel alienated from the resident blacks.[28]

In the midst of these changes, free blacks drifted to the edges of colonial society, eking out a subsistence as farm workers and city laborers, living in rural hovels or along disease infested docks, sometimes barely able to survive. For many, the long passage out of bondage consumed their most productive years. Others were freed only because they were too old or too feeble to work. In Maryland, in 1755, among the 742 adult free blacks in the colony, 152 were listed as "past labour or cripples."[29] Even those few who had escaped poverty and acquired small amounts of property found avenues for advancement restricted or entirely closed. With each passing decade their proportion in the general population shrank. The 1755 census in Maryland, the single enumeration of the group in colonial America, counted only 1,800 free persons of color, 2 percent of the colony's nonslave population. In Virginia, according to various estimates, their numbers ranged between 1,800 and 2,800, while in the other southern colonies they represented only a tiny fraction of the total black population.[30] By 1770, only about 6,000 southern blacks (1.5 percent of the total black population of 411,000) could claim the status of freemen.[31]

The Era of the American Revolution

The American Revolution and its aftermath ushered in a new era for free Negroes in the South. During the last quarter of the eighteenth and the early part of the nineteenth centuries tens of thousands of slaves gained the status of freemen. Some blacks fled to British lines after being offered their freedom by Lord Dunmore, the governor of Virginia; others were promised their liberty if they fought for the Patriots; still others fled to freedom when the Continental army advanced through their neighborhoods. Following the Revolution, inspired by ideals of liberty and equality, slaveholders emancipated large numbers of bondsmen. In 1782, Virginia legalized private manumissions; within eight years, the number of free Negroes in that state alone had risen to 12,766, more than twice the number in the entire South before the war.[32] In addition, following the slave revolt in Saint Domingue led by Toussaint L'Ouverture, and the persecution of the French in Cuba during a subsequent war between Spain and France, several thousand French-speaking free persons of color fled from the Caribbean to settlements along the Gulf and the lower Mississippi River valley. These events, coupled with natural increases, resulted in a substantial expansion of the free black population. By 1790, the year of the first decennial census, the free Negro population in the southern states stood at 32,357; a decade later it had risen to 61,241, and in another ten years to 108,265. Thus, within a single generation, the number of free blacks had grown an astonishing 1,700 percent; one out of every twelve blacks in the South was free.[33]

Even at this early date there were significant differences between the black population in the Upper South and Lower South.[34] In 1810, Maryland boasted 33,927 free persons of color, Virginia 30,570, North Carolina 10,266, Delaware, the District of Columbia, Kentucky, Tennessee, and Missouri, another 19,322, for a total of 94,085, or 87 percent of the South's free blacks. They lived among 810,523 slaves. Obtaining their freedom as a result of the large-scale, indiscriminate wave of manumissions which occurred during the post-Revolutionary era, they were overwhelmingly black, possessed few skills, and enjoyed limited opportunities for advancement. In contrast, Louisiana contained only 7,585 free Negroes in 1810, South Carolina 4,554, Georgia 1,801, and Mississippi 240, for a total of 14,180 in the Lower South. Living among 353,331 slaves, they represented less than 4 percent of the Negro population. Gaining their freedom as part of a highly selective manumission process, or immigrating from the Caribbean Islands, they were largely mulatto, highly skilled, and enjoyed opportunities for economic advancement.[35]

These demographic and manumission trends had a direct impact on the ability of free blacks to acquire property. In the Upper South, working as servants, laborers, farmhands, and sailors, free Negroes

Table 1. Property Assessed to Negroes in Selected Maryland
Counties, 1783–1818 (includes county's earliest assessments)

County	Year	Owners	Assessed Value
Allegany	1793	2	$181
Anne Arundel	1793	8	1,067
Baltimore County	1818	10	571
Baltimore City	1813	59	7,843
Caroline	1813	14	930
Cecil	1804	11	2,245
Charles	1783	3	237
Frederick	1798	3	50
Kent	1804	49	3,795
Montgomery	1793	7	349
Queen Anne's	1793	2	143
Somerset	1798	13	1,333
Talbot	1793	18	1,766
Worcester	1783	5	763
Total		204	$21,273

Source: James M. Wright, *The Free Negro in Maryland, 1634–1860* (New
York: Columbia University Press, 1921; reprint ed., New York: Octagon
Books, 1971), p. 184.

eked out an existence in much the same way as those who had secured
their freedom during the late colonial period. Only a few were able
to acquire even modest amounts of property. In Maryland, the state
with the second largest number of free blacks according to the 1790
census (and the only Upper South state with race-specific tax assessment data for this early period), surveys of seven counties in 1783
and 1793 revealed only 45 propertied individuals among a free black
population of more than 3,000. Their total holdings were assessed at
$4,500. A 1798 survey of Frederick and Somerset counties showed
only 16 property owners in a free black population of 1,059, and these
16 had an average assessment of only $86. In all, according to the
earliest Maryland assessments, only 204 Negroes owned property assessed at $21,273, or $104 per wealth holder.[36]

In the Lower South, often directly related to whites or with white
antecedents, and working as carpenters, coopers, joiners, ship's caulkers, and in some instances as cabinetmakers, goldsmiths, and wheelwrights, free Negroes had better opportunities for economic advancement. In Charleston District, even before the American Revolution, a
few black artisans had begun to acquire small amounts of property.

In 1750, one Negro homeowner and builder had advertised in a local newspaper that he could undertake "all manner of carpenter's or joyner's work, or any buildings that shall be thought proper to be offered to him; and, as he is a free man, he promises, that whosoever shall please to employ him, shall find not only their work well done and handsomely finish'd, but [done] with great fidelity, justice and dispatch." In subsequent years, property-owning black craftsmen in the city included brickmaker Thomas Cole, wheelwright John Lamput, house builder John Thompson, ship carpenter David Wilson, cabinetmaker John Gough (also spelled Goff and Goffe), and carpenters Richard Peronneau, William Johnston, James Mitchell, Robert Baldwin, John Francis, and Richard Holloway.[37] Following the Revolution, as trade between the North, the Chesapeake region, and the Caribbean increased, small groups of property-owning free Negro artisans could be found in towns and cities all along the lower Atlantic coast—in Wilmington, Beaufort, Georgetown, and Savannah, as well as in the Gulf region's port cities of Pensacola, Mobile, and New Orleans. Taking advantage of their close relationship with whites, the less prejudicial racial attitudes among Spanish and French settlers, and their extremely small numbers, a few Negroes opened retail stores, mercantile establishments, restaurants, grocery stores, or became what amounted to contractors and builders. One French visitor to New Orleans in 1802 observed that "a great number" of "free mulattoes" had learned special skills as artisans. Quite a few had established small businesses, and a number of them had begun to accumulate property.[38]

Even during the late eighteenth century, a few free persons of color, especially in South Carolina and Louisiana, boasted fairly large real estate holdings. Most of them were direct descendants of whites who had granted them large tracts of land, but a few were skilled urban blacks who had gradually acquired plantations in the countryside. Charleston resident John Williams, probably the grandson of Nathaniel Williams, one of the first black landowners in the state, was listed in local court records in 1773 as a "carpenter and planter." He had, sixteen years before, purchased 400 acres on the Santee River in Craven County.[39] During the 1780s, former slave James Pendarvis, the son of a white planter and slave woman, owned a 3,250 acre estate in St. Paul's Parish. Cabinetmaker and landowner John Gough purchased 227 acres in Christ Church Parish as well as several buildings in Charleston. In 1781, during the British occupation (1780–82), he leased a mercantile building to Emanuel Abrahams, a Jewish merchant, for £350 "current money of Great Britain." Later, he bought two large tracts of farmland in Craven County—one of 642 acres and an adjoining one of 1,042 acres. James Mitchell, who lived above his carpenter's shop in Charleston, became so prosperous that he sought (in the *City-Gazette and Daily Advertiser*) to rent a six-room house with stables and outbuildings. "A Place in the suburbs, with a little Garden," he explained, "would be preferred."[40]

A similar group of property owners emerged during the late eighteenth and early nineteenth centuries in Louisiana. Usually of Spanish or French and Negro ancestry, they purchased land, buildings, residential homes, and other property. A few operated small businesses. In New Orleans, Juana and Pedro Viejo, of Negro-Spanish heritage, owned and operated a dry goods store specializing in thread, buttons, ready-made clothing, and other items. Besides her portion of their joint real estate holdings, Juana accumulated an estate of 800 silver pesos which she willed to various heirs. In several rural parishes, including St. Landry, Iberville, West Baton Rouge, and Natchitoches, free persons of color entered the planter class. An 1802 inventory of the holdings of West Baton Rouge planter Jean Baptiste Bienville (whose name suggested his connection with an early French governor of Louisiana) included "A plantation" containing twelve arpents (slightly less than twelve acres) fronting on the Mississippi River and forty arpents in depth, complete with fences, wells, outbuildings, a warehouse, "negro cabins," kitchen, and a "medium sized house." Along with cattle, horses, tools, and slaves, Bienville's estate was appraised at nearly 14,000 pesos, a sizable sum at the time.[41]

As had been the case among black freeholders in seventeenth-century Virginia, property owners in the Lower South during these early years became increasingly independent, self-confident, and self-assured. They too felt a sense of security. Even in states previously under British control, where they had never possessed political or citizenship rights, propertied blacks asserted themselves as partners in their communities. When they felt they were being treated unfairly, or their property was being put in jeopardy, they voiced their opposition, sometimes to the highest government authority. In 1791, bricklayer Thomas Cole, and butchers Peter Bassnett Mathews and Mathew Webb, of Charleston, petitioned the South Carolina Senate about their inability to sue whites who owed them money. "Your Memorialists have been and are considered Free Citizens of this State [and] hope to be treated as such," they explained, "[but] are deprived of the Rights and Privileges of Citizens by not having it in their power to give Testimony on Oath in prosecutions on behalf of the State from which cause many Culprits have escaped the punishment due to their atrocious Crimes, nor can they give their Testimony in recovering Debts due to them, . . . whereby they are subject to great losses and repeated Injuries without any means of redress." They believed that they should possess the same rights as other South Carolinians because they were hard-working and industrious persons of property (see Appendix 2).[42]

Although the rejection of the Cole-Mathews-Webb petition reflected the difficult legal position of propertied free blacks in South Carolina, along the Gulf coast and in Louisiana, free persons of color could point to laws and institutions that promised them better protection in the possession of property. While not always enforced, the French *La code noir*, extended in practice by the Spanish in *Las siete partidas*, promised free blacks the same rights and immunities as those enjoyed by other subjects of the crown: they could sue and be sued, petition the government for redress of grievances, and testify in court against whites. One Spanish statute, passed in 1795, said that free Negroes should enjoy the same advantages as other colonists in acquiring land and other property. They "may not be molested in the possession of their property, injured, or ill-treated under the penalties provided by laws for the safety and security of white persons." These were indeed unique privileges, existing nowhere in British North America, and during the early nineteenth century some of them were gradually withdrawn. But despite restrictive statutes in subsequent years, these Spanish and French traditions continued, giving free persons of color in parts of the Lower South unique opportunities for economic advancement.[43]

Early Black Slave Ownership

One opportunity for advancement was through the ownership of slaves. As early as 1646–47, Virginia's Anthony Johnson had acquired a servant named John Casor who, according to several early court documents, was his slave for life. During the colonial period, some black slaveholders were probably benevolent in their intentions. Acquiring members of their families or loved ones, and unable to free them because of laws requiring freed slaves to leave the colony, they held them in nominal bondage. A few free Negroes made remarkable sacrifices and paid substantial amounts of money to acquire relatives. By the late eighteenth century, however, a small group of profit-oriented black slaveholders was emerging in the South, especially in South Carolina, and along the Gulf Coast. Even some of those who had earlier acquired wives, children, mothers, fathers, and various other family members now began buying blacks to work on their farms or in their shops. South Carolina bricklayer Thomas Cole, for example, bought his wife and children through a white intermediary in 1761, but a short time later Cole purchased two domestic servants and an apprentice bricklayer. Other free blacks acquired stock minders, day laborers, artisans, cooks, and haulers.[44]

Precise data concerning black slaveholding during this early period are lacking, but it is apparent that black ownership of other blacks quickly became fairly widespread in the Lower South. Most of these owners were urban artisans or small businessmen who purchased skilled slaves to assist them in their various business enterprises. Among the approximately 155 free Negro families in Charleston District, South Carolina, at the time of the first United States census (1790), nearly one-third (49) had entered the slaveholding class. They owned a total of 277 bondsmen and women. Similarly in Savannah, Pensacola, Mobile, and New Orleans, free persons of color who had established small shops and stores, or who worked as carpenters or coopers, purchased slave laborers, joiners, caulkers, and stavemakers. By the time of statehood in 1812, a number of free Negroes in the Crescent City not only managed successful businesses but also owned small gangs of slave workers.[45]

Even though most free black slave owners during this early period were urban craftsmen and shopkeepers, most of the slaves owned by free blacks lived in rural areas on large plantations. As early as the 1780s and 1790s, a few free persons of color in the lower states and territories had begun to acquire large farms and plantations. They usually received their original landholdings as well as some of their slaves from their white fathers or white relatives, but those who survived into the early decades of the nineteenth century were often capable businessmen and astute planters. Most of them were accepted by their white neighbors as persons of wealth and prestige. In 1786, James Pendarvis, a planter in St. Paul's Parish, Charleston District, South Carolina, owned a 3,250-acre plantation and 113 blacks. A foreign visitor to his estate was astonished that a former slave could have acquired such wealth and achieved such acceptance by whites. Pendarvis had married a white woman and had given his daughter's hand in marriage to a white man.[46] While few could equal Pendarvis's holdings (indeed he was among the largest individual black slave owners in American history), Georgetown District rice planters John Holman, Jr., Samuel Holman, John Gardner, and Elias Collins, and in Louisiana, Iberville Parish cotton planter Zachari Honoré, and St. Landry Parish slaveholder Jean Baptiste Meullion, had either acquired sizable gangs of slave laborers or had begun to purchase what would eventually become large plantation work gangs. Thus, even during these early years, free persons of color in the lower states, like their white neighbors, were purchasing fieldhands, house servants, and skilled blacks for purely economic reasons.[47]

Profit-oriented free Negro slave ownership was far more prevalent in the Lower than in the Upper South during the late eighteenth and early nineteenth centuries.[48] Indeed, with a few exceptions, free blacks in the upper states lacked the economic resources to expand their holdings in the same manner as the planters of the lower states. They were less often directly related to whites and only rarely received large estates from whites even when they were direct descendants. While most Upper South free Negro slaveholders purchased members of their own families or loved ones, even this could and often did reveal the ambiguous and ironic nature of blacks owning other blacks.[49]

This was perhaps nowhere more clearly demonstrated than in the case of Baltimore blacksmith Jacob Guillard who had built up a comfortable estate with the assistance of slaves he had acquired over a period of more than a decade. A harsh taskmaster, Guillard was constantly plagued with rebellious bondsmen. "RAN away, on Sunday the 19th instant, from the subscriber, living near the Blue Ball, above Old-Town," Guillard announced in 1795 through the columns of a local newspaper, "a Mulatto boy, named John Chapman, about 5 feet 7 or 8 inches high, round shouldered, and has a slovenly walk, down look, and is apt to stammer when sharply spoken to."[50] The "mulatto boy" was quickly apprehended and returned, but a decade later another of Guillard's slaves made a successful break for freedom. Guillard described the runaway as "a brownish yellow Man, named Jacob Cokkey: he sometimes calls himself *Jacob Vanlear*, at other times *Jacob Guillard*. He is about 33 years of age, 5 feet 9 or 10 inches high, strait made, and well-proportioned, flat visage and full eyes, and has short nappy hair. He in general tries to speak very politely when spoke to, and can affect a smile at any time." Guillard explained that he still owed $510 on the purchase price of the slave; if forced to pay such an amount he would lose nearly everything he owned. Only then did he reveal a startling fact: the runaway was his own son. "The said man has gone off with an intention to compel me to pay the sum of 510 dollars, for which sum I have given my bond and entered security, in order to extricate him from bondage," Guillard complained bitterly. "I leave it to a generous public to judge, whether such base ingratitude in a young man towards an aged father, can pass unnoticed—

who, in his declining days, is obliged to pay a sum of money which he is unable to raise without selling part of that property which he labored hard to procure against old age." Apparently the public proved to be no more generous toward Guillard than he had been toward his slave son. In the same issue as the runaway notice, the black slave owner advertised: "For Sale, AN elegant two-story frame House, and five Lots of Ground."[51]

New Attitudes toward Property

These slave owners, as well as other free Negro property holders, had moved a great distance from the attitudes of their West African ancestors. Many of those who had gained their freedom could point to a longer heritage on American soil than the white slave owners who signed their manumission papers. Some of them had acquired skills that would be advantageous to them in a profit-oriented society. And, however much the heritage of their African past might linger in their lives, they had come to recognize the importance of property ownership. In the Upper South, only small numbers of free Negroes entered the property-holding class, but those who did, as in South Carolina and the Gulf region, differed little from whites in the types of property they possessed. Their estates and inventories listed houses, lots, farm acreage, furniture, tools, wagons, livestock, clothing, boats, and books. An inventory of George Bedon's estate about 1794, in Charleston, listed a chest of carpenter's tools, a brass mortar and pestle, four pairs of unfinished window sashes, fireplace equipment, two pine and two cypress tables, a chest of drawers, pictures, books, a cupboard, crockery, six silver teaspoons, and a safe. Other free Negroes owned fishing canoes, horses, dogs, carts, wagons, buggies, jewelry, linens, guns, and fancy clothing. One free black, for instance, owned several linen shirts with his initials embroidered on them, while his wife could choose from a wardrobe of thirteen gowns—one black bombazine, six cambrics, and six dimities.[52]

Most of these property owners were members of the small, urban elite, but rural free Negroes, even in the Upper South, were anxious to possess the same types of property. Few observers understood this better than William and Mary College law professor St. George Tucker, who called for the gradual abolition of slavery in Virginia. The number of free blacks, Tucker argued in 1796, would soon surpass the number of slaves. The vast majority of them would not be able to sustain themselves in freedom and would thus become a burden on society. To solve the problem he called for the gradual abolition of slavery and the colonization of the freed slaves in the West. But how? Free Negroes were already denied political and constitutional rights; in some ways they were no better off than those in bondage. Yet they showed no inclination to emigrate. In fact, Tucker observed, they looked upon themselves as Virginians. The only way was to stifle their economic aspirations. "Let no Negroe or mulattoe" take, hold, or acquire any "estate in lands or tenements," Tucker proposed, except in the form of a lease agreement not exceeding twenty-one years. By "incapacitating them from holding lands," he believed whites could "effectually remove the foundation of ambition." Nothing ever came of Tucker's scheme, but it revealed a unique understanding of the aspirations of emancipated slaves, aspirations that ironically helped doom any emigration plan to failure from the beginning.[53]

Even among slaves who had little or no hope of ever gaining their freedom, the values and attitudes such as those brought to the New World by Olaudah Equiano began to give way to new ideas about acquiring property. With the closing of the Atlantic slave trade to the United States in 1808, only those smuggled into the country—a tiny fraction of the total black population—could claim any direct ties with Africa. By the early nineteenth century, the vast majority of blacks in the South had been born on American soil. In some areas, they lived on plantations that were relatively small (in comparison with the huge sugar estates in the Caribbean and Brazil), and a majority belonged to masters who owned fewer than fifty slaves. As in the colonial period, a significant minority lived on small farms and worked alongside their owners. Often even those on the largest plantations were offered incentives for individual effort, particularly in the cultivation of rice and cotton along the Sea Island coast of South Carolina and in Georgia, where the quite individualistic task system continued to prevail. The cooperative work ethic did not disappear, as slaves moved across the fields in a row, hoeing side by side to the rhythm of work songs, but Sea Island blacks worked at assigned tasks and looked upon their work in a highly individualistic manner. They discovered numerous ways to acquire their own property—selling produce from their garden patches, obtaining farm animals, learning a craft, and seeking to be hired out for wages. These conditions did not prevent the transmission of certain values and attitudes from West Africa, but slaves found themselves comprehending and speaking English, discarding some African rituals and customs, and accepting new values and attitudes. Even as they yearned for a return to their old ways, they found their world view, rooted in the past, being transformed;

they began to think of themselves more and more as individuals bound together by the exploitative system of human bondage.[54]

Even some blacks with direct ties to Africa embraced new attitudes toward property. "Fourteen years ago I took to wife Patience, of the *tribe of Dan*; as we both were of African origin and of a deep jetty black, it never entered my head, that my wife would have *Patience* to listen to the persuasions of a swarthy Indian," South Carolina free Negro James Jackson explained. Not only had she run off with a "swarthy Indian," but she had also carried with her the bulk of his property, including bed and bedding, "*great and little wheel, bed cord, steel yards, pot and spider*." Jackson had followed her and tried to win her back: he "piped" to her; he "mourned with her"; he bought her a beautifully colored shawl. But to no avail. "To save the wreck of my estate, I hereby forbid all persons from harbouring or trusting said patience on my account, as I will pay no debts of her contracting, after this date."[55]

The letter of a free black preacher in Savannah, Georgia, who had friends and acquaintances in West Africa, similarly suggests the power of American values. On December 23, 1800, former slave Andrew Bryan, founder of the first black Baptist church in America, explained to a high church official in London that he was well pleased with his life in America. He enjoyed good health, headed a fine family, and although sixty-three years old, boasted a "strong body." Despite his meager earnings as a minister, he had also done very well in acquiring "worldly comforts," including a house and lot in Savannah, several rental properties, a fifty-six-acre farm in the country, and eight slaves. "P.S.," Bryan concluded the letter, "I should be glad that my African friends could hear the above account of our affairs" (see appendix 1).[56]

CHAPTER TWO

Property Ownership among Slaves, 1800–1865

Much of the recent literature on American Negro slavery emphasizes "culture" and "community." Relying on previously neglected primary sources—slave autobiographies, interviews, folktales, songs, narratives—and reacting against an older view that blacks were depersonalized victims who became "Samboes," scholars have described how black culture—an emotional religion, folk songs and folktales, dances, superstitions, language, extended kinship networks, unique customs—not only gave slaves strength to survive but also "fostered cooperation, mutual assistance, and black solidarity." As one historian explains: "slaves created several unique cultural forms which lightened their burden of oppression, promoted group solidarity, provided ways for verbalizing aggression, sustaining hope, building self-esteem, and often represented areas of life largely free from the control of whites." The more their unique culture differed from that of their masters the more they were "immune from the control of whites" and the more they "gained in personal autonomy and positive self-concepts."[1]

There is little doubt that these studies have greatly expanded our understanding of slavery and its impact on the lives of bondspeople. Yet slavery was a diverse and multisided institution. It developed differently in different sections of the South, in rural and urban areas, in black belt and up-country, in the Lower and Upper South. Within each of these areas there were contrasts between slaves who worked on large plantations and those who worked on small plantations or farms, slaves who had acquired skills as artisans and those who worked as field hands and laborers, slaves who worked under the task system, the gang system, or a combination of both, and slaves who were hired out, who hired their own time, or who achieved what contemporaries called "virtual freedom," living apart from the master and earning their own living. In addition, despite the seemingly unchanging nature of the institution of slavery especially during the antebellum era, it was in reality changing and evolving with each passing decade.[2]

The dynamic nature of the South's "peculiar institution," as well as its evolution from the early years of the nineteenth century until its demise during the Civil War, can perhaps be best understood by an analysis of slave property ownership. Of course, like other aspects of slavery, much of what occurred was hidden from view, or purposely concealed by masters and slaves alike, since it was illegal for bondsmen and women to own property; and compared with what has been described as a "protopeasant economy" in the British West Indies, especially Jamaica—where slaves grew much of their own food, produced many of their own necessities, and sold their surpluses more or less freely for their own profit—the South's internal slave economy remained relatively modest. Yet, as suggested in the previous chapter, the institutions that allowed bondspeople to accumulate property had been in place for generations; and during the nineteenth century, property ownership among slaves expanded significantly, not only in the low country of the Carolinas and Georgia, but on plantations and farms, in towns and cities, in both the Lower and Upper South. In each of these locations and regions it developed out of different circumstances and traditions and took slightly different forms. In the rural Lower South it was primarily an extension of slave gardens and livestock raising, in the Upper South primarily a result of slave hiring practices, and in urban areas it evolved from slaves being allowed to hire their own time, or in some instances, live virtually as free men and women. In both regions, as the doors to legal emancipation slowly closed during the antebellum decades, some of the most talented and ambitious slaves were able to achieve quasi-free status. Property ownership among slaves, therefore, not only tells us a good deal about cultural changes occurring in the lives of Afro-Americans but illuminates the diverse, complex, multidimensional, and evolving nature of slavery in the nineteenth century South.[3]

The Domestic Slave Economy

From the early years in colonial Virginia, blacks had been allowed to plant gardens of their own. This tradition continued during the eighteenth century, and by the early nineteenth century, the practice had spread from the tidewater of Virginia, down the eastern seaboard, and westward as slavery penetrated the areas beyond the Appalachians. Its vitality was largely due to the fact that it benefited both master and slave. From the master's perspective, blacks could use the gardens to supplement their meager diet, raising sweet potatoes, pears, pumpkins, okra, eggplant, corn, beans, collards, peas, turnips, tomatoes, and other fruits and vegetables; from the slaves' perspective this was land they could call their own and do with as they pleased. One South Carolina slave explained that while his master was cruel in many ways—seldom allowing him and the others to visit relatives on neighboring plantations, strictly forbidding the construction of a black church, and threatening to whip anyone caught reading a newspaper—he gave "every one of he plantation family so much land to plant for dey garden, and den he give em every Saturday for dey time to tend dat garden."[4]

Some slaves used this land to plant and cultivate a few acres of a cash crop—rice, cotton, sugar, tobacco. At the end of the season, they sold their harvest to either the master or a nearby merchant. Georgia black Charles Houston planted rice on four acres allotted him by his master; in addition, he built a hog pen, a fodder bin, and a chicken coop. South Carolina's Lorenza Ezell said that on her place "All de men folks" raised a few acres of cotton "for to sell in de market." "We were never given any money," Louisiana bondswoman Octavia George recalled, "but were able to get a little money this way: our Master would let us have two or three acres of land each year to plant for ourselves, and we could have what we raised on it."[5] Another black said that in his area slaves grew tobacco as a cash crop. In this way, he explained, several acquired sufficient means to purchase their freedom. One Alabama woman remembered how her uncles each planted a few acres of cotton. At the end of the season, they sold it to the master who paid them in cash. "My grandfather owned a cotton patch," former South Carolina bondswoman Mariah Calloway recalled, "and the master would loan him a mule so he could plow it at night." He had arrived directly from Africa, she said, and preferred working in the evenings when it was cool. Late in the autumn, he would journey to town, sell his cotton, and come back "loaded down" with cheese, sugar, tea, and dried fish.[6]

On some plantations this internal slave economy reached surprising proportions. A group of South Carolina planters noted that in their district "negroes have every other Saturday [off], keep horses, raise hogs, cultivate for themselves every thing for home consumption & for market that their masters do." This domestic economy included planting and selling cotton. On Julien S. Devereux's Monte Verdi estate in Rusk County, Texas, a dozen field hands used their evenings, Saturday afternoons, and Sundays to plant their own cotton. In 1850, Jesse marketed two bales weighing 1,158 pounds; Jack harvested two bales weighing about the same; Gill, Lewis, Bill, Lucius, Henry, Martin, Levin, and Stephen each raised one bale; Daniel and Scott harvested a half bale. Selling the cotton to Mt. Pleasant merchant Charles Vinzent, they purchased clothing, tobacco, hats, and other items. They also demanded partial payment in specie. "I send you $300 in gold," Vinzent wrote Devereux in 1853, "with the request to have the same distributed amongst those Negroes of yours who owned the Cotton which I bought from them." The payment to slaves for their extra crop on one plantation near Augusta, Georgia, came directly from the mistress of the estate. "Mrs. T. told me she had lately paid them [her slaves] $1,000 for their own extra crop of cotton this year—that she paid to one of the men $70," a visitor to Emily Tubman's plantation noted in 1836. "She says that there is not a more interesting set of colored people, perhaps to be found any where."[7]

It was obvious that Devereux and Tubman, like numerous planters in the Lower South, used a combination of the task and gang systems on their plantations. Where the task system was exclusively employed, as in the cultivation of rice along the Sea Island coast of South Carolina and Georgia, slaves had even greater opportunities of accumulating property. One observer in Chatham County, Georgia, said in 1822 that blacks had "as much land as they can till for their own use." Following their work in the fields, they cultivated four or five acres of rice, corn, and cotton. A few bondsmen and women planted ten or twelve acres of a cash crop. After the harvest, they sold the crops to factors, or local merchants, or to their masters. "His slaves are sometimes his creditors to large amounts," Frederick Law Olmsted noted, after visiting Richard Arnold's plantation in Georgia; "at the present time he says he owes them about five hundred dollars."[8]

The importance blacks attached to being able to raise their own crops, no matter how small the return, could be seen in the care they displayed toward these few acres, a devotion that far exceeded any concern for cultivating the broad fields beyond. Often they used a portion of the day on Saturday and Sunday tilling, planting, cultivating, or harvesting, and sometimes, even after twelve or fourteen hours in the field, they would spend time on their "own land." One Louisiana black recalled how she and her fellow slaves would return at dusk so exhausted they would sometimes fall into bed without supper, but when the moon was full they would spend a few more hours cultivating their tobacco patches, carefully plucking away dead leaves, gently turning over the soil, attentively digging out roots and weeds. When insects or drought destroyed their crops they often agonized at the sight of their withering fields in such emotional terms that it seemed as if a part of their own souls had withered away and died. Though they realized they could not own real or personal property without the consent of whites, or in any legal sense even with such consent—how could chattel property itself own property?—blacks believed they had certain rights of proprietorship over these fields. "A great deal [of real estate] was held by sufferance and their [the slaves'] right was most universally recognized and respected," one postwar observer acknowledged, "no advantage taken of even verbal agreement." Among the largest slaveholders, this was "a matter of honor." Another knowledgeable white explained that many masters allowed bondspeople to own gardens and small acreages as well as various personal possessions. These practices were so universal, he asserted, that slave owners made no claim whatsoever on this property.[9]

Some slaves on large plantations in the Lower South not only planted a few acres of a staple crop but also acquired other types of property. While this varied from plantation to plantation and region to region, blacks often owned a few personal items such as shirts, pants, shoes, watches, furniture, beehives, dogs, wagons, even firearms. "Slaves have not infrequently been known to have pistols & other dangerous weapons in their possession, and even to carry them about their persons," a Lexington District, South Carolina, grand jury explained in 1855, following the gunshot slaying of a bondsman by a fellow slave. Plantation slaves also owned hogs, cows, sometimes a horse, mule, or a few head of cattle. When Union army officers arrived in Mississippi and initiated a plan to assist former slaves in becoming independent farmers by confiscating plantation mules, horses, oxen, as well as carts, wagons, and tools, believing they belonged to the planter class, blacks protested vociferously, explaining that they had long "possessed" their own livestock and equipment. Texas slave Felix Haywood, of Bexar County, recalled how he and his father had built up a herd of seventy head of cattle by the time of the Civil War. They had begun with a few head donated to them by their owner. "My father," Haywood said proudly, "had his own brand."[10]

If owning such a large herd was very unusual, by the end of the antebellum era a large proportion of the slaves in the low country of the Carolinas and Georgia owned farm animals and other property, and a few of them, like Haywood, were slaves of considerable means. Slave driver Paris James was described by a white planter as a "substantial man before the war [and] was more like a free man than any slave." According to the same planter, James owned a horse, eight cows, sixteen sheep, twenty-six hogs, and a wagon. Another slave livestock owner was described by a black witness as "just like a white man except [for] his color. His credit was just as good as a white man's because he had the property to back it." Other low-country slaves were considered to be "more than usually prosperous," "pretty well off," and "hardworking and moneysaving." Georgia black Alexander Steele, a slave carpenter, said his estate included four horses, a mule, and two cows, as well as large quantities of fodder, hay, and corn. He had obtained these possessions by trading for himself over a period of thirty years, and when a white planter offered him $300 for one of his prized colts, Steele refused.[11]

Even more widespread than the ownership of livestock was the possession of money. Plantation slaves discovered several ways to earn small amounts of cash: telling fortunes, healing with roots and herbs, playing the fiddle at plantation dances and social gatherings, betting on cockfights and horse races, selling trinkets and others items to fellow slaves. Sometimes they sold poultry, meats, and liquor to free blacks, or peddled baskets and handicrafts to a nearby store owner. Masters found it virtually impossible to halt these market activities. To control their bondsmen and women in this regard the best most slave owners could do was to purchase slave produce, crops, poultry, and other items themselves. South Carolina planter Henry W. Ravenel, who owned nearly two hundred blacks, recalled that it was a "custom" among many planters to pay cash for various slave products. On his Pooshee plantation the overseer operated a store—he called it "an institution"—which purchased "everything the negroes wished to sell, whether wanted or not," and paid them "the market price." Ravenel said the slaves received payments for Indian and Guinea corn, pumpkins, melons, ground nuts (or "pindars"), fish, eggs, chickens, and honey. "Among the more enterprising," he said, "beehives—a dozen or more, ranged under some old peachtree—would give a supply of honey or its equivalent in cash."[12]

On a few plantations slaves could actually earn wages if they performed their tasks with extraordinary skill and dexterity. Planter James Townes was so enthusiastic about this method of creating good work habits that he urged his fellow slave owners to follow his lead. On payday, as the Negroes called it, Townes explained in an article on plantation management in the *Southern Cultivator*, his slaves were "very proud to go off with a pocket full of silver." Other slaves earned silver away from the plantation, hawking fruit to steamboat stewards, selling partridges to train conductors, peddling vegetables in a nearby town, or selling a few yards of cloth to poor whites. "Po-buckra [poor whites] come there and buy cloth from Mom," one slave in All Saints Parish, South Carolina, recalled. "Buy three and four yards. Ma sell that [and then] have to weave day and night to please obersheer." "My daddy alus had some money," a former Texas bondsman testified, "'cause he made baskets and chair bottoms and sold them."[13] One Negro who corded wood during his spare time said that when slaves in his vicinity saw something they wanted at the store they usually did like the whites. "Us bought it."[14]

An Alabama dental surgeon who traveled extensively in his home state confirmed this contention. He told a reporter that he frequently encountered slaves with cash in their pockets. At crossroads stores he witnessed them purchasing barrels of molasses, sugar, flour, and mackerel, as well as boxes of cheese and tobacco and sacks of coffee. Around his hometown of Fairfield slaves sometimes ordered a year's supply of groceries from Mobile, and once he espied a slave asking a merchant to change a fifty-dollar bill. "They do not like to lay up paper money," he explained, "and get their bills exchanged for silver and gold." Nor were they "fancy negroes" such as barbers, waiters, and stewards; they were just plain "plantation hands."[15]

Although the surgeon's proslavery zeal probably caused him to overstate his case, and although slaves could acquire only small amounts of cash (he was correct, however, about their desire to "lay up" silver and gold rather than notes and paper currency), plantation slaves in the Lower South took understandable pride in being able to acquire plots of land, a few farm animals, and small amounts of money. The feeling of self-worth and independence this engendered could be seen in the proud recollection of Texas slave Scott Hooper's son who explained that his father sold his own cotton and "Dat-away, he have money and he own pony and saddle and brung chillen candy and toys and buys coffee and tea for mammy." Another black expressed the same feeling toward his stepfather who built a log house, furnished it with tables, beds, and chairs, then purchased a cloak and gown for his mother, frocks for his sisters, and coats and hats for his two brothers and himself, "all new and good, and all with money he earned in the time allowed him for sleep." It could also be seen in the enthusiasm blacks demonstrated toward earning some extra money. When a group of sugar planters near Convent, St. James Parish, Louisiana, offered cash payments to their slaves for any wood they cut during their spare time, virtually every black on the jointly owned plantation—more than one hundred—responded. In all, as shown in the "Accounts of Wood Cut in 1854" (dated July 10, 1854), they cut 2,225 cords (284,000 cubic feet), earning nearly two thousand dollars. Among the participants were "Little Joe" (a half-cord), "Old Jacob" (ten cords), and Jack Page, who cut and piled an amazing sixty-nine cords. "Poor and dependent as most of the freemen are," John Alvord, an inspector for the Freedmen's Bureau, reported in 1866, after touring states in the Deep South, "I found that a considerable number had money." A "considerable number" also owned cattle, horses, mules, and other personal items.[16]

Slave Hiring

By the end of the antebellum era, property ownership among slaves on plantations in the Lower South was fairly widespread, especially where the task system was employed. As in the eighteenth century, some owners believed that incentives, combined with force and coercion, were the best means of labor management. Away from the plantation, in towns and cities, and in manufacturing establishments of the Upper South, another labor method evolved from the colonial period which allowed slaves opportunities to accumulate property: the hiring-out system. As with the task system, hiring out provided incentives to both master and slave. With steadily rising prices for slaves and increased demands for temporary workers, masters found themselves in an enviable position. They could hire out their bondsmen and women and obtain profits ranging from 10 to 20 percent (of the slave's price) per year. While contracts concerning clothing, food, medical attention, and treatment varied, slaves hired in such a manner could often expect to earn wages for themselves if they worked beyond what was considered a normal workday. As historians Robert Starobin and Charles Dew suggest, this "Stimulant & Reward Money," as one Tennessee turnpike owner called it, was a means of labor control rather than "a step toward freedom," but blacks responded enthusiastically to even these limited opportunities.[17] "The negroes in the swamp [cutting shingles] were more sprightly and straight-forward in their manner and conversation than any field-hand plantation-negroes that I saw at the South," one traveler said in 1856, commenting on "THE EFFECT OF PAYING WAGES TO SLAVES." There were no complaints of "'rascality' or laziness."[18]

Hired slaves gradually came to expect some type of extra compensation. Those who were employed as dining room servants, porters, draymen, and coachmen collected tips; barbers, laundresses, and market women kept some of their earnings; skilled carpenters, masons, industrial workers, and factory hands received cash payments. While their remunerations were often small, usually a few dollars a month, observers in several Upper South cities explained that virtually all hired blacks had "prerequisites" of one kind or another. If they were called upon to do extra work, labor in the evenings or at night, or if they demonstrated unusual "fidelity," they generally expected to be compensated. Frederick Olmsted explained how this worked in the tobacco industry. "In the tobacco-factories in Richmond and Petersburg, slaves are, at this time, in great demand, and are paid one hundred and fifty to two hundred dollars, and all expenses, for a year," he said. These blacks, primarily hired hands, were expected to complete a certain amount of work, a "daily quota," and once this had been finished, they received "bonus pay." Factory managers discovered that hired blacks "could not be 'driven' to do a fair day's work so easily as they could be stimulated to it by the offer of a bonus for all they would manufacture above a certain number of pounds." As a result, slaves earned for themselves from $5 to $20 dollars per month. Another observer said hired hands in tobacco factories earned an average of $120 annually, compared to the going rate of $1 a day for white workers. While this may have been an exaggeration, following the Civil War freed slaves in Richmond complained that their wages were less than half of what they had previously earned as hired slaves! [19]

By the 1850s, slave hiring was a common practice in the South's major industries—hemp manufacturing, textiles, tobacco, iron production—as well as in the cities of the Upper South. In Richmond, 62 percent of the male slave-labor force was hired, in Lynchburg, 52 percent, in Norfolk, more than 50 percent, and in Louisville, 24 percent. In the South as a whole, at least 100,000 slaves (estimates range from 60,000 to 160,000) were hired each year. One industrialist who used hired blacks was William Weaver, owner of Buffalo Forge, an iron-manufacturing establishment near Lexington, Virginia. Weaver employed slave founders, colliers, miners, teamsters, woodcutters, and furnace hands—a total of nearly 100 hired blacks each year, or nearly one-half of his labor force. And, like iron makers in Tennessee, Kentucky, North Carolina, South Carolina, Georgia, Alabama, and Missouri, he offered his hired workers cash incentives. Those who were willing to cord more than the required amount of wood received forty cents per cord, the same rate at which white woodchoppers were paid. Skilled slave ironworkers could earn overwork payments for producing more than their required quota of iron, while ore-bank hands could collect for mining and washing extra ore, colliers for tending the charcoal pits at night, shoemakers for making extra pairs of shoes, and common laborers for working extra hours. What is remarkable is the manner in which Weaver's hired hands responded to these wage incentives. Most slave hands, both skilled and unskilled, used the overwork system to earn their own money. They used their wages to purchase extra clothing, tobacco, sugar, meat, coffee, liquor, and other commodities, to acquire hogs, chickens, and horses, and to pay for extra holidays with their families. In this way, historian Charles Dew notes, "a sizable number of blacks took advantage of the system to carve out something of a private and individual life for themselves."[20]

Not all hired slaves fared as well as Weaver's ironworkers. Some were auctioned off like fieldhands and fell into the hands of harsh and oppressive masters. This was especially true of slaves turned over to the administrator of an estate following the death of a master. Others, despite extraordinary effort and diligent work habits, received only modest remunerations or did not receive the wages originally agreed upon. But even these slaves, while seeking to avoid conflict, were not completely without recourse when they felt betrayed. For three years (1799–1801), James, a slave carpenter in Norfolk, Virginia, was hired out by his owner William Walker, earning between $2.40 and $3.50 a week for himself and his master. In 1801, however, apparently dissatisfied with the amount of his wages, James ran away, remaining at large for thirteen months. But upon his return, he was neither scolded nor disciplined; rather, his wages were increased. Others attempting to negotiate in such a manner were less fortunate. In 1846, James Armstrong, a Kentucky bondsman owned by farmer James Rudd, was similarly hired out for wages and was allowed to keep everything he earned in excess of $5.00 a week. Armstrong worked diligently, rarely missing a payment to his master. Between 1846 and 1853, Rudd kept a meticulous record of "Cash Received of James," dutifully recording each week's payment. Over the eight years, he received $1,897.65, or an average of $4.60 per week. In October 1853, however, Rudd decided to raise his own share to $7.00. Incensed by this "breach of contract," Armstrong ran away, was apprehended, and made a second break for freedom. This time he was captured, severely whipped, and cast into irons. On March 4, 1854, the once conscientious and profitable slave was sold for $1,600.[21]

Self-hired Bondsmen and Women

Only a few months before, neither slave nor master would have predicted such an event, but the incident, agonizing to both, demonstrated what might happen if some sort of concession were not granted to a hired slave. To avoid this, some slaveholders (including Rudd) allowed their most trusted and skilled blacks to hire their own time. Self-hire had a long tradition in American slavery, stretching back to the earliest colonial period when some slaves, usually the most skilled and trustworthy, were allowed to contact a potential employer, make arrangements for wages and working conditions, and secure their own food and lodging. From generation to generation, the practice changed very little, in large measure because, as with hiring out, it benefited both master and slave. Owners did not have to pay for the slave's clothing or lodging and also saved the 5 to 8 percent fee charged by a hiring broker as well as the aggravation of taking care of the matter themselves. "I cannot now say whether the negroes will be exposed in hire or no [sic], that is at public auction," one Tennessee planter grumbled in 1813, expressing the sentiments of other slave owners. "I cannot possibly attend the hiring this year."[22] Slaves, while required to pay their masters a monthly or yearly fee, were allowed to keep anything they earned above and beyond that amount. The famous bondsman Frederick Douglass, when he was a self-hired Baltimore ship's caulker, explained: "I was to be allowed all my time; to make all bargains for work; to find my own employment, and to collect my own wages; and, in return for this liberty, I was required, or obliged, to pay him [Douglass's master] three dollars at the end of each week, and to board and clothe myself, and buy my own calking [sic] tools." This was a hard bargain, requiring that Douglass earn twice the amount his master required, but self-hire, he asserted, had "armed my love of liberty with a lash and a driver, far more efficient than any I had before known." It was a highly valued privilege, "another step in my career toward freedom."[23]

Unlike Frederick Douglass, most self-hired slaves were not able to extricate themselves from bondage, but they too greatly valued the privilege of managing their own time and collecting their own wages. This could be seen in their willingness to hire out despite the difficulties some of them faced in providing for themselves while continuing to make payments to their masters. During periods of economic recession or depression, and in some rural areas even during more prosperous times, slaves who lacked special skills were sometimes forced to find employment wherever they could. According to one North Carolina farmer, self-hired Negroes in his neighborhood encountered difficulties earning a decent wage. "Fact is," he said, "a man couldn't earn his board, let along his wages, for six months in the year." What did they do during the remainder of the year? "Well, they keeps agoin' round from one place to another, and gets their living somehow." Self-hired slaves who earned larger sums were sometimes forced to turn over substantial amounts to their owners. The literate North Carolina house servant and barber James Starkey, though earning a large income, was required to give most of it to his master. If allowed to work only partially for himself, he could raise his purchase price in a few years, but as long as he had wages to pay, he lamented, "it is impossible."[24] Other blacks were allowed to hire their time only after their most productive years had long since passed. The "aged" female slave Yarico, who served Virginia farmer Thomas Wells faithfully for many years, eked out an existence "principally if not entirely" by hiring "her own labor." According to other observers, some slaves, like Yarico, would have been better off working as field-hands on large plantations. On their own they ran the risks of harsh treatment, seizure by a slave trader, arrest by public authorities, and the infirmities of old age.[25]

One of the most pernicious practices connected with self-hire was a master's holding out the promise of freedom and then drawing up a contract that was virtually impossible to fulfill or reneging on the original promise. Even under the best of circumstances, purchasing one's self was an enormous and risky undertaking. During the 1820s, a young male slave could buy himself for about $350 in Virginia, and about $700 in Louisiana. A generation later, with the inflation of slave prices, these costs had nearly doubled. Although the earning power of self-hired bondsmen and women appreciated considerably during the interim, during both periods it was extremely difficult for even the most frugal and dedicated black to purchase freedom papers. Even so a number of self-hired slaves exerted great effort to pay for themselves. In 1855, Mary Carrol, a young self-hired Tennessee slave who worked as a chambermaid, signed an agreement according to which she was to be advanced $600 (her appraised value) in the form of a mortgage note, and she was not to be free until she had paid the note and interest as well as premiums on a life-insurance policy and any health expenses she might incur. Table 2 indicates the difficulties facing even the most enterprising blacks who tried to purchase themselves. After fifty-four months, she still owed nearly $400 on her purchase price. As if sinking deeper in quicksand, Mary Carrol's struggle to buy herself had ended only in desperate failure. Still, she was probably better off than Fanny Smith, a Virginia slave who made a verbal agreement with her master to pay for herself and her two children over a period of ten years. Shortly before the final payment she was sold.[26]

Despite such wrenching experiences, blacks eagerly sought to hire

Table 2. Account: Mary Carrol to Dr. W. B. Cooper, 1855–60

| | | Payments | | Amount |
Date	Earnings	Insurance	Interest	due[1]
1855[2]	$68	$13.50	$18.00[3]	$587.50
1856	100	24.96	35.25	547.75
1857	100	21.90	32.96	502.57
1858	100	20.10	30.15	452.72
1859	100	18.20	27.16	398.08
Total	$468	$98.66	$143.52	$398.08

Source: W. B. Cooper to Mary Carrol, January 7, 1860, Carter Woodson Collection, LC.
[1] Some of the "amount due" totals are slightly off but have been left unaltered.
[2] Beginning July 7, 1855; [3] plus a $24 doctor's bill

themselves out. For whites it was simple and economical to hire slaves for certain jobs; it was often simpler and more economical to deal with the slaves themselves. But for blacks it meant the ability to earn wages, provide for their families, and gain a measure of autonomy. Several types of evidence point to the success of self-hire. One was its remarkable longevity. As early as 1712 whites in Charleston noted the presence of slaves who "go whither they will and work where they please," upon condition that so much money was paid to the master. Nearly a century and a half later Charleston residents, as well as whites in virtually every town and city and many rural areas of the Upper and Lower South, described self-hired blacks in much the same manner. In addition, by the antebellum period self-hired slaves had entered a wide range of different occupations. In urban areas of the Lower South, where free blacks often worked as skilled craftsmen, self-hired slaves became porters, draymen, market women, fishermen, boatmen, and hucksters. In New Orleans, self-hired women of color sold flowers and oranges in the streets or candy and pies in small shops. In the towns and cities of the Upper South, self-hired slaves, while working as coopers, carpenters, and millers, also loaded and unloaded steamboats, labored on the docks and along riverfronts, became servants, domestics, cooks, coachmen, and found employment as tobacco twisters, woodchoppers, and day laborers.[27] Lastly, the increasing number of complaints, legislative petitions, and anti-self-hire laws formulated by whites in virtually every section of the South during the pre–Civil War generation reveals less about the ability of slave owners to curtail or even control the institution than about its continuing strength and vitality.[28]

One of the primary reasons blacks remained so eager to hire themselves out was the financial benefits that could be derived from the system. Wages varied in different periods in various parts of the South, but slaves working on their own could command between $100 (for unskilled labor in the Upper South early in the century) and $500 (for skilled workers in the Lower South on the eve of the Civil War). Fluctuations could occur to the detriment (or benefit) of these slaves, during periods of economic depression (or prosperity), but generally they could expect to earn profits of between $25 and $150 per annum. One observer in Baltimore explained that slaves "let themselves out for every kind of work," paid their masters a given sum for the loss of their services, and kept only "a trifle for themselves." But in Charleston, Savannah, and New Orleans, observers said ambitious slaves were able to "save a great deal of money." Those who managed small businesses or peddled confectionery, bread, cooked fish, rice, fruit, oysters, and other commodities, or who were highly skilled as cabinetmakers, joiners, or coopers, could sometimes earn as much as white workers. The ability of some self-hired slaves to purchase luxury items such as boats, carriages, fancy clothing, or buy relatives or themselves out of bondage (see chapter 3) testifies to the earning power of some members of this group. Several among them, including laborers, artisans, and businessmen, became slaves of considerable means.[29]

The eagerness of slaves to hire their own time was perhaps best illustrated by the bondsmen and women on John Liddell's Black River plantation in Catahoula Parish, Louisiana. "I request that you would forthwith proceed to prosecute *John S. Sullivan* of Troy, Parish of Catahoula, for Hiring four of my Negro men, secretly, and without my knowledge or permission, at *midnight* on the *12*th of Aug last 1849 (or between midnight and day)," Liddell instructed his lawyer,

> to steal away my large flatboat from my landing, and use the same in transporting lumber from Capt. Shriver's old saw Mill to his (Sullivan's) landing or store or warehouse, at troy, a distance back and forth of 6 miles, hard pulling and three miles against the current with a heavily loaded flat, thereby causing *one* of the said four negroes to become sick from . . . over exertion & exposure during the night, while striving to return home in time to prevent discovery, thereby ultimately causing death of said negro (Jake).

After Jake's death Liddell discovered to his astonishment that Sullivan had often hired his slaves, had been doing so for years, and during the past twelve months had paid them $500 in wages. "Where does this sum come from," he asked bitterly, "unless from my means, my property?"[30]

His slaves, of course, felt differently. They viewed self-hire as an opportunity to earn spending money, even if it meant working all day, stealing away at midnight, and returning to the fields at dawn the next morning. Nor were they easily deterred; three years later Liddell was still pressing for a state law "prohibiting the employing and hiring of slaves without consent of the owners under heavy penalty." But even under the best of circumstances, self-hire sometimes strained the relations between master and slave. Although the contractual terms and amount of personal earnings slaves were allowed to keep varied considerably in individual cases, self-hire usually carried with it at least a degree of financial independence. Even slaves who reported regularly to their masters were able to manage their own money, earning their own wages and paying their owners an agreed upon sum. As a result, self-hired blacks often demonstrated an independence, self-esteem, and at times arrogance which grated on whites who believed slaves should be docile, self-deprecating, and humble. "As I have hired the boy Stephen, he is no longer authorized to trade for himself," Maury County, Tennessee, slave owner Edward H. Chappin complained in 1823, "or own any property in his own name." It seems that Stephen, without authorization, had acquired a string of horses and then established a business renting them to slaves on neighboring plantations. "I do hereby authorize the bearer of this [note]," Chappin declared, "to take in possession and deliver to me all [Stephen's] horses or other property" that might be in the hands of other blacks. On a visit to Richmond during the hiring season one foreign traveler was amused by the demands of a black domestic servant who was hiring herself out for the coming year. She demanded not only high wages, but also a number of other concessions, including the right to entertain her "friends and favourites." At length, she agreed only "to visit her proposed home and see how things looked."[31]

Slaves who made their own financial arrangements not only felt a sense of power, however limited, but in some instances had merely occasional contact with their masters. Those who rented their time on an annual or semiannual basis sometimes moved into a twilight zone between bondage and freedom. The question of whether or not this was "undermining" the South's peculiar institution, as claimed by some contemporaries, was a specious argument considering the relatively small proportion of slaves who hired themselves out during a particular year. What is important is the willingness of slaves, whenever possible, to enter into such contracts, and the self-esteem, positive self-concepts, and attitudes of independence self-hire engendered in bondsmen and women. This was certainly true for the slave Lotty, owned by the famous Kentucky politician Henry Clay. Returning to his Ashland plantation in 1830 after serving as secretary of state, Clay sought the services of his bondswoman, an excellent house servant who had been "receiving her own hire" for about eighteen months. She was probably still with Martin Van Buren, he explained to a friend in Washington, D.C., but he could not be sure. "Will you do me the favor to look her out, and tell her I want her to return." If she displayed a "perverse or refractory disposition," he added, "be pleased to have her imprisoned until I can hear of it, and give the necessary directions."[32]

Virtually Free Slaves

As suggested by Lotty's tenuous ties to Henry Clay, some self-hired slaves melted into the free Negro population, living and acting as free persons of color and acquiring real estate and other property. Little is known about these "virtually free slaves." This is not surprising, since even the term seems incongruous: how could slaves also be free? In some respects, of course, they could not, and even legally emancipated blacks have been termed by some historians as "Quasi-Free Negroes" and "Slaves without Masters."[33] In addition, as their livelihoods depended upon secrecy or deception or, at the very least, a tacit illegal agreement with a prominent white slaveholder, it is extremely difficult even to identify much less uncover information about such slaves. Owners were reluctant to acknowledge that bondsmen in their charge roamed about unsupervised, undermining the controls so necessary for the slave system to function properly; the unsuspecting foreign traveler or northern visitor or southern defender of slavery believed these blacks to be either slaves or free Negroes; and free slaves themselves refused to admit, much less advertise, their situation. Consequently, the journals of the slaveholding class, descriptions by outside visitors, writings of white southerners, and to a large extent even the narratives, recollections, and autobiographical reminiscences of blacks themselves, contain only fleeting references to slaves who exercised many of the privileges of free men and women.[34]

Yet there were slaves in the South who achieved a remarkable degree of self-sufficiency. In the Lower South, they were clustered primarily in towns and cities. In Athens, Georgia, one resident said in 1859 that there were more "free negroes manufactured and made virtually free" than there were "bona fide" free blacks in Clarke and any ten surrounding counties. A visitor to New Orleans noticed "a great many loose negroes about," slaves who seemed to be hiring their own time and earning their own living without supervision from slave owners. City officials in Charleston, Savannah, Mobile, and other urban areas told about the presence of "nominal slaves," "quasi f. n.," and "virtually free negroes" who moved about the streets seemingly oblivious to any law or regulation. While the precise number of these masterless slaves remains a matter of speculation, contemporaries in some cities believed they represented a sizable population group, at least as large as the legally free Negro population. Noting that the local courts often disregarded the spirit of an 1831 law requiring special legislative action to manumit slaves, the editor of the Natchez *Mississippi Free Trader* said that at least fifty legally enslaved bondsmen and women in the area "affect to be free." It was well known by local residents that "a large number of slaves" had been illegally manumitted; and after having "gone up the river, set foot upon the soil of Ohio or some other free or abolition State, received from them certain certificates, which are called 'free papers'; forthwith they return to Mississippi, to reside as 'free people of color.'" A longtime resident of Savannah noted in 1856, "There are, you may say, hundreds of Negroes in this city who go about from house to house—some carpenters, some house servants, etc.—who never see their masters except at payday, live out of their yards, hire themselves without written permit, etc." Others were "employed without any expression of the will of the master manifested by written permit." In his estimation, self-hired and quasi-free slaves (they were often lumped together) represented at least 10 percent of the city's total Negro population.[35]

In the Upper South, increasing numbers of quasi-free bondsmen and women also congregated in urban areas—Baltimore, the District of Columbia, Norfolk, Richmond, Lexington, Louisville, and St. Louis. Some earned wages working in tobacco and hemp factories; a few were skilled artisans who contracted with whites as builders, carpenters, coopers, and mechanics; others worked as servants, barbers, and hack drivers. Among the nearly one thousand slaves hired yearly in Elizabeth City County, Virginia, nearly one hundred lived as quasi-free bondsmen and women including nominal slave William Roscoe Davis, who operated a small pleasure boat on Chesapeake Bay. In other cities, virtually free slaves established market stalls, traded produce, fish, and other goods with plantation slaves, and sold various commodities to whites. In the port cities of Baltimore and Wilmington and in smaller river towns, slave fishermen and boatmen, often quasi-free or hiring their time by the year, worked along the river systems, fishing and trading with plantation blacks. In Louisville and St. Louis, nearly free slaves were waiters, servants, barbers, and steamboat stewards.[36]

In Nashville, several hundred virtually free slaves found employment as hackmen, wagoners, hostlers, confectioners, masons, builders, barbers, and laborers. Among them during the early years of the nineteenth century was a mulatto boy named John, whose activities as a self-hired slave illustrate how some Negroes managed to move into the middle ground between slavery and freedom. Taken by his owner from Charlottesville, Virginia, to Nashville, John was allowed to hire out to barge captain Richard Rapier, who transported tobacco down the Cumberland, Ohio, and Mississippi rivers to New Orleans, carrying back to Nashville sugar, tea, coffee, raisins, molasses, rum, brandy, wines, logwood, nails, tin, glass, and other commodities. Following his owner's death, John reverted to the estate of Charles Thomas, a Virginia slave owner, but the quasi-free slave remained with Rapier and accompanied his employer to Florence, Alabama, in 1819, where he continued to work as a self-hired waiter and pole boy for a full decade, before obtaining his legal freedom (with a bequest from the barge master's estate), taking the surname Rapier, and establishing a barbershop. During the antebellum period, the number of nominal slaves grew steadily in Nashville and other cities, until by the 1850s, according to some observers, they had become "a sizeable Negro population."[37]

Although quasi-free bondsmen and women tended to congregate in towns and cities, where there were better opportunities for employment and escaping detection, some remained in rural areas as farm laborers and in a few instances as farm "owners." Usually those who became farmers did so with the acquiescence of whites since land "possession" was involved. In North Carolina, Martin County black Ned Hyman, a slave owned by John and Samuel Hyman, accumulated an estate "consisting of Lands chiefly, Live Stock, Negroes and money," worth between $5,000 and $6,000. Most of this property was listed in his free Negro wife's name. He was a "remarkably uncommon and extraordinary Negro," a group of nearly one hundred whites in his neighborhood said, and had acquired his holdings because he was "remarkably industrious, frugal & prudent." "In a word, his character stands as fair and as good—for honesty, truth, industry, humility, sobriety & fidelity[—]as any Negro they (your memorialists) have ever seen or heard of" (see appendix 2). In a sparsely settled rural area of Sullivan County, Tennessee, near the Virginia border, one white farmer noted the presence of a large family of quasi-free black farmers. "Although they are Slaves yet they have been living to themselves for about 20 years," Samuel Rhea explained. "They have supported themselves on land of their masters and are tolerable farmers." William Weston, a lifelong resident of Craven County, North Carolina, recalled on the eve of the Civil War that Rebecca Sutton and her five children had taken up residence on a deserted farm near

Pamlico Sound in 1818. Although a slave, "she always lived as a free woman and acted for herself," Weston testified. "She lived on my Father's Land for Several years & then lived on John Benston[']s Land. She acted for herself there also until she died."[38]

Few nominal slaves could boast of an estate as large as Ned Hyman's, but a number entered the property-owning class. Posing as free persons of color some purchased real estate or, acting through a white protector, acquired a member of their family, even though they themselves remained legally enslaved. Other quasi-free bondsmen and women rented houses, buildings, and other property, establishing small businesses. One Nashville woman ran a laundry from her rented house in the heart of the central business district. Over the years, she saved a considerable amount of money, including $350 in Mexican gold coins, and eventually bought one of her three slave children out of bondage. Virginia slave Billy Brown, who had purchased his freedom and found a job at Hampden-Sidney College, was required by law to leave the state. Seeking to remain near his slave family, he petitioned the General Assembly: "By the course of honest industry, and careful economy," he had "acquired property, sufficient probably, with ordinary labor," to support his family for many years to come; he prayed to remain in Virginia. When his plea was rejected, Brown was forced once again to become "the property of a gentleman," although he continued to support himself "by honest industry and prudent economy."[39] South Carolina slave Sally Patterson, the wife of a free Negro carpenter in Columbia, was listed in 1850 as a free Negro possessing $1,200 worth of real estate. In Charleston, quasi-free carpenter Joseph Elwig, who was actually owned by his father, purchased a house on Coming Street, where a number of affluent free Negroes owned homes, and was listed on the tax rolls in 1836 as a free black. Even though few of his neighbors realized that he was in reality a slave, when his father became seriously ill in 1843 Elwig was sold for $1 to his own free Negro wife so that he would not be confiscated to pay any of his father's debts. Perhaps no other act could more poignantly illustrate the anomalous condition of quasi-free bondsmen and women than a father selling his own son to ensure the son's freedom.[40]

Slave Entrepreneurs

A few partially free slaves actually established businesses. Virginia's Robert Gordon sold slack from his white father's coal yard to local blacksmiths, amassing a small fortune of $15,000 by 1846, when he purchased his freedom and moved to Cincinnati. Kentucky's Frank

McWorter set up a crude saltpeter manufactory (the principle ingredient in gunpowder) in Pulaski County at the beginning of the war with Great Britain in 1812 and expanded it considerably in subsequent years as settlers poured through the region to the West.[41] Mississippi's Benjamin Montgomery, a favorite slave of cotton planter Joseph Davis (the brother of the future president of the Confederacy), operated a retail dry goods store at Davis Bend, thirty miles south of Vicksburg, selling items to his fellow slaves in exchange for wood, vegetables, chickens, and eggs.[42] A slave named Allen drove back and forth from the Mississippi river to the Piedmont in Virginia, vending wares from his dry goods wagon.[43] Future Alabama congressman Benjamin Turner, while still in bondage, acquired a livery stable and considerable other property in Selma. Turner not only managed his own business but also conducted his owner's financial affairs as well. "I [ran] a livery-stable in Selma, and r[a]n omnibuses, hacks, etc.," Turner testified to the Southern Claims Commission in 1871, seeking restitution for the $8,000 worth of property he had lost at the hands of Wilson's raiders. "That was my business, and my boss [Dr. Gee] left me some business of his to look after, such as collecting money for him, and attending to his affairs as a matter of encouragement to me and to make me behave myself and not run away while the war was going on."[44]

In Bennettsville, South Carolina, bondsman Thomas David owned a construction business, negotiating contracts, hiring day laborers (many of whom were also bondsmen), and supervising the erection of numerous houses as well as several larger buildings. "Those who were mechanics had extra privileges," a postwar investigator explained, "some of them hiring their own time, & working as master builders—hiring labourers & teaching them—making contracts for buildings &c." As early as 1802, this practice had become so prevalent in New Hanover County, North Carolina, that a group of white mechanics signed a remonstrance to the state legislature. Despite statutes forbidding such practices, slaves worked as free mechanics and undertook contracts "on their own account, at sometimes less than one half the rate that a regular bred white Mechanic could afford to do it." Sometimes these slaves hired gangs of eight to twelve other bondsmen and women who worked entirely "for their own benefit." More than a half-century later, quasi-free slave contractors in the county still controlled a large portion of the construction business. In Charleston, South Carolina, a slightly different system emerged. House servants left with the responsibility for letting out repair and building contracts when their masters journeyed to the North during the summer months hired virtually free slaves and free blacks as carpenters, builders, and masons, who in turn maintained small work gangs of nearly free bondsmen to erect outbuildings and construct houses.[45]

Some slave entrepreneurs found it difficult to sever their ties with profit-seeking slave owners. For nearly ten years Mary Ann Wyatt of King and Queen County, Virginia, rented herself and her five children (seven others had been sold) from her master for $45 a year while establishing a business retailing oysters to local residents. Each week during this period, she journeyed to the Rappahannock River, a distance of approximately sixteen miles, purchased two baskets of oysters, and returned to sell them in the town square. Even after she had acquired a widespread reputation as an astute businesswoman and accumulated considerable property, including a rental house, Wyatt continued to pay a monthly tribute to her master. When a local representative of the credit-rating firm of R. G. Dun and Company evaluated the barbering and confectionery business of "Edwards & Carroway" in Wythe County, Virginia, during the 1850s, he noted that the two men were "slaves who hire their time" but added that they carried on the business "in name of Jas. Saunders whom they belong to." A Tennessee slave named Jack found his master equally insistent on receiving a sizable portion of his profits. For many years "Doctor Jack," as he was known, practiced medicine in sections of south-central Tennessee "with great & unparalled success" (see appendix 2). Even as his practice grew, Jack's owner, William Macon, a planter in Maury and later in Giles county, demanded the fees. Only after more than a quarter-century, perhaps after his master's death, did this gifted slave establish his own practice. An eight word advertisement in Nashville's first business directory in 1853 told of his eventual success: "Jack, Root Doctor. Office 20 N Front St."[46]

Two popular and industrious free-slave barbers in New Bern, North Carolina, similarly forfeited most of their earnings to their owner, free mulatto John Carruthers Stanly, who had himself started out as a free-slave barber. According to Stephen F. Miller, a prominent white resident of the town, Brister and Boston were always neatly dressed and kept their shop "in good reputation." "They were purchased by your Petitioner when they were quite small and reared by him and taught the trade of a barber," Stanly said in a petition to the Craven County Superior Court. "After the increase of business compelled your Petitioner to direct his attention to other matters, he left to the care of these two slaves the management of the said establishment." During this period the shop had been under the "exclusive management of the aforesaid servants" who had faithfully collected and paid to him the "money received by them from the customers to the shop." After many years of devoted service, Stanly now hoped that the two slaves would not only be permitted to retain their earnings but would also be granted freedom papers.[47]

Most slave business people were able to move out on their own in the early stages of their careers. In the same Nashville business directory that listed "Doctor Jack" an advertisement appeared for another enterprising slave, bathhouse owner and barber shop proprietor Frank Parrish, a bondsman originally owned by Catherine Parrish, the widow of a Davidson County farmer, and later by Edwin Ewing, a lawyer and politician. As early as 1836, Parrish had advertised that customers could enjoy the luxury of "the falling spray" and the "lucid coolness" of "the flood" at his bathing establishment. He promised to receive visitors from six o'clock in the morning to ten o'clock at night. "Ladies are respectfully informed that convenient apartments have been prepared, with every accommodation for their comfort, for their exclusive use, and female servants will always be in readiness [to attend] them." At his barbershop next door, Parrish sold fancy soaps, perfumes, collars, socks, suspenders, "CURLS, PUFFS, &C.," also the best CIGARS and TOBACCO." For nearly two decades prior to his formal emancipation in 1853, Parrish ran these popular and thriving businesses.[48]

A number of black women were also to be found among the slaves who started various types of businesses. In the Lower South, female plantation slaves were involved nearly as much as the men in the retailing of various crops to their masters or to local factors. They also established stalls and small stores on the edges of towns and cities, selling various products. In the Upper South, they managed businesses as seamstresses, weavers, laundresses, and shopkeepers. One former Maryland slave recalled how his mother ran two business enterprises at the same time. "After my father was sold my master gave my mother permission to work for herself," he wrote, "provided she gave him one half [of the profits]." Within a short time, she had opened a coffee shop at the federal army garrison of Fort Washington and later operated a secondhand clothing store, selling trousers, coats, shoes, caps, and stockings to marines at the base. Despite the protests of "poor whites" in the area, she "made quite a respectable living."[49]

Perhaps the South's most resourceful free slave was Anthony Weston, a South Carolina mechanic who built rice mills for various slave owners at the edge of the inland river systems. "In consideration of the good conduct and faithful valuable service of my mulatto man

Toney by trade a millwright I have for some years past given him to himself for his time say from the middle of May to the middle of November every year," Charleston planter Plowden Weston wrote in 1826, leaving instructions that six years after his death "his whole time be given up to him" and that he should be "emancipated and set free or allowed to depart from the State." But Weston was neither emancipated, nor did he leave the state. Instead, using his earnings as a builder, he invested in real estate and slaves. Between 1833 and 1845, he purchased (in the name of his free Negro wife Maria) large amounts of real property and twenty blacks, including skilled artisans who assisted him in constructing rice mills. In 1856, one planter described a Weston-built mill as "better than any on the river." By 1860, this remarkable slave owned $40,075 worth of real estate (in his wife's name) and had become one of the most affluent blacks in South Carolina.[50]

These quasi-free blacks who engaged in business and acquired property were highly unusual. They had a shrewd understanding of Southern society, an intuitive sense for anticipating danger, and the ability to earn a livelihood. They were also able, in some instances, to secure the aid and protection of whites. Ambitious, persevering, hard working, and astute, some of them were highly successful as business people, and even those who had achieved less success had gained a large measure of freedom and independence. They realized that only the most strenuous and persistent effort would be rewarded. For some the fear of discovery remained a constant threat; for others, what might be termed "freedom dues," payments to owners or others for the privilege of quasi-freedom, continued to be a financial burden. Yet, in virtually every city in the South and in some rural communities, legally enslaved blacks moved out on their own and established businesses. In a few instances, they led completely autonomous lives, comfortably maintained their families, moved about from place to place, and acquired real estate and other property.

Slave Masters and Industrious Slaves

The acquisition of property by slaves took place in a context of master-slave relations. To understand property holding among slaves the attitudes and activities of the slaveholding class are therefore no less important than the feelings of bondsmen and women. The dilemma whites faced was as old as slavery itself: how could they inculcate the work ethic in their bondspeople without also inculcating ambition, drive, and a desire for freedom? In the struggle to solve this dilemma, they became increasingly divided. Some masters argued that allowing slaves certain freedoms would undermine the entire system; others, ignoring laws and prophecies of doom, offered their slaves incentives, including the right to own property. In the end, both sides remained steadfast in their views, but the dispute itself, as seen in the growing number of planter complaints and restrictive laws on the one hand and the increasing instances of self-hire, quasi-freedom, and property ownership on the other, revealed the complex, ambiguous, and at times intensely personal nature of master-slave relations.

It had long been assumed that slaves, as chattel property themselves, could not legally own property. During the colonial and early national periods laws had been passed making it illegal for bondsmen and women to purchase, acquire, or own various goods and commodities. Slaveholders argued that granting such privileges would not only result in robberies, thefts, and increased "trafficking in stolen goods" but also could end in the far more serious problems of slave discontent and rebellion. With the increases in property ownership among slaves during the nineteenth century, slave owners enacted new, more specific statutes to deal with the problem. In 1826, Georgia prohibited blacks from buying or selling "any quantity or amount whatever of cotton, tobacco, wheat, rye, oats, corn, rice or poultry, or any other articles, except such as are known to be usually manufactured or vended by slaves." Tennessee forbade bondsmen and women from owning a pig, cow, mule, horse, "or other such like description of property." Virginia proclaimed that anyone who bought, sold, or received "any commodity whatsoever" from a slave would be subject to thirty-nine lashes "well laid on" or a fine of four times the value of the items bought, sold, or received. Later, state lawmakers made this crime punishable by a jail sentence of up to six months. South Carolina passed an act to prevent the illicit traffic in cotton, rice, corn, and wheat, between slaves and free blacks. As late as 1864, Texas passed a law to prevent slaves from exercising "pretended ownership over property." It listed horses, sheep, cattle, goats, hogs, or any other animals "over which such negro may exercise a pretended right of ownership or on which such negro slave shall have a brand or ear mark."[51]

Similarly, with the expansion of self-hire and quasi-freedom during the nineteenth century, slaveholders recast their eighteenth century laws to deal with these problems. These legal codes bore witness not only to the existence of these phenomena but also to the increasing importance slave owners attached to curtailing such activities among blacks. While most of the new statutes passed between 1818 and 1840 carried relatively small fines for each offense, some states, including Georgia, enacted laws with stiff penalties. "*Whereas* divers persons of color, who are slaves by the laws of this State, having never been manumitted in conformity to the same, are nevertheless in the full exercise and enjoyment of all the rights and privileges of free persons of color, without being subject to the duties and obligations incident to such persons, thereby constituting a class of people, equally dangerous to the safety of the free citizens of this State, and destructive of the comfort and happiness of the slave population," an 1818 Georgia law read, "*Be it therefore* enacted [that a fine of $500 shall be administered] for each and every offence." Several other states followed Georgia's lead. With a 1785 statute as a guide, North Carolina passed a law in 1831 to deal with the increasing number of slaves who went "at large as free men." Henceforth, masters who allowed slaves to "go at large as a freeman, exercising his or her own discre[t]ion in the employment of his or her time," would be subject to indictment and upon conviction "shall be fined in the discretion of the court."[52] "It shall not be lawful for any person to hire to any slave the time of such slave," an 1840 Tennessee law read; or to allow bondspeople to "trade in spirituous liquors, hogs, cows, horses, or mules as a free person of color." The South Carolina Court of Appeals ruled during the 1830s that "if the owner without a formal act of emancipation permit his slave to go at large and to exercise all the rights and enjoy all the privileges of a free person of color the slave becomes liable to seizure as a derelict." At one time or another, lawmakers in virtually every southern state enacted similar codes to control slaves who enjoyed "the rights and privileges" of free blacks.[53]

The extensive legal codes governing master-slave relations with regard to property ownership and virtually free status reflected the anxieties of whites who felt they were losing control over *their* property. The entire structure of slavery rested on the power of owners to exert complete control over their blacks. When slaves acquired property or hired their own time, they became independent and ungovernable. This problem of control, ever present in the minds of whites, was not confined to one section of the South or one type of "domestic economy" but was as deeply rooted as slavery itself. There was a direct connection between black property ownership, black initiative, and black theft, one Louisiana planter proclaimed, and on his plantation slaves would never be allowed to have anything they could call their own. When blacks possessed "stocks of horses and hogs" and exercised "all the rights of ownership in such stock," a group of Virginians noted, they were not adverse to stealing farm animals and fodder, thefts which were virtually impossible to trace.[54] A group of Tennessee slave owners echoed these same sentiments: pass some law to prevent Negroes from "selling meats, chickens, fruits, etc., upon public days at public places," they instructed the legislature. They had experienced firsthand "the evil effects of the system now prevailing." "Every measure that may lessen the dependence of a Slave on his master ought to be opposed as tending to dangerous consequences," Edward Dudley, Timothy Barton, Jonathan Nichols, Jacob Hare, and a group of other South Carolina cotton planters explained. "The more privileges a Slave obtains, the less depending he is on his master, & the greater nuisance he is likely to be to the public." Two of the privileges they pointed to included allowing blacks to cultivate their "own cotton fields" and "trade in their own name." Forty-three years later, in 1859, a group of Hays County, Texas, slave owners offered the same opinion. "The undersigned, Grand Jurors, of the County aforesaid, Now in Session, Would Most respectfully Solicit your particular attention and ask the passage of an act of the present Legislature," J. C. Watkins, James M. Malone, John H. Cocks, and seventeen others said in a petition to the General Assembly, "to forbid Negro slaves *the right* to hold in their own name and for their own use, as property, Horses, Cattle, Land, and Stock of every description, as we see daily the baneful influence and effects on the Slave population."[55]

But despite the web of legal restrictions, and the outcries of slave owners concerning the "baneful influence and effects" of property ownership and quasi-freedom, these practices not only continued during the antebellum period but also grew and expanded. This was due largely to the acquiescence and in numerous instances the active support of the slaveholding class. Some masters believed that encouraging initiative and individual enterprise among slaves was the best means of control, since it gave blacks something to strive for and allowed them to provide for their families. Others granted bondsmen and women certain liberties for personal, ideological, and economic reasons. Some whites who had fathered slave children felt compassion for their offspring and, though finding it difficult to manumit their progeny, did allow them to accumulate property. Though antislavery sentiments were virtually silenced following the Nat Turner rebellion, a few whites, including North Carolina Quakers and others, continued to own slaves while allowing them to "go at large as free men." One jurist called this "custom" in effect "a species of *quasi* emancipation." A substantial number of slaveholders in Maryland, Virginia, and other Upper South states, and in a few Lower South states, practiced what was referred to as "deferred manumission," allowing bondsmen and women several years to adjust to a new life and acquire property before granting them complete freedom.[56]

Some whites who strongly defended slavery and publicly denounced quasi-freedom and self-hire found it was profitable to send blacks out on their own to earn a living. Those who owned especially talented and industrious bondsmen and women whom they trusted to be "strictly obedient to heredity" were often not adverse to sending them to towns and cities to work in various capacities. By the 1840s and 1850s many of these masters were earning good returns from their blacks who found employment in Baltimore, Norfolk, Louisville, Nashville, St. Louis, Savannah, Charleston, New Orleans, and smaller urban areas. Furthermore, it was whites who hired and paid these slaves. In 1856, a group of white builders in Smithfield, North Carolina, complained that they were constantly being outbid by free Negroes and self-hired slaves to build "houses, vessels &c." They were not only bitter about the competition from blacks but also criticized the whites who hired these construction gangs. The same was true of a group of Sumter District, South Carolina whites, who noted in 1849 that the state statute forbidding self-hire did not even apply to female slaves, yet they were often hiring themselves out and accumulating property. "The law in relation to Slaves hiring their own time is not enforced with sufficient promptness, and efficiency," a group of rural residents in the same state added a decade later, "as to accomplish the object designed by its enactment."[57]

Not only did they flaunt the laws prohibiting property ownership and self-hire, but some masters went to great lengths to protect especially industrious slaves. "This man has served his time in my neighbourhood, and has always maintained an excellent character," Virginia planter Samuel Anderson wrote concerning one quasi-free slave. "He is a good workman and an honest and industrious man. I have no doubt that he can obtain the sanction of every man in the neighbourhood." The distinguished Virginian John Wise wrote a glowing letter in behalf of the slave Jingo of Accomac County. "His Character while a slave was a good one in every respect as far as I ever knew or heard," Wise explained. "Since he has been considerd and acted as a free man it has sustained no diminution; he has lived for the last ten years within a mile of me and has supported a spotless character & one far above the generality of people of his colour for honesty, Sobriety and orderly deportment." Another black who secured similar praise was Parlour Washington, "a good industrious mechanic in the arts & trades of tanner & currier of leather and also a good shoe, boot and harness maker." Nearly one hundred Hamilton

County, Tennessee, residents explained that his services were "much needed and required by the Citizens of the section of the County where he now resides." In Nashville, Ephraim Foster, a lawyer, Whig politician, and United States senator, not only allowed a few of his most trusted blacks quasi-free status but also appeared in court in behalf of his bondsmen and women. In 1818, Foster testified that the African-born Simon, who was "sober, industrious, hard working, and a firm believer in the Christian religion" should be manumitted; later, he posted bond of $1,000 for Anna, a slave who was honest, temperate, and "strictly obedient to heredity"; in 1851, he presented a petition to the court for the emancipation of his virtually free slave James Thomas, a barber, property owner, and businessman who had always maintained "an exemplary character."[58]

In states where legal emancipations were rare, whites sometimes entered into trust agreements, promising to hold legal title to slaves while allowing them to move about freely, or purchased family members so they could remain near loved ones. South Carolina slave owner Robert Howard (not to be confused with a black slave owner of the same name) did both, when, in 1823, he purchased James Marsh's slave mother, Abby Hopton, from him for $5 (her market value was about $800) and then promised, in a deed of trust, to allow her the same rights as a free person of color. Such agreements were extralegal, or illegal, but this did not deter whites from evading or breaking the law. Even Charles C. Jones, Jr., a man of the highest probity, advised his father not to prosecute the person who had illegally hired one of his father's runaway slaves. "A prosecution would be unpleasant, tending to make the matter notorious, and would in every probability be unaccompanied by conviction," he explained. "Unless there be an obligation resting upon one for purposes affecting the general good, order, and well-being of society, the less said and done in cases of this kind the better." One southern jurist went so far as to rule (to the consternation of many slaveholders) that until illegally freed blacks were actually seized and brought to trial they must be allowed to "stand on the footing of any other free negro." Another argued that "a common reputation of freedom" was prima facie evidence of free status. "It is difficult to suppose a case," he declared, "where common reputation would concede to a man the right of freedom if his right were a groundless one."[59] Indeed, such rulings and activities on the part of slave masters were as much a part of the fabric of antebellum race relations as the punitive and repressive laws designed to control every aspect of Negro life.

Slave Property Ownership in the South

It was a clear, bright morning, the second day of winter 1864, as General William T. Sherman, heading an entourage of Union soldiers, rode slowly down Bull Street in Savannah, Georgia, to the customhouse. Climbing several flights of stairs to the roof, he scanned the city—the small brick houses, the grilled gateways and half-concealed gardens, the sluggish, rust-colored Savannah river, and a smoldering, half-sunken ironclad in the navy yard—the only vestige that the city had been occupied less than twenty-four hours before by the Confederate Army. Sherman felt a sense of relief and triumph.[60] He had led his men on one of the most successful campaigns of the war; he had reached his destination with very few casualties (only 764 men killed, missing, or wounded in an army of 65,000); he had confiscated large herds of livestock. "We started out with about five thousand head of cattle, and arrived with over ten thousand," he reported to Ulysses Grant, "of course consuming mostly turkeys, chickens, sheep, hogs and the cattle of the country."[61] In addition, he had captured fifteen thousand first-rate mules and at least thirty thousand horses. Before his final assault northward, through the Carolinas to Richmond, he would rest his men and stock his supply wagons. In the weeks that followed Union barges, carrying thousands of hogs, sheep, horses, mules, and huge quantities of cornmeal and potatoes, moved steadily up the Ogeechee River to the narrow road at King's bridge.

Even the most loyal Savannahian had probably forgotten Sherman's month-long occupation when, some eight years later, another representative of the United States government, Special Agent Virgil Hillyer of the Southern Claims Commission,[62] arrived in the city. Under a mandate from Congress to identify and provide restitution to Union loyalists who had lost personal property to Sherman's pillaging troops, Hillyer remained in the city nearly a year, listening to the testimony of thousands of witnesses, taking depositions from hundreds of claimants.[63] "I know it is hard for some to realize or imagine how it was possible for slaves to own property," he wrote after several months, "[but there] are colored persons in Savannah worth their [sic] thousands; some in our market who can buy 50 or 300 head of cattle at a time, and did so before and during the war." Among them were cotton factor Monday Habersham, hostler John Butler, livery keeper Henry Wane, butcher Abram Steward, and cotton farmer Prince Kendy. These blacks had become as prosperous as many whites. Steward, for example, had leased five hundred acres from his master, owned between three and four hundred head of cattle, and had been, according to Hillyer, "the largest and most successful butcher in the Savannah market." Kendy had also rented land from his master but planted it in cotton. It was well known that Kendy's father had been the richest slave in Georgia, worth between $18,000 and $20,000, and that Kendy himself sold several bales of cotton at market each year. As if to allay any doubts about these findings, Hillyer explained that cattle and hogs multiplied rapidly, doubling in number every four or five years, and that blacks near the coast had tended livestock for many generations. Moreover, he had made every effort to verify each claim. He was convinced that most black families in southern Georgia owned a horse, mule, cattle, or other property; and that such ownership was widespread "all through the Southern States."[64]

Coming as it did from a northern-born Unionist who was sympathetic toward freedmen and women such a report might have been viewed with suspicion, but subsequent investigators, including Virginia-born William W. Paine, a former captain in the First Georgia Volunteer Regiment, confirmed Hillyer's findings.[65] Paine corroborated the claims of ex-slaves with the recollections of former masters. "I will [say] that if I can aid him in any degree in making the necessary proofs, I will cheerfully do so," former slave owner Charles C. Jones, Jr., wrote from New York City, concerning John Monroe's claim that he had lost cattle and horses worth $2,642. "He was one of the best Negroes I ever knew. His industry was ceaseless. He was always adding to his possessions, and surrounding himself with comforts unusual for one in his station. He had, of his own means, purchased his own and his wife's freedom prior to the emancipation proclamation."[66] When the statements of former masters could not be procured, Paine interviewed neighbors, friends, and local residents. It took him nearly a year and a half to verify the claim of former bondswoman Linda Roberts. On January 30, 1875, she had testified that she had recently lost her husband and relied on her children and grandchildren for support, but before the war she had owned 20 head of cattle (valued at $400), 30 hogs ($150), 40 beehives ($80), 18 ducks ($9), 50 chickens ($10), 20 bushels of corn ($30), 100 bushels of rice ($200), a saddle and bridle ($20), and a horse and buggy ($260).

"I owned the property in my petition [valued at $1,159] because my husband bought it. In the first place my husband bought a mare colt which was the beginning of his raising. He planted corn & sold it to buy the mare. We raised this colt till she had a colt, she had three colts, one died. Master bought one & we kept one which we swapped for a gray mare, which the Yankees took from us. He got the cattle same as he did the horse; bought a cow and raised off her. He got the hogs in the same way, bought a sow & raised from that. He got the other things mentioned in his petition by buying, raising, & trading."[67]

After a lengthy investigation Paine concluded, as had Hillyer, that significant numbers of slaves had owned property.

Working within the task system low-country blacks discovered many ways to accumulate property. But in various other parts of the South, on large and small plantations and in towns and cities, slaves used other means to acquire a few head of livestock, extra clothing, and small amounts of cash. Some planted staples and sold them to the master; others earned wages when they were hired out or hired themselves out; and a few gained quasi-free status. Property ownership among slaves remained small during the eighteenth century, but by the eve of the Civil War—according to the comments of slaveholders, increasing enactments to halt "pretended ownership," the recollections of former slaves, and the reports of postwar investigators— considerable numbers of slaves had become property owners. They possessed cattle, milk cows, horses, pigs, chickens, cotton, rice, tobacco, gold and silver coin, wagons, buggies, fancy clothing, and in rare instances even real estate.

While this coincided with a declining African influence in the slave population, the motives and attitudes of slaves toward accumulating property were complex. Even those who never left the plantation saw the symbiotic relationship between ownership and autonomy, wealth and prestige, earnings and freedom. Some of them were motivated by the work ethic or a competitive impulse: they spoke of "getting ahead" and "accumulating"; they were described as "very acquisitive" or having "a passion for ownership." Yet others acquired property for show (e.g., fancy clothes), for practical reasons (a horse for visiting family members on a neighboring plantation), or as an expression of status. The drudgery and despair of perpetual enslavement aroused in some a special yearning for possessing even a few things they could call their own. In rural areas with the largest concentrations of blacks—eastern North Carolina, the Sea Islands of South Carolina and Georgia, the black belt of Alabama, the Mississippi Delta, and the sugar parishes of Louisiana—the dominant motive was probably the desire for autonomy. Indeed, by planting crops, raising farm animals, hunting and fishing, blacks could distance themselves not only from the impersonal forces of the marketplace but from their overseers and masters as well. These goals—subsistence and independence—as historian Philip Morgan suggests, were "nothing more than the central priorities of peasants throughout the world."[68] Yet even in these regions, and more so in towns and cities and in areas with smaller concentrations of slaves (or larger numbers of free Negroes)—as in Maryland, Virginia, Tennessee, and Missouri—bondsmen and women demonstrated not only the need for autonomy but also a determination to improve themselves and provide their families with more than bare necessities. In any case, black attitudes toward property ownership had changed dramatically in only two generations.

Standing on the roof of the customhouse and looking out over a conquered city, General Sherman felt a sense of euphoria on that December day during the waning months of the Civil War. At that very moment, his troops were making their way across sluggish streams, down through cane brakes, and into cypress swamps as they marauded to accumulate provisions for a final assault against the dying Confederacy. Little did he realize, however, that some of the provisions and livestock being seized belonged to the very slaves he had marched to the sea to liberate.

CHAPTER THREE

Free Negro Property Owners, 1800–1860

Beginning in 1913, with the publication of John H. Russell's *The Free Negro in Virginia, 1619–1865*, three generations of scholars have examined the plight of free Negroes in the South. The pioneer historians in the field—Howard Rosser, James Wright, Ralph Flanders, Charles Syndor, Luther Porter Jackson, and John Hope Franklin— produced an important body of literature, analyzing the social, religious, and economic strivings of a people who were neither accepted as equals in the society in which they lived nor wanted as friends and neighbors.[1] As indicated in the Introduction to this work, Jackson and Franklin were especially concerned about the economic plight of free blacks, investigating "The Free Negro Farmer and Property Owner," "The City Property Owner," "Property in Slaves," and "The Free Negro in the Economic Life of North Carolina." While their methodologies and to some extent their conclusions differed slightly, both recognized this area of free Negro life as being of vital importance. "The span of time in which the free Negro is thought to have suffered the most severe restrictions is that treated in this study," Jackson said in the introduction to his classic study of Virginia between 1830 and 1860, but these restrictions were legal and political in nature. "Favorable economic conditions mitigated the force of the law and enabled the free Negroes to advance along with the general upward movement in the state."[2]

For nearly a generation the books of Jackson and Franklin, meticulously researched and forcefully written, stood as the last major publications on the subject. Yet, even at the time, and a few years later in 1947, the black sociologist E. Horace Fitchett was writing some important articles on free persons of color in Charleston, South Carolina, and a few other scholars were publishing essays about this group in other locales. During the 1950s and 1960s, some of the most significant work on the subject, including Donald E. Everett's doctoral dissertation on free people of color in New Orleans, remained unpublished.[3] Then, within a two-year span during the early 1970s, three published dissertations appeared on free persons of color in the nation's capital, Louisiana, and South Carolina. These studies examined the social, political, and economic conditions of free Negroes in a variety of different settings, ranging from urban centers of the Upper and Lower South to the rural back country of the Piedmont in the Carolinas. While some attention was devoted to black wealth holding—Letitia Brown, for example, listed all the black taxpayers in the District of Columbia between 1824 and 1845—these authors were primarily concerned with other subjects—origins, status, lack of citizenship rights, manumissions, and the growing sectional conflict.[4]

The second generation of research drew to a close in 1974 with the publication of Ira Berlin's influential *Slaves without Masters: The Free Negro in the Antebellum South.* Virtually every scholar who has subsequently written on the subject is indebted to Professor Berlin's gracefully written and broad-ranging analysis of what he termed "masterless slaves," the first comprehensive study of free blacks in the South. For the first time historians had a clear picture of the subregional differences in the Upper South and the Lower South, the demographic changes that occurred from decade to decade, and the paradoxical and ambiguous nature of race relations. In addition, he portrayed free Negroes as a diverse and heterogeneous group, with different social, political, economic, and cultural strivings.[5]

Following the publication of *Slaves without Masters,* a third generation of scholars has begun to look more deeply into various aspects of free Negro life in the South. In his economic profile of free blacks in antebellum Savannah, Whittington B. Johnson contends that this group did not experience "insuperable difficulties earning a living with the restrictions defined by laws and social customs" and that economically free blacks were not "slaves without masters." Entering a range of occupations—as artisans, barbers, draymen, tailors, seamstresses, and pastry cooks—they earned good wages, purchased real estate, and owned slaves. In his investigation of urban free blacks, Leonard Curry uncovered that they were "roughly one-half" as likely as other city dwellers in 1850 to own real estate, but given their "economic deprivation" and limited opportunities for employment, he believed this was truly "remarkable." Indeed, it was "a monument" to their "energy, enterprise, and frugality."[6]

Despite this considerable scholarship, the themes suggested nearly a half-century ago by Luther Porter Jackson and John Hope Franklin have only been hinted at in the literature. Wealth accumulation among free blacks in the South—perhaps the best key to understanding their attitudes as well as their position in Southern society—remains largely unexplored. We still know little about the origin, growth, and regional variations of free black property ownership, the subtle economic changes occurring in the Lower South during the 1840s, and the surge into the property-owning class in the Upper South during the 1850s. In addition, many questions remained unanswered: What were the barriers to economic advancement? How did free blacks confront these obstacles? How did property ownership differ in various sections of the Lower and Upper South, among men and women, blacks and mulattoes, among those living in urban and rural areas? How did it change over time? In seeking answers to these questions, this chapter will also analyze the relations between free blacks and whites, discuss the guardianship systems, both formal and informal, and examine the responses of free black property owners to the emigration movement. Since the first precise statistical evidence for the region's property owners is not available until the 1850 census, the tables and charts will be skewed toward the latter antebellum period, but comparative data from earlier periods will be used in every section of the chapter. By focusing on the quest of blacks for an economic foothold, and by analyzing their successes and failures, we can perhaps more fully understand the ambiguous and anomalous condition of a people striving for economic betterment in a society dominated by a slaveholding aristocracy.

Barriers to Advancement

That all except a few free blacks became property owners seems remarkable considering the social, political, legal, and economic barriers they confronted during the first six decades of the nineteenth century. In fact, no other group in American history (excluding slaves) faced more seemingly insurmountable obstacles to advancement. Following the wave of emancipations and the liberalizing of the legal codes during the post-Revolutionary era, slave owners tightened the laws governing free blacks. With each passing decade, but especially during the 1820s, following the Denmark Vesey conspiracy in South Carolina, and the 1830s, following the Nat Turner revolt in Virginia, southern whites enacted new legislation and initiated new controls to curtail the activities of a group that seemed to pose a threat to the stability of the "peculiar institution." In at least one state free Negroes who were considered "idle" could be turned over to local authorities and then bound out to planters, and if they entered the state "illegally," they could be "sold."[7] During the late 1850s, several states enacted statutes requiring free persons of color—even those who had accumulated considerable amounts of property—to leave the state or find a suitable master and return to bondage.[8]

Some of these laws and controls struck directly at the opportunities of free Negroes to acquire property. While only a few of them went so far as the plan advocated by St. George Tucker in 1796—to stifle completely the aspirations of freedmen and women—Tucker would have been pleased with the economic restrictions enacted in various states and locales. South Carolina granted certain communities the privilege of taxing free blacks—a prerogative generally reserved to the state; in response, the Georgetown Town Council levied a duty of up to $100 on each adult free person of color who did not live under the direct supervision of a white (at the same residence) or who wished to open a shop or store. Maryland denied Negroes the right to put their savings in homestead and building associations, institutions designed to promote "economy and frugality among the people." At the same time, Maryland lawmakers tried but failed to pass a law denying slaves emancipated after 1831 the right to purchase real estate.[9] Florida made it a crime for anyone to purchase items from a free black without written authorization.[10] In 1843, Louisiana authorized local authorities in New Orleans to arrest free persons of color born outside of the state, even longtime residents who owned large amounts of property. Shortly after its passage one observer noted that the new law was forcing some free Negroes to sell their homes at a substantial loss. At the state's Constitutional Convention in 1852, several delegates unsuccessfully attempted to forbid free Negroes from acquiring real estate by inheritance or purchase. In Mississippi, free blacks emancipated outside the state, or entering the state without legal permission, were prohibited from owning real estate or any other property.[11]

In other states authorities prohibited free Negroes from selling certain foods and beverages (beer, whiskey, wine, fruit, cake, candy), managing certain types of businesses (coffee houses, billiard parlors, retail liquor stores), or entering skilled occupations without obtaining a special permit (barbering, bricklaying, butchering).[12] In some towns and cities, freemen and women were required to register at the courthouse, wear badges verifying their status, and post "good behavior" bonds. But no state went so far as Georgia in seeking to stifle the economic aspirations of free blacks. In 1818, the state legislature passed a law denying them the right to acquire property. "No free person of colour within this state, (Indians in amity with this state excepted) shall be permitted to purchase or acquire any real estate, or any slave or slaves," the law stated, either by direct conveyance, will, deed, contract, agreement, or stipulation; nor could anyone establish a trust "reserving to such free person of colour the beneficial interest therein." Any property acquired in such a manner would be confiscated by the state and sold at public auction, with 10 percent of the proceeds going to the informant. Although this enactment did not cover property held at the time of its passage, and though a year later, except in Augusta, Darien, and Savannah, the 1818 law was repealed so far as it related to real estate, Georgia lawmakers had gone to extraordinary lengths to keep free Negroes in a subordinate economic position.[13]

Besides the web of legal restrictions, free blacks confronted other obstacles to economic advancement, not the least of which were the years, sometimes decades, it had taken many of them to save enough merely to purchase themselves out of slavery. Often these years represented the most productive ones of their lives. While some of them would later become property owners, if they had been able to include the amount they had paid for themselves as "tangible assets" they would have been able to boast much larger estates. "He was 7 years in laying up his freedom-money," an acquaintance of South Carolina slave George Moss said, "and during the whole of this time, he performed the ordinary labor of a slave for his master." Allowed to work for himself on Sundays, holidays, and in the evenings, Moss strung baskets and fashioned brooms. He sold these items and used the earnings to make small loans to whites.[14] Another slave carved wooden trays and bowls for a number of years before eventually saving enough to purchase his freedom.[15] It took Godfrey Brown twenty-three years to purchase himself, his wife, and his nine children. "I have no hesitation in saying," stated Virginia slave owner John T. Bowdoin after receiving $2,375 from Brown, "that I was influenced [to free him] by the high character which he supported for honesty and industry, and inoffensive behavior."[16]

Although there were few Godfrey Browns in the South, a significant proportion of blacks who gained the status of freemen and women did so by purchasing themselves. According to a local survey, among the 1,129 former slaves in Cincinnati, Ohio, in 1839, 476, or 42 percent, had purchased themselves. They paid a total of $215,522, or an average of $453 each, and in addition, there was still a "large number in the city who are working out their own freedom,—their free papers being retained as security." A census of two other southern Ohio communities revealed that almost 20 percent of the local black population had been freed through purchase by blacks or self-purchase. Usually in their thirties, they tended to be artisans, cooks, servants, or barbers if men, and laundresses if women. Among the 1,077 ex-slaves in Philadelphia, during the late 1840s, 275, or 26 percent, had bought themselves, paying a total of $63,034. Some blacks who acquired their freedom in Adams County, Mississippi, purchased themselves; the same was true in Cole County, Missouri, Henrico County, Virginia, and various other locales.[17]

The economic burdens of self-purchase, and its subsequent effects on earning power and property accumulation, were no less economically draining than the substantial sums free blacks put out to buy members of their families. Maryland preacher Noah Davis paid several thousand dollars over a period of seventeen years for his wife and six of his nine children. In 1826, former slave Alethia Tanner, of the District of Columbia, bought her sister and five nieces and nephews. While still a slave the District's Sophia Browning bought her husband who then bought Sophia's freedom. In Virginia, Frank Gowen, Mosby Shepherd, Samuel Johnston, Charles Cousins, Henry Carter, and others, purchased wives, sons, daughters, and relatives. Nearly three times as many free blacks in Petersburg in 1827 owned slaves as owned real estate (69 compared with 25). Most of them owned family members or relatives. Virginia's Elizabeth Cromwell spent several decades earning $3,000 to pay for herself, her husband, and her eight children. One of her grandchildren, editor and educator John Wesley Cromwell, explained that the family was by all rights free before the purchases since one of the first Cromwells had been emancipated before the American Revolution but later reenslaved. One former Tennessee slave recalled how her grandfather had saved $800 to buy himself, another $800 to purchase her grandmother, and $350 to buy her mother. "Now mind you, for his own child, they charged him $350," she exclaimed, "just think of that." John Berry Meachum, pastor of the African Baptist Church in St. Louis, not only purchased his own freedom, but also bought his wife, children, and father, as well as twenty other slaves, allowing them to purchase their freedom after learning a trade.[18]

Even in the Deep South, where black slave ownership was primarily commercial, some free Negroes purchased relatives, friends, and family members, holding them in nominal bondage. In 1828, Moses

Irvine, a Charleston shoemaker, bought his wife Harriet and their two children. Shortly afterward, he petitioned the state legislature for their freedom. The petition was rejected, but the family remained together. Several years later, Irvine again petitioned the general assembly, this time to allow his slave family the right to inherit his real and personal property. The granting of this petition was a rare instance of slave property ownership receiving the sanction of law. Between 1803 and 1815, South Carolina carpenter Titus Gregorie purchased his sons Aberdeen and Titus, Jr., his daughters Elizabeth and Eleanor, and his wife Nelly. Gregorie, too, was unable to free the members of his family, holding them virtually as free slaves. In Georgia, Florida, Alabama, Mississippi, and Louisiana, a few free blacks, like Irvine and Gregorie, acquired members of their families. In New Orleans, during the 1830s and 1840s, though constituting only a small fraction of the city's slaveholders, free persons of color entered nearly one-third of all the emancipation petitions (501 of 1,553), often for relatives they had purchased out of slavery. While it is not possible to put a dollar value on freedom such efforts represented substantial earnings and payments. Without the burden of buying themselves and their families, and the years of effort it took, some self-acquired blacks would have accumulated handsome estates. Indeed, a few did anyway.[19]

Struggling against repressive legal codes, spending substantial sums to purchase themselves or their loved ones out of slavery, facing competition from slaves and whites in various occupations, and entering freedom, especially in the Upper South, with few skills to sustain themselves in a competitive economic order, blacks found the acquisition of even modest amounts of real estate and personal holdings extremely difficult. In addition, they were denied employment in some instances because whites believed that free Negroes were indolent, lazy, and ignorant. Considering these difficulties, it is not surprising that a majority remained propertyless. What is striking is that with each passing decade increasing numbers of free Negroes entered the property-owning class.

Free Black Property Ownership before 1830

It was a slow, tedious process. From the early decades of the nineteenth century to 1830 the entry rate into the propertied group in most areas was only slightly greater (and in some sections less) than the proportional growth of the free black population. This was true nearly everywhere in the South, except for a few sections in the Lower

South where traditions of ownership had already been firmly established. In the Upper South, many free blacks had only recently emerged from bondage. Working as farm laborers, dockhands, domestic servants, day workers, laundresses, and in various other menial capacities, a majority of them found it difficult to provide for their families, much less accumulate land or become farm owners. In 1798, in Frederick County, Maryland, out of a total free Negro population of nearly 473, only 3 owned property, with an assessed total value of only $50; nearly three decades later, in 1825–26, while the free black population had increased to an estimated 2,300, only 47 free Negroes were assessed a total of $1,025, or $22 per wealth holder. In 1804, in Kent County, Maryland, with a population of approximately 1,800 free Negroes, 49 persons held an aggregate of $3,795; more than two decades later in 1825–26, with the population rising to about 2,100, 85 family heads held $9,152 in assessed property, or $108 per wealth holder. Considering the fact that during the period there was some inflation in land values, the increased average in Kent County from $77 to $108 was even less than it would appear. In other Maryland counties the numbers were much the same; only a tiny proportion of the free black population was able to accumulate even the most modest amounts of property.[20]

Similar property assessment records are not available for other Upper South states, but contemporary observers and scattered tax assessments tell much the same story. "The last census [1820] disclosed the melancholy truth," one group of Virginia whites noted, pleading for state action to "return" free Negroes to West Africa, "[that in] Maryland and Virginia together [there are] more than 76,000 free people of color." As to their "actual condition," it was doubtful that more than a few hundred in each state were landholders. Their situation in Virginia was "perhaps sufficiently illustrated" by the fact that "although not debarred from holding lands, not two hundred of 37,000, are proprietors [of the land]."[21] A decade later, in the ten largest towns and cities in the state, including Richmond, Petersburg, Norfolk, Portsmouth, Alexandria, and Fredericksburg, 120 free Negroes owned property valued at $63,860, or $532 per owner. In Richmond, only one out of fifteen family heads was a property holder; in Petersburg, only one out of twenty. "The main explanation for this condition," Luther Porter Jackson observed, "lay in the fact that the [pre-]1830 generation of free Negroes had not been free long enough to establish themselves as property owners." In North Carolina, and to the west, in Kentucky, Tennessee, and Missouri, the same profile existed. In 1830, the tax assessor in St. Genevieve County, Missouri, failed even to record the surnames of the five free black property owners, merely listing "Bastian," "Isaac," "Letty," "Molly," and "Portorique," as owners of between $25 and $150 worth of property.[22]

This did not deter free blacks from exerting every effort to enter the property-holding class. Even those who failed to do so often revealed by their actions that they held the acquisition of land in the highest regard. One individual who demonstrated this desire was Virginia carpenter Daniel Ellett, who, for the use of a small farm in Norfolk County, signed a remarkable lease with white farmer John Hodges: "[I agree to] build and compleat thereon [the leasor's land] Houses after the following dimentions[,] to wit A dwelling house after the following dimentions[,] viz to be Eighteen feet square of proper and proportionable hight and form in every other aspect, with a Window in each side and one end below [the] stairs to consist each of eight lights of Sash to [be] finished with proper and suitable Glass, . . . with a good brick Chimney and underpinned flush with bricks, Two floars to be made and laid in said house both tounged and grooved, also a pair of Stairs, all to be compleat and finished in a workman like manner, also a Meat house." It is not known whether or not Ellett ever became a farm owner himself, but such an agreement, however exploitative it might have been, illustrated the determination of free blacks to begin the ascent toward economic independence.[23]

Opportunities to acquire property were better in the Lower South. The comparatively small number of free persons of color, their close association with whites, and their higher skill levels were advantages not possessed by their brethren in the border states. But even in the Lower South, a majority of the free Negro property owners were able to accumulate only small amounts of property. A rare surviving "Register of Free Persons of Color" in Chatham County, Georgia— indicating name, age, place of residence, occupation, name of white guardian, and "property owned"—suggests the difficulties facing this anomalous group in acquiring an economic stake during this early period. Between 1817 and 1829, a total of 140 free persons of color in the county had acquired some type of property. Since it was against the law for blacks in the city of Savannah to own either real estate or slaves, free Negroes were forced to "possess" their estates in the name of whites or purchase buildings on someone else's land. Seamstress Polly Baptiste owned a building on lot number five in Greene Ward; street vendor Nelly Dolly held the "improvements" on half a lot in Trustees Garden; carpenter John Johnson owned one small building on lot number thirteen in Washington Ward; cooper Benjamin Reizne owned buildings on one-fourth of a lot in Yamacraw; huckster Leah

Beard owned a small house on the lot of M. H. McAllister, a white resident; and barber Alexander Debross possessed the "improvements" on a lot in Liberty Ward. While the proportion of free Negroes who "owned" a building on someone else's land, or a house, or some other property, including slaves, was higher in Chatham County than in various counties in Maryland and Virginia, the value of the property in both sections remained very small. In 1826, among 184 adult men and women in Chatham County, 67 owned property, or approximately one out of three, but only a few—Anthony Odingsells, Louis Mirault, John Gibbons, Polly Spein, Susan Jackson, Hannah Leron, and Andrew Marshall—controlled property valued in excess of $500.[24]

Only in Charleston, New Orleans, and a few rural areas in South Carolina and Louisiana did free Negroes acquire more than modest property holdings prior to 1830. As suggested previously, many of these owners were direct descendants of early white settlers, had received land grants and other assistance from their white fathers, or had arrived in the United States from the Caribbean with property as well as experience in financial matters. Often highly skilled, and representing only a small proportion of the total black population (3.4 percent in the Lower South in 1830), they seemed to pose no threat to the South's "peculiar institution." Indeed, a significant number of them were themselves slave owners (see chapter 4). Under such conditions, some free persons of color accumulated comfortable amounts of property.

During the first three decades of the nineteenth century, skilled artisans in Charleston, South Carolina, continued to purchase houses, buildings, town lots, and rural tracts of farmland. Among the largest property owners were carpenters Robert Baldwin, George Bendon, Thomas Davis, John V. Francis, Richard Holloway, Robert Hopton, George Logan, George Matthews, James Mitchell, and Smart Simpson, cabinetmakers Thomas Charnock and Charles DuBois, turner William Eden, and tinsmith Manuel Pincell.[25] They owned not only city property and rural acreage, but also a few acquired herds of cattle and livestock, shares in the Charleston Planters and Mechanics Bank, and handsome residential homes. James Mitchell's house, for example, was described as a "two & half story brick dwelling with kitchen and stables."[26]

Similarly, during the same thirty-year span, free Negroes in several Louisiana parishes emerged as sizable property owners.[27] Luc Ricard and Augustin Dubuclet of Iberville Parish, Augustin and Louis Metoyer of Natchitoches, Louise Oliver of Plaquemines (see appendix 3),

Henry Collin of Pointe Coupée, and Honoré Dumony and Agnes Mahier of West Baton Rouge acquired farms, plantations, and small
gangs of slaves. Like their white neighbors, they planted rice, cotton,
corn, and vegetables, owned farm equipment, livestock, and machinery, and sold their crops to commission merchants in New Orleans.[28]
An inventory of Agnes Mahier's estate in 1833 showed that she owned
two separate tracts of land, one of sixty and the other of eighty acres,
fronting on the Mississippi River. Her other possessions included a
large house, four pair of oxen, several horses, ten cows, and fourteen
slaves.[29]

The largest group of property owners in the South during this period was located in the Crescent City. Often directly related to whites,
or mulatto or quadroon women living with white men, free persons
of color in the city boasted a long history of economic prosperity.
Taking advantage of their acceptance by the French and Spanish during the early years, and of the continuing traditions of black enterprise after statehood, they acquired lots, houses, stores, buildings, and
other property. "These men, sir, for the most part, sustain good char-
acters," Louisiana governor C. C. Claiborne explained to General Andrew Jackson in 1814, describing free persons of color in the city.
"Many of them have extensive connections and much property to defend and all seem attached to arms." Those with "much property"
included, among others, Augustin Ben, Louis Canal, Francois Durant, Edmond Rillieux, and Augustin Ricard, who ran small businesses or worked as skilled craftsmen. As the city grew and expanded
during the 1820s and early 1830s, becoming one of the nation's leading commercial and trading centers, hundreds of free colored people
entered the property-holding ranks. Securing employment not only
as skilled artisans and craftsmen but also as merchants, retailers,
brokers, and traders, by 1836, according to one assessment list,
855 free persons of color in the city paid taxes on property worth
$2,462,470—a total exceeding the value of black-owned property
anywhere else in the United States.[30]

Expansion in the Upper South

Indeed, the value of the property owned by blacks in Crescent City
was probably greater than the total value of black-owned property in
the entire Upper South, but during the next generation—1830 to
1860—free Negroes in the upper states closed the gap considerably
between themselves and free persons of color in the lower states. The
relative improvement among free black property owners in the Up-

per South was due to a number of complex and interrelated forces. As Luther Jackson suggested, it sometimes took a generation of freedom for former slaves to become economically independent. Thus, with the wave of emancipations completed by the first decade of the nineteenth century, it took until the 1830s for the newly freed men to enter the tax rolls. This is borne out by the first race-specific age data among property owners in the 1850 census, when the mean age among Negro realty owners stood at forty-eight, with nearly half of them fifty or older, 23 percent sixty or older, and nearly one out of ten threescore and ten years. In addition, there were a number of economic forces at work in this growth—increased demand for workers, higher wages, easier access to markets for farmers, growing demand for skilled artisans, and in some sections, with the migration of whites to cities or to the western states, better opportunities to purchase land at reasonable prices. At the same time, for reasons discussed later, there was a leveling off of free Negro wealth holding in the Lower South, and in some areas, by the 1850s, a relative decline, especially among property owners with modest holdings. While even on the eve of the Civil War, free blacks in the Upper South remained behind their brethren in the lower states in the average value of their land holdings, during the generation before the war they made notable advances.

These gains were widespread, occurring in every state from Virginia to Missouri, in rural and urban areas, among men and women, blacks and mulattoes, skilled and unskilled workers. The rate of increase among property owners was many times greater than the general increase in the free Negro population (approximately 16 percent per decade), and the value of their holdings outstripped the general property inflation rate (which varied, but in areas where free blacks were concentrated rarely exceeded 4 or 5 percent annually) in nearly every state. While Upper South blacks improved their general skill levels, both in the numbers of craftsmen, shopkeepers and tradesmen, and service-related businessmen and women and in relation to their counterparts in the Lower South, most property owners remained unskilled or semi-skilled workers even by the eve of the Civil War. Thus the expansion was primarily a result of the relentless drive on the part of former slaves and their children to gain an economic foothold. Even during the late antebellum era some blacks journeyed from slavery to freedom to land proprietorship in a single generation.

Despite these widespread increases, opportunities for economic advancement varied in urban and rural areas, and in some rural areas compared with others. The most significant expansion among rural land and farm owners in the Upper South occurred in four states: Delaware, Maryland, Virginia, and North Carolina. Following the depression of 1837–43, with the continued migration of some whites and large numbers of slaves to the West, free blacks along the eastern seaboard could more easily purchase rural farm land at reasonable prices. Then, during the 1850s, with generally prosperous times (except for the recession of 1857–58), they witnessed a rise in the value of their holdings. In 1830, free Negro farmers in Virginia owned 31,721 acres of land appraised at $184,184; thirty years later they owned 60,045 acres valued at $369,647. During the same period the number of rural land holders rose from approximately 678 to 1,316. In 1832–33, excluding the city and county of Baltimore, freedmen and women in Maryland owned $172,848 in total assessed property (real estate, buildings, houses, lots, livestock, farm tools, furniture, wagons, carriages, boats, etc.); in 1860, rural blacks owned $1,270,000 in real estate and $618,700 in personal holdings for a total of $1,888,700, an increase—taking into account an assessment ratio of less than 50 percent of the actual value—of nearly 450 percent in one generation. During the same period the number of rural landowners in the state rose from approximately 500 to 2,124. In North Carolina, in 1850, free Negroes controlled $165,400, and in Delaware, $163,000 worth of rural land; a decade later those in North Carolina owned $452,200, and those in Delaware controlled $318,500 worth. The number of rural realty owners in North Carolina rose from 502 to 844, in Delaware from 290 to 522. Thus, while the rural free Negro population in the northeastern portion of the Upper South grew very slowly—less than 10 percent per decade—the number and property holdings of rural free blacks in this area rose significantly.[31]

The vast majority of these farm owners were either former slaves themselves or the children of former slaves. Although color—black vs. mulatto—is not a precise gauge of previous condition, the fact that the great majority of these landowners in the seaboard states of the Upper South were listed in the censuses of 1850 and 1860 as "black" suggests a close proximity to slavery. In Virginia, one-third of all the Negro farm owners in the state in 1860 lived in a cluster of eight Coastal Plain counties where blacks outnumbered mulattoes in the free Negro population by more than three to one (compared to three to two in the state as a whole). These counties contained sizable concentrations of slaves and relatively large free Negro populations. What set them apart was the black component in the free Negro farm-owning class. In Maryland, the proportion of rural land holders more nearly approximated the black-mulatto breakdown in the free Negro population, but four out of five free Negro farm owners in the state were listed in the censuses as black. In the two Eastern Shore counties where the number of farm owners rose most precipitously during the 1850s—Dorchester, from 119 to 490; and Kent, from 58 to 196—blacks outnumbered mulattoes in the free Negro population by nearly twenty to one (the ratio in the state was four to one). As in Virginia, these counties contained significant slave and free Negro concentrations, but they stood apart because of the large concentrations of blacks who had entered the farm-owning group.[32]

This, of course, is only suggestive with regard to former status, but the fact that between 85 and 90 percent of the slave population in Virginia and Maryland was black in 1860 (compared with 59 and 81 percent of the free Negro population) and the proportion of blacks in the rural land-holding class equaled or exceeded their proportion in the free Negro population indicates that most of these property owners were either former slaves or the children of former slaves. Even in areas with proportionally larger numbers of free mulattoes, property owners were often former bondsmen and women who had saved many years to acquire land. Faquier County, Virginia, mulatto Samuel Johnston had purchased his freedom, acquired his wife and daughter, and over a long period of time accumulated "comfortable real estate." "I have Known Samuel Johnson thirty years," a local white physician said, "during that time I have not Know [sic] a more honest man; his industry aided by his very superior character" allowed him to purchase a house and farmland (see appendix 2). As the following table indicates, the largest increases in rural land ownership during the 1850s occurred along the Atlantic seaboard states of the Upper South, a region where many free blacks had vivid memories of slavery.[33]

At the same time it should be emphasized that, despite these gains, the great majority of rural free Negroes in the upper states remained propertyless. Even in Maryland and Virginia, only approximately one out of six family heads (3,440 of 20,784) became landowners. Those who did usually owned only small acreages, worth a few hundred dollars. Yet, considering the distance they had traveled in a single generation, the increased number of property owners and their expanded holdings represented a significant achievement.

A significant minority of free blacks in the Upper South—nearly one out of three—lived in towns and cities. During the early years of the century thousands of freed slaves had poured into the urban centers of the region. The journey, usually only a few miles, and almost always in their home state, represented a sharp break with the past.

Table 3. Rural Free Negro Realty Owners in the Upper South, 1850/1860

State	Total	Arph	Trph
Delaware	290/522	$562/610	$163,000/318,500
District of Columbia	6/34	350/718	2,100/24,400
Kentucky	501/464	604/751	302,600/348,600
Maryland	1,035/2,124	450/598	466,100/1,270,000
Missouri	66/98	603/682	39,800/66,800
North Carolina	502/844	329/536	165,400/452,200
Tennessee	169/213	535/1,060	90,400/225,800
Virginia	762/1,316	473/557	360,500/732,700
Total	3,331/5,615	$477/612	$1,589,900/3,439,000

Source: Computed from USMSPC, 1850, 1860.

For many it served as a reminder of the distance they had moved away from slavery; for others it offered a new social and cultural milieu, a chance for anonymity, an opportunity to attend a black church, or send their children to school. The cityward movement, so vigorous early in the century, slowed considerably during the 1840s and 1850s, due, at least in part, to rising expectations for property ownership in rural areas. Nevertheless, as trading centers, with opportunities for employment and increasingly higher wages, urban areas provided unique possibilities for the accumulation of wealth.[34]

At mid-century, among 1,030 propertied free blacks living in 42 towns and cities in the Upper South—Wilmington, Delaware, the District of Columbia, Baltimore, Richmond, Louisville, Nashville, St. Louis, and Wilmington, North Carolina, among others—the mean real estate holding stood at $933, nearly twice the $477 average held by the region's 3,331 rural property-owning blacks. Comprising only 24 percent of the black real estate owners, and approximately 30 percent of the family heads, they controlled 38 percent of the black-owned realty ($960,800 of $2,550,700). A decade later, among the 1,706 urban real estate owners (a 66 percent increase) in various towns and cities, the average real property holding stood at $1,340 (a 44 percent rise), representing more than twice the $612 average held by the Upper South's 5,615 rural property owners. Still comprising 23 percent of the real estate owners, and about the same proportion of the family heads, urban property owners now controlled 40 percent ($2,285,900 of $5,724,900) of the region's black-owned real estate.

Table 4. Urban Free Negro Realty Owners in the Upper South, 1850/1860

| City | Total Owners | Average Age | Percentage | | Arph | Percentage | |
			Born Instate	Literate		Mulatto	Male
Baltimore	102/169	45/48	91/92	68/68	$1,327/1,324	41/33	91/90
District of Columbia	194/497	45/47	24/31	48/45	659/1,242	37/37	86/77
Louisville	59/59	46/44	56/70	64/75	1,554/1,800	49/46	75/75
Nashville	31/44	47/46	52/57	61/50	1,977/2,714	52/48	81/61
Richmond	92/211	42/43	100/100	47/62	1,174/877	48/55	65/54
St. Louis	20/94	43/43	20/35	90/66	4,530/4,560	60/67	85/80
Wilmington, North Carolina	33/42	45/44	91/100	[1]/33	1,306/1,324	55/91	73/55

Source: Computed from USMSPC, 1850, 1860; Luther Porter Jackson, *Free Negro Labor and Property Holding in Virginia, 1830–1860* (Washington: American Historical Association, 1942), p. 138.

[1]Data not available

While there was an inflation in urban property values, in most cities these increases far exceeded the rise in the value of lots, houses, and other property. In the District of Columbia, in 1825, only 46 black realty owners paid taxes on $23,764 worth of property, an average of $517 each; they represented about 1 out of every 22 family heads. In 1850, 194 real estate owners controlled $127,900, or $659 each; they represented about 1 out of 10 family heads. By 1860, 497 owners controlled $617,200, or $1,242 each, constituting about 1 out of 4.5 heads of family. During the 1850s, as the free Negro population in the city rose a modest 11 percent, the number of real estate owners increased 156 percent and the value of their holdings shot up 383 percent. Between 1830 and 1860, the number of lot owners in Richmond, Virginia, jumped from 50 to 211, in Petersburg from 25 to 246, and in other towns in the state from 82 to 236, while the total value of these holdings rose from $74,543 to $463,016, or 521 percent. By 1860, in Richmond, 1 out of 4 free black family heads owned at least some city property; in Petersburg, about 1 out of 3. During the 1850s, both Nashville and St. Louis witnessed an increase in the number of property owners and a rise in their average holdings, in Nashville from 31 to 44 and from $1,977 to $2,714, in St. Louis from 20 to 94 and from $4,530 to $4,560. In the Gate City, the total value of black-owned realty grew from $90,600 in 1850 to $428,600 in 1860, or 373 percent. Although, in the same decade, cities such as Baltimore, Louisville, and Wilmington, North Carolina, experienced more gradual changes, in each of these urban centers either the number or the mean holdings of black property owners were on the rise.[35]

Of course compared with the holdings of whites these gains were modest. By 1860, in Baltimore, for example, free blacks comprised 12 percent of the city's population but controlled only $628,000 in total wealth—real and personal holdings—compared to $127,000,000 for whites. Nonetheless, in a single generation, urban free blacks in the Upper South had increased their property holdings to a remarkable extent. Like their predecessors in seventeenth-century Virginia, and eighteenth-century South Carolina, former slaves and their children in the towns and cities of the Upper South firmly believed that the possession of property would help them to protect their families, assert their rights in court, and secure the goodwill of whites. The significance that William Butcher, a black pressman in Frankfort, Kentucky, attached to the acquisition of a house (purchased before his twenty-second birthday) could be seen when he divided the property, valued at $600, among his mother, two brothers, and two sisters, deeding each of them a $100 share. By 1860, nearly one out of seven black family heads in the cities of the Upper South (1,706 of 12,153) owned real estate.[36]

This occurred despite the fact that comparatively few free persons of color in the region were highly skilled. In Kentucky and Virginia, only a handful of free Negroes entered the building trades as carpenters and joiners, while in Maryland, among real property owners in 1850, only two were listed as brickmasons. In these states, free blacks tended to work in the service trades as coachmen, draymen, laundresses, painters, porters, or, merging with slaves and quasi-free blacks, as tobacco twisters, iron moulders, coal miners, wood haulers, and cattle tenders. Yet the ability of free Negroes to find work was enhanced by the relatively few European immigrants in the Upper South, the drain of slave laborers to the Deep South as a result of rising slave prices, and the reluctance of whites to engage in certain types of employment. "No white man would ever do certain kinds of work (such as taking care of cattle or getting water or wood to be used in the house)," Frederick Law Olmsted observed, "and if you should ask a white man you had hired to do such things, he would get mad and tell you he wasn't a nigger." These attitudes, coupled with a continued demand for unskilled or semi-skilled workers in the Upper South, gave some blacks an opportunity to advance, despite a lack of job skills.[37]

This could be clearly seen during the 1850s by the significant surge into the property-owning class of a number of blacks who worked in unskilled occupational categories. During this decade in the Upper South, growing numbers of laborers, both rural and urban, as well as coachmen, draymen, laundresses, painters, porters, seamstresses, servants, and waiters, acquired small amounts of real estate. Between 1850 and 1860, the number of laborers who owned real property in the upper states rose from 921 to 2,054 and the value of their holdings from $316,000 to $838,900; the number of washerwomen from 4 to 330 and their holdings from $900 to $195,400; and the number of servants from 17 to 164, with their realty going from $10,200 to $151,500. They also increased their average holdings—coachmen from $691 to $1,944, draymen from $530 to $1,088, painters from $664 to $925, and servants from $600 to $924.

Whenever possible free blacks in the Upper South struggled to improve their occupational standing. In Frankfort, Kentucky, they labored as butchers, plasterers, and home builders; in the District of Columbia, as tanners, coppersmiths, coopers, tinsmiths, cutters, and slaters; in St. Louis, as barbers, carpenters, and stewards. In the Upper South, at mid-century, census takers listed 94 different occupations for black real estate owners. These included 93 blacksmiths, 44 brickmasons, 140 carpenters, 29 coopers, 23 masons, 20 mechanics, 56 shoemakers, and 18 plasterers. A decade later, in the same category, they listed 147 different occupations, a 56 percent increase, and among them were 109 blacksmiths, 69 brickmasons, 221 carpenters, 50 coopers, 39 masons, 32 mechanics, 70 shoemakers, and 26 plasterers, as well as a few caulkers, clergymen, cooks, dairymen, gaugers, livery stable owners, musicians, salesmen, and shopkeepers. Despite such gains, they remained far behind free persons of color in the Lower South: with six times the free black population (224,963 compared to 36,955 in 1860) they boasted only about half the skilled workers. Yet blacks in the Upper South were gradually closing the gap. Among the 344 free Negro carpenters who owned real estate in the South as a whole in 1850, 140 lived in the Upper South; a decade later among the 431 carpenters, 221 lived in the same region, a rise from 41 to more than 51 percent of the total. Similar changes occurred in other skilled occupations as well as among storekeepers, butchers, grocers, merchants, and tailors.[38]

Changing Profile in the Lower South

During the prewar generation, free persons of color in the Lower South, while still the largest property-owning group, lost ground compared with blacks in the upper states. This decline was relative, and in some instances was apparent only in relation to rising land values, but by the 1850s a definite leveling was occurring among the lower region's property owners. Some suffered from the depression during the late 1830s and early 1840s; others, who had obtained their property during the early 1800s, died, and when their estates were divided, creditors took a share of their holdings; still others struggled against droughts, floods, crop failures, price fluctuations, and in urban areas, against competition from whites in certain skilled occupations. As the sectional controversy intensified, some free persons of color found it increasingly difficult to combat the web of legal restrictions and the growing hostility of whites. Yet this decline was gradual, and it did not affect all property owners in the same manner. A few of the most prosperous free Negroes lost ground, but others greatly expanded their holdings (see chapter 4); a larger proportion of those with smaller estates, who were often less insulated from the economic and political turmoil of the period, suffered financial reversals.

By the 1850s, these changes were clearly visible. In the rural areas of the region, some free Negro farm owners, especially in states where they were few in number and relatively isolated—Georgia, Mississippi, Arkansas, and Texas—either lost their holdings, experienced a relative decline in the value of their land, or fled from the state in the face of mounting violence and intimidation. The situation was especially perilous in Mississippi and Arkansas where laws were passed during the late antebellum period to remand free blacks to slavery or force them to leave the state. Some groups of black property owners emigrated, others went into hiding, while still others waged pitched battles with whites. By the eve of the Civil War, the Negro property-holding class in Mississippi had declined; in Arkansas, it had been virtually eliminated. In rural Louisiana, where more than half of the free Negro farmers and planters in the Lower South resided, the 23 percent increase in the average value of real property did not keep pace with rising land values. In Natchitoches Parish, despite some increases in the number of land owners, the total value of land owned by free people of color dropped from $386,200 to $253,700, and the average per realty owner from $4,300 to $2,400. In several other parishes there were similar declines, and if the few wealthy planters who expanded their holdings are excluded, these declines would be even greater. There was genuine improvement in only one state—South Carolina. As was the case in Maryland and Virginia, free blacks found that the migration of whites to the West left some land (often the least desirable) available and at reasonable prices. During the 1850s, the number of rural landowners in the Palmetto State rose from 182 to 304, and the value of their holdings increased from $102,400 to $251,400. But even with this increase, the total number of rural realty owners in the Deep South was increasing at one-fourth the rate of those in the upper states. While the average value of their holdings remained several times larger, the total value of their rural realty holdings had, by 1860, dropped below the total for free blacks in the Upper South.[39]

In a similar way free persons of color in the towns and cities of the Lower South made few economic gains during the late antebellum period. In Savannah, Georgia, in 1823, a total of sixty-four free blacks owned their own homes; a quarter-century later, in 1848, the number remained almost exactly the same, at sixty-five. Some black homeowners lost their properties through defaulting on their taxes during the panic of 1837, while others, including Henry Cunningham, Richard Houston, and Rose Galineau, did not pass their wealth on after their deaths. In 1852, according to a Chatham County (Savannah) tax assessment list, blacks controlled real estate appraised at only $18,500 and personal property appraised at only $20,015, slightly more than

Table 5. Rural Free Negro Realty Owners in the Lower South, 1850/1860

State	Total	Arph	Trph
Alabama	58/89	$712/1,267	$41,300/112,800
Arkansas	38/2	632/600	24,000/1,200
Florida	7/23	500/1,083	3,500/24,900
Georgia	50/47	552/617	27,600/29,000
Louisiana	543/567	3,829/4,709	2,078,900/2,669,800
Mississippi	28/17	646/2,653	18,100/45,100
South Carolina	182/304	563/827	102,400/251,400
Texas	10/17	2,050/1,871	20,500/31,800
Total	916/1,066	$2,529/2,970	$2,316,300/3,166,000

Source: Computed from USMSPC, 1850, 1860.

$125 per wealth holder. In 1846, the tax assessment list for Pensacola, Florida, contained the names of four free Negro realty owners and three other black property owners who controlled a total wealth of $3,050; thirteen years later, in 1859, the same list included the names of three real estate owners and four other property owners, who owned slaves, city lots, improvements, cash, horses, cattle, and household furniture worth an estimated $6,360.

The same type of evidence is not available for Charleston, but by the time of the secession crisis, free persons of color in the city were experiencing economic difficulties. During the early 1860s, the number of free Negroes who paid municipal taxes dropped from 371 to 258, or 30 percent, with the largest decline occurring among those who owned less than $2,000 in taxable property. Even more precipitous, though over a longer period, was the decline in the city of New Orleans, where, as noted previously, free colored people born outside of Louisiana found themselves and their property holdings in jeopardy during the late antebellum era. Between 1836 and 1860, the number of realty owners in the city dropped from 855 in 1836, to 642 in 1850, to 581 on the eve of the Civil War, a total decline of 32 percent. The total value of the realty during the 1850s went from $2,465,000 to $2,628,200, significantly less than the rising prices of city real estate. In all, at least as roughly judged by tax assessment lists and census estimates, a significant number of urban realty owners in the Lower South, especially those with smaller estates, witnessed a steady erosion of their holdings, or found it virtually impossible to expand their wealth.[40]

They also experienced a slow decline of their previously high oc-

Table 6. Occupations among Upper and Lower South Black Real Estate Owners, 1850/1860

Occupation	1850				1860			
	US Total	LS Total	US Arph	LS Arph	US Total	LS Total	US Arph	LS Arph
farmers	1,343	247	$613	$2,107	2,044	386	$908	$1,476
laborers	921	54	343	596	2,054	102	408	1,126
planters	4	199	600	5,761	5	214	1,200	9,708
craftsmen								
blacksmiths	93	22	528	1,182	109	13	895	962
brickmasons	44	40	584	1,278	69	42	652	2,455
carpenters	140	204	662	1,763	221	210	885	1,300
coopers	29	3	455	1,100	50	9	494	989
masons	23	11	513	1,427	39	14	505	1,521
mechanics	20	21	525	833	32	20	903	3,005
plasterers	18	3	694	3,833	26	4	904	900
shoemakers	56	19	668	3,274	70	25	709	2,016
shopkeepers and tradesmen								
barbers	91	14	1,538	1,293	114	18	2,866	1,750
boardinghouse keepers	*	3	*	6,667	2	19	1,900	2,700

butchers	3	18	13,833	2,211	12	23	1,242	1,657
grocers	6	24	1,417	5,067	8	17	1,388	9,747
merchants	11	13	2,045	8,585	7	18	6,629	9,833
restaurateurs	2	5	350	3,520	8	4	1,100	1,125
storekeepers	7	7	1,943	6,786	15	4	1,960	725
tailors	4	26	950	3,385	9	24	1,689	13,954
service								
coachmen	11	*	691	*	39	3	1,944	1,600
draymen	54	18	530	1,011	115	34	1,088	1,303
laundresses	4	3	225	300	330	78	592	772
painters	22	5	664	1,120	55	9	925	2,122
porters	14	3	621	3,067	32	11	1,453	1,773
seamstresses	1	*	600	*	54	59	713	1,527
servants	17	1	600	700	164	13	924	1,031
stewards	11	2	1,155	2,250	17	1	3,194	1,200
mariners	41	7	363	2,171	89	2	496	1,400
ministers	14	2	1,493	900	24	7	1,133	1,114
physicians	2	1	800	4,000	3	3	2,167	9,333
teachers	3	2	1,733	550	5	5	1,960	1,080

Source: Computed from USMSPC, 1850, 1860.

* = none

cupational standing. In the midst of new restrictive laws, racial hostility, and increasing competition from Irish and German immigrants in some skilled and semiskilled jobs, the proportion of free black property owners in the most lucrative occupations declined. In 1850, approximately one out of five real property owners in the region worked as a carpenter or builder (19 percent); a decade later, while the number of carpenters and builders remained nearly the same (204 and 210), the proportion had declined to one out of eight (13 percent). The same relative decline occurred among blacksmiths, brickmasons, mechanics, shoemakers, and tailors. The number of grocers, 24 in 1850, representing 2.2 percent of the realty owners, dropped to 17 in 1860, only 1 percent of the owners. The average amount of real estate held by blacks in some occupations also declined (despite rising property values). Among blacksmiths it went from $1,182 in 1850 to $962 in 1860; among carpenters from $1,763 to $1,300; and among shoemakers from $3,274 to $2,016. In short, what represented improvement in the Upper South—the movement of unskilled laborers into the property-owning class—represented "downward mobility" in the Lower South, as skilled artisans and small businessmen found it difficult to maintain their previously high occupational standing, and among those who did their average wealth, in some occupations, dropped despite rising land values. In only a few occupational areas, including keeping boardinghouses, was there substantial improvement during the 1850s. Even among free women of color who operated rooming houses there was a tendency to rent or lease rather than purchase their establishments.

Free Women of Color

From the early years of the century, in both sections of the South, a significant portion of free black wealth was controlled by women. For a variety of reasons free women of color remained circumspect about committing themselves to marriage. Those who had saved some money, acquired real estate, or operated a business could lose everything by the wrong choice of a mate, since the courts invariably recognized the property rights of men. Those who were trying to purchase a loved one out of bondage often did not wish to assume additional family responsibilities. Some black women chose to live with a partner without formalizing marital vows. This could have the ironic effect of a woman losing all she had sought to preserve by not marrying. In 1827, Nancy Munford, a Virginia slave, was purchased by her husband and emancipated, but the couple never legalized their union. In subsequent years, they built up a substantial estate, but in 1845, Nancy's husband, Thomas Walden, a carpenter, was murdered. To her surprise, Nancy discovered that she was not entitled to any of their jointly acquired property—a house, three lots, and 150 acres of farmland—all listed in her husband's name.[41] Although she eventually petitioned the state legislature and was awarded the property others were not so fortunate.

Such difficulties prompted some black women to take extra precautions to protect their estates. Even those who chose to formalize their marital vows made prenuptial arrangements concerning their holdings. Charleston's Sophia Smith demanded that her future husband, Caribbean-born goldsmith Francis C. N. LeFond, sign "a conveyance in trust" promising not to disturb her real estate holdings.[42] Free mulatto Hannah Norman turned her thirteen slaves over to Richard and Margaret Singleton prior to marrying free black James Miles and stipulated that if she should die childless the slaves were to be transferred to the Singletons permanently.[43] Some of the more than 400 free Negro women listed in the 1850 and 1860 censuses as having separate property holdings though living with a male head of family probably had made similar premarital arrangements.

Concerned about their property, cautious about "marrying" slaves, forbidden by statute from marrying whites, and in some communities unable to find a suitable husband, a substantial number of free Negro women remained single, or lived alone. Although census takers rarely noted their occupations, among those who owned property approximately half earned their living as seamstresses and laundresses. Others found employment as domestic servants, waitresses, and farm laborers. As was the case with free black men they were often forced to take the most menial jobs or enter occupations shunned by whites, and even the small number who acquired special skills worked in relatively low-paying jobs, as bakers, cooks, milliners, nurses, and midwives. Yet, even at these tasks, energetic women could earn as much as their male counterparts—day laborers and farm workers. In Frankfort, Kentucky, Winny Lewis and Sally Chiles, though described in 1842 as "washerwomen," actually ran small laundry businesses. Each was able to save enough to purchase her own home valued at $1,000.[44]

In most large cities, and in some small towns, free women of color were able to establish themselves in service enterprises. They managed eating houses, hairdressing shops, fruit and vegetable stands, confectioneries, bakeries, and grocery stores. It was ironic that white men sometimes deemed it inappropriate for white women to enter the business world (and in some instances passed laws to this effect) but did not forbid black women from establishing enterprises. In Savannah, Susan Jackson ran a pastry shop in Reynolds Ward, the leading business section of the city, and eventually purchased her place of business, a brick building appraised at $10,000.[45] Her neighbor, free mulatto Ann Gibbons, the descendant of a West African Ibo chieftain, lived comfortably on the income from her various rental properties.[46] During the 1820s Amelia Gallé managed a popular bath house in Petersburg, Virginia, advertising in local newspapers that customers would be treated to refreshing baths as well as relaxing elixirs. During the 1850s, free black Susan Mahaly owned a popular candy store in Annapolis, Maryland.[47]

Not only did a few free women of color establish small businesses, but as a group they also controlled a substantial proportion of the total black wealth. In 1850, they owned $2,033,500 worth of real estate, or 27 percent of the total $7,668,100; in 1860, they owned $2,782,700 of the $12,841,600 in real property, or 22 percent. As with men there was a sharp contrast between the Lower South, where, according to the census, 561 free women of color owned a total of $1,671,400 in 1850, or $2,979 per realty holder, and the Upper South, where 695 black women controlled only $362,100, or an average of only $521 each. In 1860, 694 women in the Lower South owned $1,870,200, or $2,695 per owner, while in the Upper South 1,223 owned $912,500, or $746 apiece. Some of these women—especially in Louisiana and Virginia where half of them lived—were widows of prosperous free men of color or former mistresses of wealthy whites, but in the Upper South most were simply industrious women who had spent many years accumulating small amounts of property. In both sections a few Negro women had made the journey from slavery to freedom to landownership in a single lifetime. This was reflected in the fact that as a group they were extremely old—an average of fifty years—and 44 percent of them at mid-century were listed by census takers as black, and 56 percent as being unable to read and write. Two out of five had no children living at home—a reflection of the age differential—but even among younger women with children most had only one or two in the same household. Yet, despite these difficulties, free black women accumulated significant amounts of property. In addition, they owned more real estate, on average, than Negro men: in 1850, their average realty holding stood at $1,619 compared with $1,144 for men; a decade later the gap had narrowed but women still possessed larger average estates than their male counterparts. By then, one out of five Negro real estate owners in the South was female.

White Guardians and Protectors

Whether male or female, skilled or unskilled, black or mulatto, rural or urban, free black property owners were very often dependent on the goodwill and assistance of whites. In the midst of racial violence, restrictive laws, and antiblack prejudices, free Negroes were forced to seek out whites who might serve as guardians and protectors. If Georgia plantation owner Charles C. Jones's admonition that whites "live and die in the midst of negroes and know comparatively little of their real character" was true for masters of large plantations, like himself, it did not apply to whites who served as guardians to free blacks.[48] Even the most virulent anti-free Negro demagogue could, and often did, provide assistance to an individual free black, especially if the person had achieved a degree of economic success. Tennessee judge and politician John Catron, who castigated free Negroes as "indolent," "thieving," and "depraved," for example, allowed several of his slaves quasi-free status, emancipated several other blacks, and assisted free Negroes in acquiring land. In a similar manner, a group of North Carolinians, including lawyer William H. Haigh and banker W. G. Broadfoot, wrote about Matthew Leary, Jr., who had requested a travel pass to Ohio. "He is a free man of color, born and raised in the Town of Fayetteville, N. Carolina, of free parents and is now about twenty four years old, of bright copper complexion, rather above the ordinary hight [sic], well made, very good looking and quite intelligent," they explained. Leary was a man of "excellent character," honest and industrious, "in every respect worthy of the confidence of the people."[49]

Once a free person of color had acquired such a reputation, whites in the vicinity would make every effort to provide protection. Nearly one hundred residents of Stewart County, Tennessee, both slaveholders and nonslaveholders, petitioned the state legislature in 1851, defending a group of property-owning free blacks who, despite longtime residency, were being forced to put up a substantial bond, enter "into a recognizance" with two or more "good and sufficient sureties," or face deportation. "Good conduct, good citizenship, and good industry should be encouraged wherever found, whether among white or colored," the petitioners exclaimed, describing boatman Elijah Davis and farmers Edward Moore and Daniel Brown as native-born, quiet, law-abiding, and hardworking. Their sober and industrious habits were the best guarantee that they would never became a nuisance to the state or community.[50] Although the legislature could not exempt industrious free blacks from the law, it could and did grant concessions to those who had been born in the state.

No less important was the willingness of a few whites to assist blacks in economic matters. They rented, leased, and sold them real estate, loaned them money, vouched for their credit, and countersigned their mortgage notes and property deeds. They also served as estate administrators, employers, and, when the law required it, as legal guardians. In Georgia, planter-businessman Farish Carter signed guardianship papers for more than one hundred free persons of color.[51] Carter and other whites testified in open court about the ability of free blacks to find employment and earn a living. Their comments sometimes meant the difference between freedom and returning to slavery. "The following named free Negroes & Mulattoes come into court on citation, and having satisfied the court of their right to freedom, and of their good character and ability to maintain themselves," a Missouri judge ruled in 1836, echoing the words of hundreds of similar decrees, "the court orders that licenses [be] issued to them in form of law."[52] At Georgetown Crossroads, in Kent County, Maryland, Cornelius Comegys, a white farmer, became what amounted to a trustee for every black landowner in his community (more than 75 in number) when he cosigned their mortgage notes.[53] In Natchitoches Parish, Louisiana, white farmers and planters, including Shelborne Cambell and Narchisse Prud'homme, loaned free persons of color sums ranging from a few hundred to a few thousand dollars.[54] During the 1820s the president and the board of trustees of the Bank of New Bern (North Carolina) authorized several loans to free Negro John Carruthers Stanly.[55] In 1831, Robert C. Hataway, a farmer near Wadesboro, North Carolina, journeyed 500 miles, to Gibson County, Tennessee, to purchase a farm for his friend and neighbor, free Negro Zachariah Roberson.[56]

Whites who employed free Negroes in various capacities often recommended them to their friends and neighbors. Those who contracted the services of North Carolina carpenter and builder James Boon were typical in this regard. During the late 1830s and 1840s, Louisburg merchants Augustus Lewis and John King, Wake County businessmen D. Cosby and Brian Green, and Halifax entrepreneur R. H. Mosby, among others, praised Boon as an excellent workman, honest, diligent, industrious. He was straightforward, hardworking, a "gentleman" of "strictest propriety." "I write this to say to you or to any other person who may wish to get his services that he is an orderly and well behaved man and attentive to his business," Mosby said in praise. "His work is executed better and with more taste than any persons within my knowledge in this section of the country." Anyone who needed a highly proficient builder, explained another, could do no better than employing him. Such recommendations meant the difference between regular work and being out of a job. For his part, Boon considered these whites as "protectors." He carried their letters in his coat pocket as he moved about from one job to the next.[57]

Occasionally whites went to great lengths to offer assistance and protection to property-owning free blacks. This was certainly true when a group of six whites, including three Virginians, intervened in 1833 in behalf of District of Columbia Navy Yard worker Michael Shiner, a free person of color who learned that his wife and three children had been kidnapped from an alley near their home and sold into slavery. Shiner had nearly lost hope when he learned that his family, though legally free, had been purchased by John Armfield and Isaac Franklin, owners of the largest slave-trading firm in Virginia, and were being readied for sale to the Deep South. "i am under ten thousand obligation," Shiner wrote in his diary. Having crossed "the long bridge" to Alexandria, three times in one day, it was not until his "white friends" had come to his assistance by posting a $10,000 bond that his family was transferred to the county jail, and eventually released. Shiner found it difficult to put into words his heartfelt appreciation for those who were willing "to help me out of my distresses in an honest and up right way."[58]

Even during periods of mass hysteria, a few whites were willing to defend industrious free Negroes "in an honest and up right way." Following the discovery of the South Carolina slave insurrection plot by Denmark Vesey, a free Negro property owner, local authorities in Charleston deported forty-three blacks, and sentenced thirty-five others, including Vesey, to be hanged, but when some panic-stricken residents demanded a general retribution against all free Negroes, Edwin C. Holland, a leading editor, quickly came to their defense. Free mulattoes, he argued, provided a buffer between whites and blacks, and in cases of revolt, despite Vesey's betrayal, they would align themselves with the master class. "Most of them are industrious, sober, hardworking mechanics, who have large families and considerable property," he said, "and so far as we are acquainted with their temper and disposition of their feelings abhor the idea of association with blacks in any enterprise that may have for its object the revolution of their condition."[59] Nine years later, in the wake of the bloodiest slave revolt in American history, led by Nat Turner, several Virginia slave owners provided protection to free Negroes who were fleeing from their homes as bands of vengeance-seeking whites scoured the country-side. "There are about 200 Free People of Colour anxious to obtain a chance of Emigrating," John McPhail, an officer of the American Colonization Society, wrote from Norfolk, Virginia, a month after the revolt. They were "honest, industrious people," but had suffered severely at the hands of "white people of low character" who had taken advantage of the situation and violently accosted them. Indeed, they would not have made it to the port city at all had it not been for several white planters who, despite the frenzied atmosphere, had allowed them to hide on their plantations.[60] In the Carolinas, Georgia, Tennessee, and other states, sympathetic whites provided the same type of protection during the frantic months following the revolt. In one instance, an entire community came to the defense of Robert Roderick, a hardworking, well-known brickmaker. "He is a member of the Methodist Society," Wallace Bordan, the founder of Bordansville, North Carolina, said, "and is every way a good citizen, if necessary he can get recommendations from our best citizens as to character."[61] Bordan's counterpart in Charleston was Thomas S. Grimké;[62] and in Savannah, Shadrack Winkler, who, according to free Negro Philip Moor, "is my Guardian and will do me evry justice."[63]

Even on the eve of the Civil War, in the midst of agitation to strip free Negroes of their liberty, some whites continued to serve as patrons to property owners. In 1860, a group of South Carolina planters, including William Grayson and Benjamin Huger, vigorously protested against a bill to drive free colored people from the state "under heavy penalties." In a petition to the state senate, they said such a law would unfairly penalize many industrious, sober, and respectable men "who are good citizens."[64] In the same year, twenty-one Wilkinson County, Mississippi, residents came to the defense of Titus Hill after the General Assembly passed a law remanding free Negroes to slavery or requiring them to leave the state. "We approve of the policy of the general law prohibiting free negroes from remaining in this state," Peter Katcliff, James A. Stewart, Joseph B. Hoff, Enoch McLain, Nolan Dickson, and others wrote, but they had known Hill for twenty-five years, and "during the whole of this time, have never known him to be guilty of a single mean, or dishonest act (see appendix 2)." Furthermore, he had acquired property "worth about Four, or Five Thousand Dollars."[65]

Property Owners and the Emigration Movement

Yet, even those worth "Four, or Five Thousand Dollars" could sometimes feel threatened, and despite their reliance on white protectors, some free Negro property owners seriously considered emigrating from the South.[66] Perhaps none was more energetic or enthusiastic in this regard than Alabama-born Shandy Jones, a Tuscaloosa barber who acted as an unofficial agent of the American Colonization Society. "I am proud to be able to inform you that colonization is growing in favor rapidly in this state, both among black and white," Jones said in an unsigned, undated letter to an official in Washington, D.C. Among the whites who were "strong Friends of the cause" he listed Alabama Supreme Court Chief Justice H. W. Collier, a local pastor of the Methodist Episcopal church, two other prominent churchmen, Reverends Samuel Jennings and N. H. Cobbs, and a number of Tuscaloosa civic and business leaders, including Alexc Glascock, J. P. Turner, and George and John Purcell. Among the free blacks who "seemed anxious to Emigrate" were Huntsville's John Robinson, a livery stable owner who headed a family of seventeen, and Charles Sampson, a blacksmith whose wife's brother (M. H. Smith) had already left and become a member of the Liberian legislature. Jones had also spoken to many slaves, especially those who hired their own time, earned wages, and might be able to convince their masters to allow them to purchase themselves. In one letter Jones professed that he would do everything in his power to arouse his brethren to "go forth" and build a great black nation in Africa where blacks would have their own towns and cities, their own laws and institutions, their own army and navy, their own schools and colleges, and their own doctors and lawyers; in a word, he wrote, blacks would "cease to be 'hewers of wood and drawers of water,' and be men" (see appendix 1). So confident was Jones in the power of these words that he predicted within a few years that "there will not be a free man of color left in the southern or slave-holding States."[67]

Among those who let "national pride be kindled" in their hearts were a number of black property owners. Ironically, the most poverty-ridden free blacks, like the hundreds of farmhands in Westmoreland County, Virginia, who signed long-term contracts (up to twenty years), in return for food, clothing, and shelter, were unable to venture beyond their own locales, much less journey across the Atlantic. Property owners, on the other hand, at least had the means to begin the emigration process, and some of those who actually migrated, or seriously considered doing so, had saved enough money to establish themselves in a new country. Among a group of emigrants from Frankfurt, Kentucky, in 1839, each family started out with $200 in cash, money they had acquired by selling their land and unneeded personal belongings;[68] another group, leaving from Lynchburg, Virginia, had put aside "funds to defray their own expenses."[69] When he set out from Maryland in 1827, Joseph Dickinson, a free black farmer and carpenter, took with him "a very valuable" stock of tools: ploughs, hoes, picks, hatchets, saws, planes, angle bars, and gimlets; he also carried rope, tobacco, "domestic cloth," blankets, school books, a double barrel shotgun, and two rifles.[70] In 1848, a resident of Savannah said that everyone he had observed asking about passage to Liberia was either a skilled artisan—engineer, machinist, blacksmith—or a property-owning farmer.[71]

Similarly, observers in Mobile and New Orleans mentioned how "men of worth" and "men of property" were joining the colonization movement.[72] "Several men of property, ie., 2 to \$3000, desire to go out to Liberia," Crescent City free Negro J. B. Jordan informed William McLain, secretary of the American Colonization Society. "Some are anxious to purchase a Saw Mill to be put up there." But they needed to know what type of buildings would be most suitable—brick, stone, or wood? What would be the best location for a steam sawmill? How much would it cost to erect such a structure? Would it be difficult to procure horses or oxen to work in a horse-powered mill? "What think you of Sugar? Can it be raised in Liberia to advantage with the Aid of steam and the proper apparatus under the management of a man of industry, skill and practice?"[73] The same kinds of questions were posed by 150 Charleston free Negroes who were contemplating leaving the United States: How should they carry their money to the colony—in notes, cash, or supplies? What articles were in greatest demand for trade with the native population? Could colonists purchase as much land as they wished? Would they be provided with "fee simple titles" to the land? Could they sell, mortgage, and divide their property as they saw fit?[74]

A few property owners actually did emigrate to the North, Canada, West Africa, or the Caribbean. A brief note in the *Niles Register* in 1821 mentioned free mulatto slaveowner George Creighton of South Carolina who had purchased the schooner *Calypso* and set sail for Africa. "He had accumulated considerable wealth and had begun to feel that it would be better for him to spend his remaining days in a land of freedom." During the 1830s, following the wave to anti-Negro sentiment and oppressive laws, Charleston tailor Jehu Jones, Jr., the son of a free Negro hotel owner (see chapter 4), sailed for Liberia, as did William N. Colson, one of the most prosperous free Negroes in Petersburg, Virginia, and his business partner, Virginian J. J. Roberts, who later became the first president of the country.[75] In 1837, the prosperous North Carolina merchant Louis Sheridan, worth an estimated \$20,000, sought "deliverance" from his "present bondage." "I would die tomorrow," Sheridan cried out shortly before leaving his home state, "to be free today." Some years later, following a visit to Haiti, white emigrationist James Redpath said he had encountered a number of "Louisiana exiles." "There are among them," Redpath noted, "some of the richest colored planters of Louisiana."[76]

Many who emigrated, including Colson, Roberts, Sheridan, and others, thought that it would only be a matter of time before the movement would gain widespread support among black property owners. One former Georgia slave, Samuel Benedict, who had purchased his freedom, bought his family out of bondage, and saved several thousand dollars, said he was delighted that so many propertied blacks were "coming forward" and having "their names entered as candidates for Liberia." Shortly before departing Benedict predicted, like Shandy Jones, that it would not be long before "every intelligent person of colour will [accept] the propriety of emigrating to the land of our forefathers."[77]

In the end, however, despite the strenuous efforts of colonizationists—black and white—and despite the seemingly convincing arguments favoring emigration, only a small number of property-owning free Negroes left the South. Skeptical of the motives of Pan Africanists, they hoped to improve economic, social, and political conditions within the United States; they valued, as did most whites, independence, legal redress, and the ownership of property; and they felt a sense of loyalty to their communities and families. Some had relatives—sisters, brothers, grandmothers, grandfathers, aunts, uncles, nieces, nephews, cousins—living nearby or in neighboring counties; others had family members still in slavery. Shandy Jones himself, despite repeated assurances that he would sail for Liberia "within a fortnight," remained in Alabama.[78] During the 1850s and 1860s, he increased his real estate holdings from $500 to $7,000; and by age fifty, in 1870, he had become one of the richest blacks in the state.[79] Nor did Shandy Jones convince many of his brethren that they should return to West Africa and build a great black nation. During the years of his most active involvement in the movement (the 1840s and 1850s) a total of 103 of the state's blacks were listed as emigrants sent to Liberia by the American Colonization Society and its auxiliaries. Many of them, including 23 in 1848, 30 in 1852, and 15 in 1853, were probably emancipated slaves. Among the approximately 2,300 free Negroes in the state, fewer than 50 emigrated to Liberia, about 2 each year. The comparative numbers were even smaller for the South as a whole. During the 1820s, the society sent out 116 emigrants per year to Liberia; the next decade, 255; during the 1840s, 189; and in the 1850s, 470. Under the program "Maryland in Liberia," the Maryland State Colonization Society, the most active state organization, sent out 1,200 emigrants. Among the 12,000 blacks transported to West Africa during the antebellum era, more than 6,000 had been recently freed slaves, and more than 1,000 had originated in New England, the West, or the Caribbean. Thus, as the region's free Negro population grew from 134,000 in 1820, to 216,000 in 1840, to 262,000 in 1860, only 4,300 chose to emigrate to Liberia, 100 per year, or in any given year, about 1 out of 2,000.[80]

A few of those who did leave the South became so disenchanted that they returned to the United States. Perhaps no returnee expressed his feelings more poignantly than Jehu Jones, Jr., who, with his wife and children, left in 1832 for Monrovia, Liberia, having been promised a teaching position with a $600-a-year salary, as well as town lots and "a farm of valuable lands in the country." When these things did not materialize, he found himself "among strangers jealous of new commers, without friends, without funds & without employment." He would have immediately returned to his native state, but the law forbade free Negroes from leaving the state and returning under penalty of being sold into slavery. "I at once made up my mind to search for a Home & locate myself in some desirable situation where I could maintain my wife & family," he wrote from Philadelphia, petitioning the South Carolina legislature to permit him to return to the state of his birth and "once more mingle with & embrace the Friends & associate[s] of my youth." Despite his plea to once more "visit the grave of my Father, the Spot where I was Born, and grew up & lived respectably for nearly half a cent[u]ry," the petition was denied.[81]

Starting a new life in a strange land, leaving family and friends, abandoning white patrons, adjusting to a new climate and a new work routine could dissuade even the most adventuresome from striking out on his or her own. Those who had never ventured more than a few miles from home felt comfortable in familiar surroundings; and those who had purchased their own freedom felt grateful to their guardians or former owners. Over a forty-five-year period, among blacks sent out by the American Colonization Society, only 344, less than 1 percent, had purchased their own freedom.[82] The failure of ships to depart on schedule, the lack of information about supplies, and the difficulties paying for board while awaiting a ship's departure persuaded some free Negroes that leaving was a bad idea. Waiting in Baltimore for a packet to Liberia, a Charleston free Negro named Tucker, described as "a very intelligent" carpenter, was forced to sell his wagon, building materials, and tools, to pay for several months' lodging. Eventually, he returned to South Carolina.[83]

Other property owners heard rumors about prolonged voyages, unproductive land, hostile natives, high mortality, government corruption, inept bureaucrats, disease, and poverty.[84] "We have found nothing here as it was told us in America," one emigrée wrote back home to his family after a few months in Liberia. "A man has to work very hard here to make a living and then can just live; and as for becoming Rich [that] is out of the question unless he come[s] out well provided with such things as will enable him to trade with the native[s]; otherwise he must forever Remain poor."[85] Another colonist told relatives that he "was forced by poverty" to wade through three miles of swamp gathering wood to trade for food, despite "a severe attack of fever." "The substance of his letter," a white observer noted, "appears to be lamentation, mourning, and woe: he appears still quite desirous to get back to America."[86] Virginia free mulatto James Winn, who distributed books, maps, and pamphlets about Liberia to his neighbors, felt betrayed when he learned that "a great many people" had died of "the fever" within a few months after their departure. White colonizationists had assured him, he said bitterly, that blacks were immune to African diseases.[87] Such information prompted a group of Kentucky blacks to appoint an agent to visit Liberia and return with information "acquired by observation on the spot."[88]

But the vast majority of propertied free blacks simply did not want to leave the South. Bound by family, kin, culture, and attitude to the land of their birth they resisted any attempt to convince them that their future lay elsewhere. This was reflected by the remarkably high proportion of realty owners who had been born in the same state where they held their property. In Virginia, in 1850, 97 percent had been born in state (1,000 of 1,029); in Maryland, 99 percent (1,139 of 1,154); in North Carolina, 92 percent (599 of 654); in South Carolina, 96 percent (272 of 284). Even farther west, where many free blacks had arrived as slaves, a majority of the landholders, by 1860, were native born: in Alabama, 55 percent (78 of 142), in Tennessee, 62 percent (169 of 271), in Kentucky, 68 percent (413 of 605), and in Louisiana, 83 percent (1,053 of 1,262, with 34 missing cases). Thus, at a time when white southerners, often leading coffles of slaves, moved restlessly from one section to another, propertied blacks, relying on white guardians, closely tied to family and friends, fearing the unknown, and having achieved a measure of economic success, remained bound to communities where they had been born and had lived all their lives.

Articulating the sentiments of others on this subject were several free persons of color in Virginia who sought exemption from a law requiring recently emancipated slaves to leave the state. Elvira Jones, a free woman of color in Richmond who had purchased her two children and acquired a small house on the outskirts of town, explained in a petition to the state legislature: "Tis with anxious and trembling forebodings then that your Petitioner presents herself before the Legislature to supplicate of their liberality and clemency, permission to herself and children to live and die in the Land of their nativity." She had acquired, through great effort and frugality, "some small pecuniary resources"; in addition, she named several known whites from whom she could obtain references. It was her opinion that "endearments of kindred and of home" were more important to the "humble and obscure" than to persons "more elevated in life." Virginia boat captain John Dungee and his recently emancipated wife Lucy Ann similarly supplicated the state's lawmakers: "An enumeration of the disastrous effects of the enforcement of the law in this case is almost unnecessary to your enlightened body," they said through a white friend, "but they will briefly state, that if they are compelled to leave this land, your petitioner, John, in a moment loses the labour of a lifetime spent in acquiring an accurate knowledge of the Chesapeake Bay and the rivers which disembark themselves therein, . . . and the legacy [of $1,000] bequeathed to Lucy Ann [by her white father] will be lost or of little value to them." Having deep "feelings and attachments" to Virginia, they would be "torn from their parents, relatives and friends and driven in a state of destitution to migrate to a foreign land."[89]

Most property-owning free blacks shared these sentiments. They felt ties to the land of their birth. Cautious and circumspect by nature, they sought to preserve the few privileges they had already achieved. Not only did they reject the nationalism of men like Shandy Jones; they also felt bound to their communities. During the antebellum years they had made significant economic advances. That their success was not complete was to be expected at a time of social, political, and racial turmoil. Yet, despite oppressive laws, arguments of racial inferiority, and intermittent violence, they had established themselves as productive members of their communities. In all, by 1860, 16,172 free persons of color in the fifteen slave states (and the District of Columbia) had accumulated $20,253,200 worth of property, or $1,252 per individual property holder—an extraordinary accomplishment considering that some of them, only a generation before, had worn shackles as slaves.

Affluent Free Persons of Color, 1800–1861

"There are also, in the vicinity, a large number of free-colored planters," Frederick Law Olmsted wrote in 1856, a few years after a steamboat trip down the Cane River in Louisiana. They had stopped at several of the plantations to take on cotton, and the captain had told him that "in fifteen miles of a well-settled and cultivated country on the bank of the river, beginning ten miles below Nachitoches [*sic*], he did not know but one pure blooded white man." In describing these "GALLIC AND HISPANO-AFRIC CREOLES," Olmsted noted that they were slaveholding descendants of "old French or Spanish planters, and their negro slaves." Other contemporary observers, including free Negro Cyprian Clamorgan of St. Louis, and white abolitionist James Freeman Clarke, both of whom wrote pamphlets about the economic condition of blacks in the South, also commented on the presence of creoles of color[1] who owned slaves and had acquired substantial amounts of property.[2]

Nearly a half-century elapsed, however, before the first historical treatment of this group appeared. In 1905, Calvin Dill Wilson, an amateur historian, wrote a brief essay for the *North American Review* titled "Black Masters: A Side-Light on Slavery." During the next two decades Wilson wrote a second essay titled "Negroes Who Owned Slaves," historian John Russell examined "colored slave owners" in Virginia, and the noted black scholar Carter G. Woodson published "Free Negro Owners of Slaves in the United States in 1830," a directory drawn from the population census listing every free black head of family in the country who owned slaves (or at least had a slave or slaves listed in the same household). Although the head of household did not always own the blacks listed, Woodson's article (later published in book form) was the first serious effort to examine the subject. Except for a few sketchy chapters in more general studies, very little appeared to advance our knowledge in this area for many, many years, but since 1977, four books have been published examining various aspects of free Negro slaveholding and wealth accumulation: Gary B. Mill's illuminating study of the Metoyer and other families in Natchitoches Parish, Louisiana; David O. Whitten's entrepreneurial study of Plaquemines Parish sugar planter Andrew Durnford; Michael P. Johnson and James L. Roark's biography of South Carolina cotton gin maker William Ellison; and Larry Koger's detailed analysis of free black slave masters in South Carolina.[3]

Despite the observations of contemporaries and the various historical studies, we still know very little about free Negroes who reached the highest economic levels in the pre-Civil War South, how they acquired their wealth and maintained or failed to maintain their standing, how the group changed over time, how it differed in various parts of the Lower South and the Upper South. In describing this group some authors have used such terms as "the colored aristocracy," "wealthy men of color," "the free Negro elite," and "the mulatto elite," but as noted earlier, these terms are often only vaguely defined. What constituted free Negro "affluence?" What proportion of the free black population attained this level? How many affluent free blacks owned slaves? How did this ownership change from one decade to the next? How did black masters compare with white owners in their treatment of bondspeople? What effect did the repressive laws enacted at various times have on this group? What were their social and cultural activities? What was their relationship with whites? In short, despite our glimpses of various members of this group, at different times in specific locations, we have only begun to understand the complex motives, attitudes, and values of free people of color who acquired significant amounts of wealth.

Perhaps the best way to answer these questions is to focus on individuals who possessed at least $2,000 worth of real estate. These property owners represented only a tiny proportion of the total free Negro population, approximately one family in sixty (compared to one in eight for whites), and some of them, with realty valued between $2,000 and $5,000, could probably be more accurately described as "prosperous" rather than "affluent." There were, in addition, those who controlled very little real property, yet possessed substantial personal holdings, but their numbers were so small as to be inconsequential in any general analysis. At mid-century, those who owned this seemingly small amount of real estate, whether white or black, had reached the top 13 percent among all families in the United States.

They had reached the top 10 percent among the South's black property owners.[4]

This chapter, unlike those preceding it, focuses on the Lower South, especially Louisiana. As suggested by recent studies, the great majority of affluent free persons of color lived in this region. This was especially true during the early decades of the nineteenth century, but even later, when they lost ground compared with the same group in the Upper South, a majority of the most prosperous Negroes were residents of South Carolina, Louisiana, and a few other Deep South states. By 1850, when the first precise profile of the group is possible, nearly three out of four lived in this section of the South. In 1860, among those who were truly wealthy, with realty valued in excess of $20,000, five out of six lived in the Lower South, and two out of three in Louisiana. This chapter, unlike others, also has several shifts in its chronological framework. Since the group's wealth accumulations grew steadily until the late 1830s and then began to level off, the first several sections—focusing on origins, economic expansion, and slave-holding—examine rural and urban sections of the Lower and Upper South prior to 1840 (rather than 1830 as in the previous chapter) and then turn to the same topics during the two decades prior to the Civil War. This chronology, however, is less appropriate when discussing the group's social and cultural values and its relations with the dominant race. Consequently, the final three sections, while continuing to analyze regional differences, focus on the entire antebellum era.

Interracial Mixing in the Lower South

The origin of the affluent group stretched back to the late eighteenth and early nineteenth centuries, when some white men took black women as sexual partners and bequeathed them, or their mulatto children, land and slaves. In South Carolina and Georgia, where English customs and racial prejudices made such unions rare, the number of Negroes who acquired landed estates from whites remained small, but along the Gulf coast and in Louisiana, where Spanish and French traditions (as well as a scarcity of white women and a lack of color prejudice) encouraged interracial unions, the number of free blacks who received property from whites was fairly large. While the marriage of whites to slaves, or free blacks, was illegal in every state, mixed racial couples became so common in Louisiana that an institution called *placage*—white men contracting to live with black women and providing them with financial support—became firmly established. In some sections of the Lower South, white immigrants from the Caribbean arrived in the United States with Negro wives, or, upon their their arrival, took free women of color or slaves as their partners. In other sections, a few white plantation owners felt so strongly toward their slave mistresses, or their mulatto children, that they emancipated them and bequeathed them a portion of their estates.[5]

Whatever the specific circumstances, and despite the different traditions in various sections of the Lower South, prior to 1840, most free people of color who reached the upper economic levels were of mixed racial ancestry and had received assistance from whites. Often they were the children of white planters or merchants. In South Carolina, the father of free mulatto plantation owner Robert Collins was a white landowner in St. Thomas Parish; the father of farmer Henry Glencamp was a white planter in St. Stephens Parish; Charleston hotel owner Jehu Jones, described as "almost white," tinner William Penceel, and barber Thomas Inglis claimed white ancestry; the father of Sumter County cotton gin maker William Ellison was probably Fairfield District planter and slave owner Robert Ellison.[6] Charleston slaveholder Margaret Noisette and other members of the Noisette family were children and grandchildren of French-born Philip Stanislas Noisette and his Haitian-born slave wife.[7] In Georgia, fisherman and farmer Anthony Odingsells, one of the largest Negro property holders, received his land and nine slaves from Charles Odingsells, an officer in the American Revolution, a state legislator, and the owner of three plantations. The most prominent "colored creole family" in Florida, the Pons family, who engaged in various business activities, claimed descent from two Spanish officers. In Alabama, the two largest Negro slaveholders, cattle ranchers Zeno and Basile Chastang, were the children of Dr. John Chastang, a prominent Mobile surgeon who had served as a medical consultant at the Spanish fort of San Esteban de Tombecbe. In Mississippi, the plantation and slaveowning Barland brothers—Andrew, David, and John—and probably the Natchez barber William Johnson, the wealthiest Negroes in the state, were children of white slave owners and slave women.[8]

Similarly, affluent free persons of color in Louisiana were often directly related to whites. In New Orleans, among the approximately 535 successions (estates) probated for free blacks in the District Court between 1805 and 1846, nearly two-thirds were for women. Their names—Marie Allemand, Charlotte Burle, Marguerite Beaudouin, Charlotte Colbert, Catherine Lachiapella, Magdeleine Jourdain, Marie Pierre, Madeleine Rillieux—bore witness to their relationship with white Creoles. At the same time, a majority of the city's property-holding free men of color, including prosperous merchants Leon Sindoz and Erasme Legoaster and speculator Francois Edmond Dupuy, were of mixed African and Spanish or French heritage.[9] Similar interracial family backgrounds existed among affluent free persons of color in rural parishes, including those of Plaquemines Parish sugar planters Andrew Durnford, Louise Oliver, and Adolphe Reggio; St. John the Baptist Parish slave owner Louisa Ponis; Pointe Coupée Parish cotton planters Zacharie Honoré and Antoine Decuir; Iberville Parish slave owners George Deslonde, Cyprien Ricard, and Antoine Dubuclet; St. Landry Parish planters Adolphe Donatto and Jean Baptiste Meullion; and Natchitoches Parish slave masters Nicholas Augustin Metoyer, Marie Suzanne Metoyer, and Dominique Metoyer. Meullion was the son of white planter Luis Augustin Meullion, and his slave Maria Juana, while the Metoyers were the children of French immigrant and planter Claude Thomas Pierre Metoyer, and his slave mistress Marie Thereze Coincoin.[10]

Even when there were no direct kinship ties prosperous free persons of color often received some assistance from whites. Alabama bridge builder Horace King, emancipated in 1829 by Georgia slaveholder John Godwin, was assisted by his former master when he constructed a bridge across the Chattahoochee River, and later the two became partners in a construction company. In New Orleans, Pierre A. D. Casenave, who worked for many years as a clerk in the office of philanthropist Judah P. Touro, was given a bequest of $10,000 by his employer to start a mercantile firm. Later, Casenave established the first large-scale, black-owned undertaking business in the South. Between 1828 and 1832, Plaquemines Parish sugar planter Andrew Durnford purchased St. Rosalie plantation from New Orleans merchant-planter John McDonogh, a friend of Durnford's white father, who allowed Durnford to pay the $72,000 purchase price over a period of more than twenty years, at 6 percent interest, when mortgage notes for such amounts usually called for lump sum payments over a period of three or four years at 8 or 10 percent. By 1840, with rare exceptions, affluent free persons of color in the Lower South were directly related either to whites or mulattoes who had been assisted by white benefactors.[11]

Drive and Ambition

Even so, it took energy, industry, and business acumen to maintain or expand these property holdings. The careers of three free mulattoes—Richard Holloway of Charleston, Eulalie d' Mandeville Macarty of New Orleans, and Jean Baptiste Meullion of St. Landry Parish—illustrate these qualities as well as the diverse economic activities of Lower South free persons of color. Born of mixed racial ancestry in 1776, Holloway was apprenticed as a carpenter during his early years. In 1803, at age twenty-seven, he married seventeen-year-old Elizabeth Mitchell, the daughter of James Mitchell, also a mulatto carpenter in the city. That same year, he was admitted as the thirty-fourth member of the Brown Fellowship Society, a prestigious mutual aid and burial association of free mulattoes. A man of enormous energy and vitality, Holloway preached regularly at the African Methodist Episcopal Church, attracting hundreds of converts to the fold with his spirited sermons. He began acquiring small amounts of property in Charleston District as early as 1806, and over the years, as his reputation as a master builder and carpenter grew, he bought several slaves and additional real estate.[12] In 1842, at the age of sixty-six, Holloway drew up his Last Will and Testament. To his wife, he bequeathed two slaves (Cato and Betty), their home on Beaufain Street, and two rental houses; to his daughter-in-law, the widow of his son James, he gave a small house; to his son Richard he bequeathed a townhouse, a workshop, and several rental properties; and to each of his other sons—Charles, Edward, Isaac, John, and Samuel—he presented a house or rental property. Three years later, in 1845, having amassed an estate in excess of $20,000, Richard Holloway died. A group of fellow Methodists, including mulattoes Samuel and Jacob Weston, lamented "That in the death of Richard Holloway Senr. The church have lost a pious and useful member, a sound and Zealous exhorter, and a faithful leader, The poor have lost a true friend, Society an ornament, The community an Honest, Upright, Industrious, intelligent member."[13]

The most successful free mulatto businesswoman in the prewar South, Eulalie d' Mandeville Macarty, was for many years the mistress of white businessman Eugene Macarty of New Orleans, but Eulalie managed her own business affairs. Establishing a wholesale mercantile and dry goods store, she purchased various manufactured goods from abroad, housed them at her depot in Plaquemines Parish, and distributed them, through a network of slaves, to various retail outlets, some as far away as Attakapas. She used her profits to purchase stocks, real estate, and discounted bank notes. By the mid-1840s she had built up a personal fortune exceeding $155,000. When Eugene Macarty died, however, several white relatives, citing a law prohibiting a white man from leaving more than 10 percent of his estate to his black mistress, argued that Eulalie was not entitled to this property. After listening to the testimony of many witnesses, a Louisiana judge ruled that "all the property in the possession of the defendant belongs exclusively to her, . . . the result of her industry and economy during half a century." He found no cause for "disturbing her in the enjoyment of the fruits of the labor and thrift of a long life."[14]

Emancipated by his white father, and later marrying the daughter of free mulatto planter Martin Donatto, Jean Baptiste Meullion of St. Landry Parish began acquiring real estate the same year Louisiana became a possession of the United States, purchasing 400 arpents on Bayou Teche in 1803. Later, in 1819, he added another 840 arpents "lying in the Prairie Laurent fronting on B[a]you Teche." Contracting with various New Orleans merchants, he purchased supplies, seed, and machinery, and planted crops of sugar and cotton. In 1834, he sold his sugar crop for $1,418, and in 1838, at the beginning a national depression, he sold 41 bales of cotton for $19,349. His credit rating among merchants in Opelousas, Natchez, Mississippi, and New Orleans was excellent, and at various times during the 1830s he borrowed up to $5,000, while keeping an account open of almost $1,000 in order to purchase coffee, whiskey, pork, and other supplies. Meullion was a devout Catholic and made frequent contributions to the parish church, including donations for the construction of a new building in 1826, where, fourteen years later, he received his last rites.[15]

Other free persons of color in the region were also able to expand their wealth holdings during the early years of the nineteenth century. In towns and cities, they took advantage of the continued demand for service-type businesses, the relatively small number of skilled whites and immigrants, and the appreciation in city property values. In rural areas, they took advantage of the economic expansion to the west, rising prices for slaves, and increasing real estate values. Some speculated in city property or expanded their farm acreage, while others watched as the value of the land they had acquired years before appreciated dramatically in value. Improved farm acreage in Louisiana, for example, especially along a river or bayou, went from $2, to $10, $25, and $50 and more an acre. They also witnessed a rise in the value of their personal holdings, including inventories, tools, machinery, livestock, and slaves. Those who astutely managed their businesses, or expanded their farm acreage, were able to increase their wealth holdings substantially; and by the late 1830s, small clusters of free persons of color could be found in various parts of the

Lower South, especially in South Carolina and Louisiana, whose realty and personal-property holdings were appraised in excess of $15,000, $25,000, even $50,000.[16]

Slave Ownership and Treatment of Slaves

To sustain their various economic activities, free persons of color acquired increasing numbers of slaves. Urban artisans—carpenters, bricklayers, stonemasons, mechanics—purchased slave apprentices, hod carriers, and helpers; merchants and businessmen and women bought haulers, carters, and stock boys; plantation owners purchased house servants, cooks, mechanics, and field hands. South Carolina rice planters James Peagler, Margaret, Elias, and Robert Collins, and John Garden owned large contingents of blacks. Garden, who ran Hermitage Plantation on the Pon Pon River in Colleton County, maintained a slave labor force of sixty-two. In Georgia, two free mulattoes, drayman Andrew Marshall and fisherman Anthony Odingsells, used slaves to assist them in their businesses. Maximillian Collins and Zeno Chastang, both large landowners and children of white fathers, gradually acquired forty-five blacks to work on their farms in Mobile County, Alabama, including stockmen, herdsmen, and field hands. Eventually the two men held personal assets, principally in human chattel, worth $45,000, before distributing some slaves to various family members. Though once a slave himself, Jean Meullion purchased Negroes on a regular basis, traveling to the slave market in Natchez, Mississippi, or making arrangements with a slave-trading firm in New Orleans. Cotton planter Dominique Metoyer of Natchitoches Parish steadily increased the number of slaves he owned, working them on land he originally acquired in a grant from the Spanish government. Eventually, he owned a 500-acre plantation on the Red River and thirty-two slaves (see appendix 3).[17]

By 1830, approximately 1,556 Negro masters in the Deep South owned a total of 7,188 slaves. Representing about 42 percent of the Negro owners in the entire South, they owned 60 percent of the black-owned slaves (7,188 of 11,912). In Charleston District, 407 owners possessed 2,195 blacks, and in the state of South Carolina, 450 free Negro masters owned 2,412 slaves. In New Orleans, there were 753 Negro owners, including 25 who owned at least 10 bondsmen and women and another 116 who owned between 5 and 9 slaves. In eight rural Louisiana sugar and cotton parishes (Iberville, Natchitoches, Ouachita, Point Coupée, St. John the Baptist, St. Landry, St. Martin, and West Baton Rouge), 43 creoles of color (1.2 percent of the South's total number of slaveholders) owned a total of 1,327 blacks, or 1 out of 9 slaves owned by Negroes. Some had received their first slaves from white relatives. Others had built up their plantations through shrewd management. In St. John the Baptist Parish, 3 plantation owners held 139 blacks in bondage—an average of 46 slaves each; in Point Coupée Parish, 8 plantation owners held 297 slaves, an average of 37 slaves each; and in Iberville Parish, 6 planters owned 184 bondsmen and women—an average of 31 slaves each.[18] In 1830, approximately 1 free Negro family in 4 in the region was a slaveholder.

While occasionally manumitting a bondsman or woman for long years of service, or, as in the case of Cyprien Ricard of Iberville Parish who paid $1,570 in 1819 for Nigerette and her two-year-old son, purchasing slaves for personal reasons, free mulatto slave owners generally bought and sold blacks as a matter of economic necessity. Plaquemines Parish sugar planter Andrew Durnford, the mulatto son of English-born Thomas Durnford, an early settler in Louisiana, journeyed all the way to Richmond, Virginia, in 1835, to acquire a coffle of blacks. His comments during the trip revealed much about his attitudes toward fellow blacks: "I have two or three bargains on hand, butt so high, that I dare nott come to a conclusion, woman of 32, her daughter of 12, a boy of 7, a boy of 3 for 1,350. I have made the offer of 1,000$." "Blacks are getting higher every day, even the Negro traders are surprised at the prices demanded." "Young men boys & girls is as high here or more than in New Orleans; out of what I bought, there is at least twelve or fourteen that will be able to do good work." Complaining about "rotten" people and diseased blacks, he confessed that "They all say that I wish to have people cheap. I tell them that I must have something for my money, or send my money back to New Orleans in drafts." After several weeks, he secured twenty-five bondsmen, women, and children, for a total of $6,786 and arranged for their passage to his plantation twenty-seven miles below New Orleans on the Mississippi River.[19]

In their treatment of their bondspeople, they differed little from white slave owners. Some felt compassion for those in bondage, reduced the work load of women, kept families together, granted their blacks special privileges, and provided slaves with adequate food, clothing, and living quarters. In Charleston, New Orleans, Natchitoches Parish, and a few other areas, a few Negro masters allowed their bondsmen and women quasi-free status or purchased a slave's relatives and friends. But most owners considered their blacks primarily as chattel property. They bought, sold, mortgaged, willed, traded, and transferred fellow Negroes, demanded long hours in the workshops and fields, and severely disciplined recalcitrant blacks. As had been the case during the colonial period, a few seemed as callous as the most profit-minded whites. As early as the 1790s, two African-born mulatto brothers, John and Samuel Holman, Sr., and their half-brother, William Holman—sons of English slave trader John Holman and two African women—established a "factory" on the Rio Pong River, north of Sierre Leone. For nearly a quarter-century, they reaped huge profits buying and selling fellow Africans. Using their father's inheritance, the two eldest sons, John, Jr., and Samuel, purchased a rice plantation near Charleston, and later one in Georgetown District, acquiring more than one hundred slaves.[20] By 1807, they had amassed a substantial fortune.

With the closing of the Atlantic slave trade, the Holmans lost the most lucrative part of their operations, but the end of the trade allowed free Negro A. F. Edwards to expand his business activities. Purchasing blacks in Maryland, Virginia, and North Carolina, he sold them in Mobile, New Orleans, and Natchez, sometimes at twice their purchase price. "I have a regular correspondence with gentlemen in the market where Negroes are bought as well as where they are sold," Edwards informed potential customers through the columns of the Mobile *Advertiser* in 1835. "Persons desirous of selling may rest assured that those entrusted to my care, particular attention will be paid to them and will please call at my office in Hitchcock's building."[21] South Carolina free mulatto Thomas Inglis acquired most of his small fortune ($19,303) speculating in slaves, buying when prices were low, selling when they rose: in 1817, he sold a twenty-two-year-old slave named Alex for $1,000; a few years later, he auctioned off "Mary and her children"; and in 1830, he sold a domestic servant. Perhaps the most hardened black master was George Wright, described as a "coal black free born nigger," who, according to Alabama slave Angie Garrett, sold his own children. "Dey was his own chillun, and he could sell 'em under law," she said. "De names was Eber, Eli, Ezekiel, Enock, and Ezra, an' he sole 'em ter de highes' bidder right yonder ont [steps] of de Pos' Office for cash."[22]

While few would go so far as to sell their own children, most mulatto owners seemed more interested in profits than in the sanctity of the black family. Following the death of her husband in the late 1830s, Marie Marguerite Le Comte, a free woman of color in Natchitoches Parish, sold two children away from their mothers, disposed of an elderly woman for $50 and tried in vain to sell several other blacks described as "sickly" and "infirmed." On sugar estates, where the harvesting and pressing of the cane demanded, as it did in the Caribbean, sixteen- and eighteen-hour workdays, mulatto owners pushed their slaves incessantly; and, when women were unable to work such long hours, they stocked their plantations with young men. Among the twenty-eight field hands on Louise Oliver's Plaquemines Parish sugar estate the men outnumbered the women three to one; in the age group fifteen to thirty-six, the ratio was four to one; only two women, Martha, age thirty-five, and Pauline, age twenty-five, had any children. Mulatto owners were not adverse to selling off a few blacks for a quick profit, despite the effect this might have on slave families. Seeing such an opportunity, the heirs of St. Landry Parish slave owner Felicite Oursol auctioned off several of her field hands, including thirty-five-year-old Charles, appraised at $1,100 but bringing $1,850, forty-year-old Eugene, appraised at $1,200 but bringing $1,730, and thirty-seven-year-old Hypolite, appraised at $1,200 but bringing $1,950. Similarly, following Francois Allain's death in Point Coupée Parish in 1839, a group of relatives auctioned off his slave property. One laconic sentence told of the fate of each slave:

> Jean Louis, African negro man, aged about 39 years, was set up for sale and after crying him for some time and receiving frequent bids, therefor was finally struck off to Celrina Patin.
> Christine, American negro woman aged about 40 years, was set up for sale and after crying her for some time and receiving frequent bids, therefor was finally struck off to Adolphe Graugard.
> St. Luke, American negro man aged about 28 yrs., was set up for sale and after crying him for some time and receiving frequent bids, therefor was finally stuck off to Celrina Patin.
> Desires, American negro girl aged about 15 years, was set up for sale and after crying her for some time and receiving frequent bids, therefor was finally Struck off to Joseph B. Bourgeat [Bourgue].[23]

"You might think, master, dat dy would be good to dar own nation; but dey is not. I will tell you de truth, massa; I know I'se got to answer; and it's a fact, they is very bad masters, sar," one anonymous slave told a white traveler. "I'd rather be a servant to any man in de world, dan to a brack man. If I was sold to a brack man, I'd drown myself. I would dat—I'd drown myself! dought I shouldn't like to do dat nudder; but I wouldn't be sold to a colored master for anything." Even those few "colored masters" who had some compassion for their brethren found it difficult to maintain productive plantations without considering slaves primarily as property. Andrew Durnford, who saw the "back-to-Africa" movement as a "glorious cause," allowed his slaves many privileges, and emancipated several bondsmen and women, purchased only "likely" black men and women, and put one "wicked fellow" named Jackson in irons. Once, when Jackson stole away to New Orleans, Durnford angrily threatened to "fix him so the dogs will not bark at him." Other owners, in need of cash or credit, used slaves as collateral for loans, precariously balancing the future of individual Negroes with fluctuating market conditions. Even the most benevolent masters believed that their slaves should labor arduously and diligently in the fields. "He was good to all de slaves on de place, but he mean for dem to wuk w'en he say wuk. He ain' never 'low none of them to be famil'ar wid him," one free born black said, describing St. Mary Parish planter Romaine Verdun. "Dey war a big diff'rence mek between de slave niggers and de owner niggers. Dey was as much diff'rence between dem as between de white folks and de culled folks."[24]

Prosperous Blacks in the Upper States

In the Upper South, prior to 1840, only a tiny number of free Negroes—probably fewer than one hundred families—acquired more than $2,000 worth of real estate. Fewer still—not more than a few dozen families—accumulated enough property to be considered wealthy. As suggested in the previous chapter, free blacks in the region were part of a large scale manumission process. They entered freedom unskilled and with few resources to accumulate significant amounts of wealth. Those who did gain a measure of affluence were in some respects similar to their counterparts in the Lower South: they were most likely persons of mixed racial origin; they were often the children or grandchildren of whites; they usually received some assistance from white benefactors. The two wealthiest farmers in Virginia, Priscilla Ivey and Frankey Miles, lived with white slave owners. Two others, Francis and Alfred Anderson, were children of a white planter and his slave mistress, while Christopher MacPherson, a mulatto bookkeeper in Richmond, received his freedom and financial assistance from his owner. North Carolina barber-planter John Carruthers Stanly of New Bern was the son of the wealthy white shipping merchant John Wright Stanly and an African-born Ibo woman who had been brought to America on one of Wright Stanly's ships. He was emancipated by Alexander and Lydia Carruthers Stewart, Stanly's friends and neighbors. Other prosperous North Carolina free Negroes —cabinetmaker Thomas Day of Milton, merchant Louis Sheridan of Bladen County, and contractor James D. Sampson of Wilmington— had similar mixed racial backgrounds, while slave-born Julius Melbourn of Wake County received a bequest of $20,000 from the widow of a British army official who legally adopted Julius after her only son was killed in a duel. In Tennessee and Kentucky, the few free Negroes who acquired large estates, including Nashville hotel owner Robert Rentfro, received assistance from their former owners.[25]

With its early Spanish, French, and creole traditions, St. Louis was similar to the Gulf region in many respects. By the 1830s, the four richest families of color in the city—the Clamorgans, Labadies, Mordecais, and Rutgers—were all descendants of early white settlers and black women. Louis, Henry, Louisa, and Cyprian Clamorgan were the grandchildren of Jacques Clamorgan, a Spanish fur trader, merchant, and land speculator, and his mulatto mistress Susanne, or Anna. The prosperous cattle dealer Antoine Labadie was described as being "nearly white," and it was well known that merchant Samuel Mordecai was the son of a Jewish man and a Negro woman. Louis Rutgers was the son of Dutch immigrant Arend Rutgers, who had received a land grant from the French government. After being emancipated by his father, Louis married slave-born mulatto Pelagie Clamorgan, the widow of one of Jacques's children, Eutrope Clamorgan, who had died at a young age. Eventually, after Louis's death, Pelagie Rutgers inherited the property that had been originally bequeathed to her husband by her white father-in-law. As Cyprian Clamorgan noted some years later, the most affluent free persons of color in the city were often "separated from the white race by a line of division so faint that it can be traced only by the keen eye of prejudice—a line so dim indeed that, in many instances that might be named the stream of African blood has been so diluted by mixture with Caucasian, that the most critical observer cannot detect it."[26]

Yet, as was the case in the Lower South, those who received such assistance would not have been able to maintain their economic standing without a shrewd understanding of business affairs. Some benefited from gradually increasing land and property values and periods of general prosperity, but others aggressively expanded their holdings. In 1829, Joseph Jenkins Roberts and William Nelson Colson of Petersburg, Virginia, established a business partnership to trade in West Africa. They secured a schooner, obtained credit with mercantile firms in Philadelphia and New York, and began buying finished goods to sell and trade for ivory, cane, wood, and palm oil. Even as a slave, John Stanly had "acquired considerable real and personal property." Once free, he built up a large clientele, turned his barbershop over to two slaves, and began investing in real estate. Between 1805 and 1817, he purchased three plantations, including one of 602 acres on Bachelor's Creek south of the Neuse River. Using similarly aggressive tactics, several other Upper South businessmen and women, including Missouri cattle dealer and merchant Louis Charleville (who was listed in local records as white), greatly expanded their property holdings during the same period.[27]

Some large property owners acquired gangs of slaves, but unlike those in the lower states, only a few free black slave owners in each state—Priscilla Ivey in Virginia, Louis Sheridan and John Stanly in North Carolina, Sherod Bryant, a farmer in Tennessee—controlled relatively large numbers of laborers. Some of them were harsh masters, purchasing, mortgaging, and selling bondsmen and women away from their families, demanding long hours in the fields or shops, harshly disciplining workers, but others were well known for their benevolent attitudes toward their human property. Contractor and builder James D. Sampson, who owned a work force of twenty blacks in New Hanover County, North Carolina, granted his slaves many privileges, including quasi-freedom, while arranging for them to attend night classes and to learn to read and write, despite laws prohibiting such practices.[28]

Yet the ownership of slaves carried with it responsibilities for control and punishment. Consequently, as in the Deep South, large slave owners often found it difficult to consider their slaves other than a species of property. Even free black masters who had once been slaves themselves were forced to demand that their bondsmen and women produce as much wealth as possible or found it necessary to sell or mortgage them for ready cash. This was perhaps nowhere more apparent than in the career of slave-born John C. Stanly, who emerged during the 1820s as the largest Negro slave owner in the South. From the early years of the nineteenth century, Stanly had begun acquiring blacks to work in his barbershop and on his cotton and turpentine plantations. A regular bidder at local slave auctions, by 1820 Stanly had acquired 32 city slaves, including several who worked in his barbershop or as house servants, and another 95 blacks, including 36 adult men and 13 adult women, who labored on his plantations. Within eight years, through various purchases, sales, mortgages, trades, and speculations, he had added another 36 blacks to his labor force, owning a total of approximately 163 slaves, mostly field hands, unskilled workers, and children who were under the supervision of his three white overseers. With adult men, including several born in Africa, outnumbering adult women by a significant margin, most of Stanly's slaves toiled long hours in the fields or, along with gangs of hired blacks, labored from dawn to dusk in his pine forests producing turpentine. While Stanly did present a number of emancipation petitions to the Craven County Court, the pleas most often involved various members of his wife's family or slaves belonging to white neighbors. As one local resident recalled, Stanly was a "hard taskmaster" who demanded long hours in the fields and "fed and clothed indifferently."[29]

The great majority of black slave owners in the region, however, possessed only a few bondspeople, usually family members or loved ones. In 1830, a total of 2,128 free Negroes owned 4,728 slaves, slightly more than two blacks per slaveholder. If one out of four families in the Lower South was a slave owner, only one out of fourteen families in the upper states was in the same category. In Virginia, 948 free blacks owned 2,235 slaves; in Maryland 653 owned 1,175; and in North Carolina 192 controlled 624. While some of those who owned only a few slaves hired them out for wages or worked them in their blacksmith shops or on their farms, Luther Porter Jackson found that in Virginia these masters represented only a tiny minority of the black slave owners. In rural counties, he listed only 26 "commercial slaveholders" in 1830, out of a total of nearly 740 free Negroes who possessed fellow blacks; while in Petersburg, among 69 owners in 1827, he found only 7 who could be designated in the same category. Even among this group, Jackson concluded, there were probably some who did not actually own the slaves listed in their households; like their white neighbors, they had probably hired these blacks as assistants and apprentices.[30]

As the statistics on slave ownership suggest, with rare exceptions, even the most affluent blacks in the region during this early period controlled only modest amounts of property. In 1825, the richest black in the District of Columbia, Charles King, owned real estate assessed at only $4,088, while other members of what was called the city's "colored upper class," including bank messenger William Costen, War Department messenger Francis Datcher, and hackman William Wormley, owned city lots assessed at between $784 and $1,348. In Petersburg, Virginia, the leading free Negro property owners included shoemaker Graham Bell, cooper Shadrack Brander, barbers James and William Colson, and blacksmith Jack Cooper. Their holdings rarely exceeded a few thousand dollars. Brander's property included 1,300 barrel staves, cooper's tools, a wagon, plows, cows, three horses, and a lot in the city, but his entire estate was appraised at only $1,533. The most prosperous free Negroes in Frankfort, Kentucky, in 1842, included grocer John Ward, who owned a house and lot worth $4,000, plasterer Harry Mordicai, who owned a house worth $3,000, and drayman Tom Bacon who was worth $2,500.[31]

The same was true in rural areas. Some of the largest farm owners in Delaware, Maryland, Virginia, Kentucky, and Tennessee controlled acreage worth only a few thousand dollars. The wealthiest free Negro in Virginia, William Jarvis, for example, left the members of his family an estate valued at $6,656 in 1825. Between 1800 and 1814, Lewis Turner, a Sussex County farmer, bought several tracts of land ranging in size from twenty-eight to ninety acres, but even with several subsequent additions, by 1818, the land was worth less than $4,000. Amelia County farmers Alfred and Francis Anderson, and Frankey Miles, owned realty worth slightly more, but they had inherited most of their property from whites. Tennessee farmers Sherod Bryant, York Freeman, and Peter Lowery of Davidson County, Joseph Harris and Milly Price of Shelby County, P. A. Stewart of Macon County, and Henry Dickerson of Wilson owned land, livestock, and machinery that placed them among the most prosperous free Negroes in their areas, but they were classified only as "middle-sized" farmers. In short, by the late 1830s, few free Negroes in the Upper South could match the substantial holdings among free persons of color in the lower states, and even the most prosperous controlled comparatively small amounts of property.[32]

Transition in the Lower South

During the 1840s and 1850s, this began to change as free blacks in the border region significantly expanded their property holdings, and free persons of color in the Lower South experienced increasing difficulties in maintaining their former levels of prosperity. The change was gradual, due more to an expansion in the Upper South than to any precipitous decline among free people of color in the lower states. Yet some free persons of color in the areas of greatest free Negro wealth holding did feel the effects of the prolonged depression during 1837–43, the increasing political turbulence, and the rise of anti-free black legislation. The restrictions on the movement of Negroes, especially in Louisiana, for example, hampered the economic activities of affluent businessmen and women as well as small farmers. Moreover, some prosperous artisans in urban areas faced increasing competition from white mechanics who sought to improve their competitive edge by raising the race question, while successful farmers suffered periodically from droughts, flooding, fluctuating prices, and currency depreciation.[33]

These economic and political problems coincided with a generational change among the Lower South's most prosperous group. By the 1840s, a number of free persons of color who had acquired their holdings during the early years of the century had reached their six-ties and seventies. As they died, their estates were broken up and distributed among their heirs. While this did not necessarily result in economic decline, some of the heirs did not possess the same drive and business acumen as their forebears. When, in 1847, South Caro-lina plantation owner John Garden died at the age of seventy-five, his 382-acre, sixty-two-slave estate was sold at public auction, and the pro-ceeds were distributed to his wife and five children. Three years later, the most prosperous among the children, Elias William Garden, the estate's executor, owned only $4,000 worth of real estate and eight slaves. As early as 1824, Savannah drayman Andrew Marshall, the nephew of preacher Andrew Bryan, owned property valued at $8,400, but when he died in 1857 (see appendix 3), at the age of one hundred, his holdings had diminished, and in 1860, his relatives, in-cluding Anna, Joseph, Louisa, and Sarah Marshall, owned only small amounts of real and personal property.[34]

By the late antebellum period, there were no property owners in Florida who claimed descent from the Pons family, and only one land-holding Barland in Mississippi, among an earlier clan of thirteen families whose wealth in land and slaves at one time had exceeded that of all free blacks in the state combined. In Natchitoches Parish, Louisiana, after the deaths of Marie Suzanne Metoyer in 1838, and Dominique Metoyer in 1839, their land and other holdings, worth in excess of $104,000, were distributed among various children, grand-children, and relatives. In subsequent years, not only did individual holdings among the Metoyers decline (though they remained one of the richest free families of color in the South) but their slaveholdings and farm acreage dropped off as well. To a lesser extent this was true for the Meullion family in St. Landry Parish. Though several of Jean Baptiste Meullion's heirs maintained large plantations, others, includ-ing Antoine and Susanne Meullion, owned real estate valued in 1850 at between $1,500 and $2,500.[35]

The difficulties prosperous free persons of color confronted in seeking to maintain their economic position were reflected by a de-cline in slave ownership. Since, except in a few rural areas of South Carolina and Louisiana, free Negroes invested most heavily in real estate, and since such investments increased substantially during the inflationary late 1840s and 1850s (free blacks were not immune from the speculative "land fevers" that swept various areas during the pe-riod), the decline in the slaveholding class did not necessarily indicate economic decline. Moreover, several black masters, including William Ellison, Pierre and Madam Ricard, and Antoine Decuir, Jr., substantially expanded their slave labor force during the period. But others, especially in Charleston, New Orleans, and Natchitoches Parish, sold their slaves. Some of them had overextended themselves during the early 1830s and were caught without sufficient capital to maintain their businesses or plantations during the depression of the late 1830s and early 1840s. Consequently, they sold some of their slaves to pay creditors. Others suffered economic reversals during the downturn in the economy in the late 1850s. Still others decided to sell their slaves and invest in notes and bonds, or stocks, often at a loss. Thus, when the number of free Negroes who owned slaves in Charleston District, including the rural areas of St. James Santee Parish, St. James Goose Creek Parish, St. Stephen's Parish, St. Thomas Parish, and St. Dennis Parish, as well as in the city, declined from 402 in 1840, to 266 in 1850, to 137 in 1860, and the number of slaves they owned fell from 2,001 in 1840 to 544 twenty years later, a drop in personal property holdings was evident. The sharp drop in New Orleans, and the more gradual decline among slaveholders in the Cane River colony, also indicated economic decline among some wealth holders.[36]

During the 1850s, free persons of color faced not only fluctuating economic conditions but also increasing political pressures and legal enactments designed to curtail their activities. This combination made it more difficult for them to obtain loans, receive credit, and settle land disputes amicably with their white neighbors. Some businessmen and women were ostracized by their white customers; some farmers and planters lost a portion of their property to creditors. Consequently, in some areas of the Lower South free persons of color who had previously accumulated more than $2,000 worth of realty either dropped below that level, lost their holdings, or found the political atmosphere so hostile that they decided to leave the United States. This was especially true in several Louisiana parishes. Between 1850 and 1860, the number of prosperous farmers and planters in Jefferson Parish dropped from sixteen to seven and their realty holdings from $98,000 to $69,000; in Natchitoches Parish, from forty-one to twenty-seven and their holdings from $351,700 to $204,500; in St. John the Baptist Parish, from six to four, and from $128,000 to $70,000; and in St. Tammany Parish, from ten to one, and from $41,400 to $12,000. A significant decline also occurred in the Crescent City: in 1850, 311 prosperous businesspeople and landholders owned $2,188,000 in realty; a decade later, 263 owned $2,317,300. The rise in city property values greatly exceeded the 6 percent valuation increase, and did little to offset the 15 percent decline in the number of free persons of color who had reached the upper wealth levels. Several of the city's richest creoles of color, including Leon Sindoz, an apartment house owner worth $60,000 in 1850, were absent from the tax rolls a decade later. A few of them were probably among the 291 emigrés described in local newspapers as "literate and respectable free colored people," who left New Orleans in 1859 and early 1860 bound for the Negro republic of Haiti.[37]

Despite these difficulties, to describe the late antebellum period as one of economic decline among prosperous free persons of color in the Lower South would be inaccurate. While some experienced losses, others purchased new land, acquired additional slaves, and started new businesses. If whites made inroads in some skilled occupations, blacks still maintained a monopoly in others, especially the building trades. If some farmers and planters witnessed a devaluation of their land holdings, others experienced a continued appreciation in the value of their real estate. To some extent, the wealthiest free Negroes were less susceptible to the vagaries of the marketplace and the hostile legislative acts. In addition, outside South Carolina and Louisiana, increasing numbers of free blacks were able to take advantage of the general prosperity of the 1850s and entered the most prosperous group for the first time. In all, despite the political turbulence and economic troubles, prosperous free Negroes (unlike those at lower wealth levels) generally held their own during the period. A few greatly improved their economic position.

In South Carolina, despite a drop in the number of black slaveholders, some free persons of color significantly expanded their holdings during the two decades before the Civil War. Most of this expansion occurred in the Charleston District, where free Negroes had dominated certain skilled trades for many years. Those who were most successful in accumulating substantial amounts of property were members of families who had begun acquiring houses and rental property during the 1820s and 1830s—shoemakers Malcolm Brown and John Mishaw, hairdressers Francis and Edward Lee, barber Peter Brown, and various members of the Holloway, Mathew, McKinlay, Howard, and Weston families. During the 1850s Samuel and Jacob Weston, who managed thriving tailoring establishments, purchased various city properties and increased the value of their real estate holdings from $8,000 to $24,500. While their achievements were not quite as spectacular, hairdressers John Frances and Edward Lee, stable keeper Jacob Green, boardinghouse keeper Sally Graham, wood dealers Richard Dereef and Robert Howard, and land speculator Joseph Dereef (Richard's brother was listed as an Indian, though he was part Negro), and bricklayer Paul Wigfall substantially increased their wealth holdings. In all, between 1850 and 1860, the number of prosperous free persons of color in the city rose 227 percent, from 37 to 121, and the average value of their holdings rose from $4,541 to $5,115, despite a slight drop in the city's free Negro population.[38]

In rural areas of the state, while the numbers of those who rose to the upper levels remained smaller than in the Charleston District, some farmers and planters accumulated substantial profits after 1840. Rice planter Margaret Mitchell Harris, who inherited twenty-one slaves from her father, Robert Michael Collins, and sixteen slaves from her mother, Elizabeth Holman Collins, more than doubled the value of her estate during the 1840s. By 1849, she was producing 240,000 pounds of rice each year and reaping 18 percent annual profit. Between 1846 and 1850, she increased the value of her real estate possessions from $4,050 to $9,000. The most striking example of wealth expansion was that of Sumter County plantation owner and cotton gin manufacturer William Ellison, who increased the value of his holdings several times over during the late antebellum period. Opening a gin shop in Stateburg in 1817, Ellison gradually purchased slave artisans, plantation hands, and farm acreage, until by the early 1840s he had become one of the most prosperous residents of his community, black or white. Along with the continued success of his manufacturing company—Ellison cotton gins could be found as far west as the state of Mississippi—he substantially increased his cotton acreage and slave labor force. In 1852, he paid $9,560 for "Keith Hill" and "Hickory Hill," plantations totaling 540 acres, bringing his land holdings to more than 1,000 acres; during the 1850s, he increased his slave labor force (including children) from 36 to 63, or 75 percent. Assisted by his three sons, William, Jr., Henry, and Reuben, Ellison marketed between 80 and 100 bales of cotton annually. By 1860, with personal assets worth an estimated $53,000, and real estate worth another $15,000, he had become, outside of Louisiana, the wealthiest free person of color in the South.[39]

Only a small proportion of the affluent free Negroes in the Lower South—in 1860 approximately 10 percent—were residents of Georgia, Florida, Alabama, Mississippi, and Texas, but in these states, too, a few prosperous free persons of color expanded their wealth holdings. Zeno Chastang and Maximillien Collins, Alabama farmers and cattle ranchers, more than doubled the value of their landholdings during the 1850s, and in addition they each deeded tracts of land to various members of their families. In Mississippi, despite the death of her husband in 1851, William Johnson's wife Ann increased the value of his realty holdings from $8,000 to $10,000, and by 1860, a member of the Barland family controlled realty valued at $17,000. Despite being forced to flee from their ranches during a period of racial violence in 1856, the Ashworth family of Texas returned to a different county, and by 1860, with one exception, they had increased their land holdings, including Aaron, who went from $3,800 to $4,900 in realty, and Rosella (Abner's wife), who went from a few thousand dollars to $11,400.[40] In addition, several families entered the affluent group for the first time, including Georgia farmer James Williams, worth an estimated $5,500 in 1860, Florida farmer William Dempsey, worth an estimated $7,000 in 1860, and Alabama livery stable keeper and omnibus driver John Robinson, worth an estimated $12,000. In Florence, Alabama, free Negro barber John Rapier increased the size of his total estate from a few hundred to more than $7,000 during the 1850s. In all, the number of realty holders with more than $2,000 rose from 32 to 72 in these states, and their real property increased in value from $131,000 to $287,000.[41]

The great majority of the area's affluent free persons of color—in 1860 nearly two out of three—were residents of Louisiana. Despite declines in New Orleans and a few other parishes, they remained by far the richest group of African descent in the United States, controlling substantially more property than prosperous free Negroes in the other states of the Lower South combined. Their mean real estate holdings stood at $10,311, slightly more than twice that of their nearest rival. Among them were merchants and landlords, businessmen and brokers, planters and successful farmers. Even though they came under increasing economic and political pressures during the 1840s and 1850s, and some either lost a portion of their wealth or decided to leave the South, most of the state's wealthiest free Negroes sustained their previous wealth levels. And a few, with a sharp eye for future values, greatly enhanced their estates. Even in New Orleans, where anti-free black sentiment seemed most pronounced, this was true. According to the credit reports of R. G. Dun and Company, Pierre Casenave, who invented a secret embalming process, was able to increase his income during the period 1850–57 from $10,000 to $40,000 each year. At the same time, dry goods broker Drausin McCarty, the son of Eulalie Macarty, was listed in Dun's credit ledgers in 1848 as being worth $30,000; twelve years later he had real estate valued at $25,000 and personal possessions at $10,000. Between 1850 and 1860, McCarty's brother-in-law, merchant and exchange broker Bernard Soulié, doubled the estimated value of his real estate possessions, from $50,000 to $100,000. Soulié's brother, Albin Soulié, a partner in the business, was also very prosperous. Together they were described in 1854 as "very wealthy, est. w[orth] from 250–300m." An R. G. Dun investigator exclaimed in 1857, they "are rich, w $500m." Equally impressive were the property expansions of slave owner and landlord Francis Ernest Dumas, who was said to be worth $250,000, and tailor Francois Lacroix, who, between 1845 and 1860, speculated in various city properties and increased his real estate holdings from $30,000 to $242,600.[42]

By 1860, five of the ten wealthiest free persons of color in the South—Bernard Soulié, Dumas, Lacroix, grocer J. Camps, worth an estimated $86,000, and landlord Francois Edmond Dupuy—claimed the Crescent City as their place of residence.[43] The financial career of Francois Dupuy suggests some of the qualities necessary for economic success during the period. Astute, aggressive, with a keen eye for future appreciation in property values, between 1828 and 1854 he purchased more than a dozen buildings in the First and Second wards. Following each purchase he would personally supervise the renovation and improvement of the property, directing plasterers, painters, carpenters, and builders as they repaired walls, leveled floors, erected outbuildings, added kitchens, and made various other enhancements. In one description of his property on Basin Street he said that "improvements comprise a one story and attic brick house with four rooms, two cabinets, and closed gallery on the ground floor, two rooms in the attic, a two-story brick building with three rooms on the ground floor, three rooms in the first story; another building fronting Franklin street, shed, privies, water works, etc." Another nearby lot was described as having a one-story brick house with four rooms, and a two-story brick kitchen with two rooms on the ground floor, two rooms on the second floor, water closets, waterworks, etc. Dupuy also bought 267 shares of capital stock in the New Orleans City Railroad Company and purchased United States Land Warrants and 73 shares of capital stock in the New Orleans Insurance Company, but like most other wealthy free Negroes he put the bulk of his investments in realty. During the 1840s and 1850s the estimated value of Dupuy's realty holdings in the city rose 584 percent, from $25,000 to $171,000.[44]

Few could equal Dupuy's impressive ascent, but in some rural parishes wealthy creoles of color, taking advantage of improving cotton and sugar prices, expanded their property holdings. At mid-century, exactly one out of three rural free Negro landowners in Louisiana (181 of 543) owned at least $2,000 worth of real estate. These farmers and plantation owners controlled a total of $1,850,000 worth of land, 24 percent of the property owned by Negroes in the entire South.

Figure 1. Leading Black Wealth-holding Parishes in Louisiana, 1860
Source: *Louisiana, 1950: Census Index* (Bountiful, Utah: Accelerated
Indexing Systems, 1981), n.p.

Typically, they cultivated a few hundred acres, owned several slaves,
and tended small herds of livestock. The widow P. Olivier of Plaquemines Parish, for example, owned 280 acres of land, worth $4,000, and
a few head of cattle and horses. She worked a small gang of slaves. St.
Mary Parish planter Leon Frilot farmed 60 acres, owned another 560
acres of woodland and pasture, and boasted 50 mules and 8 oxen.
He, too, owned a small gang of blacks. But also among them were
some of the richest free mulattoes in the United States: St. John
the Baptist Parish's Louisa Ponis, who owned 1,300 acres valued at
$35,000 and produced several hundred hogsheads of sugar in 1849;
Plaquemines Parish's Adolphe Reggio, who owned 700 acres valued
at $40,000, with sugar-refining machinery worth $20,000; his neighbors Louise Oliver, who owned 600 acres, some of them fronting
along the Mississippi River, and 31 slaves, worth a total of $53,185,
and Andrew Durnford whose 2,660-acre St. Rosalie plantation, with
large herds of livestock and 70 slaves, was worth $161,300; Madam
Cyprien Ricard, who, along with her son Pierre, owned a 1,050-acre
plantation in Iberville Parish valued at $80,000, stocked in 1849 with

Table 7. Prosperous Farmers and Planters in Louisiana, 1850/1860
(rural free persons of color with real estate worth $2,000 or more)

Parish	Owners	Erph	Arph
Avoyelles	/1	/$2,500	/$2,500
Caddo	/2	/7,000	/3,500
Calcasieu	1/1	$2,500/4,500	$2,500/4,500
Catahoula	1/	3,000/	3,000/
Iberville	7/9	269,500/646,000	38,500/71,778
Jefferson	16/7	98,000/69,000	6,125/9,857
Lafayette	1/	2,000/	2,000/
Lafourche	1/1	6,000/2,000	6,000/2,000
Livingston	1/	8,400/	8,400/
Natchitoches	41/27	351,700/204,500	8,578/7,574
Orleans	4/	100,000/	25,000/
Plaquemines	26/24	284,000/157,500	10,923/6,563
Pointe Coupée	37/46	408,000/746,000	11,027/16,217
Rapides	1/4	2,000/52,300	2,000/13,075
St. Bernard	1/	25,000/	25,000/
St. Charles	1/2	4,000/38,000	4,000/19,000
St. John the Baptist	6/4	128,000/70,000	21,333/17,500
St. Landry	8/23	40,100/117,700	5,013/5,117
St. Martin	4/4	15,900/76,000	3,975/19,000
St. Mary	7/13	44,500/111,000	6,357/8,538
St. Tammany	10/1	41,400/12,000	4,140/12,000
Terrebonne	2/1	4,000/12,500	2,000/12,500
West Baton Rouge	5/7	12,000/74,000	2,400/10,571
Total	181/177	$1,850,000/2,402,500	$10,221/13,573

Source: Computed from USMSPC, Louisiana, 1850, 1860. Wealth estimates for nine property owners were taken from USMSAC, 1850; Robert C. Reinders, "The Free Negro in the New Orleans Economy, 1850–1860," *LH* 6 (Summer 1965), 273–85; David C. Rankin, "The Origins of Black Leadership in New Orleans During Reconstruction," *JSH* 40 (August 1974), 417–40; Herbert E. Sterkx, *The Free Negro in Ante-Bellum Louisiana* (Rutherford, N.J.: Fairleigh Dickinson University Press, 1972).

6 horses, 27 mules, 10 milk cows, 16 oxen, 25 head of cattle, and 85 sheep; and her neighbor Antoine Dubuclet, whose wealth in land and slaves exceeded $87,000.[45] In Pointe Coupée Parish, thirty-seven planters controlled $408,000 worth of real estate, or $11,027 per family; in Natchitoches, forty-one landowners had property valued at $351,700, or $8,578 per family; in Plaquemines, twenty-six planters owned $284,000, or $10,923 per household; and in Iberville, seven plantation owners controlled $269,500, or $38,500 per planter. In 1850, the average realty holdings among these affluent mulattoes

were worth $10,221, more than ten times the average for whites (including nonproperty owners) in the nation.

During the 1850s, some mulatto planters substantially increased their holdings. They acquired new land, diversified their crops, and experimented with fertilizers; they purchased the most up-to-date machinery, erected gin mills and grist mills, built storage houses and stables. "Dey uster call us de Free Mulattoes from crost de Boyous," the nephew of one black planter recalled. "De plantation support' a gris' mill and a raw sugar mill. Dey mek de sugar, dark, big grain' 'cause dey ain' no refinery in dem days. Dey put de sugar in big 500-pound hogsheads. Den dey tek it by boat down de Tecke [Bayou Teche] to New Orleans and sell it." Another free mulatto slaveowner, Antoine Decuir, Jr., of Pointe Coupée Parish, who owned 112 blacks, built stables, a sugar house, a row of slave cabins, several outbuildings, and a comfortable house on his 1,248-acre plantation. Decuir planted cotton, sugar cane, and corn, while raising hogs, cattle, and horses. His holdings eventually grew to include more than $160,000 worth of property.[46] In Iberville Parish, by 1860, nine plantation owners were listed as having $646,000 in real estate, or $71,778 per family. Census takers probably included some personal property in these valuations, but even so Zacharie Honoré increased his land holdings from $20,000 to $60,000; Antoine Dubuclet, from $87,500 to $200,000; George Deslonde (and his wife), from $65,000 to $155,000; and Madam and Pierre Ricard, from $80,000 to $200,000. In 1859, one observer described the Ricard family as "doubtless the richest black family in this or any other country."[47]

Expansion in the Upper States

After 1840, the profile of affluent free blacks in the Upper South changed dramatically. In part, like other free Negroes in the region, they were able to take advantage of the general upturn in the economy from the mid-1840s onward—improved roads and river transportation systems, rising industrial development, new techniques in replenishing the land, improved wages and a growth in demand for skilled workers—but it was more than the general prosperity that saw the number of prosperous free Negroes rise by more than 100 percent during the 1840s, and by nearly 200 percent during the next decade. Nor was this change reflected in the relatively small (29 percent) increase in the free black population. Now a generation removed from bondage, free blacks had acquired a considerable degree of experience in dealing with economic matters. Some shrewdly began purchasing land when prices were low and then either sold or improved their holdings during periods when land values were on the rise. Others gradually added to their holdings. In rural areas, they expanded their livestock herds, farm acreage, and personal property; in towns and cities, they purchased lots, unimproved land, buildings, and business property. A few entered more highly skilled occupations, or started new businesses, but most continued their farming and small business activities as before, but with a much better understanding of how to expand their estates.

A majority of those who reached the upper-wealth levels had spent many years expanding their property holdings. The careers of three prosperous free Negroes—Baltimore barber Thomas Green, Virginia farmer William Epps, and St. Louis cooper John Berry Meachum—indicate the qualities it took to move ahead in the border states as well as the differences between wealthy blacks in the Upper South and their counterparts in the various regions of the Lower South. Green arrived in Baltimore from Barbados about 1813 and opened a small barbershop on Light Street. As time passed, he built up a large clientele, primarily of white business and professional people, and by 1838 he had begun to acquire rental properties. Gradually adding to his holdings, by the 1850s he owned seven buildings on Hill, Little, Hughes, Montgomery, and Rash streets, as well as several vacant lots, which he rented to thirteen people, mostly black. His rental income was small, about $175 a month, and with taxes, insurance, and repairs, the net profits did not exceed $100 a month. But he kept a close eye on his earnings, and at the time of his death in 1858, at the age of seventy-one, Green had become the wealthiest free Negro in the state of Maryland, with a total estate of $17,139, a significant portion of which, about $5,923, he kept in cash. Over the course of forty-five years, he saved and invested between $300 and $400 a year.[48]

Although not obtaining an estate equal to that of Green, Halifax County, Virginia, farmer William Epps made a remarkable economic ascent during the period. Beginning with a single horse, Epps gradually began purchasing real estate. Between 1830 and 1842, he obtained 595 acres of land for $2,966. Steadily improving these holdings, and acquiring machinery and livestock, he became a fairly large-scale tobacco farmer. In 1850, the forty-nine-year-old Epps was listed in the census as a "planter." By 1859, the value of his livestock, including fifty hogs, was $650, and in addition to his tobacco harvest, his crops and other yields included 120 bushels of wheat, 525 bushels of corn, 280 bushels of oats, 20 bushels of Irish potatoes, 300 bushels of sweet potatoes, 400 pounds of butter, and 100 pounds of honey. He owned no slaves, but his wife Nancy and his two sons, James and Nathaniel, and their families assisted him during the long grueling hours in the fields. By the eve of the Civil War, with real estate valued at an estimated $5,900, and personal property worth $1,800, Epps operated one of the most profitable black-owned farms in the Upper South.[49]

Born a slave in Virginia about 1790, John Berry Meachum purchased his own freedom, moved to Kentucky, and, after marrying a slave and purchasing her from her master, journeyed to St. Louis, arriving with a few dollars in his pocket about 1815. Meachum used the carpenter's skills he had been taught in bondage to find work as a cooper. Within a few years, he had opened a small cooper's shop and, like Thomas Green, began purchasing small amounts of city real estate. Described as dark in color, and listed in the census as "black," Meachum conceived of an idea to help slaves attain their freedom. He would purchase bondsmen, teach them how to make barrels, and allow them to earn money to reimburse him for their liberty. Over the years, he acquired twenty slaves in this manner and set them free. In addition, he became a Baptist minister and kept two black schools, one after a state law prohibited such practices. By 1850, he owned two brick buildings in St. Louis and a farm in Illinois, and his $8,000 in real estate holdings, according to the census, placed him as the third wealthiest free Negro in Missouri. Despite his substantial wealth, Meachum lived modestly. An inventory of his estate in 1854 included a few cane-seated chairs, a parlor carpet valued at $7, and thirty-five or forty books worth $8. A few years before, in 1850, twelve people lived at his residence, including his wife Mary, his two grandchildren, John and William Meachum, several other adults and children, and two black coopers who were apparently working to repay Meachum for their freedom.[50]

As the careers of Green, Epps, and Meachum suggest, those who reached the upper economic levels in the region were quite different from the affluent groups in the Lower South. At mid-century, according to the census, Epps was the only planter (among the $2,000-plus group) in the entire Upper South. There were a few large farmers who owned a moderate number of field hands—North Carolina's Enoch Evans (Evins) and Lydia Mangum; Virginia's Rebecca Matthews, Frankey Miles, and Alfred Anderson—but, compared to rural Louisiana, they represented only a tiny proportion of the free black affluent class. In Delaware, Maryland, and the District of Columbia, by 1860, the phenomenon of free blacks owning slaves had nearly disappeared. In North Carolina, only a handful of free Negroes still owned slaves, and in Virginia, the same was true. In Petersburg, between 1830 and 1860, the number of owners dropped from 70 to 9, and though in the latter year, several owners, including livery keeper Robert Clark, contractors Thomas Scott and Christopher Stephens, and blacksmith Armistead Wilson, owned helpers, apprentices, and carpenters, at no time during the antebellum era did free Negro ownership in the state approximate "a system of slave bondage."[51]

In the Upper South, among those with more than $2,000 in real estate in 1850, there were nearly three times as many laborers as merchants, and next to farmer, the largest single occupational category was that of barber. Unlike the Lower South, where there were fewer than a dozen barbers listed in the census as part of the most prosperous group, in the Upper South one out of eight who reached this wealth level owned a barbershop. Nearly every city had its cadre of affluent "tonsorial artists"—Green in Baltimore, Reuben West in Richmond, Washington Spradling in Louisville, John Thomas and James Thomas (not related) in Nashville, Joseph Clauston (also spelled Clouston) in Memphis, and Henry Clamorgan, Barriteer (also spelled Byertere) Hickman, William Johnson, and Albert White in St. Louis. Some of them owned cigar stores or bathing establishments or ran small shops selling wigs, ties, lotions, and hats. Most of them invested heavily in city real estate. By 1860, their average realty holdings exceeded $6,500, two and a half times the average for their counterparts in the lower states.

In the Upper South there were a few merchants, including Moses Spencer, of Lexington, Kentucky, but most of the other prosperous free Negroes worked as blacksmiths, bricklayers, builders, and shoemakers, or owned small shops. Some acquired sizable holdings even though working as waiters, stewards, plasterers, and painters. Meachum was the only cooper listed as having large wealth holdings, and there was only one grocery store owner. In 1860, unskilled and semiskilled workers still outnumbered store owners by a considerable margin, and farm owners and barbers still constituted more than half of the affluent class. There were slight increases in the proportion of more highly skilled artisans (carpenters went from 3 percent to 3.6 percent), but those at the lower occupational levels, including laundresses and seamstresses, continued to constitute a significant proportion of the more prosperous group in the Upper South.[52]

Despite the limited business and job opportunities, and despite the fact that only a tiny number of families accumulated at least $2,000 worth of real estate—one of seventy-three in 1860, compared with about one of ten in the Lower South—between 1850 and 1860 afflu-

Table 8. Real Estate Holdings among Affluent Free Persons
of Color in the Upper South, 1850/1860

	Number	Arph	Trph
Delaware	13/38	$5,000/$3,076	$65,000/$116,900
District of Columbia	8/89	2,375/3,082	19,000/274,300
Kentucky	41/71	3,668/3,875	150,400/275,100
Maryland	53/167	3,857/3,825	204,400/638,700
Missouri	15/65	6,407/6,515	96,100/423,500
North Carolina	14/32	4,329/5,538	60,600/177,200
Tennessee	21/56	3,719/4,780	78,100/267,700
Virginia	48/101	3,581/3,601	171,900/363,700
Total	213/619	$3,969/4,099	$845,500/2,537,100

Real Estate Holdings among Affluent Free Persons
of Color in the Lower South, 1850/1860

	Number	Arph	Trph
Alabama	12/32	$3,817/$3,691	$45,800/$118,100
Arkansas	4/*	2,500/*	10,000/*
Florida	2/8	4,000/3,825	8,000/30,600
Georgia	5/13	5,200/3,585	26,000/46,600
Louisiana	504/472	7,922/10,311	3,992,500/4,867,000
Mississippi	6/13	4,033/4,685	24,200/60,900
South Carolina	47/162	4,411/4,723	207,300/765,100
Texas	3/6	5,667/5,133	17,000/30,800
Total	583/706	$7,428/8,384	$4,330,800/5,919,100

Source: Computed from USMSPC, 1850, 1860.
*none

ent free blacks in the border states made considerable advances compared to their counterparts in the lower tier of states. Their numbers nearly tripled, from 213 to 619; they increased their overall real estate wealth from $845,000 to $2,537,100, or 200 percent. This included a slight rise in their average holdings, from $3,969 to $4,099. Most of those who entered the affluent group during this decade owned relatively modest amounts of real estate, or increased their holdings by only a few thousand dollars. Typical among them were William Addison, a farmer in Baltimore County, Maryland, who increased his holdings from $1,000 to $3,000; Dorchester County farmer James Clash, who increased his wealth from $2,000 to $3,000; Alexandria, Virginia, carpenter George Seaton, who went from $500 to $4,000; Louisville drayman Allen Peggen, who went from $400 to $2,000; and

Nashville laborer Thomas Pincham, who went from $1000 to $2,500. But there were also among them a few who had obtained substantial estates, with realty worth from $8,000 to $50,000. This truly wealthy group included, among others, Baltimore caterer Henry Jakes, Georgetown livery stable owner and feed merchant Alfred Lee, North Carolina farmers J. Freeman and John Burchett and merchant-farmer Hardy Bell, Tennessee gardener Lewis Doxey, and St. Louis tobacconist William Deaderick. While still behind in total wealth and average holdings, free blacks in the Upper South had reached a near parity with those in the Lower South in the number of those who could be classified as affluent.[53] Despite limited opportunities, they had made remarkable advances in the two decades before the Civil War.

Clans and Friendship Networks

During the antebellum era, the social and cultural values of the Lower South's prosperous free persons of color reflected their unique position in society. On the one hand they admonished themselves and their children to "Settle debts" and "Save money," "Stay away from liquor" and "Stick closer to work." "A man should Settle down [and] Should use industry, economy, Keep Sober, and mind his own business," an Alabama barber told one of his children, "and the way to get Rich, is to lay out some money in the west for land, near Some growing town with natural advantages." They deeply believed that honesty, frugality, sobriety, hard work, and the accumulation of property were keys to a better life. At the same time, they also developed certain mores and customs to protect themselves from the periodic hostility of whites, or the possibility of being mistaken for slaves. Primary among them was their determination to separate themselves from less fortunate free Negroes, and whenever possible from whites as well, by forming tightly knit social and family clans. They socialized with one another, attended church together, provided an education for one another's children, and arranged for the marriage of their children within the clan. Whenever possible they clustered together in the same residential neighborhoods and farming districts. The wealthiest free Negro families in three states—the Odingsells of Georgia, Chastangs of Alabama, and Metoyers of Louisiana—felt so strongly about isolating themselves that they took up residency on islands.[54]

As with other persons of means, prosperous free Negroes engaged in a rich and varied social life. In cities, they attended the opera, theater, horse races, cockfights, and circuses. In rural areas, they hunted, fished, rode horses, danced, shot at targets, gambled, and traveled to nearby towns for sporting events. In New Orleans, on Grand Opera nights, Tuesdays and Thursdays, a portion of the gallery at the Theatre d'Orleans was occupied by *gens de couleur*, including several patrons of the theater. The same type of accommodations were provided for a few affluent free persons of color at the local theater in Natchez where some of the nation's leading actors appeared periodically. Most of their leisure time, however, was spent visiting, dining, and conversing with family members and friends. Despite their contacts with whites, they felt most comfortable with others of their own status. In nearly every state small groups of affluent free persons of color formed close friendships with one another. In South Carolina, the social network included the Ellison, Bonneau, Johnson, McKinlay, Mishaw, and Weston families; in Alabama, the Collins, Chastang, Rapier, and Robinson families; in Mississippi, the Johnson, McCary, Barland, and Fitzgerald families; in New Orleans, the Soulié, Dupuy, and Macarty families; in Natchitoches Parish, the Metoyer, LeComte, Rachel, and Rocques families; and in East Baton Rouge Parish, the Mathers, Bienville, and Ricard families. One local court judgment described the Decuirs, Deslondes, Honorés, and Dubucelets of West Baton Rouge and Pointe Coupée parishes as being "all free persons of colour, Relations & friends."[55]

This exclusiveness was most apparent in the linking of families through intermarriage. To perpetuate their property holdings, parents arranged for their children to marry in families of equal wealth and status. In South Carolina, the Holman and Collins families were related by ties of kinship and marriage, as were the Ellison, Weston, Holloway, Johnson, and Bonneau families. Henry and Reuben Ellison married Mary Elizabeth and Harriett Ann Bonneau, daughters of Thomas S. Bonneau, a member of the Brown Fellowship Society and a respected teacher and property owner. Another of Ellison's sons, William, Jr., married Mary Mishaw, the daughter of John Mishaw, a prosperous mulatto shoemaker. After the death of her first husband, Eliza Ann Ellison, a daughter, married James M. Johnson, the son of another member of Charleston's free mulatto elite, James Drayton Johnson, a tailor. The other affluent families united by marriage in the city of Charleston included Cole-Seymour, Cole-Desverney, Garden-Mitchell, Inglis-Glover, Lee-Seymour, Lewis-Pinceel, and McKinlay-Huger. "For the most part, the free Negro with status, in this community," one student of Charleston's free blacks wrote, "considered it demeaning to marry a slave." Rather, they chose marital partners according to economic position, "cultural status," and free, mixed-blood ancestry.[56]

Even in areas where the tiny free Negro population made it extremely difficult to find a suitable mate, one with the correct "cultural status," prosperous free Negroes sought out those with correct "lineage." In 1844, Mississippi's John Barland, the son of a white planter, married Mary E. Fitzgerald, the daughter of a prosperous free mulatto in Natchez. A few years later, in 1850, William McCary, the son of Robert McCary, a property-owning free Negro barber in Natchez, married Lavinia Miller, daughter of James Miller, a brother-in-law of another free Negro barber in the city, William Johnson, a large property holder. McCary and Johnson, who helped arrange the marriage, were closest friends. They loaned money to one another, attended social events together, and usually dined together on Saturday evenings.[57]

Occasionally, the wishes of parents and inlaws were ignored, as children ran off with slaves, propertyless free blacks, or whites, but even in families with modest property accumulations the rule of marrying "one's own kind" was generally respected. The marriage contract between Marie Llorens and Joseph Metoyer, signed January 28, 1840, in Natchitoches Parish, for example, stipulated that the future bride, "a free lady of color, a native of this parish, and a minor," contribute a dowry of $517, money she had inherited from her grandmother Suzanne Metoyer; and that the future groom, "for and in consideration of the projected marriage," contribute eight slaves. Any previous indebtedness should be paid "from their own particular funds." Among wealthy creoles of color in Louisiana, endogamous marriages were almost universal. Antoine Decuir and Antoine Dubuclet, the richest blacks in Point Coupée Parish, signed formal contracts concerning their children. In the case of Decuir's son, Antoine, Jr., and Dubuclet's daughter, Josephine, they drew up a four-page document (in French) specifying the date of the wedding, the size of the dowry, and arrangements for the distribution of property. Decuir contracted for his second son, Augustin, to marry the granddaughter of Iberville Parish planter Cyprien Ricard, at the time the wealthiest free person of color in Louisiana. Similar arrangements were made by the Donatto, Meullion, Simien (Simon), Guillory, and Lemmelle families in St. Landry;[58] the Conant, Metoyer, Rogues, and Llorens families in Natchitoches; the Reggio, Oliver, and Leonard families in Plaquemines; the Bienville, Ricard, Turpin families in East Baton Rouge; and the Honoré and Decuir families in West Baton Rouge. Indeed, by 1860, the genealogies of prosperous families in Louisiana and other parts of the Lower South were as intertwined as clusters of fine-haired roots.[59]

Not only did these families marry among themselves, but they also placed a great emphasis on educating their children. Some, like James M. Bland of Charleston, provided tutors for their sons, while others sent their boys away to school. "Study your Book well and try and give your father satisfaction," an Alabama barber wrote his eldest son in New York. "I am in hopes you will show me that you have not Been in Buffalo all this time for nothing and that I can hold you up as an example to your little Brothers." One of the "little Brothers" was attending school in Nashville: "he writes very plain for a boy of his age and practice," the father proudly noted, "and has [as] much taste for reading as any child I know off [sic] and very good in arithmetic." In Louisiana, a few creoles of color with strong attachments to the land of their forefathers sent their children abroad for schooling. New Orleans investment broker John Francis Clay, for example, sent three of his daughters to Paris and Bordeaux for an education. One of them, Charlotte, remained in France permanently. Eulalie Macarty's son, Victor-Eugene, was admitted to the Imperial Conservatoire of music in Paris where he studied harmony and composition.[60]

Whenever possible, affluent free persons of color established their own schools. They rented buildings, hired teachers, even acted as instructors. In Charleston, until an 1834 law forbade free Negro schools, Thomas Bonneau and William McKinlay, both wealthy slave owners (Bonneau owned a plantation in St. Thomas and St. Dennis Parish), operated schools. In Savannah, Julien Fromontin, a native of Santo Domingo, started a Negro school, continuing it for many years after a state law prohibited teaching black children to read and write. As early as 1813, free mulattoes in New Orleans had opened a school, offering instruction in French, Latin, Greek, geography, reading, writing, mathematics, and accounting; and the city's Couvent School, founded in 1847 with a bequest from a wealthy free woman of color, boasted several hundred "scholars." "The method of instruction is very good, and the progress of the pupils does honor to the teachers," one observer said. "Some of the pupils have mastered the principal rules in arithmetic, and progressed as far as the square and cube root." By 1850, 1,000 free children of color attended school in the Crescent City—23 percent of the South's total number of black schoolchildren.[61] In rural St. Mary Parish, Romaine Verdun built a school and hired a full-time teacher for his children and those of his neighbors. Mulatto planters in St. Landry and several other parishes erected school buildings, or secured "classrooms [in] the principal houses," and employed instructors on a yearly basis. "Out of nearly two hundred colored families who were free before the war," one observer in Pointe Coupée Parish noted in 1866, "only one family is unable to read and write while among the white people from twenty to twenty-five percent are in ignorance." Such an observation was not far from the truth. By 1860, the literacy rate among affluent free persons of color in the Lower South stood at 87 percent, higher than that for southern whites.[62]

Next to the family and the school, the church was the most important cultural institution for affluent free persons of color in the Lower South. A majority of those who reached the upper wealth levels were conscientious churchgoers. Since separate free Negro churches were rarely allowed during the antebellum era, they attended church with whites, sitting at the rear, or in the balcony, or in a special pew. In Charleston, most prosperous free mulattoes attended St. Philip's Episcopal Church, but a few others joined St. Michael's, St. Mark's, St. John's, St. Luke's, St. Paul's, and Grace Episcopal. William Ellison and his family worshiped at the Church of the Holy Cross, an Episcopal church in Stateburg, where by 1844, he had rented a pew at the rear on the main floor. In Georgia, Mississippi, and Alabama, prosperous free people of color joined Baptist and Methodist churches, while in Florida and Louisiana, most creoles of color became practicing Catholics. Some of the wealthy families in New Orleans attended St. Louis Cathedral Church, others St. Augustin's Catholic Church, while in Natchitoches, the Metoyer family built its own Catholic church. "The Church of St. Augustin of Natchitoches was built [here] by me and my family, principally for our usage," Augustin Metoyer explained in 1839, "except that I desire, and such is my wish that [white] outsiders professing our holy, catholic, apostolic, and Roman religion will have the right to assist at the divine office in the said chapel and shall enjoy, moreover, all the rights and privileges which I and my family are able to have there."[63]

Race Relations in the Lower South

Perhaps no single statement better captured the ambiguous nature of the race relations in the Lower South than Augustin Metoyer's expressed wish that white "outsiders" be allowed to worship at the Church of St. Augustin. However much they sought to lead isolated and separate lives, they remained inextricably bound to their white neighbors. Since there were many areas of possible mixing between the races—religious, economic, legal, social, sexual—and since when they did occur such contacts were sometimes kept secret, it is extremely difficult to make accurate generalizations about this subject. Yet, affluent free people of color understood both the complexities

and intricacies of southern racial mores, they recognized the importance of acting in a way so as not to offend whites, and they made
every effort to avoid racial conflict.[64]

For most, maintaining a reputation for honesty, frugality, and "upright behavior" was a matter of economic necessity. Those who owned
butcher shops, grocery stores, mercantile establishments, or tailor
shops, or ran businesses as contractors, carpenters, masons, or mechanics, even those who owned large farms and plantations, often
dealt with whites on a daily basis. Virtually every business in the
Lower South was sustained by the patronage of white customers. In
Charleston, the free Negro bootmakers, tailors, hairdressers, and
butchers catered to whites; in Stateburg, Ellison repaired the cotton
gins of the up-country gentry; in Macon, Georgia, grocer-merchant
Solomon Humphries sold his hardware, cutlery, dry goods, and groceries to local white residents; in Savannah, Susan Jackson sold her
cakes, bread, and sweet rolls to white citizens; and in various other
communities across the Lower South, free Negro barbers, store owners, shopkeepers, and merchants catered to a white clientele.

Among those who sometimes patronized Negro-owned businesses
were prominent local planters and businessmen and political and civic
leaders, including mayors, judges, state legislators, Congressmen, and
United States senators. One of Natchez barber William Johnson's loyal
customers was Adam L. Bingaman, a graduate of Harvard who
served as the speaker of the Mississippi House of Representatives and
made an unsuccessful bid for the United States Senate. Among the
customers at Ellison's cotton gin establishment were various members
of the Singleton family who had extensive slave and land holdings in
Sumter County. Among those who frequented Nathan Warren's two-
story confectionery store on Markham street in Little Rock, Arkansas,
were some of the town's leading citizens who sought his assistance in
providing refreshments at weddings and social events. Customers at
Shandy Jones's barbershop in Tuscaloosa included politicians, clergymen, business leaders, and probably Alabama Supreme Court Justice
H. W. Collier, one of the several prominent whites with whom Jones
discussed the emigration question. Similarly, Negro farmers and
planters had constant dealings with whites, purchasing machinery, securing supplies, borrowing money, acquiring slaves, ordering equipment, marketing crops, and buying land. For most affluent free persons of color in the Lower South, success in business and farming
depended not only on favorable economic conditions, but also on tact
and humility in dealing with whites.[65]

The economic ties that bound prosperous free persons of color and whites together continued even as the sectional crisis intensified. "Their labor is indispensable to us in this neighbourhood," a group of prominent Charleston residents, including James Rose, William J. Grayson, Benjamin Huger, and others, said in a petition to the South Carolina State Senate in 1860. "They are the only workmen who will, or can, take employment in the Country during the summer. We cannot build or repair a house in that season without the aid of the coloured carpenter or bricklayers" (see appendix 2). Also "indispensable" to whites in the city were the shops of free Negro bootmakers, barbers, butchers, wheelwrights, millwrights, and tailors. "We know many among them who command the respect of all respectable men, many who are good citizens, [demonstrating] patterns of industry, sobriety, and irreproachable conduct," Rose and the others concluded; "there can be no better proof of this than the fact that they hold property in the City of Charleston to the value of more than half a million of Dollars."[66]

The dynamics of race relations and the ability of free persons of color to carve out a special niche in a local economy, and in doing so gain a measure of affluence, was perhaps nowhere more evident than in the hotel and rooming house business in Charleston and New Orleans. As early as 1816, Jehu Jones, a Charleston tailor, purchased the Burrows-Hall Inn, changed the name to Jones Inn, later to Jones Hotel, and began a seventeen year career as an hotelier, acquiring a reputation for excellent cuisine and unsurpassed service. Following his death in 1833, the hotel was taken over by Jones's stepdaughter Ann Deas, and later by John Lee and his wife Eliza Seymour Lee, who had previously operated a boardinghouse. The guests at these establishments included white slaveholders, merchants, businessmen, and virtually every distinguished foreign visitor to the city. English actress Frances Kemble, who visited Charleston in 1839, was highly complimentary to Eliza Lee, "a very obliging and civil colored woman who is extremely desirous of accommodating us to our minds." Kemble praised her hostess for providing the best lodgings in the city.[67] Lee's counterparts in the Crescent City during the 1850s included Lucy Ann Cheatham, Elizabeth Reid, Mary Harby, Martha Johnson, and several other free women of color who kept clean, comfortable, and attractively decorated rooming- and boardinghouses. They catered to southern white businessmen and other visitors. In 1860, the registrants at Reid's boarding establishment included Alabama-born Cornelius Wykoff, Kentuckian George Thomas, and a French-born broker, Levi Nathans; a few doors away, at Harby's, the guests included North Carolina commission merchant William Atwood, Georgia mer-

chant George Anderson, and South Carolina cotton broker Thomas
Siexas; at Martha Johnson's the visitors included, among others, Louisiana businessman John Poindexter.[68]

The relationship between "obliging and civil" free Negroes like
Eliza Lee and southern aristocrats was generally one of goodwill and
mutual respect. "Among our inside passengers, in the stage-coach,
was a free coloured woman," Frederick Law Olmsted said during a
trip "through the Carolinas"; "she was treated in no way differently
from the white ladies." This was customary in the South, asserted
Olmsted, and "no Southerner would ever think of objecting to it."[69]
Occasionally, there was sincere warmth and understanding, even
admiration and affection. When Georgia free Negro Anthony Odingsells, a large landowner, asked Liberty County planter Charles
O. Screven, the descendant of a distinguished Georgia family, to serve
as his guardian, as the law required, the response was neither patron-
izing nor impersonal. "I have not visited my plantation across the
river for more than a year past—nor have I visited Savannah for four
or five years past," Screven explained. "The affliction of my eye is the
cause of my confinement."[70] Unable to travel, or adequately care for
himself, he admitted he would be "utterly incompetent" to attend to
Odingsells's concerns. Under ordinary circumstances he would be
more than happy to comply with the request, and he deeply regretted
his inability to do so. Such an apology from a southern slave owner to
a free black suggested that, whatever the public professions concerning an "inferior and servile caste," on a personal and individual basis
there could be trust, honesty, and genuine concern.

Affluent free persons of color often counted whites among their
close acquaintances and occasionally ignored the code forbidding interracial social relationships. A visitor to Macon, Georgia, in 1833 was
surprised to learn that businessman Solomon Humphries, who had
purchased himself out of slavery, had actually entertained "some of
the wealthiest people of the city" at his home. Humphries acted with
respect and deference toward his white visitors, waiting on them himself rather than allowing his bondsmen and women to do so. After
winning a raffle, William Johnson of Natchez celebrated the occasion
by treating local whites to free champagne. Later, he invited a local
dentist to his farmhouse for supper.[71] In New Orleans, some families
became so close that the children grew up unmindful of racial prejudice. "I used to go every day in her yard when she lived on Dauphin
Street," said Rose Necaud, a white woman who managed a coffeeshop
in the French Quarter, recalling her childhood playmate Zuline Aubry Evans, a free person of color, "and she use to visit me [as] we lived

nearly opposite each other." Visitors to the city were frequently surprised by such cordiality. Shortly after his arrival in New Orleans,
John William De Forest, a Union army officer, was invited to supper
by a black man named Dumas, the brother of the rich landowner
Francis Dumas. "Our entertainer is a man of about thirty who looks
like a West Indian; his brother has the complexion of an Italian and
features which remind one of the first Napoleon," De Forest said; the
supper was "a collation of cakes, confectionery, creams, ices and
champagne, followed by *cafe noir*, cognac and delicious cigars." De
Forest and several of his fellow officers, Negro and white, played the
piano, sang patriotic songs, and danced with "very pretty ladies."[72]
Such social occasions were rare, even in New Orleans, but whites
and free persons of color, especially those with substantial property,
occasionally disregarded the prevailing taboos against interracial
mixing.

Although on the decline during the late antebellum period, some
mixed "marriages" remained as a reminder of an earlier period when
interracial unions were relatively common in some parts of the Lower
South. A substantial majority of free women of color who lived openly
with property-owning white men in 1850 were residents of Louisiana
(158 of 199 or 79 percent). In New Orleans, sixty-four women lived
in such households, including Lucy Ann Hagan (Cheatham), who was
the mistress of the wealthy cotton merchant John Hagan, worth an
estimated $160,000. In Plaquemines Parish, ten free women of color
cohabited with white planters and farmers, including thirty-eight-
year-old Antoinette Angelette who lived with sixty-year-old sugar
planter Sylvestre Dobard, Harriett Burlard who lived with farmer
Etienne Burlard, and Molly Thompson who lived with seventy-year-
old slaveowner C. C. Forsyth.[73] A number of similar relationships
were probably kept secret, but the census revealed fourteen such
couples in South Carolina, six in Georgia, four in Florida, eight in
Alabama, three in Mississippi, and four in Arkansas. As in Louisiana,
the men in these unions were often individuals of substantial wealth.
Little Rock businessman Joseph Fenno, worth an estimated $20,000,
for example, lived with a black woman named Mary and their two
mulatto children for many years.[74]

Only about one-third as many propertied Negro men in the Lower
South cohabited with white women. With few exceptions they were
listed as mulattoes by census takers and tended to cluster together
with a few other mixed couples in rural areas (more than four out of
five lived in the country), seeking to avoid contact with the outside
world. Small enclaves of these mixed families could be found in every

Deep South state, but they were especially prevalent in Chesterfield, Edgefield, and Orangeburg counties, South Carolina. In Orangeburg County, more than half of the property-owning Negro men— Abraham and Josiah Chavis, John Jacobs, V. J. Rickenbacker, and William Williamson, among others—were listed in the census as having white women as probable spouses in their households. In addition, the patriarch of the largest and wealthiest mulatto family in Texas, rancher William Ashworth, as well as several of his brothers, took white wives. In a few instances, as had been the case for South Carolina's James Pendarvis during the 1790s, the heads of these families seemed to merge with the dominant society. "Your Petitioner Humbly Showeth That he is the offspring of a white man by a mulatto woman," John Barland of Jefferson County, Mississippi, explained, "that he was born in Adams County and is now about thirty-nine years of age, that his father gave him a decent education and property enough to be independant [sic], that he intermarried with a respectable white family by which said wife he has two children." Barland noted that he had served on grand and petit juries, voted in local elections, testified in court against whites, and was treated in most respects as if he were "a white man and of fair character."[75]

Despite such rare acceptance, affluent mulattoes could never escape the legacy of slavery. Even on his own 650-acre plantation, the refined, sophisticated, highly educated Romaine Verdun, who sported Scotch side-whiskers and finely tailored suits, was mistaken for a house servant by one undiscerning visitor. During periods of political tension, or rumored slave unrest, such a mistake could result in tragedy. On December 7, 1829, shortly after the publication of an antislavery tract calling for slaves to rise up against their masters, Jean Baptiste Meullion petitioned the St. Landry Parish court to issue deeds of emancipation for his ten grandchildren and two great grandchildren. Though a large slave owner himself, Meullion feared that "some recent occurrences" might result in some members of his family being "reduced to slavery." This never occurred, but Meullion's fears were more than justified. On several occasions free persons of color were sold into slavery. "I was taken up bodily by a white man," M. S. Fayman, the granddaughter of a French-born planter and Haitian black, recalled, "carried on the boat, put in a cabin and kept there until we got to Louisville, Kentucky." Sold to slave trader/planter Pierce Haynes, Fayman recalled that her father, Henry de Sales, and her mother, Marguerite Sanchez De Hayne, had been creoles "of wealth and prestige in their day," possessing a large farm and raising pelicans for the New Orleans market. She remained in bondage several years before escaping to Ohio during the Civil War.[76] On the eve of the conflict, despite the economic connections between the races, some of the most prosperous free persons of color feared for their safety. "Since my absence the agitation has been so great as to cause many to leave who were liable to the law of 1822[77] & the panic has reached those whom the law cannot affect," James M. Johnson, of Charleston, wrote his friend Henry Ellison, on August 20, 1860; some free persons of color, even those who could prove that their grandmothers had been bona fide free mulattoes, had been rounded up and sold into slavery.

Although few were actually enslaved, even the most prosperous bona fide free mulattoes were constantly reminded that the slightest miscalculation, the most innocent breach of racial etiquette—an ill-chosen word, an offhand remark, an improper gesture—could result in a violent confrontation. Two free women of color in Natchitoches Parish, Magdelaine Lecomte and Augustine St. Denis, apparently offended community mores when they visited the home of a white man, Marc Sompayrac, and remained there until the middle of the evening. Returning to her home Augustine found one of Sompayrac's relatives standing outside her gate. Without saying a word, the man brandished a whip, threw her to the ground, and began thrashing her about the head and shoulders. When she wriggled free and ran into her house, he pursued her and, according to an eyewitness, "hit her on the temple, which caused her to fall on the table." Exactly what prompted this assault was never revealed, but a complaint lodged in the same parish some years later suggests what might have been the cause. Free Negro Manuel Llorens, a member of the Metoyer clan by marriage, testified that a local white man had threatened to hog-tie and whip his daughter because she had refused to bid him good day.[78] Most affluent free persons of color were able to avoid such incidents, carefully tailoring their behavior so as not to offend racial mores, but the violent confrontation and threats against young women of color in Natchitoches Parish pointed to the fragile nature of the relationship between whites and affluent blacks.

Black Communities in the Upper South

Prosperous free blacks in the Upper South and their brethren in the lower states shared many of the same cultural values: they believed in honesty, frugality, sobriety, and hard work; they believed in providing an education for their children, and in the importance of family and friends, religious piety, and sustaining amicable relations with the dominant race. They, too, were convinced, as had been their predecessors in the seventeenth and eighteenth centuries, that the ownership of property would help them protect their families and defend their rights. Yet, the origins, growth, and makeup of the prosperous group in the Upper South contrasted sharply with its counterpart in the lower states. As a result, some of the social and cultural values of affluent free Negroes in this region developed differently and they maintained a different type of relationship with whites.

Rarely separating themselves into small, exclusive groups (except perhaps in St. Louis), they maintained social and cultural contacts with a wide variety of other blacks, including those in bondage. In a number of instances affluent blacks themselves had been born in slavery or had slave parents. They had grown up mingling with other slaves and free blacks. When they reached adulthood they continued to maintain these old friendships. Nashville barber James Thomas, a slave until age twenty-three, counted among his best friends slave barber Frank Parrish, slave preacher Alfred Williams, and free blacks Solomon Porter, Anderson Cheatham, and Julia Sumner as well as several of the most prosperous free Negroes in St. Louis, including barbers William Johnson and Henry Clamorgan. Thomas and other prosperous blacks sometimes attended slave barbecues, Christmas dances, and New Year's celebrations, or frequented tippling houses, grocery stores, and eateries. They also joined various benevolent associations, friendship societies, and fraternal organizations whose memberships included less prosperous free Negroes and occasionally slaves—Baltimore's African Friendship Benevolent Society for Social Relief, Wilmington's African Benevolent Association, and Virginia's Beneficial Society of Free Men of Color. The class conscious and color conscious friendship networks so prevalent in the Gulf region were more subtle and far less widespread in the Upper South where, in 1860, a majority of the affluent group was listed in the census as black (compared with 14 percent in the lower states).

The late emergence of the most prosperous group in the Upper South, its close connection with slavery, and the much larger general free Negro population affected the family structure. Some wealthy free Negroes, including John Stanly and John Berry Meachum, had purchased their wives out of slavery, while others had married former slaves. In other cases they had married propertyless free women of color. Even if they had wished to separate themselves into family clans or networks of "Relations & friends," the number of affluent free blacks remained so small, and their wealth holdings so modest until the late antebellum era, that it would have been virtually impossible to do so. Except in St. Louis, and to a lesser degree in the District of Columbia, few parents insisted that their children marry others of their own economic status. Among both parents and children marital partners were most likely to be drawn from diverse economic and social backgrounds. It was not uncommon for even the largest property owners to marry ex-slaves or to purchase some of their children out of bondage.[79]

Yet, like their counterparts in the lower states, prosperous free blacks in the Upper South were determined to provide an education for their children. Charles Augustus Hodges, a farmer near Blackwater, Virginia, employed a tutor—"a professor of several languages and a man without prejudice or respect for color"—to instruct his eleven children. In areas where tutors were not available, free blacks sometimes taught their children themselves. How much they valued educating their families was revealed in the last will and testament of Thomas Braddock, a carpenter and builder in Alexandria, Virginia, who owned several rental houses as well as a small "library of books." Braddock instructed the administrators of his estate to "attend to the Education of my children, the boys untill they arrive to the age of sixteen then I wish my executors to bind them to some useful and propper trade, and the girls I wish them to be put to the milliners or mantua-making business, but I wish them to be kept regular at school until they are put to propper trades." He insisted that his boys should not be "bound to Sea, as it is not [a] trade for them."[80]

Despite such efforts, it was far more difficult than in the Lower South for affluent free blacks to educate their children. Even among the adults in the most prosperous group a near majority (41 percent in 1860) remained illiterate (compared to 13 percent in the Lower South), and although schools were maintained at various times in Virginia, North Carolina, Kentucky, Tennessee, Missouri, and other states, they were far inferior to those in the Gulf region. Except for John Francis Cook's Union Seminary school in the District of Columbia, where the curriculum included reading, composition, recitation, sculpture, physiology, and health, the courses offered in black schools were of a rudimentary nature. Most of these schools, in addition, were kept open only a few months a year and sometimes they were closed by local authorities. In the census schedules, only rarely were the sons and daughters of affluent free blacks listed as "attending school."[81]

By the late antebellum period, prosperous free blacks in the Upper South were more likely than their brethren in the lower states to attend separate churches. In both sections whites viewed large gatherings of blacks with alarm and suspicion, but in the Upper South, especially in urban areas, they found it more difficult to control black religious activities. Moreover, some whites either condoned or encouraged separate Negro churches. Consequently, in a number of cases prosperous free blacks became members of separate black congregations. In Baltimore, they attended (and contributed generously to) the Bethel African Methodist Episcopal Church and the Madison Street Presbyterian Church; in the District of Columbia they formed their own Presbyterian church in 1841 after complaining that "the colored members of the several Presbyterian and other evangelical churches in good standing do not enjoy, in our white churches, [equal] privileges." In several Virginia cities, including Norfolk and Petersburg, prosperous Negroes purchased church buildings, elected their own deacons, clerks, and trustees, and listened to their own preachers. It was against the law for blacks to be completely autonomous in their religious activities in Virginia, but white preachers, whose salaries were sometimes paid by the congregates, often turned the meetings over to Negro "chairmen." In Richmond, the gradual lessening of white control over Negro congregations and the significant expansion in the number of African Baptist churches, as Luther Porter Jackson has pointed out, were intricately connected with the financial contributions of the free black property-holding class, including those described as "well-to-do." The same was true in Louisville, Nashville, and St. Louis, where free persons of color who had reached the upper economic levels took an active role in establishing separate churches.[82]

Not only did they more often attend and support black religious institutions than free persons of color in the lower states, but the congregations also included a cross-section of blacks, from the economically most prosperous, to free Negroes of modest means, to plantation and city slaves. Among the congregates of the Gillfield Baptist Church in Petersburg were some of the most well-off free Negroes in the city, but the membership also included a number of bondspeople. In Nashville, various groups of blacks attended several Baptist and Methodist churches. What "was know as the African church," a former slave recalled, attracted large numbers of blacks every Sabbath, including prosperous free Negroes and city slaves. One could observe "all the styles" as well as people who "possessed the so called extravagant deportment."[83]

While few among the upper-economic group entered the clergy or became preachers, most of the South's property-owning free Negroes who were listed as ministers or clergymen in the population census lived in various communities of the border region—Jacob Bell and

Shadrack Boyer in Delaware, Levin Lee in Maryland, Samuel Brown and Daniel Jackson in Virginia, James Harper and Austin Woodfolk in Kentucky, and John Meachum in Missouri. The son of a Baptist preacher, Meachum joined the St. Louis Mission Church as early as 1816, and when it became an independent black church in 1827 he became its pastor. A decade later his congregation included two hundred slaves and twenty free blacks, while the name of his steamboat—"Temperance"—symbolized his work as a minister and as a community leader. Meachum and others, one former slave recalled some years later, preached "the straight old time sermons." Christ had been crucified to save all the sinners; God accepted blacks and whites on an equal basis; everyone had the same opportunity for salvation.[84]

This independence in social and religious life was also reflected in race relations. There were, of course, similarities between the upper and lower states with regard to the relations between prosperous free Negroes and whites. In both sections, some whites castigated free Negroes, even the wealthiest, as indolent, thieving, and ungovernable. "[It] would be wholly absurd to expect from them any attachment to our laws and institutions," a group of Virginia slave owners said, echoing the sentiments of others in various sections of the South, "or any sympathy with our people." In both sections, free Negroes found it necessary to seek cordial relations with prominent whites who might vouch for them during periods of racial unrest. And in both sections, free blacks were dependent on white customers in their various business pursuits. Yet the paternalistic ties binding free persons of color and whites together were much weaker in the upper states than in the Lower South. The origin, size, and makeup of the free black populace, with its close ties to slavery and its largely black rather than mulatto membership, contrasted sharply with South Carolina and the Gulf region. In the border states, prosperous free Negroes were three times more likely to be of pure African descent. Even those of mixed ancestry were often generations removed from their white forebears. Some of them had lived their early years in bondage. Free black women only rarely lived openly with white men, and those who did, unlike those in New Orleans, resided in isolated rural districts.

At the same time, white attitudes toward prosperous free Negroes differed in the two sections. In the upper states, whites rarely defended free persons of color as a group, although they did come to the assistance of especially industrious free blacks. The petitions to various state legislatures concerning an "industrious and honest people," "generally respected by the white population," such as those sent by whites in South Carolina and Louisiana, were largely absent in the upper states, where planters and slaveholders were more likely to condemn all free Negroes, including those who had acquired substantial amounts of property, as a threat to the South's "peculiar institution."

This tended to push prosperous free Negroes even more toward seeking friendships and maintaining social and cultural contacts with various groups of other blacks, both slave and free. Unlike the free persons of color in the Lower South, those who reached the higher economic levels in the upper states revealed a marked indifference or sardonic humor toward their white customers and guardians. They mentioned them only in passing. Independent and self-reliant, they secured white protectors as a matter of necessity, but found greatest satisfaction in commingling with a remarkable array of friends, acquaintances, and relatives in various black communities. They perceived themselves as fortunate free Negroes who had been able, through hard work and good luck, to accumulate substantial amounts of property, rather than a privileged group seeking to occupy a middle ground between slaves and the white aristocracy.[85]

Those who rose to the top of the economic spectrum in both sections remained precariously balanced between the dominant whites and the masses of their brethren. Yet those in the Lower South, more closely tied to whites, owning larger numbers of slaves, accepting some of the values and attitudes of the planter class, and seeking to separate themselves socially and culturally from other Negroes, found their position and wealth holding inexorably connected with the plantation aristocracy, while free blacks in the Upper South, more independent, owning fewer slaves, and often only a generation removed from bondage themselves, discovered new opportunities during the intense years of sectional conflict. On the eve of the Civil War, however, few realized the wrenching changes that were about to occur, even among free persons of color who had reached the highest economic station in the South.

CHAPTER FIVE

Property Ownership
among Southern Blacks,
1860–1915

Most of the literature by economic historians dealing with the post-emancipation period emphasizes either "competition" or "coercion." Those who argue that the competitive free-market forces were at work in the southern states discuss how freedmen and their children made significant economic progress following the Civil War. Despite efforts of whites to control freedmen through intimidation, violence, and "restrictive cartels," black per capita income rose at an annual rate of 2.7 percent; housing, diet, and living conditions improved; ownership of property increased; and material well-being improved significantly. Competition "prevented the general emergence of racial discrimination in wage payments or farm rental agreements," one author asserts, and consequently "economic progress did occur [among blacks]."[1] Those who argue that coercion was predominant emphasize economic repression, the crop lien system, indebtedness, and poverty.[2] One study of the Cotton Belt in the Lower South concludes that the blacks' economic, political, and social freedom was "under constant attack by the dominant white society determined to preserve racial inequalities." "The economic institutions established in the post-emancipation era effectively operated to keep the black population a landless agricultural labor force, operating tenant farms with a backward and unprogressive technology." What little income was earned above the bare subsistence level was often "exploited by monopolistic credit merchants."[3]

At the same time revisionist historians concerned with Reconstruction and its aftermath have emphasized the failure of government programs (local, state, and federal) to assist former slaves and their children in securing an economic stake.[4] They often paint a bleak picture of failed programs, oppressive laws and institutions, corruption, political wrangling, and lost opportunities.[5] If Congress had acted differently, if President Andrew Johnson had not been so opposed to helping freedmen, if former plantation owners had not been allowed to regain control of their old plantations, and if, at the moment of defeat, the conquered South had been forced to grant radical economic concessions, one historian asserts, the specter of "perpetual debt" and virtual bondage would have been eliminated.[6]

Despite this substantial literature, few of these studies systematically examine black property ownership. When they do discuss this subject they either ignore changes over time, capture them at particular moments, or focus primarily on rural black-belt regions.[7] This chapter seeks to broaden our understanding of black property ownership by focusing on the changes that occurred in various sections of the South over a period of more than fifty years. By analyzing land acquisition after the war, comparing it with prewar holdings, viewing the South's towns and cities as well as its agricultural regions, and looking at both the Upper and the Lower South, and subregions within each, we can not only utilize a new and more revealing conceptual framework but also gain a clearer picture of the economic activities of postemancipation blacks. How successful were former slaves and their children in acquiring land and other property in different regions of the South? during different periods from the Civil War era to the early twentieth century? How did the profile of Negro property owners— their location, color, gender, occupational status, average wealth— change from the antebellum to the postbellum eras? from the 1870s to the early 1900s? How did property accumulations among blacks compare with those of whites and how did this change over time? How did former free black property owners fare during Reconstruction and afterward? What were the attitudes of freedmen toward the acquisition of property? To answer these questions, the crucial period of the 1860s, where our knowledge is so impressionistic, will be examined in some depth—first in the Lower South (in terms of rural and urban real property holding, total estate holding, and profile of owners), then in the Upper South (covering the same topics). The post-1870 period will be examined in a broader context by viewing changes in farm ownership, home ownership, and black-owned business enterprises.

Freed Slaves as Property Owners in the Lower South

Perhaps no Americans better understood the meaning of owning property than those who had been considered a "species of property" themselves. "If I was free, massa; *if I was free*," one Louisiana slave told Frederick Law Olmsted on the eve of the Civil War, "I would go to work for a year, and get some money for myself,—den—den—den—den, massa, dis is what I do—I buy me, fus place, a little house, and little lot of land." These sentiments were shared almost universally by those who had spent their lives in bondage. When freedom came, they expressed again and again how they hoped to buy a "little lot of land." "What's de use of being free," an old man informed the journalist Whitelaw Reid in 1865, "if you don't own land enough to be buried in? Might juss as well stay [a] slave all yo' days." "The freedmen have a passion for land," one observer in South Carolina said. "Where a little can be obtained they are always purchasers." The sole ambition of freed slaves, another observer noted, seemed to be a desire to become the "owner of a little piece of land" where he could build a small house and live "in peace and security at his own will and pleasure."[8]

It was natural for blacks to have a passion for the land. For generations they had worked the soil, planting, cultivating, harvesting, tending gardens, and raising livestock. Like most rural people who derived their sustenance from the soil, they respected the land and its bounty. Some of them had felt a certain "proprietorship" over their garden plots and, to some extent, over the provision grounds beyond. As freedmen they saw the possession of land as a symbol of a new beginning, a new independence. Some believed ownership would release them from the control of their former masters. Others believed that they deserved a portion of the land that they had worked on all their lives—whites should be forced to relinquish their old plantations as punishment for holding a people in bondage. As was the case during the antebellum period, some blacks spoke of "getting ahead," taking advantage of new opportunities, and becoming "acquisitive." Whatever the mixture of motives, former slaves saw land ownership as a symbol of freedom.[9]

It quickly became apparent, however, that the path to ownership would be a long and difficult one. In the Lower South, where 2.4 million slaves had been released from bondage, whites mounted a determined campaign to keep freedmen in an economically subordinate and dependent position. In 1865, Mississippi prohibited "any freedman, free negro or mulatto" from renting or leasing "any land or tenements" except within the limits of "incorporated titles or towns" where local authorities could control and oversee such rental and lease agreements. While this law was overturned in 1867, in various parts of the Lower South white landowners signed agreements not to hire one another's black workers. They demanded that freedmen and women labor in much the same way as they had in slavery and refused to sell or lease them land. During his travels, Whitelaw Reid noted that in many sections of the Mississippi Valley if a white man or woman sold land to a black he or she might be physically attacked. Every effort was made "to prevent negroes from acquiring lands," Reid said; "even the renting of small tracts. . . ." "The nigger is going to be made a serf, sure as you live," one Alabama planter boasted during the early months after the war. "It won't need any law for that. Planters will have an understanding among themselves: 'You won't hire my niggers, and I won't hire yours'; then what's left for them? They're attached to the soil and we're as much their masters as ever." Texas freedman Toby Jones recalled the validity of this boast: "I don't know as I 'spected nothin' from freedom," he said, "but they turned us out like a bunch of stray dogs, no homes, no clothin', no nothin', not 'nough food to las us one meal." [10]

The strong opposition of whites to black land ownership in the rural areas of the Lower South would have long lasting effects. Only in places where military authorities or northern missionaries assisted freedmen or women, or in remote and infertile back-country regions, did significant numbers of former slaves acquire small tracts of land. Between December 10, 1862, and September 23, 1869, members of the South Carolina Direct Tax Commission and northern philanthropists sold land certificates to more than 2,234 Negroes on St. Helena, Our Ladies, and Port Royal islands. Most of the purchasers acquired from ten to forty acres at $1.25 per acre. While some of these owners were subsequently forced to return the land to its former white proprietors, others eventually received title to the prop-

Table 9. Rural Negro Landowners in the Lower South, 1870

State	Trph	Arph	Owners	Rural Families	Ratio
Alabama	$916,700	$523	1,752	90,075	1:51
Arkansas	660,300	476	1,388	23,379	1:17
Florida	334,900	348	961	17,089	1:18
Georgia	1,085,100	390	2,784	101,072	1:36
Louisiana	1,972,700	855	2,308	61,646	1:27
Mississippi	1,495,900	745	2,009	85,788	1:43
South Carolina	1,827,100	508	3,598	76,594	1:21
Texas	503,900	370	1,361	47,952	1:35
Total	$8,796,600	$544	16,161	503,595	1:31

Source: Computed from USMSPC, 1870. To obtain property owners with estates valued at from $100 to $900, a sample of 7,855 propertied blacks (from every twentieth printed page in the manuscript census) was used. See An Essay on Sources and Methodology.

erty. By 1870, with average holdings worth about $600, approximately 1,200 freedmen and women in Beaufort County owned their own land, the highest number of any county in the entire South. In remote areas of Duval and Marion counties, Florida, and Desha and Union counties, Arkansas, several hundred former bondsmen and women secured small tracts of unimproved land. Even with these pockets of ownership only a tiny number of former slaves in rural areas of the Lower South had acquired their own land by 1870. In Alabama, the ratio was one family in 51, in Mississippi, one family in 43, and in Georgia, one family in 36.[11]

In the immediate aftermath of the war, thousands of freed people tested their freedom by abandoning their old plantations and migrating to the nearest town or city. Many became disillusioned with the overcrowding, disease, and poverty, returning to rural areas, but a small number remained, seeking to start a new life. In 1870, only 7 percent of the Lower South's black population lived in urban areas, and with the exception of Charleston, Savannah, Mobile, and New Orleans, where more than half of the urban Negroes of the region lived (103,616 of 194,231), they were scattered in dozens of smaller urban centers. Most of these "urban areas" were hardly cities at all, having only a few dozen dirt streets stretching back from the central business district. In Columbia, South Carolina, for example, even after its restoration following the destruction by Sherman's troops, residents could walk from the Capitol building to the outskirts of town in less than ten minutes.[12]

Yet urban blacks enjoyed economic advantages not possessed by their brethren in the countryside. They usually earned wages that were paid to them directly, and though the payments were often small they were able to avoid high interest rates and crop liens that took so much of the rural blacks' earnings. They were able to take advantage of the rising demand for skilled and unskilled workers, especially to rebuild buildings or construct new homes, and the continued importance of small towns as trading and merchandising centers. Property values generally remained below prewar levels, but unlike their counterparts in rural areas, urban whites, in need of capital and less fearful of blacks, were often anxious to sell them property. Consequently, freedmen and women in Charleston, Savannah, Mobile, New Orleans, and in smaller towns such as Columbia, South Carolina, Valdosta and Augusta, Georgia, Jacksonville, Florida, Selma, Alabama, Pine Bluff and Little Rock, Arkansas, and various other commercial and trading centers acquired realty at a rate three-and-a-half times faster than did blacks in rural areas. By 1870, one out of nine blacks in towns and cities of the region (4,313 of 38,846 families) had acquired a total of $5,299,600 in realty, or an average of $1,229 per real estate owner. While some of these property owners, especially among the more affluent in Charleston and New Orleans, had been antebellum free Negroes (see chapter 6), the great majority were former slaves.[13]

Although the masses of former slaves in rural and urban areas of the Deep South remained landless, the number of black land owners and the value of their holdings increased significantly after the war. This rise was all the more important since it occurred despite the generally hostile attitudes of whites, the rise of the Ku Klux Klan and other terrorist groups, and the refusal of whites in some areas to sell land to freedmen and women. It also occurred despite a substantial drop in land values—in rural areas of South Carolina, Georgia, Alabama, Mississippi, and Louisiana, between 55 and 70 percent—and despite various other economic problems: a general indebtedness, scarcity of money, lack of capital, and "unsettled conditions."

Ironically, some of the postwar difficulties may have been actually beneficial to former slaves. If improved farmland sold for between $15 and $25 per acre before the war, it now sold for between $2 and $8 per acre. In addition, during the war nearly one out of five southern white males aged thirteen to forty-three had died, and tens of thousands of others had returned home physically disabled or mentally impaired. Neither the lower land prices nor the wartime deaths necessarily resulted in better opportunities for former slaves; yet the number of real estate owners in South Carolina rose from 680 in 1860 to 3,977 in 1870; in Georgia, from 116 to 3,729; in Alabama, from

Table 10. Black Realty Owners in the Lower South, 1860/1870

State	Erph	Arph	Total Owners
Alabama	$195,200/1,536,700	$1,375/636	142/2,417
Arkansas	3,200/833,500	800/538	4/1,548
Florida	55,500/455,900	895/390	62/1,170
Georgia	113,000/1,746,300	974/468	116/3,729
Louisiana	5,514,500/4,343,600	4,370/1,336	1,262/3,250
Mississippi	73,200/1,979,700	2,091/689	35/2,875
South Carolina	1,124,300/2,615,100	1,653/658	680/3,977
Texas	37,800/585,400	2,100/388	18/1,508
Total	$7,116,700/14,096,200	$3,069/688	2,319/20,474

Source: Computed from USMSPC, 1860, 1870.

142 to 2,417; in Mississippi, from 35 to 2,875; and in Texas and Arkansas, from 22 to 3,056. The value of their holdings, despite depressed prices, rose nearly 100 percent, from $7.1 million to $14 million. Still, by 1870, one Negro family in twenty-six in the region was a realty owner.[14]

Unfortunately, census takers in 1870 did not ask questions about former status (e.g., "Were you born in slavery?" "Did you ever live in bondage?" "Were you or your parents free born?"). But a profile of these owners in 1870, including a comparison of occupational groupings and occupational wealth holdings and an examination of the "persistence" rate among antebellum free Negroes, suggests that the vast majority of the Lower South's landholders were now ex-slaves. Following the war there was almost an entire reversal in the proportion of Lower South real estate owners listed in the census as "black" compared with those listed as "mulatto": in 1860, 80 percent were of mixed ancestry; a decade later, 76 percent were black. An even more dramatic change occurred among property-owning women. On the eve of the Civil War, nearly one out of three realty owners in the region was female. As a group they controlled 26 percent of the real and 27 percent of the total wealth. In 1870, they represented less than 8 percent of the realty owners and owned only 12 percent of the real and 7 percent of the total wealth. There was also a precipitous drop among both sexes in the average value of realty holdings, from $3,069 in 1860 to only $688 a decade later, greater than the depreciation in land values.

The changes in the occupational structure and the decline in the average property held by those in certain occupations similarly point to an infusion of freedmen and women into the ranks of real estate owners. Prior to the Civil War, the occupational skills among free Negroes in the Lower South, especially in Charleston and New Orleans, were far superior to those of blacks anywhere else in the country. After the war, however, there was a marked shift. A much larger proportion of Lower South real estate owners in 1870 than in 1860 earned their livelihoods as draymen, porters, peddlers, servants, laundresses, whitewashers, and unskilled workers. N. J. Shaler, a visitor to Charleston in 1870, observed that it was "a rare thing" to see blacks engaged in skilled trades, such as carpentry; most of them, he asserted, toiled as manual laborers and dock hands. Although Shaler's observations did not accurately reflect the occupational structure in the city, there was little doubt that Charleston—a center for black artisans since the 1790s—had lost its former status as a mecca for skilled Negroes.

In other areas of the Lower South there were similar increases among property owners who worked at lower-paying jobs as well as a relative decline—at least when compared with the huge increase in the number of free black families (from approximately 7,391 to 542,442)—among craftsmen, artisans, and tradesmen. The two skilled occupations where substantial improvements occurred—blacksmithing and barbering—prior to the war (unlike those in the Upper South), had been largely dominated by propertyless free blacks and slaves. In addition, in many skilled occupational categories the average real property holdings dropped sharply during the 1860s: brickmasons from $2,455 to $720, carpenters from $1,300 to $558, mechanics from $3,005 to $730, and shoemakers from $2,016 to $523. The same was true for blacks engaged in businesses: among grocers it went from $9,747 to $1,624, among tailors from $13,954 to $2,125 (see appendix 5).[15]

These various changes—the juxtaposition of blacks versus mulattoes, the decline among women, the drop in mean realty holdings, the changing occupational structure—suggest not only that increasing numbers of freedmen and women were entering the property-owning class (though their numbers remained very small) but also that some former free persons of color were experiencing economic difficulties. Facing increased competition from both whites and newly freed blacks, and finding it difficult to adjust to rapidly changing conditions, some highly skilled, former free Negroes took jobs as domestic servants, laborers, and laundresses. Others who worked in the same occupations as before suffered substantial property losses during the war years: Charleston carpenter Phillip Thorne, Alabama seamstress Josephine Hassel, and Louisiana farmer Antoine Rachel lost significant portions of their estates, while Georgia carpenter Richard Lamar, Louisiana farmer Carroll Jones, and New Orleans grocer Anthony Purnas lost nearly everything they owned.[16] In all, only approximately one out of five prewar realty owners could be found on the census rolls a decade later, and while some of those not listed could have been missed by census takers, this low "persistence" rate suggests that only a small proportion of the 1870 realty owners in the Lower South had been part of the free Negro property-holding group.

If purchasing a small farm or even a town lot was beyond the means of the vast majority of freedmen and women, it was much easier to acquire a few personal items. The quest for property ownership among blacks during the early postwar years can best be seen by viewing the changing profile of those who accumulated at least $100 worth

Table 11. Black Property Owners in the Lower South, 1860/1870

State	Etph	Atph	Owners
Alabama	$468,300/5,060,300	$2,072/330	226/15,317
Arkansas	4,500/2,419,400	1,125/340	4/7,113
Florida	168,400/1,052,100	1,604/317	105/3,315
Georgia	256,200/5,237,000	896/295	286/17,739
Louisiana	8,159,300/7,530,200	3,674/517	2,221/14,569
Mississippi	210,500/8,248,100	3,972/349	53/23,665
South Carolina	1,895,200/4,628,700	1,760/421	1,077/10,997
Texas	53,800/3,049,800	1,681/243	32/12,535
Total	$11,216,200/37,225,600	$2,801/354	4,004/105,250

Source: Computed from USMSPC, 1860, 1870.

of real and/or personal property. Some former slaves had preserved the small personal holdings they had acquired in slavery, but most simply found it easier to acquire a few personal items than to purchase a plot of ground. Consequently, they bought horses, mules, cattle, wagons, plows, machinery, tools, furniture, carts, carriages, and sometimes watches, jewelry, and clothing. One observer in Augusta, Georgia, in 1865, was surprised to discover that freedmen and women were so anxious to begin the ascent toward property ownership: "A Government sale of horses and mules brought large numbers to the city to-day. It is estimated that no less than 10,000 persons attended the sale, two-thirds of whom were freedmen. The stock brought enormous prices, one team, six mule, selling for $1,265— much higher than previous to the war. Freedmen bid lively and bought largely." By 1870, the two Deep South states with the largest antebellum slave (and among the smallest free black) populations, Mississippi and Georgia, led all states in the total number of property owners—Mississippi with 23,665, and Georgia with 17,739. In the other states of the Lower South, approximately 63,846 had become property owners with $100 or more, for a regional total of one family in five.[17]

Freed Slaves as Property Owners in the Upper South

In some ways the Upper South was similar to the lower states. In areas where whites supported the idea of black proprietorship some freedmen and women moved with little difficulty from slavery to land ownership, but in sections of Delaware, Maryland, and Virginia and in other areas where whites refused to sell land to blacks or mounted campaigns of violence and intimidation, landholding among former slaves was extremely rare. Some planters were determined to maintain the status quo antebellum so far as their black labor force was concerned and, like white landholders in Georgia, Alabama, and Mississippi, they signed agreements among one another not to hire their neighbor's tenants or sharecroppers. In 1865, an official of the Bureau of Refugees, Freedmen, and Abandoned Lands, established by Congress to assist former slaves, observed that "former rebels" in Virginia had reclaimed their plantations within a few months after the end of hostilities. Resisting efforts of the bureau to secure equitable labor contracts for freedmen and women, white landowners, he explained, offered only subsistence wages, refused to sell or rent acreage to blacks, and adopted nonemployment agreements for any former slave who left his former owner. In portions of Delaware and Maryland, white vigilante groups scoured the countryside, burning black churches, schools, and farmhouses. In regions of dense Negro population the same fears that prompted whites in the Lower South to control the access of freedmen and women to the land were prevalent in the Upper South. In addition, especially in Virginia where so much fighting had occurred during the war, blacks confronted many of the same economic problems faced by freed slaves in the Lower South.[18]

The areas of the Upper South which most resembled the lower states with regard to black landholding were sections of the eastern seaboard states. In Delaware and in portions of Maryland and Virginia, white hostility made it extremely difficult for freedmen and women to gain an economic foothold. Most planters in the area saw them as a threat to economic stability if they were not "regulated" and if they did not remain dependent on their former masters. Despite the huge increases in the rural free black populations after emancipation—in Maryland from 56,000 to 130,657, and in Virginia from 48,000 to 451,108—the number of rural landowners in some areas actually declined: in the state of Delaware from 522 in 1860 to 439 in 1870, in Dorchester and Harford counties, Maryland, from 642 to approximately 350, and in Prince George, Southampton, and Surry counties, Virginia, from 76 to fewer than a dozen. The small increases in Kent County, Maryland, were primarily due to former free Negroes breaking up their holdings and parceling out a few acres to their children and relatives. In Maryland, while the rural black population grew 133 percent, the number of landholders rose only 29 percent, from 2,124 to 2,730; in Virginia, with an 840 percent population growth, the number of realty owners increased 100 percent, from

1,316 to 2,633. While the ratios of landholders to the total rural population in Delaware and Maryland remained the highest in the South (one out of nine and one out of ten families, respectively) the proportion of landowners had dropped considerably from the antebellum period; in Virginia, by 1870, only one out of thirty-four rural black family heads was a landowner, about the same ratio as in Georgia and Texas.[19]

Yet, in rural areas of the Trans-Appalachian West, former slaves in the upper tier of states possessed advantages over their brethren in the Deep South. In some areas, whites were not opposed to black proprietorship. Some even assisted freedmen and women in their quests for self-sufficiency. In other sections, the momentum toward property ownership that had begun during the 1850s continued during the postwar period, allowing former free Negroes to hold on to their land and to sell small tracts to friends and relatives who had once been held in slavery. In addition, there was a continuing demand for unskilled workers on the countryside which gave former slaves better employment opportunities.[20] With smaller rural populations, less opposition from whites, and greater demand for wage laborers, some freedmen and women moved with little difficulty from bondage to farm ownership. In Kentucky, Tennessee, and Missouri, the number of rural landholders did not keep pace with the large increases in the number of free Negro families in rural areas following emancipation, but the number of realty owners rose from 775 in 1860 to 6,538 in

Table 12. Rural Negro Landowners in the Upper South, 1870

State	Trph	Arph	Owners	Rural Families	Ratio
Delaware	$579,800	$1,321	439	3,917	1 : 9
District of Columbia	51,900	2,163	24	724	1 : 30
Kentucky	1,456,800	580	2,513	37,713	1 : 15
Maryland	1,947,400	713	2,730	26,131	1 : 10
Missouri	968,400	693	1,397	16,844	1 : 12
North Carolina	950,500	369	2,573	74,785	1 : 29
Tennessee	1,863,700	709	2,628	58,164	1 : 22
Virginia	1,515,400	576	2,633	90,222	1 : 34
Total	$9,333,900	$625	14,937	308,500	1 : 21
Total in rural South	$18,130,500	$583	31,098	812,095	1 : 26

Source: Computed from USMSPC, 1870.

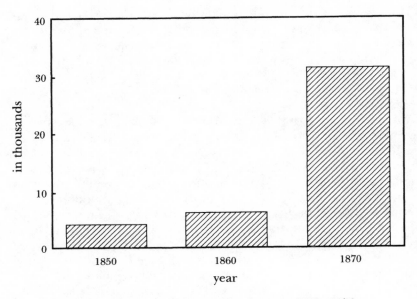

Figure 2. Rural Black Realty Owners, 1850–1870

1870, or 744 percent. Some of them were only part-time farmers who worked as harvest hands, woodcutters, rail splitters, and day laborers. Charles Christopher, James Warren, Harrington Bruce, and Jesse Jones of Boyle County, Kentucky, for example, were listed in the census as common laborers, but they each owned small acreages for farming. Similarly, Thornton Washington, Ned Holloway, and Frederick Ball of Pike County, Missouri, were listed as hired hands and a blacksmith, although they each owned small farms and land valued at between $800 and $1,000. Although the holdings of these rural blacks remained small—averaging between $580 in Kentucky and $709 in Tennessee—by 1870 freedmen and women in this section of the South were accumulating real estate at a much faster pace than rural blacks along the eastern seaboard in the Upper South; and they were nearly twice as likely to own land as their rural counterparts in the Lower South.[21]

The shift among urban property owners that had begun before the Civil War continued during the early years of the postbellum period. In the towns and cities of the Upper South, the number of realty owners rose significantly between 1860 and 1870: in Baltimore, from

169 to approximately 435; in the District of Columbia, from 497 to 1,019; in Lexington, from 44 to 671; and in Wilmington, North Carolina, from 42 to 408. In the District of Columbia, in 1870, one out of eight Negro family heads owned real estate. Its value exceeded $2,305,900 (excluding land outside the city but in the district), or $2,263 per realty holder, more than the value of the property held by the entire urban free black population in the upper states prior to the war. Although this did not compare favorably to the figure for whites, who made up 68 percent of the city's population but owned 98 percent of the property, the total realty holdings among urban blacks in the Upper South had almost quadrupled (from $2,285,900) in only ten years. This expansion nearly kept pace with the significant increases in the urban free black population following emancipation. In Wilmington, North Carolina, 42 free Negroes owned $55,600 worth of land in 1860; a decade later, 408 blacks owned real estate valued at $247,900. In Nashville, Tennessee, there were 44 antebellum land-owners who owned property worth $119,400; in 1870, 65 owners controlled $245,300. In St. Louis, 94 real estate owners controlled $428,600 before the war, and afterward approximately 128 owners controlled $765,100 worth of property. Representing only 15 percent of the Upper South's black population (265,132 of 1,808,655) city dwellers comprised 34 percent of the realty owners and controlled 49 percent of the black wealth ($8,863,500 of $18,197,402).

This growth was due primarily to rapidly improving occupational opportunities. In some of the border cities, economic activity had increased substantially during and after the war. While cities such as Columbia, Charleston, Mobile, and Selma had experienced the brunt of Union artillery, Baltimore, the District of Columbia, Lexington, Louisville, Nashville, and St. Louis had witnessed an economic boom during the war which continued during the late 1860s. Moreover, with large numbers of whites going off to fight in the war, and a significant number not returning, there was a rising demand for laborers and skilled workers. Although most black property owners still worked as day laborers, waiters, servants, haulers, dock hands, and laundresses, a growing number now worked as blacksmiths, brick-masons, carpenters, coopers, mechanics, shoemakers, small shop-keepers, and tradesmen. "There are over thirty thousand colored people in Baltimore," the editor of the Baltimore *American* observed as early as 1864. "They have or can have constant employment, for there is no lack of demand for the kind of labor which for the most part they can perform." The "kind of labor" included working on the

Table 13. Occupations among Upper and Lower South
Urban Black Realty Owners, 1860/1870

Occupation	Upper South		Lower South	
	Total	Arph	Total	Arph
laborers	341/2,617	$748/$591	51/701	$1,243/$537
craftsmen and skilled workers				
blacksmiths	22/223	1,555/728	2/98	2,150/769
brickmasons	35/196	891/906	29/230	3,090/754
caulkers	17/17	653/1,512	5/20	1,200/300
carpenters	67/546	1,552/926	140/511	1,646/759
coopers	12/50	533/626	5/29	1,220/1,259
masons	12/112	683/544	8/1	1,675/1,500
mechanics	12/12	1,100/3,958	12/73	4,633/905
plasterers	16/184	1,200/807	2/48	1,250/617
shoemakers	22/133	859/877	19/102	2,384/611
shopkeepers and tradesmen				
barbers	78/218	3,467/2,566	13/72	2,069/1,639
boarding house/ hotel keepers	2/12	1,900/12,083	17/3	2,888/2,233
butchers	6/28	1,883/1,271	16/57	1,863/1,172
grocers	6/74	1,583/2,014	16/116	10,263/1,764
merchants	5/11	7,380/5,882	13/34	13,285/5,259
restaurateurs	5/53	1,320/1,857	4/15	1,125/1,973
storekeepers	10/11	2,650/1,982	3/1	667/4,500
tailors	8/3	1,800/1,667	22/39	15,173/1,785
service				
coachmen	36/94	2,033/1,021	3/1	1,600/1,000
cooks	28/98	1,257/1,053	5/23	780/335
draymen	75/365	1,379/1,000	29/228	1,441/741
laundresses	157/126	871/933	49/88	800/461
painters	36/97	1,167/851	8/38	2,350/837
porters	28/198	1,496/1,574	11/76	1,773/424
seamstresses	30/27	1,037/2,159	39/39	1,938/1,818
servants	103/240	1,213/1,185	5/101	1,760/675
stewards	16/23	3,300/4,757	1/6	1,200/1,917
mariners	11/17	945/1,888	2/1	1,400/500
ministers	9/167	1,722/1,452	4/71	825/1,346
physicians	2/6	2,900/2,883	3/3	9,333/2,000
teachers	4/9	2,425/2,478	3/8	1,167/1,838

Source: Computed from USMSPC, 1860, 1870.

docks, waiting tables, cleaning clothes, transporting goods, cooking, whitewashing, and carting, but *Woods City Directory* for 1867–68 also listed sixty-four Negro blacksmiths and carpenters, thirty-one grocers, twenty-five confectioners, eighteen restaurateurs, fourteen engineers, eleven boardinghouse keepers, and ten cabinetmakers, as well as bakers, barkeepers, wheelwrights, and bricklayers. Some of these skilled workers and small businessmen began to seek out black customers, but the most successful ones continued to rely on a white clientele. Most towns and cities in the Upper South states now boasted similar lists of skilled artisans as well as a few blacks who owned grocery stores, saloons, restaurants, barbershops, and boardinghouses.

In a number of these occupational categories the growth rate was substantially greater than the 336 percent rise in the urban free black population (12,153 to 53,026 families) following emancipation. There was a 833 percent increase among property-owning urban black stonemasons (from 12 to 112), 914 percent among blacksmiths (from 22 to 223), 460 percent among brickmasons (from 35 to 196), 715 percent among carpenters (from 67 to 546), and 1,050 percent among plasterers (16 to 184). In 1860, there were 6 black-owned grocery stores in the Upper South; a decade later there were 74. Even with these rises and a decline in property values in some areas Upper South urban brickmasons, coopers, mechanics, shoemakers, boardinghouse keepers, grocers, and restaurateurs increased the average value of their real estate holdings. This, coupled with the changes in the Lower South, resulted in Border South blacks surpassing their counterparts in the Deep South in average realty holdings in six of nine occupations listed under skilled craftsmen, a remarkable reversal in a single decade.[22]

Following the Civil War, Upper South blacks also surpassed their counterparts in the Lower South in a number of other wealth-holding categories: total value of real estate owned, average value of realty per property owner, and proportion of real estate owners among family heads. This, too, was a remarkable change from the antebellum period when free persons of color in Louisiana alone controlled nearly as much real estate as free blacks in the entire upper tier of states. In Kentucky, where substantial numbers of ex-slaves had joined the Union army during the Civil War, and where northern missionaries encouraged landownership, black real estate owners increased more rapidly than in any other state. By 1870, nearly one of nine Negro heads of family in the state owned land with an average value of $684. Freedmen and women in several Virginia towns and cities, and in Tennessee and Missouri, also substantially expanded their holdings. During his travels, journalist John Trowbridge observed "a thrifty village" of freedmen and women in Virginia. "Every house had its woodpile, poultry and pigs, and little garden devoted to corn and vegetables," he said. "Many a one had its stable and cow, and horse and cart." In Tennessee, Union General George H. Thomas, a commander of black troops during the war, noted how freed blacks

Table 14. Black Realty Owners in the Upper South, 1860/1870

State	Erph	Arph	Total Owners
Delaware	$404,700/859,000	$611/1,138	662/755
District of Columbia	641,600/2,357,800	1,208/2,261	531/1,043
Kentucky	564,700/3,296,800	933/684	605/4,818
Maryland	1,541,300/2,960,900	661/888	2,332/3,333
Missouri	501,900/2,187,500	2,561/904	196/2,419
North Carolina	578,000/1,433,700	548/419	1,055/3,421
Tennessee	411,500/2,537,800	1,518/835	271/3,039
Virginia	1,081,200/2,563,900	648/646	1,669/3,966
Total	$5,724,900/18,197,400	$782/798	7,321/22,794
Total South	$12,841,600/32,293,600	$1,332/746	9,640/43,268

Source: Computed from USMSPC, 1860, 1870.

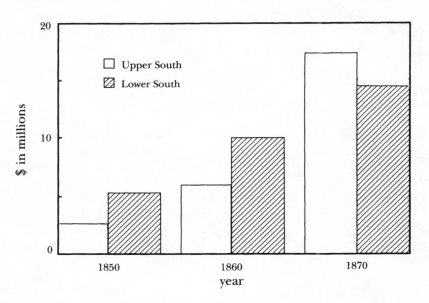

Figure 3. Total Value of Black-owned Real Estate: Upper and Lower South

were disposed to work and take care of themselves. Some of them were constructing new homes; others were working for wages and "leasing and buying farms." By 1870, 22,794 blacks in the upper tier of states controlled $18,197,400 worth of real estate. Both in the average value of their holdings—$798—and in the proportion of families who claimed landowning status—one out of sixteen—they had surpassed their brethren in the Deep South.[23]

Similarly, among those with at least $100 worth of real and/or personal property, Upper South blacks surged ahead of Negroes in the Lower South. Comprising 40 percent of the South's total black population in 1870, they controlled 46 percent of its total black wealth ($31,302,600 of $68,528,200). During the antebellum era, they had owned about the same proportion of the total wealth, but had constituted 86 percent of the free black population. In their average holdings, which in 1860 had been about one-fourth the amount held by free persons of color in the lower states, they had moved ahead of Lower South blacks by a significant margin, $499 as compared with $354. Much of this difference, as will be shown in the final chapter, was the result of the loss of slave and other property by free persons of color in the Lower South, but it was also due to the more favorable economic conditions in the upper states. The most striking contrast between the two regions can be seen in the proportion of their total estates in realty vs. personal holdings. Upper South blacks had 58 percent of their total wealth in real estate; Lower South blacks, denied access to the land, had only 38 percent in realty. Although a slightly lower proportion in the Upper than in the Lower South controlled at least some property—approximately one family in 5.8 compared to

Table 15. Black Property Owners in the Upper South, 1860/1870

State	Etph	Atph	Owners
Delaware	$595,100/1,108,000	$562/899	1,059/1,232
District of Columbia	788,500/2,702,300	1,109/1,712	711/1,578
Kentucky	976,200/5,564,500	832/479	1,173/11,629
Maryland	2,581,500/4,389,800	643/701	4,013/6,262
Missouri	637,800/4,416,500	1,787/558	357/7,914
North Carolina	1,073,800/2,759,500	640/329	1,679/8,375
Tennessee	638,300/6,514,400	1,244/385	513/16,904
Virginia	1,745,800/3,847,600	656/433	2,663/8,890
Total	$9,037,000/31,302,600	743/499	12,168/62,784
Total South	$20,253,200/68,528,200	$1,252/408	16,172/168,034

Source: Computed from USMSPC, 1860, 1870.

one family in 5.2—blacks in the upper tier of states, taking advantage of opportunities not available to freedmen and women in the heart of the Deep South, made substantial economic gains during the Civil War decade. They increased the total value of their wealth from $9,037,000 to $31,302,600. The sharpest rises came in the District of Columbia, Kentucky, Tennessee, and Missouri.

A profile of Upper South real estate owners in 1870 indicates that, while the great majority of new landowners were former slaves, there was more continuity from the antebellum period than in the lower states. The proportion of blacks compared with mulattoes remained high, but it increased only from 63 to 77 percent between 1860 and 1870. The proportion of women in the property-owning group dropped at a much slower rate than in the Lower South, from 17 percent to 11 percent. A number of antebellum free women of color in the region, including, among others, North Carolina seamstress Martha Armstrong, District of Columbia laundress Elizabeth Bean, and Kentucky housekeeper Milly Lewis, survived the war with their holdings intact or slightly improved. The same was true for men. Delaware blacksmith Prince Colwell, Maryland shoemaker George Adams and sawyer Alexander Allen, District of Columbia teacher-physician Enoch Ambush, Virginia laborer John Lambert, Kentucky drayman Edward Alexander, Tennessee hauler-coachman William Napier, and Missouri wagoner Adam Taylor were among more than 1,800 antebellum real-estate owners who sustained or improved their position after the war. They represented approximately one out of four antebellum real estate owners in the Upper South.[24] Only estimates can be made of propertyless antebellum free Negroes who acquired real estate after the war, but perhaps as many as one out of five landholders in the region in 1870 were former free Negroes, a ratio far greater than in the lower states.

Compared to whites, and considering that there were 4.5 million blacks in the South in 1870, approximately 900,000 families, the property accumulations among blacks remained very small. Only 4.8 percent of the black families (or household heads) owned real estate with an average value of $746 in 1870, and, including the property-less, the average per black family stood at only $36. At the same time 43 percent of the white adult males in the nation owned realty and, including the propertyless, they owned an average of $1,782. Thus one-ninth as many southern blacks owned one-fiftieth as much real property as the average white American. Even when the analysis shifts to the number of blacks who controlled at least $100 worth of real and/or personal property, freedmen and women and former free Negroes still remained far behind in their ability to accumulate wealth. Including the propertyless, blacks controlled an average of only $76 worth of wealth in 1870, compared to $2,034 for southern whites, and proportionally less than one-third as many blacks owned at least some property. Even when property values for whites are adjusted to 1860 prices, giving them an average total holding of $1,440, the huge gap remains. Representing one-third of the region's population, blacks controlled 1.3 percent of its real and personal wealth.[25]

But such comparisons tend to ignore the unique conditions confronting former slaves as they emerged in freedom. Besides the economic dislocations caused by the war and the other economic problems of the postwar era, Negroes in many regions faced white landholders who were determined to keep them in a subordinate position. The political currents of the time, with proposals for confiscating and redistributing land to blacks, only strengthened the resolve of former slave owners that freedmen and women should remain dependent on the old master class. Northerners who came South either shared this resolve or discovered that selling land to freed blacks was not acceptable to other whites.[26] The legacy of slavery, the lack of assistance from federal and state authorities, the continued hold of whites on the land, the emergence of vigilante groups, and the increased competition in some areas from white workers were only some of the obstacles blacks faced in seeking to gain an economic foothold during the years just following the Civil War. Under such circumstances it was not surprising that relatively few blacks moved from slavery to land ownership. Yet, by 1870, especially in towns and cities of the Upper South, and in rural areas where some whites supported black proprietorship, tens of thousands of former slaves had begun the long journey toward self-sufficiency and economic independence.

After 1870 in the Rural Lower South

After 1870, during the first generation-and-a-half of freedom, blacks in rural areas of the Lower South continued to face numerous obstacles to economic advancement. They struggled against oppressive white landlords, the debilitating effects of the crop lien system, discrimination in wage rates, seemingly endless debt, and an increasingly hostile racial climate. As W. E. B. Du Bois explained in 1906, the ability of former slaves to become property owners depended on their "character and . . . attending circumstances." "Thrifty negroes in the hands of well-disposed landowners and honest merchants early became independent landholders; shiftless, ignorant negroes in the power of unscrupulous landowners and merchants sank to a condition hardly better than slavery." What Du Bois failed to add was that even the most diligent, persistent, frugal, and industrious blacks were often unable to overcome the ironlike grip of whites on the land, or the low wages. Most observers of blacks in the rural Deep South during these decades were struck by the continuity with the prewar era: Negroes laboring in the fields on white-owned plantations in much the same manner as they had during slavery. They were also struck by the deplorable living conditions. In parts of Georgia, Du Bois lamented in his classic 1903 study, *The Souls of Black Folk*, black sharecroppers lived under conditions worse than those endured by the most poverty-ridden tenement dweller in New York City. "The size and arrangements of a people's homes are no unfair index of their condition," Du Bois explained. "All over the face of the land is the one-room cabin,—now standing in the shadow of the Big House, now staring at the dusty road, now rising dark and sombre amid the green of the cotton-fields." The "cabin," built with rough-hewn lumber, was nearly always dark, dingy, and dilapidated, without windows, light, or proper ventilation. It smelled of must, eating, and sleeping. Containing eight to ten people, it stood as a silent symbol of the degradation of landless blacks in the Deep South.[27]

In the post-1870 rural Lower South, freed parents and their children only gradually acquired small amounts of land. Even after an especially good harvest, rising prices for their crops, and other favorable conditions, former slaves often lost most of their profits to landlords who charged as much as 100 percent interest for goods and supplies and took most of their crops as payment for the use of the land. Fifteen years after the Civil War, only 9.8 percent of the acreage under cultivation in the most densely populated counties of the "Cotton South" (an agricultural region designated by Ransom and Sutch stretching mainly across Louisiana, Mississippi, Alabama, Georgia, and South Carolina) was owned and operated by blacks, although they comprised more than half the agricultural population. At the same time, they comprised only 7.3 percent of the farm owners. Freedmen and women in less densely populated regions, especially in Florida, Arkansas, and Texas, were able to purchase farmland more easily, but it was often of poor quality or located in remote sections. Even the few who did acquire land found it difficult to expand their farm acreage, continuing to hold a disproportionate share of their wealth in cash, household furniture, livestock, tools, and other personal possessions. In Georgia, in 1876, black landowners held only

21.6 percent of their total wealth in rural land.[28] By 1890, while farm ownership had increased in every Deep South state, in Georgia, Alabama, and Mississippi, it had reached only 13 percent of the black farming population. During the next two decades this changed only slightly. Although Georgia witnessed a 40 percent increase in the number of farm owners during the 1890s, and a 38 percent rise in the first decade of the twentieth century, still only 13 percent of the black farmers owned their own land. In the Lower South as a whole, fewer than one out of five Negro farmers boasted land ownership a half-century after freedom.

Even in some areas where land ownership had become widespread some blacks continued to live in poverty and backwardness. By 1890, 72 percent of the farms in Beaufort County, 71 percent in Colleton County, South Carolina, and 81 percent in Bryan County, Georgia, were owner-operated, the vast majority by the children of former slaves. Yet, as Eric Foner and others have pointed out, the low-country "peasantry" lived at a bare sustenance level, raising their own poultry and vegetables, fishing, hunting, and cultivating a few acres of rice or cotton to raise necessary cash. Although impervious to the oppressive crop lien system, and able to exercise local political authority, low-country blacks suffered from "the same debilitating disadvantages that afflict peasant agriculture throughout the world, among them a credit system that made direct access to capital impossible, an inability to invest in fertilizer or machinery, vulnerability to the vagaries of the national and international markets, and the demands for taxation of an oppressive state."[29] Though they were more independent and autonomous their lives had changed little from the early nineteenth century when, as slaves, they had used the task system to acquire various types of property. Moreover, their original holdings, sometimes in excess of one hundred acres, had been subdivided so many times among family members that by the early twentieth century the average size of their plots had dwindled to only a few acres.[30]

As in South Carolina, most Lower South farm owners controlled very small amounts of property. In his analysis of rural wealth holders in Georgia, Du Bois noted that in 1899 approximately 8,450 black farmers owned land assessed at $1,795,416. Though failing to equate assessed with market values, he observed that more than half of the owners controlled land assessed at less than $200, and only 113 had acreage worth $1,500 or more. Landowning black families in South Carolina, Florida, Arkansas, and Texas similarly possessed only a few hundred dollars' worth of property. In Louisiana, in a number of rural parishes, the total value of black-owned property, including

Table 16. Black Farm Owners in the Lower South, 1870–1910, by Total Number and Percentage of Owners

State	1870		1890		Percentage of increase 1870–90	1900		Percentage of increase 1890–1900	1910		Percentage of increase 1900–1910
Alabama	1,152	1.3	8,847	13	668	14,110	15	59	17,047	15	21
Arkansas	1,203	5.2	8,004	24	565	11,941	25	49	14,660	23	23
Florida	596	3.5	4,940	38	729	6,551	48	33	7,286	50	11
Georgia	1,367	1.4	8,131	13	495	11,375	14	40	15,698	13	38
Louisiana	1,107	1.8	6,685	18	504	9,378	16	40	10,681	19	14
Mississippi	1,600	1.9	11,526	13	620	20,973	16	82	24,949	15	19
South Carolina	3,062	4.0	13,075	21	327	18,970	22	45	20,356	21	7
Texas	839	1.8	12,513	26	1,391	20,139	31	61	21,182	30	5
Total	10,926	2	73,721	18	575	113,437	20	54	131,859	19	16

Sources: Computed from USMSPC, 1870. Includes only realty owners designated as "farmer" or "planter." Percentage of owners in 1870 = percentage of rural family heads. Percentage of owners in 1890–1910 = percentage of farmers listed in census as "owners." Excludes those listed as "managers." Tabulated from U.S. Dept. of the Interior, *Report on Farms and Homes: Proprietorship and Indebtedness in the United States* (Washington, D.C.: GPO, 1896), pp. 566–70; *Negro Population 1790–1915* (Washington, D.C.: GPO, 1918), pp. 607, 625–26.

land, town lots, horses, cattle, mules, sheep, wagons, carts, stock, merchandise, household goods, jewelry, and various personal items, remained below antebellum figures more than a generation after the Civil War. In several other rural parishes, the increases between 1870 and 1901 did not keep pace with population increases or rising land values. Facing problems of drought (especially in 1893 and 1894), the disadvantages of small-scale farming, the onset of a severe depression, and after 1907, the infestation of the boll weevil, some rural landowners in the Lower South were forced off the land, while even those who tenaciously continued to put in a crop year after year were often little better off than the masses of sharecroppers and tenant farmers (see appendix 4).[31]

Seeking to overcome these and other problems, a few Lower South blacks sought to separate themselves from whites by forming all-Negro farming communities. The most famous of these was at Davis Bend, Mississippi (see chapter 6), but virtually every state had a few such communal efforts—Promiseland, South Carolina; Burroughs, Harrisburg, and Gullinsville, Georgia; Eatonville, Florida; Kowaliga and Klondike, Alabama; Mound Bayou and Renova, Mississippi; and Thomasville, Arkansas. In some cases, freedmen and women pooled their savings to purchase land. In South Carolina, the Charleston Land Company and the Atlantic Land Company, organized by former slaves and free blacks, acquired land to be distributed to their members. In other cases, a few energetic leaders appealed to racial pride, self-help, and economic chauvinism, or, as in the case of Paul and Jim Hargress, founders of a black farming community in Hale County, Alabama, used the ownership of land to ensure the continuation of family and kinship ties that had been formed during slavery. Although most of these separate communities lasted only a generation or less, a few of them prospered for brief periods of time. Founded in 1888 by Isaiah Montgomery, in the Yazoo Delta of Mississippi, about halfway between Vicksburg and Memphis, Mound Bayou started out with a few settlers in an area densely forested with "cane and heavy timber." Within a few years, the all-black settlement boasted several hundred farm owners, and by 1907 the village had become the center of a thriving agricultural colony of some eight hundred families. But Mound Bayou was unique, and it, too, would later experience a decline.[32]

The vast majority of rural black landholders in the Lower South lived in areas with neighboring white farmers; and though their numbers rose steadily during the late nineteenth and early twentieth centuries, they never represented more than a small portion of the rural black population. Yet, despite the small percent who became farm owners and the small size of their farms, rural blacks in the Lower South increased their holdings significantly during the period from 1870 to 1910. Five years after the Civil War the estimated value of real estate owned by Negro farmers in the eight Deep South states included the following: in Alabama, 1,152 farmers owned $661,300 worth of land, an average of $574; in Arkansas, 1,203 owned $559,600, or $465; in Florida, 596 owned $219,500, or $368; in Georgia, 1,367 owned $605,500, or $443; in Louisiana 1,107 owned $1,239,500, or $1,120; in Mississippi 1,600 owned $971,200, or $607; in South Carolina 3,062 owned $1,508,800, or $493; and in Texas 839 owned $284,900, or $340. In the Lower South, 10,926 blacks controlled land worth $6,049,800, or $554 per average farm owner. Forty years later, in Alabama, 17,047 farm owners (including those listed as "owners, free," "owners, mortgaged," and "part owners") controlled $17,285,502 worth of real estate (including buildings), an average of $1,014[33] per farm owner; in Arkansas, 14,660 owned $20,694,215, or $1,412; in Florida, 7,286 owned $6,786,810, or $931; in Georgia, 15,698 owned $20,540,910, or $1,309; in Louisiana, 10,681 owned $12,779,570, or $1,196; in Mississippi, 24,949 owned $34,317,764, or $1,376; in South Carolina, 20,356 owned $22,112,291 or $1,086; and in Texas, 21,182 owned $30,687,272, or $1,449. Thus, by 1910, 131,859 black farm owners controlled real estate worth $165,204,000, or $1,253 per farm owner. While, considering changes in land values, their average holdings had increased only slightly, and the proportion of owners had remained small, the total value of their land had risen substantially.

After 1870 in the Urban Lower South

After 1870, freedmen and women and their children in the Lower South continued to abandon the countryside and take up residence in towns and cities. With each passing decade, census takers recorded that urban blacks constituted a larger portion of the total black population—12 percent in 1890, 13 percent in 1900, and 18 percent in 1910—and a larger portion among the region's city dwellers. As had been the case before the war, former slaves and their children migrated to the city for a variety of reasons—political, social, cultural, educational, and economic. By the the late nineteenth century, nearly every city in the Lower South had either witnessed steady increases in the number of their black residents or had experienced substantial influxes of blacks. By the early twentieth century, in several cities, including Savannah and Montgomery, a majority of the residents were black.[34]

Despite periodic harassment, racial segregation, the lack of public services, and anti-Negro feelings, blacks who lived in towns and cities continued to have better job and business opportunities than their counterparts in the countryside. The extent of these opportunities varied in different urban areas, and by the 1870s and 1880s it was apparent that the cities of the Old South—Charleston, Augusta, Savannah, Mobile, Natchez, New Orleans—were gradually losing ground compared with the cities of the New South—Atlanta, Jacksonville, Birmingham, Little Rock, and Galveston and Houston, Texas. In general the property-owning antebellum class of skilled artisans and small shopkeepers who had fared so well economically in Charleston, Savannah, Mobile, and New Orleans found it increasingly difficult to compete with freedmen and women and their children, especially as time passed and former slaves gained experience in economic matters. These were subtle shifts, sometimes difficult to detect, but in Charleston the occupational decline is clear, while in New Orleans the decline of foreign-born in the city's population and the ability of some blacks to continue working as shoemakers, masons, bakers, butchers, carpenters, and coopers masked the changes that were occurring. As the former creoles of color, who generally lived below Canal Street in the downtown area, declined, other blacks, largely former slaves who were living uptown, moved into the more skilled occupations or started small businesses.

The most significant occupational improvements occurred in New South cities. "All the draying and trucking are done by colored men," New York newspaperman T. Thomas Fortune explained after visiting Jacksonville, Florida, in 1890. "Street car[t] drivers, train hands, freight handlers, stokers on engines, stevedores, masters and workmen—all are in the main, colored." Although a great majority of city blacks worked as handlers, laborers, and day workers, growing numbers in Jacksonville and other New South cities entered more highly skilled occupations, including "masters," brickmasons, carpenters, and mechanics. Some established small service-type businesses, such as restaurants, barbershops, grocery stores, coffee houses, saloons, and tailor shops. Negro women operated rooming houses, boardinghouses, millinery shops, and laundries. By the 1880s and 1890s, most of these enterprises were located in Negro business districts, and most businessmen and women were now seeking to attract a Negro clientele. At the same time, a few blacks became involved in small-scale manufacturing as brickmakers, cigarmakers, shinglemakers, harnessmakers, and wagonmakers. While even skilled workers earned lower wages than whites, and while most of these business ventures were capitalized at a few hundred or a few thousand dollars, during the post-1870 decades most New South cities had a growing number of blacks who worked as skilled artisans or owned small businesses. In 1876, even the Atlanta *Constitution*, a newspaper that often carried articles hostile to freedmen, took notice of the growing number of Negro boot and shoemakers, undertakers, restaurant owners, livery stable operators, and grocers in the city. By 1891, among the 450 retail grocery stores in Atlanta, 75 were black owned.[35]

The gradually improving occupational levels allowed New South urban blacks to increase their real estate and other property holdings at a much more rapid rate than could their brethren on the countryside. One investigator reported in the early twentieth century that the aggregate value of taxable property owned by blacks in Fulton County, Georgia (Atlanta), rose from $256,450 in 1878, to $655,505 a decade later, to $1,443,712 in 1893, before declining to $1,109,030 following the depression of the 1890s. By 1900, the assessed value of real estate held by blacks in the state's towns and cities stood at $4,361,390, up from $1,203,202 in 1875. Representing approximately 16 percent of the Negro heads of family, city blacks controlled 31 percent of the black real estate wealth. Another observer, a longtime resident of Jackson, Mississippi, wrote early in the twentieth century: "Statistics of the condition of property ownership among Negroes of twelve years ago are not available, and only the citizen acquainted with the situation at that time can appreciate the great advance on the part of the Negroes." The tax books, he said, revealed that 566 blacks (in a total of 8,000) owned real estate assessed at $581,580. More than one-third of the assessments were for realty in excess of $1,000; a sizable portion of the black families owned their own homes. This, too, represented a disproportionate share of Mississippi's black wealth.

The comparative rise of urban property holding (compared to that of rural areas) as well as the relative decline of black wealth holding in cities of the Old South were reflected by the changing profile of property owners in Little Rock and Charleston. In 1906, John E. Bush, for many years the receiver in the United States Land Office in Little Rock, estimated that Negroes paid taxes on $2,500,000 worth of property. A significant proportion of the blacks in the city, he explained, owned their own homes, and some managed small businesses. Comprising 4 percent of the state's black population, Little Rock Negroes controlled 8.3 percent of the state's aggregate black wealth. At the same time, William D. Crum, a longtime South Carolina resident, noted that "The Colored citizens" of Charleston controlled an aggregate wealth of $1,000,000 in real and personal property. "There is hardly a street in the city," Crum asserted, "that they do not possess and pay taxes on from one to thirty thousand dollars worth of real estate." Although this, too, represented a significant proportion of the state's black wealth, Crum's estimate showed how much black wealth holding had shifted in the urban Lower South by the early twentieth century. With only half as many Negro residents as Charleston, blacks in Little Rock boasted more than twice the total wealth holdings.[36] Indeed, as will be more clearly seen in the final chapter, Charleston's blacks (excluding slaves) were significantly better off economically during the late antebellum era than they were more than a generation after the Civil War.

Other indicators of urban property holding were census tabulations on home ownership. Census takers, regrettably, did not differentiate between urban and rural homeowners in their 1890 through 1910 tabulations, but they did differentiate between "farm homes" and "other homes." Although some of the "other homes" were on the outskirts of cities, or in the country, most of them were in towns and cities. The statistics on home ownership, while not precise, do provide at least a rough gauge of the number of blacks, primarily urban, who owned real estate, how this changed over time, and how it compared with farm ownership. Although, in 1870, the number of urban home owners can only be estimated from real-estate holdings, probably not more than 1,665 Negroes (those with at least $700 erph) owned their own homes in the urban Lower South. In Florida, Mississippi, Arkansas, and Texas combined only 267 blacks owned homes. Two decades later, 58,061 Negroes in the region boasted home ownership, with most of their homes unencumbered with mortgages. This was 13 percent of the nonfarm black heads of families. In Alabama, the number had risen from 215 to 6,898, in Georgia from 232 to 11,874, in Texas from 27 to 8,367, and in Louisiana, from 639 to 7,917. Despite the depression of the 1890s, the number of homeowners in the Lower South rose 117 percent during the next two decades, more than keeping pace with the increasing black population. Noting this trend, one observer in the early twentieth century said: "I am informed by large and responsible real estate dealers of both races that the great activity, so generally manifested by Afro-Americans in buying homes, is not spasmodic, but steady and firm; further, that the pride of owning their homes is rapidly growing, and daily the man of color is becoming less improvident."

The most significant increases occurred in the western states of Texas and Arkansas. Traveling through Arkansas in 1905, a reporter for the New York *Evening Post* was struck by the "progressive Western spirit" that prevailed among blacks. "We are here in a certain way upon the frontier, and one feels the bracing optimism that prevails where people are doing things," he wrote; there seemed to be "a hopeful readiness" to look to the future rather than the past for solutions to racial problems. He was especially impressed with the blacks living in Pine Bluff, a trading and commercial center on the Arkansas River with 9,000 black inhabitants. "It is said that there is a larger portion of negroes owning their homes in Pine Bluff, than in any other city in the United States."

The reporter erred in this conclusion (indeed Jefferson County ranked only twenty-fourth among Arkansas counties in 1910), but he had correctly observed the ability of some urban and nonfarming blacks to acquire small amounts of real estate. By 1910, about the same proportion of blacks throughout the Lower South (one out of five) had bought their own home as had become farm owners. The reporter had also unwittingly pointed to new areas of black wealth—Jacksonville, Florida, Jackson, Mississippi, Houston, Texas, and Little Rock and Pine Bluff, Arkansas, where between 21 and 34 percent of the black families owned their own homes, compared to Charleston and New Orleans, where only 11 percent claimed home ownership. Five years after the Civil War, Louisiana had claimed

Table 17. Black Homeowners in the Lower South,
1870–1910 (excluding farm homes)

State	1870* Total	1870* Percentage	1890 Total	1890 Percentage	1910 Total	1910 Percentage
Alabama	215	4.3	6,898	11	16,714	17
Arkansas	56	5.3	3,840	17	9,802	27
Florida	46	3.7	5,709	28	13,581	22
Georgia	232	2.9	11,874	12	22,544	16
Louisiana	639	5.7	7,917	11	16,160	16
Mississippi	138	4.5	5,430	11	13,783	20
South Carolina	312	4.8	8,026	11	12,730	15
Texas	27	1.0	8,367	22	20,443	26
Total	1,665	3.1	58,061	13	125,757	19

Sources: Computed from USMSPC, 1870; Calculated from *Report on Farms and Homes: Proprietorship and Indebtedness in the United States* (Washington, D.C.: GPO, 1896), pp. 566–70; *Negro Population, 1790–1915* (Washington, D.C.: GPO, 1918), pp. 470, 475–500. Percentage = percentage of "other homes" listed in returns as "owned."

*Those in towns and cities with erph of $700 and more.

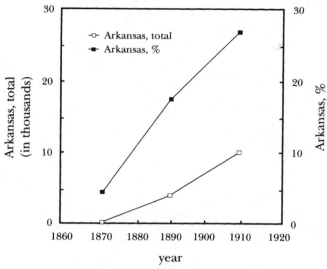

Figure 4. Black Home Ownership in Arkansas, 1870–1910
(excluding farm houses)

nearly 40 percent of the homeowners in the entire lower tier of states. Most of them had been residents of the Crescent City. Now, four decades later, there were only 2,410 Negroes in the city who claimed home ownership, 2 percent of the total in the Lower South.[37]

After 1870 in the Rural Upper South

In some sections of the rural Upper South, former slaves and their children confronted the same obstacles to land ownership as blacks in the Lower South during the post-1870 period. They continued to find difficulty in obtaining credit, low prices for farm products, and whites who refused to sell them land. And, as in the Sea Islands of South Carolina and Georgia, land ownership did not necessarily bring with it economic independence. In Charles, Frederick, and Kent counties, Maryland, freedmen and women continued to break up their holdings, worked long hours in the fields, and often went into debt to white merchants and brokers. The average value of owner-cultivated farms in these three counties in 1880 was less than $660, while the average value for black share tenancies in Frederick and Kent (the census taker did not record data for Charles) was more than $3,800. By that year, the average black landholder in Kent County controlled only sixteen acres. In Delaware, sections of North Carolina and Missouri, and western Tennessee, black farm owners suffered from low prices for their cotton and tobacco, small acreages under cultivation, and exorbitant costs to gin and sell their crops. After merchants and middlemen took their "cut," some black landowners were left with scarcely enough to sustain their families through the winter. As historian Barbara Fields suggests, however much land ownership "enhanced black people's sense of freedom, independence, and accomplishment," for some it meant little more than living at a bare subsistence level.[38]

Despite such difficulties, rural blacks in most sections of the Upper South maintained their advantages over their brethren in the lower states. In some sections, after initial hostility toward black proprietorship, whites gradually became less resistant to the idea of selling farmland to blacks. "The whites own a great deal of land and they want money," Thomas C. Walker, a graduate of Hampton Institute and a successful lawyer in Gloucester County, Virginia, explained in 1894. "If a colored man has got money and wants land he can get it." For his own part Walker had researched the land-deed records of his home county and found that former slaves had increased their holdings from less than 100 acres shortly after the war to more than 10,000 acres, one-fifth of all the land in the county. White farmers were eager to sell to blacks in part because they were discovering higher-paying jobs in manufacturing and industry, jobs that were generally not available to Negroes. At the same time, with the founding of the True Reformers Bank in Richmond, and the Capital Savings Bank in the District of Columbia, in 1888, black farmers were better able to finance land purchases. This was even more true after 1900 when a large number of white banks in Virginia began competing for black customers. In addition, the rural Negro population grew very slowly, or actually declined in some areas, allowing those who remained behind better opportunities to purchase their own farms.[39]

But none of these conditions fully explains the remarkable expansion of black farm ownership in the Upper South during the period. Even under the best of circumstances it took extraordinary effort for former slaves to enter the landholding class. Such was the case for the illiterate North Carolina black Isaac Forbes, a former slave who saved his extra earnings for nearly a decade before acquiring his first farm. On December 14, 1872, at the age of fifty, Forbes put his mark on an "Indenture" between himself and Francis T. and Hanna G. Hawks:

> Witnesseth That said Hawks & wife for & in consideration of Five thousand dollars to them in hand paid by the said Forbes, have granted bargained & sold and by these presents do grant bargain & sell unto the said Isaac Forbes, his heirs & assignees, a body of land lying on Brices Creek in Craven County, bounded by the Creek on the west, by Boleyns

swamp on the south, by the lands of Henry R. Bryan on the North, and by the lands of G[.] Moye & others on the east, being the entire body of lands owned by the late Judge Gaston on the north side of Boleyns Swamp, containing twelve hundred acres more or less, To have & to hold the said lands with all privileges and appurtenances thereunto belonging to him the said Isaac his heirs, and assignees forever.[40]

While few freedmen and women did as well as Isaac Forbes, blacks in rural Virginia steadily entered the farm-owning ranks until, by the early 1900s, they constituted a large majority of the state's Negro farmers. A combination of unique conditions, complex and inter-woven, paved the way for this expansion: the long tradition of black proprietorship going back to before 1800; the increasing availability of mortgage money; the growth of mutual benefit and insurance so-cieties such as the Knights of Pythias, True Reformers, and the Order of St. Luke; the ideas of enterprise and self-sufficiency promoted at Hampton Institute; and the efforts of black leaders—Congressman John Mercer Langston, editor John Mitchell, and banker Maggie Wal-ker—in promoting property ownership. As a result, former slaves and their children in Virginia became almost obsessed with the idea of acquiring their own land. As had been the case before the Civil War, it took a generation of freedom before the momentum gained its greatest strength, but once it did the results were startling. By 1891, blacks owned 698,074 acres of improved and unimproved farmland; by 1895, this had risen to 833,147, by 1900 to 993,541, by 1905 to 1,292,697, and by 1910 to 1,551,153. One visitor to the state was so impressed with the Negro farming community around Chris-tianburg that he proclaimed it one of the most prosperous in the South. Nearly every farmer lived in a comfortable, two-story frame house, surrounded by gardens "and numerous out buildings," and there was a "genuine air of comfort and contentment." Observers were equally impressed with the farming communities in Gloucester, Middlesex, Essex, King and Queen, and other counties, describing them in much the same way. Between 1900 and 1910, black farm owners in the state increased their acreage by one-third (compared to 7 percent for whites) and in the latter year more than one-half of the total farm acreage tilled by blacks was on black-owned farms. By then, 32,168 Negro farmers—67 percent of the rural family heads—owned land and buildings worth $28,059,534, or $872 per farm owner. Even considering the appreciation in land values, and the relatively low per capita wealth, they owned considerably more property than had the entire free Negro population in the South on the eve of the Civil War.[41]

While no other state could equal Virginia's growth in rural land-

Table 18. Black Farm Owners in the Upper South, 1870–1910, by Total Number and Percentage of Owners

State	1870		1890		Percentage of increase 1870–90	1900		Percentage of increase 1890–1900	1910		Percentage of increase 1900–1910
Delaware	154	4.0	288	35	87	331	41	15	406	44	23
District of Columbia	1	*	16	31	*	5	29	*	8	67	*
Kentucky	1,336	3.5	4,110	40	208	5,391	48	31	5,916	51	10
Maryland	884	3.4	2,150	43	143	3,262	56	52	3,949	62	21
Missouri	695	4.1	2,745	50	295	2,657	54	−3	2,104	58	−21
North Carolina	1,628	2.2	10,494	26	545	16,834	31	60	20,707	32	23
Tennessee	1,301	2.2	6,378	23	390	9,414	28	48	10,698	28	14
Virginia	860	1.0	13,678	43	1490	26,527	59	94	32,168	67	21
Total	6,859	2.2	39,859	33	481	64,421	41	62	75,956	44	18
Total South	17,785	2.2	113,580	21	539	177,858	24	57	207,815	24	17

Sources: Computed from USMSPC, 1870. Includes only realty owners designated as "farmer" or "planter." Percentage of owners in 1870 = percentage of rural family heads. Percentage of owners in 1890–1910 = percentage of farmers listed in census as "owners." Excludes those listed as "managers." Tabulated from U.S. Dept. of the Interior, *Report on Farms and Homes: Proprietorship and Indebtedness in the United States* (Washington, D.C.: GPO, 1896), pp. 566–70; *Negro Population 1790–1915* (Washington, D.C.: GPO, 1918), pp. 607, 625–26; U.S. Dept. of Commerce, Bureau of the Census, *Thirteenth Census of the United States Taken in the Year 1910*, 11 vols. (Washington, D.C.: GPO, 1913), 5 :219.

*Fewer than 100 cases not computed.

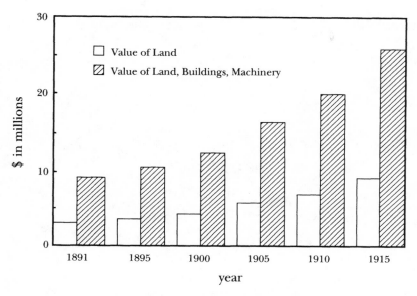

Figure 5. Black-owned Farm Property in Virginia

ownership—between 1870 and 1910 black farm ownership in the
state rose a remarkable 3,641 percent—rural blacks in the Upper
South greatly expanded their holdings during the first generation-
and-a-half of freedom. In 1870, the estimated value of real estate
owned by black farmers in the Upper South included the following:
in Delaware, 154 farmers owned $352,100 worth of land, an average
of $2,286; in Kentucky, 1,336 owned $865,200, an average of $648;
in Maryland, 884 owned $998,800, or $1,130; in Missouri, 695 owned
$533,000, or $767; in North Carolina, 1,628 owned $658,500, or
$404; in Tennessee, 1,301 controlled $1,010,200, or $776; and in Vir-
ginia, 860 owned $637,900, or $742 per farm owner. By 1910, in
Delaware, 406 farm owners controlled $547,551, or $1,349; in Kentucky, 5,916 owned $7,154,168, or $1,209; in Maryland, 3,949 owned
$3,924,773, or $994; in Missouri, 2,104 owned $5,645,438, or $2,683;
in North Carolina, 20,707 owned $22,810,089, or $1,102; in Tennessee, 10,698 owned $12,179,780, or $1,139; and in Virginia, 32,168
owned $28,059,534, or $872. In 1910, including a few in the District
of Columbia, 75,956 black farm owners controlled real estate (and
buildings) worth $80,369,733, or $1,058 per farm owner.
After 1870, rural blacks in the region acquired land at better than

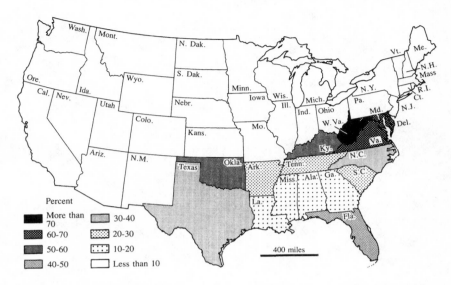

Figure 6. Percentage of Black-owned Farms by States in the South: 1910
Source: *Negro Population 1790–1915* (Washington, D.C.: GPO, 1918, p. 573.)

twice the rate of their brethren in the Lower South. In 1890, one out of three farmers in the region worked on his or her own land. Despite numerous economic difficulties on the farm during the next two decades, by 1910 nearly half the black agriculturists in the Upper South had become landholders (compared with 19 percent in the Lower South). With one-fourth of the South's rural black population, Upper South blacks controlled one-third of the Negro farm wealth in land and buildings. This expansion during the 1890s and early 1900s was all the more impressive since it occurred at a time of depression when the number and proportion of white farm owners was steadily declining.[42]

After 1870 in the Urban Upper South

The flood of migrants to the towns and cities of the Upper South following the Civil War continued unabated during the post-1870 period. With each passing decade the number and proportion of the region's urban population expanded significantly until by 1890 nearly one out of four blacks lived in cities. Two decades later, this had grown to nearly one out of three. Two border cities—the District of Columbia and Baltimore—replaced New Orleans as having the largest urban black populations in the nation. By the early twentieth century six of the nation's ten urban centers with the largest concentrations of Negroes were in the Upper South. While the rural population remained fairly stable during the postwar era and afterward, cities such as Richmond, Louisville, Nashville, Memphis, and St. Louis expanded rapidly, as the Upper South's urban black population grew from 577,987 in 1890, to 713,592 in 1900, to 840,625 by the end of the first decade of the twentieth century.

Many of these migrants were young, and they included a disproportionate share of women—in 1890, Baltimore, the District of Columbia, Richmond, and Nashville contained 125 females to every 100 males. According to some observers the new black immigrants were attracted by the "glare and glitter of city life," but they also came, as had free blacks prior to the Civil War, to improve their social, cultural, and economic situation. "It may occasion some surprise to note that more than half of the Negro population of Missouri, two-fifths that of Maryland, and more than a third of that of Kentucky are found in cities," one observer said in 1902. He believed that the "sense of social loneliness," where Negroes were "thinly scattered among whites," was perhaps the most important cause that drove them to seek a "more congenial companionship with their own kind and color in towns and cities."[43]

The cityward movement put great strains on the Upper South's urban blacks. Since most of them were propertyless when they arrived, the black migrants were forced to live in rundown neighborhoods and in congested, increasingly all-black sections—the Eleventh Ward in Baltimore, southeast Washington, Jackson Ward in Richmond, the California District in Louisville, Black Bottom in Nashville, and along Twelfth, Wash, and Morgan streets in St. Louis. These areas lacked effective police and fire protection, lighting, paved streets, and sanitary facilities. They also contained dilapidated and dangerous housing. In 1877, the Nashville Board of Health reported that most of the city's blacks lived in "old stables, situated upon alleys in the midst of privy vaults, or in wooden shanties a remnant of war times, or in huts closely crowded together on the outskirts." Thirty-one years later a Civic League Survey of St. Louis found that more than half of the structures in the predominately Negro section were not fit for human habitation. A few years after the survey one building simply collapsed, killing one resident and injuring six others.[44]

Although Upper South blacks were twice as likely to live in towns and cities as their brethren in the lower states, there were some important similarities between the two sections with regard to occupational trends and urban black business activity. As in the Lower South, city blacks increasingly entered more highly skilled occupations. Except in Baltimore, where competition from immigrants and antiblack unions pushed Negroes out of bricklaying, carpentry, painting, tinning, smithing, and other profitable jobs, there were steady increases among brickmasons and stonemasons, carpenters, bootmakers and shoemakers, and blacksmiths. Also similar to the Lower South was the emergence during the 1880s of an increasing number of black-owned businesses catering to a black clientele. Even during the early postwar period some businessmen had envisioned the possibility of reaping large profits from such race-oriented ventures. Baltimore merchant Stansbury Boyce moved his dry-goods store five times during the 1870s before "getting to the locality I desired which was the thoroughfare for my race." But the time was not right, and his "warm friends" only peered through his display windows and upon discovering the proprietor was black "sauntered away." "I have for many years been an ardent advocate of business among our people," he said bitterly at the end of his life. "I have grown weary of the struggle and am leaving the fight to younger men." But during the next two decades, as in the cities of the lower states, the growth of black neighborhoods, increasing competition from immigrants and others for the patronage of affluent whites, worsening race relations, and the expansion of Negro property ownership created new business opportunities. By the 1890s, in most towns and cities, small Negro business districts had emerged, typically including a grocery store, saloon, restaurant, dry goods establishment, rooming house, small hotel, barbershop, undertaker, and livery stable.[45]

While most of these enterprises were capitalized at only a few thousand dollars, and the failure rate, due to inexperience, lack of capital, and injudicious extension of credit, remained high, black businessmen in the urban Upper South possessed several advantages over their brethren in the lower states. These included a higher urban-population density, greater expansion of the black property-owning class, a larger black wealth-holding group, and in a few locations less opposition from whites. In some cities, especially Richmond, Durham, and Nashville, a growing professional class and expanding credit opportunities (see chapter 6) facilitated the expansion of business enterprises. Consequently, the black entrepreneurial class grew more rapidly in the towns and cities of the upper states. By 1910, with 30 percent of the South's black population, the Upper South contained 45 percent of the 2,090 blacks listed in the census as building contractors, 40 percent of the 1,198 "manufacturers," including most of the publishing and hair products companies, 45 percent of the bankers and brokers, and 42 percent of the South's 16,179 retailers and merchants. The cities of the Upper South also contained a disproportionate share of Negro insurance companies, wholesale merchants, morticians, restaurant owners, boardinghouse and hotel proprietors, and barbershop owners. "Many colored people are going into business here," a correspondent for the *Colored American* wrote from Baltimore, in 1894, describing what was happening in other Upper South cities. "Four more small stores were opened this week." It seemed as if Negroes had contracted a "business fever." "They are ready to argue," he added, "that business will solve the race question."[46]

With this expansion—the number of black-owned businesses rose in excess of 1,000 percent between 1870 and 1910 in the upper states—came a rise in black home ownership. As in the Lower South, the number of freedmen and women who purchased their own homes during the early postwar period remained very small. Only approximately 6 percent of the Upper South urban Negroes had acquired homes by 1870. Within twenty years the number of homeowners had risen from approximately 3,177 to 58,465, or 1,740 percent, with substantial increases coming in most towns and cities, and by 1910, nearly one out of four blacks, excluding farmers and farm owners, owned their own homes, about 25 percent greater than the ratio in the Lower South. These percentage increases coincided with substantial population increases in most towns and cities. While by the early twentieth century the actual numbers and the percentage of homeowners was declining in the District of Columbia, in most other cities the reverse was true, and in several urban areas of the Upper South the ratio of home ownership rose precipitously. Among cities with between 25,000 and 50,000 blacks, Nashville led the entire South in this wealth category; among cities with 10,000 to 25,000 blacks, Petersburg, Virginia, and Wilmington, North Carolina, ranked first and second, ahead of Little Rock, Arkansas. Richmond was also high in the rankings.

If inflated property values and the huge influxes of younger blacks from the countryside made it difficult for the proportion of black homeowners to rise in cities like Baltimore, the District of Columbia, Louisville, and St. Louis, in other urban areas, the founding of black banking institutions, the growth of mutual aid associations and black insurance companies, the availability of mortgage money from

Table 19. Black Homeowners in the Upper South,
1870–1910 (excluding farm homes)

State	1870*		1890		1910	
	Total	Per-centage	Total	Per-centage	Total	Per-centage
Delaware	136	21.2	976	22	1,065	19
District of Columbia	778	10.0	2,116	15	2,062	11
Kentucky	768	11.4	8,767	22	13,697	27
Maryland	462	5.2	6,446	19	7,977	20
Missouri	238	3.5	6,149	26	7,974	23
North Carolina	199	5.6	9,516	15	19,627	26
Tennessee	187	3.0	8,285	16	16,070	23
Virginia	409	3.3	16,210	20	24,405	27
Total	3,177	6.0	58,465	19	92,877	24
Total South	4,842	5.3	116,526	16	218,634	21

Sources: Computed from USMSPC, 1870; Calculated from *Report on Farms and Homes: Proprietorship and Indebtedness in the United States* (Washington, D.C.: GPO, 1896), pp. 566–70; *Negro Population, 1790–1915* (Washington, D.C.: GPO, 1918), pp. 470, 475–500. Percentage = percentage of "other homes" listed in returns as "owned."
*Those in towns and cities with erph of $700 and more.

white banks and the increasing effectiveness of black realtors in advertising property resulted in a substantial expansion of black home ownership. Nashville's leading black realtor, Richard Hill, asserted that owning a home was no more difficult than paying rent. "Do you want to buy a home or lot?" he asked through the columns of the Nashville *Globe* in 1908. "If so, why not let me help you? If you are married and sometimes find it hard to pay rent, I will help to so place you that you will have NO MORE RENT TO PAY. If you are single you could with so much more ease ask you sweetheart to share your joys and your sorrows IF YOU HAD A HOME OF YOUR OWN. Make your start now on my easy plan; make your home your Savings Bank." By 1910, 92,877 blacks in the Upper South, primarily residents of various towns and cities, had purchased their residences or were buying them over a period of a few years.[47]

As in the Lower South, only approximations of urban black wealth holdings can be made for the post-1870 decades. It is clear that in most cities property holding among blacks rose appreciably during the period and that urban dwellers continued to hold a share disproportionate to the total wealth. A prominent Baltimore editor estimated that the "aggregate wealth" of blacks in the city in 1890 was between "three and four millions." This represented a 142 percent rise from Baltimore's 1870 total estate holdings of $1,648,100 among Negroes. In the District of Columbia, the assessed value of black-owned property in 1890 exceeded $8,000,000, and city blacks had increased their proportion of the total wealth in the city from 2 percent to 5 percent in twenty years. According to an 1891 state auditor's report, Negroes in sixteen Virginia cities owned real estate assessed at $3,207,069. The list of cities included, among others, Richmond with $986,736, Lynchburg with $425,908, Petersburg with $440,840, Norfolk with $232,250, Danville with $194,171, and Manchester (South Richmond) with $178,564. While constituting 18 percent of the total black population, urban blacks controlled approximately 36 percent of the assessed real estate. By 1897, the estimated true value of property held by Richmond's Negroes had increased to $1,918,821, and by 1915, to $3,180,662, more than 400 percent greater than in 1870, while the city's black population had increased about 100 percent during the same period. One Virginia town not listed among the sixteen was Hampton, in Elizabeth City County, but the success of blacks in acquiring property was not less impressive there than in Richmond. With black civic, religious, political, and business leaders, including a number of Hampton Institute graduates, pressing the children of slaves to become economically self-sufficient and independent, the number of property owners and the value of their property rose dramatically. In 1870, 121 blacks in the county owned property assessed at $52,000; twenty-six years later, 1,619 owned property assessed at $468,927 including 884 who owned city lots in Hampton and the adjoining townships of Chesapeake City (Phoebus) and Wythe.

In two other Upper South cities—Nashville and Durham, North Carolina—blacks greatly enhanced their wealth holdings. Between 1870 and 1886, Nashville Negroes increased the value of their landholdings from $245,300 to $1,000,000. Subsequently, with the founding of a black bank and a Negro publishing company, and with Fisk University graduates entering business and professional fields, black property ownership expanded even more. In Durham, the founding of the North Carolina Mutual Life Insurance Company in 1898 and its growth as a leading black-owned business in the state were primarily responsible for the expansion of the property-holding group in the area. Between 1887 and 1909, Durham blacks increased their assessed property holdings (at about 50 percent of the market value) from $8,696 to $583,036, and by 1916, to $866,207, a remarkable expansion in slightly less than three decades. In both cities, the growth rate exceeded population increases and their proportional holdings exceeded those of rural Negroes.[48]

The Quest for Property Ownership

This expansion of black property holding did not go unnoticed by contemporary observers. Travelers, journalists, editors, authors, and politicians pointed to the progress blacks had made during the first generation of freedom. While few attempted to analyze the differences between the Lower and the Upper South, rural and urban areas, farm and home ownership, they were impressed with the ability of former slaves and their children to accumulate real estate and other property. It was a "great pleasure" for the editor of the New York *Age* to reprint two editorials from the *Progressive Farmer*, published in Raleigh, North Carolina, on "how colored people in the South are buying property at [an] enormous rate." "We are sure that the figures given by this Southern white paper," the editor beamed, "will surprise even our best friends."[49]

Black leaders similarly praised the ability of freedmen and women to accumulate wealth and establish businesses. "Suddenly becoming citizens, without shelter or food, they have struggled in a land where they receive little assistance from the courts and where the juries are systematically formed to oppress them; where they work often on the promise to pay; where they receive no protection from the labor law," South Carolina Congressman Thomas E. Miller declared in 1891, in a speech to the House of Representatives, "yet they have achieved a success founded upon material prosperity and accumulated wealth the equal of which has never been accomplished by pauperized serfs or peasants in any part of the universe." While not as euphoric, both Du Bois and Booker T. Washington shared some of the same sentiments. "It is hardly possible to place too great stress," Du Bois said in 1898, "[upon] the deep significance of business ventures among American Negroes." "As I have travelled through the country," Booker T. Washington opined a few years later, in a typical statement, "I have been constantly surprised to note the number of colored men and women, often in small towns and remote districts, who are engaged in various lines of business."[50]

Few of these espousers of racial progress took a deeper, more cynical look at the dire conditions facing many blacks in the South. They often failed to describe the subsistence farmers who eked out a living in backward rural areas, or the urban day laborers who were periodically without jobs and lived in dilapidated "nigger sections." One of the most astute observers was Du Bois, who, while noting increases in wealth holding, lamented the nearly insurmountable obstacles most blacks confronted in seeking to provide for themselves and their families. Sometimes even landowners who expanded their wealth holdings saw their actual economic position worsen with declining prices for cotton and increasing interest rates. As job discrimination became more intense and the population expanded, urban blacks found their economic opportunities increasingly limited. Most remained at the bottom of the occupational spectrum, and in some cities their position deteriorated during the late nineteenth and early twentieth centuries.

Yet facile arguments about the reemergence of slavery or the failure of freedmen and women to acquire property fail to appreciate how former bondspeople perceived their freedom and the significant advances they made in accumulating wealth. Even compared with whites, Negroes made some substantial gains in certain respects. During the first decade and a half after the war, some whites, lacking capital and forced into debt by increased taxation, lost their land, while others migrated from the up-country to become renters and laborers in more fertile areas. At the same time a number of freedmen and women, by hard work, thrift, and good luck, purchased land. By 1880, about one-fifth of the black farm "operators" in the South had become landowners. Living primarily in the Upper South, and in a few peripheral regions of the Lower South, they owned less than half the average acres of whites, and black-owned real estate was worth less per acre than white-owned real estate. Nevertheless, as historian James McPherson points out, for a people emerging from bondage "to have done this well by 1880 was a significant achievement, all the more remarkable because it occurred while many whites were losing their land."

In subsequent decades their estates remained below those of whites—the mean value of black-owned farm property, including livestock, stood at $779 in 1900 and $1,588 in 1910, compared with $2,140 and $3,911 for southern whites—but in the portion of those who owned their own land, the relative distribution of their acreage, and their portion of total farm wealth, blacks slowly narrowed the gap between themselves and whites. Between 1890 and 1910, the number of blacks who owned their own farms rose from 21 to 24 percent, while the number of whites dropped from 65 to 60 percent in the South. During the first decade of the century, the relative distribution of acreage on black owner-operated farms increased at a slightly faster rate (6.5 percent) than on white farms (6.3 percent). Comprising 14 percent of the farm owners in 1900 and 1910, blacks increased their proportional farm wealth (including real estate, buildings, equipment, and machinery) from 5 to 6 percent.[51]

It is difficult to view this period without being struck by the remarkable expansion of black property owning. In rural and urban areas, in the Lower and in the Upper South, former slaves and their children continued to purchase land, homes, and businesses during periods of depression, racial hostility, and violent intimidation. Considering the political, economic, and institutional barriers they faced, the prejudices of whites, and the general backwardness of the South itself, it is not surprising that most Negroes remained landless, but it is surprising that by the early twentieth century at least 426,449 blacks in the South were farm owners and homeowners, 25 percent of the family heads, while others owned town lots, rural acreage, and small businesses. These post–Civil War gains, even in the heart of the rural black belt, prompted comments from some of the most skeptical observers. What Du Bois said concerning one southern state at the turn of the century was true for every state in the region: "It seems clear that the Georgia Negro is in the midst of an unfinished cycle of property accumulation. He has steadily acquired property since the war, and in fully 100 counties he has continued this steady increase in the last decade."[52] While this "unfinished cycle of property accumulation" had reached a significant segment of the population by the early twentieth century, only a small number were able to acquire substantial amounts of wealth. It is to this group that we turn in the last chapter.

CHAPTER SIX

Prosperous Blacks in the South, 1862–1915

In 1891, a newspaper reporter set out to describe the Negro upper class in the South. Under the title "Colored Aristocracy," he explained that entry into this group had nothing to do with material possessions. Rather, it was predicated on educational attainments, proper dialect, membership in certain social clubs, attendance at the right churches, and residency on particular streets. "The more educated drift into one set and form an exclusive circle of their own," he wrote. "It is almost impossible for one who is not of that set to obtain invitations to its entertainments or gain admittance to its clubs and societies." In "colored society," he added, money has very little weight, "education being the chief requisite." The anonymous journalist could have added a number of other criteria to his list: free status before the war, light skin color, professional occupational standing, leadership in politics, "correct" behavior, membership in "old families."[1]

When more than a generation later sociologists and anthropologists began to analyze this group more systematically, they, too, found that the Negro class structure was based not only on occupation and/or wealth, but also on several other factors, including education, family background, and skin color; and when, during the 1960s and afterward, historians turned their attention to this subject, they discussed the complex and multidimensional nature of the black elite.[2] Not only were there different patterns in various sections of the South, in different cities, in urban and rural areas, and among those who lived in predominately white or predominately black areas, but the path to "respectability" included, as one historian explained, "sobriety, ambition, education, hard work, stable family life, and church membership."[3] Discussing "Aristocrats of Color" in the North and South during the post–1880 period, one recent scholar noted that the "colored aristocracy," or "upper-class," could be identified by its "self-image, ideology, and strategies and relationship to the larger society," as well as by its social exclusiveness, pride in ancestry, and light skin color.[4]

If such definitions perhaps have some validity, particularly for ante-bellum free Negroes who had lost their property as a result of the war but sought to maintain their privileged status, they hardly provide an adequate means for understanding the dynamic changes that were occurring among upper-wealth-level blacks during the postwar era. By using a "wealth model" we can systematically analyze the impact of the Civil War on affluent free persons of color, trace the regional differences in various sections of the South, and analyze the changing profile of the most affluent group during the 1880s and 1890s. What happened to the prosperous group of antebellum free Negroes during the postwar era? How did the profile of blacks who reached the upper-wealth levels change between 1860 and 1870? How did this vary in the Lower and Upper South, in rural and urban areas, among men and women, blacks and mulattoes? And how had the most prosperous group changed by the early twentieth century?

Like previous chapters, this chapter will also examine the values and attitudes of this group, their social and cultural life, and their relations with whites. The 1870 census provides a good gauge for analyzing those who reached the higher wealth levels after the war and comparing them with the same group during the prewar period. Unfortunately, there is no similar primary source for subsequent decades. It is therefore necessary to draw information from a biographical data list compiled from various sources, both primary and secondary, on blacks who acquired significant amounts of property. As noted in the Introduction, this list contains information on 241 blacks who acquired at least $20,000 during and after the 1870s, a group admittedly more select than the one taken from the census, but one that will provide at least a crude comparison with prosperous blacks who lived during earlier periods (see appendixes 6 and 7 and An Essay on Sources and Methodology). While the rapid changes occurring during the Civil War era can best be understood by focusing on the two sections of the South that have formed the analytical framework for previous chapters, the declining significance of the Upper-Lower South dichotomy among prosperous blacks after 1870 requires a switch to a broader perspective—to the South as a whole. As the final portion of this chapter reveals, by the early twentieth century the differences among prosperous blacks in the Lower and Upper South— in residency, background, occupational status, wealth accumulations, and relations with whites and other blacks—had nearly vanished.

Free Persons of Color and the Confederate Cause

The morning of April 24, 1862, began much the same as those preceding it on St. Rosalie plantation. Following Andrew Durnford's death in 1859, the management of the 2,000-acre estate had become the responsibility of his older half-brother Joseph, his thirty-six-year-old son Thomas, and his widow, Marie Charlott Remi Durnford. Early that morning, the fieldhands, with hoeing rakes over their shoulders, moved slowly from the quarters to the cane fields; the river, stretching nearly a mile to the distant shore, moved placidly toward the Gulf; the bright-green cane stalks, not yet waist high, drooped slightly in the still morning air; even the dark fringe of the distant forest seemed pleasant and unforeboding. Late that afternoon, however, the quietude was shattered by the throbbing pistons of Admiral David Farragut's Union Navy steamships as they moved relentlessly against the current toward New Orleans. The entire slave community—seventy-seven men, women, and children—as well as the Durnford family, lined the riverbank to watch the spectacle. Neither the slaves, nor the Durnfords, nor perhaps even Farragut himself, however, realized the profound changes this intrusion of Union gunboats would bring to the Deep South. The unique and privileged position of affluent free persons of color would be lost forever.[5]

Twenty-seven miles up the Mississippi River in New Orleans, church bells had already sounded the alarm. The streets and alleys quickly filled as soldiers and civilians, astride horses and mules, driving wagons, carts, and carriages, moved frantically from one place to another. The roads became so clogged that Confederate troops, seeking to join Pierre Beauregard, at Corinth, Mississippi, found it difficult to evacuate the city. At dusk a rear-guard cavalry unit galloped along the lower levee throwing lighted torches on the bales of cotton awaiting shipment. Clouds of thick, black smoke swirled slowly skyward, under them an orange-red glow, and as darkness descended, bright yellow flames shot into the night sky. When the Union gunboats finally arrived about midnight, a large portion of the lower levee was ablaze. Along the edge of the Crescent thousands of residents crowded the banks to observe the fleet as it approached. They stood silently, viewing the silhouetted ships, one onlooker recalled, "with inexpressible sorrow, shame, and anger."[6]

Among those witnessing the intrusion of Union gunships were some of the most prosperous free Negroes in the Lower South. They, too, felt a sense of sadness and sorrow. Only a year before they had organized two splendidly equipped battalions, modeled after the

French *Chasseurs d'Afrique*, to fight for the Confederacy. In all, more than 3,000 Louisiana Negroes—three out of four adult free men of color in the state—joined colored military or militia units to fight for the South. Once the war broke out, though generally excluded from the regular army, they were, one observer noted, as strongly in favor of the rebellion "as the veriest fire-eater [from] South Carolina." Many of them owned slaves and defended the South's peculiar institution "as zealously as any of the disciples of [John C.] Calhoun." Even after Farragut turned the city over to Union General Benjamin Butler, on May 1, 1862, a mulatto schoolteacher refused to hoist the American flag above his schoolhouse. One postwar investigator in Louisiana noted that despite numerous professions of Union loyalty by free persons of color it was virtually impossible to prove such claims. Having compared the muster rolls of free colored militia—the Home Guard that had so enthusiastically offered its services to the "rebel government"—with the list of claimants who were now professing the utmost loyalty to the Union, he found them virtually identical. A few young men from prosperous families, including St. Landry Parish's Charles Lutz, Jean Baptiste Pierre-Auguste, and Lufroy Pierre-Auguste, actually fought for the Confederacy, seeing action at Manassas, Fredericksburg, Shiloh, Vicksburg, and in other battles.[7]

In other Lower South states, affluent free persons of color also sympathized with the Confederate cause. Those who owned slaves wished to protect their property; others feared the consequences of a general emancipation. Few went so far as a group of Charleston, South Carolina, free Negroes who professed in a memorial to the governor that their allegiance to the South was so great that they would "offer up our lives and all that is dear to us," but many either tacitly hoped the South would be preserved or openly backed the new government by purchasing Confederate bonds, donating money to soldier relief organizations, or providing slaves to work on fortifications. Following the death of William Ellison in 1861, William, Jr., and Henry Ellison made every effort to prove themselves loyal to the new government: they paid their taxes, offered corn, fodder, and bacon to the army, and purchased treasury notes, 4 percent certificates, and Confederate notes.[8]

As the war progressed, however, and it became increasingly clear that the old regime might crumble in the wake of Union advances, prosperous free Negroes in the Lower South grew fearful and apprehensive. Like white aristocrats, they looked longingly toward the past. Few expressed their feelings more poignantly than Catherine

Johnson, the eldest daughter of the wealthy Mississippi barber William Johnson, who had been brutally murdered in 1851 by a free black during a boundary dispute. Part of her despair was personal—the girlhood memories of her father, the growing insanity of her brother, and the financial sacrifices of her mother—but these problems seemed to be only symptomatic of a much deeper anguish, an anguish caused by the incomprehensible changes taking place as a result of the war. At first she remained optimistic, hoping that things would turn out for the best, but as time passed, and the war dragged on month after month, year after year, she grew increasingly resentful and bitter, eventually melancholy and despondent. Three entries in her diary reveal her growing despair. On August 16, 1864, she wrote:

> To day we received papers stating that another large Battle has been fought in which the [Union soldiers] had been literally cut to pieces. God grant that the life of one who has become dear to us may be spared. Just two short months and 17 day[s] since he was with us full of life and hope. Now he is far away engaged in a cruel and bloody strug[g]le, the issue of which no mortal can tell. And to night who knows but that he may be among the fated one[s] that fell Eleven day[s] ago.

Several months later, on New Year's day, she added:

> Our Christmas past quietly enough; our table lacked not many of its accustomed luxuries; yet some how they were [not] partaken of with the same zest as in former years. Ah it is useless to sigh for the past. things change every year; aye every day and we are of the world and must expect to bear its changes however sad. . . . I wonder where Mr. Gardner and Mr. Reed and the rest of them are to night, though if [the] post be true they are at Savan[n]ah; and the Confederacy has received another blow. Oh when will this cruel and bloody war end and how. We can only prey God [it] will be done. . . . why it was sent upon the land none can tell. it is a subject that baf[f]les me completely. Oh the miserable thought that is conjured up by the mere mention of war.

The following year, she confessed:

> My head aches and I feel so unhappy. It seems that the times grow harder instead of better and I do so dread poverty. And another thing, every body seems so changed, and most of all I grieve over the change that has taken place in My self. to the present the past seems so Bright, so bright that I dare not call up its memories, for it makes me wretched to think that in reality I can never live them again, and I know that it is wrong but sometimes I do long to die. I feel so useless and so hopeless. I strug[g]le for the right, but my strength and nature are both weak and fail me in the strug[g]le. God help me. I know not what I shall do.[9]

Once it became clear that the North would prevail free Negro support for the Confederacy in the Lower South quickly evaporated. Those who had served in the home guard units or professed loyalty to Jefferson Davis now asserted that they had acted out of fear of retaliation. How could any black, one of them queried, support a government set up for the distinctly avowed purpose of holding his brethren and kindred in eternal slavery? "But now, we see that our future is indissolubly bound up with that of the negro race in this county," a free person of color who had previously held himself aloof from blacks and taken great pride in his French ancestry explained to northern journalist Whitelaw Reid. "We have no rights which we can reckon safe while the same are denied to the fieldhands on the sugar plantations." Echoing these sentiments an Alabama creole of color exclaimed: "We are all tarred with the same stick, knit together by bonds of common sympathy and suffering, and must rise or fall together." Louis Roudanez, owner of the first black daily newspaper in America, the *New Orleans Tribune*, urged free men and women and freedmen and women to work together for the common cause of black equality.[10]

Decline in the Lower South

Despite such professions of "common sympathy," the war and its aftermath spelled disaster for the great majority of affluent free persons of color in the Lower South. This was especially true in rural areas that had experienced the brunt of Union attacks, but even in towns and cities, despite the ability of some wealthy families to maintain their real estate holdings, there was a marked decline in the wealth holdings of the majority. Following three successive postwar crop failures, South Carolina rice planter Robert Collins, who had once owned a 3,100-acre plantation and seventeen bondsmen and women, was forced to borrow money from the Freedmen's Bureau to purchase supplies for his former slaves. Collins's sister, Margaret Mitchell Harris (both children of Elias Collins), owner of 44 slaves and a 981-acre rice plantation in Georgetown District, had a premonition of the coming disaster. In 1860, she sold her slaves, disposed of her plantation, and invested $35,000 in stocks and bonds, only to lose everything as her stock certificates became worthless during the war. Andrew Anderson, who owned the 663-acre Bulls Head Plantation in St. Thomas and St. Dennis and had produced 13,200 pounds of rice in 1860, sold his holdings in 1867 for a meager $1,333. In Sumter County, the once proud Ellison family experienced a more gradual decline. William, Jr., and Henry Ellison held on to their father's gin-making business and plantation, and when these failed to produce a profit they opened a small mercantile store in Stateburg. But the value of their land plunged—in 1865, 760 acres being assessed at $7,600, a year later at $5,334, and in 1867 at $2,280—and eventually they sold off a portion of their holdings. During the 1870s, R. G. Dun and Company estimated their wealth at between $2,000 and $8,000. In 1879, the Ellisons, once among the dozen wealthiest free mulatto families in the South, harvested six bales of cotton.[11]

"When war commence it purty hard on folks," a free Negro in St. Mary Parish, Louisiana, recalled. First came the Confederates who swept up the slaves, including those owned by blacks, and took them away to build fortifications. "Dey line my daddy up with de others, but a white man from town say, 'Dat a good, old man. He part Indian and he free'. . . . So dey let him go." Then Yankee raiding parties rode through, burning, pillaging, and looting. "Dey tak a whole year crop of sugar and corn and horses." Everywhere the Union army advanced free blacks told of death and destruction. "The road all the way to Natchitoches," one observer said, describing the region where some of the wealthiest free persons of color in America owned their plantations, "was a solid flame." His heart was "filled with sadness" at the sight of those lovely plantations being burned to the ground. While some of the Metoyer family plantations escaped destruction, in St. Landry Parish, despite declarations of loyalty to the United States, Antoine Meullion lost 30 head of cattle, 150 sheep, 26 hogs, and 5,000 fence rails to a band of Union soldiers under the command of Nathaniel Banks. Pierre and Cyprien Ricard, descendants of the wealthiest free person of color in the state, lost virtually everything during the war. In 1868, a final 161 acres was seized by the Iberville Parish sheriff for nonpayment of debts and sold at public auction. Similarly, the Ponis family in St. John the Baptist Parish, the Verdun family in St. Mary Parish, the Deslonde in Iberville Parish, and the Porche family in Pointe Coupée Parish witnessed the disintegration of their antebellum fortunes during the war.[12]

Those who somehow sustained themselves, and, still possessing large tracts of fertile soil, hoped to rebuild, discovered that the wartime destruction was only a harbinger of things to come. As with their white neighbors, the problems in securing farmhands, the flooding and crop failures in 1866 and 1867, and the difficulties in obtaining credit forced many landholders off the land, while pushing others to the brink of disaster. Within a few years after the war the vast majority of the wealthiest rural Negroes in antebellum America—

Louisiana's creoles of color—had lost not only their slaves, farm machinery, livestock, buildings, and personal possessions, but their land as well. During the war, Antoine and Josephine Decuir, once among the richest free mulattoes in America, were forced to mortgage their house, the adjoining land, and even their crops. Following Antoine's death in 1865, his wife was beset by creditors, and on March 23, 1871, her 840-acre plantation in Point Coupée Parish, worth $160,000 before the war, was sold by the local sheriff to satisfy debts amounting to $34,967. The Metoyer family in Natchitoches Parish, declining since the 1850s, experienced a final economic disaster during the depression of the 1870s. In the first year of the depression, 1873, forty-four members of the family were listed as having had their land sold at "tax sales." Often these sales were conducted for nonpayment of assessments amounting to only a few dollars. Following the death of their mother in 1866, Andrew Durnford, Jr., and his sister Rosema Durnford struggled desperately to regain the antebellum production of sugar that had made their father one of the richest free Negroes in the United States, but in 1874, besieged by creditors, they were forced to sell St. Rosalie plantation for a few thousand dollars. In St. Mary Parish, once affluent mulattoes eked out a subsistence on small plots of their old plantations. During the 1860s the mean value of real estate held by black "planters" in the Lower South dropped from nearly $10,000 to less than $2,000, significantly more than the general depreciation in the value of land.[13]

Only a few affluent free persons of color escaped the war years unscathed. Those who did had usually invested heavily in urban real estate (rather than slaves) or maintained profitable businesses. In Charleston and New Orleans, despite occupational declines and wartime destruction, a few prosperous free blacks actually improved their economic standing following the Civil War. Charleston engineer Anthony Weston, wood dealers Richard Dereef and Robert Howard, butcher George Shrewsberry, and realtor William McKinlay, among the richest antebellum mulattoes, either maintained their estates or improved their economic position. In 1867, Weston's city real estate was valued at $20,300, and when he died nine years later, he still possessed much of his antebellum estate. In the late 1870s, Dereef divided his estate among members of his family, leaving four houses and stock in the Charleston Gas Light Company. His rental houses, located on Calhoun, Meeting, Coming, and Spring streets, were appraised at $7,400, and his stocks, bonds, and mortgage notes at $4,797. Although losing twelve slaves, valued at $10,800, Howard (Dereef's business partner) still owned real property worth $30,000 in 1870, only $3,900 less than a decade earlier; and Shrewsberry, who had acquired his first house in Charleston as early as 1843, and by 1859, controlled $7,500 in real estate, expanded his total estate after the war; by 1875, the year of his death, he paid city taxes of $446 on more than $10,000 worth of real estate, and his total wealth, including a large savings account, amounted to $28,845. McKinlay, at the time of his death in 1873, owned eleven pieces of rental property worth $23,900, and South Carolina Stock Certificates worth $6,200. A few other members of Charleston's mulatto elite—James D. Johnson (also spelled Johnston), Richard Holloway, Jr., Joseph A. Sasportas, Francis Wilkinson, and Samuel Weston—despite wartime difficulties, were able to sustain their antebellum economic standing after the war.[14]

A similar situation existed in the Crescent City. Land speculator Thomy Lafon, who became a large contributor to various black charities, increased his wealth from $10,000 to $55,000 by speculating in swamplands during the Union occupation. Money broker John Racquet Clay added $16,500 to his estate during the 1860s, and another broker, Drauzin Barthelemy McCarty, increased his fortune from $45,000 to $77,300 during the same period. Between 1860 and 1870, real-estate dealer Aristide Mary acquired $70,000 worth of property, while antebellum plasterer Oscar James Dunn, builder Jean Baptiste Roudanez, and tailor Sidney Thezan entered various professional and business fields to enhance their holdings. Several other prosperous free persons of color in the city, while not increasing their wealth, maintained their high prewar economic standing: merchant Bernard Soulíe, who had loaned the Confederate government $10,000, kept the bulk of his $100,000 estate, as did landlord Edmond Dupuy, whose $200,000 worth of real estate made him the second wealthiest Negro in the South.[15]

But those who survived the war in such a manner represented only a small proportion of prewar wealth holders in the two centers of free Negro affluence. In 1860, 121 Negro real-estate owners in Charleston (including a few near the city but in the county) boasted holdings of more than $2,000; they owned a total of $618,900, or $5,115 per property owner. A decade later, only 81 realty owners were listed in the same category; they held $423,000, still $5,222 per owner, but a large majority of the 1870 group—two out of three—had acquired their holdings during the postwar era. In addition, free persons of color in the city lost an estimated $216,900 in slave property when they were forced to free their bondsmen. In New Orleans, a close study of creoles of color in the Fourth, Fifth, and Sixth wards, the heart of the free mulatto community, reveals a similar decline. Among

the 98 free persons of color listed in the 1860 and 1870 census returns, nearly half experienced losses, only one of four kept their holdings intact, and 23 expanded their wealth. Musician Nicholas Dabron
saw his real estate drop from $11,000 to $5,150, grocer Felix Roberts
from $5,600 to $1,000, and carpenter Casimir Labat from $3,000
to no wealth at all in 1870. Labat was joined by 31 other propertied antebellum men and women in the three wards who had lost
everything.[16]

Even those who had survived the war with their estates intact sometimes found it impossible to adjust to the rapid changes occurring in
the wake of emancipation. Saddened by the passing of the old regime,
disheartened by their loss of status, and angered at being mistaken
for ex-bondsmen, they ignored their business obligations and allowed
their real-estate holdings to evaporate. One of the wealthiest free persons of color in antebellum America, Francois Lacroix, worth an estimated $242,600 in 1860, seemed not to care about the decline of his
wealth. Even after the war, Lacroix, a tailor and realtor, maintained
control over 198 separate pieces of real estate in the city and surrounding areas. Nor was he without funds to pay the taxes which he
ignored until the sheriff confiscated his property. In 1874, the once
vibrant Lacroix, wearing a vacant smile, stood silently as the "splendid
creation of his industry" crumbled before the auctioneer's gavel. According to one witness, Lacroix seemed "forlorn and sorrowful." Two
years later he was dead. Three other rich creoles of color, Aristide
Mary, John Racquet Clay, and Jean Baptiste Jourdain, men who had
not only distinguished themselves in various business ventures but
had also gained stature as the "most intelligent and well educated
colored creoles" in the Crescent City, suffered similar financial reversals. Depressed and unable to cope, one by one each of them
ended his own life, Clay by putting a pistol to his temple and pulling
the trigger.[17]

Such extreme responses were rare, but few affluent mulattoes escaped the postwar years unscathed. Illustrating this loss of prestige,
self-esteem, and economic standing was the career of Adolphe Donato (Donatto), a member of one of the richest black slave-owning
families in the South. In 1883, Donato was working as a body servant
to a white man. Accompanying his employer on a trip to the nation's
capital, he saw streets "as smooth as glass" and buildings "more magnificent than I ever dreamed of." "My room is small but I have a good
bed and a stove and, what is better than any thing else, a servant
comes in every morning to make my fire." Just think, he explained to
a friend in Opelousas, how much of a luxury it was to be waited on

"but then you Know 'folks of fashion are bound to put on airs.'" Dressing in the latest styles, strolling along Pennsylvania Avenue, window shopping at the downtown stores, he feigned being a "distinguished colored gentleman." Each morning, however, he was expected to serve his employer coffee and then wash the cups and saucers. "But I do this so quietly," he confessed, "that the servant never supposes for a moment that I am other than a 'gentleman of leisure.'"[18]

Rapidly emerging in the postwar Lower South was a new economic elite, one quite different from its antebellum predecessor. If prior to the war two out of three among those with at least $2,000 worth of real estate resided in Louisiana, and nine out of ten in Louisiana and South Carolina, by 1870 there was a much broader distribution among prosperous blacks, with 44 percent residing in Georgia, Florida, Alabama, Arkansas, and Texas. Some of them had been property owners before the war, but they represented a relatively small portion of the postwar realty owners. Only about one out of four prosperous antebellum free Negroes in the region survived the war as realty owners, a "persistence" rate substantially lower than for whites in the black belt of Alabama. Among the postwar prosperous group only about one out of nine had owned property in 1850 and/or 1860. Not only had there been a reshuffling and redistribution by state and former status, but significant increases also occurred in the number of upper-wealth blacks in smaller cities and towns—Columbia, South Carolina; Savannah and Augusta, Georgia; Jacksonville, Florida; Montgomery and Mobile, Alabama; Jackson, Mississippi; and Little Rock, Arkansas. During the Civil War decade the percentage of the Lower South's affluent group living in Charleston and New Orleans dropped from 54 percent to 25 percent, while the proportion living in smaller urban areas more than doubled, from 11 percent to 24 percent, a trend that would continue in subsequent decades.

Not only was the postwar prosperous group in the Lower South more small-town than its antebellum predecessor, but it had also changed considerably in other respects. Nearly a third of the prewar group had been female (32 percent); by 1870 this had declined to less than one-fifth (18.9 percent). During the antebellum period slightly more than half lived in stable, monogamous families, while after the war this had risen to nearly two-thirds. According to the population census, the proportion who were mulattoes, compared with blacks, decreased dramatically during the 1860s, from 86 percent to only 56 percent. Although a majority were still listed as farmers, skilled artisans, and retail merchants, they were now entering new occupations, including coach making, contracting and building, cotton sampling, dentistry, jewelry retailing, wine and liquor wholesaling, "inspecting," and other business and professional fields. There were also significant changes in various wealth-holding categories among the most prosperous group: their mean real estate holdings dropped from $8,384 to $4,971, and the proportion with at least $10,000 worth of real estate dropped from 16 to 6 percent. At the same time the proportion of those with between $2,000 and $5,000 rose from 63 to 83 percent. Among the postwar economic elite were several former free Negroes, including South Carolina carpenter Israel Smith and salesman Joseph Taylor, Georgia farmer William Higginbotham, Louisiana planters Antoine Dubuclet, Zacharie Honoré, and Charles Reggio, and printer Paul Commagere, and Arkansas resident Mary Fenno. But as the changes in color, gender, and wealth groupings indicate, even among the most prosperous Negroes in the postwar Lower South there were increasing numbers of former slaves.[19]

Perhaps the best known ex-slave to amass substantial wealth during the period was Benjamin Thornton Montgomery, formerly the property of Mississippi plantation owner Joseph Davis, the older brother of Jefferson Davis, president of the Confederacy. On November 19, 1866, despite a law prohibiting blacks from acquiring rural land holdings, Montgomery purchased from Joseph Davis two plantations at Davis Bend, Mississippi, for $480,000, to be paid over a period of ten years. The two men kept the transaction a secret until the spring of 1867 when former slaves were legally allowed to own rural property in the state. Working with his sons, William and Isaiah, Montgomery set about making Davis Bend, with its 1,600 black inhabitants, an ideal black community, where both tenant farmers and the Montgomerys would reap large profits. During the early years, despite flooding, declining cotton prices, and hostile white neighbors, Davis Bend was a decided success. In 1870, the Montgomerys sold 6,141 bales of cotton; the following year they added 1,557 acres of fertile bottom land to their holdings; and in 1872, their mercantile business received the coveted "A 1 +" rating from R. G. Dun and Company. By then, with assets of more than $350,000, they had become the wealthiest black family in the entire South. Yet Benjamin kept the title to the land in his own name, and like white merchants, he charged tenants high interest rates for supplies. By the mid–1870s, poor crops, the continued decline in cotton prices, and credit losses pushed the Montgomerys to the edge of bankruptcy, and following Benjamin's death in 1877, creditors foreclosed on the Montgomerys' mercantile firm. In 1881, the land was sold at public auction to the family of Jefferson Davis and the grandchildren of Joseph Davis.[20]

Expansion in the Upper South

Nearly as precipitous as the decline of affluent free persons of color in the Lower South was the rise of prosperous free blacks in the Upper South during the Civil War and the Reconstruction era. As previously noted, unlike their brethren in the lower states, Upper South blacks had owned few slaves; they were often far removed from the fields of battle (except in Virginia and North Carolina); and they did not witness a severe depreciation in the value of their holdings. Indeed, in some areas, especially border cities, property values actually rose during the 1860s. Not only were former free Negroes in a better position to expand their wealth holdings, but the increasing demand for certain skilled and semiskilled workers, less fear by whites of "Negro domination," at least compared to the densely populated black belt regions of the Lower South, and the momentum toward property ownership gave some former slaves opportunities to accumulate more than $2,000 worth of property. Those who reached the top of the economic spectrum still remained part of a very small group, unevenly distributed in rural and urban areas, in the eastern and western states, but in virtually every wealth category, including the total value of their real estate, prosperous blacks in the Upper South surged ahead of their brethren in the lower states.

Even so, the few large slave owners, like free people of color in the Gulf region, experienced a sharp decline in their economic fortunes. In Amelia County, Virginia, Alfred and Francis Anderson, slaveholding brothers who had managed thriving farms, watched helplessly as their livestock and crops were carried off by Union soldiers. Over a period of three days they lost everything—horses, mules, sheep, 1,500 pounds of bacon, 1,200 pounds of fodder, wheat, corn, and twenty hogs. Another member of the family, James P. Anderson, recalled how, in April 1865, Philip H. Sheridan's men confiscated his horses "and Carried them off"; and a short time later, a Union "Wagon Train Stopped on [my] premises and took all the rest of [my] property." A neighbor, Frankey Miles, the largest Negro slave owner in Virginia, lost not only nineteen slaves, but everything else on her 1,100-acre plantation, including mules, cattle, sheep, a few hogsheads of tobacco, 2,000 pounds of bacon, and 3,000 pounds of fodder.[21] In North Carolina, the wealthy slaveholder James D. Sampson lost more than twenty bondsmen and women during the early 1860s (valued at $10,000) and saw his real estate holdings plummet in value. Following his death about 1862, his wife and two sons were left with real estate worth about one-third of Sampson's antebellum estate. Several other North Carolina blacks who had owned slaves, including members of the Evins, Mangum, and Alston families in Wake County, lost substantial amounts of property during the 1860s, as did the family of Sherod Bryant, the largest free Negro slaveholder in neighboring Tennessee. Though Bryant himself had died before the war, none of his three sons was able to maintain more than $1,000 worth of real estate during the postwar era.[22]

Many former free Negroes, even in rural areas, however, were able to improve their economic standing during these years. This was especially true in the western states of Kentucky, Tennessee, and Missouri, where wartime destruction had been slight and the relatively low density of blacks in the total population allayed the anti-black proprietorship attitudes of whites. Now entering the most prosperous group were free blacks who prior to the war had owned only modest amounts of real estate or had owned no property at all—among Kentucky farmers, Dennis Lane increased his realty from $300 to $6,000, John Shaw, from no real estate to $4,000, and Alfred Ewell, from $755 to $4,500; among Tennessee landholders, Rubin (Reuben) Caldwell went from $800 in 1850, to $3,000 in 1860, to $5,000 in 1870, Michael Archer, from no real property in 1860 to $4,000 a decade later, Fleming Higgins, from $1,500 to $3,000; and among Missouri farmers, Moses Logan increased his holdings from $1,500 to $2,500, Lewis Mitchell, from $800 to $2,000, and Samuel Smith went from no property to $5,700 after the war. While containing only 37 percent of the Upper South's rural Negroes, these three states boasted nearly half of the farmers who had, by 1870, accumulated at least $2,000 worth of realty, a significant portion of whom had been free prior to the Civil War.[23]

In the rural northeast—North Carolina, Virginia, Maryland, and Delaware—former free Negroes were less successful in maintaining or improving their position. Not only did the few large slave owners in North Carolina and Virginia lose much of their property, but other free Negroes, like their white neighbors, also suffered from wartime destruction. By 1870, with more than half of the region's rural black population, these two states contained only one of five prosperous farm owners. Since Maryland and Delaware remained under Union control during the war, conditions in rural areas of these two states were slightly better, and some former free Negroes moved into the upper-wealth group for the first time or significantly expanded their holdings. During the 1860s, for example, Kent County farmer Alexander Wilson moved to the outskirts of Baltimore, purchased a farm, and by 1870 managed a thriving operation. His real estate was valued at nearly $6,000. But Wilson was unusual, and despite a modest rise in the total number of farmers who owned property valued $2,000 or more, the proportion of the most prosperous group in these two states, compared with other states in the Upper South, declined from slightly more than half in 1860 to less than a third a decade later.[24]

Not only did former free blacks fare better in the rural Upper than in the rural Lower South, but freedmen and women also had better opportunities to acquire property. Although the number of ex-slaves who acquired at least $2,000 worth of real estate within a half-decade after freedom cannot be ascertained precisely, the changing profile of the most prosperous group in rural areas shows that even among this higher-wealth group some members had formerly been slaves. The proportion of those listed as black rose from 61 percent to 72 percent; the proportion of those designated as farm workers and laborers rose slightly, while there was a slight drop among those designated as farmers, from 76 to 71 percent. The mean value of their holdings also went down slightly, from $3,713 to $3,682. Among the most prosperous group in 1860 a majority were literate, but a decade later more than 60 percent were described as illiterate or semiliterate. Granted these changes were not pronounced, in part due to the continuity among former free blacks, but the slight shifts indicate that even among the most prosperous group of farmers some had been slaves only five or six years before.

Compared with the massive increase of the rural free black population in the wake of emancipation (about ninefold) only a tiny minority of the rural blacks in the Upper South, approximately one family in 369, accumulated real estate worth at least $2,000 during the early years after the war. Yet, despite some land devaluations, prosperous rural Negroes in every state expanded their property holdings between 1860 and 1870: in Delaware from $105,600 to $341,000, in Maryland from $497,000 to $711,800, in Virginia from $209,200 to $427,500, in North Carolina from $143,700 to $178,400, in Kentucky from $140,500 to $410,600, in Tennessee from $114,800 to $690,200, and in Missouri from $16,400 to $283,100. In all, including the few blacks living in rural portions of the District of Columbia, they increased their total realty holdings from $1,240,200 to $3,078,300, or 148 percent. This was almost exactly the same as the increase in their numbers, from 334 to 836, or 150 percent. Remarkably, by 1870, in the total value of their real estate (within $600) rural landholders in the upper states had pulled even with prosperous rural blacks in the Lower South, who, only two decades before, had controlled more than five times as much realty.

The most dramatic change among prosperous blacks occurred in the towns and cities of the Upper South. During the Civil War decade a number of urban areas in the region, unlike those in the Lower South, had experienced substantial economic growth. Serving as transportation and merchandising centers, providing services for the Union army and civilians, cities like Baltimore, the District of Columbia, Lexington, Louisville, and St. Louis expanded their commercial and business activities significantly during and immediately after the war. Even cities under federal or Confederate control—Nashville and Richmond—either witnessed a wartime boom or quickly recovered in its aftermath. By the late 1860s, with the beginning of railroad expansion, increased manufacturing, and rising government services, most towns and cities in the region were centers of bustling economic activity.

In contrast to their counterparts in the Lower South, urban free blacks in the upper states were in a much better position to improve their economic standing. Those who had previously carved out a niche in the local economies as artisans, draymen, livery operators, stewards, and barbers were often able to expand their operations, as were those who managed various small business concerns. There were also improved employment opportunities in the professions and government service. In addition, the rapid urban population growth stimulated new demands for service-related employment. As a result, former free Negroes, some of them with modest prewar holdings, surged into the most prosperous group—Wilmington, Delaware's Charles Agnes improved the value of his real estate from $1,000 in 1860 to $17,000 during the 1860s; Baltimore barber Augustus Roberts went from no real estate to property valued at $12,000; District of Columbia laborer and coachman William Cole, from $600 to $6,000; Alexandria, Virginia, butcher William Gray from $1,700 to $5,000; Richmond boilermaker James Woodson, from $700 to $4,000; Goldsboro, North Carolina, blacksmith Charles Winn, from $1,500 to $3,000; Shelbyville, Kentucky, drayman and later merchant Thomas Ballard, from $200 to $6,200; Louisville barber Nathaniel Rogers, from $1,800 to $8,000; Memphis barber and later grocer Joseph Clauston, from $700 in 1850 to $10,000 in 1870; and St. Louis steward James Young, from no realty to $5,000 a decade later. In all, former property-owning urban free Negroes in the Upper South were far more likely to enter the highest economic strata for the first time than were their brethren in the lower states.[25]

These changes were perhaps nowhere more visible than in Lexington, Kentucky, a town that had grown considerably in population and economic vitality during the war years and shortly afterward. While hemp, tobacco, and thoroughbred horse breeding remained the community's principal economic activities, there was also a marked expansion in construction, retailing, and transportation. In these latter pursuits ex-free Negroes who had established businesses before the war, or during the early 1860s, were in a position to expand their economic activities during the postwar era. Even with the town's rapid black population expansion, from about 3,100 (free and slave) to more than 7,000, the number of Negroes with more than $2,000 worth of real estate rose at a faster pace, from four in 1860 to twenty-four a decade later. As in other Upper South cities, the new prosperous group included a large proportion of former free blacks who had greatly expanded their wealth holdings during the war years. Forty-year-old James Turner, worth $1,000 in 1860, became one of the most successful plasterers in Fayette County, employing a highly proficient crew and winning contracts on a number of large jobs. By 1870, he had increased his real estate holdings by 700 percent. Similarly, livery stable owners John and William Taylor acquired a reputation of excellent service and high-quality teams of horses. With a combined realty wealth of $3,500 in 1860, they acquired additional lots and buildings until their combined estate stood at $14,380 during the postwar period. Another livery operator, free Negro Denis Seals, became nearly as prosperous, while Moses Spencer, who owned and operated a secondhand furniture store on Main Street, increased the value of his holdings from $2,000 (assessed value) in 1858 to nearly $20,000 during the 1870s. By then, Spencer had become the wealthiest black in Lexington.[26]

Not only did urban free Negroes with relatively modest antebellum estates significantly improve their economic standing, but free blacks with larger holdings before the war also often added significantly to their property holdings. Unlike the majority of affluent free people of color in the Lower South, prosperous free Negro businessmen—merchants, grocers, barbers—as well as a few professionals and government employees—could boast of steadily increasing assets. Some of them who owned rental property before the war now found time to improve their properties while others with steadily rising profits and incomes invested in new real estate holdings. As with free Negroes who entered the prosperous group for the first time, each city had a group of prosperous antebellum free blacks who remained as leading wealth holders after the war. Indeed, some of them were able to add significant amounts of property to their estates. Among those who before the war had owned between $2,000 and $6,000 in realty, but by 1870 had increased their holdings to more than $10,000, were

Baltimore blacksmith Remin Adams, District of Columbia wheel-wright James Jackson and merchant Alfred Jones, Louisville steward Marshall Woodson, Paris, Kentucky, confectioner and grocer Jefferson Porter, Nashville barber John Thomas and schoolteacher Peter Lowery, and St. Louis salesman Ludwell Lee and barber Barriteer [Byertere] Hickman. In addition, several of the richest families in the postwar Upper South were descendants of prosperous urban wealth holders who had died shortly before or during the Civil War. These included, among others, Thomas Green's family in Baltimore, feed merchant Alfred Lee's family in Georgetown, and Antoine Labadie's family in St. Louis. For most affluent free Negroes in towns and cities of the Upper South the war years were marked by significant economic progress.[27]

At the same time the changing urban profile of the most prosperous group suggests that a few among them, primarily those with wealth holdings between $2,000 and $5,000 by 1870, had recently emerged from slavery. Not only had the number of prosperous Negroes in various cities risen sharply—from 285 to 978, or 243 percent—but nearly one out of five in 1870 also worked in lower occupations such as waiters, servants, porters, day laborers, hackmen, laundresses, occupations often relegated to slaves prior to the war. In addition, the portion of upper-wealth level individuals listed by census takers as black had risen from 40 percent to 55 percent during the decade. Indeed, by 1870 there were nearly twice as many prosperous urban blacks in the Upper South as there had been affluent blacks and mulattoes combined before the war. As in rural areas, the proportion of illiterate persons in the upper-wealth group had also risen during the decade, from 33 percent in 1860 to 43 percent in 1870 (including those listed as semiliterate). While none of these comparisons proves the prewar status of postwar affluent blacks, and some ex-free Negroes could be found in each of the above categories, taken together they strongly suggest that some members of the upper-wealth group had only a few years before been held in bondage.

Thus, whether freedman or woman or former free black, the number of prosperous Negroes in the Upper South's cities rose rapidly during the decade of the 1860s. So, too, did the value of their real-estate holdings. In Wilmington, Delaware, the number of prosperous blacks increased from 4 to 32, and their total real-estate possessions increased from $11,300 to $112,100; in Baltimore, from 24 to 115, and from $120,200 to $530,500; in the District of Columbia, from 83 to 339, and from $261,300 to $1,701,000; in Richmond from 23 to 52, and from $74,100 to $229,200; in Louisville, from 16 to 61, and from $67,500 to $261,100; in Nashville, from 19 to 38, and from $91,800 to $211,500; in Memphis, from 6 to 25, and from $43,000 to $184,500; and in St. Louis, from 57 to 79, and from $403,100 to $708,600. In most cities there was also a jump in the mean value of their holdings, ranging from nearly $1,900 per realty owner in the District of Columbia ($3,148 to $5,018), to $1,200 in Richmond ($3,222 to $4,408), to more modest rises in other cities. Only in Baltimore was there a drop, and that was relatively slight (from $5,008 to $4,613), especially considering the increase in the number of prosperous Negroes in the city. In all, prosperous Upper South urban blacks increased their wealth holdings 275 percent between 1860 and 1870, from $1,296,900 to $4,857,300, and along with the sharp rise in their numbers came an increase in the average value of their holdings, from $4,551 to $4,967. By 1870, constituting less than 2 percent of the region's Negro urban families, they controlled more than 61 percent of the Upper South's black urban realty wealth.

The South's new center of affluent blacks, surpassing Charleston and New Orleans, was the District of Columbia. During the postwar years opportunities for economic advancement were probably better in the nation's capital than in any city in the South. Some Negroes obtained government clerkships or teaching positions; others started small businesses or continued the businesses they had managed before the war; a few entered the professions as doctors, lawyers, and ministers; and after 1870 blacks were employed as tellers and cashiers at the Freedmen's Savings Bank, as professors at Howard University, and as editors and printers at the *New National Era*, a newspaper founded by Frederick Douglass. There were also profits to be made in the building trades, as the city witnessed a rapid expansion of its population, which in turn stimulated a growth of home construction and home renovation. In addition, unlike rural areas, the new demands for real estate drove District of Columbia property values spiraling upward, higher than in any other city except perhaps St. Louis. Free blacks who had acquired buildings before or during the war, especially in the First Ward, witnessed a marked appreciation in the value of their holdings.[28]

As in other Upper South cities, the postwar prosperous group consisted of former free blacks who had improved their estates, formerly affluent free Negroes who had maintained their economic standing, and a few industrious former slaves. But to a greater degree than in any other city, the new economic elite was comprised of ex-free Negroes of modest means who substantially expanded their wealth holdings during the 1860s. Before the war, Edward Crusoe owned a small grocery store and his real estate was valued at $2,000; by 1870, he had risen to become a large-scale grain merchant and had increased his realty holdings more than tenfold. Although the census listing of banker William Wilson's holdings at $71,000 in 1870 was probably inflated, he was nonetheless a man of substantial means who prior to the war had owned only $1,000 worth of real estate. It was not uncommon for former free blacks to double or triple the size of their estates. Among those who increased the value of their holdings from less than $2,000 to more than $5,000 were barber Robert Booker, Capitol building employee Philip Nolan, restaurant owner Richard Francis, salvager Palmer Briscoe, plasterer Richard Sanders, milkman Charles Dyson, laborer William Cook, and government messengers Edward Watson, William Myers, Garden Snowden, and William Pierre. In addition, most free Negroes who had been well-to-do prior to the war—boardinghouse owner Andrew Henson, furniture dealer Isaac Johnson, barber James Wright, messenger Lindsay Muse; or had been members of affluent families—William Syphax, Harriett Lee, Ellen Datcher; or who had migrated to the city from the North were able to improve their economic standing during the war decade. In all, the District witnessed a more than 300 percent rise in the number of blacks who owned at least $2,000 worth of real estate, and a 551 percent rise in the value of their holdings.[29]

Unlike the antebellum period, when all except a few of the South's wealthiest blacks were residents of the Lower South, by the 1870s a number of the region's richest Negroes lived in urban areas of the Upper South. District of Columbia hotel owner and restaurateur James T. Wormley, who began as a steward and caterer, established one of the finest hotels in Washington in 1871. Tall, well built, with piercing dark eyes, Wormley was a man of consummate business skills and innate intelligence. "The fame of his table spread far and wide," one observer said, "and a supper at Wormley's was one of the experiences which every visitor to Washington thought he must not miss." By 1870, he had amassed a small fortune of $87,000.[30] Another hotel owner, slave-born Henry Harding, worth $35,000 in 1870, lost a large portion of his wealth with the collapse of the Freedmen's Bank in 1874, but went on to establish a successful secondhand furniture store and real estate business. At the time of his death in 1888 Harding was one of the largest black taxpayers in Nashville, with holdings of $80,000. Former bondsman James Thomas, a barber in St. Louis who married Antoinette Rutgers, the daughter of Pelagie Rutgers, the wealthiest black woman in Missouri, amassed a fortune speculating in real estate, some of it belonging to his late mother-in-law. While continuing to work as a barber, he bought, sold, leased, rented, and mortgaged property. By the 1870s, he owned nearly two entire blocks in downtown St. Louis, rented forty-eight apartment units (thirty-eight on Rutger Street, six on Jefferson Avenue, and four on Phoenix Street), and controlled real estate as far away as Memphis and Nashville. In 1870, his assets totaled $165,000, the third largest estate controlled by a black in the South; at the height of his financial career in the 1880s Thomas's property was valued at $400,000.[31]

Thus, within a short period of ten years the configuration of the most prosperous group in the South had changed dramatically. In the Lower South, the small group of free persons of color who owned large plantations and gangs of slaves—once the richest group of Negroes in the United States—lost most of their holdings. Even in Charleston and New Orleans, where postwar economic activity quickly revived, the number and average wealth holdings of free Negroes who had been at the top of the economic pyramid dropped off sharply. By 1870, the affluent class in Louisiana and South Carolina, which had previously controlled $5,632,100 worth of real estate, 44 percent of the black-owned real property in the entire South, owned land worth only $3,851,100, slightly less than 12 percent of the total holdings. With their economic decline and the loss of their plantations came a loss of prestige and self-esteem. Within a short time they had become, as one historian has noted, a "forgotten people."

As affluent free persons of color in the Lower South found it impossible to maintain their unique status and economic standing in the postwar era, free blacks in the Upper South, especially in towns and cities, moved in increasing numbers into a group of prosperous skilled artisans and small businessmen. Perhaps the most revealing measurement of these changes was the rapid fluctuations in median real estate holdings (at the 50th percentile) and standard deviation (dispersion about the mean) in the Lower South compared with the figures for the upper states during the decade. Between 1860 and 1870, the median for Lower South blacks dropped from $1,000 to $300 while in the upper states it remained the same at $400; the standard deviation dropped from 121, or 8 times that of the upper states, to 31, or 1.5 times that in the Upper South. This leveling between the sections was in part the result of former slaves and propertyless free blacks acquiring real estate, but primarily it revealed the marked decline among the most prosperous group of antebellum free persons of color and the rise of a new group of affluent postwar blacks (see appendix 5). By 1870, approximately 1,814 blacks in the upper region had acquired at least $2,000 worth of real estate, a threefold rise

Table 20. Prosperous Blacks in the Lower South, 1860/70 (those with at least $2,000 in erph)

| State | Number | Percentage | | | Arph | Trph |
		Mulatto	Female	Urban		
Alabama	32/149	91/46	25/13	47/48	$3,691/$4,401	$118,100/$655,700
Arkansas	*/61	*/41	*/7	*/38	*/4,641	*/283,100
Florida	8/22	100/36	50/14	50/36	3,825/4,977	30,600/109,500
Georgia	13/127	92/43	46/19	92/47	3,585/3,624	46,600/460,200
Louisiana	472/510	85/79	31/27	63/57	10,311/5,730	4,867,000/2,922,400
Mississippi	13/162	77/24	31/15	38/27	4,685/5,335	60,900/864,300
South Carolina	162/206	87/48	32/12	81/56	4,723/4,508	765,100/928,700
Texas	6/41	83/41	33/10	17/24	5,133/3,134	30,800/128,500
Total	706/1,278	86/56	32/19	66/49	$8,384/$4,971	$5,919,100/$6,352,400

* = none

Prosperous Blacks in the Upper South, 1860/70 (those with at least $2,000 in erph)

| State | Number | Percentage | | | Arph | Trph |
		Mulatto	Female	Urban		
Delaware	38/103	21/21	5/10	11/31	$3,076/$4,399	$116,900/$453,100
District of Columbia	89/350	54/44	15/18	93/97	3,082/4,962	274,300/1,736,700
Kentucky	71/259	51/44	13/15	44/60	3,875/4,051	275,100/1,049,200
Maryland	167/320	27/28	7/9	17/41	3,825/4,092	638,700/1,309,300
Missouri	65/172	65/26	26/12	91/52	6,515/6,100	423,500/1,049,200
North Carolina	32/89	91/39	6/15	13/43	5,538/3,238	177,200/288,200
Tennessee	56/292	61/36	21/9	50/29	4,780/4,011	267,700/1,171,200
Virginia	101/229	59/51	25/14	47/47	3,601/3,837	363,700/878,700
Total	619/1,814	49/38	15/13	46/54	$4,099/$4,375	$2,537,100/$7,935,600

Source: Computed from USMSPC, 1860, 1870.

in a decade, and a figure that now exceeded the number of affluent Negroes in the Lower South by a substantial margin. Compared with whites, with twenty-two out of every one hundred families at this wealth level, even in the Upper South this group remained tiny, with only about one-half percent of the region's black families having acquired such wealth, but as the following table demonstrates a remarkable shift among upper-wealth level blacks had occurred in only ten years.[32]

A New Black Economic Elite in the Rural South

Between the 1870s and 1915, the rapid changes that had occurred as a result of the Civil War slowed considerably. In the Lower South, the decline of the antebellum affluent class, especially in rural areas, gave way to the rise of a new economic elite, one increasingly urban and with its roots in slavery. In the Upper South, the surge into the upper-wealth group stabilized, and a new economic upper class, though with a higher proportion of former free blacks than in the lower states, became predominately urban and largely ex-slave, or of slave ancestry. By the late 1880s and 1890s, the Lower-Upper South dichotomy, so important in understanding affluent blacks during the pre- and early postwar eras, had nearly disappeared. In both regions prosperous blacks were largely urban, male, and of mixed-racial-slave-ancestry; they engaged in the same types of economic activities as wholesalers, retailers, undertakers, manufacturers, real estate speculators, contractors, builders, and large-scale farmers; and they had begun to establish new businesses and economic enterprises catering to a black clientele. While some of their values and attitudes remained much the same as their antebellum predecessors, especially with regard to property ownership, educating their children, and seeking amicable relations with whites, few of them sought to separate themselves from other blacks, or demonstrated the same class-conscious attitudes as had affluent free persons of color.

While historians have sketched, at least in outline form, some of the changes that were occurring among the most prosperous blacks in the South during the late nineteenth and early twentieth centuries, few scholars have attempted to analyze these changes from the perspective of black wealth holding. During a period of growing racial violence and hostility how did some blacks continue to acquire substantial amounts of wealth? What changes occurred in rural areas? in towns and cities? How and why did the differences in various sections of the South become increasingly less important? What were the attitudes of prosperous blacks toward becoming involved in politics, assisting their less fortunate brethren, involving themselves in various ways with whites? How did they achieve their high economic standing? In short, what was the profile of prosperous blacks in the South during this latter period, and how and why did it differ from previous periods? To answer these questions, as previously noted, the pages that follow will examine the entire South, focusing on a small group of prosperous Negroes who acquired the bulk of their estates during and after the 1870s.

In the rural South, the rapid decline of affluent free persons of color during the postwar years represented the most precipitous shift among upper-wealth-level blacks during the nineteenth century. By the 1870s and 1880s, the families of the once prosperous free Negro farmers and planters had virtually disappeared from the landholding class. By the early twentieth century, among the most prosperous farmers in the South, only one, strawberry farmer Joseph Noisette, who clung tenaciously to the original sixteen acres he had inherited from his white grandfather, remained as a wealthy landholder. In most areas of Virginia, North Carolina, South Carolina, and Louisiana, where free Negro farmers had once owned large farms or plantations, black tenant farmers and sharecroppers eked out an existence on small plots of infertile soil, suffering from the vagaries of the market and the exploitation of white landholders. By 1910, in Natchitoches Parish, Louisiana, where once the Metoyer, Rocques, Lecomte, and other families controlled vast plantations, and large amounts of property, a total of only 469 blacks owned farmland—compared with 2,169 share tenants, 179 cash tenants, and 46 "share-cash" tenants— and their plots averaged only twenty-six "improved" acres apiece. Among those who owned their farms outright the total value of their land was only $237,481, less than the value of the holdings controlled by free persons of color prior to the war.[33]

Despite this decline, during the closing decades of the nineteenth century the affluent antebellum group was slowly being replaced by another group of prosperous Negro farmers. They were most often former slaves who had gradually accumulated their acreage over a period of many years, sometimes decades, until eventually they had acquired substantial land holdings. Former North Carolina slave William Mangum labored for sixteen years mauling fence rails, digging wells, and stringing cotton baskets before saving enough to purchase his first thirty-nine-acre farm in 1881 for $400. Planting cotton, fruits, vegetables, and tobacco, Mangum sold homemade wine and beer, while marketing lumber. Gradually adding to his holdings, by the early twentieth century his farm was the envy of many of his white neighbors.[34] Following emancipation, Tennessee freedman Benjamin Carr did farm work for $30 a year before acquiring a small tract of land and two mules. Three decades later he owned a 400-acre farm near Hartsville, complete with pastures, fruit orchards, and herds of horses, mules, sheep, cattle, and hogs. It took Anthony Crawford, a farmer near Abbeville, South Carolina, nearly as long to acquire 427 acres of "the prettiest cotton land in the county." He did so, one observer said, "by dint of hard work and thrift." "I is a nigger what has sure been prosperous in my life," Prince Johnson, a former Mississippi slave, declared late in his life, explaining how he had gradually acquired 360 acres of Delta land, 60 hogs, 30 head of cattle, and 14 mules. Johnson had marketed 125 bales of cotton each year.[35] Another ex-Mississippi slave, Scott Bond, who had moved to Arkansas during the 1860s, worked as a plow hand, woodcutter, wood hauler, and tenant farmer for more than a decade before purchasing his first tract of land.[36] "I worked from can't to can't—from 'can't see in the mornin'' till 'can't see at night,'" he explained, and eventually expanded his holdings until his farm, located in the St. Francis River valley forty miles west of Memphis, was the envy of his white neighbors.[37] Most other prosperous Negro farmers in the South— Virginia's James A. Field, Tennessee's H. W. Key, South Carolina's John Stokes Thorne, Georgia's Elbert Head, and Alabama's Thomas Ruffin—recounted similar stories. "I have worked hard for the past 35 years or more," one black planter in Mississippi said, "and farming has yielded me good returns."[38]

But it took more than working from daybreak to dusk for blacks to earn "good returns" as farmers during a period of declining farm prices, rising interest rates, and increasing racial unrest. While most of these farmers planted a cash crop, primarily tobacco or cotton, they also diversified their holdings by cultivating various other crops and raising herds of livestock. South Carolina plantation owner Jonas W. Thomas, known as the "Cotton King of Marlboro County," not only planted several hundred of acres of cotton each spring, but also harvested corn, vegetables, tobacco, "some garden truck," while raising horses, mules, cattle, and hogs. Another South Carolina planter, Lewis Duckett, who owned a 796-acre plantation near Newberry, harvested in 1881, 61 bales of cotton, 1,200 bushels of corn, 800 bushels of oats, and boasted a herd of cattle, ten milk cows, four yearlings, and twenty-five hogs. In the heart of rural Georgia, a region described by W. E. B. Du Bois as "forlorn and forsaken," Cody Bryant of Jasper County, acclaimed as "one of the richest colored farmers in the United States," harvested in 1905, 415 bales of cotton, 4,000 bushels of corn, 1,200 bushels of wheat, 900 bushels of oats, 1,000 bushels of potatoes, and 475 bushels of peas, and produced 6,335 gallons of syrup. Bryant employed twenty black wage hands on his 1,650-acre estate. Deal Jackson, of Dougherty County, Georgia, who marketed the first bales of cotton east of the Mississippi for fourteen consecutive years, tended large herds of livestock and planted oats, corn, and vegetables. Even Du Bois was impressed by this "great, broad shouldered, handsome black man (called "Jack Delson" in *The Souls of Black Folk*), intelligent and jovial," the most prosperous Negro farmer in the region.[39]

Several successful rural blacks devoted their farms almost exclusively to producing fruits and vegetables, or raising poultry and livestock. District of Columbia truck farmer Lewis Jefferson, who began operations in the 1880s, soon employed "a great army of colored people" to transport his fresh vegetables to market. Tennessee freedman Lewis Winter, who began after the war selling eggs and poultry in Davidson County, was described in 1889 as the richest Negro in the state with real estate worth $70,000, "to say nothing of his bank account." A few years later, he owned the largest business of its kind in the entire South, shipping sixty-five boxcar loads of poultry and produce to New York and Philadelphia during one six-month period. Another Tennessee black, Philip Nicholson, competed successfully with Italian truck farmers in Shelby County for thirty-five years, amassing a considerable fortune in the process.[40] In 1905, Florida farmer J. D. McDuffy, who owned 800 acres near Ocala, shipped 101 carloads of cantaloupes, watermelons, tomatoes, cabbage, and other fruits and vegetables to the North. He also owned seventy head of horses, a large herd of cattle, hundreds of hogs, a slaughterhouse, and a packing establishment, employing forty-six hands year around. Former Texas slave Daniel Webster Wallace, who began in 1885 as a homesteader in Mitchell County, eventually became one of the largest cattle ranchers in his area and acquired more than 10,000 acres of pasture land.[41]

This economic diversity among prosperous rural blacks could also be seen in the variety of rural businesses they established. Several started country stores, erected gin houses, and acquired sawmills. Others owned blacksmith shops, grist mills, and mercantile firms. One farmer, E. F. Scott, of Clifton Forge, in western Virginia, owned eighteen rental houses and lots, a Negro hotel, a coal yard, and an amusement hall, while nearby William Hamilton Johnson, of Baynesville, ran a grocery store, and invested heavily in walnut forests. During the 1880s, Johnson started a business shipping walnut logs to Germany, and though the business failed in 1896, he started it again a few years later, and, after acquiring several schooners, expanded his operations into Maryland. Prior to moving to Massachusetts in 1907, North Carolina Negro George Blacknall, who lived at Port Cross Roads in Franklin County, conducted what was described as "the largest contracting and building business of any colored man in [the state]." Besides his truck farm, Lewis Jefferson managed the *Jane Mosely*, a Potomac River tourist boat for blacks, acquired several houses and lots in the District of Columbia, and started a fertilizer business. Jonas Thomas purchased a mercantile store and built a hotel in nearby Bennettsville. "I have a reputation," he boasted, "of owning the best Negro hotel in the state of South Carolina." J. T. Henderson, who farmed 900 acres in De Soto Parish, Louisiana, ran a wood yard and manufactured soft drinks for local consumption. It was indeed unusual for those who acquired substantial farmlands in the rural South during the late nineteenth century to concentrate on a single crop or even a single rural enterprise.[42] Most engaged in a wide range of economic activities.

Several of these prosperous farmers and planters were also politicians. Slave-born John Roy Lynch, who became a Mississippi congressman, purchased his first parcel of land in Natchez, in 1869, at the age of twenty-one. In subsequent years, he acquired eleven more city lots, and four plantations. Blanche Kelso Bruce, a former slave who served in the United States Senate, acquired a Mississippi plantation occupying 640 acres in Bolivar County. In addition, Bruce speculated in town lots in Floreyville (later Rosedale), Mississippi, and purchased a house in the District of Columbia. Florida Congressman Josiah Walls paid $5,620 in 1870 for Harrison's Landing Plantation in Alachua County (named after a former Confederate general) and later added 4,000 acres to his original purchase. Alabama Congressman James T. Rapier was an active businessman when not engaging in political canvasses and the duties of office. During the 1870s, Rapier rented or leased seven plantations in Lowndes County (near Montgomery). Louisiana State Representative Theophile T. Allain, the son of a white planter and a slave woman, was a highly successful merchant and plantation owner in West Baton Rouge and Iberville parishes. These planter-politicians were men of substantial business acumen. Indeed, the same characteristics that led to success in the turbulent political contests of the day—shrewd judgment, foresight, and courage—were also needed for economic advancement. In addition, most of them had formed alliances with prominent white Re-

1. Mercantile firm owned by Scott Bond [portrait on next page], Madison, Ark., c. 1916. From Daniel A. Rudd and Theophilus Bond, *From Slavery to Wealth: The Life of Scott Bond* (Madison, Ark.: Journal Printing Co., 1917), p. 239.

2. Richard B. Hudson (1866–?), coal dealer, Selma, Ala., and wife, Irene, daughters E. Leola (on Irene's lap) and Bernice, c. 1906. From Booker T. Washington, *The Negro in Business* (Chicago: Hertel, Jenkins, and Co., 1907; reprint ed., AMS Press, 1971), following p. 236.

3. Scott Bond (1852–c. 1940), Madison, Ark., merchant farmer, c. 1909. Hartshorn, p. 426. (Unless otherwise stated, all photographs are from W. N. Hartshorn, ed., *An Era of Progress and Promise, 1863–1910* [Boston: Priscilla Publishing Co., 1910].)

4. John Edward Bush (c. 1856–1916), banker and realtor, Little Rock, Ark., c. 1909. Hartshorn, p. 449.

5. Home of John Merrick, founder of North Carolina Mutual Life Insurance Company, Durham, N.C., c. 1910. From Walter Weare, *Black Businesses in the New South: A Social History of the North Carolina Mutual Life Insurance Company* (Urbana: University of Illinois Press, 1973), following p. 148.

6. Alonzo Franklin Herndon (c. 1858–1927), barber and insurance company founder, Atlanta, Ga., c. 1909. Hartshorn, p. 500.

7. John Mitchell, Jr. (1863–1929), banker and editor, Richmond, Va., c. 1909. Hartshorn, p. 437.

8. James Carroll Napier (1845–1940), banker and realtor, Nashville, Tenn., c. 1909. Hartshorn, p. 415.

9. Anthony Crawford (1865–1916), farmer, Abbeville, S.C., c. 1915. From Roy Nash, "The Lynching of Anthony Crawford." *The Independent* 88 (December 11, 1916).

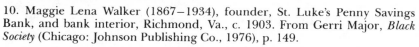

10. Maggie Lena Walker (1867–1934), founder, St. Luke's Penny Savings Bank, and bank interior, Richmond, Va., c. 1903. From Gerri Major, *Black Society* (Chicago: Johnson Publishing Co., 1976), p. 149.

publicans, both northerners and southerners, and found it easier to deal with them in matters other than party politics.[43]

During the first generation of freedom a remarkable change had occurred among the most prosperous blacks in the rural areas of the South. Now widely scattered—in thirteen states and forty-six counties—they were, for the most part, former slaves or the children of slaves who had painstakingly added to their holdings over many years. Even the few who had been born free prior to the war, or had been children of free parents, usually began their ascent to prosperity with little or no property during the immediate postwar period. Compared to the size of the rural population, freedmen and women and their children were far less likely to accumulate large landholdings during the early decades after the Civil War than had free persons of color during the antebellum era. Indeed, the actual number of those with holdings of $20,000 or more, while dropping in the 1860s and 1870s, rose to the prewar level only by the early 1900s. During the entire period only approximately fifty-five blacks in rural areas of the South entered this large landholding class. Among them only fourteen controlled assets in excess of $100,000, while 58 percent of the group owned land and other property worth from $20,000 to $49,999. If population increases and land appreciation are taken into account, the group's size and wealth holdings remained much the same in 1900 as they had been during the antebellum period. This reflects the overwhelming difficulties confronting even the most ambitious former slaves as well as the unique and privileged position of affluent free persons of color. Despite this, the property accumulations of this tiny group of postwar blacks served as silent testimony to their extraordinary achievements.

A New Black Economic Elite in the Urban South

For ambitious and enterprising blacks the city offered many more opportunities than the countryside. Between 1870 and 1915, though the South's urban black population grew with each passing decade, it never surpassed 22 percent of the total. Yet, during the same period, fully 77 percent of the wealthiest blacks lived in towns and cities. The proportion was slightly higher in the Upper than in the Lower South, and there was, among them, a slightly higher proportion of former free blacks than in rural areas, but in both regions, and among former slaves and former free persons, cities became the centers for the small black economic elite. During the 1870s and early 1880s, some blacks continued to engage in the same types of businesses and service trades that had allowed a small group of antebellum free Negroes to achieve a measure of prosperity, operating livery stables, grocery stores, dry goods establishments, and barbershops. With the expansion of black property ownership and the rising tide of Jim Crow laws in subsequent years, however, Negro entrepreneurs began to exploit new markets among fellow blacks. They established undertaking, insurance, manufacturing, banking, and construction businesses, and offered professional services. Yet, even at the dawn of the twentieth century, some of the most prosperous urban blacks operated businesses as wholesalers, retailers, contractors, builders, and restaurateurs catering to whites. In either case, blacks with energy, foresight, and business acumen managed to take advantage of the economic opportunities in an urban environment.

The occupational transition from the antebellum to the postbellum periods was symbolized by the decline among prosperous barbers. In 1860, among realty owners in the South with at least $5,000 worth of property, 5 percent were barbers, and among those with at least $20,000, 10 percent practiced the same trade. By 1870, while the proportion with more than $5,000 remained about the same, those with the larger amount dropped from 10 to 5 percent. Concentrated more in the Upper than in the Lower South, in both regions they catered to white clienteles, often well-known white businessmen and politicians. During the 1870s and later decades, the number and proportion of prosperous Negro barbers dropped off sharply to less than 1.7 percent of the most prosperous group. Former free Negro John A. Fernandis continued to operate a shop in Baltimore that he had taken over from his Brazilian-born father sixteen years before the Civil War, expanding his operations and increasing his clientele during the postwar era, while Alfred Billingslea of Montgomery, Alabama, started a shop after the war and by the 1880s had amassed a small fortune. A few others, including Atlanta's Alonzo Herndon and St. Louis's James Thomas, maintained barbering establishments while engaging in other economic activities. But increasingly, the "old time barbershop," run by a black and catering to whites, became an anachronism in the New South, as prosperous urban blacks moved away from personal service enterprises to other types of business endeavors.[44]

Beginning in the late 1880s, and continuing into the early twentieth century, Negro businessmen increasingly sought to exploit new markets among fellow Negroes. This change was perhaps nowhere more visible than in the proliferation of prosperous Negro undertakers. Prior to the Civil War there had been only one large undertaking establishment in the entire South, Pierre Casenave's New Orleans company, and even during the 1870s, most of those who started such businesses did so as a side occupation. Former free Negro John W. Locks ran a "hack and funeral business" in Baltimore, but the bulk of his $30,000 estate at the time of his death in 1884 had been derived from other business ventures. By the 1890s, however, virtually every large urban area in the South boasted a large-scale undertaking establishment. In some cities, including the District of Columbia, Richmond, Atlanta, Mobile, Memphis, and St. Louis, several companies competed against each other for the business that had previously been the responsibility of relatives, church groups, burial societies, or fraternal associations. In some respects the career of William Claud Gordon of St. Louis was typical. When he established his company in 1894, at the age of twenty-six, he had very little capital and virtually no entrepreneurial experience, having worked as a quarryhand, domestic servant, and Pullman porter. Within a decade, he had become one of the wealthiest Negroes in St. Louis, and his gross returns exceeded $43,666 annually. Advertising rolling stock "second to none," a beautiful mortuary chapel, and the most "up-to-date" embalming facilities, Gordon had capitalized on providing a much needed service to blacks in his community.[45]

In other areas besides undertaking urban blacks sought to exploit new markets among their brethren. Two of the potentially most profitable were banking and insurance. Following the establishment of the Capital Savings Bank in the District of Columbia, and the Savings Bank of the Grand Fountain of the United Order of True Reformers in Richmond in 1888, the first black banks, Negroes opened financial institutions in a dozen other cities by the early 1900s. These included, among others, William Pettiford's Alabama Penny Savings and Loan Company in Birmingham, James Napier's One Cent Savings Bank in Nashville, and Charles Banks's Bank of Mound Bayou in Mississippi. In insurance, the three founders of the North Carolina Mutual Life Insurance Company—John Merrick, Dr. Aaron McDuffie Moore, and Charles Clinton Spaulding—had all been successful businessmen in Durham prior to launching the first black-owned operational legal reserve insurance company in the nation. As their company expanded selling policies to blacks between 1898 and 1910, other black entrepreneurs founded insurance companies in Atlanta, Birmingham, Mobile, New Orleans, and other cities.[46]

The rising tide of legal segregation and the increasing profits of a few successful Negro companies presented blacks with other opportunities. Baltimore entrepreneur John Henry Murphy, who ran a feed and produce business during the 1870s, purchased a printing plant and acquired, in 1899, the *Afro-American*, which became one of the most successful black newspapers in the country. District of Columbia architect and builder John Anderson Lankford designed and constructed a number of large buildings for blacks, including Richmond's True Reformers Hall. The building was the headquarters for the United Order of True Reformers, founded in 1881 by former slave William Washington Browne, who had amassed a fortune providing sick and death benefits to freedmen and women. Another Richmond fraternal order, St. Luke's, was founded in 1903 by Maggie Lena Walker, who served as president of St. Luke's Bank and Trust Company. Within a short time, Walker, one of only two women among the most prosperous urban blacks, employed 145 field workers and 54 clerks. In other towns and cities, blacks established amusement parks, restaurants, saloons, theaters, racetracks, and retail or wholesale operations catering to a black clientele. In Louisville, restaurateur Thom Cole not only catered to Negroes in his eating establishment, but owned a saloon and several entertainment enterprises, including the *Louisville Giants*, a black baseball team. Similarly, Knoxville's Calvin F. Johnson owned two popular saloons (one with a partner named Scott) and a racetrack. Former slave Richard Henry Boyd, a Nashville minister, established the National Baptist Publishing Board in 1896. Manufacturing and distributing church books, furniture, Sunday school magazines, and Negro dolls, within eight years he employed 132 workers, boasted company assets exceeding $300,000, and oversaw one of the most successful black enterprises in the South.[47]

The careers of two businessmen illustrate how a few of the most enterprising blacks could reap substantial profits from exploiting a market among their brethren. Slave-born Robert Reed Church, the son of a white steamboat owner, opened a saloon and billiard hall in Memphis, shortly after the Civil War. Frugal and hard working, he saved large amounts of cash, and when the city was depopulated following the 1878 and 1879 yellow fever epidemics, he invested heavily in city lots, a risky speculation that paid off handsomely when property values rose as the city returned to normal. By the early twentieth century, he had acquired an amusement park for blacks on Beale Street, described as "one of the most attractive [areas] in the city." With its large auditorium, Church's Park quickly became a center for black political activity. Church also sponsored an annual Thanksgiving supper for the city's poor blacks, and while maintaining amicable relations with leading whites, he provided financial assistance to local political aspirants. At the time of his death in 1912, at the age of seventy-three, his estate had reached nearly $1,000,000, the second largest for a black in the South.[48]

A second slave-born black entrepreneur, Alonzo Franklin Herndon, worked as a hired hand for his former master in Walton County, Georgia, during the early years after the war. Later, he moved to Covington, hired out as a barber, and in 1882, traveled to Atlanta, where he found work at the city's Markham House hotel. After a fire destroyed the hotel in 1896, he established his own barbershops; and in 1904, he opened a magnificent establishment on Peachtree Street, complete with twenty-five chairs and forty employees. He was already one of the most prosperous blacks in Georgia when, in 1905 at the age of forty-seven, he founded Atlanta Life, which eventually became one of the most successful black life insurance companies in the nation. Contemporaries described him (and Church) as hard-driving, astute, personable, honest, intelligent, and shrewd. By the time of his death in 1927, he had accumulated personal assets, including large amounts of urban real estate, valued at more than $500,000.[49]

Yet some of the most successful businesses—approximately one out of four—continued to cater to whites, or to whites and blacks. Among the thirty-two businesses in Williamsburg, Virginia, owned by blacks or whites, in 1895, only one equaled and none surpassed Samuel Harris's mercantile store, which boasted some of the town's leading white citizens as customers. Following Harris's death his wife kept the business at the forefront. Among the 1,125 concerns listed by R. G. Dun and Company in the city of Jacksonville, Florida, only 53 were rated as being worth more than Charles Anderson's fish and produce company, while Berry O'Kelly, a Raleigh, North Carolina, builder and brickmaker, boasted an "Estimated Pecuniary Strength" which put him among the ten wealthiest businessmen in the city. Both men catered primarily to whites. Similarly, Atlanta contractor Alexander Hamilton, Selma, Alabama, coal dealer Richard B. Hudson, and Corpus Christi, Texas, merchant D. N. Leathers catered to both races or to whites. Most black contractors and builders, coal and wood dealers, manufacturers, and wholesalers were in the same category. One observer described Lexington, Kentucky, contractor Henry A. Tandy as one of the most successful builders in the region. Awarded the contract for the Fayette County Court House, Tandy had overseen the construction of "stately buildings and handsome residences" on nearly every main thoroughfare in the city.[50]

Clothiers Dominique, Ernest, and A. Mercier of New Orleans not only relied on a white clientele, but also employed white workers in their retail and wholesale stores. Described as "a mulatto from an old colored family," Dominique Mercier had established a small clothing store in the Crescent City before the war, and while not wealthy, he had earned a good living retailing ready-made clothing primarily to a white clientele. During the 1860s he expanded his business, and by 1870 his store and other properties were worth $15,000. Following Dominique's death in 1876, his two sons transformed their father's retail store into a wholesale outlet, specializing in hats, boots, shoes, and suits for men. By 1885, they had acquired substantial amounts of real estate, including what was known as "the Christ Church property" on Canal Street (the site of the first Protestant church in the Mississippi Valley), described by one observer as "the finest business block in the city." "The Merciers who control perhaps the largest clothing business in the New Orleans, and who have a hundred or more white men in their employ," one newspaper reporter said, "are colored—true representatives of the old free people of color of [the city]." In 1895, R. G. Dun and Company rated "D. Mercier's Sons" as having good credit and estimated their "pecuniary Strength" in excess of $300,000; two decades later, the two brothers controlled assets in excess of $1,000,000, and had become the wealthiest Negroes in the South.[51]

As in rural areas, blacks who reached the upper-wealth levels during the last third of the nineteenth century engaged in a wide range of economic pursuits. Baltimore and District of Columbia property owner William E. Matthews was a lawyer, money broker, real estate agent, post office employee, mortgager, and financier. Hampton businessman R. R. Palmer, born a slave, operated a dry goods store and a carriage factory, but owned a paint shop, small printing office, and blacksmith shop. William T. Hightower of Nashville, who purchased a junkyard during the early 1880s, later became a dealer in eggs, hides, wool, feathers, and pig iron. "Not a week passes," the Nashville *Globe* observed in 1908, "that he does not make one or two car loads shipment to the Northern and eastern factories and foundries." In Sumter, South Carolina, William Trent Andrews amassed his considerable wealth as a lawyer, notary public, schoolteacher, restaurateur, insurance agent, and director of a Negro development company. For more than thirty years Charles C. Leslie operated a retail and wholesale fish, oyster, game, and poultry company in Charleston, while William Reuben Pettiford had various careers as a teacher, preacher, realty agent, and banker in Birmingham, Alabama. Other urban blacks not only established a variety of business enterprises—saloons, theaters, retail stores for lumber, coal, drugs, leather goods, furniture, and clothing, small manufactories for tin, cottonseed oil, textiles, and bricks—but also often engaged in several of these enterprises at once while maintaining a professional career.[52]

Despite this diversity, prosperous urban blacks rarely invested heavily in "liquid assets"—stocks, bonds, silver, gold, jewelry, cash, bank savings. Like their predecessors during the antebellum era, they invested the bulk of their profits in real estate. It seemed as if the assertion of one of the first Negro landholders in the South—"I know myne owne ground"—remained as dominant in the minds of blacks in the late nineteenth and early twentieth centuries as it had been among those early colonists in Virginia. Whatever the merits of such an investment strategy, affluent city Negroes found themselves wedded to the idea of landownership. District of Columbia realtor Whitefield McKinlay, besides managing properties for such well-known blacks as Archibald Grimké, Robert H. Terrell, Charles Purvis, and Robert R. Church, Sr., gradually acquired about $200,000 worth of real estate. Former slave John Merrick, who worked as a barber before founding North Carolina Mutual, gradually purchased 162 rental homes in Durham, as well as two store buildings and a thirty-three-acre tract on Goose Creek. His realty holdings were appraised at $135,310. Raleigh merchant and brick manufacturer Berry O'Kelly acquired fifty-five tracts of land in Wake County, an office building in Raleigh, and several thousand acres of farmland in Virginia, real estate worth $155,516 when it was inventoried during the Great Depression.[53] Jacksonville developer and builder J. H. Blodgett, who built 200 homes after "the great fire" in 1901, owned 121 rental houses in Duval County. In New Orleans, philanthropist Thomy Lafon, whose estate reached $413,000 during the 1890s, owned large amounts of real property, as did Walter Cohen, who controlled nearly $31,624 worth of city property. Arkansas brickmaker and later organizer of the National Order of Mosaic Templers, John E. Bush, controlled a block of buildings in the business district and fifteen rental homes in Little Rock. The largest Negro taxpayer in Texas, John Brown Bell, purchased fifty rental houses and a large store in Houston. "Seize opportunity," Bell asserted in one speech, "and buy lands."[54]

Typical of those who responded to this injunction was slave-born Wiley Jones of Pine Bluff, Arkansas, who, during his career as a barber, saloon keeper, liquor wholesaler, and amusement park owner, purchased more than 100 separate pieces of real estate. In 1904, an appraisal of his holdings in Pine Bluff and surrounding areas took three full, single-spaced pages on legal-size paper: "The North half of block one, Western Addition to the city of Pine Bluff," "Block two, Western Addition," "Fifty feet off West side lot one, block two, Taylor's addition," "Block eighteen, Reed's Addition," "50x154 feet off the East side of lot two, block thirty, Old Town," "Block four, Harrisons's Addition," "Lot three, block one, Wiley Jones Addition," and a fifty-five-acre tract known as Wiley Jones Park one mile from Main Street. Jones also owned the streetcar line to his amusement park and investment properties in Illinois, the Oklahoma Territory, and several Arkansas counties. His total estate, primarily in real property, amounted to $131,157.[55]

By the early twentieth century, most prosperous urban backs, such as Wiley Jones, had either been born in slavery or claimed slave parents. During the 1860s and early 1870s, some former free Negroes in Baltimore, the District of Columbia, Lexington, Nashville, St. Louis, and even in New Orleans and Charleston, had substantially increased their property holdings compared to the antebellum period, but by the late 1870s and 1880s most of them had passed from the scene, through either retirement or death. Only a few among them, including Baltimore's Thomas Bradford, who died in 1886 at the age of seventy-two, and District of Columbia's James Wormley, who died in 1884 at age sixty-five, were able to pass on estates large enough for their children to remain among the most prosperous group of blacks. It also seems that the children of prosperous former free blacks, except in rare cases, lacked the drive and ambition for material success that their parents possessed. The second generation was more likely to value educational and intellectual achievement. Thus, by the 1890s, only a few members of the "old elite" families remained as leading property holders. The decline was more gradual in urban than in rural areas, and in the Upper than in the Lower South, but it was observable everywhere. It could be seen in the rise of new centers for prosperous blacks—Atlanta, Jacksonville, Little Rock, Houston, Nashville, Richmond—and in the fact that by 1900, including the District of Columbia, a substantial majority of those who reached the upper-wealth levels in the urban South had direct ties to antebellum slavery.[56]

Despite this heritage, a large majority of prosperous urban Negroes from the 1870s to 1915 were of mixed racial ancestry. Some scholars have argued that during the closing decades of the nineteenth century the "black elite" was becoming increasingly dark-skinned, as former slaves and their children entered this group. This was not true for those who reached the highest wealth levels. They were most often described as mulatto, being of "mixed racial origin," or as having features generally associated with mixed ancestry—wavy hair, brown, yellow, or light skin, Caucasian features. Complete genealogical information, including color of parents, could be gathered on less than half of the group, but among them a very high proportion—65 percent—were partially white, and a remarkably high proportion—29 percent—had white fathers. Within this latter group were some of the richest Negroes in the urban South: Durham's John Merrick; Concord, North Carolina, merchant and cotton mill owner Warren Clay Coleman; Nashville pharmacist James Dallas Burrus; Memphis businessman Robert Reed Church; St. Louis barber James Thomas; Charleston physician William Dermos Crum; Atlanta dentist Roderick D. Badger and funeral director-insurance company founder David Tobias Howard; Pine Bluff capitalist Ferdinand Havis; and Houston stevedore-businessman and politician Norris Wright Cuney. They had benefited from being more assimilated than the majority of slaves as well as from the kinds of learning experiences they had received from white relatives. But unlike the prewar period, when free people of color had often inherited their property, mixed racial ancestry in later years seems to have been an asset, primarily in dealings with whites in various business undertakings. With few exceptions, the curt comment of James Thomas about the financial assistance provided him by his white father, a famous Tennessee judge, could have been repeated by most mulatto property owners during the last third of the nineteenth century: "He gave me twenty five cents once. If I was correctly informed that was all he ever did for me."[57]

Some of those who reached the upper-wealth levels, as in rural areas, took an active role in politics. During Reconstruction, a number of prominent Republican leaders, especially in the Lower South, were men of substantial wealth and property. In South Carolina, eleven members of the state's constitutional convention, including Richard Cain, Francis Cardozo, Robert Delarge, William and William J. McKinlay (father and son), of Charleston, and William Beverely Nash and Charles Wilder, of Columbia, possessed at least $5,000 worth of real estate. Twenty-two New Orleans Republican leaders, including, among others, wealthy landowners Edmond Dupuy, Bernard A. Soulié, and Aristide Mary, were in the same category.[58] After Reconstruction, prosperous blacks served on Republican state committees, gained patronage appointments as collectors of customs, internal revenue officers, and post office officials, attended local, state, and national Republican political conventions, and occasionally ran for elective office. Among the most prominent businessmen who became actively engaged in politics were Baltimore financier William Matthews, a spokesman for racial equality; Richmond editor John R. Mitchell, Jr., a city alderman; Virginia educator John Mercer Langston, who won a seat in the Fifty-first Congress; Henderson, Kentucky, merchant Aaron Cabell, who attended several national Republican conventions; Nashville banker James Napier, Langston's son-in-law, who became register of the treasury; St. Louis manufacturer John Milton Turner, who served as minister to Liberia; Charleston physician William Crum and Savannah editor John Deveaux, who became collectors of customs; Mobile undertaker Andrew N. Johnson, an internal revenue officer and Republican nominee for Congress; New Orleans saloon keeper Walter Cohen, a collector of customs; Little Rock businessmen John Bush and Mifflin Gibbs, receivers in the U.S. Land Office; and Galveston, Texas, entrepreneur Norris Cuney, collector of customs.[59]

Some of these leaders had begun their business activities as slaves, and except in New Orleans, few among them had owned large amounts of property prior to the Civil War. Most of them were hard-headed, sometimes opportunistic businessmen who entered the political arena to advance their own cause as well as to improve conditions among fellow blacks. Their prominence in the Republican party and the prestige of the offices they held not only gave them opportunities for securing loans and buying land on credit, but also provided most of them with relatively good salaries during their tenure in office. Some of these politician-entrepreneurs sustained their wealth long after retiring from the political arena, but a number of others, including South Carolina Congressman Robert Brown Elliott, Florida's Josiah Walls, Alabama's James Rapier, and Selma, Alabama, livery owner Benjamin Turner, who for many years ran the same business he had begun as a slave, died in poverty. "It is sad that his last days were clouded by debts," the Huntsville *Gazette* lamented, noting the death of Turner in 1894, "which swept away his all."[60]

Thus, in some ways, including mixed ancestry, a profile of the most prosperous Negroes in the urban South had changed little from the prewar period. But in most respects those who reached the top of the economic ladder had changed dramatically by the early twentieth century. Now engaged in a remarkable variety of business, political, and professional activities, they were largely "self-made" men who had risen from slavery to acquire large amounts of property. They were scattered in fifty-two towns and cities in fourteen states, with the largest concentrations in the District of Columbia, Richmond, Durham, Atlanta, and Nashville. Having invested heavily in urban real estate, they gradually added to their holdings as cities grew and expanded, until 53 city Negroes controlled estates in excess of $100,000, and another 133 had assets of between $20,000 and $99,999. While few among them became involved in cooperative economic ventures, a number established businesses catering to the growing markets among blacks. An increasingly smaller proportion were descendants of antebellum free Negroes, and by 1915, the number of the most prosperous urban blacks who had inherited their holdings from free ancestors could be counted on one hand. In relation to the black urban population, they remained a tiny group, but compared with rural areas and compared with affluent free persons of color before the war, prosperous urban blacks in the New South had significantly advanced their economic position.

Race Relations in the New South

Yet, despite the group's changing profile, there were continuities with the past. Like those who had achieved economic success in the generation before the Civil War, prosperous blacks during the late nineteenth and early twentieth centuries found it necessary to maintain cordial relations with dominant whites. Even with the wave of new businesses catering to blacks, most who had risen to the top had been assisted along the way by whites, had served white patrons before turning to a black clientele, or continued to rely on white customers. In North Carolina, John Merrick, a founder of the North Carolina Mutual Life Insurance Company, Richard B. Fitzgerald, who owned the brick manufacturing company, and Warren Clay Coleman, a merchant in Concord who founded the Coleman Textile Manufacturing Company, had received financial assistance, credit references, and encouragement from tobacco magnets Benjamin and Washington Duke as well as from Julian S. Carr, a well-known white businessman. When Booker T. Washington visited Durham in 1910, he noted that some of the leading Negro-owned businesses had white patrons "among their most substantial purchasers." Washington and others probably overstated or misrepresented the true picture of race relations, but their statements revealed how much importance they attached to maintaining amicable relations with the dominant race. "My relations with my white fellow-citizens are most pleasant and cordial," Texas merchant D. N. Leathers explained in 1912, "and the white men and women of [my] section respect me as an individual and trade with me and cooperate with me in civic affairs and in business." Another black explained that this was also true in Mississippi where the "better class of Negroes and the better class of whites are coming closer together on purely economic grounds."[61]

There was also a continuity of many shared values and attitudes among prosperous blacks. When Andrew Bryan said in 1800 that he had, through diligence, hard work, and piety, done very well in acquiring "worldly comforts," including a home, rental buildings, and a fifty-six-acre farm, he was articulating the beliefs of his counterparts a century later, who also believed that frugality, patience, hard work, diligence, fortitude, education, and piety were the keys to a better life. Even in the midst of race riots, lynchings, racial violence, and brutal murders, prosperous Negroes exalted these precepts. In 1900, Chattanooga businessman G. W. Franklin told a convention of fellow blacks that "Character building should commence early," "An honest man is the noblest work of God," "Idleness, not work, is the curse of mankind," and "All who accomplish much in any sphere of life have been noted for their perseverance." Franklin and others had established businesses, acquired real estate and other property, and founded black institutions by relying on the same character traits as whites who had achieved economic success. They truly believed, like other Americans of their day, that a life of personal sacrifice, self-improvement, and upright behavior would be rewarded by economic success. "By always giving close attention to the minor details, ever striving to give satisfaction (believing that a satisfied customer is the very best advertisement to be had) and above all things, by dealing in a straight forward, honest and upright manner," Montgomery, Alabama, grocer and confectioner Victor Tulane said in 1907, "I have succeeded in gaining the respect and good will of the public at large, together with the support of the majority of the colored people and many of the white[s] of my city."[62]

"Respect and good will" from whites, as had been the case prior to the Civil War, however, were fragile commodities, even for those who had achieved economic success. Prosperous blacks were expected to act deferentially toward whites, to address white men as "Mister" and white women as "Miss" or "Missus," and to respond to "Uncle," "Boy," and "nigger." They were expected to step aside for whites when entering buildings and walking along sidewalks, to eschew politics, and to avoid direct contact with white women. Thus the characteristics that successful blacks brought to their economic activities—ambition, drive, aggressiveness, acquisitiveness, self-confidence, sometimes arrogance—had to be quickly reversed to humility and submission when dealing with the dominant race. Whatever such a transformation did to one's self-esteem, most prosperous blacks were able to quickly change their personalities when dealing with whites. Scott Bond, who spoke perfect English despite a lack of formal schooling, usually addressed whites in dialect. On one occasion when a business-

man from the North addressed him as "Mr. Bond," he quickly replied
that in Arkansas addressing a black man in such a manner was not
appropriate. "Why?" the gentleman queried. "In de fus' place you
know you don' mean it," Bond replied. "And if you does you can't
afford to call niggers 'mister' in dis part of de country. You must be
one of dem 'publicans fum de North." "Well, what'll I call you then?"
the stranger asked. "Call me cross-eyed nigger," Bond, who suffered
from strabismus, replied, "dat's what dy says behind my back. And if
you wants to do beter'n dat—why call me Unc Scott—dey calls me
Unc Scott round hyer."[63]

As had been the case during the antebellum period those who refused to act respectfully and deferentially toward whites could find
themselves in precarious circumstances. Merely becoming involved in
politics, or accumulating significant amounts of property, or owning
successful and highly competitive businesses could be deemed disre-
spectful to certain elements of the white population. In some instances these successful blacks received threats against their lives, had
their businesses destroyed, or suffered assaults and beatings. In September 1878, Raford Blount of Natchitoches Parish, Louisiana, a
Baptist minister and large landowner who was active in politics, was
driven from the parish by a band of armed whites when he refused
to stop "agitating" among the freedmen. A few years later, William
Mangum, the hard-driving North Carolina farmer, was buried alive
by a group of whites. Mangum's life was saved when his dog brought
the family to the spot where he had been interred. Others were not
so fortunate. When three Memphis blacks, Thomas Moss, Calvin Mc-
Dowell, and William Stewart, opened a grocery store across the street
from a white grocer and began taking business away their competitor,
they precipitated what one author described as a "minor riot." In
1892, an angry mob took the three proprietors from jail and murdered them. During the bloody race riot in Atlanta in 1906, when
twenty-five Negroes lost their lives, rampaging whites went out of
their way to attack property owners and destroy black homes. "The
negroes with property, then, those who had children to bring up and
who desired to live in peace for their sakes, if not for their own, sold
what they had, at great sacrifice, and went to other more friendly
cities," a correspondent for the New York *Evening Post* reported a few
weeks after the riot. Joining the exodus were some of the city's most
affluent blacks.[64]

Their desire to "live in peace" and care for their children could be
seen in the emphasis they placed on education. During the 1870s and
later, only a small proportion of those who rose to the top in wealth

accumulations remained illiterate, mostly rural landowners who had been born in slavery. An increasing number finished high school or its equivalent, and fully 36 percent had attended college for at least a few years. A few lawyers, physicians, teachers, and race leaders who owned large amounts of property were among the best-educated members of their communities. Even though expending most of their time and energy acquiring wealth and property, they, as had free Negroes, placed a great emphasis on providing an education for their children. Benjamin Montgomery not only hired a tutor for his daughter, Mary Virginia, but also urged her to undertake a daily regimen of self-study. "I read Well's *Self Culture*," Mary noted in her diary in 1872, adding in subsequent entries: "I have spent my leisure studying Phrenology," "I re[a]d *Self Education* tonight," "I busied myself studying *Ten Commandments*," "After completing my office work [she was a clerk in her father's mercantile firm] I resumed my study of ancient and sacred history," "Pa and the remainder of us engaged ourselves in the Tribune, Times, and Politics until midnight," "Pa brought out a short essay on Science and Theology. After breakfast we talked, read or sang, as best suited our feelings."

Other parents sent their children to primary, secondary, and post-secondary schools, to normal colleges, and to universities—Lincoln, Oberlin, and Wilberforce in the North, Hampton, Tuskegee, Fisk, Atlanta, and Howard in the South. One well-to-do Arkansas Negro boasted that he had not only educated his own six children, three of whom had graduated from college, but had also paid for the schooling of his younger brothers and sisters as well as his wife's brothers and sisters and one adopted son—"fifteen in all." Atlanta grocer and merchant Willis Murphy, described as one of the richest blacks in the city, paid for the college educations of his five grandchildren (after his thirty-nine-year-old son and business partner had been committed to an insane asylum), sending them to Oberlin in Ohio, and Atlanta University. Robert R. Church educated his son, Robert Jr., with private tutors and in an Episcopal parochial school in Memphis before sending him to Oberlin College. Not only did they provide for the schooling of their children, grandchildren, and various relatives, but they also often advised them to enter the professions rather than business.[65]

In spite of these shared values and the continued relationship they maintained "on purely economic grounds," most prosperous blacks separated themselves from whites in other areas of their lives. While there were exceptions, they usually lived in black neighborhoods, or on all-black blocks. During the 1870s, they sometimes lived side-by-side with poorer blacks, or as was the case for livery keeper Robert Johnson in Lexington's Third Ward, next to white brothels, but gradually they moved to more affluent segregated areas—Druid Hill Avenue in Baltimore, LeDroit Park in the Northwest District of Columbia, College Street in Richmond, Fayetteville Street in Durham, Chestnut Street in Louisville, and Auburn Avenue in Atlanta. Observing this trend, one St. Louis resident said in 1904 that the most "cultured" Negroes were "withdrawing more and more into separate localities." In addition, prosperous Negroes joined black fraternal organizations, attended black churches, socialized with other blacks, and formed black business associations. One such organization, the National Negro Business League, founded in 1900 by Booker T. Washington, expanded rapidly until there were several hundred local leagues in various communities. Except for occasional financial transactions, journalist Ray Stannard Baker observed in 1907 after touring the South, prosperous Negroes (which he called "the new negro") and the "better class of whites" (which he called "the new southerner") rarely engaged in interracial discussions or even exchanged views. It were "as if they lived in different countries."[66]

It would have been perhaps more accurate to say that the hardening of racial animosities made it extremely difficult for either group to cross the color barrier. Even after 1890 there were exceptions to Baker's stark portrayal. Most prosperous Negroes continued to have economic dealings with whites; a few joined white organizations—John Mitchell was the lone black member of the American Bankers Association—attended white churches, and continued to reside in predominately white neighborhoods. In 1908, one Nashville realtor noted that a few well-off blacks could be found even in "the most exclusive neighborhoods" adjacent to Vanderbilt University, despite strenuous efforts by whites to keep them out. Several wealthy Negroes even socialized with whites. Former United States Senator Blanche K. Bruce, who married Josephine Wilson, the beautiful daughter of a prominent mulatto dentist in Cleveland, Ohio, gained acceptance in white society circles in the District of Columbia. The light-skinned, well-educated Bruce and his lovely wife entertained white guests in their home, attended the white First Congregational Church, with its antebellum antislavery tradition, and mingled with prominent politicians, businessmen, and government officials. On one occasion, during a grand tour of the Continent, the Bruces enjoyed the company of former President Ulysses Grant during a stay in Paris. At various times, P. B. S. Pinchback, a successful businessman and for a brief period acting governor of Louisiana during the impeachment trial of

Henry Clay Warmoth, socialized with whites in New Orleans and the District of Columbia, though unlike Bruce he did not gain entry into white society. "To all intents and purposes he was an educated, well-to-do, congenial white man, with but a few drops of Negro blood," Du Bois said of Pinchback, "which he did not stoop to deny, as so many of his fellow whites did."[67]

Yet these were rare exceptions. Most prosperous blacks recognized that their future was in large measure tied to the future of the black masses. Even those who relied on a white clientele privately felt the injustice of racial oppression in the South. Some years after the event, Francis Grimké recalled how James Wormley, during a supper conversation with Pan-African leader and president of Liberian University Edward Wilmot Blyden, had expressed himself in the "most forceful language" and "got wrought up" when discussing the economic and political plight of blacks. Others privately criticized the federal government for failing to protect blacks from violence and intimidation, decried the exclusion of blacks from voting and political participation, and lamented the economic condition of black tenant farmers. Someone seemingly as accommodationist as John Merrick, who had worked as barber for whites and had personal contacts with the leading men of Durham, expressed his disgust at the ways in which whites oppressed blacks. Merrick "continually expended time and money to promote the interest of colored people," a friend noted, "aiding them in securing homes and in establishing organizations of protection." "No matter how intelligent, wealthy, or prominent the Negro may be," one disgusted black said in 1899, "he is made to feel his inferiority of race in the presence of Southern people."[68]

As a result, despite public professions, some well-to-do Negroes became angry, bitter, and hostile about conditions in the South. A few became relatively militant, especially in view of the hostile racial climate. During his annual Emancipation Day speeches, Savannah's John H. Deveaux expressed his hope that the two races could work out their problems together, but at the same time he urged Savannah blacks to boycott white businesses if they felt discriminated against. Known simply as "Bill" to his white customers, William Trent Andrews, who managed a popular restaurant in Sumter, South Carolina, for more than thirty years, bitterly resented how he and other blacks were treated. "Conditions are growing damned near intolerable," he confessed, "and I am tired of it." Sometimes what they said in public masked their inner feelings. "The white people, as a whole, take pride in encouraging and uplifting their brother in black, both by advice, their counsel and money," John Bush of Little Rock said in one address. "The two races are living side by side, each striving as best it can to make the very best citizens." Whatever the motives of Bush and others for making such statements—to calm the rising tide of white hostility, allay white jealousy about their economic achievements, perhaps actually hoping to improve race relations—to a friend he bitterly complained that it was "virtually impossible to please the white man." The future for blacks in the South would always be bleak, a struggle for manhood with nothing to look forward to but "death, hell and the grave."[69]

These caustic words symbolized the growing disgust of those who had reached the highest wealth levels in the South. It seemed that no matter how prosperous they became, no matter how much they accepted American values of hard work, initiative, and enterprise, no matter how much property and wealth they accumulated, and no matter how much they struggled to enter the mainstream of American life, they would always remain something less than a man in the minds of whites. Yet remarkable changes had occurred among the most prosperous group of blacks by the early twentieth century. The old antebellum economic elite had virtually disappeared, and in its place was a tiny new group, aggressive, highly educated, articulate, and independent. They were less class-conscious and color-conscious than their predecessors; they engaged in a far wider range of economic activities; and they lived in virtually every southern state. Many of them were either children of emancipated blacks or had experienced slavery themselves, and while a few sought to distance themselves from their less fortunate brethren, most felt a compassion for oppressed blacks and a significant number worked in various ways for racial uplift. Struggling against race hatred, segregation, oppressive laws, and economic barriers, their personal achievements made a mockery of the notion of racial inferiority. If at times they lauded the South as a land of opportunity, where even former slaves could rise to wealth and prosperity, they could never rid themselves of the gnawing fear that the slightest misjudgment could result in violent retribution.

Epilogue

Nestled on the fringe of the Piedmont near the Georgia border, the small town of Abbeville, South Carolina, was best known for being the site of one of the first secessionist meetings and the location of the final gathering of the Confederate cabinet. Thus the town was sometimes referred to as "the cradle and grave of the Confederacy." The feeling of pride in the Lost Cause was still strong among many residents on the morning of October 21, 1916, as Anthony Crawford guided his wagon slowly into town, along the broad public square, to the mercantile store of W. D. Barksdale, a local businessman who purchased cotton seed from nearby farmers and sold them various items on credit. Crawford was well known to Barksdale, indeed to nearly every resident of the county where blacks slightly outnumbered whites in a total population of about 15,000. Not only was Crawford the wealthiest black farmer in the county, but his holdings also comprised nearly 10 percent of the total property owned by all blacks in the area. He was one of only a few hundred Negro landowners (compared with more than 3,000 tenant farmers) and had established himself as a pillar in the black community, hard working, thrifty, self-taught, and for nineteen years secretary of the Chapel African Methodist Episcopal Church. While raising a family of twelve sons and four daughters, he had added to his landholdings until he owned 427 acres of the best cotton land in the county. At age fifty-one, with nine of his children married and living nearby, Crawford was still a vigorous, energetic, and independent man. His large forehead, broad mustache and side whiskers, and handsome features seemed to add dignity and stature to a countenance that imbued success and achievement.

Precisely how the dispute between himself and the white merchant erupted was never told, but rumor had it that Barksdale offered Crawford eighty-five cents a pound for his seed and the black man refused to accept it, saying that he had been made a better offer. When the white man called him a liar, Crawford cursed the store-keeper and said he was trying to cheat him out of a fair price. Soon word spread through town that a black man had cursed a white, and an angry crowd gathered. Hearing the shouts and cries, Crawford made for the boiler room in a nearby gin house, went down into a partially covered pit, where he took off his coat, and picked up a four-pound sledge hammer. Once he had told a friend, "The day a white man hits me is the day I die," and as the crowd poured into the pit Crawford raised the hammer and smashed the skull of McKinny Cann, described as "a rough chap" who sold buggies and feed for a local merchant. Then a rock caught him on the back of the head, and he went down; staggering to his feet he began to run, but once again found himself on the ground and felt a warm almost painless twinge in his back as a knife was thrust downward through his ribs. He lost consciousness as the mob, like a pack of wild dogs, tore and kicked at his body.

Even as these events were unfolding Abbeville sheriff R. M. Burts rushed to the scene and tried to restore order. He begged the leaders of the mob not to kill the black man; he pleaded with them to "con-sider him and his duty." It would put him "in a terrible hole." Finally, with the promise that Crawford would be kept in jail until it could be determined whether or not Cann would live, the whites disbursed. Burts then carried Crawford, still alive, back to the jail where he was treated by a physician. Despite a severe loss of blood, Crawford re-gained consciousness and instructed a friend to retrieve his coat from the gin house and to make sure that his family received the bank book that was in one of the pockets. To his friend he murmured: "I thought I was a good citizen."

To anyone arriving on the noon train it appeared as if the most important matter in town was the slow march of the boll weevil, now about one hundred miles away in Georgia, but in mid-afternoon a rumor began to spread that Sheriff Burts was planning to "take the nigger away on the four o'clock train." A second mob quickly formed, rushed into the jail, carried Crawford into the square, tied a rope around his neck, and began dragging him through the streets. As they arrived on the edge of a white residential district, they threw their victim onto the top of a passing load of slabs; shouting, jeering, laughing, yelling, they went back and forth, past stately homes, beau-tifully manicured lawns, and flower beds adorned with marigolds in bloom and "lovely old-fashioned princes feather." Although Crawford was dead long before they arrived at the fairgrounds on the edge of town, they hanged him from a towering southern pine and riddled his swaying body with several hundred bullets. The ravaged and mutilated "mass of bloody pulp," one observer said, remained strung up for some time before finally being cut down and buried.

While the brutal murder drew national attention and was condemned by South Carolina's governor Richard Manning and a number of business and professional people, the sentiments of many whites were summed up in the comments of a local resident. "I reckon the crowd wouldn't have been so bloodthirsty," he said, "only it's been three years since they had any fun with the niggers, and it seems as tho they just have to have lynching every so often." To this a leading editor added: "Crawford was worth around $20,000 and that is more than most white farmers are worth down here. Property ownership always make the negro more assertive, more independent, and the poor whites can't stand it." They hated to see "a 'nigger' forge ahead of them, and they lay for a chance to jump him." A short time later, after a coroner's jury reported that the murder had come at the hands of person or persons unknown, the Crawfords packed up their belongings and left Abbeville County, where they and their ancestors had lived for many generations.[1]

During those generations blacks in the South had moved a great distance from their West African heritage. Most of those who had arrived in slave ships during the seventeenth and eighteenth centuries had come from societies where everything had been held in common and the land could no more be "owned" than could the rivers, ocean, or sky. Struggling to adjust to a new and hostile environment, their attitudes toward property slowly began to change. From the beginning a few had somehow loosened the shackles of bondage, gained privileges as slaves, and begun to accumulate property. Others had secured their freedom and acquired small farms or lots in the towns that had sprung up along the Atlantic seaboard, and later along the Gulf coast. As early as the 1670s there was already at least one black family in its third generation of land ownership, and by the early nineteenth century, increasing numbers of both slaves and freemen and women had become property owners. They were unevenly distributed in various sections of the South, and worked at different tasks, but everywhere their desire to acquire land and own property was strongly evident. By the eve of the Civil War, black property ownership had expanded enormously. In some sections of the Lower

South, substantial numbers of bondspeople had accumulated small estates, while a few free persons of color had themselves become large slave owners. In the Upper South, free Negroes had greatly expanded their landholdings. While often struggling, as did their white neighbors, against various economic problems and the ravages of natural disaster, and having to contend with oppressive laws and increasing white hostility, by 1860 fully one out of five free Negro heads of families had become real property owners, a remarkable achievement considering that two generations before most of them had worn shackles as slaves.

With the coming of freedom, the masses of blacks were released from slavery with "virtually nothing they could call their own," but even within five years after the war, as revealed in the United States population census, thousands of former bondspeople had begun the ascent toward property ownership. The barriers they confronted during the early postwar period were enormous, and with little or no assistance from local, state, or federal authorities the masses of freedmen remained propertyless. But they exhibited an unceasing determination to become landholders. Within a generation after the war, the same proportion of blacks in the region owned land or city property as had free Negroes on the eve of the conflict. As during the antebellum era, they remained unevenly distributed, with relatively few landholders in the rural Lower South and larger numbers in the cities of the Lower and Upper South and in the rural areas of the Upper South. Working in a wide range of occupations, and often able only to acquire small estates, by the early twentieth century blacks in some areas of the South were obtaining land more rapidly than whites, and in Virginia, where for various reasons whites were less opposed to black proprietorship, the rapid rise in Negro landownership was nothing less than spectacular. "In the sixty years of freedom the Negroes of Virginia have managed to attain [a] place of primacy in ownership of land," one twentieth-century observer said. "The various stages of effort by which the Negroes acquired this land made a story as wonderful as the tale of Aladdin and the 'Wonderful Lamp,' and more so, too, because it is true."[2]

Viewing the black experience during the nineteenth and early twentieth centuries we see that one of the most striking developments was the effort of Negroes to enter the mainstream of American life by becoming property owners. Nothing in their African heritage prepared them for the New World emphasis on land ownership and economic individualism, but by 1915 most blacks in the South had only dim memories of the attitudes of their African ancestors toward the land. Despite slavery, racism, war, emigration, colonization, lynchings, and brutal murders, most blacks continued to view the South as their home and clung to the values and attitudes that they had grown to accept: that acquiring land and property would somehow free them from the burdens of the past. Their tragedy, and the region's tragedy, was that it never would.

A Note on Appendixes

The following appendixes seek to convey the richness and texture of primary sources used in this study, to give illustrations of the various types of sources used, and to provide additional statistical data which could not be conveniently integrated into the text. The correspondence of Andrew Bryan, Shandy Jones, and David Imes, all born in the South though Imes resided in southern Pennsylvania, eloquently articulates the values and attitudes of property-owning blacks as they struggled to reconcile the duality of their existence as blacks and as Americans. The petitions in behalf of Ned Hyman, Doctor Jack, and others not only tell us about the ability of a few privileged slaves to achieve a measure of freedom but also suggest a certain respect on the part of whites toward the most talented blacks. The wills and inventories of Andrew Marshall, Richard Dereef, Dominique Metoyer, and Louise Olivier point to the life style of affluent free persons of color in the Deep South. The compilations from tax assessment rolls for Louisiana and Georgia indicate the usefulness of this type of evidence when the assessment volumes are extant. The statistical profiles of property held among different occupational groups, blacks and mulattoes, men and women, between 1850 and 1870, show again the unique value of computations from the United States population censuses in understanding black wealth holding (some data are taken from tax and probate records as well as from reliable secondary sources, thus the missing cases). The final two appendixes demonstrate how collective biography can allow historians to gain unique comprehension of a particular group, in this case those who emerged as the most prosperous blacks in the South during the late nineteenth and early twentieth centuries.

Appendix One

Correspondence

A LETTER
FROM THE NEGROE BAPTIST CHURCH IN SAVANNAH
ADDRESSED TO THE REV. DR. RIPPON
Savannah, Georgia, U.S.A., Dec. 23, 1800

MY DEAR AND REV. BROTHER,

AFTER a long silence, occasioned by various hindrances, I sit down to answer your inestimable favour by the late dear Mr. White, who I hope is rejoicing, far above the troubles and trials of this frail sinful state. All the books, mentioned in your truly condescending and affectionate letter, came safe, and were distributed according to your humane directions. You can scarcely conceive, much less can I describe, the gratitude excited by so seasonable and precious a supply of the means of knowledge and grace, accompanied with benevolent proposals of further assistance. Deign, dear sir, to accept our united and sincere thanks for your great kindness to us, who have been so little accustomed to such attention. Be assured our prayers have ascended, and I trust will continue to ascend to God, for your health and happiness, and that you may be rendered a lasting ornament to our holy religion, and a successful Minister of the Gospel.

With much pleasure, I inform you, dear sir, that I enjoy good health, and am strong in body, tho' 63 years old, and am blessed with a pious wife, whose freedom I have obtained, and an only daughter and child, who is married to a free man, tho' she, and consequently, under our laws, her seven children, five sons and two daughters, are slaves. By a kind Providence I am well provided for as to worldly comforts, (tho' I have had very little given me as a minister), having a house and lot in this city, besides the land on which several buildings stand, for which I receive a small rent, and a fifty-six acre-tract of land, with all necessary buildings, four mules in the country, and eight slaves; for whose education and happiness, I am enabled, thro' mercy to provide.

But what will be infinitely more interesting to my friend, and as to much more prized by myself, we enjoy the rights of conference to a valuable extent, worshiping in our families, and preaching three times every Lord's-day, baptizing frequently from 10 to 30 at a time in Savannah, and administering the sacred supper, not only without molestation, but in the presence, and with the approbation and encouragement of many of the white people. We are now about 700 in number, and the work of the Lord goes on prosperously. An event which has had a happy influence on our affairs was the coming of Mr. Holcombe, late pastor of the Euhaw Church, of this place, at the call of the heads of the city, of all denominations, who have remained for the 13 months he has been here, among his constant hearers, and liberal supporters. His salary is 1000 [dollars] a year. He has just had a baptistery, with convenient appendages, built in his place of worship, and has commenced baptizing.

Another dispensation of Providence has much strengthened our hands, and increased our means of information: Henry Francis, lately a slave to the widow of the late Col. Leroy Hammond, of Augusta, has been purchased, by a few humane gentlemen of this place, and liberated to exercise the handsome ministerial gifts he possesses amongst us, and teach our youth to read and write. He is a strong man, about 49 years of age, whose mother was [mulatto], and whose father was an Indian. His wife and only son are slaves.

Brother Francis has been in the ministry 15 years, and will soon receive ordination, and will probably become the pastor of a branch of my large church, which is getting too unwieldly [sic] for one body. Should this event take place, and his charge receive constitution, it will take the rank and title of the 3d Baptist Church in Savannah.

With the most sincere and ardent prayers to God for your temporal and eternal welfare, and with the most unfeigned gratitude, I remain, reverend and dear sir, your obliged servant in the gospel.

Andrew Bryan*

P.S. I should be glad that my African friends could hear the above account of our affairs.

*This letter was written perhaps by the Rev. Mr. Holcombe

Source: Andrew Bryan to John Rippon, December 23, 1800, in *The Baptist Annual Register for 1797–1801*, 3 vols., ed. John Rippon (London: n.p., 1801), 3:366–67.

Tuskaloosa, Alabama
Dec. 29, 1851

Rev. and Dear Sir: Colonization is rapidly growing in favor in this State. Ere this, doubtless you have heard of the formation of a State Colonization Society in Alabama, having for its object the colonizing her free people of color on the west coast of Africa, or in other words, sending them to Liberia. And I doubt not that the day is not distant when there will be an uprising of the free people of color—not only in Alabama—not only in the much persecuted South, where it is said by the fanatics that we are sorely oppresst, and inhumanly treated, but in the liberal and philanthropic North. We are treated about as well here, at least those who behave themselves, and conduct themselves as they should, as the same class of persons in the North. You ask the question, are you ever going to Liberia? My answer is, yes, without hesitation. I heartily thank you and the society which you represent for your kind and liberal offer of a free passage, and six months support. I regret exceedingly that I shall not be able to avail myself of the offer tendered at so early a day as the 10th January, but trust you will keep the privilege open a few months at least; and I think myself and several others will accept the proffered boon. We would most certainly go now, if we had our little matters closed, but those of us who want to go to Liberia are men who have been striving to do something for ourselves, and consequently have more or less business to close up. I think, however, that we will be able to leave here in a few months. There will be a handsome company from Alabama, I think, about next spring or fall. I have been informed by a correspondent at Huntsville, in the north end of this State, that there is several about there that have in part made up their minds to go, and they only want a little encouragement to settle them fully in favor of Liberia. The day is coming, and I trust is not far distant, when every free person of color in this country will esteem it a privilege to be sent to Liberia.

I am rejoiced to see that the free people in the great North is coming to their right minds at last. I was much pleased with the letter of Mr. Washington, of Harford, on the subject of the condition of the colored people in this country. I trust there will be found ere long many Washingtons in the field laboring in behalf of Colonization. I was also pleased to see an account of a meeting of the colored people of New York, not long since, to take into consideration the expediency of emigrating to Liberia. I trust that these meetings will be gotten up in every State in the Union. Let the free colored people of every State meet in convention in their respective States, and exchange opinions, and make their views known to each other, and if needs be, hold a grand convention of all the States at such time and place as they may think proper; and let those State conventions send delegates to Liberia, or if they should think proper to have a general convention, let that convention send delegates. There is upwards of two thousand free colored people in Alabama; and if each of these would contribute but twenty-five cents a piece, we could have a fund sufficient to send two delegates to Liberia. Now, it does seem to me, if we, as a people, do feel any interest in our own welfare and that of our children, we will have no objection to inquiring into a matter of so much moment to us, at so small cost.

I trust my brethren will think of this matter, and arouse themselves, and let national pride be kindled up in their hearts, and go to and make us a great nation of our own, build our own cities and towns, make our own laws, collect our own revenues, command our own vessels, army and navy, elect our own governors and law makers, have our own schools and colleges, our own lawyers and doctors, in a word, cease to be "hewers of wood and drawers of water," and be men.

Believe me, yours, and Colonization's devoted friend,

S. W. Jones

Source: Shandy Wesley Jones to William McLain, December 29, 1851, in *JNH* 10 (April 1925), 222–24.

Pleasent view, Juniata Co. Pa.
March 29, 1869

Dear Sir

having been loned a book, the Narration of Frederick Douglass up til 1855, which gave me an anxiety to try to know more of the man and if this letter finds you i have no dout you will ans it. it has often ben askd are you not a brother of Fred douglass. i replied not. do you know him. i do not. but i have read a good many of his Speeches. Robert Gamble was to see us from cowa this winter and said mr. douglass had made a speach in their town Washington, some 2 years ago and it was the best oration he had ever herd by a coulerd man. he says you ought to try to become acquainted with the man as you are the best Farmer, coulerd man, and he is the best orator i have ever seen in my travels and you look so much alike that you ought to be made to known to each other. i have traveld very little more than teaming to Baltimore & to Pittsburg a few times in the years of 1837 to 41, from welsh run, Franklin Co. pa where i was raisd. i was born in Washington Co. Md. where my father was a Slave til i was 3 years old and he was 50. he is living with me yet, now 95 years old. he was born in Baltimore County, on Elk ridge. his father was his master, so his mother told him. his masters name was William imes and he has the same name. one of the things that most interest me is to know the rest of the narritive, how you got to new yourk and as Slavery is dead we would be glad to hear that part of your adventure.

as i said i never travelld much as i commenced in 43, when evry thing was very low and seeing all the coulerd men that had been farming before in our nabourhood break up i was determind to try my luck, but i took a different plan. thay rented their land and i bought on credit. Such land as other men would not have, i paid in 43, 900 dols, nine hun, for 53 acres of land, and in 1853 i sold it for three thousand and came to Juniata and Bought 110 acres for three thousand and in 63 i sold it to A K Mclure, of Chambers, for five thousand. in 58 i bought a tract of land from John Gray for 25 hundred, 148 acres, that i have yet. after seling to col. A K McLure i bought a farm up tuscarara Creek, 10 miles from miflin Station, on the Central railroad and county seat of Juniata Co, for 5 thou 5 hundred dols, 270 acres. this farm i have improvd and live comfortably which cost me a good [d]eal. my house is 2 story with basement, 36 by 28. my barn is 40 by 80 with wagon sh[ed] 20 feet wide 40 long, with corncrib, tool house 22 feet square, blacksmith shop, 18 by 20, in short all the nesesery buildings here. i have though this to be my last earthly home. but as times are so changeing i will wait the isue.

when i came to this valley there was very few coulerd people here and all very poor, except my brother. he came here in 42. he now owns 114 acres with good buildings. it is valued at ten thous dols. since i came out here there is some 15 or 20 famleys came here and are doing well. nearly all farming. it is Said by the travlers that we are the most enterprizing Farmers in the state. i would be ashamed to write such a letter to a stranger if it was not that you know how hard it is to accumulate where there is nothing to begin with and when evrything was as dark as night in behalf of the coulerd race. but thanks to him whose name i am not worthy to mention he has given us the key to knolege and whosoever is found worthy will be able to open the Book and look thereon. the days of fugitives slave laws and missouri comprimises and dread scots deciscions are things of the past and the sheading of Blood was their doom. it is a truth that cannot be denied that without the sheading of blood there is no remission of sin. god grant that there may be no more sheding of blood amongst the american people. the only encouragement i had in the days of continual night was the coulerd people trying to improve their condition. there is no healthyer sighn of improvement than to see any people trying to do right. a great many are trying to do the very best and so long as thay continue we have nothing to fear. there is still lingering in the minds of our coulerd Brethren a weekness that ought to be remo[v]ed. there is not respect enough for our women and so long as any race of men can be temted by strange woman and lost, conceivd prosperity cannot be great. we must respect our own wives & daughters & Sisters if we want to be a great people. lust always jenders to Bondage. o but could i go to evry hous of coller[d] and say to the father, respect your own wife more than any other woman on earth, and say to the young men marry your own couler for thay will make you most happy and prosperous and will make you an independent & virtuous people, no more to go back in Slavery, no more to have the curse of god upon us, but blesings without number will follow our race.

i am the father of 12 children, 8 Sons & 4 daughters, all healthy and well formed, all capable of retaining a good ample supply of knowlege and so far as thay are old enough have a good common english education. thay are all industrious and doing well. i have always been careful to show good example, begining at home and it is swelling into large proportions. it indeed is remarcable what one man do when he has a cultivated mind and is careful, onnest, and fine in his motives. and as the good lord has blesd me in the times when all was so dark i do trust him that he will still continue hise blesing forever on all my ofsprings and our race for all time to come.

David imes

Source: David Imes to Frederick Douglass, March 29, 1869, Frederick Douglass Papers, reel 2, LC.

APPENDIX TWO

Petitions

To the Honorable Davis Ramsay Esquire, President
and to the rest of
Honorable New Members of the Senate of the State
of South Carolina

The Memorial of Thomas Cole, Bricklayer,
P. B. Mathews and Mathew Webb, Butchers,
on behalf of themselves & other Free Men of Colour,
Humbly sheweth

That in the Enumeration of Free Citizens by the Constitution of the United States for the purpose of Representations of the Southern States in Congress, Your Memorialist have been considered under that description as part of the Citizens of this State. Although by the Fourteenth and Twenty ninth [sections] in an Act of Assembly made in the Year 1740 and entitled ["]an Act for the better ordering and Governing Negroes and other Slaves in this Province["], commonly called The Negroe Act now in force, Your Memorialist are deprived of the Rights and Privileges of Citizens by not having it in their power to give Testimony on Oath in prosecutions on behalf of the State from which cause many Culprits have escaped the punishment due to their atrocious Crimes, nor can they give their Testimony in recovering Debts due to them, or in establishing Agreements made by them within the meaning of the Statutes of Frauds and Perjuries in force in this State except in cases where Persons of Colour are concerned, whereby they are subject to great losses and repeated Injuries without any means of redress.

That by the said clauses in the said Act, they are debarred of the

Rights of Free Citizens by being subject to a Trial without the benefit of a Jury and subject to Prosecution by Testimony of Slaves without Oath by which they are placed on the same footing.

Your Memorialist shew that they have at all times since the Independence of the United States contributed and do now contribute to the support of Government by chearfully paying their Taxes proportionable to their property with others who have been during such period and now are in full enjoyment of The Rights and Immunities of Citizens Inhabitants of a Free Independent State.

That your Memorialist have been and are considered as Free Citizens of this State they hope to be treated as such. They are ready and willing to take and subscribe to such Oath of Allegiance to the States as shall be prescribed by this Honorable House and are also willing to take upon them any duty for the preservation of the Peace in the City or any other occasion if called on.

Your Memorialist do not presume to hope that they shall be put on one equal footing with the [white population, but] only humbly solicit such indulgence as the Wisdom and Humanity of this Honorable House shall dictate in [this matter] by repealing the clauses the Act before mentioned and substituting such a clause as will efectually Redress the grivences which your Memorialists humbly submit in this their Memorial but under such restrictions as to your Honorable House shall seem proper.

May it therefore please your Honors to take your Memorialists care into tender consideration and make such Acts or insert such clauses for the purpose of relieving your Memorialists from the unmeritted grievance they now Labour under as in your Wisdom shall seem [just].

And as in duty bound your Memorialists will ever pray

Signed Jan 9, 1791

> Thos. Cole
> Peter Bassnett Mathews
> Mathew Webb

Source: Records of the General Assembly, Memorial of Thomas Cole, Peter Bassnett Mathews, and Mathew Webb, to the South Carolina General Assembly, January 13, 1791, #181, SCDAH.

To the Honorable General Assembly
of the Commonwealth of Virginia

Your petitioner Samuel Johnston, a free man of Colour, Humbly Sheweth that in the year [c. 1815] upon the recommendation of divers respectable Citizens of this Commonwealth & in Consideration of faithful Services and Singular good Conduct, an act of your honourable body was passed authorizing the emancipation of your petitioner. That Subsequent to the passage of said act, the deportment of your petitioner has been uniformly upright, industrious, & Moral, that by honest exertions, he has accumilated [sic] a tolerable estate consisting of real and personal property; that he has acquired ownership of three slaves to wit his wife Patty, aged [not given], his daughter Lucy, aged [not given], & his son Samuel, aged [not given]. That the Conduct of said slaves, and the management of your petitioner toward them has merited and met with the approbation of all the most sober and prudent part of the Community.

Your petitioner farther [sic] sheweth that from feelings incidental to all men and peculiar to those who have led the harmless and unexceptionable [sic] life of your petitioner, he is desirous and anxious to Let free the said Slaves & would long ago have executed a Deed of emancipation had he not been intimidated by the penalties of the Statute which requires their speedy departure from the Commonwealth. Your petitioner therefore humbly seeks from your honourable body the passage of an act whereby the said Slaves, when emancipated, will be permitted to Continue [as] inhabitants of this Commonwealth; by which your petitioner in his declining years will be secured in the enjoyment of those natural blessings and domestic Comforts; to which from his long and faithful Services as well as his Virtuous course of life he trusts he is entitled.

And your petitioner will ever pray &c November 1820

Samuel Johnston

Warrenton, Fauquier County, Virginia

We the undersigned, Having been Called upon by Saml. Johnson [sic], a freeman of Collour [sic] living in this place to make a correct estimate of his property both real & Personal, do hereby Certify that we believe it to be worth Three Thousand Six hundred dollars. given under Our hands & Seals this Twenty Seventh day of October 1820

Nelson S. Hutchinson
William H. Digges
Wm. W. McNeale

To the General Assembly of the Commonwealth of Virginia

Your Petitioner Samuel Johnston Humbly represents that some years past by his industry & faithful services he procured his emancipation, that afterwards by a life of activity & honesty he procured the means & became the owner of his wife Patty & Daughter Lucy, that at this time he has no other child & his wife from her advanced age can bear [*sic*] no more, that the habits & course of life pursued by his said wife & daughter are such as to recommend them to the favor and good opinion of all citizens of this county who know them, that your petitioner is anxious & desirous to have them freed with liberty to remain in the county of Fauquier where he has acquired comfortable real estate for their maintenance, that he thinks the exemplary conduct of himself & his wife & daughter entitles them to the kindness of your honorable body, he therefore prays that an act may be passed to authorize the emancipation & permanent residence in Fauquier County of his said wife & daughter & your petitioner will ever pray &c

Samuel Johnston

Source: Legislative Records, Petitions of Samuel Johnston to the Virginia General Assembly, Fauquier County, December 14, 1820, December 4, 1823, VSL.

To the Hon The Legislature of the State of Tennessee

The subscribers* having understood and learnt that an act was passed at the last Session of your Hon. body, Entitled "An act to amend the laws of This State in relation to the government of slaves and free persons of color," one section of which makes it an indictable offense for "any owner or other person having charge of any slave or slaves,["] to "permit him or them to go about the Country under pretext of practicing medicine or healing the sick." Without pretending to question the [necessity] of this law, or one of [its] general character or denying that in its general operation it may be productive of much good, yet we would most respectfully ask of your Hon. body to [make an exception in] its general operation so far as to permit a negro man named Jack, the property of Mr. William H. Macon of Maury County, to practice [medicine] as he has been heretofore doing. We ask this from a full Knowledge of the Character of this boy; though he may be a *slave*, yet in the opinion of the undersigned, his character for honesty and correct deportment, is fair and not often excelled by many who possess more than he does. In his profession we speak from our knowledge of his practice. We are free & happy to say that he has practiced with great & unparalled success, for many years, none having any cause to complain of either a want of fidelity or success among his patients. We are residents the Several Counties of Maury, Bedford, Giles, Hickman, Williamson, and Lincoln, and ask that passage of this Law, granting permission to this boy to practice, with a firm belief that the public good will be advanced by its passage & from our Knowledge of the character of this boy, and his practice for several years.

> A. L. Prickard
> Johnston Craig
> Reuben Reynolds
> Milledge Durham
> Ezekiel Boggs

*In this and subsequent petitions, only the first five legible signatures have been included.

To the Legislature of the State of Tennessee

The undersigned citizens of Tennessee respectfully petition the Honorable Legislature of the State to repeal, amend or so modify the Act of 1831, chap. 103, S[ect]. 3, which prohibits Slaves from practicing medicine, as to exempt from its operation a Slave named Jack, the property of William H. Macon, Esq., of Fayette County.

The undersigned are acquainted with the Slave Jack and his medical attainments (some of us have known him for 20 years & some for a shorter period) and state, that in his disposition he is humble, unobtrusive, peaceable and quiet; and in his morals altogether irreproachable, possessing great medical skill, particularly in obstinate diseases of long standing, and capable of great usefulness to the community in which he may reside. Doctor Jack is about 60 years of age, and has been a public practitioner of medicine 16 years, giving offense to no one, creating no disturbance and until recently meeting no disturbance in the quiet pursuit of business.

For these reasons the undersigned request that the Laws of the State may be so changed as to permit "Doctor Jack" to continue the practice of the healing art.

The undersigned would further petition the Hon Legislature to remit any fine or penalty that may be imposed by the Circuit Court of Fayette County upon the Master of said slave for permitting sd. slave to practice medicine contrary to Law, for the people are as much in fault as the master. August 1843.

> Duke Williams
> Whitfield Boyd
> B. H. Henderson
> Wm. L. Lacy
> D. I. Henderson

To the Legislature of Tennessee

The undersigned Ladies residing in Tennessee respectfully petition the Honorable Legislature of the State to repeal, amend, or so modify the Act of 1831, c. 103, S. 3, which prohibits slaves from practicing medicine as to exempt from its operation a slave named Jack the property of William H. Macon, Esq., of Fayette County.

We believe "Doctor Jack" to be honest, honorable & skilful, especially in obstinate cures of long standing; and that the people ought not to be denied the privilege of commanding his services. August 1843

> Mary M. Williams
> Lucinda Henderson
> Lockey M. Boyd
> Mary J. Henderson
> Julia A. Lacy

Source: Legislative Papers, Petition of the Residents of Maury, Bedford, Giles, Hickman, Williamson, and Lincoln counties, to the Tennessee General Assembly, c. 1832, TSLA; Petition of the Citizens of Fayette County to the Tennessee General Assembly, August 1843, #189-1843-1, ibid.; Petition of the Women of Fayette County to the Tennessee General Assembly, August 1843, #189-1843-4, ibid.

To The Honorable The General Assembly of North Carolina

The petition of Ned Hyman (a slave) humbly complaining sheweth unto The Honorable The General Assembly that your petitioner now residing in the Town Williamston in the County of Martin and by occupation a farmer was born some fifty four or five years ago[,] the property & slave of one Jno. Hyman of Bertie County, that Jno. Hyman died when your petitioner was about the age of fourteen, that your petitioner then became the property of his then young Master Samuel Hyman—during three years (the minority of his young master) he was hired out to the highest bidder, that after three years of hired service he was taken home by his master Saml. in whose possession and under whose control you petitioner lived and served from that time up to the death of his Master Samuel, which happened some time in the year 1828. Since that time your petitioner has been under the control of the Executor of his decd. Master. Your petitioner would further state that during this long period and through every change of master or service your petitioner has been a faithful and an honest servant to the interest of him or her whom it was his duty to serve, and of this he hopes he can give the most satisfactory testimonials.

Your petitioner would further state that some time about his Twenty-seventh year he intermarried with one Elizabeth Hagans[,] a free woman of Colour with whom he has lived in friendship and harmony with little or no exceptions ever since (and altho your petitioner has been informed that the sd union or marriage did not constitute your petitioner & Sd Elizabeth "husband & wife" in the Legal acceptation of that phrase—yet your humble petitioner would ask the indulgence of your Honorable body and hope that it will not be considered at all presuming to use these words, through out the remainder of this petition and the other writings accompanying it, when ever there may be necessity for them or either of them, instead of words of like import). Your petitioner would further state that through the indulgence and advantages which his kind & benevolent master extended to him, aided by his own industry, prudence and frugality and seconded by the virtues and exertions on the part of your petitioners wife, Elizabeth, your petitioner has had the good fortune to accumulate an estate worth from five to six thousand dollars, consisting of Lands chiefly live stock negroes and money, the right & title to all which except the money is vested in your petitioners wife Elizabeth. Your petitioner would further state that it was the wish of his decd Master Saml. Hyman expressed to his family often times during his last illness that your petitioner after his death should do service as a slave to no person, but that as far as was consistent with the Laws of the State he wished him to be free, alleging as the reasons that your petitioner had been a truely faithful and obedient servant to him through a long period of years; that your petitioner was getting old, and that for the future he wished him to serve himself or language to that amount. Your petitioner would further state that in furtherance of this kind and benevolent wish of your petitioners decd Master for your petitioners future freedom and happiness, his Executor Jno. S. Bryan has (at your petitioners request) sold your petitioner to your petitioners sd wife Elizabeth, that your petitioner by his sd. wife Elizabeth has three children Penny[?], Sarah and Ned, the Two daughters are of full age, the son nearly so, that your petitioner has been informed that by either the death of his sd. wife Elizabeth or a change in her feelings or disposition towards your petitioner, your petitioner might not only lose his whole estate but even that portion of freedom and happiness which, by the Kindness of his wife he is now permitted to enjoy. But your petitioner in justice to his kind and affectionate wife Elizabeth would further state, that she is not disposed at all to abridge in the least degree the liberty or happiness of your petitioner but wishes and desires (if consistent with the will of the Honorable The Genl. Assembly) that the same may be enlarged & increased that she is therefore perfectly willing and anxiously desires to give up her sd. title to your petitioner to the Honorable Genl. Assembly that they may confer the same (by an act of manumission) together with such other liberties and privileges & immunities as other free persons of Colour now by law enjoys, upon your petitioner—that to this end & for this purpose Elizabeth the wife of your petitioner will unite with your petitioner in praying The Honorable Genl. Assembly that they would take his case into consideration and pass such an act in favor of your petitioners manumission as they in their wisdom may deem meet and proper, that in confirmation of the sd Elizabeths sincerity in this prayer and request she will most willingly sign this petition with your petitioner. Your petitioner considers that further enlarging might be trespassing to much upon the time of The Honorable the Genl. Assembly aforesaid. But in conclusion however your petitioner would further state that from the facts already stated it must be apparent in what an unpleasant and grievous situation your petitioner is placed. He has by laboring in the nights and at such other spare times as his master would give him and by his prudence and frugality acquired an estate which (say nothing of the uncertainties of life) he has not the assurance of enjoying even for a day, that he in a single hour might be placed in a worse condition than the day he began this life, that your petitioner has by his faithfulness and extraordinary attention to his masters business and interest secured his esteem and favor and obtained his sincere wishes that your petitioner should be freed & the nearest your petitioner has been able to approach an end so desirable to his decd Master is to have had the title to your petitioner vested in your petitioners wife, that it must be evident to the Honorable The Genl. Assembly from these facts in what a precarious condition stand the property, and more the happiness itself of your petitioner. Your petitioner, together with his wife Elizabeth therefore pray the Genl. Assembly aforsd in under consideration of his unhappy and grievous condition to pass such an act for his benefit and relief as in their wisdom may seem meet & in their justice may seem right & proper & your humble petitioners as in duty bound will ever pray &c—— signed

Test Wm. B. Benning

his
Ned x Hyman
mark

E. S. Smithwick

her
Elizabeth x Hagans
mark

Williamston October 10th 1833

The Honorable The Genl. Assembly
of North Carolina for 1833–1834

Your memorialists beg leave to State to your Honorable Body that for many years they have been well acquainted with Ned Hyman a humble petitioner to the Genl Assembly foresd for an act of Manumission to be passed by your Honorable Body in his favor and for his benefit. Your Memorialists would further state that they have read the petition of sd Ned, and they believe that all the facts therein stated are substantially true. Your memorialists would further state that the sd Ned has been, and still is, a very uncommon and extraordinary Negro, that he is remarkably industrious, frugal & prudent, that he has acquired a very pretty Estate, at least to the Amount of what he has stated in his petition, mostly by farming. Your memorialists further say that the sd Ned is a humble, peaceable and well [behaved] negro to all persons; that they believe him to be a sincere and devoted friend to good order and a strenuous supporter among those of his own colour and condition of their being faithful & sincere to the interests of their Masters. Your memorialists further say they believe the sd Ned to be upright and honest in all his dealings, that in a word his character stands as fair and as good for honesty, truth, industry, humility, sobriety & fidelity, as any negros they (your memorialists) have every seen or ever heard of. In conclusion your memorialists would say that altho they know of no extraordinarily meritorious services performed by Ned in saving the life of his owners in imminent peril, or other extraordinary service, Yet your memorialists believe from what they know of Ned that no person, slave or free-man, would scarcely go further to deserve the good opinion of the public in any act that he could do than your petitioner Ned, that your memorialist would further state to the Honorable Genl Assembly that if it be within the Policy of the State to pass acts of manumission at all (and your memorialists would say [in] entire submission to the Genl Assembly that in Neds case they think there is ample cause to justify the passing such an act in his favor) that your memorialists know of no case which has arisen or can arise upon grounds merely meritorious in which the benevolence of Manumission has been or can be now justly and beneficially administered than in the case of your petitioner Ned. Neds situation is truly as he has stated in his petition to your Honorable Body an unpleasant & precarious one, and in the humble opinion of your Memorialists merits the attention and assistance of the Honorable The Genl. Assembly aforsd—All which however Your Memorialists most cheerfully & respectfully submit.

Jno. L. Bryan
Jas. S. Bryan
John Hyman
Ann G. Hyman
Frances H Hyman

Source: General Assembly, Session Records, Petition of Ned Hyman and Elizabeth Hagans to the North Carolina General Assembly, November 23, 1833, NCDAH; Petition of John S. Bryan, James L. Bryan, John Hyman, et al., to the North Carolina General Assembly, 1833, ibid.

To the Honorable the Legislature of the State of Mississippi

We the undersigned neighbors and acquaintances of Titus Hill, a free man of color, of Wilkinson County, respectfully petition your Honorable Body to pass a special act granting him leave to remain in the State of Mississippi, and enjoy all the rights and privileges which have heretofore been secured to him. Many of us have known Titus Hill for Twenty and Twenty five years, and during the whole of this time, have never known him to be guilty of a single mean, or dishonest act; he has always been an honest, peaceable, industrious and good citizen, and has always secured, and now [main]tains, the good opinion of all good Citizens who have known him. He is almost Sixty years of age, and by his energy and industry, has honestly acquired property worth about Four or Five Thousand Dollars. We approve of the policy of the general law prohibiting free negroes from remaining in this state, but think, that in consideration of Titus Hill's old age, his honesty and energy as a man and his good behavior as a citizen, a special act should be passed for his benefit.

Peter Ratcliff
Joseph B. Hoff
Enoch B. McLain
Henry G. Langmen
Charles Ratcliff

Source: Legislative Records, Petition of Residents of Wilkinson County to the Mississippi Legislature, c. 1860, box 29, MDAH.

To the Honble The President and Members of the Senate
of South Carolina

The petition of the undersigned citizens of Charleston respect fully sheweth, That they have seen with regret in the papers, the draught of a bill proposing to drive our free coloured people from the State under the heaviest penalties.

Your petitioners can find no reason for such severity, on the contrary, they believe the project one of wrong and injustice to a class of our inhabitants who ought to be objects of our care and protection.

We know many among them who command the respect of all respectable men, many who are good citizens, [demonstrating] patterns of industry, sobriety, and irreproachable conduct. There can be no better proof of this than the fact that they hold property in the City of Charleston to the value of more than half a million of Dollars.

Their labour is indispensable to us in this neighbourhood. They are the only workmen who will, or can, take employment in the Country during the summer. We cannot build or repair a house in that season without the aid of the coloured carpenter or bricklayers.

But we put their claim to protection on a higher ground. In their humble station they are equitably entitled to the rights which the laws of their native place have secured to them. These may be properly called vested rights, which neither justice, nor humanity, nor christian charity can wantonly assail.

We are the strong and they the feeble. Let us not begin now for the first time in our history to subject ourselves to the charge of oppressing the weak and unresisting.

If there are evil persons among them as there are all classes let the laws punish those who deserve punishment. But let us refuse to involve innocent and guilty, virtuous and vicious, industrious and vile, in one indiscriminate ruin.

There are individuals among them to whom the safety of the community may be confidently intrusted. They are sincere friends, why alienate them, however humble.

Your petitioners respectfully solicit the attention of your Honorable body to these objections to the proposed bill, and as in duty bound will ever pray.

James Rose
Wm. J. Grayson
Benj Huger
E N Fuller
Oney Harleston

Source: Records of the General Assembly, Petition of James Rose, William J. Grayson, Benjamin Huger, et al., to the South Carolina Senate, 1860, ND #2801, SCDAH.

Probate Court Records

Georgia, Chatham County

In the Name of God Amen! I Andrew Marshall, a free man of color, of the City of Savannah, being of sound and disposing mind and memory, do make and publish this my last Will and Testament

Item First. I commit my soul unto God, hoping for happiness in the world to come, and desire that my body be buried in my family vault in the grave-yard in Savannah.

Item Second—I give devise and bequeathe to my wife Sarah Marshall the Southern Half of Lot Number Nineteen (19) situate on the corner of Farm and Bryan streets in the City of Savannah, with the improvements thereon, also my household and Kitchen furniture, my four wheeled carriage and one horse, to have and to hold the same for and during the term of her natural life, and after her death to be equally divided between my sons Joseph and George, their heirs executors & administrators forever (Grand-Children to represent their parents and stirpes and not per capita) and after the death of either of the survivor, his heirs, executors, Administrators and assigns forever.

Item Third—I give devise and bequeathe unto my son George Marshall the Northern Half of said Lot Number Nineteen (19) containing a double Stone building on Farm Street and a wooden building back of it in the lane, with all the improvements thereon, to have and to hold the same to him, his heirs, executors, Administrators and assigns forever. But should my said son George depart this life without leaving a child or children or representative of children living at the time of his death, then immediately after his death, to my wife Sarah.Marshall, and to my son Joseph, so long as they both shall live, and after the death of my said wife Sarah, to my son Joseph, his heirs, Executors, Administrators and Assigns forever.

Item Fourth—I give devise and bequeathe to Georgiana, the daughter of Crissy Houston, Four shares of Stock in the Marine and Fire Insurance Bank of the State of Georgia.

Item Fifth, I give devise and bequeathe unto my son Joseph Marshall, Lot Number Eleven (11) in that part of the City of Savannah, known as the village of St. Gall, with the improvements thereon, to have and to hold the same to him, his heirs, executors, Administrators and assigns forever.

Item Sixth, I give devise and bequeathe my silver watch with all my wearing apparel unto my cousin Andrew, a slave now owned by Dr. Kollock.

Item Seventh, All the rest and residue of my property not herein specifically bequeathed (and out of which I desire that all my debts may be paid) after the payments of my debts, I give devise and bequeathe unto my wife Sarah and to my sons Joseph and George, to be equally divided between them, to them, their Heirs, Executors, Administrators and assigns forever. But should either of them die, without leaving a child or children or representatives of children, living at the time of their death then to the survivors, a survivor of them, their and his heirs, executors, Administrators and assigns forever.

Item Eighth, I nominate constitute and appoint Frederick A. Tupper, John W. Anderson, and Wylly Woodbridge Esqrs., Executors of this my last Will and Testament.

In witness thereof I have hereunto set my [signature] this 30th day of July in the year of Our Lord One thousand eight hundred and fifty two.

[signed]   Andrew Marshall

Signed, Sealed, Published and Declared as his last Will and Testament by the said testator, in our presence who in his presence, and in the presence of each other, at his request have signed our name as witnesses hereto

[signed]   Valentine Stanton
[signed]   Joseph Fet [?]
[signed]   John E. Ward

Source: RCPC, Chatham County, Ga., Estates, #M-359, April 6, 1857.

The State of South Carolina
The Last Will and Testament of Richard E. Dereef, of Charleston in the State aforesaid—
In the name of God! Amen! I Richard E. Dereef, of the City and State aforesaid, being of sound and disposing mind, and understand-

ing, but mindful of the uncertainty of life, do hereby declare this to be my last Will and Testament—hereby cancelling and revoking all former or other wills, and Testaments, by me at any time heretofore made.

First: I commend My Soul to Almighty God, and my body, I request, may be decently buried, under the direction of the members of the Brown Fellowship Society, and Humane and Friendly Society, and the [Trinity] Union Society.

Second—I order and direct that all my just and lawful Debts, if any, may be paid by my executors, and Executrix, hereinafter named, as soon after my decease as may be convenient.

Third—I give and devise my House and Lot, no 103 (one Hundred and Three) Calhoun Street, to my three Daughters, Mrs. E. C. Miller, Mrs. Isabella F. Maxwell, and Mrs. C. K. Sampson, their heirs and Assigns forever.

Fourth—I give and devise my House and Lot, no 222 (Two hundred and Twenty-two) Meeting Street, to my two Daughters, Mrs. J. H. Eggart, and Mrs. Harriet A. C. Foy, their heirs, and Assigns forever.

Fifth—I give and devise my house and Lot, no 29 (Twenty nine) at the corner of Montagn and Coming Street, and my House, and Lot, no 24 (Twenty Four) Spring Street, to my beloved wife Mrs. Margaret A. Dereef, and her heirs and assigns forever. I also give and bequeath to my said wife, my shares in the Charleston Gas Light Company, and all my Six per cent Stock of the City of Charleston, that is not hereinafter otherwise disposed of.

Sixth—I give and bequeath to my Son R. E. Dereef junior, Three Hundred dollars.

Seventh—I give and bequeath to my Son J. M. F. Dereef, Three Hundred dollars.

Eighth—I give and bequeath five Hundred Dollars, to be taken at the par value of the Stock, out of my Six Per Cent Stock of the City of Charleston, to Mrs. Rebecca Dereef, Daughter of Mrs. Sarah Drayton.

Ninth—I give and bequeath to St. Mark's Church, of which I am a member, to be taken at the par value of the Stock, Two Hundred dollars, out of my Six per cent Stock of the City of Charleston.

Tenth—I give and bequeath to the Christian benevolent Society, of which I am a member, to be taken, at the par value of the Stock, Two Hundred dollars, out of my Six per cent Stock, of the City of Charleston.

Eleventh—The Residue of the Six per cent Stock of the City of Charleston, I give and bequeath to my beloved wife Mrs. Margaret

Ann Dereef, as hereinbefore mentioned in the fifth clause of this my will.

Twelfth—I give and bequeath my gold watch to my Son James Legg Dereef.

Thirteenth—I give and bequeath my [large] silver cup to my Daughter Mrs. C. K. Sampson.

I give, devise, and bequeath all the Rest and residue of my Estate, Real and personal, of every kind whatsoever, and wheresoever, to my beloved wife, Mrs. Margaret Ann Dereef, and my youngest two Children, James Legg Dereef, and the Infant named Isabella Maxwell Dereef, to them and their heirs, Executors and Administrators forever, Share and Share alike.

Fifteenth—I hereby nominate, constitute and appoint my beloved and trusted friend and Brother, Joseph Dereef, my son J. M. F. Dereef, and my son in law, T. B. Maxwell Executors and my beloved wife Mrs. Margaret Ann Dereef, Executrix of this my last will and testament, and I leave it as a request, and my earnest desire of you all my children, and family, that a Kind feeling of Union, in the Bond of Peace, in the unity of the Spirit, with Kindness one to the other, and Brotherly love and Sisterly affection, should be maintained and preserved, remembering God in all things, and not forgetting your dear Sweet Mother, and the beloved Father who loves you all.

In the management of my wife['s] interest under this will I devise My Friends Messers Simons & Simons will advise her Feeling confident that they will extend the Like regard to her which they have Shown to me and which I reciprocate.

In Witness whereof I the said Richard Dereef have hereunto set my hand and seal this Second day of December, in the year of our Lord, one thousand Eight-Hundred and Seventy Four

[signed]   R. E. Dereef

Signed, Sealed, published, and declared by the above named Testator, as and for his last will and Testament, in the presence of us who at the request of the said Testator, and in his presence, and in the presence of Each other, have subscribed our names as witnesses hereto

[signed]   B. Forholden [?]
[signed]   J. Orrin Lea
[signed]   Wm. L. Campbell

Source: RCPC, Charleston County, S.C., Estates, #343–5, January 11, 1877.

Be it remembered that on the twenty sixth day of July in the year One thousand Eight hundred and thirty nine in pursuance of an order of the Court of Probates of the Parish of Natchitoches, State of Louisiana, I Charles E. Grencaux, Parish Judge and in office notary public, in and for the said parish, proceeded to take an Inventory of the property belonging to the succession of Dominique Metoyer, a free man of color, late of the said parish, deceased, in community with his widow Marguerite Lecomte.

The said Inventory was taken in presence of the said widow, in her own right, and as natural tutrix duly confirmed of the minor children of said deceased and also of the undersigned heirs who are of age

The said property was appraised by Philippe Brosset and Manuel Llorens, appraisers duly appointed and sworn to that effect.

Part of said property was appraised with a view to its being adjudicated to the widow at the price of Estimation.

Property appraised with a view to its being adjudicated to the widow at the price of Estimation, to wit:

All the furniture in the house appraised together at	$157
6 Plows	18
3 pr Traces	1.50
2 ox Carts	40
1 Grind Stone	4
1 Cross Cut Saw	2
1 Iron teeth Harrow	1
3 Spades	1
4 Axes	2
10 Hoes	2
3 pr mules	300
2 American Horses	120
1 American Mare & Colt	60
2 yoke oxen	70
6 Cows and Calves	72
1 Forge	20

Slaves

Alexander, negro boy, (Sickly) aged 14 years	500
Athanase, negro man, 48 years, afflicted with a hernia	700
Antoine, negro man, 60 years, also afflicted with a hernia	450
Henry, negro man, aged 22 years	1200

Jim,	"	"	24	"	1200
Blanc Francois	"	"	15	"	900
Alfred		"	28	"	1250
Silvy, negress,		"	28	" and	

Silvy, negress, " 28 " and
    her three children Francois   10 years
                         Manual   8 "
                         Catherine 3 "   1450

Celeste, negress, 20 years, and her child
    Estase   2   "   850

Fanny, negress, 22   "   and her child
    Lean Baptiste, 7 months   800

Clarisse, negress, 35 years, and her child
    Suzette   9   "   900

Choue, negress, 55 years [sic], infirm, and
    her two children
        Sylvain,   11
        Marcel   4   400

Lands

All that certain tract of land or plantation whereon
the deceased resided, situate on the left bank of
[the] Red River, containing about Five Hundred
arpents, more or less, bounded above by lands
belonging to Eloi Lecour and below by lands belonging to Octave Desonce, together with all the
buildings and improvements thereon, appraised at
Sixteen Thousand Dollars   16,000

The further taking of said Inventory was adjourned until 8 o'clock
tomorrow morning on Saturday, July 27, 1839
Said Inventory and appraisement continued

2 Spanish Saddles	8
1 Iron Brand	1

Amount of property appraised with a view to its
    adjudication to the widow   27,479.50

1 double barrelled gun	5
1 single " "	5
1 Knife	10
1 lot Plows	2
4 wooden Harrows	2.50
2 pr Collars & Traces	1.50

2 Spanish Plows	1
2 Pick axes & 1 axe	1.50
1 large Box containing Old Irons	2
1 small "	2
2 Hoes	.50
1 Iron axeltree	1
4 Mules	200
3 creole Horses (Black)	75
1 Yoke oxen	40
25 Head horned Cattle	100

Slaves

Raphael, negro man, 20 years	800
Ned, " 18 "	800
James, " 17 "	800
Jacques, " 17 "	600
Jean, " 50 "	400
Pierre, " 13 "	500
Fanchine, negress, 18 " pregnant	700
Marie, negress, 65 years	50
Mitaut, " 30 " and her two children Hermine, negress, 7 months, and Isaac, negro boy, 9 years	1200
Francoise, negress, 38 years	800

Lands

A tract of land situated in the parish on the right Bank of Red River in Brevelle Island, containing fifty arpents, bounded above by the lands of Manuel Llorens and below by lands of Emmanuel Dupre	1800
A tract of land on River a' Thao, in this parish, containing about 260 acres, bounded above by the lands of Louis Lecour and below by vacant lands	2600
A claim to a tract of land on Bayou Nantache, in this parish, containing Eighty acres	100
A claim to a tract of land, on Bayou Derbonne, in this Parish, containing ten arpents Grant	50

Papers

John B. Dm Metoyer's note, dated 13th May 1838, payable 1st May 1839, with ten p. c. interest after maturity	214.77

Eloi B. Lecour's note, 11th May 1837, payable march 1838, with ten pr. c. interest after due	86.79
Widow Valery B. Lecour's note, 9th July 1835, payable march 1836, with same interest	600.69
Ozeme D. Metoyer's note, 14th may 1838, payable march 1839, with same interest	70.07
Pierre Mission Rachal's notes, 7th December 1838, payable march 1st at ten p. c. pr. an. from march 1838	416.05
Widow Narcisse D[ominique] Metoyer, 1st May 1838, payable at 12 mos. with ten p. c. int. after due	769.55
Succession of Narcisse D[ominique] Metoyer, note by the widow—14th May 1838—payable march 1839, with same interest	812.24
Victor Rachal's note—22nd July 1838—due march 1839, with same interest	112
Eloi B. Lecour—Receipt from C. D. Rachal for succession Jn Bt Lecour	194.34

Recapitulation

Amount of property appraised with a view to its adjudication	$27,479. 50
Remainder of property	14,925.[50]
	$42,40[5]

There being nothing else belonging to the said succession to be inventoried, I have closed and signed these presents, in presence of the undersigned witnesses, who have signed, together with the appraisers and the undersigned parties interested, at the said parish of Natchitoches, in the day and year first above written

Witnesses: [signed] L Derbanne,
          C. E. Greneaux

        her

Marie Perine x Metoyer

      mark

Louis D[ominique] Metoyer

    his mark, x acclaiming

        he Knows not

        how to write

[and others]

Appraisers:

        his

Phillipe x Brosset

      mark

Manuel Llorens

Source: RPPC, Natchitoches Parish, La., Sucessions, #375, July 26, 1839.

Succession of Louise Oliver, F. W. C.
United States of America
State of Louisiana
Parish of Plaquemines

Be it Known that on this Twenty Sixth day of the month of March in the year of Our Lord, One thousand eight hundred and fifty seven, and the Eighty first year of the Independence of the United States of America,

At the request of Auguste Reggio of the Parish of Plaquemines [and] in pursuance to an order of the Honorable the Second Judicial District Court of the state aforesaid, sitting in and for the said Parish, bearing date the second day of March Eighteen hundred and fifty seven, issued in the matter of the Succession of Louise Olivier, F. W. C., deceased of this Parish, upon the petitions of Said Auguste Reggio, appointed Testamentary Executor by virtue of the last will and Testament Made on the 26th day of Dec. 1851 [signed by] Oscar Anyer the recorder of this Parish, praying that [herein] mentioned last will and Testament be executed [by Auguste Reggio], that the petitioner be confirmed as the Testamentary Executor of the deceased with Seizin, That letters of Testamentary Executorship be devised to him, on his taking the Oath required by law. That the Inventory within prayed for be made by J. L. Marciacy, Recorder in and for the Parish of Plaquemines, in presence of all parties interested, or [herein] duly Called, That Jules Delery and James Berthond be appointed and sworn to value the property so to be inventoried, That the whole be made as prayed for and according to Law. A duly certified copy of the Petition and order of Court is herewith for reference annexed.

I, Jean Louis Marciacy, Recorder in and for this Parish, Herein residing, duly elected, commissioned and sworn did this day, repair to the late residence of Said Louise Oliver in this Parish, and then and there having Arrived, I found the following persons, To wit:

1s Adolphe Reggio, The Son of said deceased and herein acting as one of the heirs of said deceased, 2d Ormand Reggio, also one of the sons of said Louise Oliver, and also one of the heirs of said deceased, 3d Charles Reggio, One of the Sons of said deceased, and herein acting as one of the heirs of said deceased, 4t Cornelie Reggio and her husband Alf[red] LeBlanc, herein acting as interested heir in the aforesaid Succession and duly authorized by her said husband, 5t Antoinette Reggio, one of the daughters of said Louise Oliver, 6th Mssrs Jules Delery and James Berthond both freeholders appraisers appointed in the aforesaid order of court and duly sworn by me the undersigned Recorder, to value and appraise all the property situated in this Parish, belonging to the said Succession, to the best of their knowledge and understanding. . . .

And in the presence and with the assistance of the aforesaid named persons, I proceeded to the taking of said Inventory . . . To wit:

1s   A certain tract of Land situated in this Parish on the left Bank of the River Mississippi at about twenty three miles below the City of New Orleans, having and measuring about fifteen arpents front on said River by forty arpents in depth, bounded above by the plantation of Mr. Jules Delery, and below by that of Adolphe Reggio, together with all the improvements, rights, Titles, utensils, and implements, ways, circumstances and dependencies thereon and thereunto belonging, without exception or reservation, valued and appraised at the full sum of Twenty five Thousand Dollars $25,000

2d   The following Slaves attached to said Plantation, To wit:

1s   A certain Slave named Leze, aged about forty years, valued and appraised at the full sum of six hundred dollars   600

2n   A certain slave named Billy, aged about thirty Eight years, valued and appraised at the sum of Eight hundred dollars   800

3d   A certain slave named Chodra, aged about forty years, valued and appraised at the full sum of seven hundred dollars   700

4t   A certain slave named Jules, aged about twenty three years, valued and appraised at the full sum of One thousand dollars   1000

5th   A certain slave named Onesippe, aged about Twenty years, valued and appraised at the full sum of One thousand dollars   1000

6th   A certain slave named Geo[rge], aged about forty five years, valued and appraised at the full sum of One thousand dollars   1000

7th   a Certain slave named Thomas valued and appraised at the full sum of Eight hundred Dollars   800

8th   A certain Slave named Robin, aged about

Thirty one years, valued and appraised at the sum
of One Thousand dollars   1000

9th   A certain Slave named Thom Jose, aged
about Thirty six years, valued and appraised at the
sum of Nine hundred dollars   900

10th   A certain Slave named Thom Hick, aged
about Thirty Six years, valued and appraised at the
full sum of Nine hundred dollars   900

11th   A certain slave named Jordan, aged about
fifty years, valued and appraised at the full sum of
six hundred dollars   600

12th   A certain slave named Duverley, aged
about twenty five years, valued and appraised at the
full sum of One thousand dollars   1000

13th   A certain Slave named Louis, aged about
Twenty Seven years, valued and appraised at the
full sum of One Thousand dollars   1000

14th   A certain slave named Sam Pagua, aged
about thirty five years, valued and appraised at the
full sum of One thousand dollars   1000

15th   A certain slave named Sam Martin, aged
about forty years, valued and appraised at the full
sum of One thousand dollars   1000

[Nineteen other slaves] valued and appraised at
the full sum of [twelve thousand five hundred
dollars]   [12,500]

3rd   The following lot of Animals attached also
to said plantation, To wit:

Sixteen Mules and Horses, valued and appraised
at the full sum of Two Thousand dollars   2000

Six pairs of Oxen, valued and appraised at the
full sum of Two hundred and forty dollars   240

Eight Cows & Calves, valued and appraised at the
full sum of One hundred and forty five dollars   145

The Total Amount of this present Inventory and
appraisement is Fifty Three Thousand One hun-
dred and Eighty five dollars $53,185.00

The heirs of said Estate herein appearing declare
that there is deposited in the hands of Mr. Cesaire
Olivier of New Orleans the Cash sum of Eight

Thousand eight hundred and Ninety One dollars
belonging to said estate $8891.00
    Total Amount of the Estate of said deceased [$62,076.00]

And there being no other property in this assessment belonging to
Said Succession, I have closed this present proce[edings] [recording
the] value of Inventory and appraisement to the Total sum of Sixty-
two Thousand and seventy Six dollars on aforesaid premises, the day,
month, and year above written, in presence of all the above named
persons, who herein signed their names with me the Recorder, after
due reading, . . . the heirs reserving to themselves to dispose of the
Crops now standing as they will think it better fit for their separate
interests in equal shares after it is raised and disposed of as above
said. . . .

(Original Signed) Antoinette Reggio, Ad Reggio, [name illegible],
Am. Reggio, A Regio [*sic*], James Berthond, G. Barland, Alf[red]
LeBlanc, J Delery, and J. L. Marciacy, Recorder

A true Copy of the Original, J. L. Marciacy, Recorder, Paid, April
6th 1857, Armand Lartigne, Clerk

Source: RPPC, Plaquemines Parish, La., Inventories, bk. 1846–58 (March
6, 1857), pp. 403–8.

Tax Assessment Rolls

Table 21. Leading Black Wealth-holding Parishes in Louisiana, 1860–1913

	1860	1870	1893	1901–3	1907	1913
Bienville		$65,200	$79,470	$198,880*	$278,610	$162,570
Bossier		175,500	233,143	344,530	348,854	272,530
Caddo	$13,200	229,900	n.d.	505,960	696,520	889,000
Claiborne	300	115,100	159,296	206,375	342,195	291,870
Concordia	100	68,000	109,581	196,746	251,869	80,695
De Soto		62,000	225,455	297,690	n.d.	448,700
East Baton Rouge	142,100	255,300	304,280	324,950	590,280	478,310*
East Carroll*			96,835	155,080	267,020	223,980
East Feliciana		118,000	124,975	187,735	364,460	181,905
Iberia		162,700	207,482	320,080	491,740	411,670
Iberville	665,100	104,600	196,315	158,910	193,325	169,490
Jefferson	129,400	129,000	130,190	118,725	133,870	107,700
Lafayette	33,400	93,400	129,005	169,898	307,478	325,796
Natchitoches	739,700	370,800	397,480	455,160	534,287	437,670*
Ouachita		68,800	n.d.	220,570	288,180	277,066
Plaquemines	379,700	341,000	173,545	n.d.	168,770*	144,208*
Pointe Coupée	796,000	259,600	173,005	133,765	327,465	122,327
Rapides	113,200	101,300	62,060	101,415	192,150	309,710
St. John the Baptist	214,100	49,700	49,880	54,395*	120,170*	121,045
St. Landry	609,900	236,200	n.d.	371,960*	734,470	530,870
St. Martin	188,700	140,900	197,670	310,320	335,580	332,270
St. Mary	228,700	83,100	240,296	315,046*	390,050*	434,630
St. Tammany	85,800	29,000	82,804	101,902	88,304	137,628
Tensas	100	205,600	161,840	179,770	237,560	177,810
Webster*			110,070	138,685	229,570	216,780
West Baton Rouge	88,500	20,800	89,080	103,430	133,992	82,028
West Feliciana	15,200	22,900	177,864	216,733	227,620	132,700*

Source: Computed from USMSPC, 1860, 1870; Assessment Rolls, Louisiana parishes, 1893–1916, LSA. Assessors were instructed to list the actual value of land and personal holdings. Postwar land values in the state dropped 70 percent. See U.S. Department of Agriculture, *Report of the Commissioner of Agriculture for the Year 1867* (Washington, D.C.: GPO, 1867), pp. 102–19; Roger L. Ransom and Richard Sutch, *One Kind of Freedom: The Economic Consequences of Emancipation* (London: Cambridge University Press, 1977), p. 51.

*Unfortunately, assessors in Orleans Parish did not break down property holding by race. East Carroll was formed out of Carroll Parish in 1877; Webster was created from portions of Bienville, Bossier, and Claiborne parishes in 1871. The data for Bienville are for 1892, for East Baton Rouge 1914, Natchitoches 1911, Plaquemines 1911 and 1916, St. John the Baptist 1899 and 1908, St. Landry 1900, St. Mary 1902 and 1905, and West Feliciana 1915.

Table 22. Number of Owners and Acres of Farm Land Owned by Negroes

[The total acres shown for the counties in this table do not agree in every case with the total from the tax receivers' reports, which were received several months later than the figures given in time changes were made in the ownership of property.]

Marginal number	County	Under 5 acres Owners	Under 5 acres Acres	5 or under 10 acres Owners	5 or under 10 acres Acres	10 or under 20 acres Owners	10 or under 20 acres Acres	20 or under 30 acres Owners	20 or under 30 acres Acres	30 or under 40 acres Owners	30 or under 40 acres Acres	40 or under 50 acres Owners	40 or under 50 acres Acres	50 or 75 Owners
1	Baker	1	3	1	8			1	20	1	34			9
2	Brooks	28	53	31	179	25	340	21	507	12	411	13	544	44
3	Calhoun	2	5			3	44	7	178	3	92			4
4	Campbell	3	4	3	20	3	37	8	178	6	213	6	253	8
5	Catoosa	2	5			1	15	2	47	1	35	3	120	1
6	Chattooga	2	5	2	10	2	23	2	40	2	63	2	85	5
7	Cherokee	5	11	1	5			1	20	1	35	16	640	5
8	Clay	9	16	4	28	3	32	1	25			1	49	5
9	Cobb	28	61	8	51	8	101	13	289	9	308	23	924	7
10	Columbia	16	39	10	67	7	95	11	242	7	229	1	47	10
11	Coweta	50	67	5	31	12	176	8	186	1	30	4	179	22
12	Dade	5	9	3	18	2	26	1	20					13
13	Dekalb	78	84	10	53	9	123	10	249	3	103	1	41	13
14	Dodge	28	54	12	62	18	219	10	228	6	180	3	133	28
15	Dooly	7	16	2	11	7	80	12	292	4	142	11	459	16
16	Effingham	48	91	37	222	61	741	38	893	21	700	18	775	32
17	Elbert	11	17	2	12	2	21	3	75	4	127	1	40	10
18	Floyd	3	8	8	52	19	242	28	659	6	188	29	1,175	13
19	Fulton	76	102	15	98	16	213	6	147	1	33	2	86	2
20	Glynn	110	241	84	534	135	1,617	71	1,627	25	816	23	972	23
21	Gwinnett	21	42	9	55	4	50	7	155	2	67	6	260	12
22	Hancock	93	177	32	207	17	218	9	215	6	194	5	221	30
23	Harris	14	24	2	11	7	82	12	293	2	68	5	205	22
24	Hart	3	7	1	8	2	22	5	116	3	104	3	126	9
25	Henry	8	15	3	19	4	54	3	74	3	90	3	134	22
26	Houston	28	52	7	43	14	178	9	205	5	155	8	332	27
27	Jefferson	2	6	5	32	9	117	8	180	5	170	7	298	14
28	Jones	13	33	15	103	8	97	4	100	3	108	3	120	11
29	Liberty	63	171	71	456	162	1,996	137	3,137	70	2,318	63	2,624	116
30	Lincoln					1	15			1	32	2	85	6
31	Lowndes	80	142	39	268	45	572	45	1,061	11	353	11	453	32
32	McIntosh	183	359	130	801	159	1,929	74	1,660	38	1,252	25	1,040	35
33	Macon	15	28	3	22	7	101	4	83	5	164	2	80	13
34	Marion	3	5					2	49	2	60			9
35	Monroe	155	252	9	54	12	146	6	129	1	30	9	386	31
36	Oglethorpe	3	10	5	30	2	21	1	20	5	154	3	123	10
37	Pierce	26	56	11	72	23	307	14	313	6	208	7	301	9
38	Polk	17	31	7	40	11	133	15	305	4	129	42	1,692	5
39	Putnam					1	20	2	50			2	80	2
40	Randolph	2	5	3	18	4	58	3	72	2	66	2	85	12
41	Richmond	35	85	34	219	35	460	13	301	7	230	7	305	16
42	Rockdale	3	6	2	11	2	22	2	53	3	102	1	40	6
43	Stewart	2	5	6	37	7	93	13	303	1	32	1	45	5
44	Sumter	48	105	18	118	10	137	6	143	6	209	6	260	18
45	Talbot	21	47	3	25	5	57	4	95	7	228	3	137	31
46	Taliaferro	20	48	8	52	9	122	2	44	5	169	6	240	7
47	Terrell	69	80	12	71	13	141	4	90	4	137	3	128	13
48	Thomas	105	166	42	273	51	653	54	1,211	24	788	20	872	48
49	Twiggs	4	8					2	47			1	45	8
50	Upson	18	36	2	10	2	21	2	45	5	164			4
51	Walton	9	15	4	33	4	53	5	121	2	74	1	47	9
52	Ware	26	40	11	62	20	262	12	276	8	252	1	46	17
53	Washington	8	20	6	37	9	101	8	184	4	130	8	333	21
54	Wayne	25	51	21	129	23	288	19	458	13	425	7	283	15
55	Wilkes	26	62	9	57	7	91	6	136	6	202	1	45	20
56	Wilkinson	29	65	5	36	3	41	2	42	3	95			7
	Total	1,689	3,145	773	4,870	1,025	12,803	768	17,688	385	12,698	431	17,993	929

Source: W. E. B. Du Bois, "The Negro Landholder of Georgia," in *Bulletin of the Department of*

in 56 Typical Counties of Georgia, by Classified Size of Holdings, 1899

shown for 1899 in the detailed tables. This discrepancy is due to the fact that this table is made up the detailed statements, which were taken from the comptroller-general's reports, and in this

Number of owners of farm land and total acres in each class															
under acres	75 or under 100 acres		100 or under 200 acres		200 or under 300 acres		300 or under 400 acres		400 or under 500 acres		500 acres or over		Total owners	Total acres	Marginal number
Acres	Owners	Acres	Owners	Acres.	Owners	Acres	Owners	Acres	Owners	Acres	Owners	Acres			
543	3	243	16	2,153	13	3,220	1	375	2	880	3	1,825	51	9,304	1
2,435	17	1,376	46	5,945	10	2,321	2	719	1	450	....	....	250	15,280	2
217	3	245	22	2,871	7	1,648	2	680	....	....	2	1,000	55	6,980	3
462	3	265	4	516	1	200	....	....	....	....	....	....	45	2,148	4
50	3	240	1	160	....	....	....	....	....	....	....	....	14	672	5
324	8	640	14	1,996	2	406	1	345	....	....	....	....	42	3,937	6
320	9	729	10	1,355	1	280	....	....	....	....	1	740	50	4,135	7
298	2	160	12	1,561	3	650	2	729	1	450	2	1,741	45	5,739	8
425	19	1,560	9	1,091	3	792	1	331	....	....	....	....	128	5,933	9
524	8	701	27	3,084	2	447	2	614	....	....	....	....	101	6,089	10
1,244	1	77	17	1,898	5	1,013	....	....	....	....	....	....	125	4,901	11
......	3	235	1	160	....	....	....	....	....	....	....	....	15	468	12
727	....	....	3	386	....	....	....	....	....	....	....	....	127	1,766	13
1,450	8	649	33	4,132	27	5,733	3	903	....	....	....	....	176	13,743	14
819	5	409	27	3,286	16	3,449	....	....	2	858	1	764	110	10,585	15
1,790	11	930	25	2,897	7	1,614	2	600	1	498	....	....	301	11,751	16
564	2	165	16	2,070	4	840	3	1,041	1	467	6	7,867	65	13,306	17
741	20	1,626	27	3,802	2	494	5	1,653	1	470	1	556	162	11,666	18
100	1	80	....	....	....	....	....	....	....	....	....	....	119	859	19
1,258	11	931	12	1,461	5	1,077	2	660	3	1,250	1	2,006	505	14,450	20
688	2	171	2	222	3	689	1	312	....	....	....	....	69	2,711	21
1,708	7	635	31	3,862	12	2,763	....	....	....	....	3	9,545	245	19,745	22
1,172	10	828	35	4,717	10	2,359	1	355	3	1,250	2	1,245	125	12,609	23
567	5	396	8	941	2	400	....	....	....	....	....	....	41	2,687	24
1,190	5	410	12	1,577	1	200	....	....	....	....	....	....	64	3,763	25
1,509	2	170	30	3,957	4	873	9	3,047	3	1,310	4	2,375	150	14,206	26
755	6	520	27	3,686	5	1,215	2	647	1	450	1	500	92	8,576	27
637	3	236	14	2,046	13	2,810	4	1,223	3	1,270	3	3,630	97	12,413	28
6,530	31	2,597	52	6,447	7	1,534	3	928	4	1,752	2	1,215	781	31,705	29
362	3	249	11	1,449	2	515	3	952	....	....	....	....	29	3,659	30
1,836	12	995	33	3,989	16	3,554	6	2,159	9	4,147	3	2,807	342	22,336	31
1,919	15	1,274	17	2,102	3	600	....	....	....	....	1	700	680	13,636	32
755	8	676	20	2,658	7	1,450	2	674	1	405	1	810	88	7,906	33
475	1	75	14	1,602	4	872	3	921	....	....	....	....	38	4,059	34
1,735	11	941	32	3,968	14	3,194	1	360	2	873	1	750	284	12,818	35
590	10	816	12	1,436	5	1,200	4	1,346	1	411	4	2,922	65	9,079	36
486	3	262	5	660	3	715	2	712	2	975	2	1,272	113	6,339	37
297	22	1,775	16	2,368	3	710	....	....	....	....	....	....	142	7,480	38
140	5	410	10	1,293	4	892	1	350	4	1,765	1	575	32	5,575	39
656	1	98	22	2,562	7	1,424	4	1,322	1	460	1	587	64	7,413	40
963	8	695	18	2,145	3	714	....	....	....	....	....	....	176	6,117	41
313	4	333	7	830	3	636	....	....	....	....	....	....	33	2,346	42
268	4	322	20	2,681	16	3,586	8	2,784	2	857	4	2,413	89	13,426	43
984	4	335	24	2,846	12	2,616	6	1,900	3	1,330	4	2,585	165	13,568	44
1,681	8	699	20	2,460	11	2,477	....	....	....	....	1	1,045	114	8,951	45
389	6	489	15	1,955	5	1,176	4	1,242	3	1,330	....	....	90	7,256	46
680	4	343	16	1,995	10	2,248	1	335	6	2,503	2	1,615	157	10,366	47
2,785	17	1,446	55	6,556	20	4,661	3	1,049	3	1,385	1	502	443	22,347	48
446	2	185	12	1,410	8	1,928	3	1,009	2	850	2	1,400	44	7,328	49
259	6	495	17	2,233	7	1,535	5	1,618	1	470	2	1,110	71	7,996	50
480	8	679	12	1,604	9	1,899	1	300	....	....	....	....	64	5,305	51
927	2	175	7	893	3	772	1	300	2	980	1	937	111	5,922	52
1,233	7	632	25	3,247	5	1,135	1	300	....	....	3	2,784	105	10,136	53
867	6	514	11	1,404	3	660	5	1,723	4	1,804	3	3,055	155	11,661	54
1,130	12	1,010	29	3,680	16	3,632	....	....	1	478	3	2,667	136	13,190	55
417	5	454	19	2,487	4	944	3	938	2	880	3	2,383	85	8,782	56
52,120	402	33,601	1,032	130,792	368	82,772	113	37,456	75	33,258	75	67,928	a8,065	507,124	

Labor, #35 (Washington, D.C.: GPO, 1901), pp. 672–73.

Table 23. Number of Owners and Assessed Value of Farm Land Owned by

[The total value of farm land shown for the counties in this table does not agree in every case with made up from the tax receivers' reports, which were received several months later than the figures this time changes were made in the ownership of property.]

Marginal number.	County.	Under $50.		$50 or under $100.		$100 or under $200.		$200 or under $300.		$300 or under $400.		$400 or under $500.	
		Owners.	Value.	Owners.	Value.	Owners.	Value.	Owners.	Value.	Owners.	Value.	Owners.	Value.
1	Baker........	2	$22	6	$458	16	$2,284	8	$1,923	7	$2,575	1	$450
2	Brooks......	44	1,113	49	3,152	51	6,679	37	8,508	28	9,247	12	5,044
3	Calhoun	4	134	5	385	10	1,197	8	1,885	15	4,760	4	1,680
4	Campbell	6	146	2	110	10	1,486	12	2,785	6	1,973	2	880
5	Catoosa	3	85	3	210	6	780	1	250	1	400	......	......
6	Chattooga....	4	76	10	675	10	1,256	7	1,500	3	1,000	3	1,300
7	Cherokee	9	189	14	940	14	1,815	9	1,900	2	600	1	400
8	Clay	12	290	4	279	8	1,071	9	2,100	4	1,254	1	462
9	Cobb........	2	55	22	1,405	37	4,580	15	3,440	11	3,435	10	4,270
10	Columbia	30	695	18	1,281	14	2,034	8	2,099	21	6,525	5	2,196
11	Coweta	22	488	20	1,800	17	2,250	12	2,742	10	3,242	3	1,270
12	Dade........	3	70	8	543	2	275	1	250	1	300	......	......
13	Dekalb......	22	655	16	965	44	5,473	11	2,543	10	3,230	6	2,525
14	Dodge........	35	976	28	1,759	43	5,585	28	6,371	9	3,122	21	9,507
15	Dooly	12	334	24	1,438	26	3,477	6	1,418	18	5,744	5	2,133
16	Effingham ...	119	3,070	84	5,181	69	8,229	22	4,980	3	900	1	498
17	Elbert........	9	233	7	504	10	1,376	8	1,878	4	1,245	5	2,183
18	Floyd........	19	615	27	1,792	44	5,666	24	5,285	17	5,379	10	4,230
19	Fulton........	21	600	43	2,680	101	12,575	65	14,270	54	16,865	42	17,085
20	Glynn........	201	4,917	165	9,871	96	11,928	22	4,720	10	3,200	6	2,500
21	Gwinnett	16	403	12	755	13	1,760	13	2,842	8	2,515	2	986
22	Hancock......	27	710	42	2,808	76	9,699	39	9,103	22	7,143	10	4,313
23	Harris........	19	461	19	1,339	27	3,725	12	2,669	16	5,324	10	4,286
24	Hart	5	105	4	335	10	1,464	9	2,156	6	1,922	3	1,322
25	Henry	5	139	7	450	6	844	6	1,534	19	6,042	5	2,130
26	Houston	35	830	19	1,155	24	3,420	18	4,060	10	3,125	6	2,675
27	Jefferson	5	146	15	985	32	4,290	6	1,430	12	4,080	12	5,225
28	Jones	34	690	4	300	16	2,187	7	1,654	6	1,865	5	2,155
29	Liberty	419	10,565	274	17,671	164	19,813	32	7,290	10	3,175	3	1,200
30	Lincoln......	1	45	1	80	8	1,188	4	947	7	2,274	1	441
31	Lowndes......	74	1,852	71	4,373	106	12,275	35	7,723	25	7,875	7	2,800
32	McIntosh	327	8,200	265	15,273	101	12,168	7	1,500	2	650	1	400
33	Macon	10	222	16	932	14	1,928	12	2,560	11	3,670	4	1,740
34	Marion......	3	75	2	132	13	1,865	7	1,500	5	1,550	3	1,295
35	Monroe	58	1,502	84	5,184	44	5,216	35	7,753	14	4,638	21	8,734
36	Oglethorpe...	4	95	9	577	7	948	13	3,089	9	2,829	4	1,650
37	Pierce........	19	498	26	1,670	28	3,457	16	3,325	5	1,635	7	2,925
38	Polk	24	698	36	2,170	35	4,060	20	4,311	17	5,430	3	1,300
39	Putnam......	......	......	2	150	2	322	3	662	2	640	4	1,769
40	Randolph....	2	65	7	500	12	1,465	7	1,625	8	2,645	7	2,855
41	Richmond ...	8	245	47	2,715	61	7,260	29	6,250	8	2,500	4	1,600
42	Rockdale	3	85	5	312	......	......	6	1,440	6	1,932	2	800
43	Stewart	8	200	21	1,460	12	1,525	9	2,030	6	1,850	8	3,380
44	Sumter......	26	714	28	1,826	25	3,086	21	4,792	13	4,235	10	4,000
45	Talbot	32	496	16	1,115	29	4,156	10	2,289	9	2,870	9	3,893
46	Taliaferro...	28	535	8	548	21	2,806	4	1,312	7	2,442	5	2,203
47	Terrell	24	700	38	2,120	25	3,038	12	2,760	13	4,092	3	1,200
48	Thomas......	120	3,418	110	5,891	104	12,876	43	9,918	29	9,457	14	5,863
49	Twiggs......	4	94	6	340	8	1,187	8	1,758	3	970	3	1,342
50	Upson........	18	336	4	246	10	1,410	10	2,280	4	1,203	9	3,896
51	Walton	9	237	6	387	6	828	9	2,130	9	2,938	4	1,775
52	Ware........	19	433	30	1,760	38	4,519	12	2,777	5	1,600	3	1,200
53	Washington..	13	265	9	554	24	3,229	18	4,497	11	3,738	8	3,459
54	Wayne........	68	1,689	48	2,915	26	3,239	4	986	4	1,268	3	1,290
55	Wilkes......	23	590	13	885	14	1,820	25	5,650	20	6,815	10	4,385
56	Wilkinson ...	28	715	12	690	10	1,258	14	3,438	6	1,966	3	1,248
	Total...	2,097	52,816	1,871	115,431	1,779	224,347	850	192,887	601	193,899	354	150,348

Source: W. E. B. Du Bois, "The Negro Landholder of Georgia," in *Bulletin of the Department of*

Negroes in 56 Typical Counties of Georgia, by Classified Value of Holdings, 1899

the total shown for 1899 in the detailed tables. This discrepancy is due to the fact that this table is shown in the detailed statements, which were taken from the comptroller-general's reports, and in

Number of owners and assessed value of farm land in each class.												Total owners.	Total assessed value.	Marginal number.
$500 or under $750.		$750 or under $1,000.		$1,000 or under $1,250.		$1,250 or under $1,500.		$1,500 or under $2,000.		$2,000 or over.				
Owners.	Value.	Owners.	Value.	Owners.	Value.	Owners.	Value.	Owners.	Value.	Owners.	Value.			
5	$2,514	3	$2,490	2	$2,000	.....	....	1	$1,650	.....	....	51	$16,366	1
19	10,563	6	4,938	3	3,200			1	1,650			250	54,094	2
5	2,550	1	800	3	3,140							55	16,531	3
3	1,700	1	750	2	2,000			1	1,800			45	13,630	4
.....												14	1,725	5
3	1,565	.....	....	1	1,000			1	1,932			42	10,304	6
				1	1,000							50	6,844	7
3	1,775	2	1,737	.....	....	1	$1,300	.....	....	1	$2,823	45	13,091	8
21	12,070	3	2,350	2	2,070	1	1,280	1	1,840	3	7,010	128	43,805	9
2	1,131	3	2,683									101	18,644	10
13	7,697	3	2,490	2	2,225	2	2,718	3	4,775			107	31,197	11
												15	1,438	12
12	6,450	3	2,515	1	1,000			3	4,550			128	29,906	13
12	7,142											176	34,462	14
13	7,667	3	2,357	1	1,247	1	1,332			1	2,293	110	29,440	15
3	1,600	.....										301	24,458	16
8	4,632			3	3,260	3	4,188	1	1,868	1	13,328	65	34,695	17
12	7,100	2	1,600	3	3,200	1	1,336			3	9,000	162	45,203	18
30	17,525	9	7,480	4	4,400			3	4,600	3	6,500	375	104,580	19
1	500	2	1,500	2	2,000					1	2,600	506	43,736	20
1	600	2	1,766					2	3,125			69	14,752	21
22	12,770	.....	....	3	3,148	1	1,485	1	1,500	6	45,225	245	97,904	22
14	8,582	2	1,600	3	3,275	2	2,672			1	2,980	125	36,913	23
3	1,820	1	750									41	9,874	24
9	5,397	4	3,270	3	3,459							64	23,265	25
15	8,740	6	4,850	5	5,465	3	4,100	4	7,095	5	10,740	150	56,255	26
5	2,950	2	1,770	1	1,125			1	1,500			91	23,501	27
15	9,040	4	3,480	3	3,435			1	1,880	2	9,700	97	36,386	28
4	2,355	.....	....	1	1,030							907	63,099	29
3	1,719	4	3,328									29	10,022	30
12	6,959	6	4,865	1	1,000	1	1,300	3	5,260	1	2,600	342	58,882	31
3	1,748	.....										706	39,939	32
7	4,145	4	3,368	1	1,000	1	1,415	1	1,600	1	2,170	82	24,750	33
3	1,877	2	1,833									38	10,127	34
14	8,212	9	7,262	4	4,529	2	2,690	1	1,892	2	5,450	288	63,062	35
7	3,883	1	800	6	6,433	1	1,348	1	1,945	3	7,241	65	30,838	36
7	4,100	4	3,325									112	20,835	37
2	1,060	4	3,250	2	2,350							143	24,629	38
9	5,525	4	3,318	.....		1	1,400			5	12,192	32	25,978	39
11	6,060	6	4,605	1	1,000			1	1,600	2	4,400	64	26,820	40
9	4,730	4	3,350	2	2,000	2	2,750	2	3,260			176	36,660	41
5	3,026	2	1,684	3	3,570			2	3,000			34	15,849	42
12	7,425	5	4,000	5	5,100	2	2,650	1	1,600			89	31,220	43
15	8,753	7	5,903	5	5,305	2	2,800	5	8,360	10	30,057	167	79,831	44
7	4,091	2	1,550							1	2,612	115	23,072	45
7	4,199	5	4,161	.....		3	3,990					90	22,196	46
15	9,306	7	5,697	3	3,655	2	2,900	3	4,750	4	9,325	149	49,543	47
15	8,308	4	3,425	4	4,127							443	63,283	48
6	3,346	2	1,542	3	3,325					1	2,000	44	15,904	49
7	4,187	4	3,180	2	2,175	1	1,300	1	1,500	1	2,000	71	23,713	50
9	5,140	6	4,967	4	4,200							62	22,602	51
5	2,610	.....										112	14,899	52
10	5,482	5	4,437	6	6,560					2	9,186	106	41,407	53
1	500	1	856									155	12,743	54
20	12,260	7	5,805	.....				1	1,670	3	9,055	136	48,935	55
5	3,013	2	1,595	2	2,190			2	3,466	1	2,000	85	21,579	56
479	278,099	173	142,542	100	107,938	33	44,954	48	79,668	65	212,487	a8,450	1,795,416	

Labor, #35 (Washington, D.C.: GPO, 1901), pp. 674–75.

Table 24. Number of Owners and Assessed Value of Town and City Real Estate Owned

[The total value of town and city real estate shown for the counties in this table does not agree in that this table is made up from the tax receivers' reports, which were received several months later reports, and in this time changes were made in the ownership of property.]

Marginal number	County	\$ Under \$50. Owners.	Value.	\$50 or under \$100. Owners.	Value.	\$100 or under \$200. Owners.	Value.	\$200 or under \$300. Owners.	Value.	\$300 or under \$400. Owners.	Value.	\$400 or under \$500. Owners.	Value.
1	Baker			1	\$50	1	\$100						
2	Brooks	11	\$360	30	1,910	33	4,225	6	\$1,275	5	\$1,650	2	\$800
3	Calhoun	7	180	17	1,120	24	3,265	6	1,315	6	1,800	2	800
4	Campbell	9	213	12	695	23	2,815	16	3,270	3	900	3	1,200
5	Catoosa	4	140	5	300	7	940						
6	Chattooga	6	115	3	205	7	875	3	640				
7	Cherokee	4	120	4	255	3	425	2	487				
8	Clay	4	120	17	1,110	22	2,950	5	1,095	1	350		
9	Cobb	2	85	22	1,425	30	3,740	37	7,900	22	6,915	15	6,550
10	Columbia	8	119										
11	Coweta	22	570	73	4,610	76	9,685	37	7,840	10	3,100	9	3,740
12	Dade					1	150						
13	Dekalb	13	357	20	1,270	28	3,500	23	4,885	11	3,430	4	1,600
14	Dodge	14	445	30	1,787	19	2,205	3	700	1	800		
15	Dooly	79	2,140	65	4,253	75	9,720	23	4,980	5	1,563	1	400
16	Effingham	1	25	2	100	2	250						
17	Elbert	1	40	7	475	20	2,625	11	2,525	7	2,290	3	1,200
18	Floyd	24	562	52	3,495	62	8,082	43	9,728	38	12,150	19	7,772
19	Fulton	1	35	5	310	30	3,490	86	18,985	140	42,595	153	62,130
20	Glynn	18	440	15	895	55	7,085	53	12,010	57	18,010	26	10,720
21	Gwinnett	15	416	19	1,175	7	945	2	450			1	445
22	Hancock							2	430	1	300	2	800
23	Harris	5	148	6	375	4	550	8	1,760	1	350		
24	Hart	12	308	13	865	6	660	2	415				
25	Henry	8	180	28	1,640	10	1,340	5	1,100	1	300	1	400
26	Houston	54	1,565	66	4,245	33	4,245	9	2,050	4	1,250		
27	Jefferson	4	86	27	1,745	35	4,225	7	1,550	3	900		
28	Jones	11	310	2	155	7	935	1	200				
29	Liberty	1	35	4	255	3	305	3	630				
30	Lincoln												
31	Lowndes	11	350	42	2,620	77	10,045	33	7,466	28	8,675	11	4,600
32	McIntosh	41	1,228	56	3,410	103	12,908	38	8,475	23	7,275	7	2,900
33	Macon	27	677	46	3,009	62	7,995	22	4,872	11	3,500		
34	Marion	13	290	41	2,645	44	5,710	15	3,250	5	1,550	1	450
35	Monroe	4	90	26	1,665	16	1,930	6	1,300	3	950		
36	Oglethorpe	5	170	13	795	8	1,125			1	350	1	400
37	Pierce	8	243	9	560	18	2,420	2	500	2	600	3	1,290
38	Polk	15	395	9	560	13	1,750	7	1,550	3	900	4	1,675
39	Putnam					12	1,930	16	3,745	8	2,680	2	880
40	Randolph	21	640	59	3,780	67	8,690	22	4,785	13	4,030	4	1,625
41	Richmond	23	555	161	8,385	211	26,230	234	52,830	173	55,860	116	48,680
42	Rockdale	6	110	10	590	17	2,160	9	1,950	3	900	4	1,640
43	Stewart	46	1,290	36	2,275	35	4,015	8	1,700	2	600	1	400
44	Sumter	20	500	30	1,815	95	12,240	89	19,888	65	20,745	43	17,820
45	Talbot	16	425	31	1,870	23	2,775	4	925	1	300		
46	Taliaferro	4	90	1	75	4	575	1	250				
47	Terrell	2	70	11	684	18	2,394	15	3,238	9	2,710	2	818
48	Thomas	29	716	66	4,278	146	19,063	72	15,827	20	6,525	11	4,625
49	Twiggs	1	20			1	100						
50	Upson	15	297	23	1,395	14	1,760	3	600	3	900		
51	Walton	11	250	11	610	18	2,310	9	1,964	4	1,300	1	400
52	Ware	10	333	17	1,080	48	6,172	42	9,440	26	8,035	13	5,450
53	Washington	14	385	22	1,450	29	3,615	7	1,590	6	1,900	1	450
54	Wayne	7	125	7	375	12	1,385	12	2,500	5	1,550	2	850
55	Wilkes	19	585	46	2,790	83	11,000	40	8,915	15	4,600	10	4,110
56	Wilkinson	5	130	9	545	5	650			1	300		
	Total	711	19,078	1,327	81,981	1,802	230,279	1,099	243,780	746	234,888	478	197,620

Source: W. E. B. Du Bois, "The Negro Landholder of Georgia," in *Bulletin of the Department of*

by Negroes in 56 Typical Counties of Georgia, by Classified Size of Holdings, 1899

every case with the total shown for 1899 in the detailed tables. This discrepancy is due to the fact than the figures shown in the detailed statements, which were taken from the comptroller general's

Number of owners and assessed value of town and city real estate in each class.													Mar-ginal number.
$500 or under $750.		$750 or under $1,000.		$1,000 or under $1,250.		$1,250 or under $1,500.		$1,500 or under $2,000.		$2,000 or over.		Total owners.	Total assessed value.
Owners.	Value.	Owners.	Value.	Owners.	Value.	Owners.	Value.	Owners.	Value.	Owners.	Value.			
1	$500					1	$1,350					2	$150	1
1	600					1	1,300					89	12,070	2
												64	10,380	3
		1	$800									67	9,893	4
												16	1,380	5
1	700	1	800									21	3,335	6
2	1,100											15	2,387	7
1	600											50	6,225	8
25	13,950	8	6,350	4	$4,200	2	280			2	$10,000	169	63,995	9
												8	119	10
9	5,200	5	4,265	3	3,175					1	2,100	245	44,285	11
												1	150	12
12	6,975	1	800	4	4,000							116	26,817	13
												67	5,437	14
6	3,195	2	1,720									256	27,971	15
												5	375	16
6	3,200	3	2,600									58	14,955	17
18	10,050	8	6,950	2	2,200	1	1,300	1	$1,600	2	6,975	270	70,864	18
324	186,390	114	93,100	98	105,400	16	21,625	44	72,100	52	187,750	1,063	793,910	19
40	22,975	13	10,600	9	9,270	5	6,620	5	8,300	4	16,290	300	123,215	20
												44	3,431	21
1	550							1	1,700			7	3,780	22
1	500			1	1,000							26	4,683	23
												33	2,248	24
												53	4,960	25
1	500											167	13,855	26
				1	1,000							77	9,506	27
1	724											22	2,324	28
												11	1,225	29
														30
9	4,600	1	900	1	1,000			1	1,600	1	3,000	215	44,856	31
11	6,225	5	4,100	2	2,200			1	1,700			287	50,421	32
3	1,700	1	800									172	22,553	33
2	1,150											121	15,045	34
3	1,500			1	1,075							59	8,510	35
												28	2,840	36
												42	5,613	37
		1	775									52	7,605	38
9	5,320	1	900									48	15,455	39
5	2,845			1	1,000	1	1,300			1	2,500	194	31,195	40
176	101,820	70	58,510	34	37,200	16	21,630	25	44,830	30	136,460	1,269	592,990	41
1	700	1	825									51	8,875	42
2	1,100											130	11,380	43
47	26,150	29	23,490	13	13,815	6	7,925	6	10,225	6	29,915	449	184,528	44
												75	6,295	45
1	600											11	1,590	46
3	1,800			1	1,050							61	12,764	47
20	11,705	2	1,700	2	2,100					1	2,200	369	68,739	48
												2	120	49
1	500	2	1,650	1	1,200							62	8,302	50
												54	6,834	51
16	9,045	8	6,925					1	1,670	1	3,100	182	51,250	52
4	2,125											83	11,515	53
7	3,600											52	10,385	54
13	7,900	2	1,600	1	1,000			1	1,500			230	44,000	55
												20	1,625	56
783	448,094	279	230,160	179	191,885	49	65,930	86	145,225	101	400,290	7,640	2,489,210	

Labor, #35 (Washington, D.C.: GPO, 1901), pp. 678–9.

The Manuscript Population Censuses

Table 25. Distribution Analysis of Black Real Estate
Owners in the Lower South, 1850

Value	Frequency	Percentage	Cum Percentage
$100–200	288	15.8	15.8
300–400	236	13.0	28.8
500–600	212	11.6	40.4
700–900	147	8.1	48.5
1,000–1,900	355	19.5	68.0
2,000–2,900	174	9.6	77.5
3,000–4,900	166	9.1	86.7
5,000 or more	243	13.3	100.0
Total	1,821	100.0	100.0

Mean = $2,810   Median = $1,000   Std Dev = 78.93
Minimum = $100   Maximum = $150,000

Table 26. Distribution Analysis of Black Real Estate
Owners in the Upper South, 1850

Value	Frequency	Percentage	Cum Percentage
$100–200	1,678	38.5	38.5
300–400	1,109	25.4	63.9
500–600	659	15.1	79.0
700–900	283	6.5	85.5
1,000–1,900	419	9.6	95.1
2,000–2,900	105	2.4	97.5
3,000–4,900	75	1.7	99.2
5,000 or more	33	.8	100.0
Total	4,361	100.0	100.0

Mean = $585   Median = $300   Std Dev = 12.81
Minimum = $100   Maximum = $40,000

Table 27. Distribution Analysis of Black Real Estate
Owners in the Lower South, 1860

Value	Frequency	Percentage	Cum Percentage
$100–200	246	10.6	10.6
300–400	259	11.2	21.8
500–600	307	13.2	35.0
700–900	197	8.5	43.5
1,000–1,900	604	26.0	69.6
2,000–2,900	246	10.6	80.2
3,000–4,900	196	8.5	88.6
5,000 or more	264	11.4	100.0
Total	2,319	100.0	100.0

Mean = $3,069   Median = $1,000   Std Dev = 121.25
Minimum = $100   Maximum = $250,000

Table 28. Distribution Analysis of Black Real Estate
Owners in the Upper South, 1860

Value	Frequency	Percentage	Cum Percentage
$100–200	2,349	32.1	32.1
300–400	1,577	21.5	53.6
500–600	1,197	16.4	70.0
700–900	620	8.5	78.4
1,000–1,900	959	13.1	91.5
2,000–2,900	284	3.9	95.4
3,000–4,900	193	2.6	98.1
5,000 or more	142	1.9	100.0
Total	7,321	100.0	100.0

Mean = $782   Median = $400   Std Dev = 15.83
Minimum = $100 Maximum = $50,000

Table 29. Distribution Analysis of Black Real Estate Owners in the Lower South, 1870

Value	Frequency	Percentage	Cum Percentage
$100–200	8,286	40.5	40.5
300–400	4,455	21.8	62.2
500–600	3,192	15.6	77.8
700–900	1,419	6.9	84.8
1,000–1,900	1,844	9.0	93.8
2,000–2,900	541	2.6	96.4
3,000–4,900	406	2.0	98.4
5,000 or more	331	1.6	100.0
Total	20,474	100.0	100.0

Mean = $688   Median = $300   Std Dev = 30.86   Minimum = $100
Maximum = $300,000

Table 30. Distribution Analysis of Black Real Estate Owners in the Upper South, 1870

Value	Frequency	Percentage	Cum Percentage
$100–200	6,054	26.6	26.6
300–400	5,689	25.0	51.5
500–600	4,370	19.2	70.7
700–900	1,949	8.6	79.2
1,000–1,900	2,918	12.8	92.0
2,000–2,900	837	3.7	95.7
3,000–4,900	536	2.4	98.1
5,000 or more	441	1.9	100.0
Total	22,794	100.0	100.0

Mean = $798   Median = $400   Std Dev = 20.10   Minimum = $100
Maximum = $150,000

Table 31. Occupations among Propertied Blacks in the South, 1850 and 1860

Occupation	1850 Total percentages			1860 (real) Total percentages			1860 (te) Total percentages		
			Arph			Arph			Ateh
farmers	1,590	36.8	$845	2,430	30.6	$998	3,707	27.3	$1,211
laborers	975	22.6	357	2,156	27.1	442	3,552	26.2	431
planters	203	4.7	5,660	219	2.8	9,514	247	1.8	12,254
craftsmen									
blacksmiths	115	2.7	653	122	1.5	902	249	1.8	792
brickmasons	84	1.9	914	111	1.4	1,334	235	1.7	937
carpenters	344	8.0	1,315	431	5.4	1,087	726	5.4	1,022
coopers	32	.7	516	59	.7	569	102	.8	518
masons	34	.8	809	53	.7	774	98	.7	732
mechanics	41	.9	683	52	.7	1,712	88	.7	1,781
plasterers	21	.5	1,143	30	.4	903	42	.3	938
shoemakers	75	1.7	1,328	95	1.2	1,053	194	1.4	916
shopkeepers and tradesmen									
barbers	105	2.4	1,506	132	1.7	2,714	263	1.9	2,114
boardinghouse keepers	3	.1	6,467	21	.3	2,624	124	.9	1,516
butchers	21	.5	3,871	35	.4	1,514	50	.4	1,640
grocers	30	.7	4,337	25	.3	7,072	30	.2	6,977
merchants	24	.6	5,588	25	.3	8,936	30	.2	10,440
restaurateurs	7	.2	2,614	12	.2	1,108	33	.2	1,133
storekeepers	14	.3	4,364	19	.2	1,700	38	.3	1,900
tailors	30	.7	3,060	33	.4	10,609	57	.4	6,611
service									
coachmen	11	.3	691	42	.5	1,919	101	.7	1,252
draymen	72	1.7	650	149	1.9	1,137	458	3.4	718
laundresses	7	.2	257	408	5.1	626	751	5.5	496
painters	27	.6	748	64	.8	1,094	122	.9	820
porters	17	.4	1,053	43	.5	1,535	145	1.1	797
seamstresses	1	.0	600	113	1.4	1,138	243	1.8	816
servants	18	.4	606	177	2.2	932	345	2.5	760
stewards	13	.3	1,323	18	.2	3,083	42	.3	1,681
mariners	48	1.1	627	91	1.1	515	140	1.0	504
ministers	16	.4	1,419	31	.4	1,129	55	.4	956
physicians	3	.1	1,867	6	.1	5,750	9	.1	4,122
teachers	5	.1	1,260	10	.1	1,520	18	.1	1,967

Source: Computed from USMSPC, 1850, 1860.

Table 32. Occupations among Upper and Lower South
Black Real Estate Owners, 1860/1870

Occupation	Upper South		Lower South	
	Total	Arph	Total	Arph
farmers	2,044/7,177	$908/742	386/10,940	$1,476/540
laborers	2,054/6,460	408/498	102/3,148	1,126/364
planters	5/none	1,200/0	214/215	9,708/1,727
craftsmen				
blacksmiths	109/582	895/691	13/356	962/531
brickmasons	69/333	652/736	42/288	2,455/720
carpenters	221/969	885/741	210/1,095	1,300/558
caulkers	21/20	571/1,450	7/20	957/300
coopers	50/73	494/662	9/33	989/1,267
masons	39/228	505/586	14/3	1,521/1,367
mechanics	32/39	903/1,508	20/122	3,005/730
plasterers	26/250	904/740	4/50	900/692
shoemakers	70/250	709/727	25/186	2,016/523
shopkeepers and tradesmen				
barbers	114/261	2,866/2,310	18/144	1,750/1,115
boardinghouse/ hotel keepers	2/15	1,900/9,827	19/9	2,700/2,800
butchers	12/53	1,242/958	23/65	1,657/1,292
grocers	8/112	1,388/1,588	17/149	9,747/1,624
merchants	7/48	6,629/2,333	18/47	9,833/10,515
restaurateurs	8/80	1,100/1,460	4/16	1,125/1,944
storekeepers	15/33	1,960/927	4/22	725/523
tailors	9/4	1,689/1,500	24/48	13,954/2,125
service				
coachmen	39/96	1,944/1,040	3/4	1,600/1,025
cooks	32/122	1,138/974	6/29	667/1,300
draymen	115/469	1,088/934	34/384	1,303/590
laundresses	330/171	592/832	78/90	772/473
painters	55/124	925/785	9/45	2,122/896
porters	32/205	1,453/1,563	11/82	1,773/473
seamstresses	54/48	713/1,540	59/41	1,527/1,827
servants	164/332	924/1,004	13/169	1,031/555
stewards	17/24	3,194/4,683	1/6	1,200/1,917
mariners	89/80	496/708	2/1	1,400/500
ministers	24/367	1,133/1,034	7/174	1,114/940
physicians	3/15	2,167/2,680	3/6	9,333/2,250
teachers	5/14	1,960/3,007	5/14	1,080/2,571

Source: Computed from USMSPC, 1860, 1870.

Table 33. Real Estate Holdings among Blacks and
Mulattoes, 1850

Variable Value Label	Mean	Cases
For Entire Population	$1,240.39	6,182
Alabama	$987.50	80
Black	$923.81	21
Mulatto	$1,010.17	59
Arkansas	$651.22	41
Black	$785.71	14
Mulatto	$581.48	27
Delaware	$505.16	446
Black	$479.75	400
Mulatto	$726.09	46
District of Columbia	$650.00	200
Black	$615.75	127
Mulatto	$709.59	73
Florida	$754.35	46
Black	$407.14	14
Mulatto	$906.25	32
Georgia	$821.62	74
Black	$376.67	30
Mulatto	$1,125.00	44
Kentucky	$710.10	584
Black	$585.07	402
Mulatto	$986.26	182
Louisiana	$3,646.22	1,244
Black	$1,364.98	217
Mulatto	$4,128.24	1,027
Maryland	$535.96	1,154
Black	$451.11	904
Mulatto	$842.80	250
Mississippi	$1,138.46	39
Black	$784.62	13
Mulatto	$1,315.38	26
Missouri	$1,516.28	86
Black	$998.18	55
Mulatto	$2,435.48	31
North Carolina	$412.08	654
Black	$385.40	226
Mulatto	$426.17	428
South Carolina	$1,102.46	284
Black	$545.68	81
Mulatto	$1,324.63	203
Tennessee	$781.25	208
Black	$873.47	98
Mulatto	$699.09	110

Table 33. (*continued*)

Variable Value Label	Mean	Cases
Texas	$1,753.85	13
Black	$1,780.00	5
Mulatto	$1,737.50	8
Virginia	$582.90	1,029
Black	$479.55	577
Mulatto	$714.82	452

Table 34. Real Estate Holdings among Men and Women, 1850

Variable Value Label	Mean	Cases
For Entire Population	$1,240.39	6,182
Alabama	$987.50	80
Male	$1,031.25	64
Female	$812.50	16
Arkansas	$651.22	41
Male	$632.35	34
Female	$742.86	7
Delaware	$505.16	446
Male	$465.36	407
Female	$920.51	39
District of Columbia	$650.00	200
Male	$675.29	170
Female	$506.67	30
Florida	$754.35	46
Male	$651.72	29
Female	$929.41	17
Georgia	$821.62	74
Male	$857.69	52
Female	$736.36	22
Kentucky	$710.10	584
Male	$755.27	465
Female	$533.61	119
Louisiana	$3,646.22	1,244
Male	$3,669.28	817
Female	$3,602.11	427
Maryland	$535.96	1,154
Male	$554.36	1,043
Female	$363.06	111
Mississippi	$1,138.46	39
Male	$1,038.46	26
Female	$1,338.46	13

Table 34. (*continued*)

Variable Value Label	Mean	Cases
Missouri	$1,516.28	86
Male	$1,688.06	67
Female	$910.53	19
North Carolina	$412.08	654
Male	$414.58	542
Female	$400.00	112
South Carolina	$1,102.46	284
Male	$1,095.18	228
Female	$1,132.14	56
Tennessee	$781.25	208
Male	$807.91	177
Female	$629.03	31
Texas	$1,753.85	13
Male	$2,050.00	10
Female	$766.67	3
Virginia	$582.90	1,029
Male	$596.48	795
Female	$536.75	234

Table 35. Total Estate Holdings among Blacks and
Mulattoes, 1860

Variable Value Label	Mean	Cases
For Entire Population	$1,252.36	16,172
Alabama	$2,072.12	226
Black	$1,300.00	47
Mulatto	$2,274.86	179
Arkansas	$1,125.00	4
Black	$900.00	1
Mulatto	$1,200.00	3
Delaware	$561.95	1,059
Black	$543.59	842
Mulatto	$633.18	217
District of Columbia	$1,109.00	711
Black	$931.59	440
Mulatto	$1,397.05	271
Florida	$1,603.81	105
Black	$637.21	43
Mulatto	$2,274.19	62
Georgia	$895.80	286
Black	$683.65	104
Mulatto	$1,017.03	182

Table 35. (*continued*)

Variable Value Label	Mean	Cases
Kentucky	$832.23	1,173
Black	$700.64	782
Mulatto	$1,095.40	391
Louisiana	$3,673.71	2,221
Black	$1,522.38	411
Mulatto	$4,162.21	1,810
Maryland	$643.28	4,013
Black	$583.30	3,198
Mulatto	$878.65	815
Mississippi	$3,971.70	53
Black	$3,833.33	15
Mulatto	$4,026.32	38
Missouri	$1,786.55	357
Black	$1,066.33	199
Mulatto	$2,693.67	158
North Carolina	$639.55	1,679
Black	$475.62	447
Mulatto	$655.24	1,222
Unknown	$6,050.00	10
South Carolina	$1,759.70	1,077
Black	$1,056.57	251
Mulatto	$1,983.21	655
Tennessee	$1,244.25	513
Black	$1,102.10	238
Mulatto	$1,367.27	275
Texas	$1,681.25	32
Black	$1,000.00	9
Mulatto	$1,947.83	23
Virginia	$655.58	2,663
Black	$551.67	1,467
Mulatto	$776.99	1,195
Unknown	$8,000.00	1

Table 36. Total Estate Holdings among Men and Women,
1860

Variable Value Label	Mean	Cases
For Entire Population	$1,249.46	16,155
Alabama	$2,072.12	226
Male	$2,360.37	164
Female	$1,309.68	62
Arkansas	$1,125.00	4
Male	$1,125.00	4
Delaware	$561.95	1,059
Male	$570.65	988
Female	$440.85	71
District of Columbia	$1,109.00	711
Male	$1,148.92	556
Female	$965.81	155
Florida	$1,603.81	105
Male	$1,013.24	68
Female	$2,689.19	37
Georgia	$895.80	286
Male	$955.93	177
Female	$798.17	109
Kentucky	$832.23	1,173
Male	$871.03	932
Female	$682.16	241
Louisiana	$3,673.71	2,221
Male	$3,832.60	1,555
Female	$3,302.70	666
Maryland	$643.28	4,013
Male	$656.02	3,649
Female	$515.66	364
Mississippi	$3,971.70	53
Male	$4,502.70	37
Female	$2,743.75	16
Missouri	$1,786.55	357
Male	$1,659.00	300
Female	$2,457.89	57
North Carolina	$607.13	1,669
Male	$631.34	1,369
Female	$496.67	300
South Carolina	$1,764.02	1,070
Male	$1,715.07	783
Female	$1,897.56	287
Tennessee	$1,244.25	513
Male	$1,245.17	414
Female	$1,240.40	99

Table 36. (*continued*)

Variable Value Label	Mean	Cases
Texas	$1,681.25	32
Male	$1,218.18	22
Female	$2,700.00	10
Virginia	$655.58	2,663
Male	$653.18	2,106
Female	$664.63	557
Missing Cases = 17 or 0.1 Pct.		

Table 37. Total Estate Holdings among Blacks and
Mulattoes, 1870

Variable Value Label	Mean	Cases
For Entire Population	$407.82	168,034
Alabama	$330.37	15,317
Black	$298.80	13,432
Mulatto	$555.33	1,885
Arkansas	$340.14	7,113
Black	$314.84	6,245
Mulatto	$522.12	868
Delaware	$899.35	1,232
Black	$825.02	1,083
Mulatto	$1,439.60	149
District of Columbia	$1,712.48	1,578
Black	$1,290.20	1,153
Mulatto	$2,858.12	425
Florida	$317.38	3,315
Black	$285.68	2,836
Mulatto	$505.01	479
Georgia	$295.23	17,739
Black	$271.36	15,490
Mulatto	$459.63	2,249
Kentucky	$478.50	11,629
Black	$429.19	9,672
Mulatto	$722.23	1,957
Louisiana	$516.86	14,569
Black	$291.86	10,941
Mulatto	$1,195.42	3,628
Maryland	$701.02	6,262
Black	$635.90	5,108
Mulatto	$989.25	1,154
Mississippi	$348.54	23,665
Black	$335.50	20,175
Mulatto	$423.87	3,490

Table 37. (*continued*)

Variable Value Label	Mean	Cases
Missouri	$558.06	7,914
Black	$516.07	6,623
Mulatto	$773.51	1,291
North Carolina	$329.49	8,375
Black	$298.48	6,710
Mulatto	$454.47	1,665
South Carolina	$420.91	10,997
Black	$368.56	9,292
Mulatto	$706.16	1,705
Tennessee	$385.38	16,904
Black	$343.49	14,721
Mulatto	$667.84	2,183
Texas	$243.30	12,535
Black	$227.07	11,397
Mulatto	$405.89	1,138
Virginia	$432.80	8,890
Black	$346.43	6,713
Mulatto	$699.13	2,177

Table 38. Total Estate Holdings among Men and Women, 1870

Variable Value Label	Mean	Cases
For Entire Population	$407.82	168,034
Alabama	$330.37	15,317
Male	$323.42	14,674
Female	$489.11	643
Arkansas	$340.14	7,113
Male	$335.04	6,920
Female	$522.80	193
Delaware	$899.35	1,232
Male	$885.07	1,139
Female	$1,074.19	93
District of Columbia	$1,712.48	1,578
Male	$1,704.29	1,328
Female	$1,756.00	250
Florida	$317.38	3,315
Male	$312.84	3,147
Female	$402.38	168
Georgia	$295.23	17,739
Male	$291.94	16,892
Female	$360.80	847

Table 38. (*continued*)

Variable Value Label	Mean	Cases
Kentucky	$478.50	11,629
Male	$469.09	10,819
Female	$604.20	810
Louisiana	$516.86	14,569
Male	$469.96	13,643
Female	$1,207.88	926
Maryland	$701.02	6,262
Male	$694.30	5,682
Female	$766.90	580
Mississippi	$348.54	23,665
Male	$347.78	22,692
Female	$366.19	973
Missouri	$558.06	7,914
Male	$554.64	7,363
Female	$603.81	551
North Carolina	$329.49	8,375
Male	$322.24	7,968
Female	$471.50	407
South Carolina	$420.91	10,997
Male	$408.82	10,490
Female	$671.01	507
Tennessee	$385.38	16,904
Male	$382.56	15,783
Female	$425.07	1,121
Texas	$243.30	12,535
Male	$245.01	11,900
Female	$211.34	635
Virginia	$432.80	8,890
Male	$413.10	8,232
Female	$679.33	658

Biographical Listing of Prosperous Blacks in the South, 1870s–1915

Black Wealth Holders with Estimated Total Estates of $20,000 to $49,999
(Acquiring bulk of estate during 1870s to 1915)

Allain, Theophile T., sugar planter and merchant, West Baton Rouge, La.

Alston, Dennis S., grocer, Norfolk, Va.

Amos, Moses, druggist, Atlanta, Ga.

Anderson, I. H., merchant, Jackson, Tenn.

Anderson, Richard D., banker, Jacksonville, Fla.

Andrews, William Trent, lawyer and restaurateur, Sumter, S.C.

Atwood, Louis K., banker, Jackson, Miss.

Avery, John Moses, insurance agent, Durham, N.C.

Badger, Roderick D., dentist, Atlanta, Ga.

Baumann, Albert, druggist, New Orleans, La.

Beckham, William, no occupation, Nashville, Tenn.

Bennett, Swinton W., lawyer, Charleston, S.C.

Benson, J. J., farmer and town builder, Kowalgila, Ala.

Blacknall, George B., contractor and builder, Franklin County, N.C.

Bostic, J. West, laundry business and restaurateur, Nashville, Tenn.

Boyd, George W., contractor and builder, Richmond, Va.

Boyd, Robert Fulton, physician, Nashville, Tenn.

Bradford, Thomas, beneficial society organizer, Baltimore, Md.

Brown, S. S., teacher, Memphis, Tenn.

Burrus, John H., lawyer, Nashville, Tenn.

Bush, John, landlord and real estate owner, Little Rock, Ark.

Butler, William N., real estate renter, Annapolis, Md.

Button, Daniel, livery stable owner, Savannah, Ga.

Cabell, Aaron Hall, grocer, Henderson, Ky.

Cain, A. C., merchant, Jackson, Tenn.

Calhoun, Moses, restaurateur, Atlanta, Ga.

Carr, Benjamin, farmer, Hartsville, Tenn.
Chandler, Henry Wilkins, lawyer and real estate speculator, Ocala, Fla.
Charles, Samuel, shoemaker and leather retailer, Pensacola, Fla.
Cohen, Walter L., saloon and insurance company owner, New Orleans, La.
Cole, Thom, restaurateur and saloon keeper, Louisville, Ky.
Cook, Elijah, undertaker, Montgomery, Ala.
Cook, George F. T., landowner, Washington, D.C.
Cox, S., farmer, Eutaw, Ala.
Cox, Wayne W., banker and insurance agent, Indianola, Miss.
Crawford, Anthony, farmer, Abbeville County, S.C.
Crum, William Dermos, physician, Charleston, S.C.
Cuney, Norris Wright, shipper and stevedore businessman, Galveston, Tex.
Dabney, James H., undertaker, Washington, D.C.
Davis, Benjamin Jefferson, builder, Atlanta, Ga.
Deveaux, John H., director savings and loan, Savannah, Ga.
Dickerson, John Henry, president building and loan, Jacksonville, Fla.
Dickson, J. H., farmer, Hancock County, Ga.
Downing, George T., restaurateur, Washington, D.C.
Drish, Lewis, farmer, Pickens County, Ala.
Duckett, Lewis, farmer, Newberry, S.C.
Dudley, Andrew, farmer, Clarksville, Tenn.
Edwards, N. L., farmer, Shelby County, Tenn.
Eskridge, Peter, merchant, Atlanta, Ga.
Evans, Z. T., mattress manufacturer, New Orleans, La.
Ferguson, Horace Stephen, restaurateur, St. Louis, Mo.
Fernandis, John A., barber, Baltimore, Md.
Franklin, G. W., Jr., undertaker, Chattanooga, Tenn.
Fulton, Jack, farmer, DeSoto Parish, La.
Gaines, Ephraim, farmer, Brunswick County, Va.
Geddes, Joseph, undertaker, New Orleans, La.
George, Randall D., merchant and shipper, Colleton County, S.C.
Giles, George, fertilizer retailer and wholesaler, Ocala, Fla.
Gilliam, G. W., grocer, Okolona, Miss.
Gordon, William Claud, undertaker, St. Louis, Mo.
Green, Benjamin, merchant, Mound Bayou, Miss.
Harvey, ?, farmer, Lamar Co., Tex.
Havis, Ferdinand, liquor wholesale merchant, Pine Bluff, Ark.
Henderson, N. H., physician, Memphis, Tenn.
Herndon, Arthur, candy manufacturer, Spartenburg, S.C.
Hightower, William T., merchant, Nashville, Tenn.
Hudson, Richard B., coal dealer, Selma, Ala.
Jefferson, E. B., dentist, Nashville, Tenn.
Jeffries, L. B., contractor and builder, Greensboro, N.C.
Johnson, Andrew N., undertaker, Mobile, Ala. and Nashville, Tenn.
Johnson, William Hamilton, wood shipping merchant, Baynesville, Va.
Johnson, William Isaac, livery owner and funeral director, Richmond, Va.

Jones, R. E., physician, Richmond, Va.
Jones, Scipio, lawyer, Little Rock, Ark.
Keatts, C. W., landlord, Little Rock, Ark.
Kelley, Henry, farmer, Belen, Miss.
Key, H. W., farmer, Davidson County, Tenn.
Knight, David L., transfer company owner, Louisville, Ky.
Lane, W. H., landlord, Birmingham, Ala.
Lankford, John Anderson, architect, Washington, D.C.
Leathers, D. H., merchant, Corpus Christi, Tex.
Leevy, I. S., clothing retailer, Columbia, S.C.
Leslie, Charles C., wholesale and retail fish dealer, Charleston, S.C.
Levy, J. R., physician, Florence, S.C.
Lewis, A. L., insurance agent, Jacksonville, Fla.
Locks, John W., undertaker, Baltimore, Md.
Love, Watt, farmer, Boydton, Va.
Lowery, Samuel, landlord, Huntsville, Ala.
McCabe, Solomon, barber, Baltimore, Md.
McCoy, Benjamin, real estate renter, Washington, D.C.
McCoy, Levy, undertaker, Memphis, Tenn.
McDuffy, J. D., truck farmer, Ocala, Fla.
McIntire, J. F., farmer, Floyd, La.
McKissack, George W., contractor and builder, Nashville, Tenn.
Mangum, William, farmer, Wake County, N.C.
Martin, D. L., editor, Nashville, Tenn.
Miller, J. J., clothier, Columbia, S.C., and Richmond, Va.
Moyer, Isaac P., grocer, Atlanta, Ga.
Murphy, John Henry, editor and publisher, Baltimore, Md.
Murphy, Willis and son William, grocers, Atlanta, Ga.
Myers, J. C., farmer, Tyler, Tex.
Owens, Joseph Alexander, farmer and merchant, Barnwell County, S.C.
Palmer, R. R., merchant, Hampton, Va.
Pearson, William Gaston, manufacturer and insurance agent, Durham, N.C.
Peters, C. W., furniture dealer, Mobile, Ala.
Pettiford, William Reuben, banker, Birmingham, Ala.
Pla[n]che, Joseph, farmer, Natchitoches Parish, La.
Price, A. D., undertaker, Richmond, Va.
Randall, C. S., contractor, Nashville, Tenn.
Ransom, James M., carriage maker, Warrenton, N.C.
Redmond, Sidney Dillon, physician, Jackson, Miss.
Reid, Frank, farmer, Macon County, Ala.
Robinson, T. J., grocer, Dyersburg, Tenn.
Royal, William H., mortician, Savannah, Ga.
Ruffin, Thomas, farmer, Hale County, Ala.
Russell, Andrew, undertaker, St. Louis, Mo.
Sanford, J. W., contractor and builder, Memphis, Tenn.
Scott, E. F., landowner and renter, Clifton Forge, Va.

Scruggs, D. C., landlord, Savannah, Ga.
Shadd, Furman, no occupation, Washington, D.C.
Sherrod, Daniel Webster, physician and druggist, Meridian, Miss.
Smith, J. M., farmer, Boyle, Miss.
Stamps, T. B., commission merchant, New Orleans, La.
Stevens, George W., grocer, Durham, N.C.
Tate, James, grocer, Atlanta, Ga.
Thomas, Cal, planter and rancher, Bastrop County, Tex.
Thomas, John Levy, restaurateur, Union Springs, Ala.
Thomas, Jonas W., cotton farmer, Bennettsville, S.C.
Tulane, Victor H., grocery merchant, Montgomery, Ala.
Turner, Benjamin, livery stable owner, Selma, Ala.
Walker, Harry, meat-shipping business, Lexington, Ky.
Walker, William, horse trainer, Louisville, Ky.
Walls, Josiah T., cotton and truck farmer, Alachua County, Fla.
Watson, William, undertaker, Louisville, Ky.
Willis, S. G., pickle wholesaler, Fredericksburg, Va.
Winston, John J., contractor and builder, New Orleans, La.
Winter, Lewis, truck farmer, Davidson County, Tenn.

Estimated Total Estates of $50,000 to $99,999

Anderson, Charles H., retail and wholesale fish dealer, Jacksonville, Fla.
Antoine, Caesar Carpetier, commission merchant, Caddo Parish, La.
Banks, Charles, banker and merchant, Mound Bayou, Miss.
Bowen, G. H., realtor, Savannah, Ga.
Boyce, Sansbury, merchant, Jacksonville, Fla.
Burruss, G. S., physician, Augusta, Ga.
Cannon, William Sherman, banker and investor, Atlanta, Ga.
Clouston, A. E., banker, Memphis, Tenn.
Coleman, Warren Clay, merchant and manufacturer, Concord, N.C.
Cook, John Francis, Jr., teacher, Washington, D.C.
Cuplantier, Charles, farmer, Buntville, La.
Field, James A., farmer, Warwick County, Va.
Fields, D. W., dentist, Memphis, Tenn.
Fitzgerald, Richard, brick manufacturer, Durham, N.C.
Forman, Zach, farmer, Fort Smith, Ark.
Francis, Richard, restaurateur, Washington, D.C.
Gibbs, Mifflin W., merchant and landlord, Little Rock, Ark.
Hale, James, contractor and builder, Montgomery, Ala.
Hamilton, Alexander, contractor and builder, Atlanta, Ga.
Head, Elbert, farmer, Americas, Ga.
Herndon, Alonzo, barber and insurance executive, Atlanta, Ga.
Howard, David Tobias, funeral director, Atlanta, Ga.
Jackson, Deal, farmer, Daugherty County, Ga.
Jefferson, Lewis, truck farmer and fertilizer dealer, Washington, D.C.

Lewey, Matthew M., restaurateur and newspaper publisher, Pensacola, Fla.
McKinley, Jake [Jacob], rock contractor, Atlanta, Ga.
Murray, Daniel Alexander Payne, landlord, Washington, D.C.
Noisette, Joseph J., strawberry farmer, Charleston County, S.C.
Peterson, James T., real estate renter, Mobile, Ala.
Pinchback, P. B. S., political leader, New Orleans, La.
Tandy, Henry A., contractor and builder, Lexington, Ky.
Taylor, Edmund Bernard, caterer, Baltimore, Md.
Thorne, John Stokes, farmer, Edisto Island, S.C.
Todd, Henry, pine land speculator, Darien, Ga.
Walker, Maggie Lena, banker, Richmond, Va.
Walton, James Tart, contractor and builder, San Antonio, Tex.
Windham, B. L., contractor and builder, Birmingham, Ala.
Wormley, William H., caterer, Washington, D.C.

Estimated Total Estates of More Than $100,000

Alexander, M. S., sugar planter, Maillard, La.
Bell, John Brown, real estate speculator, Houston, Tex.
Billingslea, Alfred, barber, Montgomery, Ala.
Black, Henry, sheep and cattle rancher, Pecos County, Tex.
Blodgett, J. H., real estate speculator and landlord, Jacksonville, Fla.
Bond, Scott, farmer, Madison, Ark.
Bosley, J. G., no occupation, Nashville, Tenn.
Bowles, George F., lawyer, Natchez, Miss.
Boyd, Richard Henry, manufacturer, Nashville, Tenn.
Brown, E. P., physician, Greenville, Miss.
Browne, William Washington, beneficial society organizer, Richmond, Va.
Bruce, Blanche Kelso, political leader and planter, Bolivar County, Miss.
Bryant, Cody, farmer, Covington, Ga.
Burrus, James Dallas, teacher, Nashville, Tenn.
Burton, Walter, planter, Fort Bend County, Tex.
Church, Robert Reed, realtor and amusement park owner, Memphis, Tenn.
Cross, J. G., merchant, Brownsville, Tex.
Dixon, Amanda, no occupation, Sparta, Ga.
Douglass, C. H., theater owner, Macon, Ga.
Eubanks, Amanda, farmer, Ga.
Gomez, F., tin manufacturer, Mobile, Ala.
Harris, Samuel, merchant, Williamsburg, Va.
Hayes, Thomas H., undertaker, Memphis, Tenn.
Henderson, J. F., farmer and wood merchant, DeSoto Parish, La.
Hutchins, James Lewis, furniture moving business, Baltimore, Md.
Johnson, Benjamin, farmer and real estate investor, Memphis, Tenn.
Johnson, C. First, banker and mutual aid organizer, Mobile, Ala.
Johnson, Calvin, saloon keeper, Knoxville, Tenn.
Jones, Charles H., grocer, merchant, landlord, Winston-Salem, N.C.

Jones, Wiley, liquor wholesaler and amusement park owner, Pine Bluff, Ark.

Judson, Elmer, planter, Judson Island, Tenn.

Lafon, Thomy, real estate speculator, New Orleans, La.

Langston, John Mercer, race leader, Washington, D.C. and Va.

Lynch, John Roy, planter and political leader, Natchez, Miss.

McGavock, W. H., undertaker, Nashville, Tenn.

McKinlay, Whitefield, realtor, Washington, D.C.

Malone, Annie M. Turnbo, manufacturer of beauty products, St. Louis, Mo.

Mansion, Lucien, cigarmaker, New Orleans, La.

Matthews, William E., real estate speculator, Washington, D.C.

Mercier, Dominique and sons, clothing merchants, New Orleans, La.

Merrick, John, barber and insurance company founder, Durham, N.C.

Mitchell, John R., Jr., newspaper publisher, realtor, banker, Richmond, Va.

Montgomery, Isaiah T., merchant, Mound Bayou, Miss.

Moore, Aaron McDuffie, physician and insurance agent, Durham, N.C.

Morton, Monroe, coal and lumber merchant, Athens, Ga.

Napier, James Carroll, banker, Nashville, Tenn.

Nicholson, Philip, truck farmer, Shelby County, Tenn.

O'Kelly, Berry, merchant and town builder, Wake County, N.C.

Onley, John E., contractor and builder, Jacksonville, Fla.

Perry, Hemon E., insurance agent, Atlanta, Ga.

Purvis, Charles B., physician, Washington, D.C.

Smith, Isaac, real estate speculator and money lender, New Bern, N.C.

Smith, John Henry, investor, Baltimore, Md.

Smith, Newton, cotton planter, Caddo Parish, La.

Spaulding, Charles Clinton, insurance executive, Durham, N.C.

Sterrett, Milton, realtor and landlord, Houston, Tex.

Suggs, Daniel Cato, physician, Winston-Salem, N.C.

Sunday, John, landlord and rentor, Pensacola, Fla.

Taylor, Preston, undertaker, Nashville, Tenn.

Terrs, J. Holmes, farmer, Marshall County, Tex.

Thomas, James P., barber and real estate speculator, St. Louis, Mo.

Thomas, Joseph, shipping merchant, Baltimore, Md.

Turner, J. Milton, politician, manufacturer, St. Louis, Mo.

Wallace, Daniel Webster, farmer and cattle rancher, Mitchell County, Tex.

Wormley, James T., hotel owner, Washington, D.C.

Wormley, W. A. A., businessman, Washington, D.C.

A Profile of Prosperous Blacks

Table 39. Black Wealth Holders with Minimum Estates of $20,000
(acquiring bulk of estate from 1870s to 1915)

	State of Residence	
State	Frequency	Percentage
Alabama	20	8.3
Arkansas	8	3.3
District of Columbia	19	7.9
Florida	14	5.8
Georgia	29	12.0
Kentucky	7	2.9
Louisiana	19	7.9
Maryland	10	4.2
Mississippi	14	5.8
Missouri	6	2.5
North Carolina	16	6.6
South Carolina	14	5.8
Tennessee	36	14.9
Texas	12	5.0
Virginia	17	7.1
Total	241	100.0

	Major Cities of Residence	
City	Frequency	Percentage (of 241 total)
Mobile, Ala.	6	2.5
Montgomery, Ala.	3	1.3
Pine Bluff, Ark.	2	.8
Little Rock, Ark.	4	1.7
District of Columbia	19	7.9
Jacksonville, Fla.	7	2.9
Savannah, Ga.	5	2.1
Atlanta, Ga.	13	5.4
Lexington, Ken.	2	.8
Louisville, Ken.	4	1.7
New Orleans, La.	10	4.2
Baltimore, Md.	9	3.8
St. Louis, Mo.	6	2.5
Durham, N.C.	7	2.9
Charleston, S.C.	5	2.1
Nashville, Tenn.	17	7.1
Memphis, Tenn.	11	4.6
Houston, Tex.	3	1.3
Richmond, Va.	8	3.3
Total	141	58.9

Urban (including small towns and cities) vs. Rural

	Frequency	Percentage
urban	186	77.2
rural	55	22.8
Total	241	100.0

Gender

	Frequency	Percentage
male	237	98.3
female	4	1.7
Total	241	100.0

Color

	Frequency	Percentage	Valid Percentage
black	37	15.4	34.6
mulatto	70	29.0	65.4
	134	55.6	missing
Total	241	100.0	100.0

Leading Occupations

	Frequency	Percentage (of 241 total)
banker	9	3.7
barber	4	1.7
contractor	15	6.2
farmer/planter	47	19.5
grocer	7	2.9
insurance agent	9	3.7
landlord	15	6.2
lawyer	7	2.9
manufacturer	11	4.6
merchant	20	8.3
physician	10	4.2
realtor	13	5.4
restaurateur	8	3.3
teacher	3	1.3
undertaker	17	7.0
Total	195	80.9

· = unknown

Wealth Estimates

	Frequency	Percentage	Valid Percentage
$20,000 to $49,999	137	56.8	56.8
$50,000 to $99,999	38	15.8	15.8
over $100,000	66	27.4	27.4
Total	241	100.0	100.0

Status at Birth

	Frequency	Percentage	Valid Percentage
slave	50	20.7	45.5
free Negro	31	12.9	28.2
post-1865	29	12.1	26.3
.	131	54.4	missing
Total	241	100.0	100.0

Education

	Frequency	Percentage	Valid Percentage
illiterate	7	2.9	4.9
primary	39	16.2	27.3
secondary	16	6.6	11.2
college	52	21.6	36.4
self-taught	29	12.0	20.3
.	98	40.7	missing
Total	241	100.0	100.0

Marital Profile

	Frequency	Percentage	Valid Percentage
married	119	49.4	92.2
single	10	4.1	7.8
.	112	46.5	missing
Total	241	100.0	100.0

Political Profile

	Frequency	Percentage	Valid Percentage
actively engaged	60	24.9	41.7
not involved	84	34.9	58.3
.	97	40.2	missing
Total	241	100.0	100.0

Status of Parents

	Frequency	Percentage	Valid Percentage
slave	51	21.2	63.0
free Negro	30	12.4	37.0
.	160	66.4	missing
Total	241	100.0	100.0

Color of Father

	Frequency	Percentage	Valid Percentage
black	20	8.3	31.7
mulatto	25	10.4	39.7
white	18	7.5	28.6
.	178	74.9	missing
Total	241	100.0	100.0

Color of Mother

	Frequency	Percentage	Valid Percentage
black	38	15.8	62.3
mulatto	22	9.1	36.1
Indian	1	.4	1.6
.	180	74.7	missing
Total	241	100.0	100.0

Color of Clientele among Businessmen

	Frequency	Percentage	Valid Percentage
black	94	39.0	61.0
white	44	18.3	28.6
both races	12	5.0	7.8
white to black	4	1.7	2.6
.	86	36.1	missing
Total	241	100.0	100.0

Notes

Introduction

1. W. E. B. Du Bois, *Black Folk Then and Now: An Essay on the History and Sociology of the Negro Race* (New York: H. Holt and Company, 1939), p. vii.

2. Lawrence W. Levine, *Black Culture and Black Consciousness: Afro-American Folk Thought from Slavery to Freedom* (New York: Oxford University Press, 1977), p. xi.

3. Carter G. Woodson, ed. and comp., *Free Negro Owners of Slaves in the United States in 1830; Together with Absentee Ownership of Slaves in the United States in 1830* (Washington, D.C.: Association for the Study of Negro Life and History, 1924); J. H. Harmon, Jr., Arnett G. Lindsay, and Carter G. Woodson, *The Negro as a Business Man* (Washington: Association for the Study of Negro Life and History, 1929); Luther Porter Jackson, *Free Negro Labor and Property Holding in Virginia, 1830–1860* (New York: D. Appleton Company, 1942), and "The Virginia Free Negro Farmer and Property Owner, 1830–1860," *JNH* 24 (October 1939), 390–439; John Hope Franklin, "The Free Negro in the Economic Life of Ante-Bellum North Carolina," *NCHR* 19 (July and October 1942), 239–59, 359–75; and *The Free Negro in North Carolina, 1790–1860* (Chapel Hill: University of North Carolina Press, 1943). Other early monographs which contain sections or chapters on property owners include: Charles H. Wesley, *Negro Labor in the United States, 1850–1925* (New York: Vanguard Press, 1927); James Hugo Johnston, *Race Relations in Virginia and Miscegenation in the South, 1776–1860* (Amherst: University of Massachusetts Press, 1970). The latter study was written as a Chicago Ph.D. dissertation in 1937. Merah S. Stuart, *An Economic Detour: A History of Insurance in the Lives of American Negroes* (New York: W. Malliet and Co., 1940); Abram L. Harris, *The Negro as Capitalist: A Study of Banking and Business among American Negroes* (Philadelphia: American Academy of Political and Social Science, 1936).

4. Du Bois, *Black Folk Then and Now*, p. 217; Lee Soltow, *Men and Wealth in the United States, 1850–1870* (New Haven: Yale University Press, 1975), and

Patterns of Wealthholding in Wisconsin since 1850 (Madison: University of Wisconsin Press, 1971).

5. Soltow, *Men and Wealth in the United States*, pp. 76, 84, 186.

6. Michael P. Johnson and James L. Roark, *Black Masters: A Free Family of Color in the Old South* (New York: W. W. Norton and Co., 1984), pp. xii, 60.

CHAPTER ONE
Beginnings: Africans in a New Land

1. Charles M. Andrews, *The Colonial Period of American History*, 4 vols. (New Haven: Yale University Press, 1934–38); John J. McCusker and Russell R. Menard, *The Economy of British America, 1607–1789* (Chapel Hill: University of North Carolina Press, 1985), pt. 2; Ira Berlin, "Time, Space, and the Evolution of Afro-American Society on British Mainland North America," *AHR* 85 (February 1980), 44–78; John Donald Duncan, "Servitude and Slavery in Colonial South Carolina, 1670–1776," (Ph.D. dissertation, Emory University, 1972); Daniel C. Littlefield, *Rice and Slaves: Ethnicity and the Slave Trade in Colonial South Carolina* (Baton Rouge: Louisiana State University Press, 1981), pp. 74–114; Clarence L. Ver Steeg, *Origins of a Southern Mosaic: Studies of Early Carolina and Georgia* (Athens: University of Georgia Press, 1975); Russell R. Menard, *Economy and Society in Early Colonial Maryland* (New York: Garland Publishing, Inc., 1985), chap. 7; Allan Kulikoff, *Tobacco and Slaves: The Development of Southern Cultures in the Chesapeake, 1680–1800* (Chapel Hill: University of North Carolina Press, 1986); Laura Foner, "The Free People of Color in Louisiana and St. Domingue: A Comparative Portrait of Two Three-Caste Slave Societies," *JSoH* 3 (Summer 1970), 406–40.

2. Olaudah Equiano, *Equiano's Travels: The Interesting Narrative of the Life of Olaudah Equiano or Gustavus Vassa the African* (London: the author, 1789; abridged ed., ed. Paul Edwards, New York: Frederick A. Praeger, 1967), pp. 7–8, 25, 68, 179.

3. John Mbiti, *African Religions and Philosophy* (New York: Praeger Publishers, 1969; Anchor Book ed., New York: Doubleday and Co., 1970), p. 32; Nathan I. Huggins, *Black Odyssey: The Afro-American Ordeal in Slavery* (New York: Oxford University Press, 1977), p. 5.

4. Philip D. Curtin, *The Atlantic Slave Trade: A Census* (Madison: University of Wisconsin Press, 1969), p. 87; Martin R. Delany, *Official Report of the Niger Valley Exploring Party* (New York: Thomas Hamilton, 1861), sec. 13; Robert Campbell, *A Few Facts Relating to Lagos, Abeokuta, and Other Sections of Central Africa* (Philadelphia: King and Baird, 1860), pp. 6, 10; R. J. M. Blackett, "Robert Campbell and the Triangle of the Black Experience," in Blackett, *Beating against the Barriers: Biographical Essays in Nineteenth-Century Afro-American History* (Baton Rouge: Louisiana State University Press, 1986), p. 164; Paul Bohannan and Philip D. Curtin, *Africa and Africans* (Garden City, N.Y.: Natural History Press, 1971), pp. 124–28; Sidney W. Mintz and Richard Price, *An Anthropological Approach to the Afro-American Past: A Caribbean Perspective* (Philadelphia: Institute for the Study of Human Issues, 1976), pp. 1–21.

5. Sidney W. Mintz, *Caribbean Transformations* (Chicago: Aldine Publishing Company, 1974), p. 155. See also Ciro Flamarion S. Cardoso, "The Peasant Breach in the Slave System: New Developments in Brazil," *Luso-Brazilian Review* 25 (Summer 1988), 49–57; Stuart B. Schwartz, "Resistance and Accommodation in Eighteenth Century Brazil: The Slaves' View of Slavery," *Hispanic American Historical Review* 57 (1977), 69–81.

6. Berlin, "Time, Space, and the Evolution of Afro-American Society," pp. 50–51, 54, 57; *The Statistical History of the United States from Colonial Times to the Present* (Stamford, Conn.: Fairfield Publishers, 1965), p. 756.

7. Allan Kulikoff, "A 'Prolifick' People: Black Population Growth in the Chesapeake Colonies, 1700–1790," *Southern Studies* 16 (Winter 1977), 406–7; Marcus Jernegan, *Laboring and Dependent Classes in Colonial America* (Chicago: University of Chicago Press, 1931), p. 22; Gerald W. Mullin, *Flight and Rebellion: Slave Resistance in Eighteenth-Century Virginia* (New York: Oxford University Press, 1972), p. 15; Berlin, "Time, Space, and the Evolution of Afro-American Society," p. 54.

8. Peter H. Wood, "'More like a Negro Country': Demographic Patterns in Colonial South Carolina, 1670–1740," in Stanley Engerman and Eugene Genovese, eds., *Race and Slavery in the Western Hemisphere: Quantitative Studies* (Princeton: Princeton University Press, 1975), p. 134; Converse D. Clowse, *Economic Beginnings of Colonial South Carolina, 1670–1730* (Columbia: University of South Carolina Press, 1971), p. 61, and *Measuring Charleston's Overseas Commerce, 1717–1767: Statistics from the Port's Naval Lists* (Washington, D.C.: University Press of America, 1981), pp. 30–33; Ver Steeg, *Origins of a Southern Mosaic*, p. 106; Legislative Records, Memorial of Thomas Cole, Peter Bassnett Mathews, and Mathew Webb to David Ramsay and Members of the South Carolina Senate, January 13, 1791, #181, SCDAH.

9. "Presentment of the [Charles Town] Grand Jury," 1733–34, in *South Carolina Historical and Genealogical Magazine* 25 (1924), 193; Thad W. Tate, *The Negro in Eighteenth-Century Williamsburg* (Williamsburg, Va.: Colonial Williamsburg, 1965), pp. 67–76; Legislative Records, Petition of the Residents of Henrico County to the Virginia General Assembly, June 8, 1782, VSL; Peter Wood, *Black Majority: Negroes in Colonial South Carolina from 1670 through the Stono Rebellion* (New York: W. W. Norton and Co., 1974), p. 207.

10. *South Carolina Gazette*, January 8, October 17, 1741.

11. *Maryland Gazette*, January 1, 1756, quoted in Kulikoff, *Tobacco and Slaves*, p. 414.

12. John Hammond, *Leah and Rachel*, in *Tracts and Other Papers Relating to the Origin, Settlement, and Progress of the Colonies in North America*, ed. Peter Force, 4 vols. (New York: Peter Smith, 1947), vol. 3, no. 14, p. 14.

13. Johann Martin Bolzius, *Reliable Answer to Some Submitted Questions concerning the Land Carolina*, trans. and ed. Paul S. Taylor et al., in *WMQ*, 3d ser., 14 (April 1957), 236.

14. Philip D. Morgan, "Work and Culture: The Task System and the World of Lowcountry Blacks, 1700–1800," *WMQ*, 3d ser., 49 (October 1982), 578–79.

15. "Scotus Americanus," *Information concerning the Province of North Carolina, Addressed to Emigrants from the Highlands and Western Isles of Scotland,* in "Some North Carolina Tracts of the Eighteenth Century," ed. William Boyd, *NCHR* 3 (October 1926), 616.

16. "An Act for the Better Ordering and Governing of Negroes," 1740, in *The First Laws of the State of South Carolina,* facsimile reprint, comp. John Cushing, 2 pts. (Wilmington, Del.: Michael Glazier, Inc., 1981), 1:172; "Presentment of the [Charles Town] Grand Jury," pp. 194–95.

17. Quoted in Allan Kulikoff, "The Origins of Afro-American Society in Tidewater Maryland and Virginia, 1700 to 1790," *WMQ,* 3d ser., 35 (April 1978), 250.

18. "An Act concerning Servants and Slaves," in *The First Laws of the State of North Carolina,* facsimile reprint, comp. John Cushing, 2 pts. (Wilmington, Del.: Michael Glazier, Inc., 1984), 1:86, 93; "An Act for Amending an Act for Making Provision for the Poor," 1779, in ibid., 2:378; "An Act to Prevent Thefts and Robberies by Slaves," 1787, in ibid., 2:609; "An Act to Amend the Several Acts of Assembly to Prevent Dealing or Trafficking with Slaves," 1788, in ibid., 2:633–34.

19. RCPC, Northampton County, Va., Deeds (July 13, 1640), in *County Court Records of Accomack-Northampton, Virginia, 1640–1645,* ed. Susie Ames (Charlottesville: University of Virginia Press, 1973), p. 32.

20. Edmund S. Morgan, *American Slavery American Freedom: The Ordeal of Colonial Virginia* (New York: W. W. Norton and Company, 1975), pp. 141–42, 154–57; Carl Bridenbaugh, *Cities in the Wilderness: The First Century of Urban Life in America, 1625–1742* (New York: Ronald Press, 1938; reprint ed., New York: Capricorn Books, 1964), p. 49.

21. For an analysis of the difficulties in ascertaining accurate population data for early Virginia, see Edmund Morgan, *American Slavery American Freedom,* pp. 396, 404, 420–23, "Slavery and Freedom: The American Paradox," *JAH* 59 (June 1972), 18, 39n, and "Headrights and Headcounts: A Review Article," *VMHB* 80 (July 1972), 361; T. H. Breen and Stephen Innes, *"Myne Own Ground": Race and Freedom on Virginia's Eastern Shore, 1640–1676* (New York: Oxford University Press, 1980), p. 69.

22. James H. Brewer, "Negro Property Owners in Seventeenth Century Virginia," *WMQ,* 3d ser., 12 (October 1955), 576–78; Breen and Innes, *"Myne Own Ground,"* p. 17; n.a., "Documents: Anthony Johnson, Free Negro, 1622," *JNH* 56 (January 1971), 71–72.

23. Quoted in Breen and Innes, *"Myne Own Ground,"* pp. 14–5.

24. Ibid., p. 6; RCPC, Northampton County, Va., Court Minutes (September 22, 1645), in *County Court Records of Accomack-Northampton,* p. 457.

25. Quoted in Morgan, *American Slavery American Freedom,* p. 156.

26. Breen and Innes, *"Myne Own Ground,"* p. 17; Ross M. Kimmel, "Free Blacks in Seventeenth-Century Maryland," *MHM* 71 (Spring 1976), 21.

27. "An Act for Suppressing Outlying Slaves," 1691, in *The Statutes at Large, Being a Collection of all the Laws of Virginia,* ed. William Hening, 13 vols. (Philadelphia: Thomas Desilver, 1823; facsimile reprint ed., Charlottesville: University of Virginia Press, 1969), 3:86–88.

28. Winthrop Jordan, *White over Black: American Attitudes toward the Negro, 1550–1812* (Chapel Hill: University of North Carolina Press, 1968), pp. 74, 125; Robert S. Cope, *Carry Me Back: Slavery and Servitude in Seventeenth Century Virginia* (Pikeville, Ky.: Pikeville College Press, 1973), p. 37; John H. Russell, *The Free Negro in Virginia, 1619–1865* (Baltimore: Johns Hopkins University Press, 1913), pp. 51, 89; James Wright, *The Free Negro in Maryland, 1634–1860* (New York: Columbia University Press, 1921), p. 94.

29. *Gentlemen's Magazine* 34 (June 1764), 261. The 1755 census of Maryland's blacks was published in this issue.

30. Ibid.; St. George Tucker, *A Dissertation on Slavery: With a Proposal for the Gradual Abolition of It in the State of Virginia* (Philadelphia: Mathew Carey, 1796; reprint ed., New York: n.p., 1861), p. 70; Russell, *The Free Negro in Virginia*, p. 11.

31. This estimate is derived from a variety of sources. See Berlin, "Time, Space, and the Evolution of Afro-American Society," p. 72, and *Slaves without Masters: The Free Negro in the Antebellum South* (New York: Pantheon Books, 1974), pp. 46–48; John Hope Franklin, *The Free Negro in North Carolina, 1790–1860* (Chapel Hill: University of North Carolina Press, 1943), p. 10; *The Statistical History of the United States*, p. 756.

32. Sylvia Frey, "Between Slavery and Freedom: Virginia Blacks in the American Revolution," *JSH* 59 (August 1983), 387; Benjamin Quarles, *The Negro in the American Revolution* (Chapel Hill: University of North Carolina Press, 1961), chap. 3; Duncan J. MacLeod, *Slavery, Race and the American Revolution* (London: Cambridge University Press, 1974), chap. 1; David B. Davis, *The Problem of Slavery in the Age of Revolution, 1770–1823* (Ithaca: Cornell University Press, 1975), chap. 6; Richard S. Dunn, "Black Society in the Chesapeake, 1776–1810," in *Slavery and Freedom in the Age of the American Revolution*, ed. Ira Berlin and Ronald Hoffman (Charlottesville: University of Virginia Press, 1983), pp. 49–52; Philip D. Morgan, "Black Society in the Lowcountry, 1760–1810," in ibid., pp. 109–16.

33. Herbert E. Sterkx, *The Free Negro in Ante-bellum Louisiana* (Rutherford, N.J.: Fairleigh Dickinson University Press, 1972), pp. 91–92; Foner, "The Free People of Color in Louisiana and St. Domingue," pp. 406–10; Berlin, *Slaves without Masters*, pp. 46–47.

34. For the purposes of this study, the Upper South includes Delaware, Maryland, the District of Columbia, Virginia, North Carolina, Kentucky, Tennessee, and Missouri; the Lower South includes South Carolina, Georgia, Florida, Alabama, Mississippi, Louisiana, Arkansas, and Texas. See Berlin, *Slaves without Masters*, pp. 46–47, 136–37, 396–402; and "The Structure of the Free Negro Caste in the Antebellum United States," *JSoH* 9 (Spring 1976), 297–318.

35. *A Compendium of the Ninth Census* (Washington: GPO, 1872), pp. 14–17; Berlin, "The Structure of the Free Negro Caste," pp. 305–7; E. Horace Fitchett, "The Origin and Growth of the Free Negro Population of Charleston, South Carolina," *JNH* 26 (October 1941), 421–36; Foner, "The Free People of Color in Louisiana and St. Domingue," pp. 406–30.

36. Wright, *The Free Negro in Maryland*, p. 184; Barbara Jeanne Fields,

Slavery and Freedom on the Middle Ground: Maryland during the Nineteenth Century (New Haven: Yale University Press, 1985), p. 13. This was true in the North as well as the South. See *Minutes of the Proceedings of the Fourth Convention of Delegates from the Abolition Societies* (Philadelphia: Zachariah Poulson, Jr., 1797), reprinted in *The American Convention of Abolition Societies*, 3 vols. (New York: Bergman Publishers, 1969), 1:133; *Minutes of the Proceedings of the Third Convention of Delegates from the Abolition Societies* (Philadelphia: Zachariah Poulson, Jr., 1796), reprinted in *The American Convention of Abolition Societies*, 1:83; Benjamin Rush to John Nicholson, August 12, 1793, in *Letters of Benjamin Rush*, ed. Lyman H. Butterfield, 2 vols. (Princeton: Princeton University Press, 1951), 2:636; Lorenzo Johnston Greene, *The Negro in Colonial New England, 1620–1776* (New York: Columbia University Press, 1942), pp. 308–9; Leon Litwack, *North of Slavery: The Negro in the Free States, 1790–1860* (Chicago: University of Chicago Press, 1961), chap. 5; Edgar J. McManus, *Black Bondage in the North* (Syracuse: Syracuse University Press, 1973), pp. 184–85, 196–97.

37. *South Carolina Gazette* (Charleston), May 23, 1750; RCPC, Charleston County, S.C., Miscellaneous Land Records, pt. 87, bks. R6–S6 (February 16, 1796), pp. 161–62; ibid., pt. 34, bk. E3 (May 16, 1765), pp. 292–99; ibid., pt. 57, bk. R4 (December 21, 1770), pp. 162–63; ibid., pt. 57, bk. S4 (February 1, 1774), pp. 83–90; ibid., pt. 66, bk. E5 (April 21, 1775), pp. 129–32; ibid., pt. 88, bks. T6-U6 (October 11–12, 1794), pp. 520–22; ibid., Wills, vol. 86A (June 5, 1759), p. 307; ibid., vol. 86B (May 5, 1763), p. 977; ibid., vol. 22 (July 27, 1785), p. 53; ibid., vol. 24 (June 27, 1791), p. 916; ibid., Letters of Administration, vol. 44 (October 1, 1799), p. 194; ibid., Mortgages, bk. AAA (April 26, 1768), p. 348, MESDA; D. E. Huger Smith and Alexander Salley, eds., *Register of St. Philip's Parish, Charles Town, or Charleston, S.C., 1754–1810* (Columbia: University of South Carolina Press, 1971), p. 83; *The South Carolina and American General Gazette* (Charleston), August 28, 1767; Philip D. Morgan, "Black Life in Eighteenth-Century Charleston," in *Perspectives in American History*, N.S., 1 (1984), 191, 193, 205, 216, 222.

38. James Robertson, ed., *Louisiana under the Rule of Spain, France, and the United States, 1785–1807: Social, Economic, and Political Conditions of the Territory Represented in the Louisiana Purchase*, 2 vols. (Cleveland: Arthur H. Clark Co., 1910–11; reprint ed., Freeport, N.Y.: Books for Libraries Press, 1969), 1:218–19.

39. RCPC, Charleston County, S.C., Miscellaneous Land Records, pt. 13, bk. E-7 (March 1, 1705–6), pp. 335–37; ibid., pt. 29, bk. TT (October 2, 1758), p. 368; ibid., Wills, vol. 62A (December 3, 1729), p. 220, MESDA; Alexander Salley, ed., *Warrants of Lands in South Carolina, 1672–1711* (Columbia: SCDAH, 1973), p. 672.

40. Brent H. Holcomb, ed., "1786 Tax Returns," *South Carolina Magazine of Ancestral Research* 9 (Spring 1981), 73; RCPC, Charleston County, S.C., Miscellaneous Land Records, pt. 57, bk. R4 (December 21, 1770), pp. 162–63; ibid., pt. 57, bk. S4 (February 1, 1774), pp. 83–90; ibid., pt. 63, bk. B5 (March 16–17, 1777), pp. 77–80; ibid., pt. 71, bk. O5 (October 20, 1778), p. 301;

ibid., pt. 89, bks. W6-Z6 (November 15–16, 1778), pp. 143–46; ibid., pt. 67, bk. G5 (March 30, 1783), pp. 465–67, MESDA; U.S. Bureau of the Census, *Heads of Families at the First Census of the United States Taken in the Year 1790, South Carolina* (Washington, D.C.: GPO, 1908), p. 44. The census listed him as "Goffe (free)." Gough was the sixth member admitted to the Brown Fellowship Society, December 2, 1790. "List of Persons Admitted Members of the Brown Fellowship Society," Brown Fellowship Society Papers, CC; *South Carolina Gazette* (Charleston), October 27, 1791; *City-Gazette and Daily Advertiser* (Charleston), January 9, 1797.

41. RPPC, Iberville Parish, La., Conveyances, bk. F (November 10, 1814), #49; ibid., bk. F (March 17, 1814, October 19, 1815), pp. 42, 171; Sterkx, *The Free Negro in Ante-bellum Louisiana*, pp. 52–53, 59; RPPC, St. Landry Parish, La., Mortgages, bk. D (May 27, 1818), p. 383, in Meullion Family Papers, Louisiana State University.

42. Legislative Records, Memorial of Thomas Cole, Peter Bassnett Mathews, and Mathew Webb to David Ramsay and Members of the South Carolina Senate, January 13, 1791, #181, SCDAH.

43. Foner, "The Free People of Color in Louisiana and St. Domingue," pp. 408–10; Donald Everett, "Free Persons of Color in Colonial Louisiana," LH 7 (Winter 1966), 38, 45, 48–49; and "Emigres and Militiamen: Free Persons of Color in New Orleans, 1803–1815," *JNH* 38 (October 1953), 377–80; Jordan, *White over Black*, pp. 77–81.

44. Jordan, *White over Black*, pp. 123–24; John H. Russell, "Colored Freemen as Slave Owners in Virginia," *JNH* 1 (June 1916), 237–40; RCPC, Charleston County, S.C., Wills, vol. 86B (May 5, 1763), p. 977; *South Carolina Gazette*, August 17, 1769, cited in *The Papers of Henry Laurens*, George C. Rogers, Jr., and David R. Chesnutt, eds., 9 vols. (Columbia: University of South Carolina Press, 1968), 7:126–27, 127n; Larry Koger, *Black Slaveowners: Free Black Slave Masters in South Carolina, 1790–1860* (Jefferson, N.C.: McFarland and Co., 1985), p. 45; James Ballagh, *A History of Slavery in Virginia* (Baltimore: The Johns Hopkins University Press, 1902), p. 485; Calvin D. Wilson, "Negroes Who Owned Slaves," *Popular Science Monthly* 81 (November 1912), 484–85; Russell, *The Free Negro in Virginia*, pp. 93–94; Franklin, *The Free Negro in North Carolina*, p. 160.

45. RCPC, Charleston County, S.C., Mortgages, vol. (May 15, 1770), 63; *South Carolina Gazette*, February 22, 1768; RCPC, Charleston County, S.C., Wills, 1786–93 (July 27, 1785), 40, MESDA; Koger, *Black Slaveowners*, pp. 14, 20–21; U.S., Department of the Interior, Census Office, *The Statistics of the Population of the United States . . . From the Original Returns of the Ninth Census* (Washington: GPO, 1872), p. 60. The Ninth Census contained county tabulations for each census between 1790 and 1870. *The Baptist Annual Register for 1797—1801*, 3 vols., ed. John Rippon (London: n. p., 1801), 3:336–37; Wilson, "Negroes Who Owned Slaves," p. 489; Peter Hamilton, *Colonial Mobile* (Boston: Houghton Mifflin Co., 1910; reprint ed., ed. Charles G. Summersell, University: University of Alabama Press, 1976), p. 368; Everett, "Free Persons of Color in Colonial Louisiana," pp. 48–49.

46. Holcomb, ed., "1786 Tax Returns," p. 73; Duke de la Rouchefoucault Liancourt, *Travels through the United States of North America the Country of the Iroquois and Upper Canada in the Years 1795, 1796, and 1797* (London: R. Phillips, 1799), p. 602. Federal census marshals and South Carolina tax collectors reported Pendarvis as white, but Larry Koger, in his exhaustive analysis of black slaveholders in the state, discovered his slave heritage. Koger, *Black Slaveowners*, pp. 13–14.

47. Legislative Records, Petition of [John Holman] to the South Carolina General Assembly, October 3, 1791, SCDAH; Koger, *Black Slaveowners*, pp. 110, 113, 211; RPPC, Iberville Parish, La., Conveyances, bk. F (November 27, 1813), #12; ibid., bk. F (March 5, 1815), pp. 130–31; RPPC, St. Landry Parish, La., Mortgages, bk. D (May 27, 1818), p. 383, copy in Meullion Family Papers, LSU; "Bill of Sale," September 9, 1822, Cane River Collection, HNOC; R. Halliburton, Jr., "Free Black Owners of Slaves: A Reappraisal of the Woodson Thesis," SCHM 76 (July 1975), 135, 142.

48. Ballagh, *A History of Slavery in Virginia*, p. 485; Russell, "Colored Freemen as Slave Owners," pp. 237–38.

49. Luther Porter Jackson, "Manumission in Certain Virginia Cities," JNH 15 (July 1930), 278–314.

50. *Federal Intelligencer, and Baltimore Daily Gazette*, April 25, 1795, MESDA.

51. *Maryland Journal, and Baltimore Advertiser*, January 12, 19, 1796; *Federal Gazette and Baltimore Advertiser*, April 11, 1805, MESDA; Leroy Graham, *Baltimore: The Nineteenth Century Black Capital* (New York: University Press of America, 1982), pp. 261–62.

52. RCPC, Alexandria, Va., Wills, bks. 1821–31 (November 25, 1829), p. 342; ibid., Charleston, S.C., Inventories, vol. C (c. 1794), p. 86; *Charleston City-Gazette and Daily Advertiser*, September 2, 1797; *Charleston Courier*, January 14, 1812, MESDA.

53. Tucker, *A Dissertation on Slavery*, pp. 91, 93–94.

54. Peter Kolchin, "Reevaluating the Antebellum Slave Community: A Comparative Perspective," *JAH* 70 (December 1983), 587; W. E. B. Du Bois, *The Suppression of the African Slave Trade to the United States of America, 1638–1870* (Cambridge: Harvard University Press, 1896; reprint ed., Baton Rouge: Louisiana State University Press, 1969), chap. 8; Mullin, *Flight and Rebellion*, p. 15, chap. 2; Lewis Gray, *History of Agriculture in the Southern United States to 1860*, 2 vols. (Washington: Carnegie Institution, 1933; reprint ed., New York: Peter Smith, 1941), 1:550–51; Philip D. Morgan, "The Ownership of Property by Slaves in the Mid-Nineteenth-Century Low Country," *JSH* 49 (August 1983), 399; Kenneth Stampp, *The Peculiar Institution: Slavery in the Antebellum South* (New York: Vintage Books, 1956), p. 31.

55. *Camden Gazette* (S.C), August 1, 1818, MESDA. The author is especially grateful to Rosemary Estes of MESDA for providing him with a printout of biographical data on the 479 free black artisans whose names appear in various county court and newspaper records in the MESDA Collection (see An Essay on Sources and Methodology).

56. Andrew Bryan to John Rippon, December 23, 1800, in *The Baptist An-*

nual Register for 1797—1801, 3:366–67; John W. Davis, "George Liele and Andrew Bryan: Pioneer Negro Preachers," *JNH* 3 (April 1918), pp. 119–27; Walter H. Brooks, "The Priority of the Silver Bluffs Church and Its Promoters," *JNH* 7 (July 1922), 172–96. As with other black Georgians who owned property, Bryan held his estate through white trustees. For example, when he bought a lot in the village of St. Gall, the deed read: "Matthew Mott (and wife) sold to William Bryan and James Whitfield In Trust for a free Black man called & Know by the name of Andrew Bryan, a Preacher of the Gospel by Lawful Authority ordain for 30 a lot . . ." RCPC, Chatham County, Ga., Deeds, n.v. (September 4, 1793), pp. 77–78, copy in Vertical File, GHS. I am very much indebted to Professor Robert Calhoon for bringing Bryan's letter to my attention.

CHAPTER TWO
Property Ownership among Slaves, 1800–1865

1. John Blassingame, *The Slave Community: Plantation Life in the Antebellum South*, rev. ed. (New York: Oxford University Press, 1979), p. 105; Eugene Genovese, *Roll, Jordan, Roll: The World the Slaves Made* (New York: Pantheon Books, 1974); Herbert Gutman, *The Black Family in Slavery and Freedom, 1750–1925* (New York: Pantheon Books, 1976); Lawrence W. Levine, *Black Culture and Black Consciousness: Afro-American Folk Thought from Slavery to Freedom* (New York: Oxford University Press, 1977); Leslie Howard Owens, *This Species of Property: Slave Life and Culture in the Old South* (New York: Oxford University Press, 1976); Thomas L. Webber, *Deep Like the Rivers: Education in the Slave Quarter Community, 1831–1865* (New York: W. W. Norton and Co., 1978); George P. Rawick, *From Sundown to Sunup: The Making of the Black Community* (Westport, Conn.: Greenwood Publishing Co., 1972); Charles Joyner, *Down by the Riverside: A South Carolina Slave Community* (Urbana: University of Illinois Press, 1984); Paul D. Escott, *Slavery Remembered: A Record of Twentieth-Century Slave Narratives* (Chapel Hill: University of North Carolina Press, 1979). See Peter Kolchin, "Reevaluating the Antebellum Slave Community: A Comparative Perspective," *JAH* 70 (December 1983), 581.

2. Kenneth Stampp, *The Peculiar Institution: Slavery in the Ante-Bellum South* (New York: Vintage Books, 1956), pp. 30–31.

3. Joyner, *Down by the Riverside*, p. 129; Lewis Gray, *History of Agriculture in the Southern United States to 1860*, 2 vols. (Washington: Carnegie Institution, 1933; reprint ed., New York: Peter Smith, 1941), 1:550–53; Philip D. Morgan, "Work and Culture: The Task System and the World of Lowcountry Blacks, 1700 to 1880," *WMQ*, 3d ser., 39 (October 1982), 565–66, and "The Ownership of Property by Slaves in the Mid-Nineteenth-Century Low Country," *JSH* 49 (August 1983), 399–401; Lawrence T. McDonnell, "Money Knows No Master: Market Relations and the American Slave Community," in *Developing Dixie: Modernization in a Traditional Society*, ed. Windred B. Moore, Jr., et al. (Westport, Conn.: Greenwood Press, 1988), pp. 31–44; Sidney W. Mintz, "The Caribbean as a Socio-cultural Area," in *Peoples and Cultures of*

the Caribbean: An Anthropological Reader (Garden City, N.Y.: Natural History Press, 1971), p. 29. For examples of this type of slave activity in other slave societies, see David Barry Gaspar, "Slavery, Amelioration, and Sunday Markets in Antigua, 1823–1831," *Slavery and Abolition: A Journal of Comparative Studies* 9 (May 1988), 1–28; Ciro Flamarion S. Cardoso, "The Peasant Breach in the Slave System: New Developments in Brazil," *Luso-Brazilian Review* 25 (Summer 1988), 49–57.

4. George Rawick, ed., *The American Slave: A Composite Autobiography*, ser. 1, 19 vols. (Westport, Conn.: Greenwood Press, 1972), vol. 7, pt. 2, p. 58. Unless otherwise indicated, future references to *The American Slave* are from this series. Ibid., vol. 5, pt. 3, pp. 36, 178; ibid., vol. 6, pt. 2, p. 107; ibid., vol. 2, pt. 1, p. 246.

5. George Rawick, ed., *The American Slave: A Composite Autobiography*, supplement, ser. 2, 10 vols. (Westport, Conn.: Greenwood Press, 1979), vol. 2, pt. 2, p. 26; ibid., vol. 7, pt. 1, p. 111.

6. John W. Blassingame, ed., *Slave Testimony: Two Centuries of Letters, Speeches, Interviews, and Autobiographies* (Baton Rouge: Louisiana State University Press, 1977), p. 353; Rawick, ed., *The American Slave*, vol. 12, pt. 1, pp. 172–73; ibid., vol. 5, pt. 3, p. 173.

7. Legislative Records, Petition of the Inhabitants of Orangeburg District to the South Carolina Legislature, December 4, 1816, #95, SCDAH; General Report of the Committee on Colored Population, c. 1858, #2848, ibid.; Report of the Judiciary Committee, 1858, #93, ibid.; Charles Vinzent to Julian S. Devereux, April 6, 21, 1853, Julien Sidney Devereux Family Papers, BTHC; Abigaile Curlee, "A Study of Texas Slave Plantations, 1822–1865" (Ph.D. dissertation, University of Texas, 1932), pp. 82, 141–43; William Allen to Ralph Gurley, December 29, 1836, RACS (on microfilm), reel 26, LC and Kent State University, Kent, Ohio.

8. Frederick Law Olmsted, *A Journey in the Seaboard Slave States, with Remarks on Their Economy* (New York: Dix and Edwards, 1856), p. 443; Thomas F. Armstrong, "From Task Labor to Free Labor: The Transition along Georgia's Rice Coast, 1820–1880," *GHQ* 64 (Winter 1980), 436; Morgan, "The Ownership of Property by Slaves," p. 415; "List of Claims," Liberty County, Ga., RCC, RTD, RG 56, reel 13, NA; Alex Lichtenstein, "'That disposition to theft, with which they have been branded': Moral Economy, Slave Management, and the Law," *JSoH* 21 (Spring 1988), pp. 413–39.

9. Rawick, ed., *The American Slave*, vol. 4, pt. 1, p. 71; Genovese, *Roll, Jordan, Roll*, pp. 535–36; Virgil Hillyer to J. B. Howell, March 22, 1873, RCC, RTD, RG 56, reel 3, NA; C. W. Dudley to Commissioners of Southern Claims, June 3, 1874, reel 4, ibid.

10. Legislative Records, Presentment of the Grand Jury of Lexington District, S.C., Fall 1855, #23, SCDAH; see ibid., Presentment of the Grand Jury of Beaufort District, S.C., Fall 1850, #3, ibid; Janet S. Hermann, *The Pursuit of a Dream* (New York: Oxford University Press, 1982), pp. 5, 44–49; Rawick, ed., *The American Slave*, vol. 2, pt. 2, p. 133.

11. "List of Claims," Liberty County, Ga., RCC, RTD, RG 56, reel 13, NA; Morgan, "The Ownership of Property by Slaves," pp. 411–12.

12. Henry William Ravenel, "Recollections of Southern Plantation Life," *Yale Review* 25 (June 1936), 751. Ravenel's recollections were written in 1876.

13. James Townes, "Management of Negroes," *Southern Cultivator* 9 (June 1851), 87–88, in *Advice among Masters: The Ideal in Slave Management in the Old South*, ed. James Breeden (Westport, Conn.: Greenwood Publishing Co., 1980), p. 259; quoted in Joyner, *Down by the Riverside*, p. 74; Rawick, ed., *The American Slave*, vol. 5, pt. 3, p. 178.

14. Rawick, ed., *The American Slave*, vol. 6, pt. 1, p. 283.

15. *De Bow's Review* 22 (1857), 632–33.

16. Rawick, ed., *The American Slave*, vol. 4, pt. 2, p. 157; Blassingame, ed., *Slave Testimony*, p. 132; "Accounts of Wood Cut in 1854," July 10, 1854, Bruce, Seddon, and Wilkins Plantation Records, LSU; McDonnell, "Money Knows No Master," p. 33; U.S. Congress, Senate, *Report of John Alvord, Inspector of Schools and Finances for Freedmen*, no. 27, 39th Cong., 1st sess., 1866, *Senate Executive Documents*, p. 141.

17. Robert Russell, *North America, Its Agriculture and Climate; Containing Observations on the Agriculture and Climate of Canada, the United States, and the Island of Cuba* (Edinburgh: A. and C. Black, 1857), p. 151; Ulrich B. Phillips, *American Negro Slavery: A Survey of the Supply, Employment, and Control of Negro Labor as Determined by the Plantation Regime* (New York: D. Appleton and Co., 1918), p. 408; Luther Porter Jackson, *Free Negro Labor and Property Holding in Virginia, 1830–1860* (Washington, D.C.: American Historical Association, 1942), p. 180; "Contract between Robert Brown and Nathaniel Leonard," March 2, 1825, Abiel Leonard Collection, folder 55, JMC-UMSHS; "Receipt," J. B. Harris to M. Leonard, January 21, 1825, in ibid.; Olmsted, *Journey in the Seaboard Slave States*, pp. 127–28, 153–56, 352–55; Robert Starobin, *Industrial Slavery in the Old South* (New York: Oxford University Press, 1970), pp. 101–3; Charles Dew, "Disciplining Slave Iron Workers in the Antebellum South: Coercion, Conciliation, and Accommodation," *AHR* 79 (April 1974), 405–8.

18. Dew, "Disciplining Slave Iron Workers," p. 405, and "David Ross and the Oxford Iron Works: A Study of Industrial Slavery in the Early Nineteenth-Century South," *WMQ*, 3d ser., 31 (April 1974), 208–9; Starobin, *Industrial Slavery in the Old South*, pp. 14–17, 134–35; Samuel Bradford, "The Negro Ironworker in Ante Bellum Virginia," *JSH* 25 (May 1959), 194–206; Robert E. Corlew, "Some Aspects of Slavery in Dickson County," *THQ* 10 (September 1951), 224–48; Barbara Green, "Slave Labor at the Maramec Iron Works, 1828–50," *MHR* 78 (January 1979), 150–64; Olmsted, *Journey in the Seaboard Slave States*, pp. 82–85; Frederick Bancroft, *Slave Trading in the Old South* (Baltimore: J. H. Furst Co., 1931), p. 405; John Stevens Abbott, *South and North; or Impressions Received during a Trip to Cuba and the South* (New York: Abbey and Abbot, 1860), p. 202.

19. Olmsted, *Journey in the Seaboard Slave States*, p. 127; John T. O'Brien,

"Factory, Church, and Community: Blacks in Antebellum Richmond," *JSH* 46 (November 1978), 151; *Richmond Dispatch*, January 16, 1857; John T. Trowbridge, *A Picture of the Desolated States and the Work of Restoration* (Hartford, Conn.: I. Sterbins, 1866), pp. 230–31; Dew, "Disciplining Slave Iron Workers," p. 407.

20. Claudia Goldin, *Urban Slavery in the American South, 1820–1860: A Quantitative History* (Chicago: University of Chicago Press, 1976), pp. 36, 72–73; Robert Francis Engs, *Freedom's First Generation: Black Hampton, Virginia, 1861–1890* (Philadelphia: University of Pennsylvania Press, 1979), p. 14; Randall M. Miller, "The Fabric of Control: Slavery in Antebellum Textile Mills," *BHR* 55 (Winter 1981), 475–90; Dew, "Disciplining Slave Iron Workers," pp. 405–7.

21. RCPC, Norfolk County, Va., Wills, bk. 2 (October 22, 1804), p. 223, MESDA; James Rudd, "Account Book," 1846–53, FC. Armstrong ran away December 11, 1853. The average payment of $4.60 per week is thus derived from the 413 weeks James hired out during the eight-year span.

22. Goldin, *Urban Slavery*, p. 36; H. C. Ewin to Benjamin H. Reeves, January 3, 1813, Abiel Leonard Collection, folder 41, JMC-UMSHS.

23. Frederick Douglass, *My Bondage and My Freedom* (New York: Miller, Orton and Milligan, 1855), pp. 328–29.

24. Frederick Law Olmsted, *The Cotton Kingdom: A Traveller's Observations on Cotton and Slavery in the American Slave States*, ed. Arthur M. Schlesinger (New York: Alfred A. Knopf, 1953), p. 397; James Starkey to William McLain, May 29, 1848, and Starkey to Gerald Hallock, May 13, 1850, in Blassingame, ed., *Slave Testimony*, pp. 82–83.

25. Legislative Records, Petition of the Citizens of Albemarle County to the Virginia General Assembly, January 31, 1835, VSL. See Phillips, *American Negro Slavery*, pp. 412–13.

26. W. B. Cooper to Mary Carrol, January 7, 1860, Carter Woodson Collection, LC; Helen T. Catterall, ed., *Judicial Cases concerning American Slavery and the Negro*, 5 vols. (Washington, D.C.: W. F. Roberts Co., 1932), 1:157.

27. Ulrich B. Phillips, "The Slave Labor Problem in the Charleston District," in Elinor Miller and Eugene Genovese, eds., *Plantation, Town and County: Essays on the Local History of American Slave Society* (Urbana: University of Illinois Press, 1974), p. 13; Legislative Records, Presentment of the Grand Jury for Sumter District, S.C., Fall 1849, #29, SCDAH; Presentment of the Grand Jury of Newberry District, S.C., Spring 1859, #45, ibid.; Presentment of the Grand Jury of Kershaw District, S.C., Fall 1857, #10, ibid.; Reports of the Judiciary Committee of the South Carolina General Assembly, 1856, #63, ibid.; Report of the Committee on the Colored Population, 1864, #6, ibid.; Presentment of the Grand Jury of York District, S.C., 1858, #43, ibid.; James Sprunt, *Chronicles of the Cape Fear River, 1660–1916* (Raleigh: Edwards and Broughton Printing Co., 1916), pp. 179–80; William L. Richter, "Slavery in Baton Rouge, 1820–1860," *LH* 10 (Spring 1969), 125–45; Raphael Semmes, *Baltimore as Seen by Visitors, 1783–1860* (Baltimore: Maryland His-

torical Society, 1953), pp. 165–66; Terry L. Seip, "Slaves and Free Negroes in Alexandria, [Louisiana,] 1850 to 1860," *LH* 10 (Spring 1969), 147–65; Roger Fischer, "Racial Segregation in Ante Bellum New Orleans," *AHR* 74 (February 1969), 926–37.

28. This interpretation differs from that set forth by Starobin, *Industrial Slavery in the Old South*, pp. 135–36. See also Stampp, *The Peculiar Institution*, p. 72; James Parton, *General Butler in New Orleans: History of the Administration of the Department of the Gulf in the Year 1862* (Boston: Houghton, Mifflin and Co., 1863), pp. 490–91; Philip D. Morgan, "Black Life in Eighteenth-Century Charleston," in *Perspectives in American History*, N.S., 1 (1984), 191–94; Lloyd Hunter, "Slavery in St. Louis, 1804–1860," *Missouri Historical Society Bulletin* 30 (July 1974), 242.

29. Morgan, "Black Life in Eighteenth-Century Charleston," p. 194; Goldin, *Urban Slavery in the American South*, p. 233.

30. John Liddell to Oran Mayo, September 4, 1849, Liddell Papers, LSU.

31. Oran Mayo to John Liddell, March 4, 1852, in ibid.; Edward H. Chappin, Authorization Note, October 4, 1823, Jill Knight Garrett Collection, TSLA; Russell, *North America, Its Agriculture and Climate*, p. 151.

32. Henry Clay to Philip R. Fendall, August 17, 1830, Miscellaneous Manuscripts, FC.

33. John Hope Franklin and Alfred A. Moss, Jr., *From Slavery to Freedom: A History of Negro Americans*, 6th ed. (New York: Alfred A. Knopf, 1987); Ira Berlin, *Slaves without Masters: The Free Negro in the Antebellum South* (New York: Pantheon Books, 1974).

34. See Clement Eaton, "Slave-Hiring in the Upper South: A Step toward Freedom," *MVHR* 46 (March 1960), 672; John Hope Franklin, "Slaves Virtually Free in Ante-Bellum North Carolina," *JNH* 28 (July 1943), 305; Richard B. Morris, "The Measure of Bondage in the Slave States," *MVHR* 41 (September 1954), 233–34; Loren Schweninger, "The Free-Slave Phenomenon: James P. Thomas and the Black Community in Ante-Bellum Nashville," *CWH* 22 (December 1976), 303; J. Merton England, "The Free Negro in Ante-Bellum Tennessee," *JSH* 9 (February 1943), 46; John Hebron Moore, "Simon Gray, Riverman: A Slave Who Was Almost Free," *MVHR* 49 (December 1962), 472–74.

35. *Southern Watchman*, April 28, 1859, quoted in E. Merton Coulter, "Slavery and Freedom in Athens, Georgia, 1860–66," *GHQ* 49 (September 1965), 265; Parton, *General Butler in New Orleans*, p. 490; Richard C. Wade, *Slavery in the Cities: The South, 1820–1860* (New York: Oxford University Press, 1964), pp. 40–43; Natchez *Mississippi Free Trader*, May 13, 1841, in Charles S. Syndor, "The Free Negro in Mississippi before the Civil War," *AHR* 33 (July 1927), 776; Charles C. Jones to Charles C. Jones, Jr., October 2, 23, November 23, 29, 1856, in *The Children of Pride: A True Story of Georgia and the Civil War*, ed. Robert Myers (New Haven: Yale University Press, 1972), pp. 243, 255, 269; Charles C. Jones, Jr., to Charles C. Jones, October 1, 1856, in ibid., p. 240; see Charles C. Jones, *The Religious Instruction of the Negroes in the United*

States (Savannah: T. Purse, 1842), pp. 6–7; Donald G. Mathews, "Charles Colcock Jones and the Southern Evangelical Crusade to Form a Biracial Community," *JSH* 41 (August 1975), 315.

36. Schweninger, "The Free-Slave Phenomenon," p. 303; Catterall, ed., *Judicial Cases concerning American Slavery*, 1:308–9, 2:161–62; Engs, *Freedom's First Generation*, pp. 16–17; Barbara Jeanne Fields, *Slavery and Freedom on the Middle Ground: Maryland during the Nineteenth Century* (New Haven: Yale University Press, 1985), p. 34; Petition of Stephen B. Forbes to the Craven County Superior Court to Emancipate Lettice, 1827, in John H. Bryan Collection, box 6–23, NCDAH; Legislative Records; Petition of A. P. Upshur, George Yerby, et al. to the Virginia Legislature, Northampton County, Dec. 6, 1831, VSL; Richard Bibb to Ralph Gurley, May 20, 1831, RACS, reel 11, LC; Wade, *Slavery in the Cities*, chap. 6.

37. RCPC, Davidson County, Tenn., Minutes, bks. 1850–53 (March 1851), p. 144; ibid., bks. 1822–24 (July 1823), p. 539; ibid., Warranty Deeds, bk. 2 (June 25, 1838), p. 542; *Nashville Republican Banner*, May 25, 1842; *Private Acts Passed at the First Session of the Twentieth General Assembly of the State of Tennessee* (Nashville: Allen A. Hall, 1833), p. 96; RCPC, Albemarle County, Va., Wills, bk. 6 (July 14, 1814), p. 28; ibid., bk. 9 (Nov. 17, 1825), p. 260; *Democratic Clarion and Tennessee Gazette* (Nashville), May 31, 1814; *Alabama Republican* (Huntsville), June 12, 1819; Jill Knight Garrett, *A History of Lauderdale County, Alabama* (Columbia, Tenn.: Jill Garrett, 1964), pp. 3–5; RCPC, Lauderdale County, Ala., Wills, vol. 6 (June 3, 1824), p. 117; Loren Schweninger, "John H. Rapier, Sr.: A Slave and Freedman in the Ante-Bellum South," CWH 20 (March 1974), pp. 23–25.

38. General Assembly, Session Records, Petition of John Bryan, James Bryan, John Hyman, Ann G. Hyman, Frances H. Hyman, et al., to the North Carolina General Assembly, October 10, 1833, NCDAH; Petition of Ned Hyman to the North Carolina General Assembly, November 23, 1833, ibid.; Joseph D. Biggs to the North Carolina General Assembly, October 1833, ibid; Samuel Rhea to Ralph R. Gurley, May 24, 1833, RACS, reel 20, LC; "Testimony of William Weston," Craven County, N.C., November 12, 1859, in Civil Actions Concerning Slaves and Free Persons of Color, 1860, NCDAH.

39. Loren Schweninger, ed., *From Tennessee Slave to St. Louis Entrepreneur: The Autobiography of James Thomas* (Columbia: University of Missouri Press, 1984), p. 28; Legislative Records, Petition of Billy Brown to the Virginia General Assembly, Prince Edward County, December 18, 1818, and December 14, 1825, VSL; James Morton, James Wood, Samuel Carter, John Hudson, et al., to the Virginia General Assembly, November 23, 1818, ibid.; William Q. Morton, Moses Tredway, et al., to the Virginia General Assembly, January 10, 1826, ibid.

40. USMSPC, Richland County, S.C., 1850, p. 11. In this and subsequent USMSPC citations the printed page numbers are generally used. The unnumbered page facing the numbered page is cited as being the same as the numbered page. If there is no printed number, readers should be guided by the numbers in the upper right-hand corner of the right-hand page. For St.

Louis County, citations are from individual census tracts. Larry Koger, *Black Slaveowners: Free Black Slave Masters in South Carolina, 1790–1860* (Jefferson, N.C.: McFarland and Company, 1985), pp. 69–70.

41. Carter Woodson, "The Negroes of Cincinnati Prior to the Civil War," *JNH* 1 (January 1916), 21; Juliet E. K. Walker, *Free Frank: A Black Pioneer on the Antebellum Frontier* (Lexington: University of Kentucky Press, 1983), pp. 35–36.

42. Hermann, *The Pursuit of a Dream*, pp. 18–19.

43. Catterall, ed., *Judicial Cases*, 1:308–9.

44. Benjamin S. Turner to Claims Commission, April 21, 1871, Deposition, Case #285, RCC, RTD, RG 56, NA. I am most grateful to Alston Fitts, of Selma, Ala., who is currently working on a biography of Turner, for sending me a copy of this deposition.

45. C. W. Dudley to Commissioner of Claims, June 3, 1874, reel 4, ibid.; General Assembly, Session Records, Petition of the Mechanical Society of Wilmington to the North Carolina General Assembly, November 29, 1802, NCDAH; Memorial of the Citizens of Smithville (Brunswick County) to the North Carolina General Assembly, 1856, ibid.; see also RCPC, Campbell County, Va. Deeds, bk. A (June 6, 1808), p. 103; ibid., Norfolk County, Va. Deeds, bk. 13 (June 15, 1815), p. 414; *Federal Gazette and Baltimore Daily Advertiser*, November 19, 1804; *American and Commercial Daily Advertiser* (Baltimore), April 28, 1812, MESDA; Catherine W. Bishir, "Black Builders in Antebellum North Carolina," *NCHR* 61 (October 1984), 424; Peter H. Wood, "Whetting, Setting, and Laying Timbers: Black Builders in the Early South," *Southern Exposure* 8 (Spring 1980), 3–7; Judith Wragg Chase, "American Heritage from Ante-Bellum Black Craftsmen," *Southern Folklore Quarterly* 42 (1978), 141–42; Legislative Records, Petition of James Rose, William J. Grayson, Benjamin Huger, et al., to the South Carolina Senate, 1860, ND #2801, SCDAH.

46. Blassingame, ed., *Slave Testimony*, pp. 454–55; Records of R. G. Dun and Company, Wythe County, Va., January 1853–December 1860, Baker Library, Harvard University Graduate School of Business Administration, Boston, Mass. The author wishes to thank Robert C. Kenzer for providing him with the above credit rating. Legislative Records, Petition of the Residents of Bedford, Giles, Hickman, Lincoln, Maury, and Williamson counties to the Tennessee General Assembly, 1832, TSLA; Citizens of Tennessee to the State Legislature, August 1843, ibid.; Ladies of Tennessee to the State Legislature, August 1843, ibid.; Certificate of Wade Barret, July 6, 1830, in Petition of the Residents of Bedford, Giles, Hickman, Lincoln, Maury, and Williamson counties to the Tennessee General Assembly, 1832, TSLA; see also Certificate of Larkin Dearen, January 5, 1831; Certificate of Thomas Stone, n.d.; Certificate of Gilbert Nichols, March 20, 1829, ibid.; *The Nashville General Commercial Directory* (Nashville: Daily American, 1853), p. 36.

47. Stephen F. Miller, "Recollections of Newbern Fifty Years Ago," typescript, 1873, p. 56, NCDAH; RCPC, Craven County, N.C., Petition of John C. Stanly to the Craven County Superior Court, c. 1829, ibid.

48. *The Nashville General Commercial Directory*, p. 68; "Reminiscences of Meritt Scott Pilcher," February 28, 1934, in Catherine Pilcher Avery Papers, TSLA; USMSPC, Davidson County, Tenn., Nashville, 6th Ward, 1840, p. 295; England, "The Free Negro in Tennessee," p. 267; *Republican Banner* (Nashville), May 25, 1842; *Davidson County, Tennessee, 1850 Census*, transcribed by Deane Porch (Fort Worth: American Reference Publishers, 1969), p. 253; *Nashville Republican*, April 21, 1836; RCPC, Davidson County, Tenn., Minutes, bk. E (October 4, 185[3]), pp. 563–64. In Edwin Ewing's emancipation petition the date is erroneously written as 1854. Parrish continued these businesses in subsequent years. *The Nashville Business Directory* (Nashville: John P. Campbell, 1855), p. 94; *Nashville Business Directory* (Nashville: Smith, Camp and Co., 1857), p. 167; RCPC, Davidson County, Tenn., Warranty Deeds, bk. 33 (June 22, 1864), pp. 368–69; *King's Nashville City Directory* (Nashville: E. Doug King, 1866), p. 257.

49. J. E. Bruce, "A Sketch of My Life," Bruce Manuscripts, Schomburg Collection, New York Public Library, in *Black Women in White America: A Documentary History*, ed. Gerda Lerner (New York: Vintage Books, 1973), pp. 33–34.

50. Koger, *Black Slaveowners*, pp. 36, 43; William Eden to Anthony Weston, March 29, 1856, in "Documents," *JNH* 11 (January 1926), 79–80; *List of the Tax Payers of the City of Charleston for 1860* (Charleston: Evans and Cogswell, 1861), p. 333.

51. *A Digest of the Laws of the State of Georgia* (Philadelphia: J. Towar and D. M. Hogan, 1831), p. 310; *Acts Passed at the First Session of the Twenty-third General Assembly of the State of Tennessee* (Nashville: J. George Harris, 1840), pp. 82–83; *A Collection of All Such Acts of the General Assembly of Virginia* (Richmond: Samuel Pleasants, Jr., 1803), p. 188; *Supplement to the Revised Code of the Laws of Virginia* (Richmond: Samuel Shepherd and Co., 1833), p. 250; Legislative Records, Report of the Judiciary Committee, South Carolina General Assembly, 1858, #93, SCDAH; *The Laws of Texas, 1822–1897*, 6 vols. (Austin: Gamble Book Co., 1898), 5:762–63.

52. *A Digest of the Laws of the State of Georgia* (Athens, Ga.: Oliver H. Prince, 1837), p. 795; Franklin, "Slaves Virtually Free in Ante-Bellum North Carolina," pp. 296, 308–9.

53. H. Bailey, ed., *Report of Cases Argued and Determined in the Court of Appeals of South Carolina*, 2 vols. (Charleston: E. Miller, 1834), 2:137–38; *Acts Passed at the First Session of the Twenty-third General Assembly of the State of Tennessee* (Nashville: J. George Harris, 1840), p. 82; David Thomas, "The Free Negro in Florida before 1865," *South Atlantic Quarterly* 10 (October 1911), 340; Ralph Flanders, "The Free Negro in Ante-Bellum Georgia," *NCHR* 9 (July 1932), 258; Marina Wikramanayake, *A World In Shadow: The Free Black in Antebellum South Carolina* (Columbia: University of South Carolina Press, 1973), pp. 43–44.

54. Edwin Davis, ed., *Plantation Life in the Florida Parishes of Louisiana, 1836–1846, As Reflected in the Diary of Bennet H. Barrow* (New York: Colum-

bia University Press, 1943), p. 409; Legislative Records, Petition of the Citizens of Charlotte County to the Virginia General Assembly, December 20, 1810, VSL.

55. Legislative Records, Petition of the Citizens of Bedford County to the Tennessee General Assembly, December 20, 1847, TSLA; Petition of the Inhabitants of Orangeburg District to the South Carolina General Assembly, December 4, 1816, #95, SCDAH; Presentment of the Grand Jury of Orangeburg District, S.C., Fall 1859, #46, ibid.; Report of the Judiciary Committee, South Carolina General Assembly, 1858, #93, ibid.; Report on Slaves Owning Cotton, South Carolina General Assembly, 1816, #125, ibid; Petition of Grand Jurors of Hays County to the Texas Senate and House of Representatives, November 30, 1859, TSA.

56. Catterall, ed., *Judicial Cases Concerning American Slavery and the Negro*, 2:161–62; Franklin, "Slaves Virtually Free in Ante-bellum North Carolina," pp. 308–9; Schweninger, "The Free-Slave Phenomenon," pp. 302–3; Jackson, *Free Negro Labor and Property Holding in Virginia*, p. 178; Eaton, "Slave-Hiring in the Upper South," p. 672; Morris, "The Measure of Bondage in the Slave States," pp. 233–34.

57. Russell, *North America; Its Agriculture and Climate*, p. 151; Richmond *Dispatch*, December 22, 1852, January 3, 1853, quoted in O'Brien, "Factory, Church, and Community," pp. 513–14. Also see O'Brien, "From Bondage to Citizenship: The Richmond Black Community, 1865–1867" (Ph.D. dissertation, University of Rochester, 1975), p. 21; Olmsted, *A Journey in the Seaboard Slave States*, p. 31; Catterall, ed., *Judicial Cases concerning American Slavery and the Negro*, 2:161–62; General Assembly, Session Records, Petition of the Inhabitants of Craven County to the North Carolina General Assembly, December 19, 1831, NCDAH; Petition of Commissioners of Raleigh (Wake County) to the North Carolina General Assembly, November 29, 1842, ibid.; Petition of the Citizens of Mecklenburg County to the North Carolina General Assembly, c. 1854, ibid.; Memorial of the Citizens of Smithville (Brunswick County) to the North Carolina General Assembly, c. 1856, ibid.; Legislative Records, Presentment of the Grand Jury for Sumter District, S.C., Fall 1849, #29, SCDAH; Presentment of the Grand Jury of Newberry District, S.C., Spring 1859, #45, ibid.

58. Samuel Anderson to Benjamin W. Womack, February 3, 1848, Carter Woodson Collection, container 15, LC; Legislative Records, Petition of John Wise to the Virginia General Assembly, Accomac County, December 1, 1810, VSL. See also Petition of Jingo to the Virginia General Assembly, December 8, 1810, ibid.; John Cropper, Jr., to the Virginia General Assembly, November 29, 1810, ibid.; John Finney to the Virginia General Assembly, January 7, 1811, ibid.; Petition of the Citizens of Hamilton County to the Tennessee General Assembly, October 1845, TSLA; see also General Assembly, Session Records, Petition of Mupendine Matthews to the North Carolina General Assembly, November 22, 1816, NCDAH; Ephraim H. Foster to Jane Foster, July 30, 1847, Ephraim Foster Papers, TSLA; RCPC, Davidson County, Tenn.,

Minutes, bks. 1816–18 (February 2–3, 1818), p. 457; ibid., Minutes, bks. 1819–21 (October 1821), p. 208; ibid., Minutes, bks. 1850–53 (March 6, 1851), p. 135.

59. Koger, *Black Slaveowners*, pp. 61, 65; Charles C. Jones, Jr., to Charles C. Jones, October 1, 1856, in *The Children of Pride*, p. 241; J. Merton England, "The Free Negro in Ante-Bellum Tennessee" (Ph.D. dissertation, Vanderbilt University, 1941), p. 206.

60. William T. Sherman, *Memoirs of Gen. W. T. Sherman, Written By Himself, with an Appendix, Bringing His Life Down to Its Closing Scenes, Also a Personal Tribute and Critique of the Memoirs*, 4th ed., ed. James G. Blaine, 2 vols. (New York: Charles L. Webster and Co., 1891), 2:217.

61. William Sherman to Ulysses Grant, December 16, 1864, in ibid., p. 208.

62. On March 3, 1871, Congress passed a law instructing the president to nominate three commissioners to receive, examine, and consider the claims of "those citizens who remained loyal adherents to the cause and the government of the United States during the war, for stores and supplies taken or furnished during the rebellion for the use of the army of the United States." Claimants had to submit their requests in writing and then prove their loyalty by answering eighty questions. Did they ever voluntarily contribute to the Confederate cause? to the Union cause? Did they ever serve in the Confederacy? Among the 22,298 claims totaling $60,258,150, Congress awarded 7,092 claimants a total of $4,636,921. The Southern Claims Commission finished its work in 1880. At first there was a question as to whether or not blacks, as slaves, could actually possess property (since they had not been citizens); but in the end they were allowed to present claims. See Introduction, in RCC, RTD, RG 56, reel 1, NA.

63. "Introduction," RCC, RTD, RG 56, reel 1, NA; "Journal of the Southern Claims Commissioners," December 4, 1877, p. 283, ibid.

64. Virgil Hillyer to J. B. Howell, March 22, 1873, ibid., reel 3; Hillyer to Asa Aldis, February 21, 1874, ibid., reel 4.

65. Report to the Commissioners of Claims, July 18, 1876, William Paine Papers, GHS; William Paine to Charles Benjamin, June 24, 1876, RCC, RTD, RG 56, reel 11, NA.

66. Charles C. Jones, Jr., to William Paine, August 19, 1876, William Paine Papers, GHS.

67. Claim #21,467, January 30, 1875, ibid.

68. Morgan, "Work and Culture," p. 596.

CHAPTER THREE
Free Negro Property Owners, 1800–1860

1. John H. Russell, *The Free Negro in Virginia, 1619–1865* (Baltimore: John Hopkins University Press, 1913); Rosser Howard Taylor, *The Free Negro in North Carolina* (Chapel Hill: University of North Carolina Press, 1920); James Wright, *The Free Negro in Maryland, 1634–1860* (New York: Columbia University Press, 1921); Ralph Flanders, "The Free Negro in Ante-Bellum Geor-

gia," *NCHR* 9 (July 1932), 250–72; Charles Syndor, "The Free Negro in Mississippi Before the Civil War," *AHR* 33 (July 1927), 769–88; Harold Schoen, "The Free Negro in the Republic of Texas," *Southwestern Historical Quarterly* 39 (April 1936), 292–308.

2. Luther Porter Jackson, *Free Negro Labor and Property Holding in Virginia, 1830–1860* (New York: D. Appleton Co., 1942), p. ix; John Hope Franklin, *The Free Negro in North Carolina, 1790–1860* (Chapel Hill: University of North Carolina Press, 1943), and "James Boon, Free Negro Artisan," *JNH* 30 (April 1945), 150–80.

3. E. Horace Fitchett, "The Traditions of the Free Negro in Charleston, South Carolina," *JNH* 25 (April 1940), 139–52, "The Origin and Growth of the Free Negro Population of Charleston, South Carolina," *JNH* 26 (October 1941), 421–37, and "The Status of the Free Negro in Charleston, South Carolina, and His Descendants in Modern Society," *JNH* 32 (October 1947), 430–51; Morris R. Boucher, "The Free Negro in Alabama prior to 1860," (Ph.D. dissertation, State University of Iowa, 1950); Donald E. Everett, "The Free Persons of Color in New Orleans, 1830–1865," (Ph.D. dissertation, Tulane University, 1952); Leonard P. Stavisky, "The Negro Artisan in the South Atlantic States, 1800–1860: A Study of Status and Economic Opportunity with Special Reference to Charleston," (Ph.D. dissertation, Columbia University, 1958); Edward F. Sweat, "The Free Negro in Antebellum Georgia," (Ph.D. dissertation, University of Indiana, 1957); John Hebron Moore, "Simon Gray, Riverman: A Slave Who Was Almost Free," *MVHR* 49 (December 1962), 472–84; Richard B. Morris, "The Measure of Bondage in the Slave States," *MVHR* 41 (September 1954), 219–40; Robert C. Reinders, "The Decline of the New Orleans Free Negro in the Decade Before the Civil War," *JMH* 24 (April 1962), 88–98.

4. Letitia W. Brown, *Free Negroes in the District of Columbia, 1790–1846* (New York: Oxford University Press, 1972), appendix 3; Herbert E. Sterkx, *The Free Negro in Ante-Bellum Louisiana* (Rutherford, N.J.: Fairleigh Dickinson Press, 1972); Marina Wikramanayake, *A World in Shadow: The Free Black in Antebellum South Carolina* (Columbia: University of South Carolina Press, 1973).

5. Ira Berlin, *Slaves without Masters: The Free Negro in the Antebellum South* (New York: Pantheon, 1974), p. 343. For a perceptive review of *Slaves without Masters* with special reference to property ownership, see Elliott Rudwick, rev., *AHR* 81 (June 1976), 665.

6. Whittington B. Johnson, "Free Blacks in Antebellum Savannah: An Economic Profile," *GHQ* 64 (Winter 1980), 428; Leonard P. Curry, *The Free Black in Urban America, 1800–1850: The Shadow of the Dream* (Chicago: University of Chicago Press, 1981), p. 40. Other recent articles include Catherine W. Bisher, "Black Builders in Antebellum North Carolina," *NCHR* 61 (October 1984), 423–58; Richard Tansey, "Out-of-State Free Blacks in Late Antebellum New Orleans," *LH* 22 (Fall 1981), 369–86.

7. Richard Morris, "The Course of Peonage in a Slave State," *Political Science Quarterly* 65 (June 1950), 244.

8. Legislative Records, Petition of Ann Archie to the Mississippi General Assembly, 1860, Box 27, RG 47, MDAH.

9. George Rogers, Jr., *The History of Georgetown County, South Carolina* (Columbia: University of South Carolina Press, 1970), p. 212; Jeffery Brackett, *The Negro in Maryland: A Study of the Institution of Slavery* (Baltimore: Johns Hopkins University Press, 1889; reprint ed., New York: Negro Universities Press, 1969), p. 188.

10. David Thomas, "The Free Negro in Florida Before 1865," *South Atlantic Quarterly* 10 (October 1911), 340.

11. Tansey, "Out-of-State Free Blacks in Late Antebellum New Orleans," p. 378; Sterkx, *The Free Negro in Ante-Bellum Louisiana*, p. 172; Syndor, "The Free Negro in Mississippi," p. 773.

12. *Public Acts Passed at the First Session of the Twenty-first General Assembly of the State of Tennessee* (Nashville: S. Nye and Co., 1836), p. 167; Ralph Flanders, "The Free Negro in Ante-Bellum Georgia," *NCHR* 9 (July 1932), 262; Johnson, "Free Blacks in Antebellum Savannah," p. 419; Robert C. Reinders, "The Free Negro in the New Orleans Economy, 1850–1860," *LH* 6 (Summer 1965), 283. There is no systematic study of free blacks and the law. Nor is there any comprehensive analysis of how effective particular codes were in controlling free Negroes. See Jonathan Beasley, "Blacks—Slave and Free—Vicksburg, 1850–1860," *JMH* 28 (February 1976), 20–24; James Browning, "The Free Negro in Ante-Bellum North Carolina," *NCHR* 15 (January 1938), 24–26; Judy Day and M. James Kedro, "Free Blacks in St. Louis: Antebellum Conditions, Emancipation, and the Postwar Era," *Bulletin of the Missouri Historical Society* 30 (January 1974), 119; Florence Beatty-Brown, "Legal Status of Arkansas Negroes Before Emancipation," *AHQ* 28 (Spring 1969), 8–12; Donnie Bellamy, "Free Blacks in Antebellum Missouri, 1820–1860," *MHR* 67 (January 1973), 204–8; Annie Stahl, "The Free Negro in Antebellum Louisiana," *LHQ* 25 (April 1942), 300–396; Wikramanayake, *A World in Shadow: The Free Black in Antebellum South Carolina*, pp. 54–55, 58–59, 63–65, 102; Syndor, "The Free Negro in Mississippi before the Civil War," pp. 775–76; Fitchett, "The Origin and Growth of the Free Negro Population of Charleston, South Carolina," p. 430.

13. *Digest of the Laws of the State of Georgia* (Middedgeville: Grantland and Orme, 1822), pp. 467–69.

14. *Memorial of the Ohio Anti-Slavery Society to the General Assembly of the State of Ohio*, by the Ohio Anti-Slavery Society (Cincinnati: Pugh and Dodd, 1838), p. 23.

15. "Diary of Mrs. William Thornton," November 20, 1800, p. 223, in William Thornton Papers, LC.

16. *Memorial of the Ohio Anti-Slavery Society*, p. 20.

17. *Condition of the People of Color in the State of Ohio with Interesting Anecdotes*, by Ohio Anti-Slavery Society (Boston: Isaac Knapp, 1839), p. 23; David A. Gerber, *Black Ohio and the Color Line, 1860–1915* (Urbana: University of Illinois Press, 1976), p. 19; *A Statistical Inquiry into the Condition of the People of*

Colour of the City and Districts of Philadelphia, by the Society for Promoting the Abolition of Slavery (Philadelphia: Kite and Walton, 1849), p. 12; Terry Alford, "Some Manumissions Recorded in the Adams County Deed Books in Chancery Clerk's Office, Natchez, Mississippi, 1795–18[5]5," *JMH* 33 (February 1971), 39–50; Lorenzo Greene, "Self-Purchase by Negroes in Cole County, Missouri," *Midwest Journal* 1 (Winter 1948), 83–85; Luther Porter Jackson, "Manumission in Certain Virginia Cities," *JNH* 15 (July 1930), 284–85; Charles Trabue, "The Voluntary Emancipation of Slaves in Tennessee As Reflected in the State's Legislation and Judicial Decisions," *Tennessee Historical Magazine* 4 (March 1918), 54. Self-purchase contracts were considered inviolable by some slaves. Mississippi black Rube Jamison, a skilled wheelwright, made a promise to pay for himself and, even after the Civil War, he continued to labor for his former master to pay off his "debt." George Rawick, ed., *The American Slave: A Composite Autobiography*, supplement, ser. 1, 12 vols. (Westport, Conn.: Greenwood Publishing Co., 1979), 8:1148.

18. "Davis, Rev. Noah," sketch of, in Daniel Murray Papers, reel 12, University of Wisconsin, Madison, Wis.; R. Halliburton, Jr., "Free Black Owners of Slaves: A Reappraisal of the Woodson Thesis," *SCHM* 76 (July 1976), 135; Calvin Dill Wilson, "Black Masters: A Side-Light on Slavery," *North American Review* 181 (November 1905), 692–96; Legislative Records, Petition of Samuel Johnston to the Virginia General Assembly, Fauquier County, December 16, 1815, VSL; Jackson, *Free Negro Labor and Property Holding in Virginia*, pp. 203–4; RCPC, Elizabeth City County, Va., Deed of Emancipation, January 10, 1849, in Carter Woodson Papers, LC; "Education, Suffrage, Progress," speech of John W. Cromwell, January 1, 1901, in ibid.; George Raick, ed., *The American Slave: A Composite Autobiography*, 19 vols. (Westport, Conn.: Greenwood Publishing Co., 1972–), 18:311–12; RCPC, St. Genevieve County, Mo., Deeds, bk. K (February 9, 1856), pp. 145–47, in St. Genevieve Archives, folder #38, JMC-UMSHS; Bellamy, "Free Blacks in Antebellum Missouri," p. 212; Benjamin Quarles, *Black Abolitionists* (New York: Oxford University Press, 1969), pp. 60–61; Calvin Dill Wilson, "Negroes Who Owned Slaves," *Popular Science Monthly* 81 (November 1912), 191. In various primary and secondary sources Meachum is spelled "Meachem," "Meacham," "Metchum," and Meachum. I have used the most common spelling. USMSPC, St. Louis, Mo., 4th Ward, 1850, p. 49; RCPC, St. Louis, Mo., Estates, #4173, April 12, 1854.

19. Legislative Records, Report of the Judiciary Committee to the South Carolina General Assembly on the Petition of Moses Irvin, December 8, 1829, SCDAH; Petition of Moses Irvin to the South Carolina General Assembly, 1836, ibid.; Larry Koger, *Black Slaveholders: Free Black Slave Masters in South Carolina, 1790–1860* (Jefferson, N.C.: McFarland Publishers, 1985), pp. 33, 39, 46–47, 59–60, 62; Carter G. Woodson, ed., *Free Negro Owners of Slaves in the United States in 1830* (Washington: Association for the Study of Negro Life and History, 1924; reprint ed., New York: Negro Universities Press, 1968), pp. 10–15; Reinders, "The Free Negro in the New Orleans Economy,"

p. 282; James McDowell to Ralph R. Gurley, October 25, 1831, RACS, reel 12, LC; Robert Brown to Millie Brown, March 8, 1854, Brown Family Papers, FC.

20. James M. Wright, *The Free Negro in Maryland, 1634–1860* (New York: Columbia University Press, 1921; reprint ed., New York: Octagon Books, 1971), pp. 88, 184, 189.

21. Memorial of the Richmond and Manchester Colonization Society, Presented January 1825, in *Annual Reports of the American Society for Colonizing the Free People of Color of the United States*, 91 vols. (Washington, D.C.: [American Colonization Society], 1818–1910; reprint ed., New York: Negro Universities Press, 1969), 8:55.

22. Jackson, *Free Negro Labor and Property Holding in Virginia*, p. 138, 145; Tax Assessments, St. Genevieve Co., Mo., 1830, folder #1455, St. Genevieve Archives, JMC-UMSHS.

23. RCPC, Norfolk County, Va., Deeds, bk. 45 (May 13, 1811), p. 144a, MESDA.

24. "Register of Free Persons of Color, Chatham County, Georgia, 1817–1829," GHS. The author wishes to thank Mary Lane Morrison, a longtime resident of Savannah, for graciously sharing the data cards she has compiled from this volume. There are three similar registers in different time periods, but only this one indicates property ownership. Flanders, "The Free Negro in Ante-Bellum Georgia," p. 267; Johnson, "Free Blacks in Antebellum Savannah," pp. 418, 422; U.S. Census Office, *Census for 1820* (Washington, D.C.: Gales and Seaton, 1821), p. 28. For examples of early black property ownership, see RCPC, Norfolk County, Va., Deeds, bk. 5 (September 15, 1798), p. 127; ibid., Wills, bk. 3 (April 26, 1814), p. 118; *Baltimore American and Commercial Advertiser*, November 15, 1806; RCPC, Charleston, S.C., Miscellaneous Land Records, bk. G6 (April 26, 1792), pp. 524–26, MESDA; Bellamy, "Free Blacks in Antebellum Missouri," p. 217. In Chatham County, Georgia, in 1806, there were 45 free persons of color listed in the tax assessment books, but most among them possessed very small amounts of property. Tax Digest, Chatham County, Ga., 1806, GDAH.

25. RCPC, Charleston, S.C., Miscellaneous Land Records, bks. W6-Z6 (July 10, 1798), pp. 275–6; ibid., bk. H9 (May 5, 1821), pp. [95]–96; ibid., bk. R7 (July 24, 1806), pp. 199–200; ibid., bk. E7 (July 24, 1801), pp. 218–19; ibid., bk. I8 (April 19, 1802), p. 260; ibid., bk. Q7 (June 18, 1803), pp. 298–99; ibid., bk. Y8 (March 1818), p. 347; ibid., bk. E8 (December 1, 1812), p. 407; ibid., bk. A8 (January 29, 1810), pp. 231–32; ibid., Wills, bks. 1826–34 (June 14, 1827), p. 394; ibid., Inventories, vol. F (September 5, 1823), p. 272; Charleston *City Gazette*, August 14, 1804, MESDA.

26. RCPC, Charleston, S.C., Miscellaneous Land Records, bk. U7 (August 18, 1804), pp. 22–23; ibid., Wills, bks. 1826–34 (June 14, 1827), p. 349; ibid., bks. 1818–26 (May 5, 1825), p. 1123; ibid., bks. 1793–1800 (June 28, 1794), p. 207; ibid., Inventories, vol. C (c. 1794), p. 86; *City Gazette and Daily Advertiser* (Charleston), June 22, 1801; Charleston *Morning Post and Daily Advertiser*, March 24, 1787; RCPC, Charleston, S. C., Miscellaneous Land Records,

pt. 91, bk. D7 (October 1, 1799), no. 403; ibid., pt. 106, bk. P8 (March 27, 1816), pp. [222–23]; ibid., bk. E9 (September 15, 1819), pp. 75–76; *Carolina Weekly Messenger* (Charleston), February 28, 1809, MESDA.

27. James Robertson, ed., *Louisiana under the Rule of Spain, France, and the United States, 1785–1807; Social, Economic, and Political Conditions of the Territory Represented in the Louisiana Purchase*, 2 vols. (Cleveland: Arthur H. Clark Co., 1910–11; reprint ed., Freeport, N.Y.: Books for Libraries Press, 1969), 1:218.

28. RPPC, Iberville Parish, La., Conveyances, bk. F (October 19, 1815), p. 171; ibid., bk. G (April 26, 1819), pp. 19–20; ibid., bk. O (November 4, 1834), n.p.; RPPC, Plaquemines Parish, La., Inventories, bks. 1846–58 (March 6, 1857), pp. 404–12; Bill of Sale, Augustin Metoyer, September 9, 1822, Cane River Collection, HNOC; Sterkx, *The Free Negro in Ante-Bellum Louisiana*, p. 53; Gary B. Mills, *The Forgotten People: Cane River's Creoles of Color* (Baton Rouge: Louisiana State University Press, 1977), pp. 108–9; RPPC, Natchitoches Parish, La., Conveyances, bk. 15 (June 24, 1824), pp. 89–90; ibid., West Baton Rouge Parish, La., Successions, #105, October 18, 1822; ibid., Successions, #2261, March 6, 1848. See also ibid., East Baton Rouge Parish, La., Successions, #460, August 14, 1855; USMSPC, East Baton Rouge Parish, La., 1850, p. 166.

29. RPPC, West Baton Rouge Parish, La., Successions, #2261, March 6, 1848. Mahier's property, listed in an inventory dated July 23, 1833, was divided among her children fifteen years later.

30. Quoted in Laura Foner, "The Free People of Color in Louisiana and St. Domingue: A Comparative Portrait of Two Three-Caste Societies," *JSoH* 3 (Summer 1970), 423; *General Index of All Successions, Opened in the Parish of Orleans, From the Year 1805, to the Year 1846*, comp. P. M. Bertin (New Orleans: Yeomans and Fitch, 1849), passim; Reinders, "The Free Negro in the New Orleans Economy, 1850–1860," p. 280; Winston, "The Free Negro in New Orleans," pp. 1080–85. Also see RPPC, New Orleans, La., Successions, #4835, January 16, 1852, NOPL; USMSPC, New Orleans, 1st Mun., 1st Ward, 1850, p. 4; ibid., 2d Ward, p. 82; ibid., 4th Ward, pp. 121, 125, 148, 150, 154; ibid., 5th Ward, pp. 190, 205; ibid., 7th Ward, pp. 376, 396; ibid., 3d Mun., 1st Ward, pp. 4, 51, 62.

31. Luther Porter Jackson, "The Virginia Free Negro Farmer and Property Owner, 1830–1860," *JNH* 24 (October 1939), p. 406, and *Free Negro Labor and Property Holding in Virginia*, 115–16; Wright, *The Free Negro in Maryland*, p. 184; computed from USMSPC, 1850, 1860. Unless otherwise noted, statistical evidence in this and subsequent sections has been computed from USMSPC, 1850, 1860.

32. Jackson, "The Virginia Free Negro Farmer," p. 406; *Population of the United States in 1860; Compiled from the Original Returns of the Eighth Census* (Washington: GPO, 1864), pp. 214, 508–13; computed from USMSPC, Maryland, Virginia, 1850, 1860.

33. Berlin, *Slaves without Masters*, p. 178; Legislative Records, Petition of Samuel Johnston to the Virginia General Assembly, Fauquier County, Decem-

ber 4, 1824, VSL; James W. Wallace to the Virginia General Assembly, November 25, 1824, ibid. See Robert Brent Toplin, "Between Black and White: Attitudes toward Southern Mulattoes, 1830–1861," *JSH* 45 (May 1979), 185–200.

34. Berlin, *Slaves without Masters*, p. 55; Richard C. Wade, *Slavery in the Cities: The South, 1820–1860* (New York: Oxford University Press, 1964), pp. 325–27.

35. Calculated from the list of "Negro Taxpayers" in Brown, *Free Negroes in the District of Columbia*, pp. 151–55; ibid., p. 11; Jackson, *Free Negro Labor and Property Holding in Virginia*, pp. 138, 154.

36. Wright, *The Free Negro in Maryland*, p. 185; "Pursuits &c of the Free People of Color in the Town of Frankfort," July 16, 1842, FC; computed from USMSPC, 1850, 1860; calculated from *Population of the United States in 1860*, pp. 1–520. My calculations of 60,766 urban and 164,197 rural Upper South free Negroes (approximately 12,153 and 32,839 families) in 1860 differ slightly from the proportion of urban Upper South free Negroes found in Berlin, *Slaves without Masters*, p. 176.

37. Frederick Law Olmsted, *A Journey in the Seaboard Slave States, with Remarks on Their Economy* (New York: Dix and Edwards, 1856), pp. 82–3.

38. Computed from USMSPC, 1850, 1860; Henry Robinson, "Some Aspects of the Free Negro Population of Washington, D.C., 1800–1862," *MHM* 64 (Spring 1969), 53; Constance McLaughlin Green, *The Secret City: A History of Race Relations in the Nation's Capital* (Princeton: Princeton University Press, 1967), pp. 43–44; Melvin R. Williams, "A Blueprint for Change: The Black Community in Washington, D.C., 1860–1870," *Records of the Columbia Historical Society of Washington, D.C., 1971–1972* (Washington, D.C.: Columbia Historical Society, 1973), p. 364; M. Ray Della, Jr., "The Problems of Negro Labor in the 1850s," *MHM* 66 (Spring 1971), p. 28; Bellamy, "Free Blacks in Antebellum Missouri," pp. 213–15.

39. Computed from USMSPC, 1850, 1860; Mills, *The Forgotten People*, p. 218. In 1850, there was a probable census undercount of free blacks in South Carolina. Even so, the increase among rural realty owners during the 1850s was significant.

40. Tax Digest, Chatham County, Ga., 1852, GDAH; Johnson, "Free Blacks in Antebellum Savannah," pp. 426–27; Tax Books, Escambia County, Fla., 1846, 1859, FSA; *List of the Tax Payers of the City of Charleston for 1859* (Charleston: Walker, Evans and Co., 1860), pp. 383–405; *List of the Tax Payers of the City of Charleston for 1860* (Charleston: Evans and Cogswell, 1861), pp. 315–34; Michael P. Johnson and James L. Roark, *Black Masters: A Free Family of Color in the Old South* (New York: W. W. Norton and Co., 1984), p. 343; Reinders, "The Free Negro in the New Orleans Economy," p. 280. The New Orleans data include a few Orleans Parish property owners living outside the city limits.

41. Legislative Records, Petition of Nancy Munford to the Virginia Legislature, City of Petersburg, January 14, 1847, VSL; Suzanne Lebsock, *The Free*

Women of Petersburg: Status and Culture in a Southern Town, 1784–1860 (New York: W. W. Norton and Co., 1984), p. 106.

42. RCPC, Charleston Co., S. C., Miscellaneous Land Records, bk. L8 (September 14, 1814), p. 31, MESDA.

43. Ibid., Marriage Records, vol. 3 (December 25, 1783), pp. 365–67, SCDAH.

44. "Pursuits &c of the Free People of Color in the Town of Frankfort," July 16, 1842, FC.

45. "Register of Free Persons of Color, Chatham County, Ga.," 1823, 1824, 1825, 1826, GHS; USMSPC, Chatham County, Ga., 1850, p. 297; RCPC, Chatham County, Ga., Estates, #J125, December 15, 1869.

46. USMSPC, Chatham County, Ga., 1850, p. 299; ibid., Savannah, 1st Dist., 1860, p. 47.

47. Lebsock, *The Free Women of Petersburg*, pp. 98–99; USMSPC, Anne Arundel County, Md., Annapolis, 1860, n. p.

48. Charles C. Jones, *The Religious Instruction of the Negroes in the United States* (Savannah: T. Purse, 1842), pp. 110–11.

49. RCPC, Davidson County, Tenn., Deeds, bk. 31 (June 11, 1860), pp. 29–30; J. Merton England, "The Free Negro in Ante-Bellum Tennessee," *JSH* 9 (February 1943), 46–47; William H. Haight, W. G. Browdfort, et al., "A Testimonal," July 20, 1857, in Carter Woodson Collection, container 9, LC.

50. Legislative Records, Petition of the Citizens of Stewart County to the Tennessee General Assembly, [December] 1851, TSLA.

51. Flanders, "The Free Negro in Ante-Bellum Georgia," p. 260n.

52. RCPC, St. Genevieve County, Mo., Minutes, vol. B (July 18, 1836), pp. 212–14, in St. Genevieve Collection, JMC-UMSHS.

53. Wright, *The Free Negro in Maryland*, p. 194.

54. Records of the Civil District Court, Natchitoches Parish, La., Petitions, #2895, October 6, 1841, #3351, March 21, 1843, #296, July 25, 1839, #3502, February 27, 1844, #3642, March 17, 1845, in Auguste Metoyer Papers, LSU.

55. RCPC, Craven County, N.C., Deeds, vol. 45 (May 8, 1828), p. 446.

56. Hataway's trip was recounted by Roberson two years later. Legislative Records, Petition of Zachariah Roberson to the Tennessee General Assembly, July 27, 1833, TSLA.

57. R. H. Mosby to Isaac Fanecon, February 22, 1842, Boon Papers, NCDAH; William Jeffreys to James Boon, March 23, 1848, ibid., quoted in Franklin, "James Boon, Free Negro Artisan," pp. 163–5.

58. Diary of Michael Shiner, June 7, 1833, LC. The "long bridge" Shiner mentioned was nearly a mile in length. It took thirty minutes to cross on foot. "Many of the planks are rotten, and it is in want of repair," a German observer noted. "It has two side-walks, one of them is separated from the road by a rail." Bernhard Karl, *Travels through North America, During the Years 1825 and 1826*, 2 vols. (Philadelphia: Carey, Lea and Carey, 1828), 1:173. For consequences when there were no white protectors, see Solomon Northrup,

Twelve Years a Slave; Narrative of Solomon Northrup, a Citizen of New-York, Kidnapped in Washington City in 1841, and Rescued in 1853 (Buffalo, N.Y.: Derby, Orton and Mulligan, 1853).

59. Edward Holland, *A Refutation of the Calumnies Circulated against the Southern and Western States, Respecting the Institution and Existence of Slavery among Them* (Charleston: A. E. Miller, 1822), pp. 84–85.

60. John McPhail to Ralph Gurley, September 23, 1831, RACS, reel 12.

61. Wallace Bordan to Ralph Gurley, November 25, 1831, ibid.

62. Thomas S. Grimké to Ralph Gurley, June 14, 1832, ibid.

63. Philip Moor to Ralph Gurley, February 22, 1832, ibid.

64. Legislative Records, Petition of James Rose, William Grayson, Benjamin Huger, et al., to the South Carolina Senate, 1860, ND #2801, SCDAH.

65. Ibid., Petition of Peter Katcliff, James Stewart, Joseph B. Hoff, et al., to the Mississippi Legislature, c. 1860, box 29, RG 47, MDAH. In the census, Hill was listed as having $2,600 worth of property. USMSPC, Wilkinson County, Miss., 1860, p. 533.

66. E. Duglas Taylor to William McLain, August 22, 1850, in "Documents: Letters to the American Colonization Society," ed. Carter Woodson, *JNH* 10 (April 1925), 224–78; see J. B. Jordan to J. W. Lugenbeel, October 1, 1850, ibid., p. 272; Thomas Grimke to Ralph Gurley, September 11, 1832, RACS, reel 15. There is a substantial literature on various phases of the emigration question. See Tom W. Shick, *Behold the Promised Land: A History of Afro-American Settler Society in Nineteenth-Century Liberia* (Baltimore: Johns Hopkins University Press, 1977); Penelope Campbell, *Maryland in Africa: The Maryland State Colonization Society* (Urbana: University of Illinois Press, 1971); Bell Wiley, ed., *Slaves No More: Letters from Liberia, 1833–1869* (Lexington: University of Kentucky Press, 1980); Floyd J. Miller, *The Search for a Black Nationality: Black Emigration and Colonization, 1787–1863* (Urbana: University of Illinois Press, 1975); Richard Blackett, *Building an Antislavery Wall: Black Americans and the Atlantic Abolitionist Movement, 1830–1860* (Baton Rouge: Louisiana State University Press, 1983); Randall M. Miller, ed., *'Dear Master': Letters of a Slave Family* (Ithaca, N.Y.: Cornell University Press, 1978).

67. Shandy Jones to William McLain, c. 1850, in "Documents: Letters to the American Colonization Society," p. 221 (see appendix 1); USMSPC, Madison County, Ala., 1850, pp. 444, 467; Shandy Jones to William McLain, April 18, 1852, in "Documents," pp. 222–25.

68. H. Wingate to Samuel Wilkeson, October 31, 1839, RACS, reel 33A.

69. E. Heldner to Ralph Gurley, November 7, 1829, ibid., reel 7A.

70. I. Merrick to Ralph Gurley, October 27, 1827, ibid., reel 13.

71. H. B. Stewart to [William McLain], July 14, 1848, in "Documents: Letters to the American Colonization Society," p. 238.

72. E. Duglas Taylor to William McLain, August 22, 1850, ibid., pp. 277–78.

73. J. B. Jordan to William McLain, August 25, 1850, ibid., p. 271; J. B. Jordan to J. W. Lugenbeel, October 1, 1850, ibid., pp. 272–73.

74. Thomas Grimke to Ralph Gurley, September 11, 1832, RACS, reel 15.

75. Luther Porter Jackson, "Free Negroes of Petersburg, Virginia," *JNH* 12 (July 1927), 376; *Annual Reports of the American Society for Colonizing the Free People of Color* (1969), 13:43; *Niles Register* 21 (1821), 163, in "Some Undistinguished Negroes," ed. Carter Woodson, *JNH* 3 (April, 1918), 196–97; Legislative Records, Petition of Jehu Jones, Jr., to the South Carolina Senate, October 1840, #47, SCDAH; J. J. Roberts to Sarah Colson, January 1, 1836, in "Documents," *JNH* 11 (January 1926), 69–72; William Colson to Joseph Gales, July 24, September 16, 1834, RACS, reel 21.

76. Louis Sheridan to Joseph Gales, May 20, 27, June 1, 17, July 22, August 8, 1836, January 6, 13, 1837, in RACS, reels 26–27; Franklin, *The Free Negro in North Carolina*, pp. 144–45; Willard B. Gatewood, Jr., "'To Be Truly Free': Louis Sheridan and the Colonization of Liberia," *CWH* 29 (December 1983), 341; Elliott Cresson to Samuel Wilkeson, April 8, 1839, in RACS, reel 32; Jehu Jones, Jr., to Ralph Gurley, April 10, 1832, ibid., reel 14; R. Finley to Ralph Gurley, March 5, 1835, ibid., reel 22B; James Redpath, *A Guide to Hayti* (Boston: Haytian Bureau of Emigration, 1861), pp. 164–65, in Myrtilla Miner Collection, LC.

77. Samuel Benedict to Ralph Gurley, May 30, 1833, RACS, reel 17; Randall Miller, "Georgia on Their Minds: Free Blacks and the African Colonization Movement in Georgia," *Southern Studies* 12 (winter 1973), 356–57.

78. Shandy Jones to William McLain, December 29, 1851, November 7, 1856, in "Documents: Letters to the American Colonization Society," pp. 222, 226.

79. USMSPC, Tuscaloosa County, Ala., 1850, p. 159A; ibid., 1860, p. 443; ibid., 6th Ward, 1870, p. 422.

80. *Annual Reports of the American Society for Colonizing the Free People of Color*, 42:53–56; ibid., 50:64; ibid., 59:27.

81. Legislative Records, Petition of Jehu Jones, Jr., to the South Carolina Senate, October 1840, #47, SCDAH; ibid, Report of the Committee on Federal Relations, c. 1840, #ND-2610, SCDAH.

82. *Annual Reports of the American Society for Colonizing the Free People of Color*, 50:64.

83. John McPhail to Ralph Gurley, October 15, 1833, RACS, reel 18.

84. *Annual Reports of the American Society for Colonizing the Free People of Color*, 19:23; G. Caesar to Ralph Gurley, June 16, 1833, RACS, reel 17; Peyton Skipwith to John H. Cocke, May 9, 1838, in *"Dear Master,"* p. 64; *DeBow's Review* 27 (1859), 67–68.

85. Charles Bullock to David Bullock, June 21, 1828, RACS, reel 4.

86. Jonathan Becraft to Ralph Gurley, September 17, 1835, ibid., reel 26.

87. James Winn to [William McLain], September 6, 1850, in "Documents: Letters to the American Colonization Society," pp. 284–85.

88. Daniel Mayes to Ralph Gurley, August 9, 1832, RACS, reel 15.

89. Legislative Records, Petition of Elvira Jones to the Virginia General Assembly, Henrico County, December 5, 1823, VSL; John Dungee to Virginia General Assembly, December 19, 1825, in James Hugo Johnston, *Race Rela-*

tions in Virginia and Miscegenation in the South, 1776–1860 (Amherst: University of Massachusetts Press, 1970), p. 278. For the migratory disposition of whites see James Oakes, *The Ruling Race: A History of American Slaveholders* (New York: Vintage Books, 1982), pp. 73–81.

CHAPTER FOUR
Affluent Free Persons of Color, 1800–1861

1. Creoles of color were persons of French or Spanish and Negro descent born in the Americas. In Louisiana, the term "creole" was also applied to whites culturally related to the original French settlers. See Ira Berlin, "Time, Space, and the Evolution of Afro-American Society on British Mainland North America," *AHR* 85 (February 1980), 45.

2. Frederick Law Olmsted, *Journey in the Seaboard Slave States, with Remarks on Their Economy* (New York: Dix and Edwards, 1856), pp. 632–33; Cyprian Clamorgan, *The Colored Aristocracy of St. Louis* (St. Louis: n.p., 1858), p. 12; James Freeman Clarke, *Present Condition of Free Colored People of the United States* (New York: American Anti-Slavery Society, 1859), pp. 12–13. See also Lester Shippe, ed., *Bishop Whipple's Southern Diary, 1843–44* (Minneapolis: University of Minnesota Press, 1937), p. 97; Alexander H. Newton, *Out of the Briars: An Autobiography and Sketch of the Twenty-ninth Regiment, Connecticut Volunteers* (Philadelphia: African Methodist Episcopal Book Concern, 1910), p. 86.

3. Calvin Dill Wilson, "Black Masters: A Side-Light on Slavery," *North American Review* 181 (November 1905), 685–98, "Negroes who Owned Slaves," *Popular Science Monthly* 81 (November 1912), 484–85; John Russell, "Colored Freemen as Slave Owners in Virginia," *JNH* 1 (June 1916), 233–42; Carter G. Woodson, ed. and comp., *Free Negro Owners of Slaves in the United States in 1830; Together with Absentee Ownership of Slaves in the United States in 1830* (Washington: Association for the Study of Negro Life and History, 1924). For other early accounts, see *Broad Ax* (Chicago), December 28, 1907; *Washington Post*, June 5, 1907; Booker T. Washington, *The Story of the Negro: The Rise of the Race from Slavery* (New York: Doubleday, Page and Co., 1909), pp. 205–7. Gary B. Mills, *The Forgotten People: Cane River's Creoles of Color* (Baton Rouge: Louisiana State University Press, 1977); David O. Whitten, *Andrew Durnford: A Black Sugar Planter in Antebellum Louisiana*, (Natchitoches: Northwestern Louisiana State University Press, 1981); Michael P. Johnson and James L. Roark, *Black Masters: A Free Family of Color in the Old South* (New York: W. W. Norton and Co., 1984); Larry Koger, *Black Slaveowners: Free Black Slave Masters in South Carolina, 1790–1860* (Jefferson, N.C.: McFarland and Co., 1985). Also see Philip J. Schwarz, "Emancipators, Protectors, and Anomalies: Free Black Slaveowners in Virginia," *VMHB* 95 (July 1987), 317–38.

4. Lee Soltow, *Men and Wealth in the United States, 1850–1870* (New Haven: Yale University Press, 1975), p. 186.

5. E. Horace Fitchett, "The Origin and Growth of the Free Negro Popu-

lation of Charleston, South Carolina," *JNH* 26 (October 1941), 425–26; Laura Foner, "The Free People of Color in Louisiana and St. Domingue: A Comparative Portrait of Two Three-Caste Slave Societies," *JSoH* 3 (Summer 1970), 408–11; James Robertson, ed., *Louisiana under the Rule of Spain, France, and the United States, 1785–1807; Social, Economic, and Political Conditions of the Territory represented in the Louisiana Purchase,* 2 vols. (Cleveland: Arthur H. Clark Co., 1910–11; reprint ed., Freeport, N.Y.: Books for Libraries Press, 1969), 1:218–19; Winthrop Jordan, *White over Black: American Attitudes toward the Negro, 1550–1812* (Chapel Hill: University of North Carolina Press, 1968), 77–81.

6. E. Horace Fitchett, "The Traditions of the Free Negro in Charleston, South Carolina," *JNH* 25 (April 1940), 141; RCPC, Charleston, S. C., Estates, #220–26, July 8, 1873; ibid., #465–11, April 20, 1906; Robert L. Harris, Jr., "Charleston's Free Afro-American Elite: The Brown Fellowship Society and the Humane Brotherhood," *SCHM* 82 (October 1981), 308; Johnson and Roark, *Black Masters,* pp. 5–6; Koger, *Black Slaveowners,* pp. 23, 165; USMSPC, Sumter County, S.C., 1850, p. 385; ibid., Charleston County, S.C., 4th Ward, 1860, p. 331; Legislative Records, Petition of John L. Wilson (Jehu Jones's guardian) to the South Carolina General Assembly, December 6, 1823, SCDAH.

7. Extract of the Will of Philip Stanislas Noisette, c. 1830, in Noisette Family Papers, SCL; Petition of the Children of Philip Stanislas Noisette to the South Carolina House of Representatives, n.d., ibid.; James L. Petigrew to John Buchanan, November 19, 1858, ibid.; John Siegling to Elias Horlbeck, March 16, 1859, ibid.; Louis Noisette to John Siegling, December 2, 1872, ibid.; Records of the Charleston District Court, Bill for Partition and Relief, Philip Lewis Noisette et al., February 7, 1867, ibid.

8. RCPC, Effingham County, Ga., Deeds, bk. G (January 1, 1806), pp. 445–46, in Charles Odingsells Papers, GHS; Julia Floyd Smith incorrectly identified Charles Odingsells as "a free Negro of Chatham County." Julia Floyd Smith, *Slavery and Rice Culture in Low Country Georgia, 1750–1860* (Knoxville: University of Tennessee Press, 1985), p. 195; David Thomas, "The Free Negro in Florida before 1865," *South Atlantic Quarterly* 10 (October 1911), 336; Jack D. L. Holmes, "The Role of Blacks in Spanish Alabama: The Mobile District, 1780–1813," *AHQ* 37 (Spring 1975), 10–11. On the Barland family see Legislative Records, Petition of L. Rowan, John Smith, et al., to the Mississippi General Assembly, c. 1830, box 19, MDAH; William Hogan and Edwin Davis, eds., *William Johnson's Natchez: The Ante-Bellum Diary of a Free Negro* (Baton Rouge: Louisiana State University Press, 1951), 15, 18–19, 334. It is highly probable that William Johnson's father was a white slave owner of the same name. Legislative Records, Petition of William Johnson to the Senate and House of Representatives of the State of Mississippi, January 21, 1820, RG 47, MDAH.

9. *General Index of All Successions, Opened in the Parish of Orleans, From the Year 1805, to the Year 1846,* compiled by P. M. Bertin (New Orleans: Yeomans and Fitch, 1849), passim; Herbert E. Sterkx, *The Free Negro in Ante-bellum*

Louisiana (Rutherford, N.J.: Fairleigh Dickinson University Press, 1972), pp. 91–92, 204; Donald Everett, "Free Persons of Color in Colonial Louisiana," *LH* 7 (Winter 1966), pp. 38, 45, 48–49, and "Emigres and Militiamen: Free Persons of Color in New Orleans, 1803–1815," *JNH* 38 (October 1953), 377–80.

10. RPPC, Plaquemines Parish, La. Inventories, vols. 1846–58 (May 6, 1857), pp. 404–9; ibid., Pointe Coupée Parish, La., Successions, #176, April 5, 1839; ibid., Pointe Coupée Parish, La., Conveyances, #1192, October 22, 1822; and #4312, January 23, 1832; Deed of Emancipation for Jean Meullion, February 21, 1776, in Meullion Family Papers, LSU; ibid., St. Landry Parish La., Successions, #1544, February 1, 1851; and #1700, February 28, 1853; ibid., Wills, bk. L-1 (September 2, 1847), pp. 75–76; ibid., Natchitoches Parish, La., Successions, #375, July 26, 1839; ibid., #362, December 15, 1838; ibid., #193–1, July 6, 1833; ibid., #355, September 7, 1838; ibid., #606, October 14, 1847; Sterkx, *The Free Negro in Ante-Bellum Louisiana*, pp. 204–7; Mills, *Forgotten People*, pp. 74–6.

11. George Rawick, ed., *The American Slave: A Composite Autobiography*, supplement, ser. 1, 10 vols. (Westport, Conn.: Greenwood Publishing Company, 1979), vol. 4, pt. 2, pp. 368, 371; USMSPC, Russell County, Ala, 1850, p. 101; Robert Reinders, "The Free Negro in the New Orleans Economy, 1850–60," *LH* 6 (Summer 1965), 279; Whitten, *Andrew Durnford*, pp. 16–7, 83.

12. "List of Persons Admitted [as] Members of the Brown Fellowship Society, from the First of November, 1790," p. 26, in Brown Fellowship Society Papers, CC; Harris, "Charleston's Free Afro-American Elite," p. 292; RCPC, Charleston County, S.C., Miscellaneous Land Records, bk. S7 (June 6, 1806), pp. 169–70; ibid., bk. C8 (August 1, 1811), pp. [438]–39; ibid., bk. H8 (April 19, 1814), p. 420; ibid. (April 21, 1814), p. 301; ibid., bk. W8 (August 13, 1817), pp. [187]–190, MESDA; South Carolina, Records of the Comptroller General, Charleston District, "Free Negro Tax Execution Book," 1816, 1823, SCDAH, and "Free Negro Tax Book," 1843, ibid.

13. Last Will and Testament of Richard Holloway, October 19, 1842, in Holloway Family Papers, CC; Jacob Weston et al., to Elizabeth Holloway, June 29, 1845, in ibid.

14. Helen Catterall, ed., *Judicial Cases concerning American Slavery and the Negro*, 5 vols. (Washington, D.C.: W. F. Roberts Company, 1932), 3:292, 589, 611–12.

15. Sterkx, *The Free Negro in Ante-Bellum Louisiana*, pp. 204–7; RPPC, St. Landry Parish, La., Conveyances, bk. H (March 22, 1830), pp. 32–33; Mortgage Bond, May 33, 1833, Meullion Family Papers, LSU; "Verification of Land Sale," August 15, 1832, in ibid.

16. RCPC, Charleston, S.C., *Miscellaneous Land Records*, bk. A8 (January 29, 1810), pp. 231–32; ibid., bk. X7 (November [1], 1808), pp. 210–13; ibid., bk. H (May 5, 1821), pp. 95–96; ibid., Charleston County, S.C., Wills, bks. 1826–34 (June 14, 1827), p. 394; *Charleston City Gazette*, August 14, 1804, MESDA; RPPC, West Baton Rouge, La., Successions, #420, October 29, 1849; ibid., #297, July 5, 1849; ibid., #292, May 2, 1838; ibid., Pointe Coupée

Parish, La., Successions, #176, April 5, 1839; ibid., St. Landry Parish, La., #1544, February 1, 1851; ibid., Natchitoches Parish, La., #362, December 15, 1838; Thomas S. Berry, *Western Prices before 1861* (Cambridge, Mass.: Harvard University Press, 1943), p. 186.

17. Koger, *Black Slaveowners*, pp. 20–21, 219–23; USMSPC, Chatham County, Ga., 1850, pp. 324, 332; Whittington B. Johnson, "Free Blacks in Antebellum Savannah: An Economic Profile," *GHQ* 64 (Winter 1980), 423–24; USMSPC, Mobile County, Ala., 1860, pp. 27, 137; USMSSC, Mobile County, Ala., 1860, pp. 11, 14; Receipt, William Shipp to Jean Meullion, February 5, 1811, Meullion Papers, LSU; Mills, *Forgotten People*, p. 57; RPPC, Natchitoches Parish, La., Successions, #375, July 26, 1839.

18. These statistics are derived from Woodson, ed., *Free Negro Owners of Slaves in the United States in 1830*; Koger, *Black Slaveowners*, pp. 11–12, 218, chap. 6; Johnson and Roark, *Black Masters*, p. 64; R. Halliburton, Jr., "Free Black Owners of Slaves: A Reappraisal of the Woodson Thesis," *SCHM* 76 (July 1976), 129–42. See An Essay on Sources and Methodology.

19. RPPC, Iberville Parish, La., Conveyances, bk. G (April 26, 1819), pp. 19–20; Andrew Durnford to John McDonogh, June 25, July 5, 1835, in David O. Whitten, ed., "Slave Buying in Virginia as Revealed by Letters of a Louisiana Negro Sugar Planter," *LH* 11 (Summer 1970), 239–40; see also Whitten, "A Black Entrepreneur in Antebellum Louisiana," *BHR* 45 (Spring 1971), 207.

20. Legislative Records, Petition of [John Holman] to the South Carolina General Assembly, October 3, 1791, SCDAH; Koger, *Black Slaveowners*, pp. 110, 119, 254.

21. Quoted in Tinsley L. Spraggins, "The History of the Negro Business Prior to 1860," (M.A. thesis, Howard University, 1935), p. 33.

22. Koger, *Black Slaveowners*, pp. 151–52; RCPC, Charleston County, S.C., Estates, #50–1, January 11, 1849; ibid., #150–1, December 16, 1862; George Rawick, ed., *The American Slave: A Composite Autobiography*, 19 vols. (Westport, Conn.: Greenwood Publishing Company, 1972—), vol. 6, pt. 1, p. 135.

23. RPPC, Natchitoches Parish, La., Successions, #375, July 26, 1839; ibid., Plaquemines Parish, La., Inventories, vols. 1846–58 (May 6, 1857), pp. 404–9; ibid., St. Landry Parish, La., Successions, #2256, September 9, 1859; ibid., Pointe Coupée Parish, La., Successions, #176, April 5, 1839, and #355, January 31, 1844; Ronald Vern Jackson, ed., *Louisiana 1850 Census Index* (Bountiful, Utah: Accelerated Indexing Systems, Inc., 1981), p. 26.

24. Frederick Law Olmsted, *The Cotton Kingdom: A Traveller's Observations on Cotton and Slavery in the American Slave States*, ed. Arthur M. Schlesinger (New York: Alfred A. Knopf, 1953), p. 262; Andrew Durnford to John McDonogh, June 25, 1835, in Whitten, ed., "Slave Buying in Virginia," pp. 239–40; Whitten, *Andrew Durnford*, p. 126; RPPC, Iberville Parish, La., Conveyances, bk. P (August 18, 1835), pp. 85–86; Rawick, ed., *The American Slave*, vol. 5, pt. 4, p. 4039.

25. Luther Porter Jackson, *Free Negro Labor and Property Holding in Virginia,*

1830–1860 (Washington: American Historical Association, 1942), pp. 123, 127, 217; Deed of Emancipation, David Ross to Christopher MacPherson, June 2, 1792, in Legislative Records, Petition of Christopher MacPherson to the Virginia General Assembly, December 10, 1810, Richmond City, VSL; RCPC, Craven County, N.C., Petition of Alexander Stewart and Lydia Stewart to Emancipate the Slave John, March 12, 1795, NCDAH; ibid., Deeds, bk. 33 (November 16, 1798), p. 503; John Hope Franklin, *The Free Negro in North Carolina, 1790–1860* (Chapel Hill: University of North Carolina Press, 1943), pp. 45, 157; Willard Gatewood, "'To Be Truly free': Louis Sheridan and the Colonization of Liberia," *CWH* 29 (December 1983), 332; Louis Sheridan to Joseph Gales, May 20, 27, June 1, 17, July 22, August 8, 1836, January 6, 13, 1837, in RACS, reels 26–27; Julius Melbourn, *Life and Opinions of Julius Melbourn* (Syracuse: Hall and Dickson, 1847), pp. 7–8, 11, 56–57; John Hope Franklin, "The Free Negro in the Economic Life of Ante-Bellum North Carolina," *NCHR* 19 (October 1942), 369; Legislative Records, Petition of Inhabitants of Davidson County to the Tennessee General Assembly, #20-1-1801, TSLA; Anita Goodstein, "Black History on the Nashville Frontier, 1780–1810," *THQ* 30 (Winter 1979), pp. 412–13.

26. Lawrence O. Christensen, "Cyrpian Clamorgan, the Colored Aristocracy of St. Louis (1858)," *Bulletin of the Missouri Historical Society* 31 (October 1974), 5, 6, 13, 14, 16, 22; RCPC, St. Louis, Mo., Deeds, bk. M (December 6, 1825), p. 421; ibid., Estates, #637, July 29, 1825; ibid., #6301, March 2, 1863; ibid., #769, October 4, 1859; ibid., Wills, #1313, March 30, 1837; Clamorgan, *The Colored Aristocracy of St. Louis*, pp. 3–4; William Foley, *A History of Missouri, 1673–1820* (Columbia: University of Missouri Press, 1971), pp. 40–41.

27. Luther Porter Jackson, "Free Negroes of Petersburg, Virginia," *JNH* 12 (July 1927), 376; J. J. Roberts to Sarah Colson, January 1, 1836, in "Documents," *JNH* 11 (January 1926), 69–72; William Colson to Joseph Gales, July 24, September 16, 1834, RACS, reel 21; Jackson, *Free Negro Labor and Property Holding in Virginia*, pp. 146–48; RCPC, Craven County, N.C., Deeds, bk. 33 (January 10, 1800), p. 495; ibid., bk. 36 (July 24, 1804), p. 622; ibid., bk. 37 (July 27, 1809), p. 684; ibid., bk. 38 (April 10, 1811), p. 102; ibid., bk. 39 (July 1, 1815), p. 503; ibid., bk. 42 (March 13, 1820), p. 241; ibid., bk. 42 (November 30, 1821), p. 381; ibid., bk. 45 (June 21, 1827), pp. 219–21; ibid., bk. 36 (December 14, 1801), p. 120; ibid., bk. 36 (February 27, 1805), p. 549; ibid., bk. 38 (March 18, 1813), pp. 455–56; ibid., bk. 40 (July 2, 1817), p. 17; ibid., bk. 40 (July 5, 1817), p. 46; ibid., bk. 40 (August 20, 1817), p. 51; ibid., bk. 40 (October 40, 1817), p. 74; Land Grant no. 1323, State of North Carolina, copy in RCPC, Craven County, N.C., Deeds, bk. 40 (April 14, 1818), p. 218; RCPC, Craven County, N.C., Deeds, bk. 53 (February 15, 1839), pp. 418–20; Christensen, "Cyprian Clamorgan," p. 23; RCPC, St. Louis, Mo., Deeds, bk. S3 (July 25, 1835), p. 304.

28. Jackson, *Free Negro Labor and Property Holding in Virginia*, pp. 122, 127, 216, 224; Schwarz, "Emancipators, Protectors, and Anomalies: Free Black Slaveowners in Virginia," pp. 323–24; Franklin, "The Free Negro in the Eco-

nomic Life of Ante-bellum North Carolina," pp. 257–58; James Browning, "The Free Negro in Ante-bellum North Carolina," *NCHR* 15 (January 1938), 32; J. Merton England, "The Free Negro in Ante-Bellum Tennessee," *JSH* 9 (February 1943), 54n; Franklin, *The Free Negro in North Carolina*, pp. 142, 157–58, 190, 216.

29. RCPC, Craven County, N.C., Deeds, 39 (March 19, 1815), p. 582; ibid., Deeds, 45 (May 8, 1828), p. 445; ibid., Deeds, 46 (April 26, 1829), pp. 332–33; *Raleigh Morning Post*, December 5, 1897; John Spencer Bassett, *Slavery in the State of North Carolina* (Baltimore: Johns Hopkins University Press, 1899), p. 44; USMSPC, Craven County, N.C., New Bern, 1820, p. 72; General Assembly, Session Records, Petition of John C. Stanly to the North Carolina General Assembly, c. 1802, NCDAH; RCPC, Craven County, N.C., Petition of John C. Stanly to the Craven County Superior Court, c. 1829, ibid; RCPC, Craven County, N.C., *Wills (Loose), A-Z, 1746–1865* (February 26, 1819), n.p., MESDA; RCPC, Craven County, N.C., *Court Minutes*, September 10, 14, 1804, September 17, 1807, September 10, 1810, December 10, 1811, March 9, 1812, December 11, 1817, MESDA; Records of the Superior Court, Craven County, N.C., Bonds, 1828, NCDAH; John C. Stanly to Ralph R. Gurley, May 12, 1838, RACS, reel 29; RCPC, Craven County, N. C., Deeds, bk. 45 (May 8, 1828), pp. 429–47; ibid., bk. 46 (April 29, 1829), pp. 273–74; ibid., bk. 53 (February 17, 1838), pp. 170–71; Wilson, "Negroes Who Owned Slaves," pp. 486, 491; Franklin, *The Free Negro in North Carolina*, pp. 23, 31–32, 76, 115, 126, 128, 160–62; Browning, "The Free Negro in Ante-bellum North Carolina," pp. 28–29; see Loren Schweninger, "John Carruthers Stanly and the Anomaly of Black Slaveholding," *NCHR* (forthcoming).

30. Woodson, *Free Negro Owners of Slaves in the United States in 1830*, p. vi, 1–78; Halliburton, "Free Black Owners of Slaves," pp. 135, 142; Russell, "Colored Freemen as Slave Owners in Virginia," pp. 239–40; Jackson, *Free Negro Labor and Property Holding in Virginia*, pp. 205–6.

31. Estimates in the District of Columbia are derived from tax assessments of 50¢ per $100. Letitia Woods Brown, *Free Negroes in the District of Columbia, 1790–1846* (New York: Oxford University Press, 1972), pp. 139, 147–50, 152–55; Jackson, *Free Negro Labor and Property Holding in Virginia*, pp. 122, 127–28, 144–47; "Pursuits &c of the Free People of Color in the Town of Frankfort," July 16, 1842, FC.

32. Jackson, *Free Negro Labor and Property Holding in Virginia*, pp. 119–20; James Hugo Johnston, *Race Relations in Virginia and Miscegenation in the South, 1776–1860* (Amherst: University of Massachusetts Press, 1970), pp. 321–22; Claim #16011, Alfred Anderson, Amelia County, Va., c. 1877, RTD, RCC, RG 56, reel 9, NA; Claim #16,012, Francis Anderson, Amelia County, Va., ca. 1877, in ibid; Claim #18,049, Henry F. Harrison, Administrator for Frankey Miles, ca. 1877, in ibid.; England, "The Free Negro in Ante-bellum Tennessee," p. 54; RCPC, Davidson County, Tenn., Wills and Inventories, vol. 9 (July 7, 1832), p. 596; ibid., Deeds, bk. 2 (March 12, 1840), pp. 389–90; ibid., bk. 7 (January 25, 1845), pp. 247–48; *Private Acts Passed at the First Session of*

the Twentieth General Assembly of the State of Tennessee (Nashville: Allen A. Hall and F. S. Heiskell, 1833), p. 96; J. Merton England, "The Free Negro in Antebellum Tennessee," (Ph.D. dissertation, Vanderbilt University, 1941), p. 49.

33. Richard Tansey, "Out-of-State Free Blacks in Late Antebellum New Orleans," *LH* 22 (Fall 1981), 378.

34. Koger, *Black Slaveowners*, pp. 128–29, 226–27; USMSPC, Charleston, S.C., 1850, p. 320; ibid., Chatham County, Ga., Savannah, 1850, p. 324; ibid., Savannah, 1st Dist., 1860, p. 42; RCPC, Chatham County, Ga., Estates, M-395, April 6, 1857; Johnson, "Free Blacks in Antebellum Savannah," p. 424.

35. USMSPC, Adams County, Miss., 1860, p. 120; RPPC, Natchitoches Parish, La., Estates, #355, September 7, 1838; ibid., #375, July 26, 1839. See also estate distributions of Jean Baptiste Louis Metoyer, Joseph Augustin Metoyer, Pierre Metoyer, and Marie Pompose Roques as follows: RPPC, Natchitoches Parish, La., Estates, #362, December 15, 1838; ibid., #692, July 25, 1851; ibid., #193-A, July 6, 1833; ibid., #606, October 14, 1847. USMSPC, St. Landry Parish, La., 1850, pp. 15, 17.

36. Koger, *Black Slaveowners*, pp. 20–21; Mills, *Forgotten People*, p. 218.

37. USMSPC, New Orleans, La., 1st Mun., 7th Ward, 1850, pp. 376, 396; Robert Reinders, "The Decline of the New Orleans Free Negro in the Decade before the Civil War," *JMH* 24 (April 1962), 95–96.

38. USMSPC, Charleston, S.C., 1850, pp. 91, 98, 110, 118, 126–28, 186, 223, 288, 320, 347, 356; ibid., 3d Ward, 1860, p. 283; ibid., 4th Ward, 1860, pp. 307–12, 327, 332, 334, 404; ibid., 5th Ward, 376, 385; ibid., 6th Ward, p. 432; ibid., 7th Ward, pp. 466, 468, 475; ibid., 8th Ward, 493, 510, 523; *List of the Tax Payers of the City of Charleston for 1860* (Charleston: Evans and Cogswell, 1861), pp. 315–34; RCPC, Charleston, S.C., Estates, #289–25, June 15, 1876; Records of the Comptroller General, Free Negro Tax Book, Charleston District, S.C., 1843, SCDAH. Here again, the probable 1850 undercount of free Negroes in South Carolina should be noted, although it does not significantly alter the general conclusion of the paragraph.

39. USMSPC, Georgetown County, S.C., 1850, p. 309; ibid., Sumter County, S.C., 1850, p. 385; ibid., 1860, p. 133. In the 1860 census, Henry, William, and Reuben were listed as having a total of $5,000 in personal holdings. I have estimated Ellison's realty at $15,000, rather than the $8,300 listed in the census. Koger, *Black Slaveholders*, pp. 37–38, 62, 121–23, 132, 136, 144–45; Johnson and Roark, *Black Masters*, pp. 70, 124–27.

40. USMSPC, Mobile County, Ala., 1850, pp. 464, 481; ibid., Southern District, 1860, p. 27; ibid., Northern District, 1860, pp. 136–37, 140; ibid., Adams County, Miss., Natchez, 1850, p. 14; ibid., 1860, pp. 44, 120; ibid., Jefferson County, Tex., 1850, pp. 481, 497, 499; Andrew Muir, "The Free Negro in Jefferson and Orange Counties, Texas," *JNH* 35 (April 1950), 186, 191, 206.

41. USMSPC, Emanuel County, Ga., 1860, p. 960; ibid., Hamilton County, Fla., 1860, p. 597; ibid., Madison County, Ala., Huntsville, p. 188; ibid., Lauderdale County, Ala., Florence, 1850, p. 293; ibid., 1860, p. 39; John Rapier, to John Rapier, Jr., December 13, 1856, Rapier-Thomas Papers, MSRC;

Loren Schweninger, "John H. Rapier, Sr.: A Slave and Freedman in the Ante-Bellum South," *CWH* 20 (March 1974), 32.

42. Juliet E. K. Walker, "Racism, Slavery, and Free Enterprise: Black Entrepreneurship in the United States before the Civil War," BHR 60 (Autumn 1986), 354, 361–62; USMSPC, New Orleans, La., 1st Mun., 7th Ward, 1850, p. 396; ibid., New Orleans, 3d Ward, 1860, p. 257; ibid., 4th Ward, p. 82; ibid., 5th Ward, p. 729; RPPC, New Orleans, La., Successions, #38,677, May 27, 1876, NOPL; Leonard Curry, *The Free Black in Urban America, 1800–1850: The Shadow of the Dream* (Chicago: University of Chicago Press, 1981), p. 42; David Rankin, "The Impact of the Civil War on the Free Colored Community of New Orleans," in *Perspectives in American History* 11 (1977–78), 396, 402; John Blassingame, *Black New Orleans, 1860–1880* (Chicago: University of Chicago Press, 1973), p. 39; Testimony of Benjamin F. Butler, Accompanying Final Report of the American Freedmen's Inquiry Commission, May 15, 1864, in Blassingame, "The Selection of Officers and Non-Commissioned Officers of Negro Troops in the Union Army, 1863–1865," *Negro History Bulletin* 30 (January 1967), 11.

43. USMSPC, New Orleans, La., 1st Mun., 4th Ward, 1850, p. 150; ibid., 1st Mun., 7th Ward, 1850, p. 376.

44. RPPC, New Orleans., La., Successions, #41,626, November 19, 1879, NOPL; Tax Receipts, no. C-530, 1845–7, in ibid.; USMSPC, New Orleans, La., 3d Mun., 2d Ward, 1850, p. 119.

45. Computed from USMSPC, La., 1850. USMSAC, Natchitoches Parish, La., 1850, p. 425; ibid., Plaquemines Parish, La., 1850, pp. 485, 549; ibid., Pointe Coupée Parish, La., 1850, p. 569; ibid., St. John the Baptist Parish, La., 1850, p. 661; ibid., St. Landry Parish, La., 1850, p. 695; ibid., St. Mary Parish, La., 1850, pp. 727–29; Lewis Gray, *History of Agriculture in the Southern United States to 1860*, 2 vols. (Washington: Carnegie Institution, 1933; reprint ed., New York: Peter Smith, 1941), 1:509; Joseph Menn, *The Large Slaveholders of Louisiana—1860* (New Orleans: Pelican Publishing County, 1964), pp. 79, 92–93; Whitten, *Andrew Durnford*, pp. 85, 88; USMSPC, Plaquemines Parish, La., 1850, p. 278; ibid., St. Mary Parish, La., 1850, p. 213; USMSAC, Iberville Parish, La., 1850, p. 81; USMSPC, Iberville Parish, La., 1850, p. 329; RPPC, Plaquemines Parish, La., Inventories, vols. 1846–58 (March 6, 1857), pp. 404–12.

46. Rawick, ed., *The American Slave*, vol. 5, pt. 4, p. 4040. See also David O. Whitten, "Rural Life Along the Mississippi: Plaquemines Parish, Louisiana, 1830–1850," *AH* 58 (July 1984), 484. RPPC, Pointe Coupée Parish, La., Conveyances, #1192, October 22, 1822; ibid., Successions, #203, July 11, 1865; USMSPC, Pointe Coupée Parish, La., 1850, p. 40; USMSAC, Pointe Coupée Parish, La., 1850, p. 567.

47. Mills, *Forgotten People*, pp. 221–23; USMSPC, Iberville Parish, La., 1850, p. 329; ibid., 1860, pp. 261, 263–64, 267, 280; Clarke, *Present Condition of Free Colored People of the United States*, p. 13.

48. *Condition of the Colored Population of the City of Baltimore* (n.p.: n.p., 1838), p. 7, in MSRC. An inventory of Thomas Green's estate and his Last

Will and Testament can be found in Records of the Baltimore County Court, Chancery Papers, 1858, Accession no. MdHr 40200-5988-1/2, MSA. Also see *Baltimore American and Commercial Advertiser*, May 18, 1864; New York *Herald*, April 1, 8, 1863; Thomas Owens and Charles W. Ridgely, executors of Thomas Green's estate, vs. Archibald George Dodson and Charles Dodson, May 1864, Records of the Baltimore Superior Court, Accession no. 40200-5988-1, MSA; Spraggins, "The History of the Negro in Business," p. 47; James Wright, *The Free Negro in Maryland, 1634–1860* (New York: Columbia University Press, 1921; reprint ed., New York: Octagon Books, 1971), p. 192; USMSPC, Baltimore, Md., 9th Ward, 1850, p. 47.

49. USMSPC, Halifax County, Va., 1850, p. 95; ibid., 1860, p. 877; Jackson, *Free Negro Labor and Property Holding in Virginia*, pp. 107, 129.

50. RCPC, St. Louis, Mo., Estates, #4173, April 12, 1854; USMSPC, St. Louis, Mo., 4th Ward, 1850, p. 49; Woodson, *Free Negro Owners of Slaves in the United States in 1830*, p. vi; Donnie Bellamy, "Free Blacks in Antebellum Missouri, 1820–1860," MHR 67 (January 1973), 216, 224.

51. Although four farm owners were listed as "planters" in the census, Epps was the only rural black with at least $2,000 worth of real estate who received this designation. Franklin, *The Free Negro in North Carolina*, p. 237; Jackson, *Free Negro Labor and Property Holding in Virginia*, pp. 225–26.

52. Computed from USMSPC, 1850, 1860; ibid., Baltimore, Md., 9th Ward, 1850, p. 47; ibid., Henrico County, Va., Richmond, 1850, p. 248; ibid., Jefferson County, Ky., Louisville, 4th Ward, 1850, p. 50; ibid., Davidson County, Tenn., Nashville, 3d Ward, 1850, p. 356; ibid., Shelby County, Tenn., Memphis, 7th Ward, 1850, p. 185; ibid., St. Louis, Mo., 2nd Ward, 1850, p. 222; ibid., 3d Ward, p. 352; ibid., 4th Ward, pp. 54, 55; Clamorgan, *The Colored Aristocracy of St. Louis*, pp. 11–13; Herbert A. Thomas, Jr., "Victims of Circumstance: Negroes in a Southern Town, 1865–1880," *The Register of the Kentucky Historical Society* 71 (July 1973), 268.

53. USMSPC, Baltimore County, Md., 1st Dist., 1850, p. 226; ibid., 4th Dist., 1860, p. 147; ibid., Dorchester County, Md., 1850, p. 421; ibid., 9th Dist., 1860, p. 1019; ibid., Alexandria County, Va., Alexandria, 1860, p. 875; ibid., Jefferson County, Ky., Louisville, 1st Ward, 1850, p. 77; ibid., 1st Ward, 1860, p. 74; ibid., Davidson County, Tenn., Nashville, 1850, p. 94; ibid., 6th Ward, 1860, p. 437; ibid., Baltimore, Md., 11th Ward, 1860, p. 560; ibid., Washington, D.C., Georgetown, 1850, p. 186; ibid., Washington, D.C., 1st Ward, 1860, p. 3; Henry Robinson, "Some Aspects of the Free Negro Population of Washington, D.C., 1800–1862," MHM 64 (Spring 1969), 52; Franklin, *The Free Negro in North Carolina*, p. 157; USMSPC, Warren County, N.C., 1860, p. 279; ibid., Davidson County, Tenn., 13th Dist., 1860, p. 225. On Doxey's life, see *Nashville Press and Times*, quoted in San Francisco *Elevator*, June 19, 1868. USMSPC, St. Louis, Mo., 7th Ward, 1860, p. 113.

54. John Rapier to John Rapier, Jr., December 13, 1856, Rapier-Thomas Papers, MSRC. See also ibid., June 26, 1857; June 18, 1858; December 28, 1858, February 14, 1859. USMSPC, Chatham County, Ga. 1850, p. 332; ibid.,

Mobile County, Ala., pp. 464, 480; ibid., Natchitoches Parish, La., pp. 465, 473, 474, 477–78. The Odingsells lived on Little Wassaw Island, the Chastangs on an island in Mobile Bay, and the Metoyers on Isle Brevelle, an island between two branches of the Cane River.

55. Loren Schweninger, "A Negro Sojourner in Antebellum New Orleans," *LH* 29 (Summer 1979), 309; Davis and Hogan, eds., *William Johnson's Natchez*, pp. 40–43, 114, 117, 755; Mills, *Forgotten People*, p. 170; USMSPC, Charleston, S.C., p. 219; John Weston to Henry and Reuben Ellison, October 12, 1848, Ellison Family Papers, SCL; Johnson and Roark, *Black Masters*, pp. 107–9, 208; Koger, *Black Slaveholders*, pp. 110, 119; RPPC, Natchitoches Parish, La., Successions, #375, July 26, 1839; ibid., #355, September 7, 1838; ibid., West Baton Rouge Parish, La., Successions, #176, July 18, 1829. For various other families in the Baton Rouge area, see: ibid., #420, October 29, 1849; ibid., #297, July 5, 1849; ibid., #292, May 2, 1838; ibid., #547, April 19, 1856; ibid., #100, September 3, 1822; ibid., #123, December 31, 1823; ibid., #460, August 14, 1855; ibid., East Baton Rouge Parish, La., #640, August 14, 1855; ibid., #1331, September 14, 1877.

56. Marriage Book, St. Phillip's Church, Charleston, South Carolina, in Fitchett, "Origin and Growth," pp. 431–32; RCPC, Charleston, S.C., Estates, #229–6, December 30, 1874; ibid., #220–6, July 8, 1873.

57. Hogan and Davis, eds., *William Johnson's Natchez*, pp. 11, 43, 334, 399; Legislative Papers, Petition of Andrew Barland to the Senate and House of Representatives of Mississippi, c. 1824, RG 47, boxes 16–17, MDAH.

58. "A Contract of Marriage Between JOSEPH METOYER and MARIE LODOISKA LLORENS," January 28, 1840, Cane River Collection, HNOC; RPPC, Pointe Coupée Parish, La., Marriage Contract, February 26, 1835. In 1860, St. Landry Parish census takers often included the maiden name of the women in each household who were probable spouses and listed them as "keeping house." Partners were usually among the most prosperous seventeen families. USMSPC, St. Landry Parish, La., 1860, passim; RPPC, St. Landry Parish, La., "Marriage Certificate," March 25, 1796, Meullion Papers, LSU; ibid., Successions, #1544–45, February 1, 1851.

59. RPPC, Natchitoches Parish, La., Successions, #344, September 7, 1838; ibid., Successions, #375, July 27, 1839; ibid., Successions, #606, October 14, 1847; ibid., Plaquemines Parish, La., Successions, #167, May 12, 1840; ibid., East Baton Rouge Parish, La., Successions, #640, August 14, 1855; ibid., West Baton Rouge Parish, La., Successions, #176, July 18, 1829. This was true, though to a lesser degree, in New Orleans. On February 24, 1851, John R. Clay signed a marriage contract with Louisa Boisdore, promising to allow his future wife complete control over the $1,800 worth of property she brought to their marriage. RPPC, New Orleans, La., Successions, #361, April 19, 1879, NOPL.

60. James M. Bland to William McLain, July 3, 1848, in "Documents: Letters to the American Colonization Society," ed. Carter Woodson, *JNH* 10 (April 1925), 227; John Rapier, Sr., to Richard Rapier, April 8, 1845, Rapier-

Thomas Papers, MSRC; RCPC, Charleston County, S.C., Wills, vol. 1793–1800 (June 28, 1794), p. 207, MESDA; ibid., New Orleans, La., Successions, #361, April 19, 1879.

61. Wikramanayake, *A World in Shadow*, p. 103; Koger, *Black Slaveowners*, p. 98; Berlin, *Slaves without Masters*, pp. 66, 74–78, 173–74, 303–6; Johnson, "Free Blacks in Antebellum Savannah," pp. 418–31; Nathan Willey, "Education of the Colored Population of Louisiana," *Harper's New Monthly Magazine* 33 (June–November 1866), 248; United States Census Office, *The Seventh Census of the United States: 1850* (Washington, D.C.: Robert Armstrong, 1853), p. 479.

62. Rawick, ed., *The American Slave*, vol. 5, pt. 4, p. 4038; Annie Stahl, "The Free Negro in Ante-bellum Louisiana," *LHQ* 25 (January–October 1942), 361; Willey, "Education of the Colored Population," pp. 248–49; Olmsted, *Journey through the Seaboard Slave States*, pp. 632–34, 641.

63. Johnson and Roark, *Black Masters*, pp. 26, 143, 227; Randall M. Miller, "Slaves and Southern Catholicism," in John B. Boles, ed., *Masters and Slaves in the House of the Lord: Race and Religion in the American South, 1740–1870* (Lexington: University of Kentucky Press, 1988), pp. 144–48; Robert L. Hall, "Black and White Christians in Florida, 1822–1861," in ibid., p. 95; Sterkx, *The Free Negro in Ante-Bellum Louisiana*, p. 257; Samuel Benedict to Richard Holloway, June 21, 1833, Holloway Family Papers, CC. According to later testimony, wealthy white planters in Natchitoches Parish became active members of the Church of St. Augustin. Mills, *Forgotten People*, p. 153.

64. Adolphe Garrigues to Charles Benjamin, January 28, 1876, in RCC, RTD, RG 56, reel 7, NA; U.S., Congress, Senate, *Report of John Alvord, Inspector of Schools and Finances for Freedmen*, no. 27, 39th Cong., 1st sess., 1866, *Senate Executive Documents*, p. 141.

65. William Ellison to Henry Ellison, March 26, 1857, Ellison Papers, SCL. The Ellison correspondence, consisting of thirty-seven letters, has been published in book form. Michael P. Johnson and James L. Roark, eds., *No Chariot Let Down: Charleston's Free People of Color on the Eve of the Civil War* (Chapel Hill: University of North Carolina Press, 1984). Carl D. Arfwedson, *The United States and Canada in 1832, 1833 and 1834*, 2 vols. (London: R. Bentley, 1834), p. 425; Johnson, "Free Blacks in Antebellum Savannah," p. 423; USMSPC, Chatham County, Ga., Savannah, 1860, p. 179; Shandy Jones to William McLain, c. 1850, in "Documents: Letters to the American Colonization Society," ed. Carter Woodson, *JNH* 10 (April 1925), 219, 221; Davis and Hogan, eds., *William Johnson's Natchez*, pp. 41, 53, 63, 67n; Margaret Ross, "Nathan Warren, A Free Negro for the Old South," *AHQ* 15 (Spring 1956), 55.

66. Legislative Records, Petition of James Rose, William Grayson, Benjamin Huger, et al., to the South Carolina Senate, c. 1860, SCDAH; Loren Schweninger, ed., *From Tennessee Slave to St. Louis Entrepreneur: The Autobiography of James Thomas* (Columbia: University of Missouri Press, 1984), pp. 89–90.

67. Bernhard Karl, *Travels through North America, During the Years 1825 and*

1826, 2 vols. (Philadelphia: Carey, Lea and Carey, 1828), 2:4–5; Thomas Hamilton, *Men and Manners in America* (London: T. Cadell, 1833), pp. 347–48; Frances Anne Kemble, *Journal of a Residence on a Georgia Plantation in 1838–1839* (New York: Harper and Brothers, 1863; reprint ed., ed. John A. Scott, Athens, Ga.: University of Georgia Press, 1984), p. 41; USMSPC, Charleston, S.C., St. Philip and St. Michael Parishes, 1850, p. 99; ibid., 4th Ward, 1860, p. 312; Albert and Harriett P. Simons, "The William Burrows House of Charleston," *SCHM* 70 (July 1969), 172–74.

68. USMSPC, New Orleans, La., 1st Mun., 2d Ward, 1860, pp. 209, 214, 265; RPPC, New Orleans, La., Successions, #22,076, March 2, 1851, NOPL.

69. Olmsted, *The Cotton Kingdom*, p. 132.

70. Charles O. Screven to Anthony Odingsells, July 30, 1828, in Joseph Parsons, "Anthony Odin[g]sells: A Romance of Little Wassaw," GHQ 55 (Summer 1971), 210.

71. Arfwedson, *The United States and Canada*, 1:425; Davis and Hogan, eds., *William Johnson's Natchez*, pp. 51–53.

72. RPPC, New Orleans, La., Successions, #34,148, November 10, 1870, NOPL; John William De Forest to wife, September 29, 1862, in *A Volunteer's Adventures: A Union Captain's Record of the Civil War*, ed. James H. Croushore (New Haven: Yale University Press, 1946), pp. 47–48.

73. USMSPC, Plaquemines Parish, La., 1850, pp. 272, 276, 279; ibid., Avoyelles Parish, La., 1850, p. 115; ibid., Caddo Parish, La., 1850, p. 355; ibid., West Feliciana Parish, La., 1850, p. 276; RPPC, New Orleans, La., Wills, vol. O (June 19, 1856), pp. 357–68; USMSPC, New Orleans, La., 1st Mun., 5th Ward, 1860, p. 710.

74. Computed from USMSPC, 1850, 1860; RCPC, Pulaski County, Ark., Estates, #184, November 17, 1866, AHCSA; USMSPC, Pulaski County, Ark., Little Rock, 2d Ward, 1870, p. 258.

75. The preceding analyses include only property owners. When it seemed highly probable that a man and woman were cohabiting, they were included even if their family names differed. It was much easier to determine mulatto men living with white women since the family name was usually the same and the children were usually listed as mulatto.

USMSPC, Orangeburg County, S.C., 1860, pp. 59, 131, 387; Frederick Law Olmsted, *Journey through Texas; or, A Saddle-Trip on the Southwestern Frontier* (New York: Dix, Edwards and County, 1857; reprinted in *The Slave States*, ed. Harvey Wish, New York: Capricorn Books, 1959), p. 164; USMSPC, Jefferson County, Tex., 1850, pp. 481, 483, 497, 499; ibid., Orange County, Tex., 1860, passim; Muir, "The Free Negro in Jefferson and Orange Counties," p. 185; Legislative Records, Petition of Andrew Barland to the House of Representatives of Mississippi, c. 1824, RG 47, boxes 16–17, MSDAH.

76. USMSAC, St. Mary Parish, La., 1850, p. 727; Rawick, ed., *The American Slave*, vol. 5, pt. 4, p. 4038; RPPC, St. Landry Parish, La., Conveyances, bk. H (March 22, 1830), pp. 32–33. Written by Boston free black David Walker, the tract, published in September 1829, was considered highly inflammatory in the South. David Walker, *David Walker's Appeal to the Coloured Citizens of the*

World (Boston: D. Walker, 1829; reprint ed., ed. Charles M. Wiltse, New York: Hill and Wang, 1965), p. vii. Rawick, ed., *The American Slave*, vol. 16, pt. 3, pp. 10–13. Creoles of color were especially vulnerable since, as slaves, they often brought the highest prices on the auction block. "The gang of slaves," one observer in New Orleans wrote in 1833, "[is] the most valuable for their number in the state (being all Mechanics and Creoles of the Country)." John Chinson to Ralph Gurley, December 16, 1833, RACS, reel 19.

77. Following the Denmark Vesey trials, South Carolina passed a law prohibiting free blacks from leaving and reentering the state on pain of imprisonment or enslavement. In Charleston, free Negroes were required to register with local officials twice a year. A record was kept of their birth place and date of entry into the state. Marina Wikramanayake, *A World in Shadow: The Free Black in Antebellum South Carolina* (Columbia: University of South Carolina Press, 1973), p. 58. Quote from James M. Johnson to Henry Ellison, August 20, 1860, Ellison Papers, SCL.

78. "Affidavit of the Negress MAGDELAINE in the case against AUGUSTINE St. DENIS for assault and battery on LOUIS SOMPAYRAC [*sic*]," March 31, 1828, Cane River Collection, MSS 182, folder 223, HNOC; "Testimony of MANUEL LLORENS" (in French), February 12, 1844, in ibid., MSS 182, folder 727, ibid.; Mills, *Forgotten People*, pp. 74, 97–98, 202–3, 213.

79. James Thomas to John Rapier, Jr., October 3, 1856, December 23, 1856, May 3, 1858, January 8, 1859, Rapier-Thomas Papers, MSRC; USMSPC, Davidson County, Tenn., Nashville, 1850, p. 155; ibid., 2d ward, 1860, p. 343; ibid., St. Louis, Mo., 2d Ward, 1860, p. 633; Schweninger, ed., *From Tennessee Slave to St. Louis Entrepreneur*, p. 6; Wright, *The Free Negro in Maryland*, pp. 250–51; Legislative Records, Petition of the Members of the African Benevolent Association to the Senate and House of Representatives of Delaware, January 1825, DHR; Jackson, *Free Negro Labor and Property Holding in Virginia*, p. 163n.

80. Willard B. Gatewood, Jr., ed., *Free Man of Color: The Autobiography of Willis Augustus Hodges* (Knoxville: University of Tennessee Press, 1982), pp. xxiv, xxviii, 23, 25–26; RCPC, Alexandria County, Va., Wills, vol. 1821–31 (November 25, 1829), p. 342, MESDA.

81. USMSPC, District of Columbia, 7th Ward, 1860, p. 767; Brown, *Free Negroes in the District of Columbia*, pp. 118, 133, 141; Robinson, "Some Aspects of the Free Negro Population of Washington, D.C.," pp. 54–56.

82. Wright, *The Free Negro in Maryland*, p. 224; Records of the Baltimore Court, Last Will and Testament of Thomas Green, 1858, in Chancery Papers, Accession no. MdHR 40200-5988-1/2, MSA; "Record of the Proceedings of the Church and Session, Subsequent to its Organization," November 21, 1841, in Carter Woodson Collection, container 11, LC; Robinson, "Some Aspects of the Free Negro Population of Washington, D.C.," pp. 57–61; Mechal Sobel, *Trabelin' On: The Slave Journey to an Afro-Baptist Faith* (Westport, Conn.: Greenwood Press, 1979; reprint ed., Princeton: Princeton University Press, 1988), pp. 206–7; W. Harrison Daniel, "Virginia Baptists and the Negro in the Antebellum Era," *JNH* 56 (January 1971), 1–16; Luther Porter Jackson,

"Religious Development of the Negro in Virginia From 1760 to 1860," *JNH* 16 (April 1931), 193–98, 221, 227, 236–37.

83. Jackson, "Religious Development," pp. 236–37n; Schweninger, ed., *From Tennessee Slave to St. Louis Entrepreneur*, pp. 66–67.

84. USMSPC, Sussex County, Del., Lewis Township, 1850, p. 64; ibid., New Castle County, Del., Wilmington, 11th Ward, 1850, p. 259; ibid., Baltimore, Md., 6th Ward, 1850, p. 177; ibid., Charles City County, Va., 1850, p. 404; ibid., Dinwiddie County, Va., Petersburg, 1850, p. 392; ibid., Jefferson County, Ky., Louisville, 4th Dist., 1850, pp. 398, 405; ibid., St. Louis, Mo., 4th Ward, 1850, p. 49; Sobel, *Trabelin' On*, p. 235; Willis Weatherford, *American Churches and the Negro; An Historical Study from Early Slave Days to the Present* (Boston: Christopher Publishing House, 1957), p. 125; R. S. Duncan, *A History of the Baptists in Missouri* (St. Louis: Scammell and County, 1882), pp. 755–56; Schweninger, ed., *From Tennessee Slave to St. Louis Entrepreneur*, pp. 66–67.

85. William Colson to Joseph Gales, September 16, 1834, RACS, reel 21; Louis Sheridan to Joseph Gales, January 13, 1837, ibid., reel 27; Journal of Reverend Sidney D. Bumpas, vol. 2, April 29, 1842, SHC; Robinson, "Some Aspects of the Free Negro Population of Washington, D.C.," p. 52; Legislative Records, Petition of A. P. Upshur, George L. Yerby, James Goffigon, et al., to the Virginia Legislature, Northampton County, December 6, 1831, VSL; ibid., Petition of James Spare, Zachariah Jones, Abner Crawford, et al., to the Delaware Senate and House of Representatives, 1832, DHR; ibid., Petition of the Citizens of King William County to the Virginia General Assembly, January 20, 1842, VSL; ibid., Memorial of R. W. Bailey to the Virginia Legislature, January 12, 1850, Miscellaneous Petitions, VSL; ibid., Petition of the Citizens of Hardeman County to the Tennessee Senate and House of Representatives, December 3, 1857, #94, TSLA; Diary of William Valentine, July 23, 1853, p. 85, SHC.

CHAPTER FIVE
Property Ownership Among Southern Blacks, 1860–1915

1. Robert Higgs, *The Transformation of the American Economy 1865–1914: An Essay in Interpretation* (New York: John Wiley and Sons, 1971), "Did Southern Farmers Discriminate?" *AH* 46 (April 1972), 325–28; and *Competition and Coercion: Blacks in the American Economy, 1865–1914* (London: Cambridge University Press, 1977), pp. 61, 134; Joseph D. Reid, "Sharecropping as an Understandable Market Response: The Post-Bellum South," *Journal of Economic History* 33 (March 1973), 106–30, and "Sharecropping and Agricultural Uncertainty," *Economic Development and Cultural Change* 24 (April 1976), 549–76; Stephen J. DeCanio, "Agricultural Production, Supply, and Institutions in the Post-Civil War South," *Journal of Economic History* 32 (March 1972), 396–98, "Productivity and Income Distribution in the Post-Bellum South," ibid. 34 (June 1974), 422–46, and *Agriculture in the Postbellum South: The Economics of Production and Supply* (Cambridge, Mass.: Massachusetts In-

stitute of Technology Press, 1974); Ralph Shlomowitz, "Planter Combinations and Black Labour in the American South, 1865–1880," *Slavery and Abolition: A Journal of Comparative Studies* 9 (May 1988), 72–84.

2. Jonathan Wiener, *Social Origins of the New South: Alabama, 1860–1885* (Baton Rouge: Louisiana State University Press, 1978), pp. 72–73, and "Class Structure and Economic Development in the American South, 1865–1955," *AHR* 84 (October 1979), 973–74; Jay R. Mandle, *The Roots of Black Poverty: The Southern Plantation Economy after the Civil War* (Durham: Duke University Press, 1978); William Cohen, "Negro Involuntary Servitude in the South, 1865–1940: A Preliminary Analysis," *JSH* 42 (February 1976), 31–60; Gerald David Jaynes, *Branches without Roots: Genesis of the Black Working Class in the American South, 1862–1882* (New York: Oxford University Press, 1986).

3. Roger L. Ransom and Richard Sutch, *One Kind of Freedom: The Economic Consequences of Emancipation* (London: Cambridge University Press, 1977), p. 198, and "Growth and Welfare in the American South of the Nineteenth Century," *Explorations in Economic History* 16 (1979), 225.

4. Leon Litwack, *Been in the Storm So Long: The Aftermath of Slavery* (New York: Alfred A. Knopf, 1979), pp. 419–20; Peter Kolchin, *First Freedom: The Response of Alabama's Blacks to Emancipation and Reconstruction* (Westport, Conn.: Greenwood Press, 1972), pp. 43–44; Edward Magdol, *The Right to the Land: Essays of the Freedmen's Community* (Westport, Conn.: Greenwood Press, 1977); Daniel A. Novak, *The Wheel of Servitude: Black Forced Labor after Slavery* (Lexington: University of Kentucky Press, 1978), p. 44; Claude Oubre, *Forty Acres and a Mule: The Freedmen's Bureau and Black Land Ownership* (Baton Rouge: Louisiana State University Press, 1978); Janet S. Hermann, *The Pursuit of a Dream* (New York: Oxford University Press, 1982); Willie Lee Rose, *Rehearsal for Reconstruction: The Port Royal Experiment* (New York: Bobbs-Merrill County, 1964; reprint ed., New York: Vintage Books, 1967), pp. 378–408.

5. Joel Williamson, *After Slavery: The Negro in South Carolina during Reconstruction, 1861–1877* (Chapel Hill: University of North Carolina Press, 1965); Carl R. Osthaus, *Freedmen, Philanthropy, and Fraud: A History of the Freedman's Savings Bank* (Urbana: University of Illinois Press, 1976); Carol K. Bleser, *The Promised Land: The History of the South Carolina Land Commission, 1869–1890* (Columbia: University of South Carolina Press, 1969); William S. McFeely, *Yankee Stepfather: General O. O. Howard and the Freedmen* (New Haven: Yale University Press, 1968); Howard Ashley White, *The Freedmen's Bureau in Louisiana* (Baton Rouge: Louisiana State University Press, 1970).

6. William S. McFeely, "Unfinished Business: The Freedmen's Bureau and Federal Action in Race Relations," in *Key Issues in the Afro-American Experience*, ed. Nathan I. Huggins et al., 2 vols. (New York: Harcourt Brace Jovanovich, Inc., 1971), 2:15, 22, 23.

7. See Harold D. Woodman, "Sequel to Slavery: The New History Views the Postbellum South," *JSH* 43 (November 1977), 523–54, and "Comment" on Jonathan M. Wiener's "Class Structure and Economic Development in the American South, 1865–1955," in *AHR* 84 (October 1979), 997–1001.

8. Frederick Law Olmsted, *The Cotton Kingdom: A Traveller's Observations on*

Cotton and Slavery in the American Slave States, ed. Arthur M. Schlesinger (New York: Alfred A. Knopf, 1953), pp. 261–62; Whitelaw Reid, *After the War: A Tour of the Southern States, 1865–66*, ed. C. Vann Woodward (New York: Harper Torchbooks, 1965), p. 564; *Nation* 1 (September 21, 28, 1865), 354, 393; U.S., Congress, Senate, *Report of John Alvord, Inspector of Schools and Finances for Freedmen*, no. 27, 39th Cong., 1st sess., 1866, *Senate Executive Documents*, p. 120. For other examples, see Raymond H. Gladding to William H. Brisbane, November 17, 1865, in Miscellaneous Letters, RSCDTC, RIR, RG 58, NA; Oliver Otis Howard, *Autobiography of Oliver Otis Howard: Major General United States Army*, 2 vols. (New York: Baker and Taylor County, 1907), 2:238–39; H. G. Judd to [Rufus] Saxon, November 23, 1865, in Miscellaneous Letters, RSCDTC, RIR, RG 58, NA; Edward Ord to Ulysses Grant, telegram, April 19, 1865, in *The Papers of Ulysses S. Grant*, ed. John Simon, 14 vols. (Carbondale and Edwardsville: Southern Illinois University Press, 1985), 14:412n.

9. Virgil Hillyer to J. B. Howell, March 22, 1873, in RCC, RTD, RG 56, reel 3, NA; Hillyer to Asa Aldis, February 21, 1874, ibid., reel 4; William Paine to Charles Benjamin, June 24, 1876, ibid., reel 11; Philip D. Morgan, "The Ownership of Property by Slaves in the Mid-Nineteenth-Century Low Country," *JSH* 49 (August 1983), 399–420; Vernon Lane Wharton, *The Negro in Mississippi, 1865–1890* (Chapel Hill: University of North Carolina Press, 1947), p. 59; Litwack, *Been in the Storm So Long*, pp. 398–404.

10. Wharton, *The Negro in Mississippi*, p. 87; Reid, *After the War*, pp. 564–65; Loren Schweninger, *James T. Rapier and Reconstruction* (Chicago: University of Chicago Press, 1978), p. 84; George Rawick, ed., *The American Slave: A Composite Autobiography*, 19 vols. (Westport, Conn.: Greenwood Publishing Co., 1972), vol. 4, pt. 2, pp. 251–52; Ransom and Sutch, *One Kind of Freedom*, pp. 81–87; *Nationalist* (Mobile, Ala.), January 11, 1866.

11. Certificates of Land Sold to Heads of Families, 1862–69, RIR, RG 58, NA; Computed from USMSPC, Duval and Marion Counties, Ark., Desha and Union Counties, Fla., 1870; Richard N. Current, *Those Terrible Carpetbaggers: A Reinterpretation* (New York: Oxford University Press, 1988), p. 43.

12. U.S. Department of the Interior, Census Office, *The Statistics of the Population of the United States . . . From the Original Returns of the Ninth Census* (Washington: GPO, 1872), pp. 77–282; ibid., *Statistics of the Population of the United States at the Tenth Census* (Washington: GPO, 1883), pp. 416–25; John W. Reps, *Views and View Makers of Urban America* (Columbia: University of Missouri Press, 1984), p. 158.

13. *Nationalist* (Mobile, Ala.), January 11, 1866; *Montgomery Daily Advertiser*, December 31, 1865; *Nation* 2 (February 15, 1866), p. 209; Howard N. Rabinowitz, *Race Relations in the Urban South, 1865–1890* (New York: Oxford University Press, 1978), p. 63; Robert E. Perdue, *The Negro in Savannah, 1865–1900* (New York: Exposition Press, 1973), p. 105.

14. Ransom and Sutch, *One Kind of Freedom*, p. 82; Maris A. Vinovskis, "Have Social Historians Lost the Civil War? Some Preliminary Demographic Speculations," *JAH* 76 (June 1989), pp. 38–39.

15. David Rankin, "The Impact of the Civil War on the Free Colored Com-

munity of New Orleans," in *Perspectives in American History* 11 (1977–78), 348; N. S. Shaler, "An Ex-Southerner in South Carolina," *Atlantic Monthly* 26 (July 1870), 58; Williamson, *After Slavery: The Negro in South Carolina during Reconstruction*, p. 162.

16. USMSPC, Charleston, S.C., 5th Ward, 1860, p. 378; ibid., 5th Ward, 1870, p. 378 [*sic*]; ibid., Montgomery, Ala., 1st Dist., 1860, p. 204; ibid., 4th Ward, 1870, p. 494; ibid., Natchitoches Parish, La., 1860, p. 500; ibid., 1870, p. 452; ibid., Richmond County, Ga., Augusta, 1st Ward, 1860, p. 758; ibid., 1870, p. 43; ibid., Rapides Parish, La., 1860, p. 80; ibid., 1870, p. 153; ibid., New Orleans, La., 5th Ward, 1860, p. 929; ibid., 7th Ward, 1870, p. 458.

17. *Nation*, 1 (September 21, 1865), 354; Rawick, ed., *The American Slave*, vol. 12, pt. 2, pp. 113, 133.

18. Oubre, *Forty Acres and a Mule*, p. 25; Testimony of Charles Watkins to Oliver Otis Howard, March 13, 1866, in *Freedom: A Documentary History of Emancipation, 1861–1867*, ser. 2, *The Black Military Experience*, ed. Ira Berlin, Joseph Reidy, and Leslie Rowland (New York: Cambridge University Press, 1982), docs. 355, 357; Barbara Fields, *Slavery and Freedom on the Middle Ground: Maryland during the Nineteenth Century* (New Haven: Yale University Press, 1985), pp. 144–45; George Campbell, *White and Black: The Outcome of a Visit to the United States* (New York: R. Worthington, 1879), p. 276; Alrutheus Ambush Taylor, *The Negro in the Reconstruction of Virginia* (Washington: Association for the Study of Negro Life and History, 1926), p. 130.

19. Fields, *Slavery and Freedom on the Middle Ground*, pp. 147–48; Taylor, *The Negro in the Reconstruction of Virginia*, pp. 81–84; U.S. Dept. of the Interior, Census Office, *Statistics of the United States at the Tenth Census* (Washington: GPO, 1883), p. 419; U.S. Dept. of Interior, Census Office, *A Compendium of the Ninth Census* (Washington: GPO, 1872), p. 14; Richard Fuke, "'Limited Access': Rural Blacks and the Land in Post-Emancipation Maryland," p. 12. The author wishes to thank Professor Fuke for permission to cite material from this unpublished manuscript. Computed from USMSPC, 1860, 1870; U.S. Dept of Interior, Census Office, *Population of the United States in 1860; Compiled from the Original Returns of the Eighth Census* (Washington: GPO, 1864), pp. 518–20.

20. John T. Trowbridge, *The Desolate South, 1865–1866; A Picture of the Battlefields and of the Devastated Confederacy* (Hartford, Conn.: I. Sterbins, 1866; reprint ed., ed. Gordon Carroll, Boston: Little, Brown, and Co., 1956), p. 153; John Dennett, *The South as It Is, 1865–66* (New York: Viking Press, 1965), p. 48.

21. USMSPC, Boyle County, Ky., 1870, p. 220; ibid., Pike County, Mo., pp. 156, 167, 180.

22. Baltimore *American*, November 14, 1864; *Woods City Directory, 1867–1868* (Baltimore: John W. Woods, 1868), passim.

23. Herbert G. Gutman, *The Black Family in Slavery and Freedom, 1750–1925* (New York: Alfred A. Knopf, 1976), pp. 167–85; Trowbridge, *The Desolate South, 1865–1866*, pp. 121, 153.

24. USMSPC, New Hanover County, N.C., Wilmington, 1860, p. 343; ibid., 1870, p. 412; ibid., District of Columbia, 7th Ward, 1860, p. 879; ibid.,

1870, p. 450; ibid., Jefferson County, Ky., Louisville, 2d Ward, 1860, p. 586; ibid., 4th Ward, 1870, p. 340; ibid., Kent County, Del., Murderhill Hundred, 1850, p. 228; ibid., 1870, p. 192; ibid., Baltimore, Md., 6th Ward, 1860, p. 541; ibid., 5th Ward, 1870, p. 159; ibid., Baltimore, Md., 2d Ward, 1860, p. 437; ibid., 2d Ward, 1870, p. 304; ibid., Washington, D.C., 7th Ward, 1860, p. 868; ibid., 7th Ward, 1870, p. 322; ibid., Prince William County, Va., 1860, p. 471; ibid., 1870, p. 436; ibid., Fayette County, Ky., Lexington, 1st Ward, 1860, p. 389; ibid., Lexington, 1st Ward, 1870, p. 183; ibid., Davidson County, Tenn., Nashville, 4th Ward, 1860, p. 400; ibid., Nashville, 4th Ward, 1870, p. 240; ibid., St. Louis, Mo., 4th Ward, 1860, p. 73; ibid., St. Louis, 5th Ward, 1870, p. 31.

25. Computed from USMSPC, 1870. The total wealth in the South in 1870 was approximately $5.5 billion. Calculated from "Valuation of Property— 1870, 1860, 1850," in U.S. Dept. of the Interior, Census Office, *A Compendium of the Ninth Census* (Washington: GPO, 1872), p. 639; see Lee Soltow, *Men and Wealth in the United States* (New Haven: Yale University Press, 1975), p. 65.

26. John Baldwin, "Fifty Years in Louisiana: Views of a Northern White Settler in the South," *Crisis* 13 (December 1916), 72; Lawrence N. Powell, *New Masters: Northern Planters during the Civil War and Reconstruction* (New Haven: Yale University Press, 1980), p. 131.

27. W. E. B. Du Bois, "The Negro Farmer," in U.S. Department of Commerce and Labor, *Special Reports: Supplementary Analysis and Derivative Tables [of the] Twelfth Census of the United States* (Washington: GPO, 1906), p. 523; Du Bois, *The Souls of Black Folk* (Chicago: A. C. McClurg and Co., 1903; reprint in *Three Negro Classics*, ed. John Hope Franklin, New York: Avon Books, 1965), p. 304; Jaynes, *Branches without Roots*, p. 173; Contracts of Edgar Dawson to Freedmen, 1870, 1873, Black History Collection, BTHC; William Parker, "The South in the National Economy, 1865–1970," *Southern Economic Journal* 46 (April 1980), 1024–28; Schweninger, *James T. Rapier and Reconstruction*, p. 164.

28. Ransom and Sutch, *One Kind of Freedom*, pp. 83–85.

29. Eric Foner, *Nothing But Freedom: Emancipation and Its Legacy* (Baton Rouge: Louisiana State University Press, 1983), pp. 108–10; Thomas F. Armstrong, "From Task Labor to Free Labor: The Transition along Georgia's Rice Coast, 1820–1880," *GHQ* 64 (Winter 1980), 443.

30. U.S. Department of Commerce and Labor, Bureau of the Census, *Census Reports: Twelfth Census of the United States, Taken in the Year 1900*, 10 vols. (Washington: GPO, 1902), 5:68–69, 118–19; W. E. B. Du Bois, "The Negro Landholder in Georgia," in *Bulletin of the Department of Labor*, #35 (Washington: GPO, 1901), pp. 648–49, "The Negro Farmer," p. 523; George Tindall, *South Carolina Negroes, 1877–1900* (Columbia: University of South Carolina Press, 1952), chap. 6.

31. Du Bois, "The Negro Landholder of Georgia," p. 777; Tax Book, Barbour County, Ala., 1893; ASDAH; Assessment List and Tax Book for Real Estate, Jefferson County, Ark., 1900, AHCSA; Tax Rolls, Louisiana, 1893– 1916, LSA.

32. *Proceedings of the Constitutional Convention of South Carolina, Held at*

Charleston, S.C., Beginning January 14th and Ending March 17th, 1868, 2 vols. (Charleston: Denny and Perry, 1868; reprint ed., New York: Arno Press, 1968), 1:117; Rawick, ed., *The American Slave,* vol. 12, pt. 2, p. 87; Elizabeth Bethel, *Promiseland: A Century of Life in a Negro Community* (Philadelphia: Temple University Press, 1981), pp. 95–96; Sydney Nathans, "Fortress without Walls: A Black Community after Slavery," in *Holding on to the Land and the Lord: Kinship, Ritual, Land Tenure and Social Policy in the Rural South,* ed. Robert Hall and Carol Stack (Athens: University of Georgia Press, 1982), pp. 56–58; Huntsville (Ala.) *Gazette,* September 28, 1889; William Benson, *Prospectus of the Dixie Industrial Company of Kowaliga, Alabama* (Boston: George Ellis, 1900), pp. 6–28; *Proceedings of the National Negro Business League; Its First Meeting, Held in Boston, Massachusetts, August 23 and 24, 1900* (Boston: J. R. Hamm, 1901), p. 115; Charles Banks, "A Negro Colony: Mound Bayou, Mississippi," typescript, c. 1912, p. 1, box 38, BTWP, LC; Booker T. Washington, "A Town Owned by Negroes," *World's Work* 14 (July 1907), 9131; August Meier, "Booker T. Washington and the Town of Mound Bayou," *Phylon* 15 (Winter 1954), 396–401; Aurelius P. Hood, *The Negro at Mound Bayou* (Nashville: AME Sunday School Union, 1910), pp. 1–10; Janet Sharp Hermann, *The Pursuit of a Dream* (New York: Oxford University Press, 1981), pp. 109–10, 148, 156–57, 160, 182, 201–3.

33. This and subsequent mean holdings differ slightly from the estimates cited in *Negro Population 1790–1915,* pp. 607, 625–26.

34. Hollis Roy Lynch, *The Black Urban Condition: A Documentary History, 1866–1971* (New York: Thomas Y. Crowell Co., 1973), pp. 422–26; *Negro Population 1790–1915* (Washington: GPO, 1918), p. 93; Howard N. Rabinowitz, "Continuity and Change: Southern Urban Development, 1860–1900," in Blaine A. Brownell and David R. Goldfield, eds., *The City in Southern History: The Growth of Urban Civilization in the South* (Port Washington, N.Y.: Kennikat Press, 1977), p. 93.

35. *New York Age,* May 17, 1890; Emma Lou Thornbrough, *T. Thomas Fortune: Militant Journalist* (Chicago: University of Chicago Press, 1972), p. 140; Rabinowitz, *Race Relations in the Urban South,* p. 78.

36. Ray Stannard Baker, "The Riddle of the Negro," typescript, 1907, pp. 9–10, box 141, Ray Stannard Baker Papers, LC; Du Bois, "The Negro Landholder of Georgia," pp. 665, 676; D. W. Woodard, "Negro Progress in A Mississippi Town; Being a Study of Conditions in Jackson, Mississippi," in Aurelius P. Hood, *The Negro at Mound Bayou* (n.p.: A. P. Hood, 1909), pp. 3–8; E. M. Woods, *Blue Book of Little Rock and Argenta, Arkansas* (Little Rock: Central Printing Co., 1907), p. 145; William D. Crum to William McKinlay, January 26, 1903, McKinlay Papers, Woodson Collection, LC. See Willard Gatewood, Jr., "William D. Crum, A Negro in Politics," JNH 53 (October 1968), 301–20; Tindall, *South Carolina Negroes, 1877–1900,* p. 142.

37. *Report on Farms and Homes,* p. 566 (see Table 16); *Negro Population 1790–1915,* pp. 270, 276, 485; Woods, *Blue Book of Little Rock,* pp. 158–59; *New York Evening Post,* November 21, 1905, clipping, bk. 1042, p. 102, BTWP, LC.

38. Fields, *Slavery and Freedom on the Middle Ground,* pp. 178–79; Lester C. Lamon, *Black Tennesseans, 1900–1930* (Knoxville: University of Tennessee

Press, 1977), pp. 111–12; Carl Kelsey, *The Negro Farmer* (Chicago: Jennings and Pye, 1903), p. 36.

39. "Proceedings of the Second Hampton Negro Conference," May 25, 1894, in *The Booker T. Washington Papers*, ed. Louis R. Harlan, 11 vols. (Urbana: University of Illinois Press, 1972-), 3:428–30; William Edward Spriggs, "Afro-American Wealth Accumulation, Virginia 1900–1914," (Ph.D. dissertation; University of Wisconsin, 1984), pp. 130, 156; Richard R. Wright, "The Colored Man and the Small Farm," *Southern Workman* 29 (November 1900), 483; Wendell Phillips Dabney, *Maggie Lena Walker and the Independent Order of St. Luke: The Woman and Her Work* (Cincinnati: Dabney Publishing Company, 1927), p. 40; Albon L. Holsey, "Negro Women and Business," *Southern Workman* 56 (August 1927), p. 345. For an examination of farm owners before and after the period under discussion, see Loren Schweninger, "A Vanishing Breed: Black Farm Owners in the South, 1651–1982," *AH* 60 (Summer 1989), 41–60.

40. RCPC, Craven County, N.C., Deeds, vol. 76 (December 14, 1872), pp. 478–79; Alan D. Watson, *A History of New Bern and Craven County* (New Bern: Tryon Palace Commission, 1987), p. 520; Eric Anderson, *Race and Politics in North Carolina, 1872–1901: The Black Second* (Baton Rouge: Louisiana State University Press, 1981), p. 22.

41. Robert Park, "Negro Home Life and Standards of Living," in *The Annals of the Academy of Political and Social Science* 49 (September 1913), 149; W. H. Brown, *The Education and Economic Development of the Negro in Virginia* (Charlottesville: University of Virginia Press, 1923), p. 89; Thomas C. Walker, "The Development of the Tidewater Counties of Virginia," *Annals of the American Academy of Political and Social Science* 49 (September 1913), 28–31; Taylor, *The Negro in the Reconstruction of Virginia*, pp. 132–36, and "The Negro in the Reconstruction of Virginia," *JNH* 11 (July 1926), 376; Samuel T. Bitting, *Rural Land Ownership among the Negroes of Virginia With Special Reference to Albemarle County* (Charlottesville: University of Virginia Press, 1915), pp. 104–5; W. T. B. Williams, "Local Conditions among Negroes: Gloucester County, Virginia," *Southern Workman* 35 (February 1906), 103–6, and "Local Conditions among Negroes: Hanover County, Virginia," ibid. 35 (March 1906), 172–75, and "Local Conditions among Negroes: Prince Edward County, Virginia," ibid. 35 (April 1906), 239–44; Spriggs, "Afro-American Wealth Accumulation," pp. 130, 156; *Report on Farms and Homes*, p. 566; *Census Reports: Twelfth Census of the United States*, 5:172; *Negro Population 1790–1915*, pp. 580, 625.

42. Computed from USMSPC, 1870; *Negro Population 1790–1915*, pp. 625–26. Mean values in 1910 differ slightly from those in the above source. U.S. Dept. of Commerce, Bureau of the Census, *Thirteenth Census of the United States Taken in the Year 1910*, 11 vols. (Washington: GPO, 1913), 5:219–21.

43. Kelly Miller, "The City Negro," *Southern Workman* 31 (April 1902), 217–22; Lynch, *The Black Urban Condition*, pp. 48–49, 422–26; George Edmund Haynes, "Conditions among Negroes in Cities," *Annals of the American Academy of Political and Social Science* 49 (September 1913), 106; Herbert A. Thomas, Jr., "Victims of Circumstance: Negroes in a Southern Town,

1865–1880," *Register of the Kentucky Historical Society* 71 (July 1973), 256; Zane Miller, "Urban Blacks in the South, 1865–1920: The Richmond, Savannah, New Orleans, Louisville, and Birmingham Experience," in Leo F. Schnore, ed. *The New Urban History: Quantitative Explorations by American Historians* (Princeton: Princeton University Press, 1975), pp. 188–89.

44. Rabinowitz, *Race Relations in the Urban South*, pp. 98, 118; George C. Wright, *Life behind a Veil: Blacks in Louisville, Kentucky, 1865–1930* (Baton Rouge: Louisiana State University Press, 1985), p. 103; Haynes, "Conditions among Negroes in Cities," pp. 105–20; Lawrence O. Christensen, "Race Relations in St. Louis, 1865–1916," *MHR* 77 (January 1984), 128–29; John Slattery, "Twenty Years' Growth of the Colored People in Baltimore, Md.," *Catholic World* 66 (January 1898), 519–27.

45. Stansbury Boyce to Carter G. Woodson, July 18, 1925, Carter Woodson Papers, LC; *Colored American* (Washington, D.C.), August 11, 1894; W. E. B. Du Bois, ed., *The Negro in Business: Report of a Social Study Made under the Direction of Atlanta University Together with the Proceedings of the Fourth Conference for the Study of Negro Problems, Held at Atlanta University, May 30–31, 1899* (Atlanta: Atlanta University, 1899), pp. 5–20; *Report of the Ninth Annual Convention of the National Negro Business League, Held in Baltimore, Maryland, August 19, 20, and 21, 1908* (Pensacola, Fla.: Florida Sentinel Printers, [1908]), pp. 260–62; Booker T. Washington, *The Negro in Business* (Chicago: Hertel, Jenkins and Co., 1907; reprint ed., New York: AMS Press, 1971), pp. 338–39.

46. *Colored American* (Washington, D.C.), August 11, 1894; tabulated from *Thirteenth Census of the United States Taken in the Year 1910*, 4:434–527; *Negro Population 1790–1915*, pp. 517–20. See An Essay on Sources and Methodology.

47. *Negro Population 1790–1915*, pp. 464, 473–77; E. C. Brown, "A Bit of Personal Experience," *Alexander's Magazine* 1 (September 1905), 36–37; *Washington Bee*, August 17, 1889; *Richmond Planet*, August 29, 1896; *Proceedings of the National Negro Business League; Its First Meeting*, pp. 35–36; *Chicago Broad Ax*, September 27, 1912; *Nashville Globe*, August 23, 1908.

48. Jeffrey R. Brackett, *Notes on the Progress of the Colored People of Maryland since the War* (Baltimore: Johns Hopkins University Press, 1890), pp. 27–28; Edward Ingle, *The Negro in the District of Columbia* (Baltimore: Johns Hopkins University Press, 1893), p. 90, in Myrtilla Miner Papers, LC; Taylor, *The Negro in the Reconstruction of Virginia*, p. 135; *Richmond Planet*, January 9, 1897; "Notes on Racial Progress," galley proof, 1915, box 856, BTWP, LC; Edward Bonekemper, "Negro Ownership of Real Property in Elizabeth City County, Va., 1860–1870," *JNH* 55 (July 1970), 177; Robert Francis Engs, *Freedom's First Generation: Black Hampton, Virginia, 1861–1896* (Philadelphia: University of Pennsylvania Press, 1979), p. 177; Rabinowitz, *Race Relations in the Urban South*, p. 96; William Boyd, *The Story of Durham: The City of the New South* (Durham: Duke University Press, 1927), p. 284; Clement Richardson, "What Are Negroes Doing in Durham," *Southern Workman* 42 (July 1913), 393; James A. Padgett, "From Slavery to Prominence in North Carolina," *JNH* 22 (October 1937), 467.

49. *Spokane Review*, January 28, 1900, clipping, bk. 1032, p. 131, BTWP,

LC; Ray Stannard Baker, *Following the Color Line: American Negro Citizenship in the Progressive Era* (New York: Doubleday, Page and Co., 1908), p. 40; *Colored American* (Washington, D.C.), August 11, 1894; *Huntsville Gazette*, October 1, 1887, March 17, 1888; *Richmond Planet*, January 9, 1897; *Savannah Tribune*, July 13, 1889, April 15, 1893; *St. Louis Palladium*, January 7, 1905, January 6, 1906; *Washington Bee*, November 27, 1886, October 22, 1887; *New York Age*, [1914], clipping, box 71, BTWP, LC; John J. Smallwood, "Colored Men Acquiring Property," *Southern Workman* 20 (October 1891), 239.

50. Howard Rabinowitz, ed., *Southern Black Leaders of the Reconstruction Era* (Urbana: University of Illinois Press, 1982), passim; Louis R. Harlan, "Booker T. Washington and the Politics of Accommodation," in John Hope Franklin and August Meier, eds., *Black Leaders of the Twentieth Century* (Urbana: University of Illinois Press, 1982), pp. 1–18; Emma Lou Thornbrough, "T. Thomas Fortune: Militant Editor in the Age of Accommodation," in ibid., pp. 19–38; Thomas C. Holt, "The Lonely Warrior: Ida B. Wells-Barnett and the Struggle for Black Leadership," in ibid., pp. 39–62; and Elliott Rudwick, "W. E. B. Du Bois: Protagonist of the Afro-American Protest," in ibid., pp. 63–84; Du Bois and Booker T. Washington, *The Negro in the South: His Economic Progress in Relation to His Moral and Religious Development* (Philadelphia: George W. Jacobs and Co., 1907), pp. 69, 103–4, 108; Du Bois, ed., *The Negro in Business*, p. 5; Washington, *The Negro in Business*, p. 15; U.S. Congress, *Congressional Record*, 51st Cong., 2d sess., 1891, 22:2693. Also see unidentified clipping, August [30], 1902, bk. 1034, p. 108, BTWP, LC; T. J. Elliott to Emmett Scott, May 25, 1914, box 852, BTWP, LC; W. H. Crogman, *The Progress of a Race; the Remarkable Advancement of the Afro-American from the Bondage of Slavery* (Atlanta: J. L. Nichols and Co., 1898); Green Polonius Hamilton, *Beacon Lights of the Race* (Memphis: F. H. Clarke and Brother, 1911); W. N. Hartshorn, ed., *An Era of Progress and Promise, 1863–1910* (Boston: Priscilla Publishing Company, 1910); G. F. Richings, *Evidences of Progress among Colored People* (Philadelphia: George S. Ferguson Co., 1905); Frank Mather, ed., *Who's Who of the Colored Race; A General Biographical Dictionary of Men and Women of African Descent* (Chicago: n.p., 1915).

51. James M. McPherson, *Ordeal by Fire: The Civil War and Reconstruction* (New York: Alfred A. Knopf, 1982), pp. 579–80. Calculated from tables in *Report on Farms and Homes*, p. 566; and *Census Reports: Twelfth Census of the United States*, 5:172; *Negro Population 1790–1915*, p. 580; Spriggs, "Afro-American Wealth Accumulation," p. 130.

52. Du Bois, "The Negro Landholder of Georgia," p. 777.

CHAPTER SIX
Prosperous Blacks in the South, 1862–1915

1. *Historic Times* (Lawrence, Kan.), August 29, 1891. See *State Capital* (Springfield, Ill.), August 8, 1891; *Huntsville* (Ala.) *Gazette*, February 25, 1882; Robert Terrell to Booker T. Washington, May 2, 1904, Container 25, BTWP, LC; *Nashville Globe*, July 10, 1908; Ray Stannard Baker, "A Colloquy [on] the Negro Problem," 1908, ms. in box 141, Baker Papers, LC.

2. Charles S. Johnson, *Shadow of the Plantation* (Chicago: University of Chicago Press, 1934), pp. 57, 89; E. Franklin Frazier, *The Negro Family in the United States* (Chicago: University of Chicago Press, 1939), p. 164, chap. 20; E. Horace Fitchett, "The Traditions of the Free Negro in Charleston, South Carolina," *JNH* 25 (April 1940), 139–52; August Meier, *Negro Thought in America, 1880–1915: Racial Ideologies in the Age of Booker T. Washington* (Ann Arbor: University of Michigan Press, 1963), pp. 150, 156. While most of the recent literature focuses on black political life there are important discussions about color and class attitudes among Negroes in a number of works. See David Rankin, "The Origins of Black Leadership in New Orleans during Reconstruction," *JSH* 40 (August 1974), 417–40; Leon Litwack, *Been in the Storm So Long: The Aftermath of Slavery* (New York: Alfred A. Knopf, 1979), pp. 530–45; Howard Rabinowitz, ed., *Southern Black Leaders of the Reconstruction Era* (Urbana: University of Illinois Press, 1982); John H. Haley, *Charles N. Hunter and Race Relations in North Carolina* (Chapel Hill: University of North Carolina Press, 1987), pp. 155–57; Joseph Cartwright, *The Triumph of Jim Crow: Tennessee Race Relations in the 1880s* (Knoxville: University of Tennessee Press, 1976); Robert Engs, *Freedom's First Generation: Black Hampton, Virginia, 1861–1890* (Philadelphia: University of Pennsylvania Press, 1979), chap. 10; Walter B. Weare, *Black Business in the New South: A Social History of the North Carolina Mutual Life Insurance Company* (Urbana: University of Illinois Press, 1973); Thomas Holt, *Black over White: Negro Political Leadership in South Carolina during Reconstruction* (Urbana: University of Illinois Press, 1977); Howard Rabinowitz, *Race Relations in the Urban South, 1865–1890* (New York: Oxford University Press, 1978), chap. 10; Eric Foner, *Reconstruction: America's Unfinished Revolution, 1863–1877* (New York: Harper and Row Publishers, 1988), pp. 396–99.

3. Engs, *Freedom's First Generation*, p. 182.

4. Willard B. Gatewood, Jr., "Aristocrats of Color: South and North. The Black Elite, 1880–1920," *JSH* 54 (February 1988), 4–5.

5. USMSPC, Plaquemines Parish, La., 1860, p. 696; RPPC, Plaquemines Parish, La., Successions, #252, April 27, 1867; "St. Rosalie Plantation Record Book," pp. 222–27, Special Collections, TU; James Parton, *General Butler in New Orleans: History of the Administration of the Department of the Gulf in 1862* (Boston: Houghton, Mifflin and Co., 1863), p. 267.

6. Parton, *General Butler in New Orleans*, pp. 263, 265–66; P. F. De Gournay, "The F. M. C.'s of Louisiana," *Lippincott's Monthly Magazine* 53 (April 1894), 516.

7. Nathan Willey, "Education of the Colored Population of Louisiana," *Harper's New Monthly Magazine* 33 (June to November 1866), 247; U.S. War Department, *The War of the Rebellion: A Compilation of the Official Records of the Union and Confederate Armies*, ser. 1, 70 vols. (Washington: GPO, 1886), 15:556; Mary Berry, "Negro Troops in Blue and Gray: The Louisiana Native Guards, 1861–63," *LH* 8 (Spring 1967), 167; Arthur W. Bergeron, Jr., "Free Men of Color in Grey," *CWH* 32 (September 1986), 248; John D. Winters, *The Civil War in Louisiana* (Baton Rouge: Louisiana State University Press, 1963), p. 21; Rodolphe Desdunes, *Our People and Our History* (originally pub-

lished as *Nos homes et notre histoire*, Montreal: Arbour and Dupont, 1911; reprint ed., trans. Dorothea McCants (Baton Rouge: Louisiana State University Press, 1973), p. 22; George S. Denison to Samuel P. Chase, August 26, 1862, in *Annual Report of the American Historical Association* (Washington: GPO, 1903), p. 311; G. B. Hauk to Charles F. Benjamin, February 28, 1874, RCC, RTD, RG 56, reel 11, NA; George Tucker to Charles F. Benjamin, February 28, 1874, ibid.; USMSPC, St. Landry Parish, La., 1860, p. 829; James E. Winston, "The Free Negro in New Orleans, 1803–1860," *LHQ* 21 (October 1938), 1081.

8. John F. Marszalek, ed., *The Diary of Miss Emma Holmes, 1861–1866* (Baton Rouge: Louisiana State University Press, 1979), p. 86; James D. Johnson to Henry Ellison, December 9, 1861, Ellison Papers, SCL; Michael P. Johnson and James L. Roark, *Black Masters: A Free Family of Color in the Old South* (New York: W. W. Norton and Co., 1984), pp. 301, 305.

9. Diary of Catherine Johnson, August 16, 1864, January 1, 1865, May 30, 1866, in William Johnson Papers, LSU.

10. Whitelaw Reid, *After the War: A Tour of the Southern States, 1865–1866* (New York: Moore, Wilstach and Baldwin, 1866; reprint ed., ed. C. Vann Woodward, New York: Harper and Row, 1965), p. 244; *The Nationalist* (Mobile), July 11, 1867; David Rankin, "The Origins of Black Leadership in New Orleans during Reconstruction," *JSH* 40 (August 1974), 433.

11. Larry Koger, *Black Slaveowners: Free Black Slave Masters in South Carolina, 1790–1860* (Jefferson, N.C., McFarland and Co., 1985), pp. 120–24, 193–95; USMSPC, Georgetown County, S.C., 1860, p. 314; ibid., Charleston, S.C., 1860, p. 85; ibid., Sumter County, S.C., 1860, p. 133; Record of General Tax Return, Sumter District, S.C., 1865, 1866, 1867, SCDAH; Johnson and Roark, *Black Masters*, pp. 314–5, 324, 330–31.

12. George Rawick, ed., *The American Slave: A Composite Autobiography*, 19 vols. (Westport, Conn.: Greenwood Press, 1972-), vol. 5, pt. 4, p. 158; quoted in Gary B. Mills, *The Forgotten People: Cane River's Creoles of Color* (Baton Rouge: Louisiana State University Press, 1977), p. 237; Petition for Relief of Antoine Meullion, December 1889, #8090, RCC, RTD, RG 56, in Meullion Family Papers, LSU; RPPC, St. Landry Parish, La., Successions, #5040, October 14, 1890; USMSPC, St. Landry Parish, La., 1860, pp. 886–87; RPPC, Iberville Parish, La., Deeds, bk. 9 (July 15, 1868), pp. 221–23; J. Ward Gurley, Jr., to Charles Benjamin, May 18, 1875, RCC, RTD, RG 56, reel 6, NA; Joseph Tournoir to J. Ward Gurley, Jr., September 5, 1874, in ibid.; USMSPC, Pointe Coupée Parish, La., 1870, pp. 324, 333, 396, 398.

13. RPPC, Pointe Coupée Parish, La., Successions, #203, July 11, 1865; USMSPC, Pointe Coupée Parish, La., 1860, p. 796; RPPC, Natchitoches Parish, La., Conveyances, vol. 69 (December 20, 1873), pp. 601–4, 637–39; Mills, *Forgotten People*, pp. 218–19; RPPC, Plaquemines Parish, La., Successions, #252, April 27, 1867; ibid., Conveyances, bk. K (May 5, 1874), pp. 791–93; USMSPC, St. Mary Parish, La., 1870, p. 574. See Loren Schweninger, "Antebellum Free Persons of Color in Postbellum Louisiana," *LH* 30 (Fall 1989), 345–64.

14. *List of Tax Payers of the City of Charleston for 1859* (Charleston: Walker,

Evans and Co., 1860), pp. 387, 389, 400; *List of Tax Payers of the City of Charleston for 1860* (Charleston: Evans and Cogswell, 1861), pp. 319, 330–32; Koger, *Black Slaveowners*, p. 197; USMSPC, Charleston, S.C., 5th Ward, 1860, p. 376; E. Horace Fitchett, "The Traditions of the Free Negro in Charleston, South Carolina," *JNH* 25 (April 1940), 139–52; RCPC, Charleston County, S.C., Estates, #243–20, December 26, 1876; ibid., #230–25, March 25, 1875; ibid., #250–24, May 4, 1878; ibid., #243–5, January 11, 1877; ibid., #220–6, July 8, 1873; ibid., #277–14, May 22, 1882; USMSPC, Charleston, S.C., 3d Ward, 1860, p. 282; ibid., 1870, p. 139; ibid., 4th Ward, 1870, pp. 211, 281, 299; Records of the Comptroller General, Charleston District, Free Negro Tax Book, 1843, SCDAH; Holt, *Black over White*, pp. 37n, 46, 57, 141n, 164–65, appendix A; Records of the General Tax Return, Charleston District, 1867, pp. 123, 143, 167, 201, SCDAH; Records of the Comptroller General, Charleston District, Free Negro Tax Book, 1833, SCDAH.

15. USMSPC, New Orleans, La., 1st Mun., 7th Ward, 1850, p. 396; ibid., 1870, 5th Ward, pp. 73, 216; ibid., 1870, 7th Ward, p. 549; RPPC, New Orleans, La., Successions, #35,055, December 2, 1871, #41,626, November 19, 1879, #38,677, May 27, 1876, NOPL; ibid., New Orleans, La., Successions, #37,326, July 28, 1874, in Louisiana Papers, 65–2, MSRC; Meier, *Negro Thought in America*, p. 140; Rankin, "The Origins of Black Leadership in New Orleans During Reconstruction," pp. 431–32; Charles E. Wynes, "Thomy Lafon (1810–93): Black Philanthropist," *Midwest Quarterly* 22 (Winter 1981), 105–9; John Blassingame, *Black New Orleans, 1860–1880* (Chicago: University of Chicago Press, 1973), pp. 57, 144, 213; Leonard Curry, *The Free Black in Urban American, 1800–1850: The Shadow of the Dream* (Chicago: University of Chicago Press, 1981), p. 42.

16. Koger, *Black Slaveowners*, p. 197; USMSPC, New Orleans, La., 6th Ward, 1860, p. 170; ibid., 1870, p. 235; David Rankin, "The Impact of the Civil War on the Free Colored Community of New Orleans," *Perspectives in American History* 11 (1977–78), 396–98.

17. *New Orleans Picayune*, September 9, 1874; RPPC, New Orleans, La., Successions, #38,677, May 27, 1876; Rankin, "The Impact of the Civil War," pp. 403–6.

18. Adolphe Donato to Jule Porudin, December 16, 1883, Miscellaneous Letters, #2946, LSU.

19. USMSPC, Richland County, S.C., Columbia, 1860, pp. 23, 58; ibid., 2d Ward, 1870, p. 108; ibid., Floyd County, Ga., Rome, 1860, p. 215; ibid., 2d Ward, 1870, p. 195; ibid., Iberville Parish, La., 1860, p. 329; ibid., 1870, listed at dwellings #675 and #700; ibid., Plaquemines Parish, La., 1850, p. 274; ibid., 1870, p. 224; ibid., New Orleans, La., 5th Ward, 1860, n.p.; ibid., 5th Ward, 1870, p. 195; RCPC, Pulaski County, Ark., Estates, #184, November 17, 1866, AHCSA; USMSPC, Pulaski County, Ark., Little Rock, 2d Ward, 1870, p. 259; Jonathan M. Wiener, *Social Origins of the New South: Alabama, 1860–1885* (Baton Rouge: Louisiana State University Press, 1978), p. 9.

20. Janet S. Hermann, *The Pursuit of a Dream* (New York: Oxford University Press, 1981), pp. 109–10, 148, 156–57, 160, 182, 201–3; RCPC, Warren

County, Miss., Estates, #3029, November 6, 1877; USMSPC, Warren County, Miss, 1870, p. 131; Vernon Lane Wharton, *The Negro in Mississippi, 1865–1890* (Chapel Hill: University of North Carolina Press, 1947), p. 42; Booker T. Washington, *The Negro in Business* (Chicago: Hertel, Jenkins and Co., 1907; reprint ed., New York: AMS Press, 1971), pp. 85–86.

21. Claim #16,011, Alfred Anderson, Amelia County, Va., c. 1877, RTD, RCC, RG 56, reel 9, NA; Claim #16,012, Francis Anderson, Amelia County, Va., c. 1877, in ibid; Claim #16,297, James Anderson, c. 1877, in ibid.; Claim #18,049, Henry F. Harrison, Administrator for Frankey Miles, c. 1877, in ibid.; USMSPC, Amelia County, Va., 1860, pp. 169, 171, 212; Luther Porter Jackson, *Free Negro Labor and Property Holding in Virginia, 1830–1860* (New York: D. Appleton Co., 1942), pp. 122, 127–28, 217, 224–25.

22. USMSPC, New Hanover County, N.C., Wilmington, 1860, p. 381; ibid., 1870, p. 161; ibid., Wake County, N.C., 1860, pp. 115, 119, 181; James Browning, "The Free Negro in Ante-Bellum North Carolina," *NCHR* 15 (January 1938), 28, 29; USMSPC, Davidson County, Tenn., 2d Dist., 1850, p. 226. For Davidson County and other parts of Tennessee, see Anita Goodstein, "Black History on the Nashville Frontier, 1780–1810," *THQ* 38 (Winter 1979), 411; May Alice Harris Ridley, "The Black Community of Nashville and Davidson County, 1860–1870," (Ph.D. dissertation, University of Pittsburgh, 1982), pp. 7–8, 15–34, 56–57; Faye Wellborn Robbins, "A World-within-a-World: Black Nashville, 1880–1915," (Ph.D. dissertation, University of Arkansas, 1980), pp. 245–52; Stephen Vaughan Ash, "Civil War, Black Freedom, and Social Change in the Upper South: Middle Tennessee, 1860–1870," (Ph.D. dissertation, University of Tennessee, 1983), pp. 592–93, 683.

23. USMSPC, Mason County, Ky., 1860, p. 279; ibid., 1870, p. 518; ibid., Hancock County, Ky., 1870, p. 212; ibid., Bracken County, Ky., 1860, p. 221; ibid., 1870, p. 276; ibid., Greene County, Tenn., 1850, p. 256; ibid., 1860, p. 368; ibid., 1870, p. 364; ibid., Rutherford County, Tenn., 15th Dist., 1870, p. 78; ibid., Davidson County, Tenn., Nashville, 1850, p. 160; ibid., Davidson County, 13th Dist., 1870, p. 431; ibid., Andrew County, Mo., 1850, p. 59; ibid., Andrew County, Mo., Nodaway Township, 1870, p. 278; ibid., Clark County, Mo., Jackson Township, 1860, p. 780; ibid., Clark County, Mo., Clay Township, 1870, p. 467; ibid., Carroll County, Mo., Wakenda Section, 1870, p. 414.

24. Barbara Fields, *Slavery and Freedom on the Middle Ground: Maryland during the Nineteenth Century* (New Haven: Yale University Press, 1985), p. 168; Donald McCauley, "The Urban Impact on Agricultural Land Use: Farm Patterns in Prince George's County, Maryland, 1860–1880," in Aubrey C. Land et al., eds., *Law, Society, and Politics in Early Maryland* (Baltimore: Johns Hopkins University Press, 1977), p. 233; USMSPC, Kent County, Del., 1860, p. 65; ibid., 1870, pp. 231, 261; ibid., Sussex County, Del., 1870, p. 613; ibid., Queen Anne County, Md., 1st Dist., 1860, p. 853; ibid., 1870, p. 317; Kent County, Md., 1860, n.p.; ibid., Baltimore County, Md., 12th Dist., 1870, p. 683.

25. USMSPC, New Castle County, Del., Wilmington, 1st Ward, 1860,

p. 699; ibid., 1870, p. 303; ibid., Baltimore, Md., 9th Ward, 1870, p. 409; ibid., Washington, D.C., 7th Ward, 1860, p. 887; ibid., 1870, p. 466; ibid., Alexandria County, Va., Alexandria, 1860, p. 841; ibid., 5th Ward, 1870, p. 134; ibid., Henrico County, Va., Richmond, 1860, n.p.; ibid., Clay Ward, 1870, p. 422; ibid., Wayne County, N. C., Goldsboro, 1860, p. 479; ibid., 1870, p. 15; ibid., Shelby County, Ky., Shelbyville, 1870, p. 415; ibid., Jefferson County, Ky., Louisville, 5th Ward, 1860, p. 107. Nathaniel Rogers's real estate was listed under his wife's name. Ibid., Louisville, 6th Ward, 1870, p. 632; ibid., Shelby County, Tenn., Memphis, 1850, 5th Ward, p. 62; ibid., 7th Ward, 1870, p. 290; James Young moved from Louisville to St. Louis. Ibid., Jefferson County, Ky., Louisville, 7th Ward, 1860, p. 427; ibid., St. Louis, Mo., 9th Ward, 1870, p. 519.

26. USMSPC, Fayette County, Ky., Lexington, 1st Ward, 1860, p. 369; ibid., 3d Ward, pp. 381, 584; ibid., 1st Ward, 1870, p. 185; ibid., 3d Ward, 1870, pp. 252, 255; Herbert A. Thomas, Jr., "Victims of Circumstance: Negroes in a Southern Town, 1865–1880," *Register of the Kentucky Historical Society* 71 (July 1973), 267–71.

27. USMSPC, Baltimore County, Md., 1st Dist., 1860, p. 881; ibid., 1870, p. 25; ibid., Washington, D.C., 4th Ward, 1860, p. 135; ibid., 1st Ward, 1870, p. 26; ibid., 1st Ward, 1850, p. 22; ibid., 1st Ward, 1870, p. 184; ibid., Jefferson County, Ky., Louisville, 8th Ward, 1860, p. 725; ibid., Bourbon County, Ky., Paris, 1860, p. 489; ibid., 1870, p. 420; ibid., Davidson County, Tenn., Nashville, 3d Ward, 1860, p. 356; ibid., 6th Ward, 1860, p. 343; ibid., Nashville, 2d Dist., 1850, p. 229; ibid., Davidson County, Tenn., 13th Dist., 1870, p. 429; ibid., St. Louis, Mo., 11th Ward, 1860, p. 111; ibid., 11th Ward, 1870, p. 462; ibid., 3d Ward, 1860, p. 84; Records of the Baltimore County Court, Chancery Papers, Last Will and Testament of Thomas Green, 1858, Accession no. MdHr 40200-5988-1/2, MSA; USMSPC, Washington, D.C., Georgetown, 1st Ward, 1860, p. 3; ibid., 1870, p. 644; RCPC, St. Louis, Mo., Estates, #15701, February 3, 1886; ibid., #6301, March 2, 1863; ibid., #18,230, May 23, 1888.

28. Computed from USMSPC, 1860, 1870. Urban data include those within city limits. Constance McLaughlin Green, *Secret City: A History of Race Relations in the Nation's Capital* (Princeton: Princeton University Press, 1967), p. 94; Henry S. Robinson, "Some Aspects of the Free Negro Population of Washington, D.C., 1800–1862," *MHM* 64 (Spring 1969), 43–64; USMSPC, Washington, D.C., 1st Ward, 1860, pp. 222, 232–33, 347, 357.

29. USMSPC, Washington, D.C., 1st Ward, 1860, p. 217; ibid., 2d Ward, 1870, p. 231; ibid., 2d Ward, 1860, p. 519; ibid., 1870, p. 270; ibid., 1st Ward, 1860, p. 318; ibid., 1870, p. 7; ibid., 4th Ward, 1850, p. 278; ibid., 1870, p. 780; ibid., 2d Ward, 1860, p. 523; ibid., 1870, p. 268; ibid., 1st Ward, 1860, p. 335; ibid., 1870, p. 53; ibid., 2d Ward, 1860, p. 595; ibid., 1870, p. 227; ibid., 1st Ward, 1860, p. 333; ibid., 1870, p. 9; ibid., 1st Ward, 1860, p. 361; ibid., 1870, p. 125; ibid., 4th Ward, 1860, p. 337; ibid., 1870, p. 683; ibid., 2d Ward, 1860, p. 110; ibid., 1870, p. 228; ibid., 2d Ward, 1860, p. 417; ibid., 6th Ward, 1870, p. 273; ibid., 1st Ward, 1860, p. 378; ibid., 1870, p. 67; ibid.,

2d Ward, 1860, p. 550; ibid., 1870, p. 300; ibid., 1st Ward, 1860, p. 324; ibid., 1870, p. 53; ibid., 1st Ward, 1860, p. 233; ibid., 1870, p. 51; ibid., 1st Ward, 1860, p. 332; ibid., 1870, p. 8; RCPC, Washington, D.C., Estates, #6605, March 2, 1895; ibid., #3152, August 3, 1888; USMSPC, Washington, D.C., 1st Ward, 1860, p. 217; ibid., 1870, pp. 3, 127; ibid., 2d Ward, 1860, p. 621; ibid., 1870, p. 285; Meier, *Negro Thought in America*, pp. 7, 28–29, 34, 35, 48; USMSPC, Washington, D.C., 5th Ward, 1870, p. 22; ibid., 1st Ward, 1870, pp. 3, 8, 13, 15, 51, 67, 125, 127, 184, 189; *Colored American* (Washington, D.C.), May 14, 1898.

30. Charles R. Douglass to Frederick Douglass, May 17, 1867, Douglass Papers, reel 2, LC; F. J. Grimke to G. Smith Wormley, August 23, 1934, container 9, Carter Woodson Papers, LC; USMSPC, Washington, D.C., 1st Ward, 1870, p. 1; RCPC, Washington, D.C., Estates, #1700, October 31, 1884; *Broad Ax* (Salt Lake City), August 31, 1895.

31. Rabinowitz, *Race Relations in the Urban South*, p. 88; USMSPC, Davidson County, Tenn., Nashville, 5th Ward, 1870, p. 266; ibid., St. Louis, Mo., 3d Ward, 1870, p. 196; RCPC, St. Louis, Mo., Deeds, bk. 405 (April 1, 1870), p. 69; *Tax Book for the Year 1879: State of Missouri*, pp. 26–29, in RCPC, St. Louis, Mo.; *New York Herald Tribune*, July 6, 1871; Loren Schweninger, ed., *From Tennessee Slave to St. Louis Entrepreneur: The Autobiography of James Thomas* (Columbia: University of Missouri Press, 1984), pp. 12–13.

32. Mills, *The Forgotten People*, p. xxv; Lee Soltow, *Men and Wealth in the United States, 1850–1870* (New Haven: Yale University Press, 1975), p. 186.

33. RCPC, Charleston, S.C., Estates, #465–11, April 20, 1906; *Negro Population 1790–1915* (Washington: GPO, 1918), pp. 723–25.

34. RCPC, Wake County, N.C., Deeds, bk. 181 (March 18, 1881), p. 119; ibid., bk. 214 (February 15, 1907), p. 54; ibid., bk. 263 (October 3, 1912), p. 263; ibid., bk. 304 (May 9, 1916), p. 225; ibid., Estates, #6103, June 11, 1948; ibid., Wills, bk. R (June 11, 1948), p. 332; *Raleigh News and Observer*, December 18, 1935. A former student, Teresa Smith, generously provided me with this information concerning her great-grandfather.

35. W. N. Hartshorn, ed., *An Era of Progress and Promise, 1863–1910* (Boston: Priscilla Publishing Co., 1910), p. 445; Lester C. Lamon, *Black Tennesseans, 1900–1930* (Knoxville: University of Tennessee Press, 1977), p. 100; Roy Nash, "The Lynching of Anthony Crawford," *Independent* 88 (December 11, 1916), p. 458; George Rawick, ed., *The American Slave: A Composite Autobiography*, supplement, ser. 1, 12 vols. (Westport, Conn.: Greenwood Press, 1979), 8:1177.

36. *Report of the Eleventh Annual Convention of the National Negro Business League, Held in New York City, New York, August 17, 18 and 19, 1910* (Nashville: A. M. E. Sunday School, 1911), pp. 88–93; *Report of the Eighteenth and Nineteenth Annual Sessions of the National Negro Business League, held at Chattanooga, Tenn., and Atlantic City, N.J.* (Nashville: National Baptist Publishing Board, 1919), pp. 42–45; Booker T. Washington to editor of *New York Times*, c. 1913, typescript, container #848, BTWP, LC; "Scott Bond," biographical sketch in Daniel Murray Papers, reel 10, University of Wisconsin.

37. *Louisville Post*, August 18, 1909, clipping, bk. 1052, p. 262, BTWP, LC; Clement Richardson, "The Man Who Turned Gravel to Dollars," *Southern Workman* 43 (April 1914), 211–16; *Lexington* (Va.) *News*, August 25, 1910, clipping, bk. 1055, p. 190, BTWP, LC; *New Orleans Times Democrat*, August 19, 1910, in ibid., p. 195; Daniel A. Rudd and Theophilus Bond, *From Slavery to Wealth: The Life of Scott Bond* (Madison, Ark.: Journal Printing Co., 1917; reprint ed., Freeport, N.Y.: Books for Libraries Press, 1971), pp. 17–18; *The Mercantile Agency Reference Book, Containing the Ratings of Merchants, Manufacturers and Traders Generally Throughout the United States* (New York: R. G. Dun and Co., 1905), Madison, Ark., p. 17, DB; George Rawick, ed., *The American Slave: A Composite Autobiography*, supplement, ser. 2, 10 vols. (Westport, Conn.: Greenwood Press, 1979), 1:25–43.

38. Alrutheus Ambush Taylor, *The Negro in the Reconstruction of Virginia* (Washington: Association for the Study of Negro Life and History, 1926), p. 133; Washington, *The Negro in Business*, p. 22; George Tindall, *South Carolina Negroes, 1877–1900* (Columbia: University of South Carolina Press, 1952), p. 105; USMSPC, Charleston, S.C., 5th Ward, 1870, p. 378; *Huntsville* (Ala.) *Gazette*, March 17, 1888; *Detroit Plaindealer*, July 3, 1891; *Jefferson County* (Ala.) *Union*, March 4, 1904; Rawick, ed., *The American Slave: A Composite Autobiography*, vol. 3, pt. 3, p. 23.

39. *Report of the Eleventh Annual Convention of the National Negro Business League*, pp. 23, 202; *Proceedings of the Twenty-second Annual Meeting of the National Negro Business League, held at Atlanta, Georgia, August 17, 18, 19, 1921* (Nashville: National Baptist Publishing Board, 1922), pp. 29–30; William Aery, "The Negro in Business: Stories of Success," *Southern Workman* 42 (October 1913), 522–25; *Montgomery* (Ala.) *Journal*, November 17, 1913, clipping, bk. 1061, n.p., BTWP, LC; Tindall, *South Carolina Negroes*, pp. 104–5; *Report of the Ninth Annual Convention of the National Negro Business League, Held in Baltimore, Maryland, August 19, 20, and 21, 1908* (Pensacola, Fla.: Florida Sentinel Printers, [1908]), pp. 49–51; *Wichita* [Kansas] *Searchlight*, February 17, 1906; *Report of the Fifteenth Annual Convention of the National Negro Business League, Held at Muskogee, Oklahoma, Wednesday, Thursday, and Friday, August 19, 20, 21, 1914* (Washington, D.C.: n.p., 1914), p. 51; *Boston Herald*, September 7, 1906, clipping, bk. 1044, p. 100, BTWP, LC; John Dittmer, *Black Georgia in the Progressive Era, 1900–1920* (Urbana: University of Illinois Press, 1977), p. 25; W. E. B. Du Bois, *The Souls of Black Folk* (Chicago: A. C. McClurg and Co., 1903; reprinted in *Three Negro Classics*, ed. John Hope Franklin (New York: Avon Books, 1965), pp. 289, 300.

40. E. E. Cooper to Emmett Scott, April 21, 1904, container 20, BTWP, LC; Cooper to Booker T. Washington, December 9, 1904, in ibid.; RCPC, Washington, D.C., Estates, #68,903, June 10, 1947; *Report of the Fourth Annual Convention of the National Negro Business League, Held at Nashville, Tennessee, August 19, 20, 21, 1903* (Wilberforce, Ohio: Charles Alexander, Publisher, 1903), p. 31; Rabinowitz, *Race Relations in the Urban South*, p. 88; *Nashville Globe*, March 25, 1910; John Hartel to Booker T. Washington, September 3, 1904, container 21, BTWP, LC; James Napier, "Opportunity and Possibility:

A Message to Young Men," *Alexander's Magazine* 1 (July 1905), 30; Green Polonius Hamilton, *The Bright Side of Memphis; A Compendium of Information Concerning the Colored People of Memphis, Tennessee, Showing their Achievements in Business, Industrial and Professional Life[,] and Including Articles of General Interest on the Race* (Memphis: n.p., 1908), p. 284.

41. "Notes on Negro Progress," galley proof, c. 1907, box 37, BTWP, LC; John Tyler to Emmett Scott, May 19, 1914, box 852, ibid.; *Wichita Searchlight*, June 12, 1909; *Report of the Ninth Annual Convention of the National Negro Business League*, pp. 49–51; Hettye Wallace Branch, *The Story of "80 John"* (New York: Greenwich Publishers, 1960), pp. 54–56; Rawick, ed., *The American Slave: A Composite Autobiography*, supplement, ser. 2, vol. 10, pp. 3938–40.

42. *Detroit Plaindealer*, August 5, 1892; J. R. E. Lee, "The Negro National Business League," *The Voice of the Negro* 1 (August 1904), 328; *Colored American* (Washington, D.C.), January 23, 1904; *Report of the Fourth Annual Convention of the National Negro Business League*, p. 35; Frank Lincoln Mather, *Who's Who of the Colored Race; A General Biographical Dictionary of Men and Women of African Descent* (Chicago: n.p.: 1915), p. xxvi; E. E. Cooper to Emmett Scott, April 21, 1904, container 20, BTWP, LC; *Report of the Eleventh Annual Convention of the National Negro Business League*, p. 202; *Nashville Globe*, October 20, 1911.

43. William J. Simmons, *Men of Mark: Eminent, Progressive and Rising* (Cleveland: Rewell Publishing Co., 1887), pp. 208–30; Vincent, *Black Legislators in Louisiana during Reconstruction*, pp. 143–44; John Hope Franklin, ed., *Reminiscences of an Active Life: The Autobiography of John Roy Lynch* (Chicago: University of Chicago Press, 1970), pp. xxvi–xxviii; Blanche K. Bruce to Roscoe Bruce, December 1, 1897, Bruce Papers, MSRC; RCPC, Bolivar County, Miss., Deeds, bk. Z (September 18, 1876), p. 307, in Bruce Papers; RCPC, Washington, D.C., Estates, #8277, April 29, 1898; Blanche K. Bruce to Josephine Bruce, December 5, 1897, Bruce Papers; Kenneth Eugene Mann, "Blanche Kelso Bruce: United States Senator without a Constituency," *JMH* 38 (May 1976), pp. 183–98; Sadie D. St. Clair, "The National Career of Blanche Kelso Bruce," (Ph.D. dissertation, New York University, 1947), pp. 60–61; Melvin Urofsky, "Blanche K. Bruce: United States Senator, 1875–1881," *JMH* 29 (May 1967), 122; William C. Harris, "Blanche K. Bruce of Mississippi: Conservative Assimilationist," in *Southern Black Leaders of the Reconstruction Era*, pp. 7–8; Peter D. Klingman, *Josiah Walls: Florida's Black Congressman of Reconstruction* (Gainesville: University of Florida, 1976), p. 52, "Race and Faction in the Public Career of Florida's Josiah T. Walls," in *Southern Black Leaders of the Reconstruction Era*, p. 59; RCPC, Lowndes County, Ala, Mortgages, bk. 5 (1877), pp. 124–27; Loren Schweninger, *James T. Rapier and Reconstruction* (Chicago: University of Chicago Press, 1978), pp. 157, 173.

44. USMSPC, Baltimore, Md., 2d Ward, 1870, p. 298; Leroy Graham, *Baltimore: The Nineteenth Century Black Capital* (New York: University Press of America, 1982), p. 203; *Huntsville Gazette*, July 3, 1886, March 17, 1888; *Atlanta Constitution*, August 27, 1893; Michael Leroy Porter, "Black Atlanta: An

Interdisciplinary Study of Blacks on the East Side of Atlanta, 1890–1930," (Ph.D. dissertation, Emory University, 1974), p. 282; Ray Stannard Baker, *Following the Color Line: American Negro Citizenship in the Progressive Era* (New York: Doubleday, Page and Co., 1908; reprint ed., ed. Dewey W. Grantham, Jr., New York: Harper Row, 1965), p. 41; RCPC, Fulton County, Ga., Estates, #15,390, June 28, 1927; St. Louis *Dispatch,* February 13, 1868, quoted in Montgomery *Weekly Advertiser,* February 25, 1868; RCPC, St. Louis, Mo., Deeds, bk. 405 (April 1, 1870), p. 489; *New York Herald Tribune,* July 6, 1871; *Tax Book for the Year 1879: State of Missouri,* pp. 26–29, in RCPC, Assessor's Office, St. Louis, Mo.

45. USMSPC, Baltimore, Md., 7th Ward, 1860, p. 596; ibid., 2d Ward, 1870, p. 427; Graham, *Baltimore: The Nineteenth Century Black Capital,* pp. 201–2; Bettye C. Thomas, "A Nineteenth Century Black Operated Shipyard, 1866–1884: Reflections upon Its Inception and Ownership," *JNH* 59 (January 1974), 4; RCPC, Washington, D.C., Estates, #30,286, February 19, 1923; *Washington Bee,* August 12, 1893, December 4, 1897; W. P. Burrell, "History of the Business of Colored Richmond," *Voice of the Negro* 1 (August 1904), 320; *Proceedings of the National Negro Business League; Its First Meeting, Held in Boston, Massachusetts, August 23, and 24, 1900* (Boston: J. R. Hamm, Publishers, 1901), p. 32; George C. Wright, *Life behind a Veil: Blacks in Louisville, Kentucky, 1865–1930* (Baton Rouge: Louisiana State University Press, 1985), pp. 95–96; *Nashville Globe,* September 4, 1908; David E. Alsobrook, "Mobile's Forgotten Progressive—A. N. Johnson, Editor and Entrepreneur," *Alabama Review* 32 (July 1979), 188; Jerry John Thornbery, "The Development of Black Atlanta, 1865–1885," (Ph.D. dissertation, University of Maryland, 1977), pp. 206–7; *Atlanta Constitution,* August 27, 1893; *Birmingham Age Herald,* August 18, 1912, clipping, box 1060, BTWP, LC; *St. Louis Palladium,* January 7, 1905.

46. Abram L. Harris, *The Negro as Capitalist: A Study of Banking and Business among American Negroes* (Philadelphia: American Academy of Political and Social Science, 1936; reprint ed., New York: Arno Press, 1968), pp. 191–92; Arnett G. Lindsay, "The Negro in Banking," in J. H. Harmon, Jr., Arnett G. Lindsay, and Carter G. Woodson, eds., *The Negro as a Business Man* (Washington, D.C.: Association for the Study of Negro Life and History, 1929; reprint ed., New York: Arno Press, 1969), pp. 60–61; W. E. B. Du Bois, ed., *Economic Cooperation among Negro Americans; Report of a Social Study Made by Atlanta University* (Atlanta: Atlanta University, 1907), pp. 150–51; [H. E. Baker], "Some Reasons for the Colored Man's Lack of Commercial Ability," *Southern Workman* 27 (September 1898), 188–89; Weare, *Black Business in the New South,* pp. 16–28; Merah Steven Stuart, *An Economic Detour: A History of Insurance in the Lives of American Negroes* (New York: Wendell Malliet and Co., 1940), pp. 117–25, 310–11.

47. Mather, ed., *Who's Who of the Colored Race,* pp. 172, 203; Gerri Majors, *Black Society* (Chicago: Johnson Publishing Co., 1976), p. 184; St. Louis *Palladium,* August 31, 1907; John Lankford, "What the Negro Builder Is Doing in Washington, D.C.," *Alexander's Magazine* 1 (September 15, 1905), 36; *Washington Bee,* September 6, 1890; *Richmond Planet,* January 8, 1898; Meier, *Negro*

Thought in America, 1880–1915, p. 137; Wendell Phillips Dabney, *Maggie Lena Walker and the Independent Order of St. Luke: The Woman and Her Work* (Cincinnati: Dabney Publishing Co., 1927), pp. 27–34, 40; Wright, *Life behind a Veil*, pp. 96, 111; The [*R.G. Dun and Co.*] *Mercantile Agency Reference Book*, Knoxville, Tenn., 1895, p. 12, DB; ibid., 1905, p. 17, DB; *Report of the Fourth Annual Convention of the National Negro Business League*, p. 24; Mather, ed., *Who's Who of the Colored Race*, p. 33; *Report of the Thirteenth Annual Convention of the National Negro Business League, Held in Chicago, Illinois, Wednesday, Thursday, and Friday, August 21, 22, 23, 1912* (n.p.: n.p., 1914), p. 116, MSRC; *Harrisburg* (Pa.) *State Journal*, December 22, 1883; *Colored American* (Washington, D.C.), March 24, 1900, June 13, 1903; Lamon, *Black Tennesseans*, pp. 188–89; Hamilton, *The Bright Side of Memphis*, p. 99; Monroe Work, "The Negro in Business and the Professions," in *Annals of the American Academy of Political and Social Science* 140 (November 1928), 143–44. The tiny number of women in the most prosperous group is probably a reflection of limitations of the sources. See An Essay on Sources & Methodology.

48. Hamilton, *The Bright Side of Memphis*, pp. 19–20, 100; *Harrisburg* (Pa.) *State Journal*, December 22, 1883; *Detroit Plaindealer*, June 13, 1890; *Colored American* (Washington, D.C.), March 24, 1900, June 13, 1903; *Syracuse Post Standard*, August 8, 1901, clipping, container 1033, BTWP, LC; Lamon, *Black Tennesseans*, pp. 188–89; Robert Church, Sr. to Whitefield McKinlay, December 16, 1904, McKinlay Papers, Carter Woodson Collection, LC.

49. RCPC, Fulton County, Ga., Estates, #15,390, June 28, 1927; Stuart, *An Economic Detour*, pp. 117–25; Dittmer, *Black Georgia*, p. 169; *Nashville Globe*, December 26, 1913; August Meier, "History of the Negro Upper Class in Atlanta, Georgia, 1890–1958," *Journal of Negro Education* 28 (Spring 1959), 131; Stephen Birmingham, *Certain People: America's Black Elite* (Boston: Little, Brown and Co., 1977), p. 92.

50. The [*R. G. Dun and Co.*] *Mercantile Agency Reference Book*, Williamsburg, Va., 1895, p. 32, DB; ibid., Jacksonville, Fla., 1915, p. 18; ibid., Raleigh, N.C., 1905, p. 24; ibid., Atlanta, Ga., 1905, p. 6; ibid., 1915, p. 8; ibid., Selma, Ala., 1905, p. 23; ibid., 1915, p. 31; ibid., Corpus Christi, Tex., 1905, p. 14; ibid., 1915, p. 18, DB; Charles Anderson to Commercial Securities Company, September 18, 1914, box 9, BTWP, LC; Records of the Superior Court, Wake County, N.C., Estate Administration, June 18, 1931; Ray Stannard Baker, "Following the Color Line," galley proofs, c. 1906, p. 33, box 141, Baker Papers, LC; Washington, *The Negro in Business*, pp. 237–39; *Boston Globe*, August 19, 1900, clipping, bk. 1032, p. 364, BTWP, LC; G. F. Richings, *Evidences of Progress among Colored People* (Philadelphia: George S. Ferguson Co., 1905), p. 321.

51. USMSPC, New Orleans, La., 5th Ward, 1870, p. 54; RPPC, New Orleans, La., Successions, #41,569, October 17, 1879; Records of the Office of the Board of Health, New Orleans, La., Certificate of Death, Dominique Mercier, August 19, 1876, in above succession; *Huntsville* (Ala.) *Gazette*, July 4, 1885; The [*R. G. Dun and Co.*] *Mercantile Agency Reference Book*, New Orleans, La., 1895, p. 13; ibid., 1915, p. 21, DB.

52. *Washington Bee*, September 18, 1888, May 4, 1894; Helen W. Ludlow,

"The Negro in Business in Hampton and Vicinity," *Southern Workman* 33 (September 1904), 496; *Nashville Globe*, September 4, 1908; *Tuskegee Student*, September 18, 1909, clipping, container 1094, BTWP, LC; William Andrews to Whitefield McKinlay, March 9, September 13, 27, 1903, box 1, Carter Woodson Papers, LC; RCPC, Charleston, S.C., Estates, #506–19, April 18, 1911; *Proceedings of the National Negro Business League; Its First Meeting*, p. 23; Giles B. Jackson, *The Industrial History of the Negro Race in the United States* (Richmond: Virginia Press, 1908), p. 87; Clement Richardson, "The 'Nestor of Negro Bankers'," *Southern Workman* 43 (November 1914), 609.

53. Whitefield McKinlay to Archibald Grimké, September 5, 1913, Archibald Grimké Papers, 30–15, MSRC; Robert Church, Sr., to Whitefield McKinlay, April 11, 1904, box 1, McKinlay Papers, Carter Woodson Collection, LC; E. H. Deas to Whitefield McKinlay, [1893], in ibid.; Charles Purvis to Whitefield McKinlay, May 3, 1906, in ibid.; RCPC, Durham County, N.C., Estates, #2227, July 6, 1919; Robert McCants Andrews, *John Merrick: A Biographical Sketch* (Durham: Seeman Printers, 1920), pp. 31–33, 56–57; Records of the Superior Court, Wake County, N.C., Inventory, June 18, 1931.

54. RCPC, Duval County, Fla, Deeds, bk. 3 (July 1, 1901), pp. 96–97; ibid., bk. 7 (August 19, 1901), pp. 214–15; ibid., bk. 11 (April 21, 1902), pp. 258–59; ibid., bk. 13 (October 18, 1902), pp. 395–96; ibid., bk. 14 (November 21, 1902), pp. 29–30; ibid., bk. 14 (January 7, 1903), pp. 787–88; ibid., bk. 19 (January 27, 1904), pp. 478–79; ibid., bk. 19 (February 17, 1904), pp. 713–14; ibid., bk. 20 (March 23, 1904), pp. 368–69; *Report of the Ninth Annual Convention of the National Negro Business League*, pp. 156–57; Wynes, "Thomy Lafon," pp. 105–12; RPPC, New Orleans, La., Successions, #189,869, January 9, 1931; *Colored American* (Washington, D.C.), October 18, 1902; Mather, ed., *Who's Who of the Colored Race*, p. 53; *Report of the Eighth Annual Convention of the National Negro Business League, Held in Topeka, Kansas, on August 14, 15, 16, 1907* (Pensacola: Florida Sentinel Print, [1908]), pp. 46–47.

55. New York *Post*, November 21, 1905; RCPC, Jefferson County, Ark., Estates, #3601, December 9, 1904.

56. Graham, *Baltimore: The Nineteenth Century Black Capital*, p. 202–3; RCPC, Washington, D.C., Estates, #1700, October 31, 1884.

57. Weare, *Black Business in the New South*, p. 51; "Warren Coleman," bio. sketch, reel 11, Daniel Murray Papers, University of Wisconsin; Joe M. Richardson, "A Negro Success Story: James Dallas Burrus," *JNH* 50 (October 1965), 274–75; *Colored American* (Washington, D.C.), March 24, 1900; Schweninger, ed., *From Tennessee Slave to St. Louis Entrepreneur*, pp. 2, 7, 60; Willard Gatewood, Jr., "William D. Crum: A Negro in Politics," *JNH* 53 (October 1968), 302; RCPC, Charleston, S.C., Estates, #522–1, December 30, 1912; Rabinowitz, *Race Relations in the Urban South*, p. 93; Clarence Bacote, "Some Aspects of Negro Life in Georgia, 1880–1908," *JNH* 43 (April 1958), 190; James W. Leslie, "Ferd Havis: Jefferson County's Black Republican Leader," *AHQ* 37 (Autumn 1978), 240–51; J. Sawyer to Benjamin Harrison, February 13, 1889, Records of Collectors of Customs, RTD, RG 56, NA; Law-

rence Rice, *The Negro in Texas, 1874–1900* (Baton Rouge: Louisiana State University Press, 1971), p. 36.

58. Richard L. Hume, "Negro Delegates to the State Constitutional Conventions of 1867–1869," in *Southern Black Leaders of the Reconstruction Era*, ed. Howard Rabinowitz (Urbana: University of Illinois Press, 1982), pp. 139–40; USMSPC, Charleston, S.C., 5th Ward, 1870, p. 539; ibid., Richland County, S.C., Columbia, 3d Ward, 1870, pp. 133, 135; ibid., 4th Ward, p. 152; ibid., Marion County, S.C., 1870, p. 190; Holt, *Black over White*, pp. 229–41; RCPC, Richland County, S.C., Inventories, bk. E (July 28, 1903), p. 364; Rankin, "The Origins of Black Leadership," p. 131; USMSPC, New Orleans, La., 5th Ward, 1870, pp. 202, 216.

59. *Washington Bee*, May 4, 1894, October 18, 1902; *Richmond Planet*, February 16, 1895, September 5, 1896; Simmons, *Men of Mark*, pp. 320–25; *Proceedings of the National Negro Business League, Its First Meeting*, p. 224; Mather, ed., *Who's Who of the Colored Race*, pp. 56, 155; *Nashville American*, October 25, 1897; John Deveaux et al. to Theodore Roosevelt, November [17], 1902, Presidential Appointments, RTD, RG 56, NA; John Deveaux to William Howard Taft, March 31, 1909, Applications for Collectors of Customs, RTD, RG 56, NA; Emmett Scott to Booker T. Washington, April 1, 1909, box 46, BTWP, LC; *Pine Bluff Commercial*, August 1, 1892; Tom W. Dillard, "Golden Prospects and Fraternal Amenities: Mifflin W. Gibbs's Arkansas Years," *AHQ* 35 (Winter 1976), 307–33; Merline Pitre, *Through Many Dangers Toils and Snares: Black Leadership in Texas, 1868–1900* (Austin, Tex.: Eakin Press, 1985), pp. 188–98; Frank R. Levstik, "Langston, John Mercer," *Dictionary of American Negro Biography*, ed. Rayford Logan and Michael R. Winston (New York: W. W. Norton, 1982), pp. 382–84.

60. RCPC, Montgomery County, Ala., Estates, bk. 5 (1883), pp. 536–45; August Meier, "Afterword: New Perspectives on the Nature of Black Political Leadership during Reconstruction," in *Southern Black Leaders of the Reconstruction Era*, p. 394; *Huntsville Gazette*, March 31, 1894.

61. Weare, *Black Business in the New South*, pp. 19–20, 32–34; Booker T. Washington, "Durham, North Carolina: A City of Negro Enterprise," *Independent* 70 (March 30, 1911), 643–44; Thomas W. Holland, "Negro Capitalists," *Southern Workman* 55 (December 1926), 537; Warren Coleman to Benjamin Duke, July 8, 14, 1896, March 8, 1899, February 21, July 10, 1900, Benjamin Duke Papers, DU; Warren Coleman to Washington Duke, June 10, 1896, February 18, 26, March 12, July 24, September 4, 1897, January 7, April 22, 29, 1898, February 20, 1900, Washington Duke Papers, ibid.; Coleman to Charles N. Hunter, June 10, 1901, Charles Hunter Papers, ibid.; J. K. Rouse, *The Noble Experiment of Warren C. Coleman* (Charlotte, N.C.: Crabtree Press, 1972), pp. 39, 88; *Proceedings of the National Negro Business League; Its First Meeting*, pp. 207–9; *Concord Times*, April 26, 1904; Allen Edward Burgess, "Tar Heel Blacks and the New South Dream: The Coleman Manufacturing Company, 1896–1904," (Ph.D dissertation, Duke University, 1977); Frenise Logan, *The Negro in North Carolina, 1876–1894* (Chapel Hill: University of North Carolina Press, 1964), pp. 114–15; *Report of the Thirteenth Annual*

Convention of the National Negro Business League, Held in Chicago, Illinois, Wednesday, Thursday, and Friday, August 21, 22, 23, 1912 (n.p.: n.p., [1913]), p. 132, in MSRC; D. W. Woodward, "Negro Progress in a Mississippi Town, Being a Study of Conditions in Jackson, Mississippi," in Aurelius P. Hood, ed., *The Negro at Mound Bayou* (n.p.: A. P. Hood, 1909), p. 8.

62. James T. Bradford to George Myers, [December 1895], George Myers Papers, LC; *National Leader* (Washington, D.C.), March 23, 1889; *Washington Bee*, March 31, 1894, September 8, 1900; *Tuskegee Student*, October 27, 1906, container 1107, BTWP, LC; *Nashville Globe*, September 23, 1910; *Proceedings of the National Negro Business League; Its First Meeting*, pp. 195–200; Washington, *The Negro in Business*, p. 260.

63. "The Nineteenth Annual Meeting of the Tuskegee Negro Conference," January 19, 1910, in bk. 52, p. 13, BTWP, LC; Richardson, "The Man Who Turned Gravel to Dollars," pp. 213–14.

64. U.S. Congress, Senate, *Report and Testimony of the Select Committee of the United States Senate to Investigate the Causes of the Removal of the Negroes from the Southern States to the Northern States*, S. Rept. 693, 46th Cong., 2d sess., 1880, 3 vols. *Senate Reports* 2:45–46; William H. Ferris, *The African Abroad, or His Evolution in Western Civilization*, 2 vols. (New Haven: Tuttle, Morehouse and Taylor Press, 1913), 2:792. It was Richard (not James) Fitzgerald who had his business vandalized. Thomas Holt, "The Lonely Warrior: Ida B. Wells-Barnett and the Struggle for Black Leadership," in John Hope Franklin and August Meier, eds., *Black Leaders of the Twentieth Century* (Urbana: University of Illinois Press, 1982), p. 42; *New York Evening Post*, December 26, 1906, bk. 1075, BTWP, LC; Dittmer, *Black Georgia*, p. 129.

65. Theophile T. Allain to D. F. Boyd, January 26, 1874, container D-10, #99, David F. Boyd Papers, LSU; Mary Church Terrell, "History of the High School for Negroes in Washington," *JNH* 2 (July 1917), 252–53; W. E. Bigglestone, "Oberlin College and the Negro Student, 1865–1940," *JNH* 56 (July 1971), 199–219; Blanche K. Bruce to Roscoe C. Bruce, December 1, 1896, folder #9–1, Bruce Papers, MSRC; *St. Louis Palladium*, June 27, 1903; Walter Cohen to Emmett Scott, November 12, 1905, box 28, BTWP, LC; *Wichita* (Kan.) *Searchlight*, February 23, 1907; *Nashville Globe*, March 18, 1910; "The Diary of Mary Virginia [Montgomery], January–December, 1872," January 23, February 1, 18, August 16, 25, 1872, Benjamin Montgomery Family Papers, LC; Rawick, ed., *The American Slave*, vol. 8, pt. 1, pp. 230–31; RCPC, Fulton County, Ga., Estates, #11,141, February 30, 1917.

66. USMSPC, Fayette County, Ky., Lexington, 3d Ward, 1870, p. 292; Rabinowitz, *Race Relations in the Urban South*, p. 118; Zane Miller, "Urban Blacks in the South, 1865–1920: The Richmond, Savannah, New Orleans, Louisville, and Birmingham Experience," in Leo F. Schnore, ed., *The New Urban History: Quantitative Explorations by American Historians* (Princeton: Princeton University Press, 1975), pp. 200–202; Paul Groves, "The Evolution of Black Residential Concentrations in late Nineteenth Century Cities," *Journal of Historical Geography* 1 (1975), 190; George Edmund Haynes, "Conditions Among Negroes in the Cities," *Annals of the American Academy of Political and Social*

Science 49 (September 1913), 109; Lilian Brandt, "The Negroes of St. Louis," *Southern Workman* 33 (April 1904), 225; *New York Times*, April [26], 1907, clipping, box 141, Baker Papers, LC.

67. Nashville *Globe*, September 4, 1908; Harris, "Blanche K. Bruce of Mississippi," p. 27; W. E. B. Du Bois, *Black Reconstruction in America, 1860–1880* (New York: Russell and Russell, 1935), pp. 469–70.

68. F. J. Grimké to G. Smith Wormley, August 23, 1934, container 9, Carter Woodson Papers, LC; William T. Andrews to Whitefield McKinlay, March 3, 1903, container 1, ibid.; Booker T. Washington, "Durham," p. 645; *Indianapolis Recorder*, January 28, 1899.

69. Robert Perdue, *The Negro in Savannah, 1865–1900* (Jericho, N.Y.: Exposition Press, 1973), p. 31; William Andrews to Whitefield McKinlay, March 9, 1903, McKinlay Papers, in Carter Woodson Collection, LC; Woods, ed., *Blue Book of Little Rock*, p. 145; John Bush to Emmett Scott, September 5, 1905, box 28, BTWP, LC.

Epilogue

1. "Anthony Crawford," *Crisis* 13 (December 1916), 67; ibid., (January 1917), p. 120; *Negro Population 1790–1915*, p. 744; U.S. Dept. of Commerce, Bureau of the Census, *Negroes in the United States 1920–1932* (Washington: GPO, 1935), p. 803; Roy Nash, "The Lynching of Anthony Crawford," *Independent* 88 (December 11, 1916), 456–62; Allen B. Ballard, *One More Day's Journey: The Story of a Family and a People* (New York: McGraw-Hill Book Co., 1984), pp. 156–57; I. A. Newby, *Black Carolinians: A History of Blacks in South Carolina from 1895 to 1968* (Columbia: University of South Carolina Press, 1973), p. 66.

2. James S. Russell, "Rural Economic Progress of the Negro in Virginia," *JNH* 11 (October 1926), 557.

An Essay on Sources
and Methodology

As the notes and various appendixes to this study suggest, I have relied on a wide range of primary and secondary sources in seeking to unravel the mysteries of black property ownership. My debt to scholars in the field, especially those writing during the period 1924 to 1943—Carter Woodson, Luther Porter Jackson, and John Hope Franklin—is extremely large. The conceptual framework advanced by Ira Berlin in the 1970s proved to be invaluable in analyzing antebellum free blacks, and economic historian Lee Soltow's provocative studies helped me to put black property ownership in a larger perspective. The numerous citations of the works of these and other authors reflect only a small portion of my substantial debt to these scholars. Most of this investigation, however, comes from a broad range of primary sources. These include the manuscript population censuses, local and state tax assessment records, probate court documents, land deed records, petitions to state legislatures, family diaries and letters, biographical works, newspapers, magazines, published government documents, and various autobiographies and reminiscences. While each of these has its peculiar strengths, each has certain weaknesses. It therefore seems appropriate to discuss in some detail how I used these various primary sources and comment on their accuracy and reliability.

In several chapters I have relied heavily on the United States manuscript census returns for 1850, 1860, and 1870. Though of unique importance for this study, the information in these volumes should be viewed with some degree of caution. "The Law requires the assistant marshal to make 'the enumeration by actual inquiry at every dwelling house or by personal inquiry of the head of every family and not otherwise,'" Assistant United States Census Marshal W. V. Bernard, of Christian County, Kentucky, wrote on the last page of his tally in 1850. "But Just as I was closing my Books a gentleman informed me of a family on his farm which he had forgotten when I was at his house." Pressed for time, Bernard obtained the data on this family from "the gentleman" who acted as an "informant." Bernard's predicament was shared by other assistant marshals, who, despite extensive canvassing, were forced to rely on information provided by neighbors, friends, relatives, business partners, family tradesmen, even family physicians. To obtain information on families in some remote areas, the director of the census lamented on one occasion, would require "that nearly every man should be commissioned as an assistant marshal." Not only was it virtually impossible to canvass every family in the United States, but census takers also misspelled names, wrote in the wrong age, color, or gender, included families outside their district, and worse, sometimes failed to complete the canvasses of their assigned districts. In the midst of the racial and political violence during the summer of 1870 they probably missed 6 to 7 percent of the black population in the South.

Despite these problems, census marshals produced a remarkable set of documents. Economist Lee Soltow described the middle period census returns as "unique" and "precious" not only in helping us understand American inequality but also in helping us comprehend the basic nature of capitalism and individualism. In his exhaustive study of Edgefield County, South Carolina, Orville Vernon Burton praised the 1870 census takers in that locale as extremely knowledgeable and conscientious. Their work, he said, provided the most detailed, accurate, and complete information available on the county's population—black and white. After an extensive investigation of several Maryland counties, Richard P. Fuke noted that a variety of different sources, including local tax assessment records and the United States agricultural census, "all lend credibility" to the reliability of the 1870 population census.

This was certainly true with regard to property ownership. No other census before or after contained such unique information about the market value of real estate and personal property. "Under heading 8, insert the value of real estate owned by each individual enumerated," the 1850 instructions read. "You are to obtain this information by personal inquiry of each head of a family, and are to insert the amount in dollars, be the estate located where it may." Enumerators were not to consider any question of lien or encumbrance, but simply to enter the value as given by the respondent. In 1860 and 1870, census takers were told to add the value of personal holdings.

"Here you are to include the value of all the property, possessions, or wealth of each individual which is not embraced in the column previous [real estate], consist of what it may; the value of bonds, mortgages, notes, slaves, live stock, plate, jewels, or furniture; in fine, the value of whatever constitutes the personal wealth of individuals." It might be difficult to obtain perfectly accurate values, "but all persons should be encouraged to give a near and prompt estimate for your information."

"Personal inquiry" had its limitations. But most respondents probably estimated their wealth as accurately as possible. In 1850, Felicite Oursol, the widow of Antoine Paillet of St. Landry Parish, Louisiana, told the census marshal that her plantation land was worth $10,600. When she died nine years later, the plantation acreage was appraised in an inventory at $13,100, almost exactly the same, considering the general appreciation of land in the area, as the census estimate. In 1860, the Durnford family in Plaquemines Parish, Louisiana, informed the census marshal that its assets amounted to $50,000 in real estate and $65,000 in other property. After an exhaustive investigation of local tax and probate records, historian David O. Whitten estimated that the family's real property was worth $51,500, and slaves $71,550. The latter did not include other personal holdings, but such an estimate by the census was perhaps as close to being exact as was possible, considering fluctuating prices, inflation and deflation, and the difficulty any individual might have in attempting to estimate his exact net worth at a given moment. The key word is *estimate*. There is little doubt that, granted a slight margin of error, the census provides a relatively accurate estimate of individual property holding.

Besides the unique valuations of property, the middle-period censuses are the only documents that consistently (as indicated in the Introduction) connect property ownership with racial identity. To obtain data on free Negroes from the 1850 and 1860 volumes (on microfilm at the University of North Carolina—Chapel Hill library) was a relatively easy task, since census takers were instructed to leave the box for "color" blank, except for blacks and mulattoes. With an MMR–1635 Dukane Microfilm Reader, and its automatic adjustment, the film rolled along from frame to frame while only an "M" or "B" had to be discerned among otherwise blank spaces. There were some obvious errors, especially when ditto marks were used in the box for color—a free black laborer in rural Virginia with property holdings listed at $60,000—but these were easily eliminated. Negroes worth more than $5,000 were usually verified in at least one other source.

To obtain information from the 1870 census was much more difficult and time consuming, since census marshals were now instructed to enter either "W" or "M" or "B" in the space for "color." Each tract had to be perused at a snail's pace, and the fancy penmanship of the time made it difficult in some instances to separate M's from W's. There was also the problem of the huge increase in the number of black families listed, from approximately 52,000 to 900,000. Biographical data from 1870 were gathered on all Negroes who owned at least $1,000 in real and/or personal property (total = 10,934). For those who controlled between $100 and $900 (rounded off to the nearest hundredth), a sampling procedure was used. Data were recorded on blacks in this category from every twentieth page (printed numbers) of the manuscript volumes (total = 7,855). (See Raymond Jessen, *Statistical Survey Techniques* [New York: John Wiley and Sons, 1978], p. 407; Frank Yates, *Sampling Methods for Censuses and Surveys*, 4th ed. [New York: Macmillan Publishing, 1981], p. 140.)

Since census takers were assigned geographic tracts, and collected data simply by going up one road, or street, and down the next (see, e.g., Robert C. Kenzer, *Kinship and Neighborhood in a Southern Community: Orange County, North Carolina, 1849–1881* [Knoxville: University of Tennessee Press, 1987], pp. 156–57), a serial sample of the population census is to some degree the same as a random sample, but to test my evidence I compared it with the data gathered by Lee Soltow who used a random sample of 1,096 adult nonwhite male household heads from the 1870 census. In their essential features our findings are nearly identical. My estimate is that 18.7 percent of the black family heads in the South owned at least $100 total estate, while Soltow's, for nonwhite males, is 18 percent. My estimate of the mean total estate of all black family heads in the South is $76; Soltow's for nonwhite males in the nation is $74 (see Soltow, *Men and Wealth in the United States, 1850–1870*, pp. 55, 144–45). Of course, I included female owners (5.6 percent of the holders), but have excluded Indians, Japanese, Chinese, and other nonwhite property owners.

To further test my sample, I gathered census data on property owners with estates of less than $1,000 in three Maryland counties and compared these data with my sampled data. Again, in its general features the sample bore up well under this close scrutiny. In Kent, Queen Anne's, and Somerset counties, according to the sample, there were 700 real estate owners; according to an actual count there were 695 realty owners; the total estate holdings in the three counties, according to the sample, stood at $366,000, while the actual total was $358,000. While there were variations in the three counties in mean holdings, total holdings, and number of property owners, these variations were relatively insignificant. In locales where there were only a few, widely scattered black property owners, however, the sampled data provide a less accurate profile. An analysis of Bienville and Calcasieu parishes, Louisiana, for instance, reveals a rather large discrepancy between the actual number of real estate owners (and to a lesser degree the value of their holdings), and the estimated number of property owners as generated by the sample. Consequently, I have used the sampled data mostly to draw state and regional comparisons, where the data are most accurate, or to analyze localities where there were significant numbers of black landowners, as in the Maryland counties mentioned above. In any case, the 1870 data for property owners, especially for towns, cities, or specific counties, should be viewed as general estimates rather than exact numbers. The sampled data were fed into a computer and analyzed with SPSSX (the most recent version of The Statistical Package for the Social Sciences). The program used to generate a profile of the lower group (thanks to Terri Kirchen, formerly of our Academic Computer Center) was the following:

```
$SPSSX
TITLE                 United States Census
subtitle              Property Owners With $100 to $900
UNNUMBERED
FILE HANDLE           census7/name = 'census7.dat'
input program
DATA LIST             FILE = census7 RECORDS = 1 FIXED /1 name
                      (columns) 1–19 (A) source 20–21 repeat 22
                      date 23–25 state 27–28 county 29–31 SC (state
                      and county) (A) 27–31 dist (town or city) 32–33
                      age 35–37 gender 39 color 41 occup 43–45
                      rprop (real property) 47–50 pprop (personal
                      property) 52–55 stateb 57–58 educ 60–61
                      marital 63 agesp 65–66 colorsp 68 progeny
                      70–71
compute               te (total estate) = rprop + pprop
do if                 (te lt $1,000 and date = 1870)
loop #I =             1 to 20
leave                 source repeat date state county sc dist age gender
                      color occup rprop pprop stateb educ marital
                      agesp colorsp progeny te
end case
end loop
else
end case
end if
end input program
```

In the categories "marital," "agesp" (age of spouse), "colorsp" (color of spouse), and "progeny," I made a deliberate decision at the outset to include this information, despite the fact that the census did not specify family relationships within each household. Marshals were asked to number "families in order of visitation," but they usually did not differentiate between "families" and "households." In a few instances—Bastrop County, Texas, Madison County, North Carolina, and Richland County, South Carolina—census takers recorded "mother," "children," "wife," "widow," "spinster," "married," but such entries were rare. I have used these family data only sparingly, but in most cases it was fairly easy to make a relatively accurate judgment concerning a family's makeup from the names, ages, occupations, and place of birth of each household member.

Census marshals were instructed to include only those with at least $100 in real or personal holdings. An analysis of local tax assessment records in South Carolina and Maryland, before and after the war, suggests that those under $100 represented perhaps 10 or 15 percent of the total. In Kent County, Maryland, in 1860, for example, 283 free blacks were listed on the tax-assessment lists, but only 253 appeared in the census as owning property valued at more than $100; the same was true in Frederick County, where assessment rolls contained the names of 291, and the manuscript census, 264 propertied blacks. Despite the importance of these small property owners, except where indicated in the text or footnotes, I have generally relied on the census returns for statistical data. (See South Carolina, Office of the Comptroller General, Records of the General Tax Return, 1865–68, SCDAH; Tax-Assessment Books, Baltimore, Frederick, Kent, Queen Anne, and Somerset counties, Maryland, 1860–66, MSA.)

Several other explanatory notes should be made regarding the use of the population censuses. To delineate between rural and urban property owners, city boundary lines have been used. In some urban counties and the District of Columbia there were rural residents living only a short distance from the city. In a few returns these lines were not clearly indicated, but generally there was some indication as to the exact location of each family. The "communal property" of Negro women living with white men has not been included in the general analyses, but the property held by the whites who headed such households is briefly examined in chapter 4. Historians are well aware of the difficulties census takers had in discerning "color" for the space reserved for "black" or "mulatto" (see Robert Brent Toplin, "Between Black And White: Attitudes towards Southern Mulattoes, 1830–1861," *JSH* 45 [May 1979], 185–200). I have not tried to correct discrepancies from one census to the next but have changed those listed as mulatto in one census and white in another to mulatto if other data showed that they were persons of color. After perusing the census returns, I occasionally ran across the name of a property owner missed by the census takers (or whom I had missed). Some of these names were added to my census data list and are cited as "Computed from USMSPC" in the statistical tables. Thus, in 1860, among the 16,172 property owners, 259 or 1.6 percent, were derived from the following sources: 178 from county tax assessment records, 40 from David Rankin's various studies of New Orleans, 10 from John Hope Franklin's works, 8 from probate court records, 7 from the Louisiana Papers collected by John Blassingame and deposited at the MSRC, and between 1 and 4 from the books and articles of Mary Berry, J. Merton England, Andrew Muir, Luther Porter Jackson, Herbert Sterkx, Herbert A. Thomas, and James Wright. For 1850 and 1870, a total of 22 names were taken from eight sources, including assessment and probate records and the publications of Donnie Bellamy, Horace Fitchett, and Thomas Holt (see A Selected Bibliography of Books and Articles).

According to Louisiana and Virginia law, slaves were supposed to be listed as real, rather than personal property. Census takers, however, applied this rule inconsistently. In 1850, as shown by comparing the property listings in the population census (which listed real property) and the agricultural census (which listed "Cash value of farm"), census takers ignored the law as much as they applied it. For a number of black planters they failed to include the valuation of slaves under real estate (Andrew Durnford and Louisa Oliver of Plaquemines Parish; Zacharie Honoré of Point Coupée; Auguste Donatto of St. Landry; and Romaine Verdun of St. Mary), but for others they did (Louisa Ponis of St. John the Baptist; Antoine Decuir of Point Coupée, and Auguste Metoyer of Natchitoches). In 1860, in thirty-four of fifty-three parishes, census takers included the value of slaves under personal holdings. For propertied blacks this inconsistency will slightly inflate the average realty holdings. I have decided, however, to leave the original census estimates for real property. (See USMSAC, Natchitoches Parish, La., 1850, p. 425; ibid., Plaquemines Parish, La., 1850, pp. 485, 549; ibid., Point Coupée Parish, La., 1850, p. 569; ibid., St. John the Baptist Parish, p. 661; ibid., St. Landry Parish, 1850, p. 695; ibid., St. Mary Parish, 1850, p. 727; Lewis Gray, *History of Agriculture in the Southern United States to 1860*, 2 vols. [Washington, D.C.: Carnegie Institution, 1933; reprint ed., New York: Peter Smith, 1941], 1:509; Joseph Menn, *The Large Slaveholders of Louisi-*

ana—1860 [New Orleans: Pelican Publishing Co., 1964], pp. 79, 92–93; David O. Whitten, *Andrew Durnford: A Black Sugar Planter in Antebellum Louisiana*, Foreword by John Hope Franklin [Natchitoches: Northwestern Louisiana State University Press, 1981], p. 85.)

Although occupational designations would seem to be self-defining, census takers were presented with new instructions from time to time. The designation "merchant," for example, is never clearly defined in the census narratives preceding the occupational listings. The 1850 census listed separately dealers, ice dealers, marketmen, grocers, storekeepers, traders, and merchants; the 1860 census added to the list hardware dealers, fancy goods dealers, provision dealers, produce dealers, furniture merchants, lumber merchants, commission merchants, and shipping merchants; the 1870 census grouped occupations by four divisions—agriculture, manufacturing, trade and transportation, and manufacturers, mechanical and mining. Traders and dealers, with articles of exchange listed beneath, were substituted for the term merchant. This was changed in 1900 and 1910 when the census replaced traders and dealers with merchants and dealers. In addition, in 1910, certain occupational categories were variously listed in different states. Saloon keepers were listed separately in four southern states; billiard hall owners in two; tailors were listed in twelve states and the District of Columbia; hotel owners were listed under female domestic and personal service occupations in nine states, and under male domestic and personal service in three others; rooming and boardinghouse keepers were listed under female personal service in most states and the District of Columbia, but under both male and female domestic service in two states.

Thus, to analyze the black occupational structure presents special problems. For the sake of simplicity, in the occupational tables presented in this study, including appendix 5, I have combined the following occupations: laborers include farm laborers, hired hands, factory hands, day laborers, sawers, woodcutters; bricklayers include brickmakers; carpenters include builders, cabinetmakers, shingle makers, ship's carpenters; masons include stone and marble cutters; mechanics include engineers, machinists, millwrights, wheelwrights; shoemakers include bootmakers, saddlers; storekeepers include confectioners, tobacconists, and shopkeepers; restaurateurs include coffee shop and saloon keepers; boardinghouse keepers include rooming house keepers and hotel owners; draymen include carters, haulers, teamsters, wagoners; painters include varnishers; mariners include seamen; servants include waiters and domestic servants. In the analysis of blacks in business in chapters 5 and 6, there are 21 different occupations combined under "manufacturers," including brickmakers, harness makers, mantua makers, shingle makers, soap makers, and others, while under retailers/merchants there are 41 occupations, including, among others, grocers, merchants, coal dealers, druggists, furniture dealers, "storekeepers," tobacconists, wood dealers, wine and liquor dealers, and undertakers. The percent is the *valid percent*, or the proportion of those whose occupations were listed. In 1850, census takers listed occupations for 70 percent of the black realty owners; in 1860, for 83 percent, and for 84 percent of all property owners; in 1870, for 98.3 percent of black property owners.

The difficulties in tracing individuals from one census to the next are obvious. The procedure used to gain an *estimate* of prewar property owners who appeared in 1870 as wealth holders was the following: the 1850, 1860, and 1870 census data lists were alphabetized according to surnames, then given names, then "sorted" according to states. These "directories" were then checked and cross-checked individual by individual. For the vast majority the matchup was obvious. For those whose names were spelled differently, or whose ages did not match exactly, the comparison was more difficult. But in all except a few cases the combination of all the variables (family name, given name, location, age, gender, color, occupation, state of birth, literacy, and, except for those between $100 and $900 in 1870, the names of those living in the same household) served as a virtual fingerprint for identification purposes. Of course, women married, or remarried, and changed their names; men died, or moved out of the South, or also changed their names (though this was rare among free blacks); some property owners were missed from one census to the next, or listed as white, and the sampled wealth holders were considered to be 5 percent (the sample size) of the postwar "repeats." Moreover, as previously indicated, census takers in 1870 probably undercounted the black population in the South. This undercount was surely less for property owners, among the most stable and well-known residents in their communities, than for nonproperty owners, but even among the propertied it could have amounted to several percentage points. Despite these considerations, the evidence strongly suggests that most antebellum property owners in the Lower South did not survive the war and its aftermath with their possessions intact. (See Loren Schweninger, "Antebellum Free Persons of Color in Postbellum Louisiana," *LH* 30 (Fall 1989), 345–64.

With the exception of scattered volumes in Maryland, Louisiana, South Carolina, and Virginia, most tax assessment books do not indicate the racial identities of property owners. As a result, while useful in some instances, they have been used only tangentially, usually for comparative purposes. In some cases, such as Orleans Parish, Louisiana, during the 1850s, the data concerning free Negroes are so uneven as to be virtually useless, except for certain individual assessments. In 1856, the assessments listed 179 free persons of color who owned property; the next year the number jumped 100 percent to 357, at a time when the emigration movement was gaining strength in the Crescent City. (See Richard Tansey, "Out-of-State Free Blacks in Late Antebellum New Orleans," *LH* 22 [Fall 1981], 384.) Even in individual cases, as historian Edward Pessen and others have pointed out, a "key" for each locality is needed to equate *assessments*, usually one-sixth, to one-third, to one-half, with *market values*. In post–1891 Virginia, even such a "key" would have to be used cautiously since there is some evidence to suggest that the average ratio for whites was one to three (assessed to actual) while Negroes were assessed at 45.3 percent of their land's sale value. (W. H. Brown, *The Education and Economic Development of the Negro in Virginia* [Charlottesville: University of Virginia Press, 1923], p. 90.) Luther Porter Jackson, however, is probably correct in his assertion that tax rolls are an excellent source when the "key" has been deciphered and the tax ledgers are extant. In chapters 1 and 3, I have used data from the "Table Showing Property Assessed to Negroes in the Counties of Maryland" in James Wright's *The Free Negro in Maryland, 1634–1860* (New York: Columbia University Press, 1921), p. 184. The 204 property owners between 1783 and 1818 are taken from the assessment lists for Allegany, Anne Arundel, Baltimore County and City, Caroline, Cecil, Charles, Frederick, Kent, Montgomery, Queen Anne, Somerset, Talbot, and Worcester counties. Wright's mid-century listing of 2,255 property owners included those listed in thirteen counties in 1852–53, and an estimate for Anne Arundel County. Although he analyzed assessment books from ten different time periods between 1793 and 1860, and though, with the exception of Virginia, these records are the best for any southern state so far as racial identity is concerned, at least eight (of the twenty-one) counties are missing for each time period. In two counties, Dorchester in 1852–53, and Anne Arundel in 1860, the data are missing for several districts within each county.

The most complete assessment volumes include *List of the Tax Payers of the City of Charleston for 1859* (Charleston: Walker, Evans and Company, 1860), and *List of the Taxpayers of the City of Charleston for 1860* (Charleston: Evans and Cogswell, 1861). Each has a section listing black taxpayers. In 1865, to support the provisional government and "raise supplies," a tax was levied in the same state on real estate, manufactured articles, liquor, town lots and buildings, and other items. Assessors were instructed to make assessments of "the *actual value* of all property taxed *ad valorem*, in reference to the market value of such property, in United States Currency, and without reference to any previous assessment." They were also told to write "P. C." (Person of Color) after the names of Negro wealth holders. In 1876, the Office of the Comptroller General in Georgia began compiling estimates of black assets in land, city and town property, money and liquid capital, furniture, horses, mules, hogs, tools, and "all other property." Two years later, Louisiana passed a law requiring that "all the real estate subject to taxation shall be estimated by the assessor at its cash value," and the same for "all personal property, and capital." Except in Orleans Parish, blacks were listed separately. In 1891, Virginia established a Tax Commission to assess the value of real estate and personal holdings for blacks and whites at five-year intervals. The ratio of assessments to true market values, however, appears to have been slightly different for blacks than for whites. These few statewide postwar assessment records provide excellent comparative data. (See Records of General Tax Return, 1865–68, SCDAH; Roger L. Ransom and Richard Sutch, *One Kind of Freedom: The Economic Consequences of Emancipation* [London: Cambridge University Press, 1977], p. 85; *Acts Passed by the General Assembly of the State of Louisiana* [New Orleans: the Democrat, 1878], p. 234; *Acts Passed by the General Assembly of the State of Louisiana at the Regular Session* [New Orleans: E. A. Brandao, 1880], p. 89; Tax Assessment Rolls, Louisiana, 1880–1916, LSA; Virginia State Auditors Reports, 1891–1916, VSL.)

For the purposes of this study, county probate estate records have proven to be far more valuable than scattered tax assessment lists. This is especially true when the data are used in conjunction with the censuses and when the economic activities of affluent free persons of color are analyzed. Unlike the tax records, probate manuscripts are generally well preserved and easily available at local courthouses. Each "packet" contains some information about the disposition and size of an estate and often includes other information—an original will (usually copied in a bound volume), an inventory of real estate and personal property, records of an estate sale, final settlements, copies of land deeds, documents concerning the distribution of property, and sometimes court transcripts of legal suits brought by creditors. The wealth estimates are usually the most accurate available since they are appraisals of actual value for the purpose of sale and/ or distribution (see appendix 3). In citing these documents, I have put them under two headings: RCPC (Records of the County Probate

Court) and RPPC (Records of the Parish Probate Court). I have not cited the specific jurisdictional court during different time periods. In East Baton Rouge Parish, Louisiana, between 1808 and 1924, for example, estates (called "successions") were probated in seven different courts, including two different parish courts, and the fifth, sixth, fifteenth, seventeenth, and twenty-second district courts.

The first chapter focuses on seventeenth-century Northampton County, Virginia, and eighteenth-century Charleston, South Carolina, where a large number of propertied blacks lived at the time. In this chapter, I have made extensive use of the collection of local records at the Museum of Early Southern Decorative Arts (MESDA), in Winston-Salem, North Carolina. These include not only estate records, but land deeds, inventories, wills, emancipation and apprenticeship decrees, court suits, newspaper notices, and various advertisements. This information is available on a MESDA computer. Among the thousands of entries there are data on 479 free Negro artisans during the period 1775 to 1825. One of the entries reads as follows:

Name/Area	Dates	Trade	Other Information
Banneker, Benjamin Baltimore Co. Md.	1796–1804	surveyor	teacher, literary talent, free black artisan, work described wares made, age, death, journeyman employed

For less illustrious free black artisans, including "Batley," a blacksmith, "Cats," a coachmaker's apprentice, and "Charles," an apprentice joiner, various other types of information are provided: inventories of tools, land purchase deeds, lease agreements, estate dispositions, bills of sale for slaves, property encumbrances, bankruptcy proceedings, runaway notices, and city directory entries. As yet untapped by scholars, the museum houses the most complete collection of national period records on the South's skilled craftsmen.

On occasion I have traced the financial activities of certain individuals in land deed records. The instruments pertaining to real property include purchase deeds, assignments, leases, mortgages, releases from mortgages, and deeds of transfer or sale. This is a time-consuming task, checking and cross-checking direct (grantor) and indirect (grantee) indexes. The most affluent blacks had literally hundreds of different entries. Consequently, for a project of this scope, I have generally confined most of my "local work" to estates and inventories. In some states, most notably Delaware, Maryland, Virginia, North Carolina, and South Carolina, certain types of local records have been preserved in the state archives, but many of these valuable documents still remain in the back rooms and basements of county court buildings. I have used documents from the following county and parish courts: Plaquemines, St. Landry, Natchitoches, East and West Baton Rouge, Opelousas, Orleans (in NOPL), Pointe Coupée, Iberville, and Rapides parishes, Louisiana; Hines and Warren counties, Mississippi; Macon, Montgomery, and Mobile counties, Alabama; Leon and Duval counties, Florida; Chatham and Fulton counties, Georgia; Charleston and Richland counties, South Carolina; Durham, Wake, and Craven counties, North Carolina; Accomac, Northampton (in Susie Ames, ed., *County Court Records of Accomack-Northampton, Virginia, 1640–1645*), Alexandria, Elizabeth City, and Norfolk counties, Virginia (at MESDA); Baltimore, Kent, Queen Anne, and Somerset counties, Maryland (at MSA); Davidson County, Tennessee; Fayette and Jefferson counties, Kentucky; St. Genevieve (at JMC-UMSHS) and St. Louis counties, Missouri; Pulaski and Jefferson counties, Arkansas; and the District of Columbia.

When appropriate, I have discussed inflationary and deflationary trends in the southern economy. Land values fluctuated in the Upper South and Lower South, in the east and west, and during various time periods. Following the Civil War, they dropped 45 percent in the South and 70 percent in the state of Louisiana but rose gradually during the 1880s. Urban property values rose significantly during the last half of the nineteenth century. The prices for other goods and commodities rose and fell during times of prosperity, recession, and depression (1830s, 1870s, 1890s). But generally improved farmland sold at from $5 to $25 per acre, and consumer prices, except during the 1860s, remained fairly stable during the nineteenth century. With 1860 equaling 100, they ranged from 98 in 1840, to 110 in 1880, to 95 in 1900, to 115 in 1915. As a result any "paradigm" to take into account *adjusted* property values would serve to confuse rather than enlighten the reader. I have not attempted to quantify a "rate of exploitation" or to analyze statistically the effects of racism. For comparative purposes over more than a century of time, I have found that average real estate holdings provide the best vehicle for analysis. The median holding—the numerical value of the case lying exactly on the 50th percentile—was, of course, lower than the mean for black property owners, but even when the median can be determined with some measure of exactness (e.g., between 1850 and 1870) it offers a less precise way of gauging changes over time among various groups of property owners than average realty holdings. In appendix 5, however, there is a distribution analysis, including mean and median holdings along with standard deviation (dispersion from the average), for black realty owners in the Lower and Upper South during the middle period. At the same time, I have relied on the works of economic historians, including Stanley Engerman, Robert Fogel, Robert Higgs, Robert Gallman, Roger Ransom, Lee Soltow, Richard Sutch, Gavin Wright, and others, to examine general economic trends in the South. (A nineteenth-century consumer price index can be found in Lee Soltow, *Patterns of Wealthholding in Wisconsin since 1850* [Madison: University of Wisconsin Press, 1971], pp. 151–52. See also Robert Gallman, "Trends in the Size Distribution of Wealth in the Nineteenth Century: Some Speculations," in *Six Papers on the Size Distribution of Wealth and Income*, ed. Lee Soltow, vol. 33, *Studies in Income and Wealth*, National Bureau of Economic Research [New York: Columbia University Press, 1969]; and Ethel D. Hoover, "Retail Prices After 1850," in *Trends in the American Economy in the Nineteenth Century* [Princeton: Princeton University Press, 1960], pp. 141–91.)

For the antebellum era, I have made extensive use of an extremely valuable, yet virtually untouched body of primary source material concerning race relations: petitions to southern legislatures. Historians have long been aware of these documents, often written by individuals seeking redress from some grievance or exemption from some law, but they have used them only sparingly, usually in narrowly focused monographic studies. Yet these petitions, several thousand in number, contain a wealth of information about white attitudes toward blacks, Negro family life, master-slave relations, self-purchase, "quasi-free" slaves, Negroes and the law, black religious activities, and white-black social and sexual relationships. Often written in response to a punitive law (freed slaves, for example, were many times required to leave their state of residence within a few months after their emancipation), the documents also tell us about black work habits, character, behavior, crime, family background, travels, attitudes toward whites, as well as free black ambition and enterprise. Though occasionally found in a collection of personal papers, petitions are usually housed in state libraries. At the Virginia State Library and the South Carolina Department of Archives and History there are more than 1,350 petitions relating to race relations, slavery, and free blacks; at the state archives in Delaware, North Carolina, Mississippi, Texas, and Tennessee (on microfilm) there are approximately 1,000 documents of a similar nature.

Since a significant portion of black property owners, especially the more prosperous, were literate, I have been able to use various letters, notebooks, diaries, autobiographies, and reminiscences. One of the purposes of this investigation has been to blend "literary" sources with demographic and statistical data. This is no easy task. Statistical evidence, so important in understanding the subject, is meaningless without a proper historical and contextual framework. It can also be misleading, since one can emphasize the wrong data or merely present numbers without proper analysis. To overcome this I have looked to the seminal works of W. E. B. Du Bois, Luther Porter Jackson, John Hope Franklin, Edward Pessen, Stephen Thernstrom, and Thomas Holt, among others. The best manuscript collections concerning property owners are the following: Cane River Collection, HNOC; Dudley Turnbull, Liddell Family, Meullion Family, Metoyer Family, and William Johnson Papers, Bruce, Seddon and Wilkins Plantation Records, and Oscar Dubreuil Day Books, 1856–58, at LSU; St. Rosalie Plantation Records, TU; Abiel Leonard Collection, JMC-UMSHS; William Wiseham Paine Papers, GHS; American Colonization Society Papers, Ray Stannard Baker, Francis Cardozo, Paul Cuffee, Frederick Douglass, Christian Fleetwood, Booker T. Washington, and Carter G. Woodson Papers, Diary of Michael Shiner, LC; Holloway Family Papers and Brown Fellowship Society Minutes and Papers, CC; Blanch K. Bruce, Roscoe Conkling Bruce, Rapier-Thomas, Mary Ann Shadd Cary, and John Francis Cook Papers, MSRC; Noisette and Ellison Family Papers, SCL; Charles Hunter and Benjamin Duke Papers, DU; Orlando Brown Papers, and James Rudd Account Book, 1846–53, FC. Also helpful have been the Records of the Bureau of Refugees, Freedmen, and Abandoned Lands (1865–72) and the Records of the Southern Claims Commission (1871–c.88), both on microfilm at NA. George Rawick, ed., *The American Slave: A Composite Autobiography*; Louis Harlan and Raymond Smock, eds., *The Booker T. Washington Papers*, as well as a few slave narratives, and John Blassingame, ed., *Slave Testimony: Two Centuries of Letters, Speeches, Interviews, and Autobiographies*, have been very helpful.

The statistics on black slave ownership in 1830 have been derived from Carter G. Woodson, ed. and comp., *Free Negro Owners of Slaves in the United States in 1830; Together with Absentee Ownership of Slaves in the United States in 1830* (Washington: Association for the Study of Negro Life and History, 1924; reprint ed., Westport, Conn.: Negro Universities Press, 1968). Woodson's listings are most accurate for Louisiana. The planters analyzed in chapter 4 have been verified in other sources. Outside Louisiana, corroborative evidence is needed to verify whether or not the head-of-household actually owned the slaves listed under his or her name. In several instances, free blacks who owned no slaves were listed as large slave owners. While beyond the scope of this study, a more accurate picture of black slave ownership during the period could be obtained by first rechecking Woodson's listings and then comparing them with the 1820 and 1840 manuscript population censuses, which list the number of slaves in each household and the racial identity of the household head in the same manner as the 1830 census. Very little is known about this group during the 1840s and 1850s. Most historians point to a sharp drop in the number of black slaveholders but offer only sketchy evidence for a number of states. As Leonard Curry has suggested, the only way to gain a true measure of the changes during the late antebellum era would be to check the manuscript population census in 1860 (which lists the dollar value of personal holdings) against the the 1860 slave schedules (which do not indicate the color of slave owners but do include the names of owners and the number of slaves they owned). My impression is that the decline in ownership during this latter period, especially in Louisiana, was not nearly so sharp as historians have suggested. (See Larry Koger, *Black Slaveowners: Free Black Slave Masters in South Carolina, 1790–1860* [Jefferson, N.C.: McFarland and Company, 1985], pp. 11–12, 218, chap. 6; Michael Johnson and James Roark, *Black Masters: A Free Family of Color in the Old South* [New York: W. W. Norton and Co., 1984], p. 64.)

In two chapters I have examined blacks who reached the upper-wealth levels. Merely defining "prosperous," "affluent," and "wealthy" presents problems since virtually any definition depends on time, location, and circumstance. To be sure there were a few blacks who were truly rich, but most of those examined in these chapters could best be described as "prospering," or "well-to-do," rather than rich. Prior to 1870, I have analyzed those who accumulated at least $2,000 in real estate as members of this prospering class. Even those at the bottom of this group were among the upper-wealth holders in their day. At mid-century, those with $2,000 in realty were among the upper 13 percent of all family heads, white or black, and those with $5,000 were among the top 4 percent. Two decades later, they were among the top 20 percent and 9 percent, respectively. Thus someone who owned farmland or city property worth $4,000 or $5,000, an amount that seems minuscule by today's standards, was doing extremely well slightly more than a century ago.

With no source comparable to the United States census for the post–1870 period, it has been necessary to shift the analysis to those who attained a higher economic standing. In this regard, I have extrapolated biographical data from the list mentioned in the Introduction on 241 blacks who accumulated property valued at $20,000 or more. This information, drawn from nearly 300 books, articles, biographical dictionaries, newspapers, estate records, tax digests, and convention reports, reflects the limitations of these sources, especially the bias toward those who were at least mentioned by contemporaries, or historians, as persons of significant wealth. The list does not purport to be *all inclusive*, merely representative. The paucity of information on Delaware has left it without representation among the most affluent Negroes, although there were surely a few blacks in that state who accumulated such estates (see Harold C. Livesay, "Delaware Blacks, 1865–1915," in Carol E. Hoffecker, ed., *Readings in Delaware History* [Newark: University of Delaware Press, 1973], pp. 121–53). While most wealth estimates have been verified in tax listings, estate inventories, credit reports, and other primary sources, a few have come from less reliable sources, including biographical dictionaries and newspaper reports. The latter have been used with extreme caution. Despite the regrettable but unavoidable lack of precision, as well as missing data in such variables as "color of parents" and "status of parents," these data (see appendixes 6 and 7 for a list of the names, occupations, locations, and a profile of these property owners; percentages are rounded off to the nearest tenth) provide at least a crude vehicle for comparing prosperous Negroes during the middle period and the late nineteenth and early twentieth centuries.

Some of these data were taken from biographical works. The *Dictionary of American Negro Biography*, ed. Rayford W. Logan and Michael R. Winston (New York: W. W. Norton and Co., 1982), usually excludes Negroes who achieved success in business or became large property owners, but several older studies contain information found nowhere else. These include: Charles Alexander, *One Hundred Distinguished Leaders* (Atlanta: Franklin Publishing Company, 1899); Samuel William Bacote, ed., *Who's Who among the Colored Baptists of the United States* (Kansas City, Mo.: Franklin Hudson Publishing Company, 1913); Green Polonius Hamilton, *Beacon Lights of the Race* (Memphis: F. H. Clarke and Brothers, 1911), and *The Bright Side of Memphis: A Compendium of Information Concerning the Colored People of Memphis, Tennessee, Showing Their Achievements in Business, Industrial and Professional Life and Including Articles of General Interest on the Race* (Memphis: n.p., 1908); W. N. Hartshorn, ed., *An Era of Progress and Promise, 1863–1910* (Boston: Priscilla Publishing Company, 1910); Andrew F. Hilyer, *The Twentieth Century Union League Directory, A His-*

torical, Geographical and Statistical Study of Colored Washington (Washington, D.C.: Union League, 1901); William Decker Johnson, *Biographical Sketches of Prominent Negro Men and Women of Kentucky* (Lexington, Ky.: Standard Print, 1897); Frank Mather, ed., *Who's Who of the Colored Race* (Chicago: n. p., 1915); William E. Mollison, *The Leading Afro-Americans of Vicksburg, Miss.: Their Enterprises, Churches, Schools, Lodges and Societies* (Vicksburg, Miss.: Biographia Publishing Company, 1908); Clement Richardson, ed., *The National Cyclopedia of the Colored Race* (Montgomery, Ala.: National Publishing Company, 1919); G. F. Richings, *Evidences of Progress among Colored People* (Philadelphia: George S. Ferguson Company, 1905); William J. Simmons, *Men of Mark: Eminent, Progressive and Rising* (Cleveland: Rewell Publishing Company, 1887); E. M. Woods, *Blue Book of Little Rock and Argenta, Arkansas* (Little Rock: Central Printing Company, 1907).

As with biographical sources Negro newspapers should be perused with caution. Usually filled with repetitious stories, accusations of political intrigue, and nonlocal news, they often failed to cover important economic activities among blacks. Typical in this regard was the *Weekly Pelican* (New Orleans, La., 1886–89), a well-edited and well-written newspaper, which included many biographical sketches of black political leaders but did not report even the most spectacular events in the Negro business world. There were exceptions, however; the *Colored American* (Washington, D.C., 1898–1904), *Huntsville Gazette* (Ala., 1881–93), *Leavenworth Herald* (Kan., 1894–98), *Nashville Globe* (Tenn., 1907–13), *Richmond Planet* (Va., 1895–1900), *Savannah Tribune* (Ga., 1875–76, 1889–92), *Washington Bee* (D.C., 1882–1922), and *St. Louis Palladium* (1903–7) provided useful articles. The *Palladium* published the financial records of W. C. Gordon's undertaking business on a yearly basis. In addition, the large files of newspaper clippings at MESDA, in the BTWP at LC, and at TI were helpful, while a few Negro periodicals contained occasional articles on black businessmen and property owners: *Alexander's Magazine* (1905–9), *Colored American Magazine* (1900–1909), *Southern Workman* (1873–1917), and *Voice of the Negro* (1904–7).

Published reports have been used extensively in several chapters, especially United States census reports on home and farm ownership, the yearly proceedings of the National Negro Business League (1900–1915), and R. G. Dun's reference books which contained financial ratings for merchants, manufacturers, and traders in the United States (1865–1915). The statistical evidence in chapter 5 concerning farm owners has been computed from *Report on Farms and Homes:*

Proprietorship and Indebtedness in the United States at the Eleventh Census: 1890 (Washington, D.C.: GPO, 1896), and *Negro Population 1790–1915* (Washington, D.C.: GPO, 1918). The aggregate farm wealth for blacks as well as the mean farm holdings for blacks compared with whites in 1900 and 1910 come from the latter volume. *The Annual Reports of the American Society for Colonizing the Free People of Colour of the United States*, 91 vols. (Washington: the Society, 1818–1910; reprint ed., New York: Negro Universities Press, 1969) contain a much broader range of information about blacks in the South than the title might suggest, as do several antislavery society reports, including *Condition of the People of Color in the State of Ohio with Interesting Anecdotes* (Boston: Isaac Knapp, 1839), *Memorial of the Ohio Anti-Slavery Society to the General Assembly of the State of Ohio* (Cincinnati: Pugh and Dodd, 1838), *The Present State and Condition of the Free People of Color of the City of Philadelphia and Adjoining Districts* (Philadelphia: Pennsylvania Society for Promoting the Abolition of Slavery, 1838), *A Statistical Inquiry into the Condition of the People of Colour, of the City and Districts of Philadelphia* (Philadelphia: Kite and Walton, 1849), and James Freeman Clarke's *Present Condition of the Free Colored People of the United States* (New York: American Anti-Slavery Society, 1859). Also useful, but marred by inflated property estimates, is Cyprian Clamorgan, *The Colored Aristocracy of St. Louis* (St. Louis: n.p., 1858). For a general description of cities in the United States, including information about location, railroads, climate, waterworks, public buildings, places of amusement, cemeteries, drainage, markets, health, city government, police, and other aspects of urban life, see George E. Waring, Jr., ed. and comp., *Report on the Social Statistics of Cities*, 2 vols. (Washington, D.C.: GPO, 1887). Several volumes of the Proceedings of the Hampton Negro Conference (at MSRC), including 1894, 1896, 1898, 1900, and 1906, contain valuable data on black farmers in Virginia.

For general population breakdowns among blacks and mulattoes, men and women, adults and children, Upper South and Lower South, rural and urban, and the number of families (c. one-fifth of the total black population), I have used *The Seventh Census of the United States: 1850* (Washington, D.C.: Robert Armstrong, Public Printer, 1853); *Population of the United States in 1860; Compiled from the Original Returns of the Eighth Census* (Washington, D.C.: GPO, 1864); *The Statistics of the Population of the United States, Embracing the Tables of Race, Nationality, Sex, Selected Ages, and Occupations* (Washington, D.C.: GPO, 1872); *A Compendium of the Ninth Census* (Washington, D.C.: GPO, 1872); *Statistics of the Population of the United States at the Tenth Census*

(Washington, D.C.: GPO, 1883); and *Negro Population 1790–1915* (Washington, D.C.: GPO, 1918). Of special value are U.S. Department of the Interior, *Report on Farms and Homes: Proprietorship and Indebtedness in the United States* (Washington, D.C.: GPO, 1896); W. E. B. Du Bois, "The Negro Farmer," in U.S. Department of Commerce and Labor, Bureau of the Census, *Special Reports: Supplementary Analysis and Derivative Tables, Twelfth Census of the United States: 1900* (Washington, D.C.: GPO, 1906); and *Thirteenth Census of the United States Taken in the Year 1910: Occupation Statistics* (Washington, D.C.: GPO, 1914). Convenient recapitulations for free blacks in the antebellum South can be found in Ira Berlin, *Slaves without Masters: The Free Negro in the Antebellum South* (New York: Pantheon Books, 1974), pp. 136–37, 176–77; Richard C. Wade, *Slavery in the Cities: The South, 1820–1860* (New York: Oxford University Press, 1964), Appendix. For the later period, see Hollis R. Lynch, ed., *The Black Urban Condition: A Documentary History, 1866–1971* (New York: Thomas Y. Crowell Co., 1973), Appendix A.

Finally, a few words should be said about time and place—the temporal and spacial dimensions as one author put it. As historians are well aware, any chronological and geographical demarkation is partially arbitrary. Yet, the data in this study have lent themselves to several unique divisions. First, the break in chapter 3 comes in 1830 since it was about that time that the second generation of property owners emerged in the Lower South and a major expansion began in the Upper South. In the next chapter, dealing with prosperous blacks, however, the demarkation is 1840. Prior to this there were only a tiny number of affluent blacks in the Upper South, and afterward the expansion of affluent free persons of color in the Lower South slowed considerably. In the final two chapters, I devote a great deal of time to the 1860s, a true watershed for black wealth holders. While the regional variation between the Lower and Upper South remains valid when the vast majority of landowners down to 1915 are considered, this was not the case for the most prosperous group. Thus, in the last half of the last chapter I examine the South as a whole during the late nineteenth and early twentieth centuries.

I have found city directories, postwar black autobiographies, and several manuscript collections, including the Daniel Murray Papers at the Wisconsin Historical Society (on microfilm), perhaps the most disappointing in the lack of accurate information they provided on property owners. City directories omit some of the largest black taxpayers, black reminiscences tend to be anecdotal and filled with misinformation, and the Murray papers, while boasting hundreds of biographical sketches, contain so many factual inaccuracies as to be virtually unusable. Yet, as scholars who seek to understand the black past realize, the sources in any undertaking are at best sketchy and eclectic. And despite the imperfect nature of the materials used in this study—the manuscript censuses, assessment rolls, government reports, county court documents, and personal papers—they reveal in stark detail the significance black Americans attached to their unfulfilled quest of the American dream.

A Selected Bibliography of Books and Articles

Books

Abbott, John S. *South and North: or Impressions Received during a Trip to Cuba and the South.* New York: Abbey and Abbot, 1860.

Arfwedson, Carl D. *The United States and Canada in 1832, 1833 and 1834.* 2 vols. London: R. Bentley, 1834.

Bacote, William, ed. *Who's Who among the Colored Baptists of the United States.* Kansas City, Mo.: Franklin Hudson Publishing Co., 1913.

Bailey, H., ed. *Report of Cases Argued and Determined in the Court of Appeals in South Carolina.* 2 vols. Charleston: E. Miller, 1834.

Ballagh, James. *A History of Slavery in Virginia.* Baltimore: Johns Hopkins University Press, 1902.

Bancroft, Frederick. *Slave Trading in the Old South.* Baltimore: J. H. Furst Co., 1931.

Basler, Roy P., ed. *The Collected Works of Abraham Lincoln.* 8 vols. New Brunswick, N.J.: Rutgers University Press, 1953.

Bell, Howard H., ed. *Search for a Place: Black Separatism and Africa, 1860.* Ann Arbor: University of Michigan Press, 1969.

Berlin, Ira. *Slaves without Masters: The Free Negro in the Antebellum South.* New York: Pantheon Books, 1974.

———, and Hoffman, Ronald, eds. *Slavery and Freedom in the Age of the American Revolution.* Charlottesville: University of Virginia Press, 1983.

———, Reidy, Joseph, and Rowland, Leslie, eds. *Freedom: A Documentary History of Emancipation, 1861–1867.* Ser. 2, *The Black Military Experience.* New York: Cambridge University Press, 1982.

Berry, Thomas S. *Western Prices before 1861.* Cambridge, Mass.: Harvard University Press, 1943.

Bethel, Elizabeth. *Promiseland: A Century of Life in a Negro Community.* Philadelphia: Temple University Press, 1981.

Bitting, Samuel T. *Rural Land Ownership among the Negroes of Virginia with*

Special Reference to Albemarle County. Charlottesville: University of Virginia, 1915.

Blackett, R. J. M. *Beating against the Barriers: Biographical Essays in Nineteenth Century Afro-American History.* Baton Rouge: Louisiana State University Press, 1986.

————. *Building an Anti-Slavery Wall: Black Americans and the Atlantic Abolitionist Movement, 1830–1860.* Baton Rouge: Louisiana State University Press, 1983.

Blassingame, John. *The Slave Community: Plantation Life in the Antebellum South.* Rev. ed., New York: Oxford University Press, 1979.

————, ed. *Slave Testimony: Two Centuries of Letters, Speeches, Interviews, and Autobiographies.* Baton Rouge: Louisiana State University Press, 1977.

Bleser, Carol K. *The Promised Land: The History of the South Carolina Land Commission, 1869–1890.* Columbia: University of South Carolina Press, 1969.

Bohannon, Paul, and Curtin, Philip D. *Africa and Africans.* Garden City, N.Y.: Natural History Press, 1971.

Brackett, Jeffery. *The Negro in Maryland: A Study of the Institution of Slavery.* Baltimore: Johns Hopkins University Press, 1889; reprint ed., New York: Negro Universities Press, 1969.

Breen, T. H., and Innes, Stephen. *"Myne Own Ground": Race and Freedom on Virginia's Eastern Shore, 1640–1676.* New York: Oxford University Press, 1980.

Bridenbaugh, Carl. *Cities in the Wilderness: The First Century of Urban Life in America, 1625–1742.* New York: Ronald Press, 1938; reprint ed., New York: Capricorn Books, 1964.

Brown, Letitia W. *Free Negroes in the District of Columbia, 1790–1846.* New York: Oxford University Press, 1972.

Brown, W. H. *The Education and Economic Development of the Negro in Virginia.* Charlottesville: University of Virginia Press, 1923.

Brown, William W. *The Black Man, His Antecedents, His Genius, and His Achievements.* New York: T. Hamilton, 1863.

Butterfield, Lyman H., ed. *Letters of Benjamin Rush.* 2 vols. Princeton: Princeton University Press, 1951.

Campbell, George. *White and Black: The Outcome of a Visit to the United States.* New York: R. Worthington, 1879.

Campbell, Penelope. *Maryland in Africa: The Maryland State Colonization Society.* Urbana: University of Illinois Press, 1971.

Campbell, Robert. *A Few Facts Relating to Lagos, Abeokuta, and Other Sections of Central Africa.* Philadelphia: King and Baird, 1860.

Campbell, Stanley W. *The Slave Catchers: Enforcement of the Fugitive Slave Law, 1850–60.* New York: W. W. Norton and Co., 1968.

Catterall, Helen T., ed. *Judicial Cases Concerning American Slavery and the Negro.* 5 vols. Washington, D.C.: W. F. Roberts Co., 1932.

Clamorgan, Cyprian. *The Colored Aristocracy of St. Louis.* St. Louis: n.p., 1858.

Clarke, James F. *Present Condition of Free Colored People of the United States.* New York: American Anti-Slavery Society, 1859.

Cope, Robert S. *Carry Me Back: Slavery and Servitude in Seventeenth Century Virginia*. Pikeville, Ky.: Pikeville College Press, 1973.

Cox, LaWanda. *Lincoln and Black Freedom: A Study in Presidential Leadership*. Columbia: University of South Carolina Press, 1981.

Crogman, W. H. *The Progress of a Race: The Remarkable Advancement of the Afro-American from the Bondage of Slavery*. Atlanta: J. L. Nichols and Co., 1898.

Croushore, James H., ed. *A Volunteer's Adventures: A Union Captain's Record of the Civil War*. New Haven: Yale University Press, 1946.

Curry, Leonard P. *The Free Black in Urban America, 1800–1850: The Shadow of the Dream*. Chicago: University of Chicago Press, 1981.

Curtin, Philip D. *The Atlantic Slave Trade: A Census*. Madison: University of Wisconsin Press, 1969.

Cushing, John, comp. *The First Laws of the State of South Carolina*. 2 pts.; facsimile reprint, Wilmington, Del.: Michael Glazier, Inc., 1981.

Dabney, Wendell. *Maggie Lena Walker and the Independent Order of St. Luke: The Woman and Her Work*. Cincinnati: Dabney Publishing Co., 1927.

Daniels, Peter. *The Shadow of Slavery: Peonage in the South, 1901–1969*. New York: Oxford University Press, 1973.

Davis, David B. *The Problem of Slavery in the Age of Revolution, 1770–1823*. Ithaca, N.Y.: Cornell University Press, 1975.

Davis, Edwin, ed. *Plantation Life in the Florida Parishes of Louisiana, 1836–1846, as Reflected in the Diary of Bennet H. Barrow*. New York: Columbia University Press, 1943.

DeCanio, Stephen. *Agriculture in the Postbellum South: The Economics of Production and Supply*. Cambridge: Massachusetts Institute of Technology Press, 1974.

Desdunes, Rodolph. *Our People and Our History*. Translated by Dorothea McCants. Foreword by Charles O'Neil. Montreal: Arbour and Dupont, 1911; reprint ed., Baton Rouge: Louisiana State University Press, 1973.

Dittmer, John. *Black Georgia in the Progressive Era, 1900–1920*. Urbana: University of Illinois Press, 1977.

Douglass, Frederick. *My Bondage and My Freedom*. New York: Miller, Orton, and Mulligan, 1855.

Du Bois, William E. B. *Black Folk Then and Now: An Essay on the History and Sociology of the Negro Race*. New York: H. Holt and Co., 1939.

———. *The Souls of Black Folk*. Chicago: A. C. McClurg and Co., 1903; reprint ed., *Three Negro Classics*. Edited by John Hope Franklin. New York: Avon Books, 1965.

———. *The Suppression of the African Slave Trade to the United States of America, 1638–1870*. Cambridge: Harvard University Press, 1896; reprint ed., foreword by John Hope Franklin. Baton Rouge: Louisiana State University Press, 1969.

———, and Washington, Booker T. *The Negro in the South; His Economic Progress in Relation to His Moral and Religious Development*. Philadelphia: George W. Jacobs and Co., 1907.

Engs, Robert F. *Freedom's First Generation: Black Hampton, Virginia, 1861–1890*. Philadelphia: University of Pennsylvania Press, 1979.

Equiano, Olaudah. *Equiano's Travels: The Interesting Narrative of the Life of Olaudah Equiano or Gustavus Vassa the African*. Abridged and edited by Paul Edwards. New York: Frederick A. Praeger, 1967.

Fields, Barbara J. *Slavery and Freedom on the Middle Ground: Maryland during the Nineteenth Century*. New Haven: Yale University Press, 1985.

Fleming, Walter L. *The Freedmen's Savings Bank: A Chapter in the Economic History of the Negro Race*. Chapel Hill: University of North Carolina Press, 1927.

Franklin, John H. *The Free Negro in North Carolina, 1790–1860*. Chapel Hill: University of North Carolina Press, 1943.

———, ed. *Reminiscences of an Active Life: The Autobiography of John Roy Lynch*. Chicago: University of Chicago Press, 1970.

———, and Meier, August, eds. *Black Leaders of the Twentieth Century*. Urbana: University of Illinois Press, 1982.

Gara, Larry. *The Liberty Line: The Legend of the Underground Railroad*. Lexington: University of Kentucky Press, 1961.

Gatewood, Willard B., Jr., ed. *Free Man of Color: The Autobiography of Willis Augustus Hodges*. Knoxville: University of Tennessee Press, 1982.

Genovese, Eugene. *Roll, Jordan, Roll: The World the Slaves Made*. New York: Pantheon Books, 1974.

Gibbs, Mifflin W. *Shadow and Light: An Autobiography with Reminiscences of the Last and Present Century*. Washington, D.C.: n.p., 1902; reprint ed., New York: Arno Press, 1968.

Goldin, Claudia. *Urban Slavery in the American South, 1820–1860: A Quantitative History*. Chicago: University of Chicago Press, 1976.

Gordon, Asa H. *Sketches of Negro Life and History in South Carolina*. n.p.: W. P. Conkey Co., 1929; reprint ed., Columbia: University of South Carolina Press, 1971.

Graham, Leroy. *Baltimore: The Nineteenth Century Black Capital*. New York: University Press of America, 1982.

Gray, Lewis. *History of Agriculture in the Southern United States to 1860*. 2 vols. Washington, D.C.: Carnegie Institution, 1933; reprint ed., New York: Peter Smith, 1941.

Green, Constance M. *The Secret City: A History of Race Relations in the Nation's Capital*. Princeton, N.J.: Princeton University Press, 1967.

Gutman, Herbert. *The Black Family in Slavery and Freedom, 1750–1925*. New York: Pantheon Books, 1976.

Hamilton, Green Polonius. *Beacon Lights of the Race*. Memphis: F. H. Clarke and Brothers, 1911.

Hamilton, Thomas. *Men and Manners in America*. London: T. Cadell, 1833.

Harlan, Louis R. *Booker T. Washington: The Wizard of Tuskegee, 1901–1915*. New York: Oxford University Press, 1983.

———, and Smock, Raymond, eds. *The Booker T. Washington Papers*. 14 vols. Urbana: University of Illinois Press, 1972–89.

Harris, Abram L. *The Negro as Capitalist: A Study of Banking and Business among American Negroes.* Philadelphia: American Academy of Political and Social Science, 1936; reprint ed., New York: Arno Press, 1968.

Hartshorn, W. N., ed. *An Era of Progress and Promise, 1863–1910.* Boston: Priscilla Publishing Co., 1910.

Hening, William, ed. *The Statutes at Large, Being a Collection of all the Laws of Virginia.* 13 vols.; facsimile reprint ed., Charlottesville: University of Virginia Press, 1969.

Hermann, Janet S. *The Pursuit of a Dream.* New York: Oxford University Press, 1981.

Herrenkohl, Roy C., and Shade, William G., eds. *Seven on Black: Reflections on the Negro Experience in America.* Philadelphia: J. B. Lippincott Co., 1969.

Higgs, Robert. *Competition and Coercion: Blacks in the American Economy, 1865–1914.* London: Cambridge University Press, 1977.

Hogan, William, and Davis, Edwin, eds. *William Johnson's Natchez: The Antebellum Diary of a Free Negro.* Baton Rouge: Louisiana State University Press, 1951.

Holland, Edward. *A Refutation of the Calumnies Circulated against the Southern and Western States, Respecting the Institutions and Existence of Slavery among Them.* Charleston: A. E. Miller, 1822.

Holt, Thomas. *Black over White: Negro Political Leadership in South Carolina during Reconstruction.* Urbana: University of Illinois Press, 1977.

Hood, Aurelius P. *The Negro at Mound Bayou.* Nashville: AME Sunday School Union, 1910.

Huggins, Nathan I. *Black Odyssey: The Afro-American Ordeal in Slavery.* New York: Oxford University Press, 1977.

Jackson, Luther P. *Free Negro Labor and Property Holding in Virginia, 1830–1860.* New York: D. Appleton Co., 1942.

Jernegan, Marcus. *Laboring and Dependent Classes in Colonial America.* Chicago: University of Chicago Press, 1931.

Johnson, Michael P., and Roark, James L. *Black Masters: A Free Family of Color in the Old South.* New York: W. W. Norton and Co., 1984.

Johnston, James H. *Race Relations in Virginia and Miscegenation in the South, 1776–1860.* Foreword by Winthrop Jordan. Amherst: University of Massachusetts Press, 1970.

Jones, Charles C. *The Religious Instruction of the Negroes in the United States.* Savannah: T. Purse, 1842.

Jordan, Winthrop. *White over Black: American Attitudes toward the Negro, 1550–1812.* Chapel Hill: University of North Carolina Press, 1968.

Joyner, Charles. *Down by the Riverside: A South Carolina Slave Community.* Urbana: University of Illinois Press, 1984.

Karl, Bernhard. *Travels through North America, during the Years 1825 and 1826.* 2 vols. Philadelphia: Carey, Lea and Carey, 1828.

Kemble, Frances A. *Journal of a Residence on a Georgia Plantation in 1838–1839.* New York: Harper and Brothers, 1863; reprint ed., ed. John A. Scott. Athens: University of Georgia Press, 1984.

Klingman, Peter D. *Josiah Walls: Florida's Black Congressman of Reconstruction.* Gainesville: University of Florida Press, 1976.

Koger, Larry. *Black Slaveowners: Free Black Slave Masters in South Carolina, 1790–1860.* Jefferson, N.C.: McFarland and Company, 1985.

Kulikoff, Allan. *Tobacco and Slaves: The Development of Southern Cultures in the Chesapeake, 1680–1800.* Chapel Hill: University of North Carolina Press, 1986.

Lamon, Lester C. *Black Tennesseans, 1900–1930.* Knoxville: University of Tennessee Press, 1977.

Levine, Lawrence W. *Black Culture and Black Consciousness: Afro-American Folk Thought from Slavery to Freedom.* New York: Oxford University Press, 1977.

Liancourt, Duke de la Rouchefoucault. *Travels through the United States of North America the Country of the Iroquois and Upper Canada in the Years 1795, 1796, and 1797.* London: R. Phillips, 1799.

Lindsay, Arnett G., and Woodson, Carter G., eds. *The Negro as a Business Man.* Washington, D.C.: Association for the Study of Negro Life and History, 1929; reprint ed., New York: Arno Press, 1969.

Litwack, Leon. *Been in the Storm so Long: The Aftermath of Slavery.* New York: Alfred A. Knopf, 1979.

Logan, Frenise. *The Negro in North Carolina, 1876–1894.* Chapel Hill: University of North Carolina Press, 1964.

Logan, Rayford W. *The Negro in American Life and Thought: The Nadir, 1877–1901.* New York: Macmillan, 1954; enlarged ed., titled *The Betrayal of the Negro: From Rutherford B. Hayes to Woodrow Wilson.* New York: Collier Books, 1965.

Lynch, Hollis. *The Black Urban Condition: A Documentary History, 1866–1971.* New York: Thomas Y. Crowell Co., 1973.

McCrary, Peyton. *Abraham Lincoln and Reconstruction: The Louisiana Experiment.* Princeton: Princeton University Press, 1978.

MacLeod, Duncan J. *Slavery, Race and the American Revolution.* London: Cambridge University Press, 1974.

McPherson, Edward. *The Political History of the United States of America During the Period of Reconstruction.* Washington, D.C.: Solomons and Chapman, 1875; reprint ed., New York: Negro Universities Press, 1969.

McPherson, James M., ed. *The Negro's Civil War.* New York: Vintage Books, 1965.

———. *Ordeal by Fire: The Civil War and Reconstruction.* New York: Alfred A. Knopf, 1982.

———. *The Struggle for Equality: Abolitionists and the Negro in the Civil War and Reconstruction.* Princeton: Princeton University Press, 1964.

Major, Gerri. *Black Society.* Chicago: Johnson Publishing Co., 1976.

Mandle, Jay R. *The Roots of Black Poverty: The Southern Plantation Economy after the Civil War.* Durham: Duke University Press, 1978.

Mbiti, John. *African Religions and Philosophy.* New York: Praeger Publishers, 1969; Anchor Book ed., New York: Doubleday and Co., 1970.

Meier, August. *Negro Thought in America, 1880–1915: Racial Ideologies in the Age of Booker T. Washington*. Ann Arbor: University of Michigan Press, 1963.

Melbourn, Julius. *Life and Opinions of Julius Melbourn*. Syracuse: Hall and Dickson, 1847.

Menn, Joseph. *The Large Slaveholders of Louisiana—1860*. New Orleans: Pelican Publishing Co., 1964.

Miller, Floyd J. *The Search for a Black Nationality: Black Emigration and Colonization, 1787–1863*. Urbana: University of Illinois Press, 1975.

Miller, Randall M., ed. *"Dear Master": Letters of a Slave Family*. Ithaca, N.Y.: Cornell University Press, 1978.

Mills, Gary B. *The Forgotten People: Cane River's Creoles of Color*. Baton Rouge: Louisiana State University Press, 1977.

Mintz, Sidney W. *Caribbean Transformation*. Chicago: Aldine Publishing Co., 1974.

———, and Price, Richard. *An Anthropological Approach to the Afro-American Past: A Caribbean Perspective*. Philadelphia: Institute for the Study of Human Issues, 1976.

Mobley, Joe A. *James City: A Black Community in North Carolina, 1863–1900*. Raleigh: North Carolina Department of Cultural Resources, 1981.

Morgan, Edmund S. *American Slavery American Freedom: The Ordeal of Colonial Virginia*. New York: W. W. Norton and Co., 1975.

Myers, Robert, ed. *The Children of Pride: A True Story of Georgia and the Civil War*. New Haven: Yale University Press, 1972.

Mullin, Gerald W. *Flight and Rebellion: Slave Resistance in Eighteenth-Century Virginia*. New York: Oxford University Press, 1972.

Newton, Alexander H. *Out of the Briars: An Autobiography and Sketch of the Twenty-ninth Regiment, Connecticut Volunteers*. Philadelphia: African Methodist Episcopal Book Concern, 1910.

Olmsted, Frederick Law. *The Cotton Kingdom: a Traveller's Observations on Cotton and Slavery in the American Slave States*. Edited by Arthur M. Schlesinger. New York: Alfred A. Knopf, 1953.

———. *A Journey in the Seaboard Slave States*. New York: Dix and Edwards, 1856.

———. *Journey through Texas or, a Saddle-Trip on the Southwestern Frontier*. New York: Dix, Edwards and Co., 1857; reprint ed., *The Slave States*. Edited by Harvey Wish. New York: Capricorn Books, 1959.

Osthaus, Carl R. *Freedmen, Philanthropy, and Fraud: A History of the Freedman's Savings Bank*. Urbana: University of Illinois Press, 1976.

Oubre, Claude. *Forty Acres and a Mule: The Freedmen's Bureau and Black Land Ownership*. Baton Rouge: Louisiana State University Press, 1978.

Owens, Leslie H. *This Species of Property: Slave Life and Culture in the Old South*. New York: Oxford University Press, 1976.

Painter, Nell Irvin. *Exodusters: Black Migration to Kansas after Reconstruction*. New York: Alfred A. Knopf, 1976.

Parton, James. *General Butler in New Orleans: History of the Administration of the Department of the Gulf in the Year 1862*. Boston: Houghton, Mifflin and Co., 1863.

Pessen, Edward. *Riches, Class, and Power before the Civil War*. Boston: D. C. Heath and Company, 1973.

Phillips, Ulrich B. *American Negro Slavery: A Survey of the Supply, Employment, and Control of Negro Labor as Determined by the Plantation Regime*. New York: D. Appleton and Co., 1918.

Pitre, Merline. *Through Many Dangers Toils and Snares: Black Leadership in Texas, 1868–1900*. Austin: Eakin Press, 1985.

Quarles, Benjamin. *Black Abolitionists*. New York: Oxford University Press, 1969.

———. *Lincoln and the Negro*. New York: Oxford University Press, 1962.

———. *The Negro in the American Revolution*. Chapel Hill: University of North Carolina Press, 1974.

Rabinowitz, Howard. *Race Relations in the Urban South, 1865–1890*. New York: Oxford University Press, 1978.

———, ed. *Southern Black Leaders of the Reconstruction Era*. Urbana: University of Illinois Press, 1982.

Ransom, Roger L., and Sutch, Richard. *One Kind of Freedom: The Economic Consequences of Emancipation*. London: Cambridge University Press, 1977.

Rawick, George, ed. *The American Slave: A Composite Autobiography*. 19 vols. Westport, Conn.: Greenwood Publishing Co., 1972.

Reid, Whitelaw. *After the War: A Tour of the Southern States, 1865–1866*. New York: Moore, Wilstach and Baldwin, 1866; reprint ed., ed. C. Vann Woodward. New York: Harper and Row, 1965.

Rice, Lawrence D. *The Negro in Texas, 1874–1900*. Baton Rouge: Louisiana State University Press, 1971.

Richardson, Joe M. *Christian Reconstruction: The American Missionary Association and Southern Blacks, 1861–1890*. Athens: University of Georgia Press, 1986.

Richings, G. F. *Evidences of Progress among Colored People*. Philadelphia: George S. Ferguson Co., 1905.

Robertson, James, ed. *Louisiana under the Rule of Spain, France, and the United States, 1785–1807: Social, Economic, and Political Conditions of the Territory Represented in the Louisiana Purchase*. 2 vols. Cleveland: Arthur H. Clark Co., 1910–11; reprint ed., Freeport, N.Y.: Books for Libraries Press, 1969.

Rogers, George, Jr. *The History of Georgetown County, South Carolina*. Columbia: University of South Carolina Press, 1970.

———, and Chesnut, David R., eds. *The Papers of Henry Laurens*. 9 vols. Columbia: University of South Carolina Press, 1968.

Rouse, J. E. *The Noble Experiment of Warren C. Coleman*. Charlotte, N.C.: Crabtree Press, 1972.

Rudd, Daniel A., and Bond, Theophilus. *From Slavery to Wealth: The Life of*

Scott Bond. Madison, Ark.: Journal Printing Co., 1917; reprint ed., Freeport, N.Y.: Books for Libraries Press, 1971.

Russell, John H. *The Free Negro in Virginia, 1619–1865.* Baltimore: Johns Hopkins University Press, 1913.

Russell, Robert. *North America. Its Agriculture and Climate: Containing Observations on the Agriculture and Climate of Canada, the United States, and the Island of Cuba.* Edinburgh: A. and C. Black, 1857.

Schweninger, Loren, ed. *From Tennessee Slave to St. Louis Entrepreneur: The Autobiography of James Thomas.* Columbia: University of Missouri Press, 1984.

―――. *James T. Rapier and Reconstruction.* Chicago: University of Chicago Press, 1978.

Sherman, William T. *Memoirs of Gen. W. T. Sherman, Written by Himself, With an Appendix, Bringing His Life Down to Its Closing Scenes, Also a Personal Tribute and Critique of the Memoirs.* 4th ed., ed. James G. Blaine, 2 vols. New York: Charles L. Webster and Co., 1891.

Shick, Tom W. *Behold the Promised Land: A History of Afro-American Settler Society in Nineteenth-Century Liberia.* Baltimore: Johns Hopkins University Press, 1977.

Shippee, Lester, ed. *Bishop Whipple's Southern Diary, 1843–1844.* Minneapolis: University of Minnesota Press, 1937.

Siebert, Wilbur H. *The Underground Railroad: From Slavery to Freedom.* New York: Macmillan Co., 1898; reprint ed., New York: Russell and Russell, 1967.

Simmons, William. *Men of Mark: Eminent, Progressive and Rising.* Cleveland: Rewell Publishing Co., 1887.

Simon, John, ed. *The Papers of Ulysses S. Grant.* 14 vols. Carbondale and Edwardsville: Southern Illinois University Press, 1985.

Smith, D. E. H., and Salley, Alexander, eds. *Register of St. Phillip's Parish, Charles Towne, or Charleston, S.C., 1754–1810.* Columbia: University of South Carolina Press, 1971.

Smith, Julia F. *Slavery and Rice Culture in Low Country Georgia, 1750–1860.* Knoxville: University of Tennessee Press, 1985.

Soltow, Lee. *Men and Wealth in the United States, 1850–1870.* New Haven: Yale University Press, 1975.

Stampp, Kenneth. *The Peculiar Institution: Slavery in the Ante-Bellum South.* New York: Vintage Books, 1956.

Starobin, Robert. *Industrial Slavery in the Old South.* New York: Oxford University Press, 1970.

Sterkx, Herbert E. *The Free Negro in Ante-Bellum Louisiana.* Rutherford, N.J.: Fairleigh Dickinson University Press, 1972.

Stuart, Merah S. *An Economic Detour: A History of Insurance in the Lives of American Negroes.* New York: W. Malliet and Co., 1940; reprint ed., College Park, Md.: McGrath Publishing Co., 1969.

Tate, Thad W., Jr. *The Negro in Eighteenth Century Williamsburg.* Williamsburg, Va.: Colonial Williamsburg, 1965.

Taylor, Alrutheus A. *The Negro in the Reconstruction of Virginia*. Washington, D.C.: Association for the Study of Negro Life and History, 1926.

Taylor, Rosser Howard. *The Free Negro in North Carolina*. Chapel Hill: University of North Carolina Press, 1920.

Tindall, George B. *South Carolina Negroes, 1877–1900*. Columbia: University of South Carolina Press, 1952.

Tocqueville, Alexis, de. *Democracy in America*. 2 vols. Paris: Charles Gosselin, 1835; reprint ed., ed. J. P. Mayer and Max Lerner. Translated by George Lawrence. New York: Harper and Row, 1966.

Towne, Laura. *Letters and Diary of Laura M. Towne: Written from the Sea Islands of South Carolina*. Edited by Rupert Holland. Cambridge: Riverside Press, 1912; reprint ed., New York: Vintage Books, 1967.

Trelease, Allen. *White Terror: The Ku Klux Klan Conspiracy and Southern Reconstruction*. London: Secker and Warburg, 1972.

Trowbridge, John T. *The Desolate South, 1865–1866; A Picture of the Battlefields and of the Devastated Confederacy*. Hartford, Conn.: I. Sterbins, 1866; reprint ed., ed. Gordon Carroll. Boston: Little, Brown and Co., 1956.

Tucker, St. George. *A Dissertation on Slavery: With a Proposal for the Gradual Abolition of It in the State of Virginia*. Philadelphia: Mathew Carey, 1796; reprint ed., New York: n.p., 1861.

Vass, L. C. *History of the Presbyterian Church of New Bern, N.C.*. Richmond, Va.: Whittet and Shepperson, 1886.

Wade, Richard C. *Slavery in the Cities: The South, 1820–1860*. New York: Oxford University Press, 1964.

Walker, David. *David Walker's Appeal to the Colored Citizens of the World*. Boston: D. Walker, 1829; reprint ed., ed. Charles M. Wilste. New York: Hill and Wang, 1965.

Walker, Juliet E. K. *Free Frank: A Black Pioneer on the Antebellum Frontier*. Lexington, Ky.: University of Kentucky Press, 1983.

Washington, Booker T. *The Negro in Business*. Chicago: Hertel, Jenkins and Co., 1907; reprint ed., New York: AMS Press, 1971.

Weare, Walter B. *Black Business in the New South: A Social History of the North Carolina Mutual Life Insurance Company*. Urbana: University of Illinois Press, 1973.

Webber, Thomas L. *Deep Like the Rivers: Education in the Slave Quarter Community, 1831–1865*. New York: W. W. Norton and Co., 1978.

Wesley, Charles H. *Negro Labor in the United States, 1850–1925*. New York: Vanguard Press, 1927.

Wharton, Vernon Lane. *The Negro in Mississippi, 1865–1890*. Chapel Hill: University of North Carolina Press, 1947.

Whitten, David O. *Andrew Durnford: A Black Sugar Planter in Antebellum Louisiana*. Natchitoches: Northwestern Louisiana State University Press, 1981.

Wiener, Jonathan M. *Social Origins of the New South: Alabama, 1860–1885*. Baton Rouge: Louisiana State University Press, 1978.

Wikramanayake, Marina. *A World in Shadow: The Free Black in Antebellum South Carolina.* Columbia: University of South Carolina Press, 1973.

Wiley, Bell, ed. *Slaves No More: Letters from Liberia, 1833–1869.* Lexington: University of Kentucky Press, 1980.

Williamson, Joel. *After Slavery: The Negro in South Carolina during Reconstruction, 1861–1877.* Chapel Hill: University of North Carolina Press, 1965.

Wood, Peter. *Black Majority: Negroes in Colonial South Carolina from 1670 through the Stono Rebellion.* New York: W. W. Norton and Co., 1974.

Woodson, Carter G. *Free Negro Owners of Slaves in the United States in 1830; Together with Absentee Ownership of Slaves in the United States in 1830.* Washington: Association for the Study of Negro Life and History, 1924; reprint ed., Westport, Conn.: Negro Universities Press, 1968.

Woodward, C. Vann. *The Strange Career of Jim Crow.* New York: Oxford University Press, 1955.

Wright, George C. *Life Behind a Veil: Blacks in Louisville, Kentucky, 1865–1930.* Baton Rouge: Louisiana State University Press, 1985.

Wright, James. *The Free Negro in Maryland, 1634–1860.* New York: Columbia University Press, 1921; reprint ed., New York: Octagon Books, 1971.

Articles

Alford, Terry. "Some Manumissions Recorded in the Adams County Deed Books in Chancery Clerk's Office, Natchez, Mississippi, 1795–18[5]5." *JMH* 33 (February 1971): 39–50.

Alsobrook, David E. "Mobile's Forgotten Progressive—A. N. Johnson, Editor and Entrepreneur." *Alabama Review* 32 (July 1979): 188–202.

Bacote, Clarence A. "Some Aspects of Negro Life in Georgia, 1880–1908." *JNH* 43 (July 1958): 186–213.

Baker, H. E. "Some Reasons for the Colored Man's Lack of Commercial Ability." *Southern Workman* 27 (September 1898): 188–89.

Beasley, Jonathan. "Blacks—Slave and Free—Vicksburg, 1850–60." *JMH* 28 (February 1976): 1–32.

Beatty-Brown, Florence. "Legal Status of Arkansas Negroes before Emancipation." *AHQ* 28 (Spring 1969): 6–13

Bellamy, Donnie. "Free Blacks in Antebellum Missouri, 1820–1860." *MHR* 67 (January 1973): 198–225.

Bergeron, Arthur W., Jr. "Free Men of Color in Gray." *CWH* 32 (September 1986): 247–55.

Berlin, Ira. "The Structure of the Free Negro Caste in the Antebellum United States." *JSoH* 9 (Spring 1976): 297–319.

———. "Time, Space, and the Evolution of Afro-American Society on British Mainland North America." *AHR* 85 (February 1980): 44–78.

Berry, Mary F. "Negro Troops in Blue and Gray: The Louisiana Native Guards, 1861–63." *LH* 8 (Spring 1967): 165–90.

Bisher, Catherine W. "Black Builders in Antebellum North Carolina." *NCHR* 61 (October 1984): 423–58.

Bonekemper, Edward H. "Negro Ownership of Real Property in Hampton and Elizabeth City County, Virginia, 1860–1870." *JNH* 55 (July 1970): 165–81.

Boyd, William, ed. "Some North Carolina Tracts of the Eighteenth Century." *NCHR* 3 (October 1926): 591–621.

Bradford, Samuel. "The Negro Ironworker in Ante Bellum Virginia." *JSH* 25 (May 1959): 194–206.

Brewer, James H. "Negro Property Owners in Seventeenth Century Virginia." *WMQ*, 3d ser., 12 (October 1955): 575–80.

Brooks, Walter H. "The Priority of the Silver Bluffs Church and Its Promoters." *JNH* 7 (July 1922): 172–96.

Browning, James. "The Free Negro in Ante-Bellum North Carolina." *NCHR* 15 (January 1938): 23–33.

Chase, Judith Wragg. "American Heritage from Ante-Bellum Black Craftsmen." *Southern Folklore Quarterly* 42 (1978): 135–58.

Christensen, Lawrence O. "Cyprian Clamorgan, The Colored Aristocracy of St. Louis (1858)." *Bulletin of the Missouri Historical Society* 31 (October 1974): 3–31.

———. "Race Relations in St. Louis, 1865–1916." *MHR* 77 (January 1984): 123–36.

Corlew, Robert E. "Some Aspects of Slavery in Dickson County." *THQ* 10 (September 1951): 224–48.

Cox, LaWanda. "The Promise of Land for the Freedmen." *MVHR* 45 (December 1958): 413–40.

Davis, John. "George Liele and Andrew Bryan: Pioneer Negro Preachers." *JNH* 3 (April 1918):119–27.

Dew, Charles. "David Ross and the Oxford Iron Works: A Study of Industrial Slavery in the Early Nineteenth-Century South." *WMQ*, 3d ser., 31 (April 1974): 189–224.

———. "Disciplining Slave Iron Workers in the Antebellum South: Coercion, Conciliation, and Accommodation." *AHR* 79 (April 1974): 393–418.

Eaton, Clement. "Slave-Hiring in the Upper South: A Step toward Freedom." *MVHR* 46 (March 1960): 663–78.

England, J. Merton. "The Free Negro in Ante-Bellum Tennessee." *JSH* 9 (February 1943): 37–58.

Everett, Donald. "Emigrés and Militiamen: Free Persons of Color in New Orleans, 1803–1815." *JNH* 38 (October 1953): 377–402.

———. "Free Persons of Color in Colonial Louisiana." *LH* 7 (Winter 1966): 21–50.

Fisher, James S. "Negro Farm Ownership in the South." *Annals of the Association of American Geographers* 63 (December 1973): 478–89.

Fitchett, E. Horace. "The Origin and Growth of the Free Negro Population of Charleston, South Carolina." *JNH* 26 (October 1941): 421–37.

————. "The Status of the Free Negro in Charleston, South Carolina, and His Descendants in Modern Society." *JNH* 32 (October 1947): 430–51.

————. "A Successful Negro Grocer." *Southern Workman* 62 (December 1933): 461–67.

————. "The Traditions of the Free Negro in Charleston, South Carolina." *JNH* 25 (April 1940): 139–52.

Flanders, Ralph. "The Free Negro in Ante-Bellum Georgia." *NCHR* 9 (July 1932): 250–72.

Foner, Laura. "The Free People of Color in Louisiana and St. Domingue: A Comparative Portrait of Two Three-Caste Slave Societies." *JSoH* 3 (Summer 1970): 406–40.

Franklin, John Hope. "The Free Negro in the Economic Life of Ante-Bellum North Carolina." *NCHR* 19 (July and October 1942): 239–59, 359–75.

————. "James Boon, Free Negro Artisan." *JNH* 30 (April 1945): 150–80.

————. "Slaves Virtually Free in Ante-Bellum North Carolina." *JNH* 28 (July 1943): 284–310.

Frey, Sylvia. "Between Slavery and Freedom: Virginia Blacks in the American Revolution." *JSH* 59 (August 1983): 375–98.

Gatewood, Willard B., Jr. "Theodore Roosevelt and Southern Republicans: The Case of South Carolina, 1901–1904." *SCHM* 70 (October 1969): 251–66.

————. "'To Be Truly Free': Louis Sheridan and the Colonization of Liberia." *CWH* 29 (December 1983): 332–48

————. "William D. Crum, A Negro in Politics." *JNH* 53 (October 1968): 301–20.

Goodstein, Anita. "Black History on the Nashville Frontier, 1780–1810." *THQ* 30 (Winter 1979): 401–20.

Green, Barbara. "Slave Labor at the Maramec Iron Works, 1828–50." *MHR* 78 (January 1979): 150–64.

Greene, Lorenzo. "Self-Purchase by Negroes in Cole County, Missouri." *Midwest Journal* 1 (Winter 1948): 83–85.

Halliburton, R., Jr. "Free Black Owners of Slaves: A Reappraisal of the Woodson Thesis." *SCHM* 76 (July 1975): 129–42.

Harris, Robert L., Jr. "Charleston's Free Afro-American Elite: The Brown Fellowship Society and the Humane Brotherhood." *SCHM* 82 (October 1981): 289–310.

Higgs, Robert. "Accumulation of Property by Southern Blacks before World War I." *AER* 72 (September 1982): 725–37.

————. "Accumulation of Property by Southern Blacks before World War I: Reply." *AER* 74 (September 1984): 777–82.

Hoffman, Edwin D. "From Slavery to Self-Reliance: The Record of Achievement of the Freedmen of the Sea Island Region." *JNH* 41 (January 1956): 8–42.

Holmes, Jack D. L. "The Role of Blacks in Spanish Alabama: The Mobile District, 1780–1813." *Alabama Historical Quarterly* 37 (Spring 1975): 5–18.

Howington, Arthur. "'A property of special and peculiar value': The Tennessee Supreme Court and the Law of Manumission." *THQ* 44 (Fall 1985): 302–17.

Hunter, Lloyd. "Slavery in St. Louis, 1804–1860." *Missouri Historical Society Bulletin* 30 (July 1974): 233–65.

Jackson, Luther Porter. "Free Negroes of Petersburg, Virginia." *JNH* 12 (July 1927): 365–88.

———. "Manumission in Certain Virginia Cities." *JNH* 15 (July 1930): 278–314.

———. "The Virginia Free Negro Farmer and Property Owner, 1830–1860." *JNH* 24 (October 1939): 390–489.

Johnson, Whittington B. "Free Blacks in Antebellum Savannah: An Economic Profile." *GHQ* 64 (Winter 1980): 418–31

Kedro, James, and Day, Judy. "Free Blacks in St. Louis: Antebellum Conditions, Emancipation, and the Postwar Era." *Bulletin of the Missouri Historical Society* 30 (January 1974): 117–35.

Kimmel, Ross M. "Free Blacks in Seventeenth-Century Maryland." *MHM* 71 (Spring 1976): 19–25.

Klebaner, Benjamin. "American Manumission Laws and the Responsibility for Supporting Slaves." *VMHB* 63 (October 1955): 443–53.

Kolchin, Peter. "Reevaluating the Antebellum Slave Community: A Comparative Perspective." *JAH* 70 (December 1983): 579–601.

Kulikoff, Allan. "The Origins of Afro-American Society in Tidewater Maryland and Virginia, 1700 to 1790." *WMQ*, 3d ser., 35 (April 1978): 225–59.

———. "A 'Prolifick' People: Black Population Growth in the Chesapeake Colonies, 1700–1790." *Southern Studies* 16 (Winter 1977): 391–428.

Leslie, James W. "Ferd Havis: Jefferson County's Black Republican Leader." *AHQ* 37 (Autumn 1978): 240–51.

McDonnell, Lawrence T. "Money Knows No Master: Market Relations and the American Slave Community." In *Developing Dixie: Modernization in a Traditional Society*. Ed. Winfred B. Moore, Jr., et al., Westport, Conn.: Greenwood Press, 1988.

Mann, Kenneth E. "Blanche Kelso Bruce: United States Senator without a Constituency." *JMH* 38 (May 1976): 183–98.

Margo, Robert A. "Accumulation of Property by Southern Blacks before World War I: Comment and Further Evidence." *AER* 74 (September 1984): 768–76.

Mathews, Donald G. "Charles Colcock Jones and the Southern Evangelical Crusade to Form a Biracial Community." *JSH* 41 (August 1975): 299–320.

Meier, August, and Rudwick, Elliott. "Negro Boycotts of Segregated Streetcars in Virginia, 1904–1907." *VMHB* 81 (October 1973): 479–87.

Miller, Randall. "Georgia on Their Minds: Free Blacks and the African Colonization Movement in Georgia." *Southern Studies* 12 (Winter 1973): 349–62.

Moore, John Hebron. "Simon Gray, Riverman: A Slave Who Was Almost Free." *MVHR* 49 (December 1962): 472–84.

Morgan, Edmund S. "Headrights and Headcounts: A Review Article." *VMHB* 80 (July 1972): 361–71.

———. "Slavery and Freedom: The American Paradox." *JAH* 59 (June 1972): 5–29.

Morgan, Philip D. "Black Life in Eighteenth-Century Charleston." *Perspectives in American History*, N.S., 1 (1984): 187–232.

———. "The Ownership of Property by Slaves in the Mid-Nineteenth-Century Low Country." *JSH* 49 (August 1983): 399–420.

———. "Work and Culture: The Task System and the World of Lowcountry Blacks, 1700–1800." *WMQ*, 3d ser., 35 (October 1982): 563–99.

Morris, Richard B. "The Course of Peonage in a Slave State." *Political Science Quarterly* 65 (June 1950): 238–63.

———. "Labor Controls in Maryland in the Nineteenth Century." *JSH* 14 (August 1948): 385–400.

———. "The Measure of Bondage in the Slave States." *MVHR* 41 (September 1954): 219–40.

Muir, Andrew. "The Free Negro in Jefferson and Orange Counties, Texas." *JNH* 35 (April 1950): 183–206.

Nash, Roy. "The Lynching of Anthony Crawford." *Independent* 88 (December 11, 1916): 456–62.

O'Brien, John T. "Factory, Church, and Community: Blacks in Antebellum Richmond." *JSH* 44 (November 1978): 509–36.

Parsons, Joseph. "Anthony Odinsells: A Romance of Little Wassaw." *GHQ* 55 (Summer 1971): 208–21.

Rankin, David. "The Impact of the Civil War on the Free Colored Community of New Orleans." *Perspectives in American History* 11 (1977–78): 379–418.

———. "The Origins of Black Leadership in New Orleans During Reconstruction." *JSH* 40 (August 1974): 417–40.

Reinders, Robert C. "The Decline of the New Orleans Free Negro in the Decade before the Civil War." *JMH* 24 (April 1962): 88–98.

———. "The Free Negro in the New Orleans Economy, 1850–60." *LH* 6 (Summer 1965): 273–86.

Richardson, Clement. "The Nestor of Negro Bankers." *Southern Workman* 43 (November 1914): 607–11.

———. "What are Negroes Doing in Durham?" *Southern Workman* 42 (July 1913): 383–93.

Richardson, Joe M. "A Negro Success Story: James Dallas Burrus." *JNH* 50 (October 1965): 274–82.

Robinson, Henry. "Some Aspects of the Free Negro Population of Washington, D.C., 1800–1862." *MHM* 64 (Spring 1969): 43–64.

Russell, John. "Colored Freemen as Slave Owners in Virginia." *JNH* 1 (June 1916): 233–42.

Schoen, Harold. "The Free Negro in the Republic of Texas." *Southwestern Historical Quarterly* 39 (April 1936): 292–308.

Schwarz, Philip J. "Emancipators, Protectors, and Anomalies: Free Black Slaveowners in Virginia." *VMHB* 95 (July 1987): 317–38.

Schweninger, Loren. "The Free-Slave Phenomenon: James P. Thomas and the Black Community in Ante-Bellum Nashville." *CWH* 22 (December 1976): 293–307.

Simons, Albert and Harriet P. "The William Burrows House of Charleston." *SCHM* 70 (July 1969): 155–76.

Smith, C. Calvin. "John E. Bush of Arkansas, 1890–1910." *Ozark Historical Review* 2 (Spring 1973): 48–59.

Stahl, Annie. "The Free Negro in Antebellum Louisiana." *LHQ* 25 (April 1942): 300–396.

Syndor, Charles. "The Free Negro in Mississippi before the Civil War." *AHR* 33 (July 1927): 769–88.

Tansey, Richard. "Out-of-State Free Blacks in Late Antebellum New Orleans." *LH* 22 (Fall 1981): 369–86.

Taylor, Alrutheus A. "The Negro in the Reconstruction of Virginia." *JNH* 11 (July 1926): 243–415.

Thomas, David. "The Free Negro in Florida before 1865." *South Atlantic Quarterly* 10 (October 1911): 335–45.

Thomas, Herbert A., Jr. "Victims of Circumstance: Negroes in a Southern Town, 1865–1880." *Register of the Kentucky Historical Society* 71 (July 1973): 253–71.

Toplin, Robert Brent. "Between Black and White: Attitudes towards Southern Mulattoes, 1830–1861." *JSH* 45 (May 1979): 185–200.

Trabue, Charles. "The Voluntary Emancipation of Slaves in Tennessee As Reflected in the State's Legislation and Judicial Decisions." *Tennessee Historical Magazine* 4 (March 1918): 50–68.

Walker, Juliet E. K. "Racism, Slavery, and Free Enterprise: Black Entrepreneurship in the United States before the Civil War." *BHR* 60 (Autumn 1986): 343–82.

Walker, Thomas C. "The Development of the Tidewater Counties of Virginia." *Annals of the American Academy of Political and Social Science* 49 (September 1913): 28–31.

Washington, Booker T. "Durham, North Carolina: A City of Negro Enterprises." *Independent* 70 (March 1911): 642–50.

———. "The Negro in Business." *Gunton's Magazine* 20 (March 1901): 209–19.

Whitten, David O. "A Black Entrepreneur in Antebellum Louisiana." *BHR* 45 (Spring 1971): 201–19.

———, ed. "Slave Buying in Virginia as Revealed by Letters of a Louisiana Negro Sugar Planter." *LH* 11 (Summer 1970): 231–44.

Willey, Nathan. "Education of the Colored Population of Louisiana." *Harper's New Monthly Magazine* 33 (June to November 1866): 244–50.

Williams, W. T. B. "Local Conditions Among Negroes: Gloucester County, Virginia." *Southern Workman* 35 (February 1906): 103–6.

———. "Local Conditions Among Negroes: Hanover County, Virginia." *Southern Workman* 35 (March 1906): 172–75.

———. "Local Conditions Among Negroes: Prince Edward County, Virginia." *Southern Workman* 35 (April 1906): 239–44.

Wilson, Calvin D. "Black Masters: A Side-Light on Slavery." *North American Review* 181 (November 1905): 685–98.

———. "Negroes Who Owned Slaves." *Popular Science Monthly* 81 (November 1912): 484–5.

Winston, James E. "The Free Negro in New Orleans, 1803–1860." *LHQ* 21 (October 1938): 1075–85.

Woodson, Carter. "The Negroes of Cincinnati Prior to the Civil War." *JNH* 1 (January 1916): 1–22.

———, ed. "Documents: Letters to the American Colonization Society." *JNH* 10 (April 1925): 154–311.

———, ed. "Some Undistinguished Negroes." *JNH* 3 (April 1918): 196–97.

Wright, Richard R. "The Colored Man and the Small Farm." *Southern Workman* 29 (November 1900): 483–85.

Wynes, Charles E. "Thomy Lafon (1810–93): Black Philanthropist." *Midwest Quarterly* 22 (Winter 1981): 105–12.

Index

Abrahams, Emanuel, 20
Adams, George, 160
Adams, Remin, 202
Addison, William, 125
Affluent free persons of color, 97–141;
  difficulties faced by, in Lower South,
  113–15
Africa: declining influence of, among
  slaves, 59; land tenure in, 10
African Benevolent Association (Wil-
  mington, Del.), 137
African Friendship Benevolent Society
  for Social Relief (Baltimore), 137
African Methodist Episcopal Church
  (Charleston), 102
Agnes, Charles, 200
Alabama Penny Savings and Loan Com-
  pany (Birmingham), 218
Alexander, Edward, 160
Allain, Francois: as slave owner, 107
Allain, Theophile T.: as merchant, 211
Allemand, Marie, 100
Allen, Alexander, 160
Alvord, John, 36
Ambush, Enoch, 160
American Colonization Society, 91–94.
  See also Emigration
Anderson, Alfred: losses of, during Civil
  War, 197; property of, 112; as slave
  owner, 123; son of white planter, 108
Anderson, Andrew, 190
Anderson, Charles, 220
Anderson, Francis: losses of, during Civil

War, 197; property of, 112; son of
  white planter, 108
Anderson, George, 133
Anderson, James P., 197
Anderson, Samuel, 55
Andrews, William Trent, 221; attitude
  of, toward whites, 231
Angelette, Antoinette, 134
Archer, Michael, 198
Armfield, John, 89
Armstrong, James, 38
Armstrong, Martha, 160
Arnold, Richard, 32
Ashworth, Aaron, 117
Ashworth, Roseila, 117
Ashworth, William, 135
Assessment value: compared with market
  value of property, 380
Atlantic Land Company (S.C.), 165
Atwood, William, 132

Bacon, Tom, 111
Badger, Roderick D., 224
Baker, Ray Stannard, 230
Baldwin, Robert, 20, 70
Ball, Frederick, 154
Ballard, Thomas, 200
Bank of Mound Bayou (Miss.), 218
Banks, Charles, 218
Banks, Nathaniel, 191
Baptiste, Polly, 69
Barbers: comparative wealth of, 82;
  in Nashville, 50; with more than

Barbers (continued)
$2,000 erph, 124; as part of economic
elite, 217
Barksdale, W. D., 233
Barland, Andrew, 100
Barland, David, 100
Barland, John, 128; white father of,
100, 135
Barton, Timothy, 54
Bean, Elizabeth, 160
Beard, Leah, 69–70
Beaudouin, Marguerite, 100
Beauregard, Pierre, 187
Bedon, George, 25
Bell, Graham, 111
Bell, Hardy, 126
Bell, Jacob, 139
Bell, John Brown, 222
Ben, Augustin, 71
Bendon, George, 70
Benedict, Samuel, 93
Beneficial Society of Free Men of Color
(Va.), 137
Bethel African Methodist Episcopal
Church (Baltimore), 139
Bienville, Jean Baptiste, 21
Billingslea, Alfred, 217
Bingaman, Adam L., 131
Blacknall, George, 211
Blacks. See also Phenotype
—culture of: in Africa, 9–10; changes in
New World, 10–11; in United States, 1
—free, 67–71; during American Revolu-
tion, 17–18; as business people in New
Orleans, 21; during colonial period,
16–17; immigrants from the Carib-
bean, 18; laws curtailing economic ac-
tivities of, 64–65; ownership of slaves
among, 104–8; population growth of,
18; in postwar Lower South, 149–50,
190–95; precautions of women about
marriage, 85; purchase of relatives, 66;
relationship with whites, 87–90; sold
into slavery, 89; views of, concerning
emigration, 91; as Virginia freeholders, 16. See also Business; Emigration;
Laws; Slave owners, black; Women
Bland, James M., 129
Blodgett, J. H., 222
Blount, Raford, 228
Blyden, Edward Wilmot, 231

Bolzius, Johann Martin, 14
Bond, Scott: moves to Arkansas, 209;
and racial etiquette, 227–28
Bonneau, Harriet Ann, 127
Bonneau, Mary Elizabeth, 127
Bonneau, Thomas S., 127; as teacher,
129
Booker, Robert, 204
Boon, James, 88–89
Bordan, Wallace, 90
Bowdoin, John T., 65
Boyce, Stansbury, 178
Boyd, Richard Henry, 219
Boyer, Shadrack, 140
Braddock, Thomas, 138
Bradford, Thomas, 223
Brander, Shadrack, 111
Briscoe, Palmer, 204
Broadfoot, W. G., 87
Brown, Billy, 47
Brown, Daniel, 87
Brown, Godfrey, 65
Brown, Malcolm, 115
Brown, Peter, 115
Brown, Samuel, 140
Browne, William Washington, 219
Brown Fellowship Society (Charleston),
102, 127
Browning, Sophia, 66
Bruce, Blanche Kelso: as plantation
owner, 211; and white society in Wash-
ington, D.C., 230
Bruce, Harrington, 154
Bryan, Andrew, 27, 227; letter of,
241–42; uncle of Andrew Marshall,113
Bryant, Cody, 209–10
Bryant, Sherod: children of, 198; prop-
erty of, 112; as slave owner, 110
Burchett, John, 126
Bureau of Refugees, Freedmen, and
Abandoned Lands, 36, 152
Burlard, Etienne, 134
Burlard, Harriet, 134
Burle, Charlotte, 100
Burroughs (Ga.), 165
Burrus, James Dallas, 224
Burts, R. M., 234
Bush, John E., 231; attitude of, toward
whites, 231–32; and black-owned
property in Little Rock, 168; political
activities of, 225; real estate of, 222

Business, black: clientele of, 131, 178, 220; free blacks engaged in, 21, 109, 131; laws prohibiting free blacks from engaging in, 64; in New South cities, 167–68; Roberts, Colson, and Company (Va. and Liberia), 109; slaves engaged in, 47–51; in Upper and Lower South, compared, 178–79. *See also* Occupations
Butcher, William, 77
Butler, John, 57

Cabell, Aaron, 225
Cain, Richard, 224
Caldwell, Rubin, 198
Calloway, Mariah, 31
Cambell, Shelborne, 88
Campbell, Robert, 10
Camps, J., 118
Canal, Louis, 71
Cane, Sebastian, 15
Cane River Creoles of color, 97; economic decline of, 113. *See also* Natchitoches Parish
Cann, McKinny, 234
Capital Savings Bank (Washington, D.C.), 172, 218
Cardozo, Francis, 224
Carr, Benjamin, 209
Carr, Julian S., 226
Carrol, Mary, 40, 41
Carter, Farish, 88
Carter, Henry, 66
Casenave, Pierre A. D., 218; bequest to, 101; prosperity of, during 1850s, 117
Casor, John, 16
Catholicism: among free blacks in Louisiana, 103, 130
Catron, John, 87
Census. *See* U.S. Population Census
Chappin, Edward H., 43
Charleston Land Company, 165
Charleston (S.C.): decline of, as center of free Negro artisans, 149; as early center of property owners, 20; free black artisans in, 70; quasi-free slaves in, 48–49; self-hire in, 13, 41, 42; white guardians in, 90, 132, 247–57
Charleville, Louis, 110
Charnock, Thomas, 70
Chastang, Bastile: white father of, 100

Chastang, John, 100
Chastang, Zeno: prosperity of, during 1850s, 116; as slave owner, 104; white father of, 100
Chavis, Abraham, 135
Chavis, Josiah, 135
Cheatham, Anderson, 137
Cheatham, Lucy Ann, 132. *See also* Hagan, Lucy Ann
Chiles, Sally, 85
Christopher, Charles, 154
Church, Robert Reed, 219; attitude of, toward education, 229; career of, 219–20; property in Washington, D.C., 222; white father of, 224
Church, Robert Reed, Jr.: early schooling of, 229
Churches. *See* Religion
Cities. *See* Urban
Civil War, 57, 60; and property owners in Lower South, 190–92; support of Confederacy among prosperous free persons of color, 187–88
Clamorgan, Cyprian: pamphlet of, 97; white ancestry of, 109
Clamorgan, Eutrope, 108
Clamorgan, Henry: as James Thomas's friend, 137; as St. Louis barber, 124; white ancestry of, 109
Clamorgan, Jacques: as Spanish fur trader, 109
Clamorgan, Louis, 109
Clamorgan, Louisa, 109
Clamorgan, Pelagie, 108. *See also* Rutgers, Pelagie
Clark, Robert, 124
Clarke, James Freeman, 97
Clash, James, 125
Clauston, Joseph, 200; as Memphis barber, 124
Clay, Charlotte, 129
Clay, Henry, 43
Clay, John Francis: sends daughter to France for schooling, 129
Clay, John Racquet: expands wealth during Civil War, 193; suicide of, 194
Cobbs, N. H. 91
Cocks, John H., 54
Cohabitation: in Lower South, 134–35
See also Interracial mixing
Cohen, Walter, 222, 225

Coincoin, Marie Thereze, 101
Colbert, Charlotte, 100
Cole, Thom, 219
Cole, Thomas, 20, 21; petition of,
   247–48
Cole, William, 200
Coleman, Warren Clay, 224; assisted by
   whites, 226
Collier, H. W., 91, 131
Collin, Henry, 71
Collins, Elias, 23; children of, 190; as
   slave owner, 104
Collins, Elizabeth Holman: prosperity of,
   during 1840s, 116
Collins, Margaret: as slave owner, 104
Collins, Maximillian: as slave owner, 104;
   prosperity of, during 1850s, 116
Collins, Robert, 190; as slave owner, 104;
   white father of, 100
Collins, Robert Michael: as slave owner,
   116
Colson, James, 111
Colson, William Nelson, 92; business of,
   109; wealth of, 111
Colwell, Prince, 160
Comegys, Cornelius, 88
Commagere, Paul, 196
Confederacy: supported by free persons
   of color in Lower South, 187–88
Cook, John Francis, 138
Cook, William, 204
Cooper, Jack, 111
Cosby, D., 88
Cousins, Charles, 66
Couvent School (New Orleans), 129
Crawford, Anthony: acquires farm, 209;
   lynching of, 233–35
Creighton, George, 92
Creoles of color: definition of, 97, 334;
   in Louisiana, 99, 100, 101. See also
   Cane River Creoles of color
Cromwell, Elizabeth, 66
Cromwell, John Wesley, 66
Crum, William Dermos: estimates value
   of black-owned property in Charles-
   ton, 168–69; political activities of, 225;
   white father of, 224
Crusoe, Edward, 203–4
Culture. See Blacks: culture of
Cuney, Norris Wright, 224; political
   activities of, 225

Dabron, Nicholas, 194
Datcher, Ellen, 204
Datcher, Francis, 111
David, Thomas, 48
Davis, Elijah, 87
Davis, Jefferson, 196
Davis, Joseph, 196
Davis, Noah, 66
Davis, Thomas, 70
Davis, William Roscoe, 45
Davis Bend (Miss.), 165; black commu-
   nity of, 196
Day, Thomas, 108
Deaderick, William, 126
Deas, Ann: as hotel owner, 132
Debross, Alexander, 70
Decaud, Rose, 133
Decuir, Antoine, 101; arranges marriage
   of son, 128
Decuir, Antoine, Jr.: economic ascent of,
   113–14, 121; losses of, during Civil
   War, 191; marriage arranged for, 128
Decuir, Josephine: marriage arranged
   for, 128; plantation sold at public auc-
   tion, 192
De Forest, John William, 134
De Hayne, Marguerite Sanchez, 135
Delany, Martin R., 10
Delarge, Robert, 224
Demographic trends: average age of Upper South property owners in 1850,
   72; decline of women among prosperous blacks in Lower South, 195–96;
   literacy rate among prosperous blacks
   in Lower South, 129–30; literacy rate
   among prosperous blacks in Upper
   South, 138; male-female ratio in cities
   of Upper South, 177; post-1870 black
   urban population growth in Upper
   South, 176–77; proportion of property owners born in-state, 95; wartime
   death rate among southern white
   males, 148. See also Blacks: free
Dempsey, William, 117
Dereef, Richard E.: as land speculator,
   115; prosperity of, during 1850s, 115;
   Last Will and Testament of, 260–62;
   wealth of, following Civil War, 192
De Sales, Henry, 135
Deslonde, George, 101
Deveaux, John H., 225, 231

Devereux, Julien S., 31
Dickerson, Henry, 112
Dickinson, Joseph, 92
Dickson, Nolan, 90
District of Columbia. *See* Washington, D.C.
Dobard, Sylvestre, 134
Dolly, Nelly, 69
Domestic slave economy. *See* Slavery: internal slave economy
Donato, Adolphe, 194–95
Donatto, Adolphe: mixed ancestry of, 101
Donatto, Martin, 103
Douglass, Frederick, 203; as self-hired ship's caulker, 39
Doxey, Lewis, 126
DuBois, Charles, 70
Du Bois, W. E. B.: on black-owned businesses, 182; on black poverty, 161; on Negro history, 1; on P. B. S. Pinchback, 231
Dubuclet, Antoine, 101; arranges marriage of daughter, 128; plantation of, 120; postwar wealth of, 196
Dubuclet, Augustin, 70
Duckett, Lewis, 209
Dudley, Edward, 54
Duke, Benjamin, 226
Duke, Washington, 226
Dumas, Francis Ernest, 118, 134
Dumony, Honore, 71
Dungee, John, 96
Dungee, Lucy Ann, 96
Dunn, Oscar James, 193
Dupuy, Francois Edmond: financial ascent of, 118; mixed ancestry of, 101; political activities of, 224; wealth of, in 1870, 193
Durant, Francois, 71
Durnford, Andrew: attitude toward slaves, 107–8; mixed ancestry of, 101; purchases St. Rosalie plantation, 101; and slave-buying trip to Richmond, 105; as sugar planter, 119; views on colonization, 107
Durnford, Andrew, Jr.: St. Rosalie sold at public auction, 192
Durnford, Joseph, 187
Durnford, Marie Charlott Remi, 187
Durnford, Rosema, 192

Durnford, Thomas, 105, 187
Dyson, Charles, 204

Eatonville (Fla.), 165
Economic elite, black, 97–141 passim, 185–232 passim, 295–300, 303–6; in antebellum St. Louis, 109; occupational diversification among, 221; in rural South, 207–8; slave antecedents of, 223; slave ownership among, 104–6
Economy: depression of 1830s, 112; postwar conditions in Lower South, 148; postwar conditions in Upper South, 197, 200; prosperity in South during 1850s, 72, 121
Eden, William, 70
Education: attitudes toward, among prosperous Upper South blacks, 138; free black schools in Lower South, 129–30
Edwards, A. F.: as slave trader, 106
Ellett, Daniel, 69
Elliott, Robert Brown, 225
Ellison, Eliza Ann, 127
Ellison, Henry: assists father, 116; marriage of, 127; and secession crisis, 136; support for Confederacy, 188
Ellison, Reuben: assists father, 116; marriage of, 127
Ellison, Robert, 100
Ellison, William: economic ascent of, 113–14, 116; as member of Church of Holy Cross, 130; probable father of, 100; white customers of, 131
Ellison, William, Jr.: assists father, 116; decline of wealth after Civil War, 190–91; marriage of, 127; support for Confederacy, 188
Elwig, Joseph, 47
Emigration, 90–96; from New Orleans in 1859–60, 115; property owners seek information about sugar industry in Liberia, 92; views of, by free black property owners, 91
Epps, James, 123
Epps, Nancy, 123
Epps, Nathaniel, 123
Epps, William: career of, 122–23
Equiano, Olaudah, 9, 26
Evans, Enoch, 123

Evans, Zuline Aubry, 133–34
Ewell, Aldred, 198
Ewing, Edwin, 50
Ezell, Lorenza, 31

Family: clans in Lower South, 126–27.
    See also Property owners
Farm owners, 16, 70–71, 73, 112; blacks
    and whites compared, 173; diversifi-
    cation among, in post-1870s South,
    209–10; former slaves among, 209;
    in Lower South, 163; in post-1870
    Upper South, 174–76; in post-1870
    Virginia, 173; statistical evidence con-
    cerning, 163–66. See also Rural
Farragut, David, 187, 188
Fayman, M. S., 135–36
Female. See Women
Fenno, Joseph, 134
Fenno, Mary, 134, 196
Fernandis, John A., 217
Field, James A., 209
Fisk University, 181
Fitzgerald, Mary E., 128
Fitzgerald, Richard B.: assisted by whites,
    226
Forbes, Isaac, 172–73
Forsyth, C. C., 134
Fortune, Timothy Thomas, 167
Foster, Ephraim, 56
Francis, John L., 115
Francis, John V., 20, 70
Francis, Richard, 204
Franklin, G. W., 227
Franklin, Isaac, 89
Franklin, John Hope, 2; scholarship
    of, 61
Freedmen: and advantages of acquiring
    land, 153–54; and difficulties in ac-
    quiring land in Lower South, 145–47;
    difficulties in acquiring land in Upper
    South, 151–53
Freedmen's Bureau. See Bureau of Refu-
    gees, Freedmen, and Abandoned
    Lands
Freedmen's Savings Bank, 203, 204
Freeman, J., 126
Freeman, York, 112
Free Negroes. See Blacks: free
Free people of color. See Blacks: free
Free women of color. See Women

Frilot, Leon, 119
Fromontin, Julien, 129

Galle, Amelia, 86
Garden, Elias William, 113
Garden, John: as planter, 104; death of,
    113
Garden plots. See Slavery: internal slave
    economy
Gardner, John, 23
Garrett, Angie, 106
Generational change: among affluent
    free persons of color in Lower South,
    113
George, Octavia, 31
Georgia: free black property owners in
    Chatham County, 62, 69; law denying
    free blacks the right to own real estate
    in, 65; slave property ownership in,
    56–60
Gibbons, Ann, 86
Gibbons, John, 70
Gibbs, Mifflin: political activities of,
    225
Gillfield Baptist Church (Petersburg,
    Va.), 139
Glascock, Alexc, 91
Glencamp, Henry: white father of, 100
Godwin, John, 101
Gordon, Robert, 47
Gordon, William Claud: career of, 218
Gough, John, 20
Gowen, Frank, 66
Graham, Sally, 115
Grant, Ulysses, 230
Gray, William, 200
Grayson, William, 90, 132
Green, Brian, 88
Green, Jacob, 115
Green, Thomas: career of, 122; family
    of, 202
Gregorie, Nelly, 67
Gregorie, Titus, 67
Grimké, Archibald, 222
Grimké, Francis, 231
Grimké, Thomas S., 90
Guillard, Jacob, 24
Gullinsville (Ga.), 165

Habersham, Monday, 57
Hagan, John, 134

Hagan, Lucy Ann: and John Hagan, 134. *See also* Cheatham, Lucy Ann
Haigh, William H., 87
Hamilton, Alexander (black contractor), 220
Hamilton, Alexander (white physician), 13
Hammond, John, 13;
Hampton Institute, 173, 181
Harby, Mary, 132
Harding, Henry, 204
Hare, Jacob, 54
Hargress, Jim, 165
Hargress, Paul, 165
Harper, James, 140
Harris, Joseph, 112
Harris, Margaret Mitchell, 190; as rice planter, 116
Harris, Samuel, 220
Harrisburg (Ga.), 165
Hassel, Josephine, 150
Hataway, Robert C., 88
Havis, Ferdinand, 224
Hawks, Francis T., 172
Hawks, Hanna G., 172
Haynes, Pierce, 135
Haywood, Felix, 33
Head, Elbert, 209
Henderson, J. T., 211
Henson, Andrew, 204
Herndon, Alonzo Franklin: as barber, 217; career of, 220
Hickman, Barriteer, 124, 202
Higginbotham, William, 196
Higgins, Fleming, 198
Hightower, William T., 221
Hill, Titus, 90; petition concerning, 256
Hillyer, Virgil, 57
Hiring out. *See* Slavery: hiring out
Hodges, Charles Augustus, 138
Hodges, John, 69
Hoff, Joseph B., 90
Holland, Edwin C., 89
Holloway, Charles, 102
Holloway, Edward, 102
Holloway, Isaac, 102
Holloway, John, 102
Holloway, Ned, 154
Holloway, Richard, 20, 101; biographical sketch of, 102; as preacher, 102; property of, 70

Holloway, Richard, Jr.: bequest from father, 102; maintains wealth after Civil War, 193
Holloway, Samuel, 102
Holman, John (white slave trader), 106
Holman, John, Jr. (free mulatto), 23; as slave trader, 106
Holman, Samuel, Sr., 23, 106
Holman, William: as slave trader, 106
Homeownership, 69–70, 77–78; in Lower South, 169–70; in Upper South, 179–80
Honoré, Zachari, 23, 101, 196; land holdings of, 121
Hooper, Scott, 35
Hopton, Abby, 56
Hopton, Robert, 70
Houston, Charles, 31
Howard, David Tobias, 224
Howard, Robert (white), 56
Howard, Robert (black): wealth of, following Civil War, 192–93; as wood dealer, 115
Hudson, Richard B., 220
Huger, Benjamin, 90, 132
Humphries, Solomon: entertains whites, 133; white customers of, 131
Hyman, John, 46
Hyman, Ned, 46; petition of, 252–54; petition concerning, 255–56
Hyman, Samuel, 46

Imes, David: letter of, 244–46
Inflation: of land values in Louisiana, 103, 113; of land values in Upper South, 72
Inglis, Thomas, 106; white ancestry of, 100
Intermarriage: among affluent free persons of color in Lower South, 127–28
Internal slave economy. *See* Slavery: internal economy
Interracial mixing, 99–101; and cohabitation in Lower South, 134–35; socially, in Lower South, 133
Irvine, Harriet, 67
Irvine, Moses, 66–67
Ivey, Priscilla: and white planter, 108; as slave owner, 110

Jack, Doctor, 49; petitions concerning, 250–52

Jackson, Daniel, 140
Jackson, Deal, 210
Jackson, James (D.C. wheelwright), 202
Jackson, James (S.C. free black), 27
Jackson, Luther Porter, 2; scholarship of,
    61, 68, 72
Jackson, Susan: pastry shop of, 86; prop-
    erty of, 70; white customers of, 131
Jacobs, John, 135
Jakes, Henry, 126
James, Paris, 33
Jarvis, William, 112
Jauna, Maria, 101
Jefferson, Lewis, 210, 211
Jennings, Samuel, 91
Johnson, Andrew N.: political activities
    of, 225
Johnson, Ann, 116–17
Johnson, Anthony, 15, 16
Johnson, Calvin F., 219
Johnson, Catherine, 188–89
Johnson, Isaac, 204
Johnson, James Drayton, 127; wealth of,
    following Civil War, 193
Johnson, James M., 127; and secession
    crisis, 136
Johnson, John (Md. farmer), 16
Johnson, John, Jr., 16
Johnson, John (Savannah carpenter), 69
Johnson, Martha, 132
Johnson, Prince, 209
Johnson, William (Natchez barber):
    friendship with Robert McCary, 128;
    probable father of, 100; relations with
    whites, 131, 133
Johnson, William (St. Louis barber),
    124, 137
Johnson, William Hamilton, 210–11
Johnston, Samuel, 66, 74; petitions of,
    248–50
Johnston, William, 20
Jones, Alfred, 202
Jones, Carroll, 150
Jones, Charles C., 87
Jones, Charles C., Jr.: advises against
    prosection of employer of runaway
    slave, 56; commends self-hired slave,
    58
Jones, Elvira, 96
Jones, Jehu: described as nearly white,
    100; as hotel owner, 132

Jones, Jehu, Jr.: emigrates to Liberia, 92;
    returns to U.S., 94
Jones, Jesse, 154
Jones, Shandy: as emigration agent, 91;
    letter of, 243–44; remains in Alabama,
    93; white customers of, 131
Jones, Toby, 146
Jones, Wiley: real estate holdings of,
    222–23
Jordan, J. B., 92
Jourdain, Jean Baptiste: suicide of, 194
Jourdain, Magdeleine, 100

Katcliff, Peter, 90
Kemble, Frances, 132
Kendy, Prince, 57
Key, H. W., 209
King, Charles, 111
King, Horace, 101
King, John, 88
Klondike (Ala.), 165
Knights of Pythias (Va.), 173
Kowaliga (Ala.), 165
Ku Klux Klan, 148. See also Violence

L'Ouverture, Toussaint, 18
Labadie, Antoine, 108; family of, 202
Labat, Casimir, 194
Lachiapella, Catherine, 100
Lacroix, Francois, 118; property losses
    of, 194
Lafon, Thomy: and land speculation
    during Civil War, 193; real estate hold-
    ings of, 222
Lamar, Richard, 150
Lambert, John, 160
Lamput, John, 20
Land owners
—black: attitudes of, toward ownership,
    25–26, 145; expansion by, in Upper
    South, 72–73; free black women as,
    85–86; during postwar period,
    148–49, 152–54; advantages of, in
    upper states, 172; difficulties of, in
    lower states, 162–63. See also Property
    owners
—white: assist free blacks, 88; opposition
    by, to black proprietorship, 17,
    145–46, 161–62
Land values: in Louisiana, 103; postwar
    depreciation of, 148. See also Inflation

Lane, Dennis, 198
Langston, John Mercer, 173, 225
Lankford, John Anderson, 219
Laws: and concessions granted to free blacks born in-state, 88; in colonial Louisiana, 22; to control free blacks, 63–64; and court testimony, 88; to curtail free black property ownership, 64; to deny blacks right to testify against whites, 21; against self-hire, excluding women, 55; and manumission, 17, 18; to prohibit freedmen from leasing land, 145; to prohibit self-hire and quasi-freedom, 52–55; to remand free blacks to slavery, 90; and reputation of freedom, 56; and slave property ownership, 15, 33, 52
Le Comte, Marie Marguerite, 106
Leary, Matthew, Jr., 87
Leathers, D. N., 220; and white customers, 226
Lecomte, Magdelaine, 136
Lee, Alfred, 126; family of, 202
Lee, Edward, 115
Lee, Eliza Seymour, 132; as hotel owner, 133
Lee, Francis, 115
Lee, Harriett, 204
Lee, John, 132
Lee, Levin, 140
Lee, Ludwell, 202
LeFond, Francis C. N., 85
Legal codes. See Laws
Legoaster, Erasme, 101
Leron, Hannah, 70
Leslie, Charles C., 221
Lewis, Augustus, 88
Lewis, Milly, 160
Lewis, Winny, 85
Lexington (Ky.), 201
Liberia: attitudes of property owners toward, 94–95. See also Emigration
Liddell, John, 42
Literacy. See Demographic trends; Education
Llorens, Marie: marriage contract of, 128
Llorens, Manuel, 136
Locks, John W., 217–18
Logan, George, 70
Logan, Moses, 198

Longo, Anthony, 15, 16
Louisiana: black real estate holdings in, 4; black slave ownership in, 107; as early center of black wealth holding, 102–4; and postwar economic decline among formerly free blacks, 191–92, 208; prosperous blacks in, 117–21. See also Blacks: free; Emigration; New Orleans
Lowery, Peter, 112, 202
Lutz, Charles, 188
Lynch, John Roy, 211

McAllister, M. H., 70
McCarty, Drauzin Barthelemy, 117, 193
Macarty, Eulalie d'Mandeville, 101; biographical sketch of, 102–3; sends son to Imperial Conversatoire in Paris, 129
Macarty, Victor-Eugene, 129
McCary, Robert, 128
McCary, William, 128
McDonogh, John, 101
McDowell, Calvin, 228
McDuffy, J. D., 210
McKinlay, Whitefield, 222
McKinlay, William: as teacher, 129; as politician, 224; wealth of, following Civil War, 193
McKinlay, William J.: as politician, 224
McLain, Enoch, 90
McLain, William, 92
Macon, William, 49
McPhail, John, 90
MacPherson, Christopher, 108
McWorter, Frank, 47–48
Madison Street Presbyterian Church (Baltimore), 139
Mahaly, Susan, 86
Mahier, Agnes, 71
Malone, James M., 54
Mangum, Lydia, 123
Mangum, William, 208–9; buried alive by whites, 228
Manning, Richard, 235
Market value: compared with assessment value, 380
Marsh, James, 56
Marshall, Andrew: death of, 113; Last Will and Testament of, 259–60; property of, 70; as slave owner, 104
Marshall, Anna, 113

Marshall, Joseph, 113
Marshall, Louisa, 113
Marshall, Sarah, 113
Mary, Aristide, 193; political involvement of, 224; suicide of, 194
Maryland State Colonization Society, 93
Mathews, Peter Bassnett, 21; petition of, 247–48
Matthews, George, 70
Matthews, Rebecca Tinsley, as slave owner, 123
Matthews, William E., 221; on racial equality, 224–25
Meachum, John, 123
Meachum, John Berry: career of, 123; as preacher, 140; purchases and frees slaves, 66; purchases wife out of slavery, 137
Meachum, Mary, 123
Meachum, William, 123
Melbourn, Julius, 108–9
Mercier, A., 220–21
Mercier, Dominique, 220–21
Mercier, Ernest, 220–21
Merrick, John, 218; assisted by whites, 226; attitude toward plight of blacks in South, 231; real estate holdings of, 222; white father of, 224
Metoyer, Augustin, 70; establishes Catholic church, 130
Metoyer, Claude Thomas Pierre, 101
Metoyer, Dominique: death of, 113; estate inventory of, 263–66; mixed ancestry of, 101; as slave owner, 104
Metoyer, Joseph: marriage contract of, 128
Metoyer, Louis, 70
Metoyer, Marie Suzanne: bequest to granddaughter, 128; death of, 113; mixed ancestry of, 101
Metoyer, Nicholas Augustin: mixed ancestry of, 101
Metoyer family: decline of, following Civil War, 192
Meullion, Antoine, 113, 191
Meullion, Jean Baptiste, 23, 102; biographical sketch of, 103; death of, 113; mixed ancestry of, 101; petition to emancipate grandchildren, 135
Meullion, Luis Augustin, 101
Meullion, Susanne, 113

Miles, Frankey: losses of, during Civil War, 197; property of, 112; as slave owner, 123; and white planter, 108
Miles, James, 85
Miller, James, 128
Miller, Lavinia, 128
Miller, Stephen F., 49
Miller, Thomas E., 182
Mirault, Louis, 70
Miscegenation. See Interracial mixing
Mishaw, John, 115, 127
Mishaw, Mary, 127
Mitchell, Elizabeth, 102
Mitchell, James, 20, 21, 70; daughter marries Richard Holloway, 102
Mitchell, John R., Jr., 225; encourages property ownership, 173; as member of American Bankers Association, 230
Mitchell, Lewis, 198
Mongum, Philip, 15
Monroe, John, 58
Montgomery, Benjamin Thornton: attitude toward education, 229; as slave entrepreneur, 48; as wealthiest black in South, 196
Montgomery, Isaiah T.: at Davis Bend, 196; as founder of Mound Bayou, Miss., 165
Montgomery, William: at Davis Bend, 196
Montgomery, Virginia, 229
Moor, Philip, 90
Moore, Aaron McDuffie, 218
Moore, Edward, 87
Mordecai, Samuel, 108
Mordicai, Harry, 111
Mosby, R. H., 88
Moss, George, 65
Moss, Thomas, 228
Mound Bayou (Miss.), 165
Mulattoes. See Phenotype
Munford, Nancy, 84
Murphy, John Henry, 218–19
Murphy, Willis, 229
Muse, Lindsay, 204
Myers, William, 204

Napier, James, 218; political activities of, 225
Napier, William, 160
Nash, William Beverely, 224

Nashville (Tenn.): virtually free slaves in, 45–46, 49, 50; black homeownership in, 180–81
Natchitoches Parish (La.), 97; black slave ownership in, 104, 106; Church of St. Augustin, 130; economic decline of free blacks in, 80, 113, 114, 208
Nathans, Levi, 132
National Baptist Publishing Board (Nashville, Tenn.), 219
National Negro Business League, 230
National Order of Mosaic Templers, 222
New Orleans: black emancipation petitions in, 67; during Civil War, 187–88; early black businesses in, 21; economic decline among free blacks in, 81, 114–15; emigration from, among free persons of color, 115; free black property ownership in, 71; free black schools in, 129; homeownership in, 195; self-hired slaves in, 41, 42
Nichols, Jonathan, 54
Nicholson, Philip, 210
Noisette, Joseph, 208
Noisette, Margaret, 100
Noisette, Philip Stanislas, 100
Nolan, Philip, 204
Norman, Hannah, 85
North Carolina Mutual Life Insurance Company, 181, 218

Occupations: artisans in Upper South, 124; among black realty owners in Upper South, 68, 72, 78–79; among blacks in New South cities, 167; and economic elite in post-1870s South, 207; among post-1870 Upper South urban blacks, 178; postwar changes among realty owners in Lower South, 149–50; postwar changes among realty owners in Upper South, 155–57; among propertied blacks in South, 285–86; among realty owners in Lower South, 81–84; among slave entrepreneurs, 48–50; among virtually free slaves, 41, 45
Odingsells, Anthony, 70; as slave owner, 104; receives bequest from white slave owner, 100; relations with whites, 133
Odingsells, Charles, 100
O'Kelly, Berry, 220; real estate holdings of, 222

Oliver, Louise, 70; estate inventory of, 267–70; mixed ancestry of, 101; as slave owner, 107; as sugar planter, 119
Oliver, P., 119
Olmsted, Frederick Law: and Cane River Creoles of color, 97; and disdain of whites for certain occupations, 78; and free women of color in Lower South, 133; and internal slave economy, 32; interviews La. slave, 144–45; and slave hiring, 36–37
One Cent Savings Bank (Nashville, Tenn.), 218
Order of St. Luke (Richmond, Va.), 173
Oursol, Felicite, 107, 373

Page, Jack, 36
Paillet, Antoine, 373
Paine, Francis, 15
Paine, William W., 58
Palmer, R. R., 221
Parish, Catherine, 50
Parker, Robert, 16
Parrish, Frank, 50, 137
Patterson, Sally, 47
Peagler, James, 104
Peggen, Allen, 125
Pencell, William, 100
Pendarvis, James, 20, 23
Peronneau, Richard, 20
Petitions, 247–57
Pettiford, William Reuben, 218, 221
Phenotype (black verses mulatto), 12, 287–88, 290–91, 292–93; black rural landholders in Upper South, 73–74; decline of mulattoes in postwar affluent class, 195; proportion of black and mulatto landowners in postwar Lower South, 149; mulattoes among late nineteenth-century economic elite, 223–24; white fathers of, 224; affluent mulattoes in Lower South, 99–101. See also Interracial mixing
Pierre, Marie, 100
Pierre, William, 204
Pierre-Auguste, Jean Baptiste, 188
Pierre-Auguste, Lufroy, 188
Pincell, Manuel, 70
Pincham, Thomas, 126
Pinchback, P. B. S., 230–31
Placage: in Louisiana, 99

Plowden, Weston, 51
Poindexter, John, 133
Politics: economic activities of black po-
litical leaders, 211–12; involvement of
prosperous blacks in, 224–25
Ponis, Louisa, 101; plantation of, 119
Porter, Jefferson, 202
Porter, Solomon, 137
Price, Milly, 112
Promiseland (S.C.), 165
Property: attitudes toward, among free
blacks, 16, 20–21, 25, 69, 77–78; attitudes toward, among slaves, 14, 35,
59–60; attitudes toward, among West
Africans, 10; meaning of, for postwar
blacks, 145, 151, 182–84; real and
personal, defined, 372–373
Property owners: blacks compared with
whites, 160–61; drive and ambition
among, 101–4; educational values of,
128–29; family values of, in Lower
South, 127–28; family values of,
in Upper South, 137–38; increases
among, in postwar Upper South,
159; in postwar rural Lower South,
146–47; among slaves in Georgia low-
country, 57–59; social and cultural
values of, Upper and Lower South
compared, 136–37
Prosperous blacks, 295–300, 303–6; attitudes of, toward education, 229; relations with whites, 130–36, 226–32;
slave ownership among, 104–8; social
life of, in Lower South, 134; wealth accumulations of, 192–97
Prud'homme, Narchisse, 88
Purcell, George, 91
Purcell, John, 91
Purnas, Anthony, 150
Purvis, Charles, 222

Quakers: in North Carolina, 54
Quasi-free slaves. See Slavery: virtually
free slaves

Race relations: attitudes of prosperous
blacks toward whites, 231–32; differences in Upper and Lower South,
140–41; fragile nature of, in Lower
South, 135–36; during late nineteenth

century, 231–32; in the Lower South,
130–36; white guardians and protectors, 87–90
Rachel, Antoine, 150
Rapier, James T., 211; looses wealth, 225
Rapier, John H., Sr.: as hired slave, 46;
prosperity of, during 1850s, 117
Rapier, Richard, 46
Ravenel, Henry W., 34
Real estate: average holdings among
prosperous Upper South urban blacks,
203; black and white holdings com-
pared, 4; compared with personal
holdings, 159, 163; investment in, by
prosperous blacks, 222–23; urban and
rural compared, 169
Redpath, James, 93
Reggio, Adolphe, 101; as sugar planter,
119
Reggio, Charles, 196
Reid, Elizabeth, 132
Reid, Whitelaw, 145, 146
Reizne, Benjamin, 69
Religion: and Andrew Bryan as
preacher, 27, 241–42; free persons of
color as churchgoers in Lower South,
130; separate black churches in Upper
South, 138–39
Renova (Miss.), 165
Rentfro, Robert, 109
Rhea, Samuel, 46
Ricard, Augustin, 71
Ricard, Cyprien, 101; purchases slave
woman and her son, 105; marriage of
granddaughter, 128
Ricard, Luc, 70
Ricard, Madam Cyprien: economic as-
cent of, 113–14; as plantation owner,
119–21
Ricard, Pierre, 113; as plantation owner,
119–21; losses of, during Civil War,
191
Richmond (Va.): free black real estate
owners in, 76–77; homeownership in,
179; self-hired slaves in, 43
Rickenbacker, V. J., 135
Rillieux, Edmond, 71
Rillieux, Madeleine, 100
Roberson, Zachariah, 88
Roberts, Augustus, 200

Roberts, Felix, 194
Roberts, Joseph Jenkins, 92; establishes trading company, 109
Roberts, Linda, 58–59
Robinson, John, 91; as livery owner, 117
Roderick, Robert, 90
Rodriggus, Manuel, 15
Rogers, Nathaniel, 200
Rose, James, 132
Roudanez, Jean Baptiste, 193
Roudanez, Louis, 190
Rudd, James, 38
Ruffin, Thomas, 209
Rural: black real estate owners, 72–75, 152–53, 171–76; ratio of black land-owners, 146–47; economic elite, 207–16. See also Farm owners; Property owners; Real estate
Rutgers, Antoinette, 204
Rutgers, Arend, 108
Rutgers, Louis: mulatto son of Dutch immigrant, 108
Rutgers, Pelagie: widow of Eutrope Clamorgan, 108; daughter marries James Thomas, 204

St. Augustin's Catholic Church (New Orleans), 130
St. Denis, Augustine, 136
St. Louis Cathedral Church (New Orleans), 130
St. Louis Mission Church, 140
St. Luke's Bank and Trust Co. (Richmond, Va.), 219
Sampson, Charles, 91
Sampson, James D.: attitude of, toward slaves, 110; family of, during Civil War, 197; mixed racial heritage of, 108; as slave owner, 110
Sanders, Richard, 204
Sasportas, Joseph A., 193
Savannah (Ga.): black property ownership in, 69, 80
Schools: maintained by free blacks in Lower South, 129; maintained by free blacks in Upper South, 138. See also Education; Property owners; Prosperous blacks
Scott, E. F., 210
Scott, Thomas, 124

Screven, Charles O., 133
Seals, Denis, 201
Seaton, George, 125
Self-hire. See Slavery: self-hire
Shaler, N. J., 149
Shaw, John, 198
Shepherd, Mosby, 66
Sheridan, Louis, 108; emigrates to Liberia, 92–93; as slave owner, 110
Sheridan, Philip H., 197
Sherman, William T., 57, 60
Shiner, Michael, 89
Shrewsberry, George, 192–93
Siexas, Thomas, 133
Simpson, Smart, 70
Sindoz, Leon, 101
Singleton, Margaret, 85
Singleton, Richard, 85
Slave owners
—black: decline of, in Upper South, 123–24; in early Virginia, 22; economic activities of, in Lower South, 102–3; economic decline of, following Civil War, 190–92; in Lower South in 1830, 104–5; in South Carolina and Lower South, 23–24; treatment of slaves by, 105–6; in Upper South, 110–11
—white, attitudes of: toward black property ownership, 54–55, 87–90; toward free persons of color, 132–33; toward industrious slaves, 51–56; toward property ownership by slaves, 33, 34; toward prosperous free persons of color in Upper and Lower South, 140–41
Slavery: response of slaves to cash payments, 34–35; response of slaves to work incentives, 32; in southern industry, 37; and task labor system, 14, 26
—hiring out: during colonial period, 13; compensation to slaves, 36; slaves' "negotiating power," 38; in tobacco industry, 36
—internal slave economy: cash crops, 31–32; in colonial British North America, 13–15; garden plots, 31; property ownership among slaves in Georgia lowcountry, 57–59; prosperous slaves, 33–34; slaves' preference

Slavery—internal slave economy
(*continued*)
for cash payments for crops, 31; types
of property owned by slaves, 33–34
—self-hire, 13, 38–39; difficulties confronted in, 39–40; financial benefits
of, for slaves, 42; longevity of practice
of, 41; slaves as entrepreneurs, 47–51;
slaves' attitudes toward, 41–42
—self-purchase, 40, 65–66; among Liberian emigrants, 94; pernicious practices concerning, 40
—virtually free slaves, 44; as businessmen and women, 45–51; in cities, 44,
45; difficulties confronted by, 49; as
property owners, 46
Smith, Elizabeth, 13
Smith, Fanny, 40
Smith, Israel, 196
Smith, M. H., 91
Smith, Samuel, 198
Smith, Sophia, 85
Snowden, Garden, 204
Social life: among affluent free people of
color in Lower South, 126–27; among
prosperous blacks in Upper South, 137
Sompayrac, Marc, 136
Soulie, Albin: as merchant, 117–18
Soulie, Bernard: as exchange broker and
merchant, 117–18; and loan to Con-
federate government, 193; political ac-
tivities of, 224
South Carolina: early black property
owning in, 20, 70; law against self-hire,
and exclusion of women, 55. *See also*
Charleston
South Carolina Direct Tax Commission,
146
Southern Claims Commission, 57, 324n
Spaulding, Charles Clinton, 218
Spein, Polly, 70
Spencer, Moses, 124; as wealthiest black
in Lexington, Ky., 201
Spradling, Washington, 124
Stanly, John Carruthers, 108; acquires
plantations, 109; borrows from Bank
of New Bern, 88; purchases wife out
of slavery, 137; seeks to emancipate his
slave barbers, 49; as slave owner, 110
Stanly, John Wright, 108
Starkey, James, 40

Steele, Alexander, 34
Stephens, Christopher, 124
Steward, Abram, 57
Stewart, Alexander, 108
Stewart, James A., 90
Stewart, Lydia Carruthers, 108
Stewart, P. A., 112
Stewart, William, 228
Sullivan, John S., 42
Sumner, Julia, 137
Sutton, Rebecca, 46
Syphax, William, 204

Tandy, Henry A., 220
Tanner, Alethia, 66
Taylor, Adam, 160
Taylor, John, 201
Taylor, Joseph, 196
Taylor, Philip, 16
Taylor, William, 201
Terrell, Robert H., 222
Thezan, Sidney, 193
Thomas, Charles, 46
Thomas, George, 132
Thomas, George H., 158
Thomas, James: emancipation of, 56;
friendships of, 137; marries Antoinette
Rutgers, 204; as Nashville barber, 124;
as St. Louis barber, 217; total wealth
of, 205; white father of, 224
Thomas, John, 124, 202
Thomas, Jonas W., 209, 211
Thomasville (Ark.), 165
Thompson, John, 20
Thompson, Molly, 134
Thorne, John Stokes, 209
Thorne, Phillip, 150
Tobacco industry: in Richmond and
Petersburg (Va.), 37
Touro, Judah, P., 101
Townes, James, 34
Trowbridge, John, 158
True Reformers. *See* United Order of
True Reformers
True Reformers Bank (Richmond, Va.),
172, 218
Tubman, Emily, 32
Tucker, St. George, 25–26
Tulane, Victor, 227
Turner, Benjamin: dies in poverty, 225;
as slave entrepreneur, 48

Turner, J. P., 91
Turner, James, 201
Turner, John Milton, 225
Turner, Lewis, 112
Turner, Nat, 63, 89–90

Union Seminary school, 138
United Order of True Reformers (Richmond, Va.), 173, 219
Urban: average real estate holdings,
compared with rural average, 75; black
property holding, 20; disproportionate
share of black wealth, 180–81; economic advantages in postwar Upper
South, 200; motives for black migration, 166–67; Old South and New
South cities contrasted, 167; prosperous blacks during postwar period,
200–205; postwar economic elite,
216–17; realty owners, 75–77, 147,
154–55; self-hired slaves, 45, 55. See
also Demographic trends
U.S. Population Census, 3, 281–94;
evaluated as source, 371–79

Values and attitudes. See Property
owners
Verdun, Romaine: attitude of, toward
slaves, 108; establishes school on plantation, 129; mistaken for house servant, 135
Vesey, Denmark, 63; as free black property owner, 89
Viejo, Juana, 21
Viejo, Pedro, 21
Vinzent, Charles, 32
Violence: Atlanta race riot of 1906, 228;
against black businessmen, 228;
against blacks in Upper South, 152;
against property owners in Lower
South, 80. See also Ku Klux Klan
Virginia: black farm owners in, 173–
75; comment on land ownership in,
236; early black freeholders in, 15–16;
expansion of antebellum property-
owning class in, 73–77
Virtually free slaves. See Slavery: virtually
free slaves

Wages: for hired slave hands, 37
Walden, Thomas, 85

Walker, Maggie Lena, 173, 219
Walker, Thomas C., 172
Walker, William, 38
Wallace, Daniel Webster, 210
Walls, Josiah, 211; looses land, 225
Wane, Henry, 57
Ward, John, 111
Warmoth, Henry Clay, 231
Warren, James, 154
Warren, Nathan, 131
Washington, Booker T., 226, 182
Washington, Parlour, 55
Washington, Thornton, 154
Washington, D.C.: as postwar center of
black wealth, 203–4
Watkins, J. C., 54
Watson, Edward, 204
Weaver, William, 37
Webb, Mathew, 21; petition of, 247–48
Wells, Thomas, 40
West, Reuben, 124
Weston, Anthony, 50–51; wealth of, fol-
lowing Civil War, 192
Weston, Jacob: and death of Richard
Holloway, 102; prosperity of, during
1850s, 115
Weston, Maria, 51
Weston, Samuel: and death of Richard
Holloway, 102; prosperity of, during
1850s, 115; wealth of, following Civil
War, 193
Weston, William, 46–47
White, Albert, 124
Whites: wealth holdings of, compared
with blacks in Baltimore, 77; attitudes
of, toward free black property owners,
89–90, 101; and violence against
blacks, following Nat Turner revolt,
90; and repression of free blacks on
eve of Civil War, 90; skilled artisans
complain about slave competition, 48,
55; attitudes of, toward freedmen and
women as landowners, 172. See also Interracial mixing; Race relations; Slave
owners: black; Slave owners: white
Wigfall, Paul, 115–16
Wilder, Charles, 224
Wilkinson, Francis, 193
Williams, Alfred, 137
Williams, James, 117
Williams, John, 20

Williams, Nathaniel, 20
Williamson, William, 135
Wilson, Alexander, 198
Wilson, Armistead, 124
Wilson, David, 20
Wilson, Josephine, 230
Wilson, William, 204
Winkler, Shadrack, 90
Winn, Charles, 200
Winn, James, 95
Winter, Lewis, 210
Wise, John, 55
Women: attitudes of, toward property ownership, 85; decline of, among postwar realty owners, 149, 195; occupations among, 85–86; and precautions about marriage, 85; property of, compared with men, 86, 288–89, 291–92, 293–94; property ownership among, 84; proportion of free black wealth held by, 86; as self-hired slaves, 41, 55; as slave entrepreneurs, 50. *See also* Demographic trends
Woodfolk, Austin, 140
Woodson, Carter G., 2
Woodson, James, 200
Woodson, Marshall, 202
Wormley, James T.: attitude of, toward plight of blacks in South, 231; fortune of, 204; passes wealth on to children, 223
Wormley, William, 111
Wright, George, 106
Wright, James, 204
Wyatt, Mary Ann, 49
Wycoff, Cornelius, 132

Young, James, 200

About the Author

Loren Schweninger is professor of history at the University of North Carolina—Greensboro. He is the author of *James T. Rapier and Reconstruction*, the editor of *From Tennessee Slave to St. Louis Entrepreneur: The Autobiography of James Thomas*, and has written numerous articles on black history in the South. He received an NEH Fellowship to complete research on *Black Property Owners in the South, 1790–1915*.

BOOKS IN THE SERIES BLACKS IN THE NEW WORLD

Before the Ghetto: Black Detroit in the Nineteenth Century
David M. Katzman

Black Business in the New South: A Social History of the North Carolina
Mutual Life Insurance Company
Walter B. Weare

The Search for a Black Nationality: Black Colonization and Emigration,
1787–1863
Floyd J. Miller

Black Americans and the White Man's Burden, 1898–1903
Willard B. Gatewood, Jr.

Slavery and the Numbers Game: A Critique of Time on the Cross
Herbert G. Gutman

A Ghetto Takes Shape: Black Cleveland, 1870–1930
Kenneth L. Kusmer

Freedmen, Philanthropy, and Fraud: A History of the Freedman's
Savings Bank
Carl R. Osthaus

The Democratic Party and the Negro: Northern and National Politics, 1868–92
Lawrence Grossman

Black Ohio and the Color Line, 1860–1915
David A. Gerber

Along the Color Line: Explorations in the Black Experience
August Meier and Elliott Rudwick

Black over White: Negro Political Leadership in South Carolina
during Reconstruction
Thomas Holt

Keeping the Faith: A. Philip Randolph, Milton P. Webster, and the
Brotherhood of Sleeping Car Porters, 1925–37
William H. Harris

Abolitionism: The Brazilian Antislavery Struggle
Joaquim Nabuco, translated and edited by Robert Conrad

Black Georgia in the Progressive Era, 1900–1920
John Dittmer

Medicine and Slavery: Health Care of Blacks in Antebellum Virginia
Todd L. Savitt

Alley Life in Washington: Family, Community, Religion, and
Folklife in the City, 1850–1970
James Borchert

Human Cargoes: The British Slave Trade to Spanish America, 1700–1739
Colin A. Palmer

Southern Black Leaders of the Reconstruction Era
Edited by Howard N. Rabinowitz

Black Leaders of the Twentieth Century
Edited by John Hope Franklin and August Meier

Slaves and Missionaries: The Disintegration of Jamaican Slave Society, 1787–1834
Mary Turner

Father Divine and the Struggle for Racial Equality
Robert Weisbrot

Communists in Harlem during the Depression
Mark Naison

Down from Equality: Black Chicagoans and the Public Schools, 1920–41
Michael W. Homel

Race and Kinship in a Midwestern Town: The Black Experience
in Monroe, Michigan, 1900–1915
James E. DeVries

Down by the Riverside: A South Carolina Slave Community
Charles Joyner

Black Milwaukee: The Making of an Industrial Proletariat, 1915–45
Edited by Joe William Trotter, Jr.

Religious Philanthropy and Colonial Slavery: The American
Correspondence of the Associates of Dr. Bray, 1717–1777
Edited by John C. Van Horne

Black History and the Historical Profession, 1915–80
August Meier and Elliott Rudwick

Paul Cuffe: Black Entrepreneur and Pan-Africanist
(formerly Rise to Be a People: A Biography of Paul Cuffe)
Lamont D. Thomas

Making Their Own Way: Southern Blacks' Migration to Pittsburgh, 1916–30
Peter Gottlieb

My Bondage and My Freedom
Frederick Douglass, edited by William L. Andrews

Black Leaders of the Nineteenth Century
Edited by Leon Litwack and August Meier

Charles Richard Drew: The Man and the Myth
Charles E. Wynes

John Mercer Langston and the Fight for Black Freedom, 1829–65
William and Aimee Lee Cheek

The Old Village and the Great House: An Archaeological
and Historical Examination of Drax Hall Plantation, St. Ann's Bay, Jamaica
Douglas V. Armstrong

Black Property Owners in the South, 1790–1915
Loren Schweninger

Reprint Editions

King: A Biography, Second Edition
David Levering Lewis

The Death and Life of Malcolm X, Second Edition
Peter Goldman

Race Relations in the Urban South, 1865–1890
Howard N. Rabinowitz, with a Foreword by C. Vann Woodward

Race Riot at East St. Louis, July 2, 1917
Elliott Rudwick

W. E. B. Du Bois: Voice of the Black Protest Movement
Elliott Rudwick

The Negro's Civil War: How American Negroes Felt and Acted during
the War for the Union
James M. McPherson

Lincoln and Black Freedom: A Study in Presidential Leadership
LaWanda Cox

Slavery and Freedom in the Age of the American Revolution
Edited by Ira Berlin and Ronald Hoffman